SPECIAL ARTICLES

Frank Butler..............
Kenny Dalglish.........

FIXTURES

Football League an
League.........
International and Cup
Scottish Cup Fixtures.
Welsh Cup Fixtures.................... 39
Irish League.................................. 46
Alliance League........................... 50
Southern League........................ 54

RUGBY LEAGUE

Fixtures..370
Principal Dates..............................376
Championship 1978–79.............376
Challenge Cup 1978–79............377
John Player Trophy......................378
Lancashire Cup..............................379
Yorkshire Cup.................................379
Australia Tour of Britain.............380
Champions.....................................381
Challenge Cup Winners.............381
County Cup Winners...................383

FOOTBALL LEAGUE

Managers...................................... 34
Referees.. 40
Football League Cup
(Past Finals)............................... 64
Honours List..................................148
Title Wins......................................153
Relegated Clubs............................154
Tables 1978–79...........................173
How Forest won the
League Cup...............................183
Arrivals and Departures.............214
League Roll Call 1978 79.........263
Playing Staffs 1979 80.............307
Results 1978 79........................357

F.A. CUP F.A. Charity Shield.... 39
1979 80 Exemptions.................. 41
The Way to Wembley.................156
F.A. Cup Wins at a Glance........158
How Arsenal won the
F.A. Cup.....................................161
Finals..163
Winners..170

...TISH CUP

The Final 1978–79.......................181

OTHER LEAGUE TABLES

Southern, Irish, League of Ireland, Northern Premier, Northern, Cheshire, Central and Welsh..... 42

INTERNATIONALS

All-time list of capped players.. 65
Home Championship
1978–79.................................. .225
Home International
Tournament..............................227
International Matches
1978–79...................................227
Results of all Matches.................237

EUROPEAN COMPETITIONS

Champion's Cup...........................134
Cup Winner's Cup........................138
U.E.F.A. Cup..................................141

CHIEF RECORDS

Club Scores...................................185
Record Crowds..............................188
Most Internationals......................189
Innovations....................................190
Players with most Caps etc.......190
Goal Scoring Records..................193 & 206
Cup Records..................................197
Record League Fines........... 201
Transfer Trail.................................212
Footballer of the Year.................216
England's Home Record.. 217
Milestones of Soccer...................220

Published by City Magazines Ltd.,
© Ring Publications Limited
1-3 Wine Office Court, Fleet Street
London EC4A 3AL.
ISBN 0 85543 018 4

CARRY ON GREENWOOD
by Frank Butler
(Sports Editor, News of the World)

As we approach football in the Eighties with the 1979-80 season hopes are high after 10 years in the wilderness of world soccer, England will prove in the European Championship Finals in Italy next June that they are at last back in business.

The last World Cup finals England took part in was back in 1970 when they failed to retain the crown they had won for the first time in 1966.

Sir Alf Ramsey stuck loyally to the 1966 squad which still gave a good account of itself. But he pressed his luck in failing to qualify for Munich by using many of his old servants.

Ramsey was sacked. Don Revie took over. The former Leeds United Manager didn't succeed. England failed to qualify for the European Championship finals in 1976 and again for the World Cup in Argentina in 1978.

Now it is Ron Greenwood's turn. Ron succeeded in ridding the England squad of a tenseness built up in Revie's short reign. He relaxed the team and brought back much lost confidence.

As the players' faith in themselves grew, so he was able to re-introduce more open attacking and entertaining football.

Though Greenwood is the first to agree that Soccer is tomorrow's game, he is wise enough to borrow many of the old tricks from the past.

Despite all the mystique and tactical discussions of today, Greenwood believes that football should be a simple game.

After all, it was played this way when talented players like Lawton, Matthews, Finney, Mannion, Carter, Mortensen led England to high scoring victories.

Greenwood also accepts that talent would survive in any generation. Matthews, Finney, DiSteffano, Best, Keegan, Puskas, Pele, Beckenbauer, Cruyff, could never be subdued.

Defensive systems, of course, change and stars of the past would have to adapt themselves to the modern game. But there is no doubt, they would cope with the situation.

Greenwood's record speaks for itself. Since he took over from Revie, England have lost only 2 games in 19 matches — early on when West Germany just pipped them at Munich and last June when they lost a thrilling game 4-3 against Austria in Vienna.

This season England will almost certainly qualify for the European championship finals in Italy in June.

They begin leading their group with games in hand. With second-leg championship matches against Denmark, Republic of Ireland and Bulgaria, all at Wembley, and one game against Northern Ireland in Belfast, England are almost home and dry.

Then the big test comes in Italy. If England do well, Greenwood's next target is to assure that England qualify for the World Cup in Spain in 1982.

All in all, Greenwood has done a splendid job and brought not only a new confidence, but a new dignity back to English football.

TEAMWORK IS THE *REAL* WINNER

KENNY DALGLISH

(LIVERPOOL AND SCOTLAND)

It appears I surprised one or two people at the Football Writers' Association's annual dinner last May. It seems that my list of "credits" when I received the coveted "Footballer of the Year" award was rather long.

But I said it how I saw it, indeed how I have always seen it. That, fine though it may be to receive praise — and I must admit to enjoying it as much as most — one must be realistic.

Football is, of necessity, a team game, an exercise in athleticism and entertainment in which one cannot operate to full effect without the assistance of everyone around you.

For me then the great honour the F.W.A. bestowed on me that evening, an occasion in which I followed some truly great names in the game — men such as Sir Stanley Matthews, Tom Finney and the rest — was an honour received by me but shared by so many.

It was primarily a recognition of the achievements of all my colleagues at the Liverpool Football Club for what they had achieved that season, just as the fact that under manager Bob Paisley, later himself to be named Manager of the Year again. The honour in regaining the League Title was a distinction shared.

That is an honour we all at Anfield wish to repeat this coming season, and along with it the recapture of the European Cup for the third time in four seasons.

Can we do it? Really, who can tell, so much lies in the lap of the gods and of lady luck. And of course the lads down the motorway at Nottingham Forest will no doubt again be wishing to put the brake upon us driving to this particular double.

Then, of course, both can expect another club to come good. If not from out of the blue than at least forward with a big new challenge. West Brom. could perhaps be placed in that category last season, and will have to be closely watched next time round.

One thing seems certain though, anyone who can beat our goals against record for last season, let alone the goals for, must have a big chance!

More seriously though, there is one honour which I gained last season which I do look upon as a personal thing, and one which brings me a feeling of sadness. That is my number of caps for Scotland, for, in creating a new record it also meant that I had to beat the previous one held by Denis Law.

I almost feel guilty about that, Denis Law is more than a footballer, he is a national institution, my hero, and the hero of thousands of Scots.

Somehow it always seemed to me that Denis and the record number of caps for Scotland went together, and should always remain part and parcel of one another.

Then I went and separated the two, a honour in a way almost sadly received. But for the rest, a season of real joy with brighter still to come one hopes. And shared all the way, naturally.

FOOTBALL LEAGUE and SCOTTISH LEAGUE FIXTURES 1979–80

Saturday, August 11
Celtic v. Morton
Dundee U. v. Dundee
Hibernian v. Rangers
Partick T. v. Aberdeen
St. Mirren v. Kilmarnock

Arbroath v. Hearts
Ayr U. v. Dumbarton
Berwick v. Airdrie
Clydebank v. Motherwell
Hamilton A. v. St. Johnstone
Raith R. v. Clyde.
Stirling A. v. Dunferline A.

Alloa v. Brechin C.
Cowdenbeath v. Montrose
Falkirk v. Stenhousemuir
Forfar A. v. East Fife
Meadowbank T. v. Stranraer
Queen of South v. Albion R.
Queen's Park v. East Stirlingshire

Wednesday, August 15
Scottish League Cup
First Round, 1st leg
Aberdeen v. Arbroath
Dumbarton v. St. Johnstone
East Stirling v. Albion R.
Forfar A. v. Berwick R.
Kilmarnock v. Alloa
Stranraer v. Dunfermline A.

Saturday, August 18
Bolton W. v. Aston Villa
Brighton & H.A. v. Arsenal
Bristol C. v. Leeds U.
Everton v. Norwich C.
Ipswich T. v. Nottingham F.
Manchester C. v. Crystal Palace
Southampton v. Manchester U.
Stoke C. v. Coventry C.
Tottenham H. v. Middlesbrough
W.B.A. v. Derby County

Birmingham C. v. Fulham
Charlton A. v. Preston N.E.
Cheslea v. Sunderland
Leicester C. v. Watford
Luton T. v. Cambridge U.
Newcastle U. v. Oldham A.
Notts County v. Cardiff C.
Orient v. Burnley
Q.P.R. v. Bristol R.
Swansea C. v. Shrewsbury T.
Wrexham v. West Ham U.

Barnsley v. Sheffield W.
Blackburn R. v. Millwall
Blackpool v. Gillingham
Grimsby T. v. Exeter C.
Hull C. v. Colchester U.
Mansfield T. v. Chesterfield
Oxford U. v. Rotherham U.
Plymouth A. v. Bury
Reading v. Brentford
Sheffield U. v. Swindon T.
Southend U. v. Carlisle U.
Wimbledon v. Chester

Bradford C. v. Crewe A.
Darlington v. Wigan A.
Doncaster R. v. Northampton T.
Hartlepool U. v. Portsmouth
Hereford U. v. York C.
Huddersfield T. v. Aldershot
Lincoln C. v. Peterborough U.
Newport Co. v. Port Vale
Rochdale v. A.F.C. B'mouth
Torquay U. v. Scunthorpe U.
Tranmere R. v. Halifax T.
Walsall v. Stockport Co.

Aberdeen v. Hibernian
Dundee v. St. Mirren
Kilmarnock v. Dundee U.
Morton v. Partick T.
Rangers v. Celtic

Airdrieonians v. Raith R.
Clyde v. Clydebank
Dumbarton v. Hamilton A.
Dunfermline A. v. Berwick R.
Hearts v. Ayr U.
Motherwell v. Arbroath
St. Johnstone v. Stirling A.

Albion R. v. Queen's Park
Brechin C. v. Forfar A.
East Fife v. Cowdenbeath
E. Stirling v. Falkirk
Montrose v. Meadowbank T.
Stenhousemuir v. Alloa
Stranraer v. Queen of South

Monday, August 20
West Ham U. v. Chelsea

Brentford v. Oxford U.

Port Vale v. Hereford U.
Stockport Co. v. Rochdale

Tuesday, August 21
Arsenal v. Ipswich T.
Coventry C. v. Bristol C.
Crystal Palace v. Southampton
Liverpool v. Bolton W.
Middlesbrough v. Manchester C.

Bristol R. v. Luton T.
Burnley v. Charlton A.
Cambridge U. v. Leicester C.
Oldham A. v. Wrexham
Preston N.E. v. Newcastle U.
Shrewsbury T. v. Notts County
Watford v. Swansea C.

Bury v. Blackpool
Carlisle U. v. Blackburn R.
Chesterfield v. Barnsley
Colchester U. v. Sheffield U.
Gillingham v. Southend U.
Millwall v. Plymouth A.
Rotherham U. v. Mansfield T.
Sheffield W. v. Hull C.
Swindon T. v. Reading

A.F.C. B'mouth v. Walsall
Aldershot v. Newport Co.
Halifax T. v. Doncaster R.
Portsmouth v. Torquay U.
Scunthorpe U. v. Hartlepool U.
York C. v. Darlington

Wednesday, August 22
Aston Villa v. Brighton & H.A.
Derby County v. Wolves
Leeds U. v. Everton
Manchester U. v. W.B.A.
Norwich C. v. Tottenham H.
Nottingham F. v. Stoke C.

Cardiff C. v. Q.P.R.
Fulham v. Orient
Sunderland v. Birmingham C.

Chester v. Grimsby T.
Exeter C. v. Wimbledon

Crewe A. v. Lincoln C.
Northampton T. v. Bradford C.
Peterborough U. v. Tranmere R.
Wigan A. v. Huddersfield T.

Scottish League Cup
First Round, 2nd Leg
Arbroath v. Aberdeen
St. Johnstone v. Dumbarton
Albion R. v. East Stirling
Berwick R. v. Forfar A.
Alloa v. Kilmarnock
Dunfermline A. v. Stranraer

Friday, August 24
Crewe A. v. Torquay U.
Rochdale v. Hartlepool U.

Saturday, August 25
Arsenal v. Manchester U.
Aston Villa v. Bristol C.
Bolton W. v. Southampton
Derby County v. Everton
Liverpool v. W.B.A.
Manchester C. v. Brighton & H.A.
Middlesbrough v. Crystal Palace
Norwich C. v. Leeds U.
Nottingham F. v. Coventry C.
Stoke C. v. Tottenham H.
Wolves v. Ipswich T.

Bristol R. v. Shrewsbury T.
Burnley v. Notts County
Cambridge U. v. Watford
Cardiff C. v. Birmingham C.
Charlton A. v. Newcastle U.
Chelsea v. Wrexham
Luton T. v. Orient
Preston N.E. v. Swansea C.
Q.P.R. v. Leicester C.
Sunderland v. Fulham
West Ham U. v. Oldham A.

Barnsley v. Reading
Carlisle U. v. Bury
Chester v. Sheffield U.
Chesterfield v. Plymouth A.
Exeter C. v. Mansfield T.
Gillingham v. Millwall
Grimsby T. v. Blackpool
Hull C. v. Oxford U.
Rotherham U. v. Colchester U.
Sheffield W. v. Blackburn R.
Swindon T. v. Brentford
Wimbledon v. Southend U.

A.F.C. B'mouth v. Newport Co.
Aldershot v. Port Vale
Bradford C. v Tranmere R.
Hereford U. v. Darlington
Huddersfield T. v. Doncaster R.
Northampton T. v. Walsall
Peterborough U. v. Halifax T.
Portsmouth v. Scunthorpe U.

Stockport Co. v. Wigan
York C. v. Lincoln C.

Celtic v. Kilmarnock
Dundee U. v. Aberdeen
Hibernian v. Dundee
Partick T. v. Rangers
St. Mirren v. Morton

Arbroath v. St. Johnstone
Ayr U. v. Clyde
Berwick R. v. Hearts
Clydebank v. Dumbarton
Hamilton A. v. Airdrieonians
Raith R. v. Dunfermline A.
Stirling A. v. Motherwell

Alloa v. Montrose
Cowdenbeath v. East Stirling
Falkirk v. Stranraer
Forfar A. v. Albion R.
Meadowbank T. v. East Fife
Queen of South v. Stenhousemuir
Queen's Park v. Brechin C.

Wednesday, August 29
Scottish League Cup
Second Round, 1st Leg
Aberdeen or Arbroath v. Meadowbank T.
Airdrieonians v. Dundee U.
Ayr U. v. Hearts
Clyde v. Rangers
Clydebank v. Hamilton A.
Cowdenbeath v. Dundee
Dumbarton or St. Johnstone v. Stranraer or Dunfermline A.
Falkirk v. Celtic
Hibernian v. Montrose
Kilmarnock or Alloa v. Forfar or Berwick R.
Motherwell v. Queen's Park
Partick T. v. E. Stirling or Albion R.
Queen of South v. Morton
Raith R. v. East Fife
Stenhousemuir v. St. Mirren
Stirling A. v. Brechin C.

Friday, August 31
Colchester U. v. Swindon T.

Darlington v. Rochdale
Tranmere R. v. Stockport Co.

Saturday, September 1
Brighton & H.A. v. Bolton W.
Bristol C. v. Wolves
Coventry C. v. Norwich C.
Crystal Palace v. Derby County
Everton v. Aston Villa
Ipswich T. v. Stoke C.
Leeds U. v. Arsenal
Manchester U. v. Middlesbrough
Southampton v. Liverpool
Tottenham H. v. Manchester C.
W.B.A. v. Nottingham F.

Birmingham C. v. Bristol R.
Fulham v. Preston N.E.
Leicester C. v. Luton T.
Newcastle U. v. Chelsea
Notts County v. Q.P.R.
Oldham A. v. Sunderland
Orient v. Charlton A.
Shrewsbury T. v. Cambridge U.
Swansea C. v. Burnley
Watford v. West Ham U.
Wrexham v. Cardiff C.

Blackburn R. v. Grimsby T.
Blackpool v. Wimbledon
Brentford v. Chesterfield
Bury v. Chester
Mansfield T. v. Hull C.
Millwall v. Carlisle U.
Oxford U. v. Barnsley
Plymouth A. v. Sheffield W.
Reading v. Gillingham
Sheffield U. v. Exeter C.
Southend U. v. Rotherham U.

Doncaster R. v. Bradford C.
Halifax T. v. Crewe A.
Hartlepool U. v. Aldershot
Lincoln C. v. Huddersfield T.
Newport Co. v. York C.
Port Vale v. Peterborough U.
Scunthorpe U. v. A.F.C. B'mouth
Torquay U. v. Northampton T
Walsall v. Hereford U.
Wigan A. v. Portsmouth

Scottish League Cup
Second Round, 2nd Leg
Meadowbank T. v. Aberdeen or Arbroath
Dundee U. v. Airdrieonians
Hearts v. Ayr U.
Rangers v. Clyde
Hamilton A. v. Clydebank
Dundee v. Cowdenbeath
Stranraer or Dunfermline A. v. Dumbarton or St. Johnstone
Celtic v. Falkirk
Montrose v. Hibernian
Forfar A. or Berwick R. v. Kilmarnock or Alloa
Queen's Park v. Motherwell
E. Stirling or Albion R. v. Partick T.
Morton v. Queen of South.

East Fife v. Raith R.
St. Mirren v. Stenhousemuir
Brechin C. v. Stirling A.

Wednesday, September 5
Airdrieonians v. Ayr U.
Arbroath v. Hamilton A.
Berwick R. v. Raith R.
Clyde v. Dumbarton
Dunfermline A. v. Motherwell
Hearts v. St. Johnstone
Stirling A. v. Clydebank

Cowdenbeath v. Meadowbank T.
East Fife v. Albion R.
East Stirling v. Brechin C.
Forfar A. v. Queen of South
Montrose v. Falkirk
Queen's Park v. Alloa
Stranraer v. Stenhousemuir

Friday, September 7
Southend U. v. Blackpool

Crewe A. v. Port Vale
Doncaster R. v. Torquay U.

Saturday, September 8
Aston Villa v. Manchester U.
Bolton W. v. W.B.A.
Derby County v. Arsenal
Ipswich T. v. Bristol C.
Liverpool v. Coventry C.
Manchester C. v. Southampton
Middlesbrough v. Norwich C.
Nottingham F. v. Leeds U.
Stoke C. v. Everton
Tottenham H. v. Brighton & H.A.
Wolves v. Crystal Palace

Bristol R. v. Watford
Burnley v. Oldham A.
Cardiff C. v. Shrewsbury T.
Charlton A. v. Wrexham
Chelsea v. Birmingham C.
Leicester C. v. Notts County
Luton T. v. Swansea C.
Orient v. Newcastle U.
Preston N.E. v. West Ham U.
Q.P.R. v. Fulham
Sunderland v. Cambridge U.

Barnsley v. Mansfield T.
Carlisle U. v. Gillingham
Chester v. Millwall
Chesterfield v. Colchester U.
Exeter C. v. Bury
Grimsby T. v. Plymouth A.
Hull C. v. Sheffield U.
Oxford U. v. Reading
Rotherham U. v. Swindon T.
Sheffield W. v. Brentford
Wimbledon v. Blackburn R.

A.F.C. B'mouth v. Wigan A.
Aldershot v. Scunthorpe U.
Bradford C. v. Lincoln C.
Hartlepool U. v. Darlington
Hereford U. v. Tranmere R.
Huddersfield T. v. Newport Co.
Northampton T. v. Halifax T.
Portsmouth v. Stockport Co.
Rochdale v. Walsall
York C. v. Peterborough U.

Celtic v. Dundee U.
Dundee v. Partick T.
Kilmarnock v. Hibernian
Morton v. Aberdeen
Rangers v. St. Mirren

Airdrieonians v. Arbroath
Ayr U. v. Hamilton A.
Dunfermline A. v. Clyde
Dumbarton v. Stirling A.
Hearts v. Clydebank
Motherwell v. Berwick R.
St. Johnstone v. Raith R.

Albion R. v. Cowdenbeath
Alloa v. Falkirk
Brechin C. v. Meadowbank T.
East Fife v. Stranraer
East Stirling v. Queen of South
Montrose v. Queen's Park
Stenhousemuir v. Forfar A.

Tuesday, September 11
Ayr U. v. Dunfermline
Clydebank v. Airdrieonians
Dumbarton v. Berwick R.
Hamilton A. v. Motherwell
Raith R. v. Hearts
St. Johnstone v. Clyde
Stirling A. v. Arbroath

Albion R. v. Alloa
Brechin C. v. Stranraer
Falkirk v. East Fife
Forfar A. v. Queen's Park
Meadowbank T. v. East Stirling
Queen of South v. Montrose
Stenhousemuir v. Cowdenbeath

Friday, September 14
Stockport Co v. A.F.C. B'mouth

Tranmere R. v. Portsmouth

Saturday, September 15
Arsenal v. Middlesbrough
Brighton & H.A. v. Ipswich T.
Bristol C. v. Stoke C.
Coventry C. v. Bolton W.
Crystal Palace v. Aston Villa
Everton v. Wolves
Leeds U. v. Liverpool
Manchester U. v. Derby County
Norwich C. v. Nottingham F.
Southampton v. Tottenham H.
W.B.A. v. Manchester C.

Birmingham C. v. Charlton A.
Cambridge U. v. Bristol R.
Fulham v. Burnley
Newcastle U. v. Leicester C.
Notts County v. Luton T.
Oldham A. v. Preston N.E.
Shrewsbury T. v. Chelsea
Swansea C. v. Q.P.R.
Watford v. Cardiff C.
West Ham U. v. Sunderland
Wrexham v. Orient

Blackburn R. v. Southend U.
Blackpool v. Rotherham U.
Brentford v. Grimsby T.
Bury v. Hull C.
Colchester U. v. Sheffield W.
Gillingham v. Chester
Mansfield T. v. Oxford U.
Millwall v. Exeter C.
Plymouth A. v. Wimbledon
Reading v. Carlisle U.
Sheffield U. v. Barnsley
Swindon T. v. Chesterfield

Darlington v. Aldershot
Halifax T. v. Hereford U.
Lincoln C. v. Doncaster R.
Newport Co. v. Bradford C.
Peterborough U. v. Crewe A.
Port Vale v. Northampton T.
Scunthorpe U. v. Huddersfield T.
Torquay U. v. Rochdale
Walsall v. Hartlepool U.
Wigan A. v. York C.

Aberdeen v. Rangers
Dundee v. Morton
Hibernian v. Celtic
Partick T. v. Kilmarnock
St. Mirren v. Dundee U.

Airdrieonians v. Dumbarton
Arbroath v. Dunfermline A.
Berwick R. v. St. Johnstone
Clyde v. Hamilton A.
Clydebank v. Ayr U.
Hearts v. Stirling A.
Raith R. v. Motherwell

Cowdenbeath v. Brechin C.
Forfar A. v. East Stirling
Meadowbank T. v. Albion R.
Montrose v. Stenhousemuir
Queen of South v. Falkirk
Queen's Park v. East Fife
Stranraer v. Alloa

Monday, September 17
Brentford v. Exeter C.

Port Vale v. Bradford C.
Stockport Co. v. Darlington
Tranmere R. v. Doncaster R.

Tuesday, September 18
Bury v. Grimsby T.
Carlisle U. v. Rotherham U.
Chesterfield v. Hull C.
Colchester U. v. Mansfield T.
Gillingham v. Wimbledon
Millwall v. Sheffield W.
Plymouth A. v. Oxford U.
Sheffield U. v. Blackpool
Swindon T v. Chester

Halifax T. v. Rochdale
Newport Co. v. Northampton T.
Portsmouth v. A.F.C. B'mouth
Scunthorpe U. v. York C.
Walsall v. Lincoln C.

Wednesday, September 19
Blackburn R. v. Barnsley
Reading v. Southend U.

Crewe A. v. Huddersfield T.
Peterborough U. v. Aldershot
Torquay U. v. Hereford U.
Wigan A. v. Hartlepool U.

Arbroath v. Clydebank
Ayr U. v. Berwick R.
Dunfermline A. v. Dumbarton
Hamilton A. v. Raith R.
Motherwell v. Hearts
St. Johnstone v. Airdrieonians
Stirling A. v. Clyde

Alloa v. Meadowbank T.
Brechin C. v. Montrose

East Fife v. Stenhousemuir
East Stirling v. Albion R.
Falkirk v. Cowdenbeath
Queen's Park v. Queen of South
Stranraer v. Forfar A.

Friday, September 21
Southend U. v. Plymouth A.

Saturday, September 22
Aston Villa v. Arsenal
Bolton W. v. Leeds U.
Brighton & H.A. v. Southampton
Bristol C. v. Nottingham F
Derby County v. Middlesbrough
Ipswich T. v. Everton
Liverpool v. Norwich C.
Manchester C. v. Coventry C.
Stoke C. v. Crystal Palace
Tottenham H. v. W.B.A.
Wolves v. Manchester U.

Burnley v. Sunderland
Cardiff C. v. Cambridge U
Charlton A. v. Shrewsbury T.
Chelsea v. Watford
Leicester C. v. Fulham
Luton T. v. Oldham A.
Newcastle U. v. Wrexham
Notts County v. Swansea C.
Orient v. Birmingham C.
Preston N.E. v. Bristol R.
Q.P.R. v. West Ham U.

Barnsley v. Millwall
Blackpool v. Blackburn R.
Chester v. Reading
Exeter C. v. Carlisle U.
Grimsby T. v. Colchester U.
Hull C. v. Gillingham
Mansfield T. v. Sheffield U.
Oxford U. v. Bury
Rotherham U. v. Chesterfield
Sheffield W. v. Swindon T.
Wimbledon v. Brentford

A.F.C. B'mouth v. Halifax T.
Aldershot v. Crewe A.
Bradford C. v. Scunthorpe U.
Darlington v. Walsall
Doncaster R. v. Newport Co.
Hartlepool U. v. Torquay U.
Hereford U. v. Wigan A.
Huddersfield T. v. Port Vale
Lincoln C. v. Tranmere R.
Northampton T. v. Peterborough U.
Rochdale v. Portsmouth
York C. v. Stockport Co.

Aberdeen v. Celtic
Dundee U. v. Partick T.
Hibernian v. St. Mirren
Morton v. Kilmarnock
Rangers v. Dundee

Ayr U. v. St. Johnstone
Berwick R. v. Stirling A.
Clyde v. Motherwell
Dumbarton v. Arbroath
Hamilton A. v. Dunfermline A.
Hearts v. Airdrieonians
Raith R. v. Clydebank

Albion R. v. Stranraer
Alloa v. East Fife
Cowdenbeath v. Forfar A.
Falkirk v. Brechin C.
Meadowbank T. v. Queen of South
Montrose v. East Stirling
Stenhousemuir v. Queen's Park

Friday, September 28
Scunthorpe U. v. Doncaster R.
Stockport Co. v. Huddersfield T.
Tranmere R. v. A.F.C. B'mouth

Saturday, September 29
Arsenal v. Wolves
Coventry C. v. Tottenham H.
Crystal Palace v. Ipswich T.
Everton v. Bristol C.
Leeds U. v. Manchester C.
Manchester U. v. Stoke C.
Middlesbrough v. Aston Villa
Norwich C. v. Bolton W.
Nottingham F. v. Liverpool
Southampton v. Derby County
W.B.A. v. Brighton & H.A.

Birmingham C. v. Newcastle U.
Bristol R. v. Cardiff C.
Cambridge U. v. Chelsea
Fulham v. Luton T.
Oldham A. v. Q.P.R.
Shrewsbury T. v. Orient
Sunderland v. Preston N.E.
Swansea C. v. Leicester C.
Watford v. Charlton A.
West Ham U. v. Burnley
Wrexham v. Notts. County

Blackburn R. v. Rotherham U.
Brentford v. Southend U.
Bury v. Wimbledon
Carlisle U. v. Chester
Chesterfield v. Sheffield W.
Colchester U. v. Barnsley

Gillingham v. Exeter C.
Millwall v. Hull C.
Plymouth A. v. Blackpool
Reading v. Mansfield T.
Sheffield U. v. Oxford U.
Swindon T. v. Grimsby T.

Crewe A. v. Northampton T.
Halifax T. v. Hartlepool U.
Newport Co. v. Lincoln C.
Peterborough U. v. Hereford U.
Portsmouth v. York C.
Port Vale v. Rochdale
Torquay U. v. Darlington
Walsall v. Aldersho
Wigan A. v. Bradford C.

Celtic v. St. Mirren
Dundee v. Aberdeen
Kilmarnock v. Rangers
Morton v. Dundee U.
Partick T. v. Hibernian

Airdrieonians v. Dunfermline A.
Berwick R. v. Arbroath
Clydebank v. St. Johnstone
Hearts v. Clyde
Motherwell v. Dumbarton
Raith R. v. Ayr U.
Stirling A. v. Hamilton A.

Albion R. v. Stenhousemuir
Cowdenbeath v. Queen's Park
East Stirling v. Stranraer
Forfar A. v. Alloa
Meadowbank T. v. Falkirk
Montrose v. East Fife
Queen of South v. Brechin C.

Monday, October 1
Mansfield T. v. Colchester U.
Southend U. v. Reading

Tuesday, October 2
Barnsley v. Blackburn R.
Grimsby T. v. Bury
Hull C. v. Chesterfield
Rotherham U. v. Carlisle U
Sheffield W. v. Millwall
Wimbledon v. Gillingham

A.F.C. B'mouth v. Portsmouth
Aldershot v. Peterborough U.
Darlington v. Stockport Co.
Doncaster R. v. Tranmere R.
Hartlepool U. v. Wigan A.
Huddersfield T. v. Crewe A.
Northampton T. v. Newport Co.
Rochdale v. Halifax T.
York C. v. Scunthorpe U.

Wednesday, October 3
Blackpool v. Sheffield U.
Chester v. Swindon T.
Exeter C. v. Brentford
Oxford U. v. Plymouth A.

Bradford C. v. Port Vale
Hereford U. v. Torquay U.
Lincoln C. v. Walsall

Friday, October 5
Colchester U. v. Reading

Stockport Co. v. Hereford U.

Saturday, October 6
Arsenal v. Manchester C.
Aston Villa v. Southampton
Coventry C. v. Everton
Crystal Palace v. Tottenham H.
Derby County v. Bolton W.
Leeds U. v. Ipswich T.
Liverpool v. Bristol C.
Manchester U. v. Brighton & H.A.
Middlesbrough v. W.B.A.
Norwich C. v. Stoke C.
Nottingham F. v. Wolves

Bristol R. v. Notts County
Burnley v. Chelsea
Cambridge U. v. Swansea C.
Cardiff C. v. Luton T.
Fulham v. Wrexham
Oldham A. v. Orient
Preston N.E. v. Birmingham C.
Shrewsbury T. v. Leicester C.
Sunderland v. Charlton A.
Watford v. Q.P.R.
West Ham U. v. Newcastle U.

Brentford v. Barnsley
Bury v. Southend U.
Carlisle U. v. Wimbledon
Chester v. Plymouth A.
Chesterfield v. Oxford U.
Exeter C. v. Blackpool
Gillingham v. Blackburn R.
Millwall v. Grimsby T.
Rotherham U. v. Sheffield U.
Sheffield W. v. Mansfield T.
Swindon T. v. Hull C.

A.F.C. B'mouth v Hartlepool U.
Aldershot v. Bradford C.
Crewe A. v. Doncaster R.

Halifax T. v. Newport Co.
Northampton T. v. Tranmere R.
Peterborough U. v. Huddersfield T.
Portsmouth v. Darlington
Port Vale v. Lincoln C.
Scunthorpe U. v. Walsall
Wigan A. v. Torquay U.
York C. v. Rochdale

Dundee U. v. Rangers
Hibernian v. Morton
Kilmarnock v. Dundee
Partick T. v. Celtic
St. Mirren v. Aberdeen

Arbroath v. Raith R.
Ayr U. v. Stirling A.
Clyde v. Airdrieonians
Dumbarton v. Hearts
Dunfermline A. v. Clydebank
Hamilton A. v. Berwick R.
St. Johnstone v. Motherwell

Alloa v. Cowdenbeath
Brechin C. v. Albion R.
East Fife v. Queen of South
Falkirk v. Forfar A.
Queen's Park v. Meadowbank T.
Stenhousemuir v. East Stirling
Stranraer v. Montrose

Monday, October 8
Wrexham v. Oldham A.

Mansfield T. v. Rotherham U.
Southend U. v. Gillingham

Tranmere R. v. Peterborough U.

Tuesday, October 9
Bolton W. v. Liverpool
Brighton & H.A. v. Aston Villa
Bristol C. v. Coventry C.
Everton v. Leeds U.
Ipswich T. v. Arsenal
Southampton v. Crystal Palace
Wolves v. Derby County

Birmingham C. v. Sunderland
Charlton A. v. Burnley
Luton T. v. Bristol R.
Notts. County v. Shrewsbury T.
Orient v. Fulham
Q.P.R. v. Cardiff C.
Swansea C. v. Watford

Barnsley v. Chesterfield
Grimsby T. v. Chester
Hull C. v. Sheffield W.
Plymouth A. v. Millwall

Sheffield U. v. Colchester U.
Wimbledon v. Exeter C.

Darlington v. York C.
Doncaster R. v. Halifax T.
Hartlepool U. v. Scunthorpe U.
Huddersfield T. v. Wigan A.
Newport Co. v. Aldershot
Rochdale v. Stockport Co.
Walsall v. A.F.C. B'mouth

Wednesday, October 10
Manchester C. v. Middlesbrough
Stoke C. v. Nottingham F.
Tottenham H. v. Norwich C.
W.B.A. v. Manchester U.

Chelsea v. West Ham U.
Leicester C. v. Cambridge U.
Newcastle U. v. Preston N.E.

Blackburn R. v. Carlisle U.
Blackpool v. Bury
Oxford U. v. Brentford
Reading v. Swindon T.

Bradford C. v. Northampton T.
Hereford v. Port Vale
Lincoln C. v. Crewe A.
Torquay U. v. Portsmouth

Friday, October 12
Southend U. v. Colchester U.

Rochdale v. Peterborough U.
York C. v. A.F.C. B'mouth

Saturday, October 13
Aston Villa v. W.B.A.
Bolton W. v. Arsenal
Brighton & H.A. v. Leeds U.
Bristol C. v. Manchester U.
Everton v. Crystal Palace
Ipswich T. v. Liverpool
Manchester C. v. Nottingham F.
Southampton v. Coventry C.
Stoke C. v. Middlesbrough
Tottenham H. v. Derby County
Wolves v. Norwich C.

Burnley v. Cardiff C.
Charlton A. v. Cambridge U.
Chelsea v. Bristol R.
Leicester C. v. West Ham U.
Luton T. v. Sunderland
Newcastle U. v. Shrewsbury T.
Notts County v. Oldham A.
Orient v. Watford
Q.P.R. v. Preston N.E.
Swansea C. v. Fulham

Wrexham v. Birmingham C.

Barnsley v. Gillingham
Blackburn R. v. Plymouth A.
Blackpool v. Brentford
Exeter C. v. Chester
Grimsby T. v. Chesterfield
Hull C. v. Carlisle U.
Mansfield T. v. Bury
Oxford U. v. Millwall
Rotherham U. v. Sheffield W.
Sheffield U. v. Reading
Wimbledon v. Swindon T.

Aldershot v. Northampton T.
Bradford C. v. Stockport Co.
Darlington v. Halifax T.
Doncaster R. v. Wigan A.
Hartlepool U. v. Port Vale
Hereford U. v. Crewe A.
Huddersfield T. v. Portsmouth
Lincoln C. v. Scunthorpe U.
Newport Co. v. Tranmere R.
Walsall v. Torquay U.

Aberdeen v. Kilmarnock
Celtic v. Dundee
Dundee U. v. Hibernian
Rangers v. Morton
St. Mirren v. Partick T.

Arbroath v. Clyde
Berwick R. v. Clydebank
Dumbarton v. Raith R.
Dunfermline A. v. St. Johnstone
Hamilton A. v. Hearts
Motherwell v. Ayr U.
Stirling A. v. Airdrieonians

Albion R. v. Falkirk
Cowdenbeath v. Queen of South
East Fife v. Brechin C.
East Stirling v. Alloa
Forfar A. v. Montrose
Queen's Park v. Stranraer
Stenhousemuir v. Meadowbank T.

Friday, October 19
Colchester U. v. Blackpool

Tranmere R. v. York C.
Stockport Co. v. Doncaster R.

Saturday, October 20
Arsenal v. Stoke C.
Coventry C. v. Brighton & H.A.
Crystal Palace v. Bristol C.
Derby County v. Aston Villa
Leeds U. v. Tottenham H.
Liverpool v. Everton
Manchester U. v. Ipswich T.
Middlesbrough v. Wolves
Norwich C. v. Manchester C.
Nottingham F. v. Bolton W.
W.B.A. v. Southampton

Birmingham C. v. Swansea C.
Bristol R. v. Charlton A.
Cambridge U. v. Orient
Cardiff C. v. Chelsea
Fulham v. Notts. County
Oldham A. v. Leicester C.
Preston N.E. v. Burnley
Shrewsbury T. v. Wrexham
Sunderland v. Q.P.R.
Watford v. Newcastle U.
West Ham U. v. Luton T.

Brentford v. Blackburn R.
Bury v. Sheffield U.
Carlisle U. v. Barnsley
Chester v. Hull C.
Chesterfield v. Wimbledon
Gillingham v. Grimsby T.
Millwall v. Mansfield T.
Plymouth A. v. Rotherham U.
Reading v. Exeter C.
Sheffield W. v. Oxford U.
Swindon T. v. Southend U.

A.F.C. B'mouth v. Huddersfield
Crewe A. v. Rochdale
Halifax T. v. Walsall
Northampton T. v. Hereford U.
Peterborough U. v. Hartlepool U.
Portsmouth v. Bradford C.
Port Vale v. Darlington
Scunthorpe U. v. Newport Co.
Torquay U. v. Aldershot
Wigan A. v. Lincoln C.

Aberdeen v. Partick T.
Dundee v. Dundee U.
Kilmarnock v. St. Mirren
Morton v. Celtic
Rangers v. Hibernian

Airdrieonians v. Motherwell
Ayr U. v. Arbroath
Clyde v. Berwick R.
Clydebank v. Hamilton A.
Hearts v. Dunfermline A.
Raith R. v. Stirling A.
St. Johnstone v. Dumbarton

Brechin C. v. Stenhousemuir
East Stirling v. East Fife
Falkirk v. Queen's Park
Meadowbank T. v. Forfar A.
Montrose v. Albion R.

Queen of South v. Alloa
Stranraer v. Cowdenbeath

Monday, October 22
Brentford v. Sheffield U.

Port Vale v. Tranmere R.
Stockport Co. v. Hartlepool U.

Tuesday, October 23
Bury v. Barnsley
Carlisle U. v. Mansfield T.
Chesterfield v. Blackpool
Colchester U. v. Wimbledon
Gillingham v. Oxford U.
Millwall v. Reading
Rotherham U. v. Hull C.
Sheffield W. v. Grimsby T.
Swindon T. v. Plymouth A.

A.F.C. B'mouth v. Hereford U.
Aldershot v. Lincoln C.
Halifax T. v. Bradford C.
Northampton T. v. Huddersfield T.
Portsmouth v. Newport Co.
Scunthorpe U. v. Darlington
York C. v. Doncaster R.

Wednesday, October 24
Chester v. Blackburn R.
Exeter C. v. Southend U.
Crewe A. v. Walsall
Peterborough U. v. Torquay U.
Wigan A. v. Rochdale

Friday, October 26
Southend U. v. Chesterfield

Doncaster R. v. Portsmouth
Rochdale v. Northampton T.
Tranmere R. v. Scunthorpe U.

Saturday, October 27
Bolton W. v. Crystal Palace
Brighton & H.A. v. Norwich C.
Bristol C. v. Arsenal
Everton v. Manchester U.
Ipswich T. v. Middlesbrough
Manchester C. v. Liverpool
Southampton v. Leeds U.
Stoke C. v. Derby County
Tottenham H. v. Nottingham F.
W.B.A. v. Coventry C.
Wolves v. Aston Villa

Birmingham C. v. Shrewsbury T.
Charlton A. v. Cardiff C.
Chelsea v. Fulham
Leicester C. v. Sunderland
Luton T. v. Preston N.E.
Newcastle U. v. Cambridge U.
Notts County v. West Ham U.
Orient v. Bristol R.
Q.P.R. v. Burnley
Swansea C. v. Oldham A.
Wrexham v. Watford

Barnsley v. Chester
Blackburn R. v. Colchester U.
Blackpool v. Swindon T.
Grimsby T. v. Rotherham U.
Hull C. v. Exeter C.
Mansfield T. v. Gillingham
Oxford U. v. Carlisle U.
Plymouth A. v. Brentford
Reading v. Bury
Sheffield U. v. Millwall
Wimbledon v. Sheffield W.

Bradford C. v. A.F.C. B'mouth
Darlington v. Peterborough U.
Hartlepool U. v. Crewe A.
Hereford U. v. Aldershot
Huddersfield T. v. York C.
Lincoln C. v. Stockport Co.
Newport Co. v. Wigan A.
Torquay U. v. Halifax T.
Walsall v. Port Vale

Celtic v. Rangers
Dundee U. v. Kilmarnock
Hibernian v. Aberdeen
Partick T. v. Morton
St. Mirren v. Dundee

Arbroath v. Motherwell
Ayr U. v. Hearts
Berwick R. v. Dunfermline A.
Clydebank v. Clyde
Hamilton A. v. Dumbarton
Raith R. v. Airdrieonians
Stirling A. v. St. Johnstone

Alloa v. Stenhousemuir
Cowdenbeath v. East Fife
Falkirk v. East Stirling
Forfar A. v. Brechin C.
Meadowbank T. v. Montrose
Queen of South v. Stranraer
Queen's Park v. Albion R.

Friday, November 2
Colchester U. v. Hull C.

Stockport Co. v. Walsall

Saturday, November 3
Arsenal v. Brighton & H.A.
Aston Villa v. Bolton W.
Coventry C. v. Stoke C.

Crystal Palace v. Manchester C.
Derby County v. W.B.A.
Leeds U. v. Bristol C.
Liverpool v. Wolves
Manchester U. v. Southampton
Middlesbrough v. Tottenham H.
Norwich C. v. Everton
Nottingham F. v. Ipswich T.

Bristol R. v. Q.P.R.
Burnley v. Orient
Cambridge U. v. Luton T.
Cardiff C. v. Notts. County
Fulham v. Birmingham C.
Oldham A. v. Newcastle U.
Preston N.E. v. Charlton A.
Shrewsbury T. v. Swansea C.
Sunderland v. Chelsea
Watford v. Leicester C.
West Ham U. v. Wrexham

Brentford v. Reading
Bury v. Plymouth A.
Carlisle U. v. Southend U.
Chester v. Wimbledon
Chesterfield v. Mansfield T.
Exeter C. V. Grimsby T.
Gillingham v. Blackpool
Millwall v. Blackburn R.
Rotherham U. v. Oxford U.
Sheffield W. v. Barnsley
Swindon T. v. Sheffield U.

A.F.C. B'mouth v. Rochdale
Aldershot v. Huddersfield T.
Crewe A. v. Bradford C.
Halifax T. v. Tranmere R.
Northampton T. v. Doncaster R.
Peterborough U. v. Lincoln C.
Portsmouth v. Hartlepool U.
Port Vale v. Newport Co.
Scunthorpe U. v. Torquay U.
Wigan A. v. Darlington
York C. v. Hereford U.

Aberdeen v. Dundee U
Dundee v. Hibernian
Kilmarnock v. Celtic
Morton v. St. Mirren
Rangers v. Partick T.

Airdrieonians v. Hamilton A.
Clyde v. Ayr U.
Dumbarton v. Clydebank
Dunfermline A. v. Raith R.
Hearts v. Berwick R.
Motherwell v. Stirling A.
St. Johnstone v. Arbroath

Albion R. v. Forfar A.
Brechin C. v. Queen's Park
East Fife v. Meadowbank T.
East Stirling v. Cowdenbeath
Montrose v. Alloa
Stenhousemuir v. Queen of South
Stranraer v. Falkirk

Monday, November 5
Mansfield T. v. Carlisle U.
Southend U. v. Exeter C.

Tranmere R. v. Port Vale

Tuesday, November 6
Barnsley v. Bury
Grimsby T. v. Sheffield W.
Hull C. v. Rotherham U.
Plymouth A. v. Swindon T.
Sheffield U. v. Brentford
Wimbledon v. Colchester U.

Darlington v. Scunthorpe U.
Doncaster R v. York C.
Hartlepool U. v. Stockport Co.
Huddersfield T. v. Northampton T.
Newport Co. v. Portsmouth
Rochdale v. Wigan A.
Walsall v. Crewe A.

Wednesday, November 7
Blackburn R. v. Chester
Blackpool v. Chesterfield
Oxford U. v. Gillingham
Reading v. Millwall

Bradford C. v. Halifax T.
Hereford U. v. A.F.C. B'mouth
Lincoln C. v. Aldershot
Torquay U. v. Peterborough U.

Friday, November 9
Charlton A. v. Oldham A.

Doncaster R. v. Peterborough U.
Rochdale v. Aldershot
Tranmere R. v. Wigan A.

Saturday, November 10
Brighton & H.A. v. Liverpool
Bristol C. v. Derby County
Coventry C. v. Leeds U.
Crystal Palace v. Arsenal
Everton v. Middlesbrough
Ipswich T. v. Aston Villa
Manchester C. v. Manchester U.
Southampton v. Nottingham F.
Stoke C. v. Wolves
Tottenham H. v. Bolton W.
W.B.A. v. Norwich C.

Birmingham C. v. Cambridge U.
Fulham v. West Ham U.
Leicester C. v. Burnley

Luton T. v. Q.P.R.
Newcastle U. v. Cardiff C.
Notts County v. Preston N.E.
Orient v. Chelsea
Shrewsbury T. v. Watford
Swansea C. v. Sunderland
Wrexham v. Bristol R.

Barnsley v. Exeter C.
Blackburn R. v. Chesterfield
Blackpool v. Sheffield W.
Brentford v. Colchester U.
Bury v. Millwall
Mansfield T. v. Swindon T.
Oxford U. v. Chester
Plymouth A. v. Carlisle U.
Reading v. Hull C.
Sheffield U. v. Gillingham
Southend U. v. Grimsby T.
Wimbledon v. Rotherham U.

Bradford C. v. Huddersfield T.
Darlington v. Northampton T.
Halifax T. v. Port Vale
Hartlepool U. v. Hereford U.
Lincoln C. v. A.F.C. B'mouth
Newport Co. v. Crewe A.
Scunthorpe U. v. Stockport Co.
Torquay U. v. York C.
Walsall v. Portsmouth

Aberdeen v. Morton
Dundee U. v. Celtic
Hibernian v. Kilmarnock
Partick T. v. Dundee
St. Mirren v. Rangers

Arbroath v. Airdrieonians
Berwick R. v. Motherwell
Clyde v. Dunfermline A.
Clydebank v. Hearts
Hamilton A. v. Ayr U.
Raith R. v. St. Johnstone
Stirling A. v. Dumbarton

Cowdenbeath v. Albion R.
Falkirk v. Alloa
Forfar A. v. Stenhousemuir
Meadowbank T. v. Brechin C.
Queen of South v. East Stirling
Queen's Park v. Montrose
Stranraer v. East Fife

Friday, November 16
Colchester U. v. Plymouth A.
Stockport Co. v. Newport Co.

Saturday, November 17
Arsenal v. Everton
Aston Villa v. Stoke C.
Bolton W. v. Manchester C.
Derby County v. Ipswich T.
Leeds U. v. W.B.A.
Liverpool v. Tottenham H.
Manchester U. v. Crystal Palace
Middlesbrough v. Bristol C.
Norwich C. v. Southampton
Nottingham F. v. Brighton & H.A.
Wolves v. Coventry C.

Bristol R. v. Newcastle U.
Burnley v. Luton T.
Cambridge U. v. Wrexham
Cardiff C. v. Orient
Chelsea v. Charlton A.
Oldham A. v. Fulham
Preston N.E. v. Leicester C.
Q.P.R. v. Shrewsbury T.
Sunderland v. Notts County.
Watford v. Birmingham C.
West Ham U. v. Swansea C.

Carlisle U. v. Sheffield U.
Chester v. Mansfield T.
Chesterfield v. Reading
Exeter C. v. Oxford U.
Gillingham v. Bury
Grimsby T. v. Wimbledon
Hull C. v. Barnsley
Millwall v. Blackpool
Rotherham U. v. Brentford
Sheffield W. v. Southend U.
Swindon T. v. Blackburn R.

A.F.C. B'mouth v. Doncaster R.
Aldershot v. Halifax T.
Crewe A. v. Darlington
Hereford U. v. Rochdale
Huddersfield T. v. Tranmere R
Northampton T. v. Hartlepool U.
Peterborough U. v. Walsall
Portsmouth v. Lincoln C.
Port Vale v. Torquay U.
Wigan A. v. Scunthorpe U.
York C. v. Bradford C.

Celtic v. Hibernian
Dundee U. v. St. Mirren
Kilmarnock v. Partick T.
Morton v. Dundee
Rangers v. Aberdeen

Airdrieonians v. Dumbarton
Ayr U. v. Clydebank
Dunfermline A. v. Arbroath
Hamilton A. v. Clyde
Hearts v. Stirling A.
Motherwell v. Raith R.
St. Johnstone v. Berwick R.

Albion R. v. Meadowbank T.
Alloa v. Stranraer
Brechin C. v. Cowdenbeath
East Fife v. Queen's Park
East Stirling v. Forfar A.
Falkirk v. Queen of South
Montrose v. Stenhousemuir

Saturday, November 24
Arsenal v. Liverpool
Aston Villa v. Leeds U.
Bristol C. v. Manchester C.
Crystal Palace v. Coventry C.
Derby County v. Nottingham F.
Everton v. Tottenham H.
Ipswich T. v. Southampton
Manchester U. v. Norwich C.
Middlesbrough v. Brighton & H.A.
Stoke C. v. Bolton W.
Wolves v. W.B.A.

Burnley v. Cambridge U.
Fulham v. Watford
Leicester C. v. Wrexham
Luton T. v. Birmingham C.
Notts County v. Chelsea
Oldham A. v. Shrewsbury T.
Preston N.E. v. Orient
Q.P.R. v. Charlton A.
Sunderland v. Bristol R.
Swansea C. v. Newcastle U.
West Ham U. v. Cardiff C.

Celtic v. Aberdeen
Dundee v. Rangers
Kilmarnock v. Morton
Partick T. v. Dundee U.
St. Mirren v. Hibernian

Airdrieonians v. St. Johnstone
Berwick R. v. Ayr U.
Clydebank v. Arbroath
Dumbarton v. Dunferline A.
Hearts v. Motherwell
Raith R. v. Hamilton A.
Stirling A. v. Clyde

Cowdenbeath v. Falkirk
East Stirling v. Albion R.
Forfar A. v. Stranraer
Meadowbank T. v. Alloa
Montrose v. Brechin C.
Queen of South v. Queen's Park
Stenhousemuir v. East Fife

Friday, November 30
Lincoln C. v. Hartlepool U.
Scunthorpe U. v. Rochdale
Stockport Co. v. Crewe A.
Tranmere R. v. Torquay U.

Saturday, December 1
Bolton W. v. Bristol C.
Brighton & H.A. v. Derby C.
Coventry C. v. Ipswich T.
Leeds U. v. Crystal Palace
Liverpool v. Middlesbrough
Manchester C. v. Wolves
Norwich C. v. Aston Villa
Nottingham F. v. Arsenal
Southampton v. Stoke C.
Tottenham H. v. Manchester U.
W.B.A. v. Everton

Birmingham C. v. Leicester C.
Bristol R. v. Burnley
Cambridge U. v. Q.P.R.
Cardiff C. v. Oldham A.
Charlton A. v. West Ham U.
Chelsea v. Preston N.E.
Newcastle U. v. Fulham
Orient v. Sunderland
Shrewsbury T. v. Luton T.
Watford v. Notts County
Wrexham v. Swansea C.

Barnsley v. Southend U.
Bury v. Chesterfield
Carlisle U. v. Brentford
Chester v. Sheffield W.
Exeter C. v. Rotherham U.
Gillingham v. Swindon T.
Hull C. v. Wimbledon
Mansfield T. v. Blackpool
Millwall v. Colchester U.
Oxford U. v. Grimsby T.
Reading v. Blackburn R.
Sheffield U. v. Plymouth A.

A.F.C. B'mouth v. Peterborough U
Bradford C. v. Walsall
Doncaster R. v. Aldershot
Huddersfield T. v. Hereford U.
Newport Co. v. Darlington
Portsmouth v. Halifax T.
Wigan A. v. Northampton T.
York C. v. Port Vale

Aberdeen v. Dundee
Dundee U. v. Morton
Hibernian v. Partick T.
Rangers v. Kilmarnock
St. Mirren v. Celtic

Ayr U. v. Raith R.
Arbroath v. Berwick R.
Clyde v. Hears
Dumbarton v. Motherwell
Dunfermline A. v. Airdrieonians
Hamilton A. v. Stirling A.
St. Johnston v. Clydebank

Alloa v. Forfar A.
Brechin C. v. Queen of South
East Fife v. Montrose
Falkirk v. Meadowbank T.
Queen's Park v. Cowdenbeath
Stenhousemuir v. Albion R.
Stranraer v. East Stirling

Friday, December 7
Colchester U. v. Carlisle U.
Southend U. v. Chester

Port Vale v. Stockport Co.
Rochdale v. Doncaster R.

Saturday, December 8
Arsenal v. Coventry C.
Aston Villa v. Liverpool
Bristol C. v. Tottenham H.
Crystal Palace v. Nottingham F.
Derby County v. Norwich C.
Everton v. Brighton & H.A.
Ipswich T. v. Manchester C.
Manchester U. v. Leeds U.
Middlesbrough v. Southampton
Stoke C. v. W.B.A.
Wolves v. Bolton W.

Burnley v. Watford
Fulham v. Shrewsbury T.
Leicester C. v. Orient
Luton T. v. Newcastle U.
Notts County v. Birmingham C.
Oldham A. v. Chelsea
Preston N.E. v. Cambridge U.
Q.P.R. v. Wrexham
Sunderland v. Cardiff C.
Swansea C. v. Charlton A.
West Ham U. v. Bristol R.

Blackburn R. v. Oxford U
Blackpool v. Reading
Brentford v. Hull C.
Chesterfield v. Millwall
Grimsby T. v. Mansfield T.
Plymouth A. v. Barnsley
Rotherham U. v. Gillingham
Sheffield W. v. Exeter C.
Swindon T. v. Bury
Wimbledon v. Sheffield U.

Aldershot v. York C.
Crewe A. v. A.F.C. B'mouth
Darlington v. Tranmere R.
Halifax T. v. Lincoln C.
Hartlepool U. v. Newport Co.
Hereford U. v. Bradford C.
Northampton T. v. Scunthorpe U.
Peterborough U. v. Portsmouth
Torquay U. v. Huddersfield T.

Walsall v. Wigan A.

Dundee v. Celtic
Hibernian v. Dundee U.
Kilmarnock v. Aberdeen
Morton v. Rangers
Partick T. v. St. Mirren

Airdrieonians v. Clyde
Berwick R. v. Hamilton A.
Clydebank v. Dunfermline A.
Hearts v. Dumbarton
Motherwell v. St. Johnstone
Raith R. v. Arbroath
Stirling A. v. Ayr U.

Albion R. v. Brechin C.
Cowdenbeath v. Alloa
East Stirling v. Stenhousemuir
Forfar A. v. Falkirk
Meadowbank T. v. Queen's Park
Montrose v. Stranraer
Queen of South v. East Fife

Tuesday, December 11
Wolves v. Liverpool

Saturday, December 15
Bolton W. v. Ipswich T.
Brighton & H.A. v. Stoke C.
Coventry C. v. Manchester U.
Leeds U. v. Wolves
Liverpool v. Crystal Palace
Manchester C. v. Derby County
Norwich C. v. Bristol C.
Nottingham F. v. Middlesbrough
Southampton v. Everton
Tottenham H. v. Aston Villa
W.B.A. v. Arsenal

Birmingham C. v. Burnley
Bristol R. v. Oldham A.
Cambridge U. v. Fulham
Cardiff C. v. Preston N.E.
Charlton A. v. Leicester C.
Chelsea v. Swansea C.
Newcastle U. v. Q.P.R.
Orient v. Notts County
Shrewsbury T. v. West Ham U.
Watford v. Sunderland
Wrexham v. Luton T.

Aberdeen v. St. Mirren
Celtic v. Partick T.
Dundee v. Kilmarnock
Morton v. Hibernian
Rangers v. Dundee U.

Airdrieonians v. Stirling A.
Ayr U. v. Motherwell

Clyde v. Arbroath
Clydebank v. Berwick R.
Hearts v. Hamilton
Raith R. v. Dumbarton
St. Johnstone v. Dunfermline A.

Scottish Cup 1st Round

Tuesday, December 18
Q.P.R. v. Chelsea

Friday, December 21
Arsenal v. Norwich C.
Aston Villa v. Coventry C.
Bristol C. v. Southampton
Crystal Palace v. W.B.A.
Ipswich T. v. Tottenham H.
Middlesbrough v. Bolton W.
Stoke C. v. Leeds U.
Wolves v. Brighton & H.A.

Burnley v. Wrexham
Fulham v. Bristol R.
Leicester C. v. Cardiff C.
Luton T. v. Charlton A.
Notts County v. Newcastle U.
Oldham A. v. Birmingham C.
Preston N.E. v. Watford
Sunderland v. Shrewsbury T.
Swansea C. v. Orient
West Ham U. v. Cambridge U.

Barnsley v. Blackpool
Bury v. Brentford
Carlisle U. v. Grimsby T.
Chester v. Rotherham U.
Exeter C. v. Colchester U.
Gillingham v. Chesterfield
Hull C. v. Blackburn R.
Mansfield T. v. Plymouth A.
Millwall v. Swindon T.
Oxford U. v. Wimbledon
Reading v. Sheffield W.
Sheffield U. v. Southend U.

A.F.C. B'mouth v. Northampton T.
Bradford C. v. Hartlepool U.
Doncaster R. v. Darlington
Huddersfield T. v. Rochdale
Lincoln C. v. Hereford U.
Newport Co. v. Peterborough U.
Portsmouth v. Port Vale
Scunthorpe U. v. Halifax T.
Stockport Co. v. Torquay U.
Tranmere R. v. Aldershot
Wigan A. v. Crewe A.
York C. v. Walsall

Saturday, December 22
Derby County v. Liverpool
Everton v. Manchester C.
Manchester U. v. Nottingham F.

Celtic v. Morton
Dundee U. v. Dundee
Hibernian v. Rangers
Partick T. v. Aberdeen
St. Mirren v. Kilmarnock

Arbroath v. Ayr U.
Berwick R. v. Clyde
Dumbarton v. St. Johnstone
Dunfermline A. v. Hearts
Hamilton A. v. Clydebank
Motherwell v. Airdrieonians
Stirling A. v. Raith R.

Alloa v. East Stirling
Brechin C. v. East Fife
Falkirk v. Albion R.
Meadowbank T. v. Stenhousemuir
Montrose v. Forfar A.
Queen of South v. Cowdenbeath
Stranraer v. Queen's Park

Wednesday, December 26
Arsenal v. Tottenham H.
Bolton W. v. Everton
Brighton & H.A. v. Crystal P.
Derby County v. Coventry C.
Liverpool v. Manchester U.
Manchester C. v. Stoke C.
Middlesbrough v. Leeds U.
Norwich C. v. Ipswich T.
Nottingham F. v. Aston Villa
W.B.A. v. Bristol C.
Wolves v. Southampton

Bristol R. v. Swansea C.
Burnley v. Newcastle U.
Cambridge U. v. Oldham A.
Cardiff C. v. Fulham
Charlton A. v. Notts County
Chelsea v. Leicester C.
Preston N.E. v. Shrewsbury T.
Q.P.R. v. Orient
Sunderland v. Wrexham
Watford v. Luton T.
West Ham U. v. Birmingham C.

Blackburn R. v. Mansfield T.
Blackpool v. Hull C.
Brentford v. Chester
Chesterfield v. Carlisle U.
Colchester U. v. Gillingham
Grimsby T. v. Barnsley
Plymouth A. v. Reading
Rotherham U. v. Bury
Sheffield W. v. Sheffield U.

Southend U. v. Oxford U
Swindon T. v. Exeter C.
Wimbledon v. Millwall

Aldershot v. A.F.C. B'mouth
Crewe A. v. Tranmere R.
Darlington v. Bradford C.
Halifax T. v. Huddersfield T.
Hartlepool U. v. York C.
Hereford U. v. Portsmouth
Northampton T. v. Stockport Co.
Peterborough U. v. Wigan A.
Port Vale v. Scunthorpe U.
Rochdale v. Lincoln C.
Torquay U. v. Newport Co.
Walsall v. Doncaster R.

Friday, December 28
Tranmere R. v. Bradford C.

Saturday, December 29
Brighton & H.A. v. Man. C.
Bristol C. v. Aston Villa
Coventry C. v. Nottingham F.
Crystal Palace v. Middlesbrough
Everton v. Derby County
Ipswich T. v. Wolves
Leeds U. v. Norwich C.
Manchester U. v. Arsenal
Southampton v. Bolton W.
Tottenham H. v. Stoke C.
W.B.A. v. Liverpool

Birmingham C. v. Cardiff C.
Fulham v. Sunderland
Leicester C. v. Q.P.R.
Newcastle U. v. Charlton A.
Notts County v. Burnley
Oldham A. v. West Ham U.
Orient v. Luton T.
Shrewsbury T. v. Bristol R.
Swansea C. v. Preston N.E.
Watford v. Cambridge U.
Wrexham v. Chelsea

Brentford v. Swindon T.
Bury v. Blackburn R.
Carlisle U. v. Sheffield W.
Chester v. Blackpool
Colchester U. v. Rotherham U.
Mansfield T. v. Exeter C.
Millwall v. Gillingham
Oxford U. v. Hull C.
Plymouth A. v. Chesterfield
Reading v. Barnsley
Sheffield U. v. Grimsby T.
Southend U. v. Wimbledon

A.F.C. B'mouth v. Darlington
Doncaster R. v. Huddersfield T.
Halifax T. v. Peterborough U.

Hartlepool U. v. Rochdale
Lincoln C. v. York C.
Newport Co. v. Walsall
Portsmouth v. Northampton T.
Port Vale v. Aldershot
Scunthorpe U. v. Hereford U.
Torquay U. v. Crewe A.
Wigan A. v. Stockport Co.

Aberdeen v. Hibernian
Dundee v. St. Mirren
Kilmarnock v. Dundee U.
Morton v. Partick T.
Rangers v. Celtic

Airdrieonians v. Raith R.
Clyde v. Clydebank
Dumbarton v. Hamilton A.
Dunfermline A. v. Berwick R.
Hearts v. Ayr U.
Motherwell v. Arbroath
St. Johnstone v. Stirling A.

Albion R. v. Montrose
Alloa v. Queen of South
Cowdenbeath v. Stranraer
East Fife v. East Stirling
Forfar A. v. Meadowbank T.
Queen's Park v. Falkirk
Stenhousemuir v. Brechin C.

Tuesday, January 1
Aston Villa v. Manchester C.
Bristol C. v. Brighton & H.A.
Coventry C. v. Middlesbrough
Crystal Palace v. Norwich C.
Everton v. Nottingham F.
Ipswich T. v. W.B.A.
Leeds U. v. Derby County
Manchester U. v. Bolton W.
Southampton v. Arsenal
Stoke C. v. Liverpool
Tottenham H. v. Wolves

Birmingham C. v. Q.P.R.
Fulham v. Charlton A.
Leicester C. v. Bristol R.
Luton T. v. Chelsea
Newcastle U. v. Sunderland
Notts County v. Cambridge U.
Oldham A. v. Watford
Orient v. West Ham U.
Shrewsbury T. v. Burnley
Swansea C. v. Cardiff C.
Wrexham v. Preston N.E.

Barnsley v. Rotherham U.
Bury v. Colchester U.
Carlisle U. v. Blackpool
Chester v. Chesterfield

Exeter C.v. Plymouth A.
Gillingham v. Sheffield W.
Hull C. v. Grimsby T.
Mansfield T. v. Brentford
Millwall v. Southend U.
Oxford U. v. Swindon T.
Reading v. Wimbledon
Sheffield U. v. Blackburn R.

A.F.C. B'mouth v. Torquay U.
Bradford C. v. Rochdale
Doncaster R. v. Hartlepool U.
Huddersfield T. v. Darlington
Lincoln C. v. Northampton T.
Newport Co. v. Hereford U.
Portsmouth v. Aldershot
Scunthorpe U. v. Crewe A.
Stockport Co. v. Peterborough U.
Tranmere R. v. Walsall
Wigan A. v. Port Vale
York C. v. Halifax T.

Celtic v. Kilmarnock
Dundee U. v. Aberdeen
Hibernian v. Dundee
Partick T. v. Rangers
St. Mirren v. Morton

Arbroath v. St. Johnstone
Ayr U. v. Clyde
Berwick R. v. Hearts
Clydebank v. Dumbarton
Hamilton A. v. Airdrieonians
Raith R. v. Dunfermline A.
Stirling A. v. Motherwell

Albion R. v. Queen's Park
Brechin C. v. Forfar A.
East Fife v. Cowdenbeath
East Stirling v. Falkirk
Montrose v. Meadowbank T.
Stenhousemuir v. Alloa
Stranraer v. Queen of South

Friday, January 4
Southend U. v. Mansfield T.

Rochdale v. Newport C.

Saturday, January 5
Blackburn R. v. Exeter C.
Blackpool v. Oxford U.
Brentford v. Gillingham
Chesterfield v. Sheffield U.
Colchester U. v. Chester
Grimsby T. v. Reading
Plymouth A. v. Hull C.
Rotherham U. v. Millwall
Sheffield W. v. Bury
Swindon T. v. Carlisle U.

Wimbledon v. Barnsley

Aldershot v. Stockport Co.
Crewe A. v. Portsmouth
Darlington v. Lincoln C.
Halifax T. v. Wigan A.
Hartlepool U. v. Tranmere R.
Hereford U. v. Doncaster R.
Northampton T. v. York C.
Peterborough U. v. Scunthorpe U.
Port Vale v. A.F.C. B'mouth
Torquay U. v. Bradford C.
Walsall v. Huddersfield T.

Celtic v. Dundee U.
Dundee v. Partick T.
Kilmarnock v. Hibernian
Morton v. Aberdeen
Rangers v. St. Mirren

Airdrieonians v. Arbroath
Ayr U. v. Hamilton A.
Dumbarton v. Stirling A.
Dunfermline A. v. Clyde
Hearts v. Clydebank
Motherwell v. Berwick R.
St. Johnstone v. Raith R.

Scottish Cup 2nd Round

Friday, January 11
Rochdale v. Darlington
Stockport Co. v. Tranmere R.

Saturday, January 12
Arsenal v. Leeds U.
Aston Villa v. Everton
Bolton W. v. Brighton & H.A.
Derby County v. Crystal Palace
Liverpool v. Southampton
Manchester C. v. Tottenham H.
Middlesbrough v. Manchester U.
Norwich C. v. Coventry C.
Nottingham F. v. W.B.A.
Stoke C. v. Ipswich T.
Wolves v. Bristol C

Bristol R. v. Birmingham C.
Burnley v. Swansea C.
Cambridge U. v. Shrewsbury T.
Cardiff C. v. Wrexham
Charlton A. v. Orient
Chelsea v. Newcastle U.
Luton T. v. Leicester C.
Preston N.E. v. Fulham
Q.P.R. v. Notts County
Sunderland v. Oldham A.
West Ham U. v. Watford

Barnsley v. Swindon T.

Carlisle U. v. Millwall
Chester v. Bury
Chesterfield v. Brentford
Exeter C. v. Sheffield U.
Gillingham v. Reading
Grimsby T. v. Blackburn R.
Hull C. v. Mansfield T.
Oxford U. v. Colchester U.
Rotherham U. v. Southend U.
Sheffield W. v. Plymouth A.
Wimbledon v. Blackpool

A.F.C. B'mouth v. Scunthorpe U.
Aldershot v. Hartlepool U.
Bradford C. v. Peterborough U.
Crewe A. v. Halifax T.
Doncaster R. v. Port Vale
Hereford U. v. Walsall
Huddersfield T. v. Lincoln C.
Northampton T. v. Torquay U.
Portsmouth v. Wigan A.
York C. v. Newport Co.

Aberdeen v. Rangers
Dundee v. Morton
Hibernian v. Celtic
Partick T. v. Kilmarnock
St. Mirren v. Dundee U.

Arbroath v. Dunfermline A.
Berwick R. v. St. Johnstone
Clyde v. Hamilton A.
Clydebank v. Ayr U.
Dumbarton v. Airdrieonians
Raith R. v. Motherwell
Stirling A. v. Hearts

Alloa v. Montrose
Cowdenbeath v. East Stirling
Falkirk v. Stranraer
Forfar A. v. Albion R.
Meadowbank T. v. East Fife
Queen of South v. Stenhousemuir
Queen's Park v. Brechin C.

Friday, January 18
Swansea C. v. Luton T.

Blackpool v. Southend U.

Newport Co. v. Huddersfield T.
Tranmere R. v. Hereford U.

Saturday, January 19
Arsenal v. Derby County
Brighton & H.A. v. Tottenham H.
Bristol C. v. Ipswich T.
Coventry C. v. Liverpool
Crystal Palace v. Wolves
Everton v. Stoke C.
Leeds U. v. Nottingham F.
Manchester U. v. Aston Villa
Norwich C. v. Middlesbrough
Southampton v. Manchester C.
W.B.A. v. Bolton W.

Birmingham C. v. Chelsea
Cambridge U. v. Sunderland
Fulham v. Q.P.R.
Newcastle U. v. Orient
Notts County v. Leicester C.
Oldham A. v. Burnley
Shrewsbury T. v. Cardiff C.
Watford v. Bristol R.
West Ham U. v. Preston N.E.
Wrexham v. Charlton A.

Blackburn R. v. Wimbledon
Brentford v. Sheffield W.
Bury v. Exeter C.
Colchester U. v. Chesterfield
Gillingham v. Carlisle U.
Mansfield T. v. Barnsley
Millwall v. Chester
Plymouth A. v. Grimsby T.
Reading v. Oxford U.
Sheffield U. v. Hull C.
Swindon T. v. Rotherham U.

Darlington v. Hartlepool U.
Halifax T. v. Northampton T.
Lincoln C. v. Bradford C.
Peterborough U. v. York C.
Port Vale v. Crewe A.
Scunthorpe U. v. Aldershot
Stockport Co. v. Portsmouth
Torquay U. v. Doncaster R.
Walsall v. Rochdale
Wigan A. v. A.F.C. B'mouth

Aberdeen v. Celtic
Dundee U. v. Partick T.
Hibernian v. St. Mirren
Morton v. Kilmarnock
Rangers v. Dundee

Ayr U. v. Berwick R.
Clyde v. Stirling A.
Clydebank v. Arbroath
Dunfermline A. v. Dumbarton
Hamilton A. v. Raith R.
Motherwell v. Hearts
St. Johnstone v. Airdrieonians

Albion R. v. Cowdenbeath
Alloa v. Falkirk
Brechin C. v. Meadowbank T.
East Fife v. Stranraer
East Stirling v. Queen of South
Montrose v. Queen's Park
Stenhousemuir v. Forfar A.

Friday, January 25
Southend U. v. Hull C.

Tranmere R. v. Rochdale

Saturday, January 26
Barnsley v. Oxford U.
Blackburn R. v. Sheffield W.
Blackpool v. Grimsby T.
Bury v. Carlisle U.
Exeter C. v. Chesterfield
Mansfield T. v. Wimbledon
Millwall v. Brentford
Plymouth A. v. Gillingham
Reading v. Rotherham U.
Sheffield U. v. Chester
Swindon T. v. Colchester U.

Bradford C. v. Doncaster R.
Darlington v. Hereford U.
Halifax T. v. Stockport Co.
Hartlepool U. v. Huddersfield T.
Lincoln C. v. Torquay U.
Newport Co. v. A.F.C. B'mouth
Peterborough U. v. Port Vale
Scunthorpe U. v. Portsmouth
Walsall v. Northampton T.
Wigan A. v. Aldershot
York C. v. Crewe A.

Scottish Cup 3rd Round

Cowdenbeath v. Brechin C.
Forfar A. v. East Stirling
Meadowbank T. v. Albion R.
Queen of South v. Falkirk
Queen's Park v. East Fife
Stenhousemuir v. Montrose
Stranraer v. Alloa

Friday, February 1
Crewe A. v. Peterborough U.
Rochdale v. Torquay U.

Saturday, February 2
Aston Villa v. Crystal Palace
Bolton W. v. Coventry C.
Derby County v. Manchester U.
Ipswich T. v. Brighton & H.A.
Liverpool v. Leeds U.
Manchester C. v. W.B.A.
Middlesbrough v. Arsenal
Nottingham F. v. Norwich C.
Stoke C. v. Bristol C.
Tottenham H. v. Southampton
Wolves v. Everton

Bristol R. v. Cambridge U.
Burnley v. Fulham
Cardiff C. v. Watford
Charlton A. v. Birmingham C.
Chelsea v. Shrewsbury T.
Leicester C. v. Newcastle U.
Luton T. v. Notts County
Orient v. Wrexham
Preston N.E. v. Oldham A.
Q.P.R. v. Swansea C.
Sunderland v. West Ham U.

Barnsley v. Sheffield U.
Carlisle U. v. Reading
Chester v. Gillingham
Chesterfield v. Swindon T.
Exeter C. v. Millwall
Grimsby T. v. Brentford
Hull C. v. Bury
Oxford U. v. Mansfield T.
Rotherham U. v. Blackpool
Sheffield W. v. Colchester U.
Southend U. v. Blackburn R.
Wimbledon v. Plymouth A.

A.F.C. B'mouth v. Stockport Co.
Aldershot v. Darlington
Bradford C. v. Newport Co.
Doncaster R. v. Lincoln C.
Hartlepool U. v. Walsall
Hereford U. v. Halifax T.
Huddersfield T. v. Scunthorpe U.
Northampton T. v. Port Vale
Portsmouth v. Tranmere R.
York C. v. Wigan A.

Celtic v. St. Mirren
Dundee v. Aberdeen
Kilmarnock v. Rangers
Morton v. Dundee U.
Partick T. v. Hibernian

Airdrieonians v. Clydebank
Arbroath v. Stirling A.
Berwick R. v. Dumbarton
Dunfermline A. v. Ayr U.
Hearts v. Raith R.
Motherwell v. Hamilton A.
St. Johnstone v. Clyde

Albion R. v. East Stirling
Alloa v. Meadowbank T.
Brechin C. v. Montrose
East Fife v. Stenhousemuir
Falkirk v. Cowdenbeath
Queen of South v. Queen's Park
Stranraer v. Forfar A.

Friday, February 8
Colchester U. v. Grimsby T.
Stockport Co. v. York C.

Saturday, February 9
Arsenal v. Aston Villa
Coventry C. v. Manchester C.
Crystal Palace v. Stoke C.

Everton v. Ipswich T.
Leeds U. v. Bolton W.
Manchester U. v. Wolves
Middlesbrough v. Derby County
Norwich C. v. Liverpool
Nottingham F. v. Bristol C.
Southampton v. Brighton & H.A.
W.B.A. v. Tottenham H.

Birmingham C. v. Orient
Bristol R. v. Preston N.E.
Cambridge U. v. Cardiff C.
Fulham v. Leicester C.
Oldham A. v. Luton T.
Shrewsbury T. v. Charlton A.
Sunderland v. Burnley
Swansea C. v. Notts County
Watford v. Chelsea
West Ham U. v. Q.P.R.
Wrexham v. Newcastle U.

Blackburn R. v. Blackpool
Brentford v. Wimbledon
Bury v. Oxford U.
Carlisle U. v. Exeter C.
Chesterfield v. Rotherham U.
Gillingham v. Hull C.
Millwall v. Barnsley
Plymouth A. v. Southend U.
Reading v. Chester
Sheffield U. v. Mansfield T.
Swindon T. v. Sheffield W.

Crewe A. v. Aldershot
Halifax T. v. A.F.C. B'mouth
Newport Co. v. Doncaster R.
Peterborough U. v. Northampton T.
Portsmouth v. Rochdale
Port Vale v. Huddersfield T.
Scunthorpe U. v. Bradford C.
Torquay U. v. Hartlepool U.
Tranmere R. v. Lincoln C.
Walsall v. Darlington
Wigan A. v. Hereford U.

Dundee U. v. Rangers
Hibernian v. Morton
Kilmarnock v. Dundee
Partick T. v. Celtic
St. Mirren v. Aberdeen

Clyde v. Airdrieonians
Clydebank v. Dunfermline A.
Dumbarton v. Hearts
Hamilton A. v. Berwick R.
Motherwell v. St. Johnstone
Raith R. v. Arbroath
Stirling A. v. Ayr U.

Albion R. v. Alloa
Brechin C. v. Stranraer
Cowdenbeath v. Stenhousemuir
East Fife v. Falkirk
East Stirling v. Meadowbank T.
Montrose v. Queen of South
Queen's Park v. Forfar A.

Friday, February 15
Rochdale v. Port Vale

Saturday, February 16
Aston Villa v. Middlesbrough
Bolton W. v. Norwich C.
Brighton & H.A. v. W.B.A.
Bristol C. v. Everton
Derby County v. Southampton
Ipswich T. v. Crystal Palace
Liverpool v. Nottingham F.
Manchester C. v. Leeds U.
Stoke C. v. Manchester U.
Tottenham H. v. Coventry C.
Wolves v. Arsenal

Burnley v. West Ham U.
Cardiff C. v. Bristol R.
Charlton A. v. Watford
Chelsea v. Cambridge U.
Leicester C. v. Swansea C.
Luton T. v. Fulham
Newcastle U. v. Birmingham C.
Notts County v. Wrexham
Orient v. Shrewsbury T.
Preston N.E. v. Sunderland
Q.P.R. v. Oldham A.

Barnsley v. Colchester U.
Blackpool v. Plymouth A.
Chester v. Carlisle U.
Exeter C. v. Gillingham
Grimsby T. v. Swindon T.
Hull C. v. Millwall
Mansfield T. v. Reading
Oxford U. v. Sheffield U.
Rotherham U. v. Blackburn R.
Sheffield W. v. Chesterfield
Southend U. v. Brentford
Wimbledon v. Bury

A.F.C. B'mouth v. Tranmere R.
Aldershot v. Walsall
Bradford C. v. Wigan A.
Darlington v. Torquay U.
Doncaster R. v. Scunthorpe U.
Hartlepool U. v. Halifax T.
Hereford U. v. Peterborough U.
Huddersfield T. v. Stockport Co.
Lincoln C. v. Newport Co.

Northampton T. v. Crewe A.
York C. v. Portsmouth

Scottish Cup 4th Round

Albion R. v. Brechin C.
Alloa v. Cowdenbeath
Forfar A. v. Falkirk
Meadowbank T. v. Queen's Park
Queen of South v. East Fife
Stenhousemuir v. East Stirling
Stranraer v. Montrose

Friday, February 22
Colchester U. v. Southend U.

Stockport Co. v. Bradford C.
Tranmere R. v. Newport Co.

Saturday, February 23
Arsenal v. Bolton W.
Coventry C. v. Southampton
Crystal Palace v. Everton
Derby County v. Tottenham H.
Leeds U. v. Brighton & H.A.
Liverpool v. Ipswich T.
Manchester U. v. Bristol C.
Middlesbrough v. Stoke C.
Norwich C. v. Wolves
Nottingham F. v. Manchester C.
W.B.A. v. Aston Villa

Birmingham C. v. Wrexham
Bristol R. v. Chelsea
Cambridge U. v. Charlton A.
Cardiff C. v. Burnley
Fulham v. Swansea C.
Oldham A. v. Notts County
Preston N.E. v. Q.P.R.
Shrewsbury T. v. Newcastle U.
Sunderland v. Luton T.
Watford v. Orient
West Ham U. v. Leicester C.

Brentford v. Blackpool
Bury v. Mansfield T.
Carlisle U. v. Hull C.
Chester v. Exeter C.
Chesterfield v. Grimsby T.
Gillingham v. Barnsley
Millwall v. Oxford U.
Plymouth A. v. Blackburn R.
Reading v. Sheffield U.
Sheffield W. v. Rotherham U.
Swindon T. v. Wimbledon

A.F.C. B'mouth v. York C.
Crewe A. v. Hereford U.

Halifax T. v. Darlington
Northampton T. v. Aldershot
Peterborough U. v. Rochdale
Portsmouth v. Huddersfield T.
Port Vale v. Hartlepool U.
Scunthorpe v. Lincoln C.
Torquay U. v. Walsall
Wigan A. v. Doncaster R.

Aberdeen v. Kilmarnock
Celtic v. Dundee
Dundee U. v. Hibernian
Rangers v. Morton
St. Mirren v. Partick T.

Arbroath v. Clyde
Ayr U. v. Motherwell
Berwick R. v. Clydebank
Dunfermline A. v. St. Johnstone
Hearts v. Hamilton A.
Raith R. v. Dumbarton
Stirling A. v. Airdrieonians

Cowdenbeath v. Queen of South
East Fife v. Brechin C.
East Stirling v. Alloa
Falkirk v. Albion R.
Forfar A. v. Montrose
Meadowbank T. v. Stenhousemuir
Queen's Park v. Stranraer

Friday, February 29
Swansea C. v. Birmingham C.

Southend U. v. Swindon T.

Lincoln C. v. Wigan A.
Newport Co. v. Scunthorpe U.

Saturday, March 1
Aston Villa v. Derby County
Bolton W. v. Nottingham F.
Brighton & H.A. v. Coventry C.
Bristol C. v. Crystal Palace
Everton v. Liverpool
Ipswich T. v. Manchester U.
Manchester C. v. Norwich C.
Southampton v. W.B.A.
Stoke C. v. Arsenal
Tottenham H. v. Leeds U.
Wolves v. Middlesbrough

Burnley v. Preston N.E.
Charlton A. v. Bristol R.
Chelsea v. Cardiff C.
Leicester C. v. Oldham A.
Luton T. v. West Ham U.
Newcastle U. v. Watford

Notts County v. Fulham
Orient v. Cambridge U.
Q.P.R. v. Sunderland
Wrexham v. Shrewsbury T.

Barnsley v. Carlisle U.
Blackburn R. v. Brentford
Blackpool v. Colchester U.
Exeter C. v. Reading
Grimsby T. v. Gillingham
Hull C. v. Chester
Mansfield T. v. Millwall
Oxford U. v. Sheffield W.
Rotherham U. v. Plymouth A.
Sheffield U. v. Bury
Wimbledon v. Chesterfield

Aldershot v. Torquay U.
Bradford C. v. Portsmouth
Darlington v. Port Vale
Doncaster R. v. Stockport Co.
Hartlepool U. v. Peterborough U.
Hereford U. v. Northampton T.
Huddersfield T. v. A.F.C. B'mouth
Rochdale v. Crewe A.
Walsall v. Halifax T.
York C. v. Tranmere R.

Aberdeen v. Partick T.
Dundee v. Dundee U.
Kilmarnock v. St. Mirren
Morton v. Celtic
Rangers v. Hibernian

Airdrieonians v. Berwick R.
Clyde v. Raith R.
Clydebank v. Motherwell
Dumbarton v. Ayr U.
Dunfermline A. v. Stirling A.
Hearts v. Arbroath
St. Johnstone v. Hamilton A.

Brechin C. v. Alloa
East Fife v. Forfar A.
East Stirling v. Queen's Park
Montrose v. Cowdenbeath
Queen of South v. Albion R.
Stenhousemuir v. Falkirk
Stranraer v. Meadowbank T.

Saturday, March 8
Arsenal v. Bristol C.
Aston Villa v. Wolves
Coventry C. v. W.B.A.
Crystal Palace v. Bolton W.
Derby County v. Stoke C.
Leeds U. v. Southampton
Liverpool v. Manchester C.
Manchester U. v. Everton
Middlesbrough v. Ipswich T.
Norwich C. v. Brighton & H.A.
Nottingham F. v. Tottenham H.

Bristol R. v. Orient
Burnley v. Q.P.R.
Cambridge U. v. Newcastle U.
Cardiff C. v. Charlton A.
Fulham v. Chelsea
Oldham A. v. Swansea C.
Preston N.E. v. Luton T.
Shrewsbury T. v. Birmingham C.
Sunderland v. Leicester C.
Watford v. Wrexham
West Ham U. v. Notts County

Brentford v. Plymouth A.
Bury v. Reading
Carlisle U. v. Oxford U.
Chester v. Barnsley
Chesterfield v. Southend U.
Colchester U. v. Blackburn R.
Exeter C. v. Hull C.
Gillingham v. Mansfield T.
Millwall v. Sheffield U.
Rotherham U. v. Grimsby T.
Sheffield W. v. Wimbledon
Swindon T. v. Blackpool

A.F.C. B'mouth v. Bradford C.
Aldershot v. Hereford U.
Crewe A. v. Hartlepool U.
Halifax T. v. Torquay U.
Northampton T. v. Rochdale
Peterborough U. v. Darlington
Portsmouth v. Doncaster R.
Port Vale v. Walsall
Scunthorpe U. v. Tranmere R.
Stockport Co. v. Lincoln C.
Wigan A. v. Newport Co.
York C. v. Huddersfield T.

Celtic v. Rangers
Dundee U. v. Kilmarnock
Hibernian v. Aberdeen
Partick T. v. Morton
St. Mirren v. Dundee

Ayr U. v. Airdrieonians
Dumbarton v. Clyde
Hamilton A. v. Arbroath
Motherwell v. Dunfermline A.
Raith R. v. Berwick R.
St. Johnstone v. Hearts
Stirling A. v. Clydebank

Albion R. v. East Fife
Brechin C. v. East Stirling
Falkirk v. Montrose

Forfar A. v. Queen of South
Meadowbank T. v. Cowdenbeath
Queen's Park v. Alloa
Stenhousemuir v. Stranraer

Wednesday, March 12
Chelsea v. Burnley

Friday, March 14
Bolton W. v. Derby County
Brighton & H.A. v. Manchester U.
Bristol C. v. Liverpool
Everton v. Coventry C.
Ipswich T. v. Leeds U.
Manchester C. v. Arsenal
Southampton v. Aston Villa
Stoke C. v. Norwich C.
Tottenham H. v. Crystal Palace
W.B.A. v. Middlesbrough
Wolves v. Nottingham F.

Birmingham C. v. Preston N.E.
Charlton A. v. Sunderland
Leicester C. v. Shrewsbury T.
Luton T. v. Cardiff C.
Newcastle U. v. West Ham U.
Notts County v. Bristol R.
Orient v. Oldham A.
Q.P.R. v. Watford
Swansea C. v. Cambridge U.
Wrexham v. Fulham

Barnsley v. Brentford
Blackburn R. v. Gillingham
Blackpool v. Exeter C.
Grimsby T. v. Millwall
Hull C. v. Swindon T.
Mansfield T. v. Sheffield W.
Oxford U. v. Chesterfield
Plymouth A. v. Chester
Reading v. Colchester U.
Sheffield U. v. Rotherham U.
Southend U. v. Bury
Wimbledon v. Carlisle U.

Bradford C. v. Aldershot
Darlington v. Portsmouth
Doncaster R. v. Crewe A.
Hartlepool U. v. A.F.C. B'mouth
Hereford U. v. Stockport Co.
Huddersfield T. v. Peterborough U.
Lincoln C. v. Port Vale
Newport Co. v. Halifax T.
Rochdale v. York C.
Torquay U. v. Wigan A.
Tranmere R. v. Northampton T.
Walsall v. Scunthorpe U.

Saturday, March 15
Aberdeen v. Dundee U.
Dundee v. Hibernian
Kilmarnock v. Celtic
Morton v. St. Mirren
Rangers v. Partick T.

Airdrieonians v. Clydebank
Arbroath v. Stirling A.
Berwick R. v. Dumbarton
Clyde v. St. Johnstone
Dunfermline A. v. Ayr U.
Motherwell v. Hamilton A.
Raith R. v. Hearts

Alloa v. Albion R.
Cowdenbeath v. Stenhousemuir
East Fife v. Falkirk
Meadowbank T. v. East Stirling
Montrose v. Queen of South
Queen's Park v. Forfar A.
Stranraer v. Brechin C.

Friday, March 21
Stockport Co. v. Scunthorpe U.

Saturday, March 22
Arsenal v. Crystal Palace
Aston Villa v. Ipswich T.
Bolton W. v. Tottenham H.
Derby County v. Bristol C.
Leeds U. v. Coventry C.
Liverpool v. Brighton & H.A.
Manchester U. v. Manchester C.
Middlesbrough v. Everton
Norwich C. v. W.B.A.
Nottingham F. v. Southampton
Wolves v. Stoke C.

Bristol R. v. Wrexham
Burnley v. Leicester C.
Cambridge U. v. Birmingham C.
Cardiff C. v. Newcastle U.
Chelsea v. Orient
Oldham A. v. Charlton A.
Preston N.E. v. Notts County
Q.P.R. v. Luton T.
Sunderland v. Swansea C.
Watford v. Shrewsbury T.
West Ham U. v. Fulham

Carlisle U. v. Plymouth A.
Chester v. Oxford U.
Chesterfield v. Blackburn R.
Colchester U. v. Brentford
Exeter C. v. Barnsley
Gillingham v. Sheffield U.
Grimsby T. v. Southend U.
Hull C. v. Reading

Millwall v. Bury
Rotherham U. v. Wimbledon
Sheffield W. v. Blackpool
Swindon T. v. Mansfield T.

A.F.C. B'mouth v. Lincoln C.
Aldershot v. Rochdale
Crewe A. v. Newport Co.
Hereford U. v. Hartlepool U.
Huddersfield T. v. Bradford C.
Northampton T. v. Darlington
Peterborough U. v. Doncaster R.
Portsmouth v. Walsall
Port Vale v. Halifax T.
Wigan A. v. Tranmere R.
York C. v. Torquay U.

Aberdeen v. Morton
Dundee U. v. Celtic
Hibernian v. Kilmarnock
Partick T. v. Dundee
St. Mirren v. Rangers

Clyde v. Motherwell
Clydebank v. Raith R.
Dumbarton v. Arbroath
Hamilton A. v. Dunfermline A.
Hearts v. Airdrieonians
St. Johnstone v. Ayr U.
Stirling A. v. Berwick R.

Brechin C. v. Falkirk
East Fife v. Alloa
East Stirling v. Montrose
Forfar A. v. Cowdenbeath
Queen of South v. Meadowbank T
Stenhousemuir v. Queen's Park
Stranraer v. Albion R.

Friday, March 28
Everton v. Arsenal

Fulham v. Oldham A.
Wimbledon v. Grimsby T.

Rochdale v. Hereford U.

Saturday, March 29
Brighton & H.A. v. Nottingham F.
Bristol C. v. Middlesbrough
Coventry C. v. Wolves
Crystal Palace v. Manchester U.
Ipswich T. v. Derby County
Manchester C. v. Bolton W.
Southampton v. Norwich C.
Stoke C. v. Aston Villa
Tottenham H. v. Liverpool
W.B.A. v. Leeds U.

Birmingham C. v. Watford
Charlton A. v. Chelsea
Leicester C. v. Preston N.E.
Luton T. v. Burnley
Newcastle U. v. Bristol R.
Notts County v. Sunderland
Orient v. Cardiff C.
Shrewsbury T. v. Q.P.R.
Swansea C. v. West Ham U.
Wrexham v. Cambridge U.

Barnsley v. Hull C.
Blackburn R. v. Swindon T.
Blackpool v. Millwall
Brentford v. Rotherham U.
Bury v. Gillingham
Mansfield T. v. Chester
Oxford U. v. Exeter C.
Plymouth A. v. Colchester U.
Reading v. Chesterfield
Sheffield U. v. Carlisle U.
Southend U. v. Sheffield W.

Bradford C. v. York C.
Darlington v. Crewe A.
Doncaster R. v. A.F.C. B'mouth
Halifax T. v. Aldershot
Hartlepool U. v. Northampton T.
Lincoln C. v. Portsmouth
Newport Co. v. Stockport Co.
Scunthorpe U. v. Wigan A.
Torquay U. v. Port Vale
Tranmere R. v. Huddersfield T.
Walsall v. Peterborough U.

Celtic v. Hibernian
Dundee U. v. St. Mirren
Kilmarnock v. Partick T.
Morton v. Dundee
Rangers v. Aberdeen

Airdrieonians v. Berwick R.
Ayr U. v. Dumbarton
Hamilton A. v. St. Johnstone
Hearts v. Arbroath
Motherwell v. Clydebank
Raith R. v. Clyde
Stirling v. Dunfermline A.

Albion R. v. Queen of South
Alloa v. Brechin C.
East Stirling v. Queen's Park
Falkirk v. Stenhousemuir
Forfar A. v. East Fife
Meadowbank T. v. Stranraer
Montrose v. Cowdenbeath

Tuesday, April 1
Coventry v. Aston Villa
Liverpool v. Stoke C.
Southampton v. Bristol City
W.B.A. v. Crystal Palace

Birmingham C. v. Oldham A.

Bristol R. v. Leicester C.
Cambridge U. v. West Ham U.
Fulham v. Cardiff C.
Orient v. Swansea C.
Shrewsbury T. v. Preston N.E.

Chesterfield v. Gillingham
Colchester U. v. Exeter C.
Plymouth A. v. Mansfield T.
Rotherham U. v. Chester
Sheffield W. v. Reading
Swindon T. v. Millwall
Wimbledon v. Oxford U.

Aldershot v. Tranmere R.
Rochdale v. Huddersfield T.

Wednesday, April 2
Leeds U. v. Middlesbrough
Manchester C. v. Everton
Norwich C. v. Arsenal
Nottingham F. v. Manchester U.
Southampton v. Bristol C.
Tottenham H. v. Ipswich T.

Chelsea v. Q.P.R.
Newcastle U. v. Notts County

Hereford U. v. Lincoln C.
Torquay U. v. Stockport Co.

Friday, April 4
Bristol R. v. Fulham
Charlton A. v. Luton T.
Wrexham v. Burnley

Blackburn R. v. Hull C.
Blackpool v. Barnsley
Grimsby T. v. Carlisle U.
Southend U. v. Sheffield U.

Crewe A. v. Wigan A.
Darlington v. Doncaster R.
Hartlepool U. v. Bradford C.
Stockport Co. v. Northampton T.

Saturday, April 5
Arsenal v. Southampton
Aston Villa v. Nottingham F.
Bristol C. v. W.B.A.
Crystal Palace v. Brighton & H.A.
Derby County v. Leeds U.
Everton v. Bolton W.
Ipswich T. v. Norwich C.
Manchester U. v. Liverpool
Middlesbrough v. Coventry C.
Stoke C. v. Manchester C.
Wolves v. Tottenham H.

Burnley v. Shrewsbury T.
Leicester C. v. Chelsea
Luton T. v. Watford
Notts County v. Charlton A.
Oldham A. v. Cambridge U.
Preston N.E. v. Wrexham
Q.P.R. v. Birmingham C.
Sunderland v. Newcastle U.
Swansea C. v. Bristol R.
West Ham U. v. Orient

Barnsley v. Grimsby T.
Bury v. Rotherham U.
Carlisle U. v. Chesterfield
Chester v. Brentford
Exeter C. v. Swindon T.
Gillingham v. Colchester U.
Hull C. v. Blackpool
Mansfield T. v. Blackburn R.
Millwall v. Wimbledon
Oxford U. v. Southend U.
Reading v. Plymouth A.
Sheffield U. v. Sheffield W.

A.F.C. B'mouth v. Aldershot
Bradford C. v. Darlington
Doncaster R. v. Walsall
Huddersfield T. v. Halifax T.
Lincoln C. v. Rochdale
Newport Co. v. Torquay U.
Portsmouth v. Hereford U.
Scunthorpe U. v. Port Vale
Tranmere R. v. Crewe A.
Wigan A. v. Peterborough U.
York C. v. Hartlepool U.

Celtic v. Aberdeen
Dundee v. Rangers
Kilmarnock v. Morton
Partick T. v. Dundee U.
St. Mirren v. Hibernian

Airdrieonians v. Hearts
Arbroath v. Dumbarton
Ayr U. v. St. Johnstone
Berwick R. v. Stirling A.
Clydebank v. Raith R.
Dunfermline A. v. Hamilton A.
Motherwell v. Clyde

Albion R. v. Stranraer
Cowdenbeath v. Forfar A.
East Fife v. Alloa
Falkirk v. Brechin C.
Montrose v. East Stirling
Queen of South v. Meadowbank T.
Queen's Park v. Stenhousemuir

Monday, April 7
Bolton W. v. Manchester U.
Brighton & H.A. v. Bristol C.

Coventry C. v. Derby County
Manchester C. v. Aston Villa
Norwich C. v. Crystal Palace
Nottingham F. v. Everton
Southampton v. Wolves
Tottenham H. v. Arsenal
W.B.A. v. Ipswich T.

Birmingham C. v. West Ham U.
Cardiff C. v. Swansea C.
Chelsea v. Luton T.
Newcastle U. v. Burnley
Watford v. Oldham A.
Wrexham v. Sunderland

Blackburn R. v. Sheffield U.
Blackpool v. Carlisle U.
Brentford v. Mansfield T.
Chesterfield v. Chester
Colchester U. v. Bury
Grimsby T. v. Hull C.
Plymouth A. v. Exeter C.
Rotherham U. v. Barnsley
Sheffield W. v. Gillingham
Southend U. v. Millwall
Swindon T. v. Oxford U.
Wimbledon v. Reading

Aldershot v. Portsmouth
Crewe A. v. Scunthorpe U.
Halifax T. v. York C.
Hereford U. v. Newport Co.
Northampton T. v. Lincoln C.
Peterborough U. v. Stockport Co.
Port Vale v. Wigan A.
Rochdale v. Bradford C.
Torquay U. v. A.F.C. B'mouth
Walsall v. Tranmere R.

Tuesday, April 8
Bolton W. v. Middlesbrough
Brighton & H.A. v. Wolves
Leeds U. v. Stoke C.
Liverpool v. Derby County

Cambridge U. v. Notts County
Cardiff C. v. Leicester C.
Charlton A. v. Fulham
Orient v. Q.P.R.
Shrewsbury T. v. Sunderland

Brentford v. Bury

Darlington v. Huddersfield T.
Halifax T. v. Scunthorpe U.
Hartlepool U. v. Doncaster R.
Northampton T. v. A.F.C. B'mouth
Peterborough U. v. Newport Co.
Port Vale v. Portsmouth
Walsall v. York C.

Wednesday, April 9
Watford v. Preston N.E.

Friday, April 11
Barnsley v. Wimbledon

Doncaster R. v. Hereford U.
Stockport Co. v. Aldershot
Tranmere R. v. Hartlepool U.

Saturday, April 12
Arsenal v. Nottingham F.
Aston Villa v. Norwich C.
Bristol C. v. Bolton W.
Crystal Palace v. Leeds U.
Derby County v. Brighton & H.A.
Everton v. W.B.A.
Ipswich T. v. Coventry C.
Manchester U. v. Tottenham H.
Middlesbrough v. Liverpool
Stoke C. v. Southampton
Wolves v. Manchester C.

Burnley v. Bristol R.
Fulham v. Newcastle U.
Leicester C. v. Birmingham C.
Luton T. v. Shrewsbury T.
Notts County v. Watford
Oldham A. v. Cardiff C.
Preston N.E. v. Chelsea
Q.P.R. v. Cambridge U.
Sunderland v. Orient
Swansea v. Wrexham
West Ham U. v. Charlton A.

Bury v. Sheffield W.
Carlisle U. v. Swindon T.
Chester v. Colchester U.
Exeter C. v. Blackburn R.
Gillingham v. Brentford
Hull C. v. Plymouth A.
Mansfield T. v. Southend U.
Millwall v. Rotherham U.
Oxford U. v. Blackpool
Reading v. Grimsby T.
Sheffield U. v. Chesterfield

A.F.C. B'mouth v. Port Vale
Bradford C. v. Torquay U.
Huddersfield T. v. Walsall
Lincoln C. v. Darlington
Newport Co. v. Rochdale
Portsmouth v. Crewe A.
Scunthorpe U. v. Peterborough U.
Wigan A. v. Halifax T.
York C. v. Northampton T.

Aberdeen v. Dundee
Dundee U. v. Morton
Hibernian v. Partick T.

Rangers v. Kilmarnock
St. Mirren v. Celtic

Arbroath v. Berwick R.
Clyde v. Hearts
Dumbarton v. Motherwell
Dunfermline A. v. Airdrieonians
Hamilton A. v. Stirling A.
Raith R. v. Ayr U.
St. Johnstone v. Clydebank

Alloa v. Forfar A.
Brechin C. v. Queen of South
East Fife v. Montrose
Meadowbank T. v. Falkirk
Queen's Park v. Cowdenbeath
Stenhousemuir v. Albion R.
Stranraer v. East Stirling

Friday, April 18
Rochdale v. Scunthorpe U.

Saturday, April 19
Bolton W. v. Stoke C.
Brighton & H.A. v. Middlesbrough
Coventry C. v. Crystal Palace
Leeds U. v. Aston Villa
Liverpool v. Arsenal
Manchester C. v. Bristol C.
Norwich C. v. Manchester U.
Nottingham F. v. Derby County
Southampton v. Ipswich T.
Tottenham H. v. Everton
W.B.A. v. Wolves

Birmingham C. v. Luton T.
Bristol R. v. Sunderland
Cambridge U. v. Burnley
Cardiff C. v. West Ham U.
Charlton A. v. Q.P.R.
Chelsea v. Notts County
Newcastle U. v. Swansea C.
Orient v. Preston N.E.
Shrewsbury T. v. Oldham A.
Watford v. Fulham
Wrexham v. Leicester C.

Blackburn R. v. Reading
Blackpool v. Mansfield T.
Brentford v. Carlisle U.
Chesterfield v. Bury
Colchester U. v. Millwall
Grimsby T. v. Oxford U.
Plymouth A. v. Sheffield U.
Rotherham U. v. Exeter C.
Sheffield W. v. Chester
Southend U. v. Barnsley
Swindon T. v. Gillingham
Wimbledon v. Hull C.

Aldershot v. Doncaster R.
Crewe A. v. Stockport Co.
Darlington v. Newport Co.
Halifax T. v. Portsmouth
Hartlepool U. v. Lincoln C.
Hereford U. v. Huddersfield T.
Northampton T. v. Wigan A.
Peterborough U. v. A.F.C. B'mouth
Port Vale v. York C.
Torquay U. v. Tranmere R.
Walsall v. Bradford C.

Dundee v. Celtic
Hibernian v. Dundee U.
Kilmarnock v. Aberdeen
Morton v. Rangers
Partick T. v. St. Mirren

Airdrieonians v. Motherwell
Ayr U. v. Arbroath
Berwick R. v. Clyde
Clydebank v. Hamilton A.
Dumbarton v. St. Johnstone
Hearts v. Dunfermline A.
Stirling A. v. Raith R.

Cowdenbeath v. Stranraer
East Stirling v. East Fife
Falkirk v. Queen's Park
Forfar A. v. Meadowbank T.
Montrose v. Albion R.
Queen of South v. Alloa
Stenhousemuir v. Brechin C.

Friday, April 25
Lincoln C. v. Halifax T.
Scunthorpe U v. Northampton T
Stockport Co. v. Port Vale

Saturday, April 26
Arsenal v. W.B.A.
Aston Villa v. Tottenham H.
Bristol C. v. Norwich C.
Crystal Palace v. Liverpool
Derby County v. Manchester C.
Everton v. Southampton
Ipswich T. v. Bolton W.
Manchester U. v. Coventry C.
Middlesbrough v. Nottingham F.
Stoke C. v. Brighton & H.A.
Wolves v. Leeds U.

Burnley v. Birmingham C.
Fulham v. Cambridge U.
Leicester C. v. Charlton A.
Luton T. v. Wrexham
Notts County v. Orient
Oldham A. v. Bristol R.
Preston N.E. v. Cardiff C.
Q.P.R. v. Newcastle U.

Sunderland v. Watford
Swansea C. v. Chelsea
West Ham U. v. Shrewsbury T.

Barnsley v. Plymouth A.
Bury v. Swindon T.
Carlisle U. v. Colchester U.
Chester v. Southend U.
Exeter C. v. Sheffield W.
Gillingham v. Rotherham U.
Hull C. v. Brentford
Mansfield T. v. Grimsby T.
Millwall v. Chesterfield
Oxford U. v. Blackburn R.
Reading v. Blackpool
Sheffield U. v. Wimbledon

A.F.C. B'mouth v. Crewe A.
Bradford C. v. Hereford U.
Doncaster R. v. Rochdale
Huddersfield T. v. Torquay U.
Newport Co. v. Hartlepool U.
Portsmouth v. Peterborough U.
Tranmere R. v. Darlington
Wigan A. v. Walsall
York C. v. Aldershot

Aberdeen v. St. Mirren
Celtic v. Partick T.
Dundee v. Kilmarnock
Morton v. Hibernian
Rangers v. Dundee U.

Airdrieonians v. Ayr U.
Arbroath v. Hamilton A.
Berwick R. v. Raith R.
Clyde v. Dumbarton
Clydebank v. Stirling A.
Motherwell v. Dunfermline A.
St. Johnstone v. Hearts

Albion R. v. East Fife
Alloa v. Queen's Park
Brechin C. v, East Stirling
Cowdenbeath v. Meadowbank T.
Falkirk v. Montrose
Queen of South v. Forfar A.
Stranraer v. Stenhousemuir

Friday, May 2
Colchester U. v. Oxford U.
Rochdale v. Tranmere R.
Stockport Co. v. Halifax T.

Saturday, May 3
Bolton W. v. Wolves
Brighton & H.A. v. Everton
Coventry C. v. Arsenal
Leeds U. v. Manchester U.
Liverpool v. Aston Villa
Manchester C. v. Ipswich T.
Norwich C. v. Derby County
Nottingham F. v. Crystal Palace
Southampton v. Middlesbrough
Tottenham H. v. Bristol C.
W.B.A. v. Stoke C.

Birmingham C. v. Notts County
Bristol R. v. West Ham U.
Cambridge U. v. Preston N.E.
Cardiff C. v. Sunderland
Charlton v. Swansea C.
Chelsea v. Oldham A.
Newcastle U. v. Luton T.
Orient v. Leicester C.
Shrewsbury T. v. Fulham
Watford v. Burnley
Wrexham v. Q.P.R.

Blackburn R. v. Bury
Blackpool v. Chester
Brentford v. Millwall
Chesterfield v. Exeter C.
Gillingham v. Plymouth A.
Grimsby T. v. Sheffield U.
Hull C. v. Southend U.
Rotherham U. v. Reading
Sheffield W. v. Carlisle U.
Swindon T. v. Barnsley
Wimbledon v. Mansfield T.

Aldershot v. Wigan A.
Crewe A. v. York C.
Darlington v. A.F.C. B'mouth
Hereford U. v. Scunthorpe U.
Huddersfield T. v. Hartlepool U.
Northampton T. v. Portsmouth
Peterborough U. v. Bradford C.
Port Vale v. Doncaster R.
Torquay U. v. Lincoln C.
Walsall v. Newport Co.

THE MANAGERS

FOOTBALL LEAGUE DIVISION ONE

Arsenal	Terry Neill
Aston Villa	Ron Saunders
Bolton Wanderers	Ian Greaves
Brighton and Hove Albion	Alan Mullery
Bristol City	Alan Dicks
Coventry City	Gordon Milne
Crystal Palace	Terry Venables
Derby County	Colin Addison
Everton	Gordon Lee
Ipswich Town	Bobby Robson
Leeds United	Jimmy Adamson
Liverpool	Bob Paisley
Manchester City	Tony Book
Manchester United	Dave Sexton
Middlesbrough	John Neal
Norwich City	John Bond
Nottingham Forest	Brian Clough
Southampton	Lawrie McMenemy
Stoke City	Alan Durban
Tottenham Hotspur	Keith Burkinshaw
West Bromwich Albion	Ron Atkinson
Wolverhampton Wanderers	John Barnwell

DIVISION TWO

Birmingham City	Jim Smith
Bristol Rovers	Bobby Campbell
Burnley	Harry Potts
Cambridge United	John Docherty
Cardiff City	Richie Morgan
Charlton Athletic	Andy Nelson
Chelsea	Danny Blanchflower
Fulham	Bobby Campbell
Leicester City	Jock Wallace
Luton Town	David Pleat
Newcastle United	Bill McGarry
Notts. County	Jimmy Sirrel
Oldham Athletic	Jimmy Frizzell
Orient	Jimmy Bloomfield
Preston North End	Nobby Stiles
Queens Park Rangers	Tommy Docherty
Shrewsbury Town	Graham Turner
Sunderland	Ken Knighton
Swansea City	John Toshack
Watford	Graham Taylor
West Ham United	John Lyall
Wrexham	Arfon Griffiths

DIVISION THREE

Barnsley	Allan Clarke
Blackburn Rovers	Howard Kendall
Blackpool	Bob Stokoe
Brentford	Bill Dodgin
Bury	Dave Hatton
Carlisle United	Bobby Moncur
Chester	Alan Oakes
Chesterfield	Arthur Cox
Colchester United	Bobby Roberts
Exeter City	Brian Godfrey
Gillingham	Gerry Summers
Grimsby Town	—
Hull City	Ken Houghton
Mansfield Town	—
Millwall	George Petchey
Oxford United	Mick Brown
Plymouth Argyle	Bobby Saxton
Reading	Maurice Evans
Rotherham United	Jimmy McGuigan
Sheffield United	Harry Haslam
Sheffield Wednesday	Jack Charlton
Southend United	David Smith
Swindon Town	Bobby Smith
Wimbledon	Dario Gradi

DIVISION FOUR

Aldershot	Tom McAnearney
Bournemouth	Alec Stock
Bradford City	George Mulhall
Crewe Alexandra	Warwick Rimmer
Darlington	Billy Elliott
Doncaster Rovers	Billy Bremner
Halifax Town	George Kirby
Hartlepool United	Billy Horner
Hereford United	Mike Bailey
Huddersfield Town	Mick Buxton
Lincoln City	Colin Murphy
Newport County	Len Ashurst
Northampton Town	Clive Walker
Peterborough United	Peter Morris
Portsmouth	Frank Burrows
Port Vale	Dennis Butler
Rochdale	Doug Collins
Scunthorpe United	Ron Ashman
Stockport County	Mike Summerbee
Torquay United	Mike Green
Tranmere Rovers	John King
Walsall	Alan Buckley
Wigan Athletic	Ian McNeil
York City	Charlie Wright

INTERNATIONAL AND CUP DATES 1979-80

AUGUST 1979

Sat 11—F.A. Charity Shield Match
Sat 11—Football League Cup First Round (First Leg)
Wed 15—Football League Cup First Round (Second Leg)
Sat 18—OPENING DAY OF FOOTBALL LEAGUE FIXTURES
Wed 29—Football League Cup Second Round (First Leg)

SEPTEMBER 1979

Sat 1—F.A. Challenge Cup Preliminary Round
Wed 5—Football League Cup Second Round (Second Leg)
Sat 8—F.A. Challenge Trophy Preliminary Round
Sat 8—F.A. Challenge Vase Extra Preliminary Round
Tue 11—England v Denmark (UEFA Under-21 Competition)
Wed 12—England v Denmark (European Championship)
Sat 15—F.A. Challenge Cup First Round Qualifying
Wed 19—European Cups Preliminary Round (First Leg)
Wed 26—Football League Cup Third Round
Sat 29—F.A. Challenge Vase Preliminary Round

OCTOBER 1979

Wed 3—European Cups Preliminary Round (Second Leg)
Sat 6—F.A. Challenge Cup Second Round Qualifying
Sun 7—F.A. Sunday Cup First Round
Sat 13—F.A. Challenge Trophy First Round Qualifying
Wed 17—N. Ireland v England (European Championship)
Wed 17—Rep.of Ireland v Bulgaria (European Championship)
Wed 17—Scotland v Austria (European Championship)
Wed 17—West Germany v Wales (European Championship)
Sat 20—F.A. Challenge Cup Third Round Qualifying
Wed 24—European Cups Second Round (First Leg)
Sat 27—F.A. Challenge Vase First Round
Wed 31—Football League Cup Fourth Round

NOVEMBER 1979

Sat 3—F.A. Challenge Cup Fourth Round Qualifying
Sun 4—F.A. Sunday Cup Second Round
Wed 7—European Cups Second Round (Second Leg)
Sat 10—F.A. Challenge Trophy Second Round Qualifying
Tue 20—England v Bulgaria (UEFA Under-21 Competition)
Tue 20—Belgium v Scotland (UEFA Under-21 Competition)
Wed 21—England v Bulgaria (European Championship)

Wed 21—Turkey v Wales (European Championship)
Wed 21—N. Ireland v Rep. of Ireland (Euro Championship)
Wed 21—Belgium v Scotland (European Championship)
Sat 24—F.A. Challenge Cup First Round Proper
Sat 24—F.A. Challenge Vase Second Round
Wed 28—UEFA Cup Third Round (First Leg)

DECEMBER 1979

Sat 1—F.A. Challenge Trophy Third Round Qualifying
Sun 2—F.A. Sunday Cup Third Round
Wed 5—Football League Cup Fifth Round
Wed 12—UEFA Cup Third Round (Second Leg)
Sat 15—F.A. Challenge Cup Second Round Proper
Sat 15—F.A. Challenge Vase Third Round

JANUARY 1980

Sat 5—F.A. Challenge Cup Third Round Proper
Sat 12—F.A. Challenge Trophy First Round Proper
Sun 13—F.A. Sunday Cup Fourth Round
Wed 16—Football League Cup Semi-Finals (First Leg)
Sat 19—F.A. Challenge Vase Fourth Round
Sat 26—F.A. Challenge Cup Fourth Round Proper

FEBRUARY 1980

Sat 2—F.A. Challenge Trophy Second Round Proper
Wed 6—England v Rep. of Ireland (European Championship)
Wed 6—Scotland v Portugal (UEFA Under-21 Competition)
Thurs 7—Scotland v Portugal (European Championship)
Sat 9—F.A. Challenge Vase Fifth Round
Sun 10—F.A. Sunday Cup Fifth Round
Wed 13—Football League Cup Semi-Finals (Second Leg)
Sat 16—F.A. Challenge Cup Fifth Round Proper
Sat 23—F.A. Challenge Trophy Third Round Proper

MARCH 1980

Sat 1—F.A. Challenge Vase Sixth Round
Wed 5—European Champion Clubs' Cup Third Round (FL)
Wed 5—European Cup Winners' Cup Third Round (FL)
Wed 5—UEFA Cup Fourth Round (First Leg)
Sat 8—F.A. Challenge Cup Sixth Round Proper
Sat 15—F.A. Challenge Trophy Fourth Round Proper
Sat 15—Football League Cup Final
Sun 16—F.A. Sunday Cup Semi-Finals
Wed 19—European Champion Clubs' Cup Third Round (SL)
Wed 19—European Cup Winners' Cup Third Round (SL)

Wed 19—UEFA Cup Fourth Round (Second Leg)
Sat 22—F.A. Challenge Vase Semi-Finals (First Leg)
Wed 26—Spain v England (Full International)
Wed 26—Spain v England ('B' International)
Sat 29—F.A. Challenge Vase Semi-Finals (Second Leg)

APRIL 1980
Wed 9—European Cups Semi-Finals (First Leg)
Sat 12—F.A. Challenge Cup Semi-Finals
Sat 12—F.A. Challenge Trophy Semi-Finals (First Leg)
Sat 19—F.A. Challenge Trophy Semi-Finals (Second Leg)
Wed 23—European Cups Semi-Finals (Second Leg)
Sat 26—F.A. Challenge Vase Final

MAY 1980
Sun 4—F.A. Sunday Cup Final
Wed 7—UEFA Cup Final (First Leg)
Sat 10—F.A. Challenge Cup Final
Tue 13—England v Argentina (Full International)
Wed 14—European Cup Winners' Cup Final
Sat 17—F.A. Challenge Trophy Final
Sat 17—Wales v England (British Championship)
Sat 17—N. Ireland v Scotland (British Championship)
Tue 20—England v N. Ireland (British Championship)
Wed 21—UEFA Cup Final (Second Leg)
Wed 21—Scotland v Wales (British Championship)
Fri 23—Wales v N. Ireland (British Championship)
Sat 24—Scotland v England (British Championship)
Wed 28—European Champion Clubs' Cup Final

JUNE 1980
Sun 1—Australia v England (Australian Soccer Federation Centenary match)
11-22—European Championship Final Tournament (in Italy)
(TO BE ARRANGED: SCOTLAND v BELGIUM (European Championship) and Scotland v Belgium (UEFA Under-21 Competition).

SCOTTISH CUP FIXTURES 1979-80

SCOTTISH CUP QUALIFYING ROUNDS

Sept 1—1st Round
Sep 15—2nd Round
Sep 29—3rd Round
Oct 13—Semi-Finals
Nov 3—Final (South) — 1st Leg
Nov 10—Final (South) — 2nd Leg
Nov 10—Final (North)

SCOTTISH CUP

Dec 15—1st Round	Mar 8, 1980—5th Round
Jan 5—2nd Round	Apr 2 and 9—Semi-Final Ties
Jan 26—3rd Round	May 10—Final Tie
Feb 16—4th Round	

WELSH CUP FIXTURES 1979-80

1979		**1980**	
Sept 1—	(Qual)	Jan 19—	
Sept 22—		Feb 16—	
Oct 27—		Mar 15—	(S/F Prov)
Nov 17—		Dates to be arranged (Final)	

F.A. CHARITY SHIELD WINNERS

Nottingham Forest 5 Ipswich Town 0

At Wembley, August 12, 1978

1908	.... Manchester United	1952	.... Tottenham Hotspur
1909	.... Newcastle United	1953	.... Manchester United
1910	Brighton and Hove Albion	1954	.... Arsenal
1911	.... Manchester United	1955	(draw) W.B.A. and Wolves
1912	.... Blackburn Rovers	1956	.... Chelsea
1913	.... Professionals	1957	.... Manchester United
1920	.. West Bromwich Albion	1958	.... Manchester United
1921	.... Tottenham Hotspur	1959	.... Bolton Wanderers
1922	.... Huddersfield Town	1960	...... Wolverhampton W.
1924	.... Professionals	1961	(draw) Burnley and Wolves)
1925	.... Professionals	1962	.... Tottenham Hotspur
1926	.... Amateurs	1963	.... Tottenham Hotspur
1927	.... Amateurs	1964	.... Everton
1928	.... Cardiff City	1965	(draw) Liverpool, West Ham
1929	.... Everton	1966	(draw) Man. U., Liverpool
1930	.... Professionals	1967	.... Liverpool
1931	.... Arsenal	1968	(draw) Man. U. and Spurs
1932	.... Arsenal	1969	.... Manchester City
1933	.... Everton	1970	.... Leeds United
1934	.... Arsenal	1971	.... Everton
1935	.... Arsenal	1972	.... Leicester City
1936	.... Sheffield Wednesday	1973	.... Burnley
1937	.... Sunderland	1974	.... Liverpool
1938	.... Manchester City	1975	.... Derby County
1939	.... Arsenal	1976	.... Liverpool
1949	.... Arsenal	1977	. (draw) Liverpool, Man U.
1950	(draw) Portsmouth, Wolves	1978	.... Nottingham Forest
1951	.... World Cup Team		

FOOTBALL LEAGUE REFEREES 1979–80

ASHLEY, N. J. (Nantwich)
BAKER, K. W. (Rugby)
BAKER, M. R. (Wolverhampton)
BANKS, R. A. (Manchester)
BATES, S. G. (Bristol)
BIDMEAD, M. J. (Chessington)
BOMBROFF, W. H. (Bristol)
BRAY, J. E. (Hinckley, Leics.)
BRIDGES, R. (Deeside)
BUNE, T. G. (Billingshurst)
BURDEN, L. F. (Corfe Mullen, Dorset)
BUTCHER, J. K. (Kendal)
CALLOW, V. G. (Solihull)
CHADWICK, R. (Darwen)
CHALLINOR, A. (Rotherham)
CHALLIS, R. C. (Tonbridge)
CIVIL, D. W. (Birmingham)
CLARKE D. E. (Accrington)
COURTNEY, G. (Spennymoor)
COX, A. D. (South Croydon)
DANIELS, B. H. (Brentwood)
DOBSON, A. (Blackburn)
DOWNEY, C. (Hounslow)
FARLEY, T. (Newton Aycliffe)
FLINT, G. E. (Kirkby-in-Ashfield)
GLASSON, A. R. (Salisbury)
GLOVER, N. H. (Chorley)
GREY, A. W. (Gt. Yarmouth)
GUNN, A. (Burgess Hill, Sussex)
HACKETT, K. S. (Sheffield)
HAMIL, A. J. (Wolverhampton)
HEATH, M. J. (Stoke)
HEDGES, D. A. (Oxford)
HILL, B. (Wellingborough)
HOUGH, J. D. (Macclesfield)
HUNTING, J. (Leicester)
HUTCHINSON, D. (Bourn, Cambs.)
LETTS, D. (Basingstoke)
LEWIS, R. S. (Gt. Bookham, Surrey)
LLOYD, D. W. (Fernhill Heath)
LOVATT, J. (Crewe)
LOWE, M. (Sheffield)
McNALLY, K. (South Wirral)
MARTIN, B. (Keyworth, Notts.)
MARTIN, J. E. (Alton, Hants.)
MASKELL, C. A. (Cambridge)
MIDGLEY, N. (Salford)
MILLS, T. (Barnsley)
MORRIS, T. L. (Leeds)
NAPTHINE, G. J. (Loughborough)
NEWSOME, C. L. (Broseley, Salop)
NOLAN, G. (Stockport)
OWEN, D. (Wirral)
OWEN, G. P. (Anglesey)
PARTRIDGE, P. (Cockfield, Co. Durham)
PECK, M. G. (Doncaster)
PHIPPS, F. (Wrexham)
PORTER, A. (Bolton)
READ, E. A. (Bristol)
REDFERN, K. A. (Whitley Bay)
REEVES, D. V. (Uxbridge)
REEVES, P. G. (Leicester)
RICHARDSON, D. (Great Harwood)
RICHARDSON, D. T. (Lincoln)
RICHARDSON, P. J. (Lincoln)
ROBINSON, A. (Portsmouth)
ROBINSON, H. R. (Norwich)
ROBINSON, L. M. (Sutton Coldfield)
SALMON, K. G. (Barnet)
SAUNDERS, A. (Newcastle)
SCOTT, M. P. (Nottingham)
SEEL, C. N. (Carlisle)
SEVILLE, A. (Birmingham)
SEWELL, J. (Birstall, Leics.)
SHAPTER, L. C. (Newton Abbott)
SHAW, D. (Sandbach)
SPENCER, T. D. (Salisbury, Wilts.)
STEVENS, B. T. (Stonehouse, Glos.)
TAYLOR, M. J. (Deal, Kent)
THOMAS, C. (Porthcawl)
TOSELAND, R. W. (Market Harborough, Leics.)
TYLDESLEY, P. A. (Stockport)
TYSON, G. M. (Sunderland)
VICKERS, D. S. (Ilford)
WALMSLEY, K. (Thornton, Blackpool)
WARNER, J. M. (Wednesbury, W. Mid.)
WEBB, D. A. (Radcliffe)
WHITE, C. B. (Harrow)
WILLIS, P. N. (Meadowfield, Co. Durham)
WORRALL, J. B. (Warrington)

THE FOOTBALL ASSOCIATION CHALLENGE CUP COMPETITION SEASON 1979-80

EXEMPTIONS

44 Clubs to the Third Round Proper

Arsenal	Everton	Orient
Aston Villa	Fulham	Preston North End
Birmingham City	Ipswich Town	Queens Park Rangers
Bolton Wanderers	Leeds United	Shrewsbury Town
Brighton & Hove Albion	Leicester City	Southampton
Bristol City	Liverpool	Stoke City
Bristol Rovers	Luton Town	Sunderland
Burnley	Manchester City	Swansea City
Cambridge United	Manchester United	Tottenham Hotspur
Cardiff City	Middlesbrough	Watford
Charlton Athletic	Newcastle United	West Bromwich Albion
Chelsea	Norwich City	West Ham United
Coventry City	Nottingham Forest	Wrexham
Crystal Palace	Notts County	Wolverhampton Wanderers
Derby County	Oldham Athletic	

52 Clubs to the First Round Proper

Aldershot	Grimsby Town	Rochdale
Altrincham†	Halifax Town	Rotherham United
Barnsley	Hartlepool United	Scarborough†
Blackburn Rovers	Hereford United	Scunthorpe United
Blackpool	Huddersfield Town	Sheffield United
AFC Bournemouth	Hull City	Sheffield Wednesday
Bradford City	Kettering Town*	Southend United
Brentford	Lincoln City	Stafford Rangers*
Bury	Mansfield Town	Stockport County
Carlisle United	Milwall	Swindon Town
Chester	Newport County	Torquay United
Chesterfield	Northampton Town	Tranmere Rovers
Colchester United	Oxford United	Walsall
Crewe Alexandra	Peterborough United	Wigan Athletic
Darlington	Plymouth Argyle	Wimbledon
Doncaster Rovers	Portsmouth	York City
Exeter City	Port Vale	
Gillingham	Reading	

*Trophy Finalists

†Occupying the place formerly allocated to the FA Amateur Cup Finalists but now to be granted to the two non-Football League Clubs considered most appropriate.

20 Clubs to the Fourth Round Qualifying

Barnet	Leatherhead	Tooting & Mitcham United
Blyth Spartans	Maidstone United	Wealdstone
Dagenham	Minehead	Weymouth
Dartford	Morecambe	Worcester City
Enfield	Nuneaton Borough	Workington
Hitchin Town	Runcorn	Wycombe Wanderers
AP Leamington	Southport	

THE SOUTHERN FOOTBALL LEAGUE

PREMIER DIVISION

	P.	W.	D.	L.	F.	A.	Pts.
Worcester City	42	27	11	4	92	33	65
Kettering Town	42	27	7	8	109	43	61
Telford United	42	22	10	10	60	39	54
Maidstone United	42	18	18	6	55	35	54
Bath City	42	17	19	6	59	41	53
Weymouth	42	18	15	9	71	51	51
A. P. Leamington	42	19	11	12	65	53	49
Redditch United	42	19	10	13	70	57	48
Yeovil Town	42	15	16	11	59	49	46
Witney Town	42	17	10	15	53	52	44
Nuneaton Borough	42	13	17	12	59	50	43
Gravesend & Northfleet	42	15	12	15	56	55	42
Barnet	42	16	10	16	52	64	42
Hillingdon Borough	42	12	16	14	50	41	40
Wealdstone	42	12	12	18	51	59	36
Atherstone Town	42	9	17	16	46	65	35
Dartford	42	10	14	18	40	56	34
Cheltenham Town	42	11	10	21	38	72	32
Margate	42	10	9	23	44	75	29
Dorchester Town	42	7	11	24	46	86	25
Hastings United	42	5	13	24	37	85	23
Bridgend Town	42	6	6	30	39	90	18

FIRST DIVISION NORTH

	P.	W.	D.	L.	F.	A.	Pts.
Grantham	38	21	10	7	70	45	52
Merthyr Tydfil	38	22	7	9	90	53	51
Alvechurch	38	20	10	8	70	42	50
Bedford Town	38	19	9	10	74	49	47
King's Lynn	38	17	11	10	57	46	45
Oswestry Town	38	18	8	12	63	43	44
Gloucester City	38	18	8	12	75	59	44
Burton Albion	38	16	10	12	51	40	42
Kidderminster Harriers	38	13	14	11	70	60	40
Bedworth United	38	13	14	11	41	34	40
Tamworth	38	15	8	15	47	45	38
Stourbridge	38	15	7	16	64	61	37
Barry Town	38	14	9	15	51	53	37
Enderby Town	38	14	8	16	46	55	36
Banbury United	38	10	13	15	42	58	33
Wellingborough Town	38	13	6	19	50	71	32
Cambridge City	38	9	9	20	37	62	27
Bromsgrove Rovers	38	6	14	18	33	61	26
Milton Keynes City	38	7	9	22	37	87	23
Corby Town	38	5	6	27	40	85	16

FIRST DIVISION SOUTH

	P.	W.	D.	L.	F.	A.	Pts.
Dover	40	28	9	3	88	20	65
Folkestone & Shepway	40	22	6	12	84	50	50
Gosport Borough	40	19	11	10	62	47	49
Chelmsford City	40	20	7	13	65	61	47
Minehead	40	16	13	11	58	39	45
Poole Town	40	15	15	10	48	44	45
Hounslow	40	16	12	12	56	45	44

Waterlooville	40	17	10	13	52	43	44
Trowbridge Town	40	15	12	13	65	61	42
Aylesbury United	40	16	9	15	54	52	41
Taunton Town	40	16	9	15	53	51	41
Bognor Regis Town	40	17	7	16	58	58	41
Dunstable	40	18	4	18	57	55	40
Tonbridge A.F.C.	40	15	10	15	43	47	40
Salisbury	40	13	10	17	46	51	36
Basingstoke Town	40	12	11	17	49	62	35
Addlestone	40	12	9	19	56	64	33
Andover	40	12	6	22	47	69	30
Ashford Town	40	10	10	20	28	53	30
Crawley Town	40	9	9	22	44	75	27
Canterbury City	40	6	3	31	31	98	15

OCS INTER-LEAGUE CUP FINAL

Sunday 13th May 1979

Southern Football League 1 Northern Premier League 0

FIAT IRISH LEAGUE CHAMPIONSHIP

	P.	W.	D.	L.	F.	A.	Pts.
Linfield	22	14	6	2	46	21	34
Glenavon	22	11	6	5	42	30	28
Ards	22	11	5	6	47	34	27
Glentoran	22	9	8	5	36	33	26
Portadown	22	10	5	7	35	27	25
Larne	22	10	4	8	43	35	24
Cliftonville	22	7	7	8	31	29	21
Coleraine	22	7	6	9	29	30	20
Crusaders	22	6	8	8	30	33	20
Bangor	22	5	8	9	28	41	18
Ballymena United	22	4	6	12	25	46	14
Distillery	22	2	3	17	19	52	7

NORTHERN PREMIER FOOTBALL LEAGUE

	P	W.	D.	L.	F.	A.	Pts.
Mossley	44	32	5	7	117	48	69
Altrincham	44	25	11	8	93	39	61
Matlock Town	44	24	8	12	100	59	56
Scarborough	44	19	14	11	61	44	52
Southport	44	19	14	11	62	49	52
Boston United	44	17	18	9	40	33	52
Runcorn	44	21	9	14	79	54	51
Stafford Ranger	44	18	14	12	67	41	50
Goole Town	44	17	15	12	56	61	49
Northwich Victoria	44	18	11	15	64	52	47
Lancaster City	44	17	12	15	62	54	46
Bangor City	44	15	14	15	65	66	44
Worksop Town	44	13	14	17	55	67	40
Workington	44	16	7	21	62	74	39
Netherfield	44	13	11	20	39	69	37
Barrow	44	14	9	21	47	78	37
Gainsborough Trinity	44	12	12	20	52	67	36
Morecambe	44	11	13	20	55	65	35
Frickley Athletic	44	13	9	22	58	70	35
South Liverpool	44	12	10	22	48	85	34
Gateshead	44	11	11	22	42	63	33
Buxton	44	11	9	24	50	84	31
Macclesfield Town	44	8	10	26	40	92	26

CHESHIRE COUNTY LEAGUE

(FIRST DIVISION)

	P.	W.	D.	L.	F.	A.	Pts.
Horwick R.M.I.	42	35	2	5	89	45	72
Witton Albion	42	30	4	8	114	38	64
Marine	42	29	5	8	104	38	63
Stalybridge Celtic	42	25	5	12	93	47	55
Burscough	42	19	15	8	59	31	53
Winsford United	42	21	11	10	74	49	53
Chorley	42	21	8	13	66	43	50
Formby	42	20	9	13	73	57	49
Leek Town	42	19	10	13	62	43	48
Droylsden	42	18	9	15	62	61	45
Nantwich Town	42	18	8	16	76	72	44
Fleetwood Town	42	17	10	15	70	68	44
Hyde United	42	15	12	15	59	57	42
St. Helens Town	42	16	9	17	59	57	41
Darwen	42	15	9	18	52	53	39
Rhyl	42	15	8	19	53	60	38
Ashton United	42	13	5	24	63	94	31
New Mills	42	9	11	22	58	82	29
Rossendale United	42	11	6	25	51	108	28
Radcliffe Borough	42	4	7	31	37	115	15
New Brighton	42	3	5	34	36	115	11
Middlewich Athletic	42	3	4	35	43	120	10

LEADING GOALSCORERS 1978/79
(League and League Cup)

Meachin, P. (Marine) 30; McClatchey, D. (Marine) 29; Keelan, K. (Stalybridge Celtic) 24; Cooke, T. (Stalybridge Celtic) 23; Walker, J. (Witton Albion) 22; Jaycock, W. (Burscough) 20; Pearson, J. (Horwich R.M.I.) 20.

CHESHIRE COUNTY LEAGUE

(SECOND DIVISION)

	P.	W.	D.	L.	F.	A.	Pts.
Bootle	34	19	9	6	61	35	47
Curzon Ashton	34	18	9	7	57	32	45
Prescot Town**	34	20	5	9	68	37	43
Kirkby Town	34	18	6	10	66	42	42
Accrington Stanley	34	18	6	10	65	43	42
Irlam Town	34	16	10	8	47	33	42
Congleton Town	34	14	13	7	52	31	41
Prescot B.I.	34	15	11	8	55	42	41
Eastwood (Hanley)	34	15	9	10	60	47	39
Prestwich Heys**	34	17	5	12	53	41	37
Maghull	34	11	7	16	41	50	29
Ford Motors	34	9	10	15	38	52	28
Anson Villa	34	10	7	17	39	60	27
Warrington Town	34	11	5	18	45	69	27
Atherton Collieries	34	8	9	17	43	56	25
Skelmersdale United	34	9	6	19	36	53	24
Glossop	34	6	6	22	42	83	18
Ashtown Town	34	3	5	26	22	84	11

**Prescot Town and Prestwich Heys have each had two points deducted.

NORTHERN LEAGUE

	P.	W.	D.	L.	F.	A.	Pts.
Spennymoor United	38	25	6	7	96	43	81
Bishop Auckland	38	25	5	8	96	38	80
Ashington	38	23	7	8	79	47	76
Crook Town	38	21	10	7	63	38	73
Blyth Spartans	38	19	12	7	81	39	69
Consett**	38	21	9	8	84	52	69
North Shields	38	21	4	13	76	55	67
South Bank	38	16	11	11	58	47	59
Horden Colliery Welfare	38	17	8	13	64	56	59
Durham City	38	15	9	14	63	62	54
Billingham Synthonia	38	12	12	14	60	55	48
Tow Law Town	38	12	8	18	54	63	44
Shildon	38	11	10	17	52	69	43
Whitby Town**	38	11	12	15	55	68	42
Whitley Bay	38	9	9	20	54	77	36
West Auckland Town	38	9	9	20	54	87	36
Ferryhill Athletic	38	10	5	23	43	74	35
Willington	38	7	10	21	41	75	31
Penrith	38	8	7	23	35	82	31
Evenwood Town**	38	4	5	29	31	112	14

** denotes three points deducted.

League Cup Winners: Blyth Spartans.
League Cup Finalists: Consett.

Durham Challenge Cup Winners: Spennymoor United.
Durham Challenge Cup Finalists: Horden Colliery Welfare.

North Riding Senior Cup Winners: Billingham Synthonia.
Northumberland Senior Cup Winners: North Shields.

BASS League of Ireland

	P.	W.	D.	L.	F.	A.	Pts.
Dundalk	30	19	7	4	57	25	45
Bohemians	30	18	7	5	53	21	43
Drogheda Utd.	30	18	6	6	60	40	42
Waterford	30	17	8	5	48	32	42
Shamrock Rov.	30	17	3	10	45	25	37
Limerick	30	14	8	8	39	25	36
Athlone Town	30	14	7	9	56	41	35
Finn Harps	30	14	6	10	56	41	34
Home Farm	30	13	7	10	47	33	33
Sligo Rovers	30	9	7	14	35	40	25
Cork Alberts	30	7	9	14	35	49	23
Thurles Town	30	9	5	16	35	62	23
Shelbourne	30	6	9	15	41	58	21
St. Patrick's Ath.	30	7	6	17	36	62	20
Galway Rovers	30	4	5	21	41	79	13
Cork Celtic	30	2	4	24	16	67	8

CENTRAL LEAGUE

	P.	W.	D.	L.	F.	A.	Pts.
Liverpool	42	30	7	5	89	34	67
Nottingham Forest	42	26	6	10	82	38	58
Stoke City	42	23	11	8	65	45	57
Manchester City	42	23	9	10	70	45	55
Wolverhampton Wanderers	42	21	11	10	79	42	53
West Bromwich Albion	42	18	12	12	80	51	48
Coventry City	42	19	8	15	87	71	46
Sheffield Wednesday	42	19	6	17	74	68	44
Leeds United	42	14	16	12	50	49	44
Aston Villa	42	16	11	15	67	54	43
Manchester United	42	17	9	16	66	58	43
Derby County	42	17	9	16	67	64	43
Everton	42	18	7	17	50	49	43
Burnley	42	15	9	18	42	56	39
Huddersfield Town	42	13	11	18	52	58	37
Blackburn Rovers	42	11	13	18	53	69	35
Bolton Wanderers	42	11	13	18	61	83	35
Sheffield United	42	12	9	21	55	88	33
Newcastle United	42	12	8	22	44	72	32
Blackpool	42	11	6	25	41	68	28
Bury	42	9	4	29	54	104	22
Preston North End	42	6	7	29	46	107	19

IRISH LEAGUE CHAMPIONSHIP

Saturday 24th November.
Glenavon v. Ards
Ballymena Utd. v. Portadown
Coleraine v. Glentoran
Crusaders v. Distillery
Linfield v. Cliftonville
Bangor v. Larne

Saturday 1st December.
Larne v. Glenavon
Ards v. Linfield
Cliftonville v. Crusaders
Distillery v. Coleraine
Glentoran v. Ballymena Utd.
Portadown v. Bangor

Saturday 8th December.
Crusaders v. Ards
Linfield v. Glenavon
Bangor v. Glentoran
Ballymena Utd. v. Distillery
Coleraine v. Cliftonville
Portadown v. Larne

Saturday 15th December
Larne v. Linfield
Glenavon v. Crusaders
Ards v. Coleraine
Cliftonville v. Ballymena Utd.
Distillery v. Bangor
Glentoran v. Portadown

Saturday 22nd December
Ballymena Utd. v. Ards
Coleraine v. Glenavon
Crusaders v. Linfield
Portadown v. Distillery
Bangor v. Cliftonville
Glentoran v. Larne

Wednesday 26th December.
Larne v. Crusaders
Linfield v. Coleraine
Glenavon v. Ballymena Utd.
Ards v. Bangor
Cliftonville v. Portadown
Distillery v. Glentoran

Saturday 29th December
Portadown v. Ards
Bangor v. Glenavon
Ballymena Utd. v. Linfield
Coleraine v. Crusaders
Glentoran v. Cliftonville
Distillery v. Larne

Tuesday 1st January.
Larne v. Coleraine
Crusaders v. Ballymena Utd.
Linfield v. Bangor
Glenavon v. Portadown
Ards v. Glentoran
Cliftonville v. Distillery

Saturday 5th January.
Distillery v. Ards
Glentoran v. Glenavon
Portadown v. Linfield
Bangor v. Crusaders
Ballymena Utd. v. Coleraine
Cliftonville v. Larne

Saturday 12th January.
Ballymena Utd. v. Larne
Coleraine v. Bangor
Crusaders v. Portadown
Linfield v. Glentoran
Glenavon v. Distillery
Ards v. Cliftonville

Saturday 19th January.
Larne v. Ards
Cliftonville v. Glenavon
Distillery v. Linfield
Glentoran v. Crusaders
Portadown v. Coleraine
Bangor v. Ballymena Utd.

Saturday 26th January.
Ards v. Glenavon
Cliftonville v. Linfield
Distillery v. Crusaders
Glentoran v. Coleraine
Portadown v. Ballymena Utd.
Larne v. Bangor

Bass Irish Cup — Round 1
Saturday 2nd February.

Saturday 9th February.
Glenavon v. Larne
Linfield v. Ards
Crusaders v. Cliftonvillle
Coleraine v. Distillery
Ballymena Utd. v. Glentoran
Bangor v. Portadown

Saturday 16th February
Ards v. Crusaders
Glenavon v. Linfield
Glentoran v. Bangor
Distillery v. Ballymena Utd.
Cliftonville v. Coleraine
Larne v. Portadown

Bass Irish Cup — Round 2
Saturday 23rd February.

Saturday 1st March.
Linfield v. Larne
Crusaders v. Glenavon
Coleraine v. Ards
Ballymena Utd. v. Cliftonville
Bangor v. Distillery
Portadown v. Glentoran

Saturday 8th March
Ards v. Ballymena Utd.
Glenavon v. Coleraine
Linfield v. Crusaders
Distillery v. Portadown
Cliftonville v. Bangor
Larne v. Glentoran

Saturday 15th March
Crusaders v. Larne
Coleraine v. Linfield
Ballymena Utd. v. Glenavon
Bangor v. Ards
Portadown v. Cliftonville
Glentoran v. Distillery

Bass Irish Cup — Semi-finals
Saturday 22nd March.

Saturday 29th March.
Ards v. Portadown
Glenavon v. Bangor
Linfield v. Ballymena Utd.
Crusaders v. Coleraine
Cliftonville v. Glentoran
Larne v. Distillery

Saturday 5th April
Coleraine v. Larne
Ballymena Utd. v. Crusaders
Bangor v. Linfield
Portadown v. Glenavon
Glentoran v. Ards
Distillery v. Cliftonville

Easter
Monday 7th or Tuesday 8th April.
Ards v. Distillery
Glenavon v. Glentoran
Linfield v. Portadown
Crusaders v. Bangor
Coleraine v. Ballymena Utd.
Larne v. Cliftonville

Saturday 12th April.
Larne v. Ballymena Utd.
Bangor v. Coleraine
Portadown v. Crusaders
Glentoran v. Linfield
Distillery v. Glenavon
Cliftonville v. Ards

Saturday 19th April.
Ards v. Larne
Glenavon v. Cliftonville
Linfield v. Distillery
Crusaders v. Glentoran

Coleraine v. Portadown	Bass Irish Cup Final
Ballymena Utd. v. Bangor	Saturday 26th April.

ULSTER CUP COMPETITION

	P	W.	D.	L.	F.	A.	Pts.
Linfield	11	8	1	2	28	12	17
Crusaders	11	6	3	2	21	16	15
Ballymena Utd.	11	6	2	3	19	14	14
Cliftonville	11	5	4	2	15	11	14
Glenavon	11	4	5	2	21	20	13
Glentoran	11	4	4	3	15	12	12
Portadown	11	2	5	4	18	19	9
Larne	11	3	3	5	16	18	9
Coleraine	11	3	2	6	19	26	8
Bangor	11	3	2	6	16	23	8
Ards	11	0	7	4	13	18	7
Distillery	11	1	4	6	9	23	6

HENNESSY GOLD CUP COMPETITION

Section A

	P.	W.	D.	L.	F.	A.	Pts.
Portadown	5	5	0	0	11	5	10
Linfield	5	4	0	1	17	6	9
Glenavon	5	3	0	2	9	11	6
Ards	5	1	1	3	8	14	3
Distillery	5	0	2	3	3	8	2
Bangor	5	0	1	4	6	12	2

Section B

	P.	W.	D.	L.	F.	A.	Pts.
Cliftonville	5	3	1	1	10	6	7
Glentoran	5	3	1	1	9	7	7
Ballymena Utd.	5	3	0	2	10	8	6
Coleraine	5	2	0	3	6	8	4
Crusaders	5	1	1	3	5	8	3
Larne	5	0	1	4	4	13	1

Final: Portadown (2) v. Cliftonville (1)
after extra time.

WEST MIDLANDS (REGIONAL) LEAGUE

Premier Division

	P.	W.	D.	L.	F.	A.	Pts.
Willenhall Town	34	23	7	4	82	32	53
Lye Town	34	21	11	2	62	33	53
Dudley Town	34	21	8	5	53	23	50
Hednesford Town	34	19	10	5	59	26	48
Tividale	34	19	6	9	63	40	44
Bilston	34	15	10	9	50	34	40

Brierley Hill Alliance	34	17	5	12	67	47	39
Brereton Social	34	17	5	12	48	40	39
Darlaston	34	15	5	14	52	51	35
Coventry Sporting	34	12	6	16	39	48	30
Hinckley Athletic	34	12	5	17	42	52	29
Ledbury Town	34	10	7	17	57	63	27
V.S. Rugby	34	9	9	16	29	41	27
Wednesfield Social	34	7	12	15	27	45	26
Halesowen Town	34	8	8	18	35	55	24
Armitage	34	7	6	21	44	69	20
Gresley Rovers	34	4	7	23	27	67	15
Gornal Athletic	34	4	5	25	21	91	13

League Cup Final — Lye Town 0 v. 2 Brierley Hill Alliance

WELSH LEAGUE

PREMIER DIVISION

	P.	W.	D.	L.	F.	A.	Pts.
Pontllanfraith	34	23	7	4	73	37	53
Cardiff Corinthians	34	20	4	10	77	45	44
Newport County	34	14	13	7	55	25	41
Afan Lido	34	17	7	10	43	37	41
Ton Pentre	34	16	8	10	62	42	40
Swansea City	34	15	9	10	61	47	39
Ammanford Town	34	14	11	9	47	42	39
Pembroke Boro'	34	16	6	12	63	50	38
Merthyr Tydfil	34	15	7	12	61	58	37
Barry Town	34	12	11	11	54	45	35
Caerau Athletic	34	13	8	13	45	55	34
Sully	34	13	7	14	42	41	33
Milford United	34	12	8	14	55	45	32
Llanelli	34	11	9	14	41	55	31
Pontlottyn	34	9	10	15	41	57	28
Treharris Athletic	34	9	8	17	43	65	26
Ferndale Athletic	34	3	6	25	36	90	12
Cardiff College	34	1	7	26	25	88	9

LANCASHIRE FOOTBALL COMBINATION

	P.	W.	D.	L.	F.	A.	Pts.
Wren Rovers	28	21	5	2	51	10	47
Leyland Motors	28	18	6	4	63	26	42
Whitworth Valley	28	15	8	5	49	35	38
Colne Dynamoes	28	13	8	7	50	32	34
Bacup Borough	28	14	6	8	48	36	34
Padiham	28	14	5	9	40	35	33
Lytham	28	11	8	9	41	34	30
Nelson	28	7	10	11	31	33	24
Blackpool Mech.	28	7	10	11	21	33	24
Chorley Res.	28	6	11	11	34	37	23
Wigan Rovers	28	6	9	13	25	40	21
Barrow Res.	28	6	8	14	25	39	20
Daisy Hill	28	5	10	13	26	45	20
Clitheroe	28	7	5	16	31	46	19
Ashton Athletic	28	3	5	20	17	67	11

THE ALLIANCE PREMIER FOOTBALL LEAGUE

FIXTURES 1979-80

Saturday 18th. August 1979.
Bangor City v A.P. Leamington
Barrow v Yeovil Town
Boston United v Bath City
Maidstone United v Scarborough
Northwich Victoria v Redditch United
Nuneaton Borough v Barnet
Stafford Rangers v Kettering Town
Telford United v Gravesend & N
Weymouth v Altrincham
Worcester City v Wealdstone

Monday 20th. August
Atrincham v. Telford United
Northwich Victoria v. Bangor City
Worcester City v. Weymouth

Tuesday 21st. August
A.P. Leamington v. Nuneaton B
Barnet v. Boston United
Gravesend & Northfleet v. Bath City
Redditch United v. Stafford Rangers

Wednesday 22nd. August
Kettering Town v. Wealdstone
Scarborough v. Barrow
Yeovil Town v. Maidstone United

Saturday 25th. August
Altrincham v. Maidstone United
A.P. Leamington v. Northwich V
Barnet v. Stafford Rangers
Bath City v. Barrow
Gravesend & Northfleet v. Bangor C
Kettering Town v. Worcester City
Redditch United v. Telford United
Scarborough v. Weymouth
Wealdstone v. Nuneaton Borough
Yeovil Town v. Boston United

Monday 27th. August
Scarborough v. Northwich Victoria
Stafford Rangers v. Nuneaton B
Wealdstone v. Maidstone United
Worcester City v. Weymouth

Tuesday 28th. August
A.P. Leamington v. Boston United
Bangor City v. Altrincham

Saturday 1st. September
Bangor City v. Redditch United
Barrow v. A.P. Leamington
Boston United v. Gravesend & N
Maidstone United v. Wealdstone
Northwich Victoria v. Bath City
Nuneaton Borough v. Kettering Town
Stafford Rangers v. Scarborough
Telford United v. Yeovil Town
Weymouth v. Barnet
Worcester City v. Altrincham

Monday 3rd. September
Bath City v. Gravesend and Northfleet
Nuneaton Borough v. A.P. Leamington
Telford United v. Altrincham
Wealdstone v. Kettering

Tuesday 4th. September
Bangor City v. Northwich Victoria
Barrow v. Scarborough
Maidstone United v. Yeovil Town
Stafford Rangers v. Redditch United

Wednesday 5th. September
Boston United v. Barnet
Weymouth v. Worcester City

Saturday 8th. September
Altrincham v. Nuneaton Borough
A.P. Leamington v. Telford United
Barnet v. Maidstone United
Bath City v. Bangor City
Gravesend & Northfleet v. Barrow
Kettering Town v. Weymouth
Redditch United v. Boston United
Scarborough v. Worcester City
Wealdstone v. Stafford Rangers
Yeovil Town v. Northwich Victoria

Monday 10th. September
Bath City v. Nuneaton Borough
Telford United v. Northwich Victoria

Tuesday 11th. September
Barrow v. Stafford Rangers

Wednesday 12th. September
Kettering Town v. A.P. Leamington

Saturday 15th. September
Maidstone United v. Kettering Town
Nuneaton Borough v. Scarborough
Stafford Rangers v. Altrincham
Weymouth v. Wealdstone
Worcester City v. Barnet

Saturday 22nd. September
Altrincham v. Yeovil Town
Barnet v. Redditch United
Barrow v. Weymouth
Boston United v. Nuneaton Borough

Kettering Town v. Bath City
Maidstone United v. Bangor City
Northwich Victoria v. Worcester City
Scarborough v. Gravesend & N
Telford United v. Stafford Rangers
Wealdstone v. A.P. Leamington

Saturday 29th. September
A.P. Leamington v. Kettering Town
Scarborough or Northwich v. Redditch
Gravesend v. Worcester or Weymouth
Altrincham v. Bangor City
Barnet v. Bath City
Boston U v. Wealdstone or Maidstone
Stafford R or Nuneaton Boro v. Yeovil
Telford United v. Barrow

Saturday 6th. October —
A.P. Leamington v. Scarborough
Bath City v. Barnet
Gravesend & N v. Wealdstone
Maidstone United v. Boston United
Nuneaton Borough v. Northwich V
Redditch United v. Altrincham
Stafford Rangers v. Bangor City
Weymouth v. Telford United
Worcester City v. Barrow
Yeovil Town v. Kettering Town

Saturday 13th. October
Altrincham v. Bath City
Bangor City v. Weymouth
Boston United v. Worcester City
Northwich Victoria v. Maidstone U
Scarborough v. Yeovil Town
Telford United v. Nuneaton Borough

Saturday 20th. October
A.P. Leamington v. Altrincham
Bath City v. Wealdstone
Gravesend & N v. Kettering Town
Maidstone United v. Telford United
Nuneaton Borough v. Barrow
Redditch United v. Scarborough
Stafford Rangers v. Northwich Victoria
Weymouth v. Boston United
Worcester City v. Bangor City
Yeovil Town v. Barnet

Saturday 27th. October
Altrincham v. Gravesend & Northfleet
Bangor City v. Nuneaton Borough
Barnet v. A.P. Leamington
Barrow v. Maidstone United
Boston United v. Stafford Rangers
Kettering Town v. Redditch United
Northwich Victoria v. Weymouth
Scarborough v. Bath City
Telford United v. Worcester City
Wealdstone v. Yeovil Town

Saturday 3rd. November
Bath City v. Telford United
Gravesend & Northfleet v. Northwich V
Redditch United v. Barrow
Scarborough v. Kettering
Yeovil Town v. Bangor City

Saturday 10th. November
A.P. Leamington v. Yeovil Town
Bangor City v. Scarborough
Barnet v. Telford United
Barrow v. Altrincham
Bath City v. Maidstone United
Boston United v. Wealdstone
Northwich Victoria v. Kettering Town
Nuneaton Borough v. Redditch
Weymouth v. Gravesend & Northfleet
Worcester City v. Stafford Rangers

Saturday 17th. November
Altrincham v. Boston United
Gravesend & Northfleet v. Worcester C
Kettering Town v. Barnet
Maidstone United v. Nuneaton Borough
Redditch United v. Weymouth
Scarborough v. Northwich Victoria
Stafford Rangers v. A.P. Leamington
Telford United v. Barrow
Wealdstone v. Bangor City
Yeovil Town v. Bath City

Saturday 24th. November
A.P. Leamington v. Bath City
Barnet v. Barrow
Boston United v. Telford United
Northwich Victoria v. Wealdstone
Nuneaton Borough v. Yeovil Town
Weymouth v. Maidstone United
Worcester City v. Redditch United

Saturday 1st. December
Altrincham v. Barnet
Barrow v. Boston United
Kettering Town v. Bangor City
Maidstone United v. A.P. Leamington
Redditch United v. Gravesend & N
Stafford Rangers v. Weymouth
Wealdstone v. Scarborough
Yeovil Town v. Worcester City

Saturday 8th. December
A.P. Leamington v. Worcester City
Bangor City v. Barnet
Bath City v. Redditch United
Kettering Town v. Barrow
Maidstone United v. Stafford Rangers
Northwich Victoria v. Boston United
Nuneaton Borough v. Weymouth
Scarborough v. Telford United
Wealdstone v. Altrincham
Yeovil Town v. Gravesend and N

Saturday 15th. December
Altrincham v. Kettering Town
Barnet v. Northwich Victoria
Barrow v. Bangor City
Boston United v. Scarborough
Gravesend & N v. Nuneaton Borough
Redditch United v. Yeovil Town
Stafford Rangers v. Bath City
Telford United v. Wealdstone
Weymouth v. A.P. Leamington
Worcester City v. Maidstone United

Saturday 26th. December
Altrincham v. Scarborough
A.P. Leamington v. Redditch United
Bangor City v. Telford United
Barnet v. Wealdstone
Bath City v. Worcester City
Gravesend & N v. Maidstone United
Kettering Town v. Boston United
Northwich Victoria v. Barrow
Nuneaton Borough v. Stafford Rangers
Yeovil Town v. Weymouth

Saturday 29th. December
Altrincham v. Northwich Victoria
Barnet v. Scarborough
Barrow v. Wealdstone
Boston United v. Bangor City
Gravesend & N v. A.P. Leamington
Redditch United v. Maidstone United
Stafford Rangers v. Yeovil Town
Telford United v. Kettering Town
Weymouth v. Bath City
Worcester City v. Nuneaton Borough

Tuesday 1st. January 1980.
Barrow v. Northwich Victoria
Boston United v. Kettering Town
Maidstone United v. Gravesend & N
Redditch United v. A.P. Leamington
Scarborough v. Altrincham
Stafford Rangers v. Nuneaton Borough
Telford United v. Bangor City
Wealdstone v. Barnet
Weymouth v. Yeovil Town
Worcester City v. Bath City

Saturday 5th. January
A.P. Leamington v. Weymouth
Bangor City v. Barrow
Bath City v. Stafford Rangers
Kettering Town v. Altrincham
Maidstone United v. Worcester City
Northwich Victoria v. Barnet
Nuneaton Borough v. Gravesend & N
Scarborough v. Boston United
Wealdstone v. Telford United
Yeovil Town v. Redditch United

Saturday 12th. January
Barnet v. Gravesend & Northfleet
Wealdstone v. Redditch United

Saturday 19th. January
Altrincham v. Wealdstone
Barnet v. Bangor City
Barrow v. Kettering Town
Boston United v Northwich Victoria
Gravesend & N v. Yeovil Town
Redditch United v. Bath City
Stafford Rangers v. Maidstone United
Telford United v. Scarborough
Weymouth v. Nuneaton Borough
Worcester City v. A.P. Leamington

Saturday 26th. January
A.P. Leamington v. Gravesend & N
Bangor City v. Boston United
Bath City v. Weymouth
Kettering Town v. Telford United
Maidstone United v. Redditch United
Northwich Victoria v. Altrincham
Nuneaton Borough v. Worcester City
Scarborough v. Barnet
Wealdstone v. Barrow
Yeovil Town v. Stafford Rangers

Saturday 2nd. February
A.P. Leamington v. Maidstone United
Bangor City v. Kettering Town
Barnet v. Altrincham
Boston United v. Barrow
Gravesend and N v. Redditch United
Northwich Victoria v. Telford United
Nuneaton Borough v. Bath City
Scarborough v. Wealdstone
Weymouth v. Stafford Rangers
Worcester City v. Yeovil Town

Saturday 9th. February
Altrincham v. Bangor City
Barrow v. Barnet
Bath City v. A.P. Leamington
Kettering Town v. Scarborough
Maidstone United v. Weymouth
Redditch United v. Worcester City
Stafford Rangers v. Gravesend and N
Telford United v. Boston United
Wealdstone v. Northwich Victoria
Yeovil Town v. Nuneaton Borough

Saturday 16th. February
A.P. Leamington v. Stafford Rangers
Bangor City v. Wealdstone
Barnet v. Kettering Town
Barrow v. Telford United
Bath City v. Yeovil Town
Boston United v. Altrincham
Northwich Victoria v. Scarborough

Chelmsford City v. Dartford
Salisbury v. Bognor Regis Town
Tonbridge v. Poole Town

Tuesday, 11th. September
Bedworth United v. Milton Keynes C
Bridgend Town v. Merthyr Tydfil
Cambridge City v. Corby Town
Gloucester City v. Barry Town
Stourbridge v. Bromsgrove Rovers
Trowbridge Town v. Cheltenham T
Witney Town v. Enderby Town

Andover v. Dunstable
Ashford Town v. Aylesbury United
Gosport Borough v. Folkestone & S
Hastings United v. Crawley Town
Hillingdon Borough v. Canterbury C
Hounslow v. Basingstoke Town
Margate v. Addlestone

Wednesday 12th. September
Alvechurch v. Wellingborough
King's Lynn v. Bedford Town

Dover v. Dorchester Town
Fareham Town v. Waterlooville

Saturday, 22nd. September
Alvechurch v. Kidderminster Harriers
Barry Town v. Cheltenham Town
Bedworth United v. Banbury United
Bridgend Town v. Bedford Town
Cambridge City v. Merthyr Tydfil
Gloucester City v. Enderby Town
King's Lynn v. Wellingborough
Minehead v. Bromsgrove Rovers
Stourbridge v. Milton Keynes City
Taunton Town v. Witney Town
Trowbridge Town v. Corby Town

Ashford Town v. Addlestone
Basingstoke Town v. Dartford
Chelmsford City v. Canterbury City
Dover v. Dunstable
Fareham Town v. Dorchester Town
Gosport Borough v. Crawley Town
Hillingdon Borough v. Bognor Regis T
Hounslow v. Folkestone & Shepway
Margate v. Andover
Salisbury v. Hastings United
Tonbridge v. Aylesbury United
Waterlooville v. Poole Town

Saturday, 29th. September
Banbury United v. Alvechurch
Bedford Town v. Stourbridge
Bromsgrove Rovers v. Barry Town
Cheltenham Town v. Cambridge City
Corby Town v. Bridgend Town
Enderby Town v. Trowbridge Town
Kidderminster H v. Taunton Town
Merthyr Tydfil v. King's Lynn
Milton Keynes City v. Minehead
Wellingborough v. Bedworth United
Witney Town v. Gloucester City

Addlestone v. Dover
Andover v. Ashford Town
Aylesbury United v. Fareham Town
Bognor Regis Town v. Hounslow
Canterbury City v. Basingstoke Town
Crawley Town v. Hillingdon Borough
Dartford v. Salisbury
Dorchester Town v. Waterlooville
Dunstable v. Tonbridge
Folkestone & Shepway v. Chelmsford C
Hastings United v. Gosport Borough
Poole Town v. Margate

Monday, 1st. October
Bedford Town v. Taunton Town
Bromsgrove Rovers v. Cambridge City
Minehead v. King's Lynn

Poole Town v. Hillingdon Borough

Tuesday, 2nd. October
Banbury United v. Trowbridge Town
Barry Town v. Witney Town
Corby Town v. Alvechurch
Merthyr Tydfil v. Stourbridge
Wellingborough v. Gloucester City

Aylesbury United v. Salisbury
Basingstoke Town v. Fareham Town
Bognor Regis Town v. Tonbridge
Canterbury City v. Andover
Crawley Town v. Margate
Dartford v. Ashford Town
Dorchester Town v. Chelmsford City
Hounslow v. Dover

Wednesday, 3rd. October
Cheltenham Town v. Bridgend Town
Enderby Town v. Bedworth United
Milton Keynes City v. Kidderminster H

Addlestone v. Gosport Borough
Folkestone & Shepway v. Dunstable
Waterlooville v. Hastings United

Saturday, 6th. October
Alvechurch v. Minehead
Bedworth United v. Merthyr Tydfil
Bridgend Town v. Milton Keynes City
Cambridge City v. Barry Town
Gloucester City v. Corby Town
Kidderminster H v. Enderby Town
King's Lynn v. Cheltenham Town

Stourbridge v. Wellingborough
Taunton Town v. Bromsgrove Rovers
Trowbridge Town v. Bedford Town
Witney Town v. Banbury United

Andover v. Folkestone & Shepway
Ashford Town v. Bognor Regis Town
Chelmsford City v. Waterlooville
Dover v. Crawley Town
Dunstable v. Canterbury City
Fareham Town v. Dartford
Gosport Borough v. Poole Town
Hastings United v. Aylesbury United
Hillingdon Borough v. Dorchester T
Margate v. Hounslow
Salisbury v. Addlestone
Tonbridge v. Basingstoke Town

Monday, 8th. October
Salisbury v. Gosport Borough

Tuesday, 9th. October
Andover v. Chelmsford City
Ashford Town v. Dover
Aylesbury United v. Hounslow
Bognor Regis Town v. Basingstoke T
Crawley Town v. Waterlooville
Dartford v. Margate
Dorchester Town v. Poole Town
Dunstable v. Hillingdon Borough
Hastings United v. Fareham Town

Wednesday 10th. October
Addlestone v. Tonbridge
Folkestone & S v. Canterbury City

Saturday 13th. October
Alvechurch v. Taunton Town
Barry Town v. Merthyr Tydfil
Bedworth United v. Kidderminster H
Bridgend Town v. Enderby Town
Bromsgrove Rovers v. Milton Keynes
Cambridge City v. Wellingborough
Cheltenham Town v. Gloucester City
King's Lynn v. Banbury United
Minehead v. Bedford Town
Stourbridge v. Corby Town
Trowbridge Town v. Witney Town

Basingstoke Town v. Dorchester Town
Canterbury City v. Addlestone
Chelmsford City v. Crawley Town
Dover v. Andover
Fareham Town v. Dunstable
Gosport Borough v. Dartford
Hillingdon Borough v. Salisbury
Hounslow v. Hastings United
Margate v. Ashford Town
Poole Town v. Bognor Regis Town
Tonbridge v. Folkestone & Shepway
Waterlooville v. Aylesbury United

Saturday, 20th. October
Banbury United v. Cambridge City
Bedford Town v. Bromsgrove Rovers
Corby Town v. Minehead
Enderby Town v. Stourbridge
Gloucester City v. Trowbridge Town
Kidderminster Harriers v. King's Lynn
Merthyr Tydfil v. Cheltenham Town
Milton Keynes City v. Alvechurch
Taunton Town v. Bedworth United
Wellingborough v. Barry Town
Witney Town v. Bridgend Town
Addlestone v. Fareham Town
Andover v. Tonbridge
Ashford Town v. Gosport Borough
Aylesbury United v. Poole Town
Bognor Regis Town v. Chelmsford C
Crawley Town v. Hounslow
Dartford v. Canterbury City
Dorchester Town v. Margate
Dunstable v. Waterlooville
Folkestone & S v. Basingstoke Town
Hastings United v. Hillingdon Borough
Salisbury v. Dover

Monday, 22nd. October
Chelmsford City v. Andover
Poole Town v. Dorchester Town
Tonbridge v. Addlestone

Tuesday 23rd. October
Basingstoke Town v. Bognor Regis T
Canterbury City v. Folkestone & S
Gosport Borough v. Salisbury
Hillingdon Borough v. Dunstable
Hounslow v. Aylesbury United
Margate v. Dartford

Wednesday, 24th. October
Dover v. Ashford Town
Fareham Town v. Hastings United
Waterlooville v. Crawley Town

Saturday, 27th. October
Barry Town v. Banbury United
Bedworth United v. Alvechurch
Bridgend Town v. Gloucester City
Bromsgrove Rovers v. Corby Town
Cambridge City v. Kidderminster H
King's Lynn v. Taunton Town
Merthyr Tydfil v. Trowbridge Town
Milton Keynes City v. Bedford Town
Minehead v. Enderby Town
Stourbridge v. Witney Town
Wellingborough v. Cheltenham Town

Basingstoke Town v. Crawley Town
Bognor Regis Town v. Canterbury C
Chelmsford City v. Hastings United
Dorchester Town v. Aylesbury United

Fareham Town v. Andover
Folkestone & Shepway v. Dartford
Hillingdon Borough v. Gosport B
Hounslow v. Salisbury
Margate v. Dover
Poole Town v. Dunstable
Tonbridge v. Ashford Town
Waterlooville v. Addlestone

Saturday 3rd. November
Alvechurch v. Stourbridge
Banbury United v. Minehead
Bedford Town v. Wellingborough
Chelthenham Town v. Bromsgrove R
Corby Town v. Barry Town
Enderby Town v. Merthyr Tydfil
Gloucester City v. Cambridge City
Kidderminster Harriers v. Bridgend T
Taunton Town v. Milton Keynes City
Trowbridge Town v. Bedworth United
Witney Town v. King's Lynn

Addlestone v. Chelmsford City
Andover v. Hillingdon Borough
Ashford Town v. Hounslow
Aylesbury United v. Canterbury City
Bognor Regis Town v. Margate
Crawley Town v. Dorchester Town
Dartford v. Waterlooville
Dover v. Folkestone & Shepway
Dunstable v. Basingstoke Town
Gosport Borough v. Fareham Town
Hastings United v. Poole Town
Salisbury v. Tonbridge

Monday, 5th. November
Salisbury v. Fareham Town

Tuesday, 6th. November
Andover v. Basingstoke Town
Ashford Town v. Chelmsford City
Bognor Regis Town v. Dover
Crawley Town v. Poole Town
Dunstable v. Aylesbury United
Gosport Borough v. Dorchester Town
Hastings United v. Tonbridge
Hillingdon Borough v. Hounslow
Margate v. Canterbury City

Wednesday, 7th. November
Addlestone v. Dartford
Folkestone & S v. Waterlooville

Saturday 10th. November
Barry Town v. Taunton Town
Bedford Town v. Corby Town
Bridgend Town v. Wellingborough
Bromsgrove Rovers v. Witney Town
Cambridge City v. Alvechurch
Cheltenham Town v. Kidderminster H
King's Lynn v. Bedworth United
Merthyr Tydfil v. Banbury United
Milton Keynes City v. Enderby Town
Minehead v. Gloucester City
Stourbridge v. Trowbridge Town

Aylesbury United v. Hillingdon B
Basingstoke Town v. Salisbury
Canterbury City v. Hastings United
Chelmsford City v. Gosport Borough
Dartford v. Bognor Regis Town
Dorchester Town v. Addlestone
Fareham Town v. Dover
Folkestone & Shepway v. Crawley T
Hounslow v. Dunstable
Poole Town v. Andover
Tonbridge v. Margate
Waterlooville v. Ashford Town

Saturday, 17th. November
Alvechurch v. King's Lynn
Banbury United v. Cheltenham Town
Bedworth United v. Bedford Town
Corby Town v. Milton Keynes City
Enderby Town v. Bromsgrove Rovers
Gloucester City v. Stourbridge
Kidderminster Harriers v. Barry Town
Taunton Town v. Cambridge City
Trowbridge Town v. Bridgend Town
Wellingborough v. Merthyr Tydfil
Witney Town v. Minehead
Addlestone v. Poole Town
Andover v. Waterlooville
Ashford Town v. Fareham Town
Bognor Regis Town v. Folkestone & S
Crawley Town v. Canterbury City
Dover v. Tonbridge
Dunstable v. Dorchester Town
Gosport Borough v. Hounslow
Hastings United v. Basingstoke Town
Hillingdon Borough v. Dartford
Margate v. Aylesbury United
Salisbury v. Chelmsford City

Monday, 19th. November
Chelmsford City v. Ashford Town
Poole Town v. Crawley Town
Tonbridge v. Hastings United

Tuesday, 20th. November
Aylesbury United v. Dunstable
Basingstoke Town v. Andover
Canterbury City v. Margate
Dartford v. Addlestone
Dorchester Town v. Gosport Borough
Hounslow v. Hillingdon Borough

Wednesday, 21st. November
Dover v. Bognor Regis Town
Fareham Town v. Salisbury
Waterlooville v. Folkestone & S

Saturday, 24th. November
Alvechurch v. Witney Town
Banbury United v. Milton Keynes City
Barry Town v. Enderby Town
Bedworth United v. Minehead
Cambridge City v. Bridgend Town
Cheltenham Town v. Corby Town
Kidderminster H v. Bromsgrove R
King's Lynn v. Gloucester City
Merthyr Tydfil v. Bedford Town
Taunton Town v. Stourbridge
Wellingborough v. Trowbridge Town

Basingstoke Town v. Waterlooville
Bognor Regis Town v. Fareham Town
Canterbury City v. Dorchester Town
Chelmsford City v. Poole Town
Crawley Town v. Ashford Town
Dartford v. Andover
Folkestone & S v. Aylesbury United
Gosport Borough v. Dunstable
Hastings United v. Addlestone
Hillingdon Borough v. Dover
Hounslow v. Tonbridge
Salisbury v. Margate

Saturday, 1st. December
Bedford Town v. Alvechurch
Bridgend Town v. Bedworth United
Bromsgrove Rovers v. Banbury United
Corby Town v. Taunton Town
Enderby Town v. Cheltenham Town
Gloucester City v. Kidderminster H
Milton Keynes City v. Merthyr Tydfil
Minehead v. Cambridge City
Stourbridge v. Barry Town
Trowbridge Town v. King's Lynn
Witney Town v. Wellingborough

Addlestone v. Bognor Regis Town
Andover v. Hastings United
Ashford Town v. Hillingdon Borough
Aylesbury United v. Dartford
Dorchester Town v. Folkestone & S
Dover v. Basingstoke Town
Dunstable v. Salisbury
Fareham Town v. Chelmsford City
Margate v. Gosport Borough
Poole Town v. Canterbury City
Tonbridge v. Crawley Town
Waterlooville v. Hounslow

Saturday, 8th. December
Alvechurch v. Corby Town
Banbury United v. Witney Town
Barry Town v. Gloucester City
Bedworth United v. Enderby Town
Cambridge City v. Bromsgrove Rovers
Cheltenham Town v. Trowbridge T
Kidderminster H v. Milton Keynes City
King's Lynn v. Minehead
Merthyr Tydfil v. Bridgend Town
Taunton Town v. Bedford Town
Wellingborough v. Stourbridge

Basingstoke Town v. Tonbridge
Bognor Regis Town v. Ashford Town
Canterbury City v. Dunstable
Chelmsford City v. Dorchester Town
Crawley Town v. Dover
Dartford v. Fareham Town
Folkestone & Shepway v. Andover
Gosport Borough v. Addlestone
Hastings United v. Waterlooville
Hillingdon Borough v. Poole Town
Hounslow v. Margate
Salisbury v. Aylesbury United

Saturday 15th. December
Bedford Town v. Barry Town
Bridgend Town v. King's Lynn
Bromsgrove Rovers v. Bedworth U
Corby Town v. Merthyr Tydfil
Enderby Town v. Taunton Town
Gloucester City v. Banbury United
Milton Keynes City v. Cheltenham T
Minehead v. Wellingborough
Stourbridge v. Cambridge City
Trowbridge Town v. Alvechurch
Witney Town v. Kidderminster H

Addleston v. Salisbury
Andover v. Canterbury City
Ashford Town v. Dartford
Aylesbury United v. Hastings United
Dorchester Town v. Hillingdon B
Dover v. Hounslow
Dunstable v. Folkestone & Shepway
Fareham Town v. Basingstoke Town
Margate v. Crawley Town
Poole Town v. Gosport Borough
Tonbridge v. Bognor Regis Town
Waterlooville v. Chelmsford City

Saturday, 22nd. December
Alvechurch v. Enderby Town
Banbury United v. Bridgend Town
Barry Town v. Minehead
Bedworth United v. Stourbridge
Cambridge City v. Trowbridge Town
Cheltenham Town v. Bedford Town
Kidderminster Harriers v. Corby Town
King's Lynn v. Bromsgrove Rovers
Merthyr Tydfil v. Witney Town
Taunton Town v. Gloucester City
Wellingborough v. Milton Keynes City

Basingstoke Town v. Aylesbury United
Bognor Regis Town v. Dorchester T
Canterbury City v. Fareham Town

Chelmsford City v. Dover
Crawley Town v. Andover
Dartford v. Dunstable
Folkestone & Shepway v. Addlestone
Gosport Borough v. Tonbridge
Hastings United v. Ashford Town
Hillingden Borough v. Margate
Hounslow v. Poole Town
Salisbury v. Waterlooville

Wednesday 26th. December
Bedford Town v. Banbury United
Bridgend Town v. Barry Town
Bromsgrove Rovers v. Alvechurch
Corby Town v. King's Lynn
Enderby Town v. Wellingborough
Gloucester City v. Bedworth United
Milton Keynes City v. Cambridge City
Minehead v. Merthyr Tydfil
Stourbridge v. Kidderminster Harriers
Trowbridge Town v. Taunton Town
Witney Town v. Cheltenham Town

Addleston v. Basingstoke Town
Andover v. Hounslow
Ashford Town v. Canterbury City
Aylesbury United v. Crawley Town
Dorchester Town v. Hastings United
Dover v. Dartford
Dunstable v. Bognor Regis Town
Fareham Town v. Hillingdon Borough
Margate v. Folkestone & Shepway
Poole Town v. Salisbury
Tonbridge v. Chelmsford City
Waterlooville v. Gosport Borough

Saturday, 29th. December
Barry Town v. Alvechurch
Bedford Town v. Witney Town
Cambridge City v. Bedworth United
Cheltenham Town v. Minehead
Corby Town v. Enderby Town
Kidderminster H v. Trowbridge Town
Merthyr Tydfil v. Bromsgrove Rovers
Milton Keynes City v. Gloucester City
Stourbridge v. King's Lynn
Taunton Town v. Bridgend Town
Wellingborough v. Banbury United

Aylesbury United v. Addlestone
Basingstoke Town v. Gosport Borough
Bognor Regis Town v. Crawley Town
Canterbury City v. Waterlooville
Chelmsford City v. Hillingdon Borough
Dartford v. Hounslow
Dorchester Town v. Andover
Dunstable v. Margate
Fareham Town v. Tonbridge
Folkestone & Shepway v. Poole Town
Hastings United v. Dover
Salisbury v. Ashford Town

Tuesday 1st. January
Alvechurch v. Bridgend Town
Banbury United v. Enderby Town
Barry Town v. Trowbridge Town
Bedworth United v. Corby Town
Cambridge City v. Witney Town
Cheltenham Town v. Stourbridge
Kidderminster H v. Bedford Town
King's Lynn v. Milton Keynes City
Merthyr Tydfil v. Gloucester City
Taunton Town v. Minehead
Wellingborough v. Bromsgrove R

Basingstoke Town v. Poole Town
Bognor Regis Town v. Waterlooville
Canterbury City v. Dover
Chelmsford City v. Aylesbury United
Crawley Town v. Dunstable
Dartford v. Tonbridge
Folkestone & S v. Ashford Town
Gosport Borough v. Andover
Hastings United v. Margate
Hillingdon Borough v. Addlestone
Hounslow v. Fareham Town
Salisbury v. Dorchester Town

Saturday, 5th. January
Bedford Town v. King's Lynn
Bridgend Town v. Cheltenham Town
Bromsgrove Rovers v. Taunton Town
Corby Town v. Cambridge City
Enderby Town v. Kidderminster H
Gloucester City v. Wellingborough
Milton Keynes City v. Bedworth U
Minehead v. Alvechurch
Stourbridge v. Merthyr Tydfil
Trowbridge Town v. Banbury United
Witney Town v. Barry Town

Addlestone v. Crawley Town
Andover v. Salisbury
Ashford Town v. Basingstoke Town
Aylesbury United v. Bognor Regis T
Dorchester Town v. Hounslow
Dover v. Gosport Borough
Dunstable v. Hastings United
Fareham Town v. Folkestone & S
Margate v. Chelmsford City
Poole Town v. Dartford
Tonbridge v. Canterbury City
Waterlooville v. Hillingdon Borough

Saturday, 12th. January
Alvechurch v. Cheltenham Town
Banbury United v. Corby Town
Bedworth United v. Barry Town
Bridgend Town v. Stourbridge
Cambridge City v. Bedford Town

Gloucester City v. Bromsgrove Rovers
Kidderminster H v. Wellingborough
King's Lynn v. Enderby Town
Taunton Town v. Merthyr Tydfil
Trowbridge Town v. Minehead
Witney Town v. Milton Keynes City

Andover v. Aylesbury United
Ashford Town v. Dorchester Town
Chelmsford City v. Dunstable
Crawley Town v. Dartford
Dover v. Poole Town
Gosport Borough v. Canterbury City
Hastings United v. Bognor Regis T
Hillingdon Borough v. Basingstoke T
Hounslow v. Addlestone
Margate v. Fareham Town
Salisbury v. Folkestone & Shepway
Tonbridge v. Waterlooville

Saturday, 19th. January
Banbury United v. Taunton Town
Barry Town v. Cambridge City
Bedford Town v. Trowbridge Town
Bromsgrove Rovers v. Stourbridge
Cheltenham Town v. King's Lynn
Corby Town v. Gloucester City
Enderby Town v. Witney Town
Merthyr Tydfil v. Bedworth United
Milton Keynes City v. Bridgend Town
Minehead v. Kidderminster Harriers
Wellingborough v. Alvechurch

Addlestone v. Margate
Aylesbury United v. Ashford Town
Basingstoke Town v. Hounslow
Bognor Regis Town v. Salisbury
Canterbury City v. Hillingdon Borough
Crawley Town v. Hastings United
Dartford v. Chelmsford City
Dorchester Town v. Dover
Dunstable v. Andover
Folkestone & S v. Gosport Borough
Poole Town v. Tonbridge
Waterlooville v. Fareham Town

Saturday, 26th. January
Alvechurch v. Gloucester City
Barry Town v. Milton Keynes City
Bedworth United v. Witney Town
Bromsgrove Rovers v. Trowbridge T
Cheltenham Town v. Taunton Town
Enderby Town v. Bedford Town
King's Lynn v. Cambridge City
Merthyr Tydfil v. Kidderminster H
Minehead v. Bridgend Town
Stourbridge v. Banbury United
Wellingborough v. Corby Town

Addlestone v. Dunstable
Basingstoke Town v. Margate
Bognor Regis Town v. Andover
Canterbury City v. Salisbury
Dartford v. Dorchester Town
Fareham Town v. Crawley Town
Folkestone & Shepway v. Hastings U
Gosport Borough v. Aylesbury United
Hillingdon Borough v. Tonbridge
Hounslow v. Chelmsford City
Poole Town v. Ashford Town
Waterlooville v. Dover

Saturday 2nd. February
Alvechurch v. Merthyr Tydfil
Bedworth United v. Cheltenham Town
Bridgend Town v. Bromsgrove Rovers
Cambridge City v. Enderby Town
Gloucester City v. Bedford Twon
Kidderminster H v. Banbury United
King's Lynn v. Barry Town
Stourbridge v. Minehead
Taunton Town v. Wellingborough
Trowbridge Town v. Milton Keynes C
Witney Town v. Corby Town

Andover v. Addlestone
Ashford Town v. Dunstable
Chelmsford City v. Basingstoke Town
Dover v. Aylesbury United
Fareham Town v. Poole Town
Gosport Borough v. Bognor Regis T
Hastings United v. Dartford
Hillingdon Borough v. Folkestone & S
Hounslow v. Canterbury City
Margate v. Waterlooville
Salisbury v. Crawley Town
Tonbridge v. Dorchester Town

Saturday, 9th. February
Banbury United v. Bedworth United
Bedford Town v. Bridgend Town
Bromsgrove Rovers v. Minehead
Cheltenham Town v. Barry Town
Corby Town v. Trowbridge Town
Enderby Town v. Gloucester City
Kidderminster Harriers v. Alvechurch
Merthyr Tydfil v. Cambridge City
Milton Keynes City v. Stourbridge
Wellingborough v. King's Lynn
Witney Town v. Taunton Town

Addlestone v. Ashford Town
Andover v. Margate
Aylesbury United v. Tonbridge
Bognor Regis Town v. Hillingdon B
Canterbury City v. Chelmsford City
Crawley Town v. Gosport Borough
Dartford v. Basingstoke Town
Dorchester Town v. Fareham Town
Dunstable v. Dover

Folkestone & Shepway v. Hounslow
Hastings United v. Salisbury
Poole Town v. Waterlooville

Saturday, 16th. February
Alvechurch v. Banbury United
Barry Town v. Bromsgrove Rovers
Bedworth United v. Wellingborough
Bridgend Town v. Corby Town
Cambridge City v. Cheltenham Town
Gloucester City v. Witney Town
King's Lynn v. Merthyr Tydfil
Minehead v. Milton Keynes City
Stourbridge v. Bedford Town
Taunton Town v. Kidderminster H
Trowbridge Town v. Enderby Town

Ashford Town v. Andover
Basingstoke Town v. Canterbury City
Chelmsford City v. Folkestone & S
Dover v. Addlestone
Fareham Town v. Aylesbury United
Gosport Borough v. Hastings United
Hillingdon Borough v. Crawley Town
Hounslow v. Bognor Regis Town
Margate v. Poole Town
Salisbury v. Dartford
Tonbridge v. Dunstable
Waterlooville v. Dorchester Town

Saturday, 23rd. February
Banbury United v. King's Lynn
Bedford Town v. Minehead
Corby Town v. Stourbridge
Enderby Town v. Bridgend Town
Gloucester City v. Cheltenham Town
Kidderminster H v. Bedworth United
Merthyr Tydfil v. Barry Town
Milton Keynes City v. Bromsgrove R
Taunton Town v. Alvechurch
Wellingborough v. Cambridge City
Witney Town v. Trowbridge Town

Addlestone v. Canterbury City
Andover v. Dover
Ashford Town v. Margate
Aylesbury United v. Waterlooville
Bognor Regis Town v. Poole Town
Crawley Town v. Chelmsford City
Dartford v. Gosport Borough
Dorchester Town v. Basingstoke Town
Dunstable v. Fareham Town
Folkestone & Shepway v. Tonbridge
Hastings United v. Hounslow
Salisbury v. Hillingdon Borough

Saturday, 1st. March
Alvechurch v. Milton Keynes City
Barry Town v. Wellingborough
Bedworth United v. Taunton Town
Bridgend Town v. Witney Town
Bromsgrove Rovers v. Bedford Town
Cambridge City v. Banbury United
Cheltenham Town v. Merthyr Tydfil
King's Lynn v. Kidderminster Harriers
Minehead v. Corby Town
Stourbridge v. Enderby Town
Trowbridge Town v. Gloucester City

Basingstoke Town v. Folkestone & S
Canterbury City v. Dartford
Chelmsford City v. Bognor Regis Town
Dover v. Salisbury
Fareham Town v. Addlestone
Gosport Borough v. Ashford Town
Hillingdon Borough v. Hastings United
Hounslow v. Crawley Town
Margate v. Dorchester Town
Poole Town v. Aylesbury United
Tonbridge v. Andover
Waterlooville v. Dunstable

Saturday, 8th. March
Alvechurch v. Bedworth United
Banbury United v. Barry Town
Bedford Town v. Milton Keynes City
Cheltenham Town v. Wellingborough
Corby Town v. Bromsgrove Rovers
Enderby Town v. Minehead
Gloucester City v. Bridgend Town
Kidderminster H v. Cambridge City
Taunton Town v. King's Lynn
Trowbridge Town v. Merthyr Tydfil
Witney Town v. Stourbridge

Addlestone v. Waterlooville
Andover v. Fareham Town
Ashford Town v. Tonbridge
Aylesbury United v. Dorchester Town
Canterbury City v. Bognor Regis Town
Crawley Town v. Basingstoke Town
Dartford v. Folkestone & Shepway
Dover v. Margate
Dunstable v. Poole Town
Gosport Borough v. Hillingdon Borough
Hastings United v. Chelmsford City
Salisbury v. Hounslow

Saturday, 15th. March
Barry Town v. Corby Town
Bedworth United v. Trowbridge Town
Bridgend Town v. Kidderminster H
Bromsgrove Rovers v. Cheltenham T
Cambridge City v. Gloucester City
King's Lynn v. Witney Town
Merthyr Tydfil v. Enderby Town
Milton Keynes City v. Taunton Town
Minehead v. Banbury United
Stourbridge v. Alvechurch
Wellingborough v. Bedford Town

Basingstoke Town v. Dunstable
Canterbury City v. Aylesbury United
Chelmsford City v. Addlestone
Dorchester Town v. Crawley Town
Fareham Town v. Gosport Borough
Folkestone & Shepway v. Dover
Hillingdon Borough v. Andover
Hounslow v. Ashford Town
Margate v. Bognor Regis Town
Poole Town v. Hastings United
Tonbridge v. Salisbury
Waterlooville v. Dartford

Saturday, 22nd. March
Alvechurch v. Cambridge City
Banbury United v. Merthyr Tydfil
Bedworth United v. King's Lynn
Corby Town v. Bedford Town
Enderby Town v. Milton Keynes City
Gloucester City v. Minehead
Kidderminster H v. Cheltenham Town
Taunton Town v. Barry Town
Trowbridge Town v. Stourbridge
Wellingborough v. Bridgend Town
Witney Town v. Bromsgrove Rovers

Addlestone v. Dorchester Town
Andover v. Poole Town
Ashford Town v. Waterlooville
Bognor Regis Town v. Dartford
Crawley Town v. Folkestone & S
Dover v. Fareham Town
Dunstable v. Hounslow
Gosport Borough v. Chelmsford City
Hastings United v. Canterbury City
Hillingdon Borough v. Aylesbury U
Margate v. Tonbridge
Salisbury v. Basingstoke Town

Saturday, 29th. March
Barry Town v. Kidderminster Harriers
Bedford Town v. Bedworth United
Bridgend Town v. Trowbridge Town
Bromsgrove Rovers v. Enderby Town
Cambridge City v. Taunton Town
Cheltenham Town v. Banbury United
King's Lynn v. Alvechurch
Merthyr Tydfil v. Wellingborough
Milton Keynes City v. Corby Town
Minehead v. Witney Town
Stourbridge v. Gloucester City

Aylesbury United v. Margate
Basingstoke Town v. Hastings United
Canterbury City v. Crawley Town
Chelmsford City v. Salisbury
Dartford v. Hillingdon Borough
Dorchester Town v. Dunstable
Fareham Town v. Ashford Town
Folkestone & S v. Bognor Regis Town

Hounslow v. Gosport Borough
Poole Town v. Addlestone
Tonbridge v. Dover
Waterlooville v. Andover

Friday, 4th. April
Bedford Town v. Cheltenham Town
Bridgend Town v. Banbury United
Bromsgrove Rovers v. King's Lynn
Corby Town v. Kidderminster Harriers
Enderby Town v. Alvechurch
Gloucester City v. Taunton Town
Milton Keynes City v. Wellingborough
Minehead v. Barry Town
Stourbridge v. Bedworth United
Trowbridge Town v. Cambridge City
Witney Town v. Merthyr Tydfil

Addlestone v. Folkestone & Shepway
Andover v. Crawley Town
Ashford Town v. Hastings United
Aylesbury United v. Basingstoke Town
Dorchester Town v. Bognor Regis Town
Dover v. Chelmsford City
Dunstable v. Dartford
Fareham Town v. Canterbury City
Margate v. Hillingdon Borough
Poole Town v. Hounslow
Tonbridge v. Gosport Borough
Waterlooville v. Salisbury

Saturday, 5th. April
Alvechurch v. Bromsgrove Rovers
Banbury United v. Bedford Town
Barry Town v. Bridgend Town
Bedworth United v. Gloucester City
Cambridge City v. Milton Keynes City
Cheltenham Town v. Witney Town
Kidderminster Harriers v. Stourbridge
King's Lynn v. Corby Town
Merthyr Tydfil v. Minehead
Taunton Town v. Trowbridge Town
Wellingborough v. Enderby Town

Basingstoke Town v. Addlestone
Bognor Regis Town v. Dunstable
Canterbury City v. Ashford Town
Chelmsford City v. Tonbridge
Crawley Town v. Aylesbury United
Dartford v. Dover
Folkestone & Shepway v. Margate
Gosport Borough v. Waterlooville
Hastings United v. Dorchester Town
Hillingdon Borough v. Fareham Town
Hounslow v. Andover
Salisbury v. Poole Town

Monday, 7th. April
Bedford Town v. Kidderminster Harriers
Bridgend Town v. Alvechurch
Bromsgrove Rovers v. Wellingborough

Corby Town v. Bedworth United
Enderby Town v. Banbury United
Gloucester City v. Merthyr Tydfil
Milton Keynes City v. King's Lynn
Minehead v. Taunton Town
Stourbridge v. Cheltenham Town
Trowbridge Town v. Barry Town
Witney Town v. Cambridge City

Addlestone v. Hillingdon Borough
Andover v. Gosport Borough
Ashford Town v. Folkestone & S
Aylesbury United v. Chelmsford City
Dorchester Town v. Salisbury
Dover v. Canterbury City
Dunstable v. Crawley Town
Fareham Town v. Hounslow
Margate v. Hastings United
Poole Town v. Basingstoke Town
Tonbridge v. Dartford
Waterlooville v. Bognor Regis Town

Saturday, 12th. April
Alvechurch v. Bedford Town
Banbury United v. Bromsgrove Rovers
Barry Town v. Stourbridge
Bedworth United v. Bridgend Town
Cambridge City v. Minehead
Cheltenham Town v. Enderby Town
Kidderminster H v. Gloucester City
King's Lynn v. Trowbridge Town
Merthyr Tydfil v. Milton Keynes City
Taunton Town v. Corby Town
Wellingborough v. Witney Town

Basingstoke Town v. Ashford Town
Bognor Regis Town v. Aylesbury U
Canterbury City v. Tonbridge
Chelmsford City v. Margate
Crawley Town v. Addlestone
Dartford v. Poole Town
Folkestone & S v. Fareham Town
Gosport Borough v. Dover
Hastings United v. Dunstable
Hillingdon Borough v. Waterlooville
Hounslow v. Dorchester Town
Salisbury v. Andover

Saturday, 19th. April
Bedford Town v. Merthyr Tydfil
Bridgend Town v. Cambridge City
Bromsgrove Rovers v. Kidderminster H
Corby Town v. Cheltenham Town
Enderby Town v. Barry Town
Gloucester City v. King's Lynn
Milton Keynes City v. Banbury United
Minehead v. Bedworth United
Stourbridge v. Taunton Town
Trowbridge Town v. Wellingborough
Witney Town v. Alvechurch

Addlestone v. Hastings United
Andover v. Dartford
Ashford Town v. Crawley Town
Aylesbury United v. Folkestone & S
Dorchester Town v. Canterbury City
Dover v. Hillingdon Borough
Dunstable v. Gosport Borough
Fareham Town v. Bognor Regis Town
Margate v. Salisbury
Poole Town v. Chelmsford City
Tonbridge v. Hounslow
Waterlooville v. Basingstoke Town

Saturday, 26th. April
Alvechurch v. Trowbridge Town
Banbury United v. Gloucester City
Barry Town v. Bedford Town
Bedworth United v. Bromsgrove R
Cambridge City v. Stourbridge
Cheltenham Town v. Milton Keynes C
Kidderminster H v. Witney Town
King's Lynn v. Bridgend Town
Merthyr Tydfil v. Corby Town
Taunton Town v. Enderby Town
Wellingborough v. Minehead
Basingstoke Town v. Dover
Bognor Regis Town v. Addlestone
Canterbury City v. Poole Town
Chelmsford City v. Fareham Town
Crawley Town v. Tonbridge
Dartford v. Aylesbury United
Folkestone & S v. Dorchester Town
Gosport Borough v. Margate
Hastings United v. Andover
Hillingdon Borough v. Ashford Town
Hounslow v. Waterlooville
Salisbury v. Dunstable

Saturday, 3rd. May
Banbury United v. Stourbridge
Bedford Town v. Cambridge City
Bridgend Town v. Taunton Town
Bromsgrove Rovers v. Merthyr Tydfil
Corby Town v. Wellingborough
Enderby Town v. King's Lynn
Gloucester City v. Alvechurch
Milton Keynes City v. Barry Town
Minehead v. Cheltenham Town
Trowbridge Town v. Kidderminster H
Witney Town v. Bedworth United

Addlestone v. Hounslow
Andover v. Bognor Regis Town
Ashford Town v. Salisbury
Aylesbury United v. Gosport Borough
Crawley Town v. Fareham Town
Dorchester Town v. Dartford
Dover v. Hastings United
Dunstable v. Chelmsford City

Margate v. Basingstoke Town
Poole Town v. Folkestone & Shepway
Tonbridge v. Hillingdon Borough
Waterlooville v. Canterbury City

FOOTBALL LEAGUE CUP FINALS

1960–61	Rotherham United 2 Aston Villa 0 Aston Villa 3 Rotherham United 0 (Aston Villa won 3–2 on aggregate)
1961–62	Rochdale 0 Norwich City 3 Norwich City 1 Rochdale 0 (Norwich City won 4–0 on aggregate)
1962–63	Birmingham City 3 Aston Villa 1 Aston Villa 0 Birmingham City 0 (Birmingham City won 3–1 on aggregate)
1934–64	Stoke City 1 Leicester City 1 Leicester City 3 Stoke City 2 (Leicester won 4–3 on aggregate)
1964–65	Chelsea 3 Leicester City 2 Leicester City 0 Chelsea 0 (Chelsea won 3–2 on aggregate)
1965–66	West Ham United 2 W.B.A. 1 W.B.A. 4 West Ham United 1 (W.B.A. won 5–3 on aggregate)
1966–67*	Q.P.R. 3 W.B.A. 2
1967–68	Leeds United 1 Arsenal 0
1968–69	Swindon Town 3 Arsenal 1
1969–70	Manchester City 2 W.B.A. 1
1970–71	Tottenham Hotspur 2 Aston Villa 0
1971–72	Stoke City 2 Chelsea 1
1972–73	Tottenham Hotspur 1 Norwich City 0
1973–74	Wolverhampton W. 2 Manchester City 1
1974–75	Aston Villa 1 Norwich City 0
1975–76	Manchester City 2 Newcastle United 1
1976–77	Aston Villa 3 Everton 2 (After 0–0 and 1–1 draws)
1977–78	Nottingham Forest 1 Liverpool 0 (After 0–0 draw)
1978–79	Nottingham Forest 3 Southampton 2

1978–79 Final Teams

Wembley (100,000), March 17, 1979

Nottm. For.—Shilton, Barrett, Clark, McGovern, Lloyd, Needham, O'Neill, Gemmill, Birtles, Woodcock, Robertson.

Southampton.—Gennoe, Golac, Peach, Williams, Nicholl, Waldron, Ball, Boyer, Hayes (Sealy), Holmes, Curran.

Scorers: Nottm. For.—Birtles 2, Woodcock. Southampton.—Peach, Holmes.

* The 1966-67 game between Q.P.R. and W.B.A. was the first League Cup Final played at Wembley.

NATIONAL HONOURS

Complete list of men who have played for England in International Championships

(**I**, the abbreviation for Ireland; **S**, for Scotland; **W**, for Wales.)

In some instances, international matches have been played in the first half of the season, but to avoid confusion, all the dates g giveven bebelow are for the second half of the season. Thus 1960 refers to season 1959-60.

Abbott, W (Everton), 1902 v. W
A'Court, A (Liverpool), 1958 v. I; 1959 v. W
Adcock, H (Leicester City), 1930 v. I & W
Alcock, C. W (Wanderers), 1875 v. S
Aldridge, A (W.B.A.), 1888 v. I; (Walsall Town Swifts), 1889 v. I
Allen, A (Stoke City), 1960 v. W & I
Allen, G (Aston Villa), 1888 v. I
Allen, H (Wolverhampton Wanderers), 1888-9-90 v. S; 1888 v. W; 1888 v. I
Allen, J (Portsmouth), 1934 v. I & W
Allen, R (West Bromwich Albion), 1954 v. S; 1955 v. W
Alsford, W (Tottenham Hotspur), 1935 v. S
Amos, A (Old Carthusians), 1885 v. S; 1886 v. W
Arnold, J (Fulham), 1933 v. S
Anderson, R. D (Old Carthusians), 1879 v. W
Anderson, S (Sunderland), 1962 v. S
Armfield, J (Blackpool), 1960 v. S; 1961 v. I, W & S; 1962 v. W, I & S; 1963 v. I, W & S; 1964 v. W, I & S
Armitage, G. H (Charlton Athletic), 1926 v. I
Armstrong, K (Chelsea), 1955 v. S
Arthur, H. J (Blackburn Rovers), 1885-6 v. S; 1885-6-7 v. W; 1885-7 v. I
Ashcroft, J (Woolwich Arsenal), 1906 v. I, W & S
Ashton, C. T (Corinthians), 1926 v. I
Ashurst, W (Notts County), 1925 v. S & W
Astle, J (West Bromwich Albion), 1969 v. W; 1970 v. S
Aston, J (Manchester United), 1949 v. S & W; 1950 v. S, W & I; 1951 v. I
Athersmith, W. C (Aston Villa), 1897-8-9-1900 v. S, 1897-8-9-1900 v. W. 1892 v. I, 1897-8-9 v. I
Austin, S. W (Manchester City), 1926 v. I
Bach, P (Sunderland), 1899 v. I
Bache, J. V (Aston Villa), 1903-4 v. W; 1904-7-10 v. I; 1905-11 v. S
Baddeley, T (Wolverhampton Wanderers), 1903-4 v. S; 1904 v. W; 1903-4 v. I
Bagshaw, J. J (Derby County), 1920 v. I & W*(I)
Bailey, H. P (Leicester Fosse), 1908 v. W
Bailey, M (Charlton Athletic), 1965 v. W
Bailey, N. C (Old Westminster), 1878-9-80-1-2-3-4-5-6-7 v. S; 17 v. W; 1884-5 v. I
Bailey, E. F (Tottenham Hotspur), 1951 v. I & W; 1952 v. W; 1953 v. I
Bain, J (Winchester), 1877 v. S
Baker, A (Arsenal), 1928 v. W
Baker, B. H (Chelsea), 1926 v. I
Baker, J (Hibernian), 1960 v. I & S; (Arsenal), 1966 v. I
Ball, A (Blackpool), 1965 v. S; (Everton), 1967 v. I, W & S; 1968 v. W & S; 1969 v. I, W & S; 1970 v. W & S; 1971 v. I & S; (Arsenal), 1972 v. S; 1973 v. I. W & S; 1975 v. I, W & S
Ball, J (Bury), 1928 v. I
Ball, W (Birmingham City), 1920 v. W*(I)
Balmer, W (Everton), 1905 v. I
Bamber, J (Liverpool), 1921 v. W

Bambridge, A. L (Swifts), 1881-3 v. W; 1884 v. I
Bambridge, E. C (Swifts), 1879-80-1-2-3-4-5-6-7 v. S; 1882-3-4-5-6-7 v. W; 1882-4-5-7 v, I
Bambridge, E. H (Swifts), 1876 v. S
Banks, G (Leicester City), 1963 v. S; 1964 v. W, I & S; 1965 v. I & S; 1966 v. I & S; 1967 v. I, W & S; (Stoke City), 1968 v. W, I & S; 1969 v. I & S; 1970 v. W, I & S; 1971 v. I & S; 1972 v. W & S
Banks, H. E (Millwall), 1901 v. I
Banks, T (Bolton Wanderers), 1959 v. I
Bannister, W (Burnley), 1901 v. W; (Bolton Wanderers), 1902 v. I
Barclay, R (Sheffield United), 1932 v. S; 1933 v. I; 1936 v. S
Barkas, S (Manchester City), 1937 v. S; 1938 v. W & I
Barker, J (Derby County), 1935-6 v. S, W & I; 1937 v. W
Barker, R. C (Herts Rangers), 1872 v. S
Barker, R. R (Casuals), 1895 v. W
Barlow, R (West Bromwich Albion), 1955 v. I
Barnes, H (Manchester City), 1920 v. W*
Barnes, P (Manchester City), 1978 v. W & S; 1979 v. I, S
Barnett, H. H (Royal Engineers), 1882 v. I
Barrass, M. W (Bolton Wnaderers), 1946 v. W*; 1952 v. W & I; 1953 v. S
Barrett, A. F (Fulham), 1930 v. I
Barrett, J. W (West Ham United), 1929 v. I
Barson, F (Aston Villa), 1920 v. W
Barton, J (Blackburn Rovers), 1890 v. I
Barton, P. A (Birmingham City), 1922-5 v. I; 1924 v. S & W
Bassett, W. I. (West Bromwich Albion), 1889-90-1-2-3-4-5-6 v. S; 1889-90-2-6 v. W; 1889-91-5-6 v. I
Bastard, S. R (Upton Park), 1880 v. S
Bastin, C. S (Arsenal), 1932 v. W; 1934 v. S, I & W; 1935 v. S & I; 1936 v. S & W; 1937 v. W & I: 1938 v. S
Baugh, R (Stafford Road), 1886-90 v. I
Bayliss, J (West Bromwich Albion), 1891 v. I
Baynham, R (Luton Town), 1956 v. I
Beasley, A (Huddersfield Town), 1939 v. S
Beats, W. M (Wolverhampton Wanderers), 1901 v. W; 1902 v. S
Beattie, K (Ipswich Town), 1975 v. S
Becton, F (Liverpool), 1897 v. W; (Preston North End), 1895 v.
Bedford, H (Blackpool), 1925 v. I
Bell, C (Manchester City), 1969 v. W; 1972 v. W, I & S; 1973 v. W & S; 1974 v. W, I & S; 1975 v. I & S
Bennett, W (Sheffield United), 1901 v. S & W
Benson, R. W (Sheffield United), 1913 v. I
Bentley, R. T. F (Chelsea), 1950 v. S; 1953 v. W; 1955 v. W
Bestall, J. G (Grimsby Town), 1935 v. I
Berry, A (Oxford University), 1909 v. I
Betts, M. P. (Old Harrovians), 1877 v. S
Betts, W (Sheffield Wednesday), 1889 v. W
Beverly, J (Blackburn Rovers), 1884 v. S, W & I
Birkett, R (Middlesbrough), 1936 v. I
Birkett, R. H (Clapham Rovers), 1879 v. S
Birley, H. F (Oxford University), 1874-5 v. S
Bishop, S. M (Leicester City), 1927 v. S
Blackburn, F (Blackburn Rovers), 1901-4 v. S; 1902 v. I
Blenkinsop, E (Sheffield Wednesday), 1929-30-1-2-2-3 v. S, W & I
Bliss, H (Tottenham Hotspur), 1921 v. S
Bloomer, S (Derby County), 1895-7-8-9-1900-1-2-3-5; (Middlesbrough), 1907 v. S; 1896-7-9-1901-2-5 v. W; 1895-6-7-9-1902-5 v. I
Blunstone, F (Chelsea), 1955 v. W & S
Bond, R (Preston North End), 1905-6 v. W; 1906 v. S; (Bradford City), 1910 v. S, W & I

Bonsor, A. G (The Wanderers), 1873-5 v. S
Booth, F (Manchester City), 1905 v. I
Booth, T (Everton, 1903 v. S; (Blackburn Rovers), 1908 v. W
Bowden, E. R (Arsenal), 1935 v. W; 1936 v. W & I
Bower, A. G (Corinthians), 1924 v. I; 1925-7 v.W
Bowers, J. W (Derby County), 1934 v. S, I & W
Bowles, S (Queens Park Rangers), 1974 v. W & I
Bowser, S (West Bromwich Albion), 1929 v. I
Boyes, W (Everton), 1939 v. W
Boyle, T. W (Burnley), 1913 v. I
Brabrook, P (Chelsea), 1959 v. I
Bradford, J (Birmingham City), 1924-9-30 v. I; 1928-30 v. S; 1929-31 v. W
Bradshaw, H (Liverpool), 1897 v. I
Bradshaw, W (Blackburn Rovers, 1910-13 v. W; 1910-12 v. ?
Brann, G (Swifts), 1886 v. S; 1886-91 v. W
Brawn, W. F (Aston Villa), 1904 v. W & I
Bray, J (Manchester City), 1935 v. W; 1936 v. S, W & I; 1937 v. S
Brayshaw, E (Sheffield Wednesday), 1887 v. I
Bridges, B (Chelsea), 1965 v. S
Bridgett, A (Sunderland), 1905-8 v. S; 1909 v. I & W
Brindle, T (Darwen), 1880 v. S & W
Brittleton, T (Sheffield Wednesday), 1912-13 v. S; 1912-14 v. W; 1912 v. I
Briton, C. S (Everton), 1935 v. S, W & I; 1937 v. S & I
Broadbent, P (Wolverhampton Wanderers), 1959 v. S, W & I; 1960 v. S
Broadis, I. A (Manchester City), 1952-3 v. S; (Newcastle United), 1954 v. S
Brockbank, J. J. B (Cambridge University), 1872 v. S
Brodie, J. B (Wolverhampton Wanderers), 1889 v. S; 1889-91 v. I
Bromilow, T. G (Liverpool), 1921-2 v. W; 1922 v. S; 1926 v. I
Brook, E. F (Manchester City), 1930 v. I; 1934-5-6 v. S, I & W; 1938 v. W & I
Brooking, T (West Ham United), 1977 v. I & W, 1978 v. W & S; 1979 v. W, S
Brooks, J (Tottenham Hotspur), 1957 v. W
Brooks, S (Wolverhampton Wanderers), 1920 v. W*(I)
Brown, A (West Bromwich Albion), 1971 v. W
Brown, A (Aston Villa), 1882 v. S, W & I
Brown, A (Sheffield United), 1904 v. W; 1906 v. I
Brown, J. H (Sheffield Wednesday), 1927 v. S & W; 1930 v. I
Brown, C. W (Corinthians), 1898 v. S; (Old Carthusianss), 1894-5 v. W; 1889 v. I
Brown, J (Blackburn Rovers), 1885 v. S; 1881-5 v. W; 1882-5 v. I & W
Brown, G (Huddersfield), 1927-9 v. S; 1927 v. I; 1927-8 v. W; (Aston Villa), 1933 v. W
Brown, K (West Ham United), 1960 v. I
Bruton, J (Burnley), 1929 v. S
Buchan, C. M (Sunderland), 1913 v. I; 1920*(I), 1920-1 v. W; 1924 v. S
Buchanan, W. S (Clapham Rovers), 1876 v. S
Buckley, F. C (Derby County), 1914 v. I
Bullock, F. E (Huddersfield Town), 1921 v. I
Bullock, N (Bury), 1926 v. W; 1927 v. I
Burgess, H (Manchester City), 1904-6 v. S; 1904 v. W & I
Burgess, H (Sheffield Wednesday), 1931 v. I & S
Burnup, C. J (Cambridge University), 1896 v. S
Burton, F (Nottingham Forest), 1889 v. I
Bury, L (Old Etonians), 1877 v. S; 1879 v. W
Butler, W (Bolton Wanderers), 1924 v. S
Byrne, G (Liverpool), 1963 v. S
Byrne, J (Crystal Palace), 1962 v. I; (West Ham United), 1964 v. S; 1965 v. W & S
Byrne, R. W (Manchester United), 1954 v. S; 1955 v. I, W & S; 1956 v. S, W & I; 1957 v. S, W & I, 1958 v. W & I
Calvey, J (Nottingham Forest), 1902 v. I

Campbell, A. F (Blackburn Rovers), 1929 v. I & W (Huddersfield Town), 1931 v. S, I & W; 1932 v. I & W
Camsell, G. H (Middlesbrough), 1930 v. I & W; 1936 v. S
Capes, A. J (Stoke), 1903 v. S
Carr, J (Middlesbrough), 1920 v. I; 1923 v. W
Carr, J (Newcastle United), 1905-7 v. I
Carr, W. H (Sheffield United), 1875 v. S
Carter, H (Sunderland), 1934 v. S; 1937 v. S & I; 1946 v. I*; (Derby County), 1947 v. S, W & I
Catlin, A. E (Sheffield Wednesday), 1937 v. W & I
Chadwick, A (Southampton), 1900 v. S & W
Chadwick, E (Everton), 1891-2-3-4-7 v. S; 1891 v. W; 1896 v. I
Chambers, H (Liverpool), 1921-3 v. S & W; 1923-4 v. I
Channon, M (Southampton), 1973 v. I, W & S; 1974 v. W, I & S; 1975 v. W & S; 1976 v. I & S; 1977 v. I, W & S
Charsley, C (Small Heath), 1893 v. I
Charlton, J (Leeds United), 1965 v. S; 1966 v. W, I & S; 1967 v. I, W & S; 1963 v. W; 1969 v. W
Charlton, R (Manchester United), 1958 v. S; 1959 v. S, W & I; 1960 v. W & S; 1961 v. I, W & S; 1962 v. W, I & S; 1963 v. S; 1964 v. W, I & S; 1965 v. I & S; 1966 v. W,I & S; 1967 v. I, W & S; 1968 v. W, I & S; 1969 v. I, W & S; 1970 v. W & I
Chedgzoy, S (Everton), 1920-1-4 v. W; 1921-3 v. S; 1921-2-5 v. I
Chenery, C. J (Crystal Palace), 1872-3-4 v. S
Cherry, T (Leeds), 1977 v. I; 1978 v. W; 1979 v. W
Chilton, A (Manchester United), 1951 v. I
Chippendale, H (Blackburn Rovers), 1894 v. I
Chivers, M (Tottenham Hotspur), 1971 v. I & S; 1972 v. S; 1973 v. I, W & S
Christian, E (Eton), 1879 v. S
Clapton, D (Arsenal), 1959 v. W
Clare, T (Stoke City), 1894 v. S; 1893 v. W; 1889-92 v. I
Clarke, A (Leeds United), 1971 v. I; 1973 v. W & S
Clarke, H. A (Tottenham Hotspur), 1954 v. S
Clay, T (Tottenham Hotspur), 1920 v. W; 1922 v. W, S & I
Clayton, R (Blackburn Rovers), 1956 v. I; 1957 v. S, W & I; 159 v. S, W & I 1960 v. W, I & S
Clegg, J. C (Sheffield United), 1872 v. S
Clegg, W. E (Sheffield United), 1873 v. S; 1879 v. W
Clemence, R (Liverpool), 1975 v. I, W & S; 1976 v. W, I & S; 1977 v. S; 1978 v. I & S; 1979 v. I, S
Clement, D (Queens Park Rangers), 1976 v. W
Clough, B (Middlesbrough), 1960 v. W
Coates, R (Burnley), 1970 v. I; (Tottenham Hotspur), 1971 v. W
Cobbold, W. N (Old Carthusians), 1883-5-6-7 v. S; 1885-7 v. W; 1883-5-7 v. I
Cock, J. G (Huddersfield Town), 1920 v. W*(I); (Chelsea), 1920 v. S & I
Cockburn, H (Manchester United), 1947 v. W & I; 1948 v. S; 1949 v. S & I
Cohen, G (Fulham), 1965 v. I, W & S; 1966 v. W. I & S; 1967 v. I, W & S; 1968 v. W & I
Coleclough, H (Crystal Palace), 1914 v. W
Coleman, J (Woolwich Arsenal), 1907 v. I
Coleman, E. G. H (Dulwich Hamlet), 1921 v. W
Common, A (Sheffield United), 1904 v. W; 1904 v. I; (Middlesbrough), 1906 v. W
Compton, D. C. S (Arsenal), 1946 v. S*
Compton, L (Arsenal), 1951 v. W
Conlin, J (Bradford City), 1906 v. S
Connelly, J (Burnley), 1960 v. W, I & S; 1962 v. W; 1963 v. W; (Manchester United), 1966 v. W, I & S
Cook, T. E. (Brighton & Hove Albion), 1925 v. W

Cooper, T (Derby County), 1928-9 v. I; 1929 v. S & W; 1932 v. W; 1933 v. S; 1934 v. S; 1935 v. W
Cooper, T (Leeds United), 1969 v. W & S; 1971 v. I, W & S
Cooper, N. C (Old Brightonians), 1893 v. I
Coppell, S (Manchester United), 1978 v. W, I & S; 1979 v. I, W, S
Copping, W (Leeds United), 1934 v. S, I & W; (Arsenal), 1935 v. I; 1938 v. S, W & I; 1939 v. W
Corbett, B. O (Corinthians), 1901 v. W
Corbett, R (Old Malvernians), 1903 v. W
Corrigan, J (Manchester City), 1979 v. W
Cottrill, G. H (Old Brightonians), 1893 v. S; 1892 v. W; 1891-3 v. ?
Cottle, J (Bristol City), 1909 v. I
Cowell, A (Blackburn Rovers), 1910 v. I
Cox, J (Liverpool), 1901 v. I; 1902-3 v. S
Cox, J. D (Derby County), 1892 v. I
Crabtree, J. W (Burnley), 1895 v. S; 1894-5 v. I; (Aston Villa), 1896-9-1900 v. S; 1896-9-1900-1-2 v. W; 1896-9-1900 v. I
Crawford, J. F (Chelsea), 1931 v. S
Crawford, R (Ipswich Town) 1962 v. I
Crawshaw, T (Sheffield Wednesday), 1896-7 v. S; 1896-7-1904 v. W; 1895-6-7-1901-4 v. I
Crayston, W. J (Arsenal), 1936 v. S & W; 1938 v. W & I
Cresswell, W (South Shields), 1921-2 v. W; (Sunderland), 1923-6 v. W; 1925-6 v. I; (Everton), 1927-30 v. I
Crompton, R (Blackburn Rovers), 1902-3-4-5-6-7-8-9-10-11-12-13-14 v. S & W; 1902-4-6-7-8-9-11-12-13-14 v. I
Crooks, S. D (Derby County), 1930-1 v. S; 1931 v. W & I; 1932 v. S, W & I; 1933 v. I & W; 1934 v. S, I & W; 1935 v. I; 1936 v. S & W; 1937 v. W
Cuggy, F (Sunderland), 1913-14 v. I
Cullis S (Wolverhampton Wanderers), 1938 v. S, W & I, 1939 v. S & I
Cuncliffe, A (Blackburn Rovers), 1933 v. I & W
Cunliffe, D (Portsmouth), 1900 v. I
Cunningham, L (West Bromwich Albion), 1979 v. W
Currie, A (Sheffield United), 1972 v. I; (Leeds United), 1978 v. W, I & S; 1979 v. I, W
Currie, E. S (Old Carthusians), 1890 v. S & W
Cursham, A. W (Notts County), 1876-7-8-83 v. S; 1879-83 v. W
Cursham, H. A (Notts County), 1882-3 v. S; 1880-2-3 v. W; 1882-3-4 v. I
Daft, H. B (Notts County), 1890 v. S & W; 1889-91-2 v. I
Danks, T (Nottingham Forest), 1885 v. S
Davenport, J. K (Bolton Wanderers), 1885 v. W; 1890 v. I
Davenport, W. E. B (Old Etonians), 1884 v. S & W
Davis, G (Derby County), 1904 v. W & I
Davis, H (Sheffield Wednesday), 1903 v. S, W & I
Davison, J. E (Sheffield Wednesday), 1922 v. W
Dawson, J (Burnley), 1922 v. S & I
Day, S. H (Old Malvernians), 1906 v. I, W & S
Dean, W. R (Everton), 1927-8-9 v. W; 1928-9-33 v. I
Devey, J (Aston Villa), 1892-4 v. I
Dewhurst, F (Preston North End), 1887-8 v. S; 1886-7-8-9 v. W; 1886-7-8 v.

Dewhurst, G. P (Liverpool Rambers), 1895 v. W
Dickinson, J. W (Portsmouth), 1950 v. S & W; 1951 v. I & W; 1952-3 v. W & S; 1954 v. W, I & S; 1956 v. W, S & I; 1957 v. W
Dimmock, J. H (Tottenham Hotspur), 1921 v. S; 1926 v. W
Ditchburn, E (Tottenham Hotspur), 1957 v. W
Dixon, H. A (Notts County), 1885 v. W
Dobson, A. T (Notts County), 1884 v. S & W; 1882-4 v. I
Dobson, C. F (Notts County), 1886 v. I
Donop, P. G Von (Royal Engineers), 1873-5 v. S

Doreel, A. R (Aston Villa), 1925 v. W; 1926 v. I
Douglas, B (Blackburn Rovers), 1958 v. W, I & S; 1959 v. S; 1961 v. I, W & S; 1962 v. W, I & S; 1962 v. S
Downs, R (Everton), 1921 v. I
Drake, E. J (Arsenal), 1935 v. I; 1936 v. W
Ducat, A (Woolwich Arsenal), 1910 v. S, W & I; (Aston Villa), 1920 v. S & W; 1921 v. I
Duckworth, F (Blackburn Rovers), 1919 v. S*(2)
Dunn, A. T. B (Old Etonians), 1892 v. S & W; 1893 v. I
Earle, S. J. G (West Ham United), 1928 v. I
Eastham, G (Arsenal), 1964 v. W, I & S
Eckersley, W (Blackburn Rovers), 1951 v. S; 1953 v. I; 1954 v. W & I
Edwards, D (Manchester United), 1955 v. S; 1956 v. S; 1957 v. S & I; 1958 v. W & I
Edwards, J. H (Shropshire Wanderers), 1874 v. S
Edwards, W (Leeds United), 1926-7-8-9 v. S; 1926-7-8-9-30 v. W; 1927-9-30 v. I
Elliot, G. W (Middlesbrough), 1913-14 v. I; 1920 v. W
Elliott, W (West Bromwich Albion), 1946 v. S*
Elliott, W (Burnley), 1953 v. I & W
Evans, R. E (Sheffield United), 1911 v. S, W & I; 1912 v. W
Fairclough, P (Old Foresters), 1878 v. S
Fenton, M (Middlesbrough), 1938 v. S; 1946 v. W*
Field, E (Clapham Rovers), 1876-81 v. S
Finney, T (Preston North End), 1947 v. W & I; 1948 v. S, W & I; 1949 v. S, W & I; 1950 v. S, W & I; 1951 v. W & S; 1952-3 v. W, I & S; 1954 v. W & S; 1956 v. S, W & I; 1957, S & W; 1958 v. W & S; 1959 v. I
Fleetwood, T (Everton), 1919 v. S*(2)
Fleming, H. J (Swindon Town), 1909-13-14 v. S; 1910-11-13 v. W; 1910-11-12 v. I
Flowers, R (Wolverhampton Wanderers), 1959 v. S & W; 1960 v. W, I & S; 1961 v. I, W & S; 1962 v. W, I & S; 1963 v. I, W & S; 1963 v. W
Forman, Frank (Nottingham Forest), 1839 v. W, I & S
Forman, Fred (Nottingham Forest), 1899 v. W, I & S
Forrest, J. H (Blackburn Rovers), 1885-6-7-9 v. S; 1884-5-6-7 v. W; 1884-5-7-1890 v. I
Foster, R. E (Oxford University), 1900-1-2 v. W; 1901 v. I & S
Foulke, W (Sheffield United), 1887 v. W
Foulkes, W (Manchester United), 1955 v. I
Francis, T (Birmingham City), 1977 v. S; 1978 v. W & S
Franklin, N (Stoke City), 1946 v. I*, W* & S*; 1947 v. S, W & I; 1949 v. S, W & I; 1949 v. S, W & I; 1950 v. S, W & I
Freeman, B. C (Everton), 1909 v. S & W; (Burnley), 1912 v. S, W & I
Froggatt, J (Portsmouth), 1959 v. I; 1951-2 v. S; 1953 v. I, W & S
Froggatt, R (Sheffield Wednesday), 1953 v. W & S
Fry, C. B (Corinthians), 1901 v. I
Garrett, T (Blackpool), 1952 v. S; 1954 v. W
Garraty, W (Aston Villa), 1903 v. W
Garfield, B (West Bromwich Albion), 1898 v. I
Gay, L. H (Old Brightonians), 1893-4 v. S; 1894 v. W
Geary, F (Everton), 1891 v. S; 1890 v. I
Geaves, R. L (Old Harrovians), 1875 v. S
Gee, C. W (Everton), 1932 v. W; 1937 v. I
Geldard, A (Everton), 1935 v. S; 1938 v. I
George, W (Aston Villa), 1902 v. S, W & I
Gillard, I (Queens Park Rangers), 1975 v. W
Gilliatt, W. E (Old Carthusians), 1893 v. I
Goodall, J (Preston North End), 1889-9 v. S & W; (Derby County), 1891-2-4-5-6 v. S; 1891-3-6-8 v. W; 1895 v. I

Goodall, F. R (Huddersfield Town), 1926-7-8-30-1 v. S; 1928-31 v. W, 1931-2 v. I; 1933-4 v, I & W
Goodhart, H. C (Old Etonians), 1883 v. S, W & I
Goodwyn, A. G (Royal Engineers), 1873 v. S
Goodyer, A. C (Nottingham Forest), 1879 v. S
Gosling, R. C (Old Etonians), 1893-5 v. S; 1892-4-5 v. W
Gosnell, A (Newcastle United), 1906 v. I
Gough, H (Sheffield United), 1921 v. S
Goulen, L (West Ham United), 1938 v. W & I; 1939 v. S & W
Graham, L (Millwall), 1925 v. S & W
Graham, T (Nottingham Forest), 1932 v. I
Grainger, C (Sheffield United), 1957 v. W & I; (Sunderland) v. S
Greaves, J (Chelsea), 1960 v. W; 1961 v. I, W & S; (Tottenham Hotspur), 1962 v. S; 1963 v. I, W & S; 1964 v. W & I; 1965 v. I & S; 1966 v. W; 1967 v. S
Green, F. T (The Wanderers), 1876 v. S
Green, G. H (Sheffield United), 1926 v. S; 1926-7 v. W; 1927 v. I
Greenhaigh, E. H (Notts County), 1872-3 v.S
Greenhoff, B (Manchester United), 1976 v. W & I; 1977 v. I, W & S; 1978 v. W, I & S
Greenwood, D. H (Blackburn Rovers), 1882 v. S & I
Grenyer, A (Everton), 1920 v. W*(1)
Grimsdell, A (Tottenham Hotspur), 1919*(2), 1920-1 v. S; 1920-3 v. W;1921-3 v. I
Grosvenor, T (Birmingham City), 1934 v. I & W
Gunn, W (Notts County), 1884 v. S & W
Gurney, R (Sunderland) 1935 v. S
Hacking, J (Oldham Athletic), 1929 v. S, W & I
Hadley, N (West Bromwich Albion), 1903 v. I
Hagan, J (Sheffield United), 1946 v. S*
Hall, A. E (Aston Villa), 1910 v. I
Hall, G. W (Tottenham Hotspur), 1930 v. S, W & I; 1939 v. S & I
Hall, J (Birmingham City), 1956 v. S, W & I; 1957 v. S, W & I
Hammond, H. E. D (Lancing Old Boys), 1889 v. S
Hampson, J (Blackpool), 1931 v. I & W
Hampton, H (Aston Villa), 1913-14 v. S & W
Hancocks, J (Wolverhampton Wanderers), 1950 v. W
Hapgood, E (Arsenal), 1934-5-6 v. S, I & W; 1938 v. S; 1939 v. S, W & I
Hardinge, H. T (Sheffield United), 1910 v. S
Hardman, H. P (Everton), 1907 v. S & I; 1905-8 v. W
Hardwick, G. F. M (Middlesbrough), 1946 v. S*; 1947 v. S, W & I; 1948 v. S, W & I
Hardy, S (Liverpool), 1907-8-9-10 v. W & I; (Aston Villa), 1912-14-20 v. I; 1913-14*-19*(2)-20 v. S; 1914-20*(1)-20 v. W
Hargreaves, F (Blackburn Rovers), 1880-1 v. W; 1882 v. I
Hargreaves, J (Blackburn Rovers), 1881 v. S & W
Harper, E (Blackburn Rovers), 1926 v. S
Harris, S. S (Cambridge University), 1904-6 v. S; 1905- v. W
Harrison, A H (Old Westminsters), 1893 v. S & I
Harrison, G (Everton), 1922 v. I
Harrow, J. H (Chelsea), 1923 v. I
Hassall, H. W (Huddersfield Town), 1951 v. S; (Bolton Wanderers), 1954 v. I
Hart, E (Leeds United), 1929-30 v. W; 1930 v. I; 1933 v. S; 1934 v. S
Harvey, A (Wednesday Strollers), 1881 v. W
Hawkes, R. M (Luton Town), 1907 v. I
Hawfrey, J. P (Old Etonians), 1881 v. S & W
Haygarth, E. B (Winchester), 1875 v. S
Haynes, J (Fulham), 1955 v. I; 1956 v. S & I; 1957 v. W; 1958 v. W, I & S; 1959 v. S & I; 1960 v. I; 1961 v. I, W & S; 1962 v. W, I & S
Healless, H (Blackburn Rovers), 1925 v. I; 1928 v. S

Headley, G. A (Sheffield United), 1901 v. I
Hegan, K. E (Corinthians), 1924 v. I
Hellawell, M (Birmingham City), 1963 v. I
Hendren, E (Brentford), 1920 v. W*(1)
Henfrey, A. G (Corinthinians), 1896 v. S; 1892-5-6 v. W; 1891 v. I
Heron, F (The Wanderers), 1876 v. S
Heron, H (The Wanderers), 1873-4-5-6-8 v. S
Hibbett, W (Bury), 1910 v. S
Hibbs, H (Birmingham City), 1930-1 v. S & W; 1931 v. I; 1932 v. S & I; 1933 v. S, W & I; 1934 v. I & W; 1935 v. S, W & I; 1936 v. W
Hilditch, C. G (Manchester United), 1920 v. W*(1)
Hillman, J (Burnley), 1899 v. I
Hill, F (Bolton Wanderers), 1963 v. I & W
Hill, J. H (Burnley), 1925-8 v. W; 1926-7 v. S; 1927-8 v. I
Hills, S. F (Old Harrovians), 1879 v. S
Hilsdon, G. R (Chelsea), 1907-8-9 v. I; 1908 v. S & W
Hine, E. W (Leicester City), 1929-30 v. I & W; 1932 v. W
Hinton, A (Nottingham Forest), 1965 v. W
Hodgetts, D (Aston Villa), 1888-92 v. S; 1888 v. W; 1888-92-94 v. I
Hodgkinson, A (Sheffield United), 1957 v. S; 1961 v. W
Hodgkinson, J (Blackburn Rovers), 1913 v. S; 1920 v. I; 1913-20* v. W
Hodgson, G (Liverpool), 1931 v. S, I & W
Hogg, W (Sunderland), 1902 v. S, W & I
Holdcroft, H (Preston North End), 1937 v. W & I
Holden, A. D (Bolton Wanderers), 1959 v. S
Holden, G (Wednesday O. A.), 1881-4 v. S; 1884 v. W & I
Holden-White, C (Swifts), 1888 v. W & S
Holford, T (Stoke City), 1903 v. I
Holley, G (Sunderland), 1909-12-13 v. S; 1909-10-12 v. W; 1912 v. I
Holliday, E (Middlesbrough), 1960 v. W & I
Holmes, R (Preston North End), 1891-2-3 v. S; 1893 v. W; 1888-1914-15 v I
Holt, J (Everton), 1891-2-3-4-5 v. S; 1890-1 v. W; 1892-4-1900 v. I
Hopkinson, E (Bolton Wanderers), 1958 v. W, I & S; 1959 v. S; 1960 v. W
Hossack, A. H (Corinthians), 1892-4 v. W
Houghton, W. E (Aston Villa), 1931 v. I & W; 1932 v. S & I
Houlker, A. E (Blackburn Rovers), 1902-3 v. S; 1903-6 v. I
Howarth, G (Accrington Stanley), 1887-8-90 v. S; 1887 v. W & I; 1906 v. W
Howarth, R (Preston North End), 1888-91 v. S; 1888 v. W; 1887-94 v. I
Howe, D (West Bromwich Albion), 1958-9 v. S, W & I; 1960 v. W & I
Howe, J. R (Derby County), 1949 v. S & I
Howell, L. S (The Wanderers), 1873 v. S
Howell, R (Liverpool), 1899 v. S; (Sheffield United, 1895 v. I
Hudson, J (Sheffield United), 1883 v. I
Hudspeth, F (Newcastle United), 1920 v. W*(1); 1926 v. I
Hughes, E (Liverpool), 1970 v. S, W & I; 1971 v. W; 1972 v. W, I & S; 1973 v. W & S; 1974 v. W, I & S; 1975 v. I; 1977 v. W & S; 1978 v. I & S; 1979 v. W
Hutton, A. E (West Ham United), 1928 v. S & I
Hulme, J. H. A (Arsenal), 1927-8 v. S; 1928-9 v. I & W; 1933 v. S
Humphreys, P (Notts County), 1903 v. S
Hunt, Rev K. R. G (Leyton Orient), 1911 v. S & W
Hunt, R (Liverpool), 1964 v. S; 1965 v. W; 1966 v. S; 1967 v. I & W; 1968 v. W & I
Hunt, G (Tottenham Hotspur), 1933 v. ?
Hunter, N (Leeds United), 1969 v. W; 1972 v. W, I & S; 1974 v. S
Hunter, J (Sheffield Heeley), 1978-80-1-2 v. S; 1880-1-2 v. W
Hurst, G (West Ham United), 1966 v. S; 1967 v. I, W & S; 1968 v. W, I & S; 1969 v. I & S; 1970 v. S, W & I; 1971 v. W & S
Iremonger, J (Nottingham Forest), 1901 v. S; 1902 v. I

Jack, D. B. N (Bolton Wanderers), 1924 v. S & W; (Arsenal), 1930 v. S; 1933 v. W
Jackson, E (Oxford University), 1891 v. W
Jarett, B. G (Old Harrovians), 1876-7-8 v. S
Jeffries, F (Everton), 1912 v. S & W
Jezzard, B (Fulham), 1912 v. S & W
Johnson, H (Sheffield United), 1900-3 v. S, W & I
Johnson, E (Saltley College), 1880 v. W; 1884 v. I
Johnson, D. (Ipswich Town), 1975 v. W & S
Johnson, J. A (Stoke City), 1937 v. S & I
Johnson, T.C (Manchester City). 1930 v. W; (Everton), 1932 v. S; 1933 v. I
Johnson, H (Blackpool), 1947-ـ v. S; 1954 v. W & I
Jones, A (Walsall), 1882-3 v. S; 1882 v. W
Jones, H (Blackburn Rovers), 1927-8 v. S; 1928 v. I
Jones, W (Bristol City), 1901 v. I
Kean, F. W (Sheffield Wednesday), 1923 v. S; 1924 v. W; 1924-6 v. I
Keegan, K (Liverpool), 1974 v. W & I); 1975 v. I & S; 1976 v. W, I & S; 1977 v. W; (SV Hamburg), 1979 v. W, S
Keen, E (Derby County), 1937 v. W & I
Kelley, R (Burnley), 1920-1-2-3-5 v. S; 1921-2-5-6 v. W; 1921-2-5-6 v. W; 1921-4-5 v. I; (Huddersfield Town), 1928 v. S
Kennedy, R (Liverpool), 1976 v. W, I & S; 1977 v. W & S
Kevan, D (West Bromwich Albion), 1957 v. S; 1958 v. W, I & S
Kidd, B (Manchester United), 1970 v. I
King, C. J. S (Falstead), 1882 v. I
Kingsford R. K (Marlborough), 1874 v. S
Kinsey, (Wolverhampton Wanderers), 1893 v. S; 1892 v. W; (Derby County), 1896 v. W & I
Kinsell, H (West Bromwich Albion), 1946 v. I* & W*
Kingsley, M (Newcastle United), 1901 v. W
Kirton, W. J (Aston Villa), 1922 v. I
Knight A. E (Portsmouth), 1920 v. I & W* (1)
Labone, B (Everton), 1963 v. I & W; 1968 v. S; 1969 v. I & S; 1970 v. S & W
Langley, J (Fulham), 1958 v. S
Langton, R (Blackburn Rovers), 1947 v. W & I; (Bolton Wanderers), 1950 v. S; 1951 v. I
Latchford, R (Everton), 1978 v. W; 1979 v. I, W, S
Latherton, E. G (Blackburn Rovers), 1913 v. W; 1914 v. I
Lawler, C (Liverpool), 1971 v. W & S
Lawton, T (Everton), 1939 v. S, W & I; 1946 v. I* & S*; (Chelsea), 1947 v. S, W & I; 1948 v. W & I; (Notts County), 1948 v. S
Leake, A (Aston Villa), 1904-5 v. S & I; 1905 v. W
Leach, T (Sheffield Wednesday), 1931 v. I & W
Lee, A (Southampton), 1904 v. W
Lee, F (Manchester City), 1969 v. I, W & S; 1970 v. W; 1971 v. I, W & S
Lee, J (Derby County), 1951 v. I
Leighton, J. E (Nottingham Forest), 1886 v. I
Lilley, H. E (Sheffield United), 1892 v. W
Linacre, H. J (Nottingham Forest), 1905 v. W & S
Lindley, T (Nottingham Forest), 1886-7-8-9-90 v. S; 1886-7-8-90 v. W; 1886-7-8-91 v. I
Lindsay, W (Winchester), 1877 v. S
Lintott, E. H (Queens Park Rangers), 1903 v. S, W & I; (Bradford City), 1909 v. S & I
Lipsham, H. B (Sheffield United), 1902 v. W
Lloyd, L (Liverpool), 1971 v. W; 1972 v. I
Lockett, A (Stoke City), 1903 v. I
Lodge, L. V (Cambridge University), 1895-6 v. S; 1894-5 v. W; 1896 v I
Lofthouse, J. M (Blackburn Rovers), 1885-7 v. S & W; 1885-8-90 v. I

Lofthouse, N (Bolton Wanderers), 1952-3 v. W, I & S; 1954 v. W & I; 1955 v. I & S; 1956 v. W & S; 1959 v W
Longworth, E (Liverpool), 1919* (2), 1920-3 v. S; 1923 v. W
Lowder, A (Wolverhampton Wanderers), 1839 v. W
Lucas, T (Liverpool), 1922 v. I
Luntley, E (Nottingham Forest), 1880 v. S & W
Lyttleton, Hon A (Old Etonians), 1877 v. S
Lyttleton, Hon E (Old Etonians), 1870 v. S
M'Call, J (Preston North End), 1913-14-19*(2)-20 v. S; 1913 v. W; 1921 v. S
McDermott, T (Liverpool), 1979 v. I, W
McDonald, C (Burnley), 1959 v. W & I
McFarland, R (Derby County), 1971 v. I & S; 1972 v. W & S; 1973 v. I, W & S; 1974 v. W & I; 1976 v. S
McGarry, W (Huddersfield Town), 1956 v. W
McGuiness, W (Manchester United), 1959 v. I
M'Inroy, A (West Bromwich Albion), 1914 v. S & W
M'Neal, M (Middlesbrough), 1961 v. I, W & S
McNab, R (Arsenal), 1969 v. I
Macaulay, R. H (Old Etonians), 1881 v. S
MacDonald, M (Newcastle United), 1972 v. W & I; 1975 v. I
Macraw, S (Notts County), 1883-4 v. S, W & I
Maddison, F. C (Oxford University), 1872 v. S
Madeley, P (Leeds United), 1971 v. I; 1972 v. W & S
Magee, T (West Bromwich Albion), 1923 v. W; 1925 v. S
Makepeace, H (Everton), 1906-10-12 v. S; 1912 v. W
Male, G. C (Arsenal), 1935 v. S & I; 1936 v. S, W & I; 1937 v. S & I
Mannion, W (Middlesbrough),, 1947 v. S, W & I; 1948 v. W & I; 1950 v. S; 1951 v. I, W & S
Mariner, P (Ipswich Town), 1977 v. I; 1978 v. W & S
Marsden, J (Darwen), 1891 v. I
Marsden, W (Sheffield Wednesday), 1930 v. W & S
Marsh, R (Manchester City), 1972 v. W, I & S
Marshall, T (Darwen), 1880-1 v. W
Martin, H (Sunderland), 1914 v. I; 1919*(2) v. S
Maskey, H (Derby County), 1903 v. I
Mason, C (Wolverhampton Wanderers), 1888 v. W; 1887-90 v. I
Matthews, R (Coventry City), 1956 v. S; 1957 v. I
Matthews, S (Stoke City), 1935 v. W; 1937 v. S; 1938 v. S & W; 1939 v. S, W & I; 1945 v. I* v. W*; 1947 v. S; (Blackpool), 1948 v. S, W & I; 1949 v. S, W & I; 1951 v. I & S; 1954 v. I; 1955 v. I, W & S; 1956 v. W; 1957 v. S, W & I
Maynard, W. J (1st Surrey Rifles), 1872-6 v. S
Meadows, J (Manchester City), 1955 v. S
Medley, L. D (Tottenham Hotspur), 1951 v. W; 1952 v. W & I
Melia, J (Liverpool), 1963 v. S
Meehan, T (Chelsea), 1924 v. I
Mercer, D. W (Sheffield United), 1923 v. I
Mercer, J (Everton), 1939 v. S & I; 1946 v. I*, W & S*
Merrick, G. H (Birmingham City), 1952 v. I & S; 1953 v. I, W & S; 1954 v. W I & S
Mew, J. W (Manchester United), 1921 v. I
Middleditch, B (Corinthians), 1897 v. I
Milburn, J. E. T (Newcastle United), 1949 v. S, W & I; 1950-1 v. W
Milne, G (Liverpool), 1964 v. W, I & S; 1965 v. I
Mills, G (Chelsea), 1936 v. W & I
Mills, M (Ipswich Town), 1976 v. W, I & S; 1977 v. I, W & S; 1978 v. W, I & S; 1979 v. I, S
Milward, A (Everton), 1891-7 v. S & W
Mitchell, C (Upton Park), 1880-3-5 v. W; 1881-3 v. S
Mitchell, J. F (Manchester City), 1925 v. I

Moffat, H (Oldham Athletic), 1913 v. W
Molyneaux, G (Southampton), 1902-3 v. S; 1903 v. W & I
Moon, W. R (Old Westminstrers), 1888-9-90-1 v. S; 1888-9-90 v. W
Moore, H (Notts County), 1883 v. I; 1884 v. W
Moore, R (West Ham United), 1963 v. I, W & S; 1964 v. W, I & S; 1965 v. I & S; 1966 v. W, I & S; 1967 v. I, W & S; 1968 v. W, I & S; 1969 v. I, W & S; 1970 v. W, I & S; 1971 v. I & S; 1972 v. W & S; 1973 v. I, W & S
Mordue, J (Sunderland), 1912-13 v. I
Morice, C. J (Barnes), 1872 v. S
Morley, H (Notts County), 1910 v. I
Morren, T (Sheffield United), 1898 v. I
Morris, F (West Bromwich Albion), 1920 v. S; 1921 v. I
Morris, W (Wolverhampton Wanderers), 1939 v. S & I
Mortensen, S. H (Blackpool), 1946 v. I*; 1948 v. W, S & I; 1949 v. S, W & I; 1950 v. S, W & I; 1951 v. S
Morton, A (Crystal Palace), 1873 v. S
Morsforth, W (Sheffield United), 1877-8-9-80-2 v. S; 1879-80-1-2- v. W
Moss, F (Arsenal), 1934 v. S
Moss, F (Aston Villa), 1922-4 v. S; 1922-3 v. I
Mosscrop, E (Burnley), 1914 v. S & W
Mozley, B (Derby County), 1950 v. W & I
Mullen, J (Wolverhampton Wanderers), 1947 v. S; 1954 v. W, I & S
Mullery, A (Tottenham Hotspur), 1968 v. W, I & S; 1969 v. I & S; 1970 v. W & I
Neal, P (Liverpool), 1977 v. W & S; 1978 v. I & S; 1979 v. I, S
Needham, E (Sheffield United), 1894-5-7-8-9-1900-1 v. S; 1897-8-9-1901-2 v. W; 1897-9-1900-1 v. I
Newton, K (Blackburn Rovers), 1966 v. S; 1968 v. W & S; 1969 v. I, W & S; (Everton), 1970 v. S & I
Nicholls J (West Bromwich Albion), 1954 v. S
Nish, D (Derby County), 1973 v. I; 1974 v. W, I & S
Norman, M (Tottenham Hotspur), 1963 v. S; 1964 v. W, I & S; 1965 v. I
Nuttall, H (Bolton Wanderers), 1928 v. W & I; 1929 v. S
Oakley, W. J (Oxford University), 1896-7-8-1900-1 v. S; 1895-6-7-8-1900-1 v. W; 1895-7-8-1900 v. I
O'Dowd, P (Chelsea), 1932 v. S; 1922 v. I
O'Grady, M (Huddersfield Town), 1963 v. I
Ogilvie, R. A (Clapham Rovers), 1874 v. S
Osborne, F. R (Fulham), 1923 v. I
Osborne, R (Leicester City), 1928 v. W
Ottaway, C. J (Oxford University), 1872-4 v. S
Owen, J. R. B (Sheffield United), 1874 v. S
Page, L. A (Burnley), 1927 v. S; 1927-8 v. W; 1928 v. I
Paine, T (Southampton), 1964 v. W, I & S; 1965 v. I; 1966 v. W
Pantling, H. H (Sheffield United), 1924 v. I
Paravacini, P. J de (Old Etonians), 1883 v. S, W & I
Parker, C. W (Stoke City), 1920 v. W* (1)
Parkinson, J (Liverpool), 1910 v. S & W
Parr, P. C (Winchester), 1882 v. W
Parry, E. H (Old Carthusians), 1882 v. S; 1879-82 v. W
Parry, R (Bolton Wanderers), 1960 v. I & S
Pawson F. W (Cambridge University), 1883-5 v. I
Peacock, A (Middlesbrough), 1963 v. I & W; (Leeds United), 1966 v. W & I
Pearson, H (West Bromwich Albion), 1932 v. S
Pearson, J (Crewe Alexandra), 1892 v. I
Pearson, S. C (Manchester United), 1948 v. S; 1949 v. S & I; 1950 v. I; 1952 v. S
Pearson, S (Manchester United), 1976 v. W, I & S; 1977 v. W & S; 1978 v. I
Pease, W. H (Middlesbrough), 1927 v. W
Pejic, M (Stoke City), 1974 v. W, I & S

Pelly, F. R (Old Foresters), 1894 v. S & W; 1893 v. I
Pennington, J (West Bromwich Albion), 1907-8-9-10-11-12-13-14-20 v. S; 1907-8-9-10-11-13-20 v. W; 1908-11-12-14 v. I
Pentland, F. B (Middlesbrough), 1909 v. S & W
Perry, C (West Bromwich Albion), 1890-1 v. I; 1893 v. W
Perry, T (West Bromwich Albion), 1898 v. W
Perry, W (Blackpool), 1956 v. I & S
Peters, M (West Ham United), 1967 v. I, W & S; 1968 v. W, I & S; 1969 v. S; (Tottenham Hotspur), 1970 v. W, I & S; 1971 v. I, W & S; 1973 v. I, W & S; 1974 v. I
Pickering, F (Everton), 1965 v. I
Pike, T. M (Cambridge University), 1886 v. I
Pilkington, B (Burnley), 1955 v. I
Phillips, L. H (Portsmouth), 1952 v. I; 1955 v. W
Plant, J (Bury), 1900 v. S
Pointer, R (Burnley), 1962 v. W
Porteous, T (Sunderland), 1891 v. W
Priest F (Sheffield United), 1900 v. I
Prinsep, J. F (Old Carthusians), 1900 v. I
Puddefoot, S. C (West Ham United), 1919 v. S*(2); 1920 v. W*(1); (Blackburn Rovers), 1926 v. S & I
Pym, R. H (Bolton Wanderers), 1925 v. S; 1925-6 v. W
Quantrill, A. E (Derby County), 1920 v. S; 1920-1 v. W; 1921 v. I
Quixall, A (Sheffield Wednesday), 1954 v. W & I
Ralkes, G. B (Oxford University), 1895-6 v. W; 1896 v. S & I
Ramsey, A. E (Tottenham Hotspur), 1950 v. S; 1951-2-3 v. I, W & S
Rawlings, W. E (Southampton), 1922 v. S & W
Rawlinson, J. F. P (Old Etonians), 1882 v. I
Rawson, H. E (Old Westminsters), 1875 v. S
Rawson, W. F (Old Westminsters), 1875-7 v. S
Reader, J (West Browmich Albion), 1894 v. I
Revie D (Manchester City), 1955 v. I & S; 1956 v. W; 1957 v. I
‡ Reynolds, J (West Bromwich Albion), 1892 v. S; (Aston Villa), 1892-4-5-7 v. S; 1893-7 v. W; 1894 v. I
Richards, C. H (Nottingham Forest), 1892 v. I
Richards, J (Wolverhampton Wanderers), 1973 v. I
Rickaby, S (West Bromwich Albion), 1954 v. I
Rimmer, E. J (Sheffield Wednesday), 1930 v. S
Roberts, C (Manchester United), 1905 v. I, W & S
Roberts, F (Manchester City), 1926 v. S & W
Roberts, H (Arsenal), 1931 v. S
Roberts, R (West Bromwich Albion), 1887 v. S; 1888-90 v. ?
Roberts, W. T (Preston North End), 1924 v. W
Robson, R (West Bromwich Albion), 1961 v. I, W & S; 1962 v. W & I
Robinson, J (Sheffield Wednesday), 1939 v. W
Robinson, J. W (Derby County), 1897; (New Brighton Tower), 1898 v. ?; (Southampton) 1899-1900 v. S; 1900 v. W; 1897-1900-1 v. I
Rose, W C (Wolverhampton Wanderers & Swifts), 1884 v. S & W; 1884-6-9 v. I
Rostron, T (Darwen), 1881 v. S & W
Rowley, J. P (Manchester United), 1950 v. I; 1952 v. S
Rowley, W (Stoke City), 1889-92 v. I
Ruddlesdin, H (Sheffield Wednesday), 1904 v. W & I; 1905 v. S
Ruffell, J (West Ham United), 1926-9 v. S; 1927-9 v. I; 1929-30 v. W
Russell, B. B (Royal Engineers), 1883 v. W
Rutherford, J (Newcastle United), 1904-7-8 v. S; 1907-8 v. I & W
Sadler, D (Manchester United), 1968 v. I
Sagar, C (Bury), 1900 v. I; 1902 v. W
Sagar, E (Everton), 1936 v. S & I
Sandford, E (West Bromwich Albion), 1933 v. W

Sandilands, R. R (Old Westminsters), 1892-4-5-6 v. W; 1898 v. I
Sands, J (Nottingham Forest), 1880 v. W
Sansom, K (Crystal Palace), 1979 v. W
Saunders, F. E (Swifts), 1888 v. W
Savage, A. H (Crystal Palace), 1876 v. S
Sayer, J. B (Stoke City), 1887 v. I
Scattergood, E (Derby County), 1913 v. W
Schofield, J (Stoke City), 1892-3 v. W; 1895 v. I
Scott, L (Arsenal), 1946 v. S*, W* & I*; 1947 v. S; W & I; 1948 v. S; W & I; 1949 v. W & I
Scott, W (Brentford), 1937 v. W
Seddon, J (Bolton Wanderers), 1927 v. W; 1929 v. S
Seed, J (Tottenham Hotspur), 1923 v. W & I; 1926 v. S
Settle, J (Bury), 1899 v. ?; (Everton), 1902 v. S; 1899 v. W; 1899-1902-3 v. I
Sewell, W. R (Blackburn Rovers), 1924 v. W
Sewell, J (Sheffield Wednesday), 1952-3 v. I
Shackleton, L. F (Bradford), 1946 v. W*; (Sunderland), 1949-50-5 v. W
Sharp, J (Everton), 1903 v. I; 1905 v. S
Shaw, G (Sheffield United), 1959 v. S & W; 1963 v. W
Shaw, G. A (West Bromwich Albion), 1932 v. S
Shea, D (Blackburn Rovers), 1914 v. W & I; 1919 v. S*(2)
Shelton, A (Notts County), 1890-1-2 v. S; 1890-1 v. W; 1889 v. I
Shelton, C (Notts Rangers), 1888-9 v. I
Shepherd, A (Bolton Wanderers), 1906 v. S; (Newcastle United), 1911 v. I
Shilton, P (Leicester City), 1971 v. W; 1972 v. I; 1973 v. I; W & S; 1974 v. W, I & S; (Stoke City), 1977 v. I & W; (Nottingham Forest), 1978 v. W
Shutt, G (Stoke City), 1886 v. I
Silcock, J (Manchester United), 1921 v. S & W
Simms, E (Luton Town), 1922 v. I
Simpson, J (Blackburn Rovers), 1911-12-13 v. S; 1911-12-14 v. W; 1911-12 v. I
Slaney, Capt Kenyon (Household Brigade), 187 v. S
Slater, W (Wolverhampton Wanderers), 1955 v. W; 1958-60 v. S
Smalley, T (Wolverhampton Wanderers), 1937 v. W
Smart, Y (Aston Villa), 1921-4 v. S; 1924-30 v. W; 1936 v. I
Smith, A (Nottingham Forest), 1891 v. S & W; 1893 v. I
Smith, A. K (Oxford University), 1872 v. S
Smith B (Tottenham Hotspur), 1921 v. S; 1922 v. W
Smith, C. E (Crystal Palace), 1876 v. S
Smith, G. O (Old Carthusians), 1894-6-7-8-9-1900-1 v. S; 1894-5-6-7-8-9-1900 v. W; 1893-6-7-8-1900 v. I
Smith, H (Reading), 1905-6 v. W; 1905 v. S; 1906 v. I
Smith, J (Bolton Wanderers), 1913-20 v. I; 1914-19*(2) v. S; 1914-20*(1)-20 v. W
Smith, J (West Bromwich Albion), 1920 v. W*(1); 1920-3 v. I
Smith, J (Portsmouth), 1932 v. I & W
Smith, J. R (Millwall), 1939 v. I
Smith, L (Brentford), 1946 v. I*
Smith, L (Arsenal), 1951 v. W; 1952 v. W & I; 1953 v. W & S
Smith, R (Tottenham Hotspur), 1961 v. I, W & S; 1962 v. S; 1963 v. S; 1964 v. W & I
Smith, S (Aston Villa), 1895 v. S
Smith, S (Leicester City), 193 v. I
Smith, T (Birmingham City), 1960 v. W
Smith, T (Liverpool), 1971 v. W
Smith, W. H (Huddersfield Town), 1922-8 v. S; 1922 v. W
Soo, F (Stoke City), 1946 v. I*; 1946 v. W*
Sorby, T. H (Sheffield United), 1879 v. W
Southworth, J (Blackburn Rovers), 1899-91 v. W; 1892 v. S
Sparks, G. J (Herts Rangers), 1879-90 v. S; 1880 v. W

Spence, J (Manchester United), 1927 v. I
Spencer, H (Aston Villa), 1897-1905 v. S; 1897-1900-5 v. W; 1908 v. I
Spencer, C. W (Newcastle United), 1924 v. S; 1925 v. W
Spiksley, F (Sheffield Wednesday), 1893-4-8 v. S; 1893-8 v. W; 1894-6 v. I
Spilsby, B. W (Derby County), 1885-6 v. ?; 1886 v. S
Spouncer, A (Nottingham Forest), 1900 v. W
Springett, R (Sheffield Wednesday), 1960 v. I & S; 1961 v. M, I & S; 1962 v. I & W; 1966 v. W
Sproston, B (Leeds United), 1937 v. W; 1938 v. S, W & I; (Tottenham Hotspur), 1939 v. W
Squire, R. T (Old Westminsters), 1886 v. S, W & I
Stanbrough, M. H (Old Carthusians), 1895 v. W
Staniforth, R (Huddersfield Town), 1954 v. S; 1944 v. W
Starling, R. W (Sheffield Wednesday), 1933 v. S; (Aston Villa), 1937 v. S
Steele, F. C (Stoke City), 1937 v. S, W & I
Stephenson, C (Huddersfield Town), 1924 v. W
Stephenson, J. E (Leeds United), 1938 v. S; 1939 v. I
Stewart, J (Sheffield Wednesday), 1907 v. S & W; (Newcastle United), 1911 v. S
Stiles, N (Manchester United), 1965 v. S; 1966 v. W, I & S; 1967 v. I, W & S; 1970 v. I & S
Stoker, L (Birmingham City), 1933 v. W; 1934 v. S
Storer, H (Derby County), 1928 v. I
Storey, P (Arsenal), 1971 v. I & S; 1972 v. W, I & S; 1973 v. I, W & S
Strange, A. H (Sheffield Wednesday), 1930-1-2 v. S; 1931-2 v. W & I; 1933 v. S & I; 1934 v. I & W
Stratford, C. W (Royal Engineers) 1887 v. S
Stratford, E. H (The Wanderers), 1874 v. S
Streten, B. R (Luton Town), 1950 v. I
Stubbins, A (Newcastle United), 1946 v. W*
Sturgess, A (Sheffield United), 1911 v. I; 1914 v. S
Summerbee, M (Manchester City), 1968 v. S; 1972 v. W & I
Sutcliffe, J. W (Bolton Wanderers), 1895-1901 v. S; 1893-1902 v. W; 1895 v. I
Swan P (Sheffield Wednesday), 1961 v. I, W & S; 1962 v. W, I & S
Swepstone, H. A (Pilgrims), 1880-2-3 v. S; 1882-3 v. W; 1883 v. I
Swift, F. V (Manchester City), 1946 v. I* & S; 1947 v. S, W & I; 1948 v. S, W & I; 1949 v. S. W & I
Tait, C (Birmingham Excelsior), 1881 v. W
Talbot, B (Ipswich Town), 1977 v. S
Tambling, R (Chelsea), 1963 v. W
Tate, J. T (Aston Villa), 1933 v. W
Taylor, E (Huddersfield Town), 1923-4-6 v. S; 1923-4 v. I; 1923 v. W
Taylor, P (Liverpool), 1948 v. W & I
Taylor, P (Crystal Palace), 1976 v. W, I & S
Taylor, T (Manchester United), 1956 v. S; 1957 v. I; 1958 v. W & I
Thickett, H (Sheffield United), 1899 v. S & W
Thomas, D (Queen's Park Rangers), 1975 v. W
Thompson, P (Liverpool), 1965 v. I, W & S; 1966 v. I; 1970 v. S
Thompson, P. B (Liverpool), 1976 v. W, I & S; 1979 v. I, S
Thompson, T (Aston Villa), 1952 v. W; (Preston North End), 1957 v. S
Thomson, R (Wolverhampton Wanderers), 1964 v. I; 1965 v. I & W
Thornley, J (Manchester City), 1907 v. W
Tilson, C. F (Manchester City), 1935 v. W; 1936 v. I
Titmui, F (Southampton), 1922-3 v. W
Todd, C (Derby County), 1972 v. I; 1974 v. W, I & S; 1975 v. I, W & S; 1976 v. I & S; 1977 v. I
Toone, G (Notts County), 1892 v. S & W
Topham, A. G (Eastbourne), 1894 v. W
Topham, R (Casuals), 1893 v. I; 1894 v. W

Towers, T (Sunderland), 1976 v. W
Townley, W. J (Blackburn Rovers), 1889 v. W; 1890 v. I
Townrow, J (Clapton Orient), 1925 v. S; 1926 v. W
Tremelling, D (Birmingham City), 1928 v. W
Tresadern, J (West Ham United), 1923 v. S
Tueart, D (Manchester City), 1975 v. I; 1977 v. I
Tunstall, F (Sheffield United), 1923-4-5 v. S; 1924 v. W; 1924-5 v. ?
Turner, A (Southampton), 1900-1 v. I
Turner, J (Bolton Wanderers), 1893 v. W; 1895-8 v. I
Turnbull, R (Bradford), 1919*(2) v. S; 1920 v. I & W*(1)
Underwood, A (Stoke City), 1891-2 v. I
Urwin, T (Newcastle United), 1926 v. W
Utley, G (Barnsley), 1913 v. I
Vaughton, H. A (Aston Villa), 1892-4 v. S & W; 1882 v. I
Veitch, C. C. K (Newcastle United), 1906-7 v. S & W; 1906 v. I; 1909 v. W
Veitch, J. G (Old Westminsters), 1894 v. W
Videl, R. W. S (Oxford University), 1873 v. S
Viljoen, C (Ipswich Town), 1975 v. I & W
Volsey, W (Millwall), 1920 v. W*(1)
Wace, H (The Wanderers) , 1878-9 v. S; 1879 v. W
Wadsworth, S. J (Huddersfield Town), 1922-3-4-5 v. S; 1924-5-7 v. I; 1926 v. W
Wainscoat, W. R (Leeds United), 1929 v. S
Waiters, A (Blackpool), 1964 v. W
Waiden, F (Tottenham Hotspur), 1914 v. S; 19derers), 1874-5-7-80 v. S
Walker, W. H (Aston Villa), 1921-5-6-7 v. 1; 1922-5-6-7 v. W; 1922-4-5-6-? v. S
Wall, G (Manchester United), 1907-10) v. W; 1908-13 v. I; 1909-10-12 v. S
Wallace, C. W (Aston Villa), 1913 v. W; 1919 v. I; 1920 v. S
Walters, A. M (Old Carthusians), 1885-6-7-9-90 v. S; 1887-9-90 v. W; 1885 v. I
Walters, P. M (Old Carthusians), 1885-6-7-8-9-90 v. S; 1886-7-9-90 v. W; 1885-6-8 v. I
Walton, N (Blackburn Rovers), 1890 v. I
Ward, J. T (Blackburn Olympic), 1885 v. W
Ward, T. V (Derby County), 1949 v. W
Waring, T (Aston Villa), 1932 v. S, W & I
Warren, B (Derby County), 1906-7-8 v. I, W & S; (Chelsea), 1909-11 v. S, I & W
Warner, C (Upton Park), 1878 v. S
Waterfield, G. S (Burnley), 1927 v. W
Watson, D (Sunderland), 1975 v. I, W & S; (Manchester City), 1977 v. I, W & S; 1978 v. W, I & S; 1979 v. I, W, S
Watson, W (Burnley), 1913 v. S; 1914-20 v. I; 1920 v. W* (1)
Watson, W (Huddersfield Town), 1946 v. W*; (Sunderland), 1950 v. I; 1951 v. W
Watson, V. M (West Ham United), 1923 v. W; 1923-30 v. S
Weaver, S (Newcastle United), 1932 v. S; 1933 v. S & I
Webb, G. W (West Ham United), 1911 v. S & W
Webster, M (Middlesbrough), 1930 v. S
Wedlock, W (Bristol City), 1907-8-9-10-11-12 v. S & I; 14 v. W
Weir, D (Bolton Wanderers), 1889 v. S & I
Weller, K (Leicester City), 1974 v. W, I & S
Welsh, R. C (Old Harrovians), 1872-4 v. S
West, G (Everton), 1969 v. W
Westwood, R. W (Bolton Wanderers), 1935 v. S & W; 1936 v. I; 1937 v. W
Whatley, O (Aston Villa), 1888 v. S, W & I; 1897 v. I
Wheeler, J (Bolton Wanderers), 1955 v. I
Wheldon, G. F (Aston Villa), 1883 v. S, W & I; 1897 v. I
Whitefield, H (Old Etonians), 1879 v. W

Whitehead, J (Accrington Stanley), 1893 v. W; (Blackburn Rovers), 1894 v. I
Whittham, M (Sheffield United), 1892 v. I
Whitworth, S (Leicester City), 1975 v. I, W & S
Widdowson, S. W (Nottingham Forest), 1965 v. W
Wilkes, A (Aston Villa), 1901-2 v. S & W; 1902 v. I
Wilkins, R (Chelsea), 1977 v. I; 1978 v. W, I & S; 1979 v. I, W, S
Wilkinson, B (Sheffield United), 1904 v. S
Wilkinson, S. R (Oxford University), 1891 v. W
Williams, B. F (Wolverhampton Wanderers), 1946 v. W*; 1950 v. S & W; 1951 v. I, W & S; 1952 v. W; 1955 v. S; 1956 v. W
Williams, O (Clapton Orient), 1923 v. W & I
Williams, W (West Bromwich Albion), 1898 v. S; 1898-9 v. W; 1897-8-9 v. I
Williamson, E. G (Arsenal), 1920 v. W*(1)
Williamson, R. G (Middlesbrough), 1905-11-13 v. I; 1911-12 v. S & W
Willingham, C. K (Huddersfield Town), 1938 v. S; 1939 v. S, W & I
Wilshaw, D (Wolverhampton Wanderers), 1954 v. W; 1955 v. S; 1956 v. W & I; 1957 v. I
Wilson, C. P (Hendon), 1884 v. S & W
Wilson, O. W (Oxford University), 1881 v. S; 1879 v. W
Wilson, G. P (Corinthians), 1900 v. S & W
Wilson, G (Sheffield Wednesday), 1921-2-3 v. 1921-3-4 v. W; 1922-3-4 v. I
Wilson, R (Huddersfield Town), 1960 v. S; 1962 v. W, I & S; 1963 v. I; 1964 v. W & S; (Everton), 1965 v. S; 1966 v. W & I; 1967 v. I, W & S; 1968 v. I & S
Wilson, T (Huddersfield Town), 1928 v. S
Winchworth, W. M (Old Westminsters), 1892 v. W; 1893 v. I
Windridge, J. E (Chelsea), 1908 v. S & W; 1908-9 v. I
Wollaston, C. H (The Wanderers), 1874-5-7-80 v. S
Wolstenholme, S (Everton), 1904 v. S; 1905 v. I & W
Wood, H (Wolverhampton Wanderers), 1890-6 v. S; 1890 v. I
Wood, R (Manchester United), 1955 v. I & W
Woodcock, A (Nottingham Forest), 1978 v. I
Woodger, G (Oldham Athletic), 1911 v. I
Woodhall, G. H (West Bromwich Albion), 1888 v. S & W
Woodley, V (Chelsea), 1937 v. S; 1938-9 v. S, W & I
Woodward, V. J (Tottenham Hotspur), 1903-4-5-7-8 v. S; 1903-5-8-9 v. W; 1903-4-5-8-9 v. I; (Chelsêa), 1910 v. I; 1911 v. W
Woosnam, M (Manchester City), 1922 v. W
Worthington, F (Leicester City), 1974 v. S
Worrall, F (Portsmouth), 1937 v. I
Wright, E. G. D (Cambridge University), 1906 v. W
Wright, T (Everton), 1970 v. W
Wright, W. A (Wolverhampton Wanderers), 1946 v. S*; 1947 v. S, W & I; 1948 v. S, W & I; 1949 v. S, W & I; 1950 v. S, W & I; 1951 v. I & S; 1952-3 v. W, I & S, 1954 v. W, I & S; 1955 v. I, W & S; 1956-7-8-9 v. S, W & I
Wylie, J. G (Shrewsbury), 1978 v. S
Yates, J (Burnley), 1889 v. I
York, R. E (Aston Villa), 1922-6 v. S
Young, A (Huddersfield Town), 1933 v. W; 1937 v. S; 1939 v. W
Young, G (Sheffield Wednesday), 1965 v. W

* Victory Internationals † Also played for Wales ‡ Also played for Ireland

SCOTTISH INTERNATIONALS

Adams, H (Heart of Midlothian), 1892 v. W; 1892-3 v. I
Agnew, W. B (Kilmarnock), 1908 v. W; 1907-8 v. I
Aitken, A (Newcastle United, 1901-2-3-4-5-6-? v. E; 1903-5 v. W; (Middlesbrough), 1907-8 v. E; 1907 v. W; (Leicester Fosse), 1910-11 v. E; 1911 v. I
Aitken, G (East Fife), 1949 v. E; 1950 v. W & I; (Sunderland), 1953 v. W & I; 1954 v. E
Aitken, R (Dumbarton), 1886 v. E; 1888 v. I
Aitkenhead, W. A. C (Blackburn Rovers), 1912 v. I
Alexander, D (East Stirlingshire), 1894 v. W & I
Allan, D. S (Queens Park), 1895 v. E; 1885-6 v. W
Allan, G (Liverpool), 1897 v. E
Allan, H (Heart of Midlothian), 1902 v. W
Allan, J (Queens Park), 1887 v. E & W
Ancell, R (Newcastle United), 1937 v. W & I
Anderson, A (Hearts), 1933 v. E; 1934-5-6-7-8 v. E, I & W; 1939 v. W
Anderson, F (Clydesdale), 1874 v. E
Anderson, G (Kilmarnock), 1901 v. I
Anderson, H (Raith Rovers), 1914 v. W
Anderson, K (Queens Park), 1898 v. E; 1896-8 v. I
Anderson, W (Queens Park), 1882-3-4-5 v. E; 1883-5 v. W
Andrews, P (Eastern), 1875 v. E
Archibald, A (Rangers), 1922-3-4-31-2 v. E; 1921-2-4 v. W; 1923 v. I
Armstrong, M (Aberdeen), 1936 v. W & I
Arnott, W (Queens Park), 1884-5-6-7-8-9-90-1-2-3 v. E; 1883-5-7 v. W; 1884 v. I
Auld, J (Third Lanark), 1887 v. E; 1887-9 v. W
Auld, R (Celtic), 1960 v. W
Baird, A (Queens Park), 1892 v. I; 1894 v. W
Baird, D (Heart of Midlothian), 1890 v. ?; 1891 v. E; 1892 v. W
Baird, J. C (Vale of Leven), 1876-80 v. E; 1878 v. W
Baird, S (Rangers), 1958 v. I
Baird, W. U (St. Bernard), 1879 v. I
Barbour, A (Renton), 1885 v. I
Barker, J. B (Rangers), 1893-4 v. W
Barrett, F (Dundee), 1895 v. W; 1894 v. I
Battles, B (Celtic), 1901 v. E, W & I
Battles, B jun (Hearts), 1931 v. W
Bauld, W (Hearts), 1950 v. E
Baxter, J (Rangers), 1961 v. I; 1962 v. I, W & E; 1963 v. W, I & E; 1964 v. W & E; 1965 v. W & I; (Sunderland), 1966 v. I, W & E; 1967 v. W & E; 1968 v. W
Baxter, R. D (Middlesbrough), 1939 v. E & W
Beattie, A (Preston North End), 1937-8 v. E; 1939 v. W & I
Beattie, R (Preston North End), 1939 v. W
Begbie, I (Heart of Midlothian), 1890 v. I; 1891-4 v. E; 1892 v. W
Bell, A (Manchester United), 1912 v. I
Bell, J (Dumbarton), 1890 v. I; 1892 v. E; (Everton), 1896-7-8-9 v. E; 1899 v. W & I; (Celtic), 1900 v. E & W
Bell, M (Heart of Midlothian), 1901 v. W
Bennett, A (Celtic), 1904-8 v. W; 1907 v. I; (Rangers), 1909-10-11 v. E; 1909-10-11 v. W; 1909-13 v. I
Bennie, R (Airdrieonians), 1925 v. W; 1925-6 v. I
Berry, D (Queens Park), 1894-9 v. W
Berry, W (Queens Park), 1888-9-90-1 v. E
Beveridge, W. W (Ayr Academicals), 1879 v. E & W; (Glasgow University), 1880 v. W
Black, D (Hurlford), 1889 v. I

Black, I (Southampton), 1948 v. E
Blackley, J (Hibernian), 1974 v. E
Blair, D (Clyde), 1929-32 v. I; 1931 v. E; (Aston Villa), 1933 v. W
Blair, J (Sheffield Wednesday), 1920 v. E & I; (Cardiff City), 1921-3 v. E; 1923-4 v. W; 1923 v. I
Blair, J (Motherwell), 1934 v. W
Blair, J. A (Blackpool), 1947 v. W
Blair, W (Third Lanark), 1896 v. W
Blessington, J (Celtic), 1894-6 v. E; 1894-5 v. ?
Blyth, J (Coventry City), 1978 v. W
Bowie, J (Rangers), 1920 v. E; 1920 v. I
Bowie, W (Linthouse), 1881 v. I
Bowman, G (Montrose), 1892 v. I
Boyde, J (Newcastle United), 1934 v. I
Brackenbridge, T (Heart of Midlothian), 1888 v. I
Bradshaw, T (Bury), 1928 v. E
Brand, R (Rangers), 1961 v. I; 1962 v. I & W
Branden, T (Blackburn Rovers), 1896 v. E
Bremner, W (Leeds United), 1966 v. E; 1967 v. W, I & E; 1968 v. W & E; 1969 v. W. I & E; 1971 v. W & E; 1972 v. I, W & E; 1973 v. E; 1974 v. I, W & E
Brennan, F (Airdrieonians), 1946 v. E*; (Newcastle United), 1947 v. W & I; 1953 v. W, I & E; 1954 v. I & E
Breslin, B (Edinburgh Hibernians), 1897 v. W
Brewster, G (Everton), 1921 v. E
Brogan, J (Celtic), 1971 v. W, I & E
Brown, A (Blackpool), 1953 v. W; 1954 v. W & E
Brown, A (Tottenham Hotspur), 1902 v. E; (Middlesborugh), 1904 v. E
Brown A (St. Mirren), 1890-1 v. W
Brown, G (Rangers), 1931 v. W; 1932 v. E, W & I; 1933 v. E; 1935-6 v. E & W; 1937 v. E, W & I; 1938 v. E & W
Brown, H (Partick Thistle), 1947 v. W
Brown, J (Cambuslang), 1890 v. W
Brown, J (Clyde), 1939 v. W
Brown, R (Dumbarton), 1884 v. W & I
Brown, R jun (Dumbarton), 1885 v. W
Brown, R (Queens Park), 1946 v. E*, W* & I*; (Rangers), 1947 v. I; 1949 v. I; 1952 v. E
Brown, W (Dundee), 1959 v. E, W & I; (Tottenham Hotspur), 1960 v. W & I; 1962 v. I, W & E; 1963 v. W, I & E; 1964 v. I & W; 1965 v. E; 1966 v. I
Browning, J (Celtic), 1914 v. W
Brownie, J (Third Lanark), 1909-10-11-12-13-14 v. E; 1910-11-12-13-14 v. W, 1909-10-11-12-13-14 v. I
Brownlie, J (Hibernian), 1972 v. I & E
Bruce, D (Vale of Leven), 1890 v. W
Buchan, M (Manchester United), 1972 v. W; 1974 v. I & W; 1978 v. I
Buchanan, J (Cambuslang), 1889 v. I
Buchanan, J (Rangers), 1929-30 v. E
Buchanan, R (Abercorn), 1891 v. W
Buckley, P (Aberdeen), 1955 v. W & I
Buick, A (Heart of Midlothian), 1902 v. W & I
Burley, G (Ipswich Town), 1979 v. W, I, E
Burns, K (Nottingham Forest), 1978 v. I, W & E
Busby, M. W (Manchester City), 1934 v. W
Cairns, T (Rangers), 1922-3-5 v. E; 1920-3-5 v. W; 1924-5 v I
Calderhead, D (Queen of South Wanderers), 1889 v. I
Caldow, E (Rangers), 1957 v. E; 1958 v. I & W; 1959 v. E, W & I; 1960 v. E, W & I; 1961 v. E, W & I; 1962 v. I, W & E; 1963 v. W, I & E
Callaghan, P (Edinburgh Hibernians), 1900 v. I
Callaghan, W (Dumfermline), 1970 v. W

Cameron, J (St. Mirren), 1904 v. I; (Chelsea), 1909 v. E
Cameron, J (Queens Park), 1896 v. I
Cameron, J (Rangers), 1886 v. I
Campbell, C (Queens Park), 1874-7-8-9-80-1-2-4-5-6 v. E; 1876-7-82 v. W
Campbell, H (Renton), 1889 v. W
Campbell, J (South Western), 1880 v. W
Campbell, J (Kilmarnock), 1891 v. I; 1892 v. W
Campbell, J (Celtic), 1893-8-1900 v. E; 1901-2-3 v. W; 1893-8-1900 v. I
Campbell, J (Sheffield Wednesday), 1913 v. W
Campbell, J (Rangers), 1899 v. E & W; 1899-1901 v. I
Campbell, K (Liverpool), 1920 v. E, W & I; (Partick Thistle), 1921-2 v. W & I; 1922 v. E
Campbell, P (Greenock Morton), 1898 v. W
Campbell, P (Rangers), 1878-9 v. W
Campbell, W (Morton), 1946 v. E*, W* & I*; 1947 v. I; 1948 v. E
Carabine, J (Third Lanark), 1939 v. E & I
Carr, W (Coventry City), 1970 v. I, W & E
Cassidy, J (Celtic), 1921-4 v. W; 1921-3 v. I
Chalmers, S (Celtic), 1965 v. W; 1967 v. I
Chalmers, W (Rangers), 1885 v. I
Chalmers, W. S (Queens Park), 1929 v. I
Chambers, T (Heart of Midlothian), 1894 v. W
Chaplin, G (Dundee), 1908 v. W
Cheyne, A (Aberdeen), 1929 v. E
Chisholm, K (Queens Park), 1946 v. I*
Christie, A. J (Queens Park), 1899 v. E; 1898 v. W; 1899 v. I
Christie, R. M (Queens Park), 1884 v. E
Clark, J (Celtic), 1967 v. W & I
Clark, R (Aberdeen), 1968 v. W; 1970 v. I; 1971 v. W, I & E; 1972 v. I, W & E
Cleland, J (Royal Albert), 1891 v. I
Clements, R (Leith Athletic), 1891 v. I
Clunas, W (Sunderland), 1924 v. E; 1926 v. W
Collier, W (Raith Rovers), 1922 v. W
Collins, R (Celtic), 1951 v. W & I; 1956 v. I & W; 1957 v. E & W; 1958 v. I & W; (Everton), 1959 v. E, W & I; (Leeds United), 1965 v. E
Collins, T (Heart of Midlothian), 1909 v. W
Colman, D (Aberdeen), 1911 v. E & W; 1911-13 v. I
Combe, R (Hibernian), 1948 v. E
Conn, A (Tottenham Hotspur), 1975 v. E
Connor, J (Airdrieonians), 1886 v. I
Connor, J (Sunderland), 1932 v. I; 1934 v. E; 1935 v. I
Cook, W (Bolton Wanderers), 1934 v. E; 1935 v. W & I
Cooke, C (Dundee), 1966 v. W; (Chelsea), 1968 v. E; 1969 v. W & I
Cormack, P (Nottingham Forest), 1971 v. W & E
Cowan, J (Aston Villa), 1896-7-8 v. E
Cowan, J (Morton), 1949 v. E & W; 1950-1 v. E. W & I; 1952 v. I & W
Cowan, W. D (Newcastle United), 1924 v. E
Cowre, D (Dundee), 1953 v. E; 1954 v. I & W; 1955 v. W & I; 1956 v. W; 1957 v. I & W
Cox, S (Rangers), 1949 v. E; 1950 v. E, W & I; 1951 v. E; 1952 v. I & W; 1953-4 v. W, I & E
Craig, A (Motherwell), 1932 v. E
Craig, J (Celtic), 1968 v. W
Craig, T (Rangers), 1927-8-30 v. I; 1930 v. E & W
Crapnell, J (Airdrieonians), 1929 v. E; 1931 v. I; 1932 v. E; 1933 v. I
Crawford, D (St. Mirren), 1894-1900 v. W; 1894 v. I
Crawford, J (Queens Park), 1932 v. I; 1933 v. E, W & I
Crerand, P (Celtic), 1962 v. I, W & E; 1963 v. W & I; (Manchester United), 1964 v. I; 1965 v. E

Cringan, W (Celtic), 1922 v. E; 1920-3 v. W; 1922 v. I
Croal, J. A (Falkirk), 1913 v. I; 1914 v. E & W
Crosbie, J (Ayr United), 1920 v. W; (Birmingham City), 1922 v. E
Cross, J. H (Third Lanark), 1903 v. I
Cruikshank, J (Hearts), 1970 v. W & E
Crum, J (Celtic), 1936 v. E; 1939 v. I
Cumming, D (Middlesbrough), 1938 v. E
Cumming, J (Hearts), 1955 v. E, 1960 v. E
Cummings, G (Partick Thistle), 1935 v. E; 1936 v. W & I; (Aston Villa), 1936 v. E; 1938 v. W & I; 1939 v. E
Cunningham, A (Rangers), 1921-3-4-6-7 v. E; 1921-3-7 v. W; 1920-2-4-6 v. I
Cunningham, W (Preston North End), 1955 v. W & E
Curran, H (Wolverhampton Wanderers), 1971 v. I & E
Dalglish, K (Celtic), 1973 v. W, I & E; 1974 v. I, W & E; 1975 v. W, I & E; 1976 v. I & E; 1977 v. W, I & E; (Liverpool), 1978 v. W & E; 1979 v. I, E
Davidson, D (Queens Park), 1881 v. E; 1878-9-80-1 v. W
Davidson, J. A (Partick Thistle), 1955 v. W, I & E
Davidson, S (Middlesbrough), 1921 v. E
Dawson, J (Rangers), 1935 v. I; 1936 v. E; 1937 v. E, W & I; 1938 v. W & I; 1939 v. E & I
Deakin, J (St. Mirren), 1946 v. W*
Delaney, J (Celtic), 1936 v. W & I; 1937 v. E; 1938 v. I; 1939 v. W & I; (Manchester United), 1946 v. E*; 1947 v. E; 1948 v. E, W & I
Devine, A (Falkirk), 1910 v. W
Dewar, G (Dumbarton), 1889 v. E; 1888 v. I
Dewar, N (Third Lanark), 1932 v. E; 1933 v. W
Dick, J (West Ham United), 1959 v. E
Dickie, M (Rangers), 1897-9 v. I; 1900 v. W
Dickson, W (Strathmore), 1888 v. I
Dickson, W (Kilmarnock), 1970 v. I, W & E
Divers, J (Celtic), 1895 v. W
Divers, J (Celtic), 1939 v. I
Docherty, T. H (Preston North End), 1952 v. W; 1953 v. E; 1955 v. W & E; 1957 v. E; 1958 v. I, W & E; (Arsenal), 1959 v. E, W & I
Dodds, E (Blackpool), 1946 v. W* & I*
Dodds, J (Celtic), 1914 v. E, W & I
Doig, J. E (Arbroath), 1887-9 v. I; (Sunderland), 1896-9-1902-3 v. E
Donachie, W (Manchester City), 1972 v. I & E; 1973 v. W & I; 1974 v. I; 1976 v. W, I & E; 1977 v. W, I & E; 1978 v. W & E
Donaldson, A (Bolton Wanderers), 1914-20 v. E; 1914 v. W; 1914-20-2 v. I
Donnachie, J (Oldham Athletic), 1913-14 v. E; 1914 v. I
Dougal, J (Preston North End), 1939 v. E
Dougal, N (Birmingham City), 1946 v. E*; 1947 v. W
Douglas, A (Chelsea), 1911 v. I
Douglas, J (Renfrew), 1880 v. W
Dowds, P (Celtic), 1892 v. I
Downie, R (Third Lanark), 1892 v. W
Doyle, D (Celtic), 1892-4-5-7-8 v. E; 1893 v. W; 1895-8 v. I
Drummond, J (Rangers), 1895-6-8-1900-1-2 v. E; 1902 v. W; 3 v. : I
Dunbar, M (Cartvale), 1886 v. I
Duncan, A (Hibernian), 1975 v. W, I & E
Duncan, D (Derby County), 1933 v. E & W; 1934 v. W; 1935 v. E & W; 1936-7 v. E, W & I; 1938 v. W
Duncan, J (Alexandria Athletic), 1878 v. W; (Rangers), 1882 v. W
Duncan, J (Leicester City), 1926 v. W
Duncanson, J (Rangers), 1947 v. I
Dunlop, J (St. Mirren), 1890 v. W
Dunlop, W (Liverpool), 1906 v. E
Dunn, J (Hibernian), 1925 v. W; 1925-7 v. I; 1928 v. E; (Everton), 1929 v. W

Dykes, J (Hearts), 1939 v. I
Easson, J (Portsmouth), 1934 v. W
Ellis, J (Mossend Swifts), 1892 v. I
Evans, R (Celtic), 1949 v. E, W & I; 1950 v. W & I; 1951 v. E; 1952 v. I; 1954 v. I, W & E; 1955 v. I; 1956 v. E, I & W; 1958 v. I, W & E; 1959 v. E; 1960 v. E, I & W
Ewart, J (Bradford City), 1921 v. E
Ewing, T (Partick Thistle), 1958 v. W & E
Farm, G. N (Blackpool), 1953 v. W, I & E; 1954 v. I, W & E
Fernie, J (Celtic), 1955 v. W & I; 1957 v. E, I & W; 1958 v. W
Ferguson, J (Vale of Leven), 1874-6-7 v. W; 1876-7-8 v. W
Ferguson, R (Kilmarnock), 1966 v. W & E; 1967 v. W & I
Findlay, R (Kilmarnock), 1898 v. W
Fitichie, T. T (Queens Park), 1905-6-7 v. W; 1906 v. I
Fleming, C (East Fife), 1954 v. I
Fleming, J (Rangers), 1930 v. E
Fleming, R (Greenock Morton), 1896 v. I
Forbes, A (Sheffield United), 1947 v. E; 1948 v. W & I; (Arsenal), 1950 v. E; 1951 v. W & I; 1952 v. W
Forbes, J (Vale of Leven), 1884-7 v. E & W; 1884 v. I
Ford, D (Hearts), 1974 v. W
Forsyth, C (Kilmarnock), 1964 v. E; 1965 v. W & I
Forsyth, T (Rangers), 1976 v. W, I & E; 1977 v. W, I & E; 1978 v. I & E
Forrest, J (Motherwell), 1958 v. E
Forrest, J (Rangers), 1966 v. W
Foyers, R (St. Bernard's), 1893-4 v. W
Fraser, E (Queens Park), 1882-3 v. E; 1880-2-3 v. W
Fraser, J (Moffat), 1891 v. I
Fraser, J (Dundee), 1907 v. I
Fraser, W. A (Sunderland), 1955 v. W & I
Fulton, W (Aberdeen), 1884 v. I
Fyfe, H. J (Third Lanark), 1895 v. W
Gabriel, J (Everton), 1961 v. W
Gallacher, H (Airdrieonians), 1924 v. I; 1925 v. E, W & I; 1926 v. W; (Newcastle United), 1926-7-8-9 v. E; 1927-8-9-30 v. W; 1926-7-9-30 v. I; (Chelsea), 1934 v. E; (Derby County), 1935 v. E
Gallacher, P (Sunderland), 1935 v. I
Galt, J (Rangers), 1908 v. W & I
Gardiner, (Motherwell), 1958 v. W
Gardiner, D. R (Third Lanark), 1897 v. W
Gardner, R (Queens Park and Clydesdale), 1872-3-4-5-8-? v. E
Gemmell, T (Celtic), 1966 v. E; 1967 v. W, I & E; 1968 v. I & E; 1969 v. W, I & E; 1970 v. E
Gemmill, A (Derby County), 1972 v. I, W & E; 1976 v. W, I & E; 1977 v. W; (Nottingham Forest), 1978 v. I, W & E
Gibb, W (Clydesdale), 1873 v. E
Gibson, D (Leicester City), 1964 v. I; 1965 v. W
Gibson, J (Partick Thistle), 1926-7 v. E; 1927 v. W & I; (Aston Villa), 1928 v. E; 1928-30 v. W; 1930 v. I
Gibson, N (Rangers), 1895-6-7-8-9-1900 v. E; 1899-1901 v. W; 1895-6-7-8-1900 v. I; (Partick Thistle), 1905 v. I
Gilchrist, J (Celtic), 1922 v. E
Gilhooley, M (Hull City), 1922 v. W
Gillespie, G (Rangers), 1881-2 v. E; 1880-1-6-90 v. W; 1891 v. I
Gillespie, J (Third Lanark), 1898 v. W
Gillespie, J (Queens Park), 1896 v. W
Gillespie, R (Queens Park), 1927-31 v. W; 1933 v. E
Gillick, T (Everton), 1939 v. W & I
Gilmour, J (Dundee), 1931 v. W

Gilzean, A (Dundee), 1964 v. W & E; 1965 v. I; (Tottenham Hotspur), 1966 v. I & W; 1968 v. W; 1969 v. W & E; 1970 v. I
Glen, A (Aberdeen), 1956 v. E & I
Glen, R (Renton), 1895-6 v. W; (Hibernian), 1900 v. I
Gordon, J. E (Rangers), 1912-13-14-20 v. E & I; 1913-20 v. W
Gossland, J (Rangers), 1884 v. I
Goudie, J (Abercorn), 1884 v. I
Gourlay, J (Cambuslang), 1888 v. W; 1886 v. I
Govan, J (Hibernian), 1948 v. E & W; 1949 v. I
Gow, D. R (Rangers), 1888 v. E
Gow, J (Rangers), 1888 v. I
Gow, J J. (Queens Park), 1895 v. E
Graham, A (Arsenal), 1921 v. I
Graham, A (Leeds United), 1979 v. W, I, E
Graham, G (Arsenal), 1972 v. I; (Manchester United), 1973 v. W & I
Graham, J (Annbank), 1884 v. I
Grant, J (Hibernian), 1959 v. W & I
Gray, D (Rangers), 1930-1 v. E; 1929-30 v. W & I; 1933 v. W & I
Gray, E (Leeds United), 1969 v. E; 1971 v. W & I; 1976 v. W & E
Gray, F (Leeds United), 1979 v. W, I, E
Gray, W (Pollockshields Athletic), 1886 v. E
Green, A (Blackpool), 1971 v. I & E; (Newcastle United), 1972 v. W
Greig, J (Rangers), 1964 v. E; 1965 v. W, I & E; 1966 v. I, W & E; 1967 v. W, I & E; 1968 v. I, W & E; 1969 v. W, I & E; 1970 v. W & E; 1971 v. I & E
Grey, A (Edinburgh Hibernian), 1903 v. I
Groves, W (Hibernian), 1888 v. W; Celtic), 1889 v. I; 1890 v. E
Guililand, W (Queens Park), 1885-6-8 v. E; 1885 v. W
Haddock, H (Clyde), 1955 v. E; 1958 v. E
Haddow, D (Rangers), 1894 v. E
Haffey, F (Celtic), 1960 v. E; 1961 v. E
Hamilton, A (Queens Park), 1885-6-8 v. E; 1885 v. W
Hamilton, A (Dundee), 1962 v. W & E; 1963 v. W, I & E; 1964 v. I, W & E; 1965 v. W, I & E; 1966 v. I
Hamilton, G (Aberdeen), 1946 v. I*, 1946 v. E; 1947 v. I
Hamilton, G (Port Glasgow Athletic), 1906 v. I
Hamilton, J (Queens Park), 1892 v. W; 1893 v. E & I
Hamilton, J (St. Mirren), 1924 v. I
Hamilton, R. C (Rangers), 1899-1901-3 v. E; 1899-1900-2 v. W; 1899-1902-3-4 v. I; (Dundee), 1911 v. W
Hamilton, T (Hurlford), 1891 v. I
Hamilton, T (Rangers), 1932 v. E
Hannah, A (Renton), 1888 v. W
Hansen, A (Liverpool), 1979 v. W
Hannah, J (Third Lanark), 1899 v. W
Harkness, J. D (Queens Park, 1927-8 v. E; 1927 v. I; (Hearts), 1929-30 v. E; 1929-34 v. I; 1929-30-2 v. W
Harper, W (Hibernian), 1923-4-5 v. E, I & W; (Arsenal), 1926 v. E
Harris, J (Partick Thistle), 1921 v. W & I
Harris, N (Newcastle United), 1924 v. E
Harrower, W (Queens Park), 1882 v. E; 1886 v. W; 1884 v. I
Hartford, A (West Bromwich Albion), 1972 v. E; (Manchester City), 1977 v. W, I & E; 1978 v. W & E; 1979 v. W, I, E
Harvey, D (Leeds United), 1974 v. I, W & E
Hastings, A (Sunderland), 1935 v. I; 1938 v. I
Haughney, M (Celtic), 1954 v. E
Hay, J (Celtic), 1905-9-10-11 v. I; 1910-11 v. E; 1910 v. W; (Newcastle United), 1912-14 v. E; 1912 v. W; 1914 v. I
Hegarty, P (Dundee United), 1979 v. W, I, E
Hay, D (Celtic), 1970 v. I, W & E; 1971 v. W & I; 1973 v. W, I & E; 1974 v. I, W & E

Heggle, C (Rangers), 1866 v. I
Henderson, G (Rangers), 1904 v. I
Henderson, J. G (Portsmouth), 1954 v. I & E; 1956 v. W; (Arsenal), 1959 v. W & I
Henderson, W (Rangers), 1963 v. W, I & E; 1964 v. I, W & E; 1965 v. E; 1966 v. I & W; 1967 v. W & I; 1969 v. I & E
Hepburn, J (Alloa Athletic), 1891 v. W
Hepburn, R (Ayr United), 1932 v. I
Herd, A. C (Hearts), 1915 v. I
Herd, D (Arsenal), 1959 v. E, W & I
Herd, G (Clyde), 1958 v. E; 1961 v. W & ?
Herriott, J (Birmingham City), 1969 v. I & E
Hewle, J (Charlton Athletic), 1956 v. E; 1957 v. E, I & W; 1960 v. I & W
Higgins, A (Kilmarnock), 1885 v. I
Higgins, A (Newcastle United), 1910-11 v. E & I
Highet, T. C (Queens Park), 1875-6-8 v. E; 1876 v. W
Hill, D (Rangers), 1881 v. E; 1881-2 v. W
Hill, D. A (Third Lanark), 1906 v. I
Hill, F (Aberdeen), 1931 v. W & I
Hill, J (Heart of Midlothian), 1892 v. W
Hogg, G (Heart of Midlothian), 1896 v. E & I
Hogg, J (Ayr United), 1922 v. I
Holm, A. H (Queens Park), 1883 v. E; 1882-3 v. W
Holton, J (Manchester United), 1972 v. W, I & E; 1974 v. I, W & E
Houlison, W (Queen of the South), 1949 v. E & I
Howden, W (Partick Thistle), 1905 v. I
Howie, H (Hibernian), 1949 v. W
Howie, J (Newcastle United), 1905-6 v. E
Howleson, J (St. Mirren), 1927 v. I
Hughes, J (Celtic), 1966 v. I; 1968 v. E
Hunter, A (Celtic), 1973 v. E
Hunter, J (Dundee), 1909 v. W
Hunter, J (Third Lanark), 1874-5-6 v. E; 1877 v. W
Hunter, R (St. Mirren), 1890 v. I
Hunter, W (Motherwell), 1961 v. W
Husband, J (Partick Thistle), 1946 v. E*; 1947 v. W
Hutchison, T (Coventry City), 1974 v. I & W
Hutton, J (Aberdeen), 1923-6 v. E & W; 1923-4-6-? v. I; (Blackburn Rovers), 1927-8 v. I; 1928 v. W
Hutton, J (St. Bernard's), 1887 v. I
Hyslop, T (Stoke City), 1896 v. E; (Rangers), 1897 v. E
Inglish, J (Kilmarnock Athletic), 1884 v. I
Ingliss, J (Rangers), 1883 v. E & W
Irons, J. H (Queens Park), 1900 v. W
Jackson, A (Cambuslang), 1886 v. W; 1888 v. I
Jackson, A (Aberdeen), 1925 v. E, W & I; (Huddersfield Town), 1926-8-9-30 v. E; 1926-7-8-9-30 v. W; 1926-7-9-30 v. I
Jackson, C (Rangers), 1975 v. W; 1976 v. W, I & S
Jackson, J (Partick Thistle), 1933 v. E; (Chelsea), 1934-5 v. E; 1936 v. W & I
Jackson, T. A (St. Mirren), 1904 v. E; 1904-5-7 v. W; 1904-7 v. I
James, A (Preston North End), 1926 v. W; 1928–9 v. E; 1929 v. I; (Arsenal), 1930 v. E, W & I; 1933 v. W
Jardine, S (Rangers), 1973 v. E; 1974 v. I, W & E; 1975 v. W, I & E; 1978 v. I
Jenkinson, T (Heart of Midlothian), 1887 v. I
Johnston, W (Rangers), 1966 v. W & E; 1968 v. W & E; 1970 v. I; 1977 v. I & E; (West Bromwich Albion), 1978 v. W & E
Johnstone, D (Rangers), 1973 v. W, I & E; 1978 v. I & W
Johnstone, J (Abercorn), 1888 v. W
Johnstone, J (Celtic), 1965 v. W; 1966 v. E; 1967 v. W; 1968 v. W; 1970 v. E; 1971 v. E; 1972 v. I; 1974 v. W & E

Johnstone, J (Heart of Midlothian), 1930 v. W; 1933 v. W & I
Johnstone, J (Kilmarnock), 1904 v. W
Johnstone, R (Hibernian), 1951 v. E; 1952 v. I & E; 1953 v. E; 1954 v. W & E; 1955 v. I; (Manchester City), 1955 v. E; 1956, E, I & W
Jordan, J (Leeds United), 1974 v. W & E; 1976 v. W, I & E; 1977 v. I & E; (Manchester United), 1978 v. I & E; 1979 v. W, I, E
Kay, J. L (Queens Park), 1880-2-3 v. E; 1882-3-4 v. W
Kellor, A (Montrose), 1891 v. W; 1892 v. I; (Dundee), 1894 v. I; 1895-6-7 v. W
Keir, L (Dumbarton), 1887-8 v. E; 1887 v. W; 1886 v. I
Kelly, J (Barnsley), 1949 v. W & I
Kelly, J (Renton), 1887-8 v. E; (Celtic), 1889-90-2-3 v. E; 1894 v. W; 1892-6 v. E
Kelso, J (Renton), 1887 v. E
Kelso, R (Renton), 1885-6-7 v. W; 1885-8 v. I; 1888 v. E; (Dundee), v. I
Kelso, T (Dundee), 1914 v. W
Kennaway, J (Celtic), 1934 v. W
Kennedy, A (Eastern), 1875-6 v. E; 1876 v. W; (Third Lanark), 1878 v. E; 1882-4 v. W
Kennedy, J (Celtic), 1964 v. W & E; 1965 v. W & I
Kennedy, J (Edinburgh Hibernians), 1897 v. W
Kennedy, S (Aberdeen), 1978 v. W & E
Kennedy, S (Partick Thistle), 1905 v. W
Kennedy, S (Rangers), 1975 v. W, I & E
Ker, G (Queens Park), 1880-2 v. E; 1881-2 v. W
Ker, W (Queens Park), 1872-3 v. E
Kerr, P (Hibernian), 1924 v. I
Key, G (Heart of Midlothian), 1902 v. I
Key, W (Queens Park), 1907 v. I
King, A (Hearts), 1896 v. E & W; 1897 v. I; (Celtic), 1889 v. W
King, J (Hamilton Academicals), 1933-4 v. I
King, W. S (Queens Park), 1929 v. W
Kinloch, J (Partick Thistle), 1922 v. I
Kinnaird, A. F (The Wanderers), 1873 v. E
Lamble, J. A (Queens Park), 1888 v. E; 1886-7 v. I
Lamble, W (Queens Park), 1894-5-6-7 v. E; 1893 v. W; 1892-5-6-7 v. I
Lamont, W (Pilgrims), 1885 v. I
Lang, A (Dumbarton), 1880 v. W
Lang, J. J (Clydesdale), 1876 v. W; (Third Lanark), 1878 v. W
Latta, A (Dumbarton Athletic), 1888 v. W; 1889 v. E
Law, D (Huddersfield Town), 1959 v. W & I; 1960 v. I & W; (Manchester City), 1960 v. E; 1961 v. E & I; (Turin), 1962 v. E; (Manchester United), 1963 v. W, I & E; 1964 v. W & E; 1965 v. W, I & E; 1966 v. I & E; 1967 v. W & E; 1968 v. I; 1969 v. I; 1972 v. I, W & E; (Manchester City), 1974 v. I
Law G (Rangers), 1910 v. E & I
Law, T (Chelsea), 1928-30 v. E
Lawrence, J (Newcastle United), 1911 v. E
Lawrence, T (Liverpool), 1969 v. W
Lawson, D (St. Mirren), 1923 v. E
Leckie, R (Queens Park), 1872 v. E
Leggat, G (Aberdeen), 1955 v. E; 1957 v. W; 1958 v. I; (Fulham), 1959 v. E, W & I; 1960 v. E, I & W
Lennie, W (Aberdeen), 1908 v. W & I
Lennox, R (Celtic), 1967 v. I & E; 1968 v. W & E
Leslie, L (Airdrie), 1961 v. W & I
Liddell, W (Liverpool), 1946 v. E*, W* & I*; 1947 v. W & I; 1948 v. E, W & I; 1950 v. E & W; 1951-2-3 v. W, I & E; 1954 v. W; 1956 v. I
Lindsay, D (St. Mirren), 1903 v. I
Lindsay, J (Dumbarton), 1880-1-4-5 v. W; 1881-4-5-6 v. E

Lindsay, J (Renton), 1888-93 v. E; 1893 v. I
Linwood, A (Clyde), 1950 v. W
Livingstone, G. T (Celtic), 1902 v. E; (Manchester City), 1906 v. E; (Rangers); 1907 v. W
Lockhead, A (Third Lanark), 1889 v. W
Logie, J. T (Arsenal), 1953 v. I
Logan, J (Ayr United), 1891 v. W
Logan, T (Falkirk), 1913 v. I
Loney, W (Celtic), 1910 v. W & I
Long, H (Clyde), 1947 v. I
Longair, W (Dundee), 1894 v. I
Lorimer, P (Leeds United), 1971 v. W & I; 1972 v. W & E; 1973-4 v. E
Low, A (Falkirk), 1931 v. I
Low, T. P (Rangers), 1897 v. I
Low, W. L (Newcastle United), 1911-20 v. E; 1911 v. W; 1912-20 v. I
Lowe, J (Cambuslang), 1891 v. I
Lowe, J (St. Bernard's), 1887 v. I
Lundie, J (Edinburgh Hibernians), 1886 v. W
Lyall, J (Sheffield Wednesday), 1905 v. E
McAdam, J (Third Lanark), 1880 v. W
McArthur, D (Celtic), 1895 v. E & I; 1899 v. W
McAtee, A (Celtic), 1913 v. W
Macaulay, A (Brentford), 1947 v. E; (Arsenal), 1948 v. E, W & I
McAulay, J (Arthurlie), 1882 v. W; 1884 v. I
McAulay, J (Dumbarton), 1883-4-5-6-7 v. E; 1883-5-7 v. W
McAulay, R (Rangers), 1932 v. I & W
McBain, E (St. Mirren), 1894 v. W
McBain, N (Manchester United), 1922 v. E; (Everton), 1923 v. I; 1924 v. W
McBride, J (Celtic), 1967 v, W & I
McBride, P (Preston North End), 1904-6-7-8 v. E; 1907-9 v. W
McCall, A (Renton), 1888 v. I
McCall, J (Renton), 1887-8-80 v. E; 1888-9 v. W
McCalliog, J (Sheffield Wednesday), 1967 v, E; 1968 v. E
McCallum, N (Renton), 1888 v. I
McCann, R (Motherwell), 1960 v. E, I & W; 1961 v. E
McCartney, W (Edinburgh Hibernians), 1902 v. I
McClean, T (Kilmarnock), 1969 v. W; 1970 v. I & W
McClory, A (Motherwell), 1925-7 v. W; 1928 v. I
McCloy, P (Ayr United), 1924-5 v. E
McCloy, P (Rangers), 1973 v. W & I
McColl, I. M (Rangers), 1950 v. E; 1951 v. W & I; 1957 v. E, I & W; 1958 v. I & E
McColl, R. S (Queens Park), 1899-1900-1 v. E; 1896-9-1900-1 v. W; 1886-7-8-9 v. I; (Newcastle United), 1902 v. E; 1908 v. I
McColl, W (Renton), 1895 v. W
McCombie, A (Sunderland), 1903-5 v. E & W
McCorkindale, J (Patrick Thistle), 1891 v. W
McCormack, R (Abercorn), 1886 v. W
McCreadie, A (Rangers), 1894 v. E; 1893 v. W
McCreadie, E (Chelsea), 1965 v. E; 1966 v. I & W; 1967 v. E; 1968 v. I, W & E; 1969 v. W, I & E
McCulloch, D (Hearts), 1935 v. W; (Brentford), 1936 v. E; 1937 v. W & I; (Derby County), 1939 v. W
McDonald, H (Edinburgh University), 1886 v. E
McDonald, J (Sunderland), 1956 v. W & I
McDougall, J (Vale of Leven), 1977-8-9 v. E; 1877-9 v. W
MacDougall, T (Norwich City), 1975 v. W, I & E
MacFadyen, W (Motherwell), 1934 v. W
McFarlane, A (Dundee), 1904-6-8-11 v. W; 1909 v. I
McFarlane, R (Greenock Morton), 1896 v. W

McGeoch, A (Dumbreck), 1876-7 v. E & W
McGhee, J (Edinburgh Hibernians), 1886 v. W
McGonagie, W (Celtic), 1933 v. E; 1934 v. E & I; 1935 v. I & W
McGowan, J (Partick Thistle), 1946 v. I*
McGrain, D (Celtic), 1973 v. W, I & E; 1974 v. E; 1975 v. W, I & E; 1976 v. W, I & E; 1977 v. W, I & E
McGregor, J (Vale of Leven), 1877-8-80 v. E; 1977 v. W
McGrory, J (Kilmarnock), 1965 v. I
McGuire, W (Beith, 1881 v. E & W
McGurk, F (Birmingham City), 1934 v. W
McHardy, H (Rangers), 1885 v. I
McInally, T ()Celtic), 1926 v. I; 1927 v. W
McInnes, T (Cowlairs), 1889 v. I
McIntosh, W (Third Lanark), 1905 v. I
McIntyre, A (Vale of Leven), 1872-82 v. E
McIntyre, H (Rangers, 1880 v. W
McIntyre, J (Rangers), 1884 v. W
Mackay, D (Celtic), 1959 v. E; 1960 v. E; 1961 v. W & I; 1962 v. I
Mackay, D (Hearts), 1959 v. W & I; (Tottenham Hotspur), ???? v. E; 1960 v. W & I; 1961 v. E, W & I 1963 v. E; 1964 v. I & W; 1966 v. I
McKay, J (Blackburn Rovers), 1924 v. W
McKay, R (Newcastle United), 1928 v. W
McKenzie, D (Brentford), 1938 v. I
McKenzie, J (Partick Thistle), 1954 v. W & E; 1955 v. E
McKeown, M (Celtic), 1890 v. E; 1898 v. I
McKie, J (East Stirlingshire), 1898 v. W
McKinlay, D (Liverpool), 1922 v. W & I
McKinnon, A (Queens Park), 1874 v. E
McKinnon, R (Rangers), 1966 v. W & E; 1967 v. W, I & E; 1966 v. I, W & E; 1970 v. I, W & E
McKinnon, W (Dumbarton), 1883-4 v. E & W
McKinnon, W (Queens Park), 1872-3-4-5-6-7-8-9 v. E; 1876 v. W
McLaren, A (St. Johnstone), 1933 v. W & I
McLaren, A (Preston North End), 1947 v. E; 1948 v. W
McLaren, J (Celtic), 1889-90 v. E; 1888 v. W
McLean, A (Celtic), 1926-7 v. W; 1926 v. I; 1927 v. E
M'Lean, D (St. Bernard's), 1896 v. W; 1897 v. I
M'Lean, D (Sheffield Wednesday), 1912 v. E
M'Leod, D (Celtic), 1906 v. E & W; 1905-6 v. I
M'Leod, J (Dumbarton), 1892 v. E; 1889-93 v. W; 1888-90 v. I
M'Leod, J (Hibernian), 1961 v. E
M'Leod, W (Cowlairs), 1896 v. I
M'Lintock, A (Vale of Leven), 1875-6-80 v. E
McLintock, F (Arsenal), 1965 v. I; 1970 v. I; 1971 v. W, I & E
M'Luckie, J (Manchester City), 1934 v. W
M'Mahon, A (Celtic), 1892-3-4 v. E; 1893-1901 v. I; 1902 v. W
M'Menemy, J (Celtic), 1910-11-14 v. E; 1910-11-12-14 v. W; 1905-9-11-14-20 v. I
M'Menemy, J (Motherwell), 1934 v. W
M'Millan, J (Airdrieonians), 1952-5 v. E
M'Millan, J (St. Bernard's), 1897 v. W
M'Millan, T (Dumbarton), 1887 v. I
M'Mullan, J (Partick Thistle), 1921-4-5 v. E; 1930-1-6 v. W; 1921-4 v. I; (Manchester City), 1926-7-8-9 v. E; 1927-8-9 v. W; 1929 v. I
M'Nab, A (Greenock Morton), 1921 v. E & I
M'Nab, A (West Bromwich Albion), 1939 v. E
M'Nab, C (Dundee), 1931 v. E & W; 1932 v. E
M'Nab, J (Liverpool), 1923 v. W
M'Nair, A (Celtic), 1908-9-12-13-14-20 v. E; 1906-8-10-11-12-20 v. W; 1907-12-14-20 v. I

M'Naught, W (Raith Rovers), 1951 v. W & I; 1952 v. E: 1955 v. I
M'Neill, H (Queens Park), 1874-5-6-8-9-81 v. E; 1876-7-9-81 v. W
M'Neill, M (Rangers), 1880 v. E; 1876 v. W
McNeill, W (Celtic), 1961 v. E; 1962 v. I & E; 1964 v. W & E; 1965 v. E; 1966 v. I; 1968 v. E; 1969 v. W & E; 1972 v. I, W & E
M'Phail, J (Celtic), 1950-1 v. W; 1951-5 v. I
M'Phail (Airdrieonians), 1927 v. E; (Rangers), 1931-3-5-7 v. E; 1929-32-8 v. W; 1931-2-3-4-8 v. I
M'Phee, J (Falkirk), 1946 v. W*
M'Pherson, D (Kilmarnock), 1892 v. I
M'Pherson, J (Cowlairs), 1889-90 v. E; 1888 v. W; (Rangers), 1894-5 v. E; 1892 v. W; 1895-7 v. I
M'Pherson, J (Clydesdale), 1875 v. E
M'Pherson, J (Vale of Leven), 1879-80-3-4 v. E; 1879-81-3 v. W; 1885 v. I
M'Pherson, J (Heart of Midlothian), 1891 v. E; 1890 v. I
M'Pherson, R (Arthurlie), 1892 v. E
M'Queen, M (Leeds United), 1975 v. W, I & E; 1977 v. W, I & E; (Manchester United), 1978 v. I & W; 1979 v. I, E
M'Queen, M (Leith Athletic), 1890-1 v. W
M'Spayden, A (Patrick Thistle), 1939 v. E
M'Stay, W (Celtic), 1925-6-7 v. E; 1921-5-6-7-8 v. W & I
M'Rorie, D (Morton), 1931 v. W
M'Tavish, J (Falkirk), 1910 v. I
M'Wattie, G. C (Queens Park), 1901 v. W & I
M'William, P (Newcastle United), 1905-6-7-9-10 v. E; 1907-9-11 v. W
Macari, L (Celtic), 1972 v. E; (Manchester United), 1973 v. E; 1975 v. W
Madden, J (Celtic), 1893-5 v. W
Main, J (Edinburgh Hibernians), 1909 v. I
Main, R (Rangers), 1938 v. W
Maley, W (Celtic), 1893 v. E & I
Marshall, H (Celtic), 1899 v. W; 1900 v.I
Marshall, J (Rangers), 1932-3-4 v. E
Marshall, J (Middlesbrough), 1921-2 v. E, W & I; (Llanelly), 1924 v. W
Marshall, J (Third Lanark), 1887 v. E; 1886-7 v. W; 1885 v. I
Marshall, R (Rangers), 1892-4 v. I
Martin, F (Aberdeen), 1955 v. E
Martis, J (Motherwell), 1961 v. W
Mason, J (Third Lanark), 1949 v. E, W & I; 1950-1 v. I
Massie, A (Heart of Midlothian), 1932 v. I & W; 1933 v. I; 1934 v. E & I; 1935 v. E, I & W; 1936 v. W & I; (Aston Villa), 1936 v. E; 1937 v. E, W & I; 1938 v. W
Masson, D (Queens Park Rangers), 1976 v. W, I & E; 1977 v. W, I & E; (Derby County), 1978 v. I & E
Maxwell, W. S (Stoke City), 1898 v. E
May, J (Rangers), 1908 v. E; 1906-9 v. W; 1906-8 v. I
Meechan, P (Celtic), 1896 v. I
Meiklejohn, D (Rangers), 1925-9-30-1 v. E; 1922-4-5-8-32 v. W; 1925-8-9-30-2 v. I
Menaies, A (Heart of Midlothian), 1906 v. E
Mercer, R (Heart of Midlothian), 1912 v. W; 1913 v. I
Middleton, R (Cowdenbeath), 1930 v. I
Miller, A (Hearts), 1939 v. W
Miller, J (Rangers), 1897-8 v. E; 1898 v. W
Miller, J (St. Mirren), 1931-4 v. E
Miller, P (Dumbarton), 1882-3 v. E; 1883 v. W
Miller, T (Liverpool), 1920 v. E; (Manchester United), 1921 v. E & I
Miller, W (Third Lanark), 1876 v. E
Miller, W (Celtic), 1947 v. E & W; 1948 v. W & I
Mills, W (Aberdeen), 1936 v. W & I; 1937 v. W
Milne, J.V (Middlesbrough), 1938-9 v. E

Mitchell, D (Rangers), 1892-3-4 v. E; 1890-3 v. I
Mitchell, J (Kilmanrock), 1910 v. W; 1908-10 v. I
Moir, W (Bolton Wanderers), 1950 v. E
Moncur, R (Newcastle United), 1970 v. I, W & E; 1971 v. W & E; 1972 v. I, W & E
Morgan, H (St. Mirren), 1898 v. W; (Liverpool), 1899 v. E
Morgan, W (Burnley), 1968 v. I; (Manchester United), 1973 v. W, I & E; 1974 v. I
Morris, D (Raith Rovers), 1924-5 v. E; 1925 v. W; 1923-4-5 v. I
Morris, H (East Fife), 1950 v. I
Morrison, T (St. Mirren), 1927 v. E
Morton, A. L (Queens Park), 1920 v. W & I; (Rangers, 8-9-30-1-2 v. E; 1922-3-4-5-8-9-30-1-2 v. W; 1923-4-5-7-8-9-30-1 v. I
Mudie, J (Blackpool), 1957 v. E, I & W; 1958 v. I, W & E
Muir, W (Dundee), 1907 v. I
Muirhead, T (Rangers), 1923 v. E; 1924-9-30 v. W; 1922-7-8-9 v. I
Mulhall, G (Aberdeen), 1960 v. I; (Sunderland), 1963-4 v. I
Munro, A (Heart of Midlothian), 1937 v. W & I
Munro, F (Wolverhampton Wanderers), 1975 v. I & E
Munro, N (Abercorn), 1889 v. E; 1888 v. W
Murdoch, J (Motherwell), 1931 v. I
Murdoch, R (Celtic), 1966 v. W & E; 1967 v. I; 1968 v. I; 1969 v. W, I & E
Murray, J (Renton), 1895 v. W
Murray, J (Vale of Leven), 1890 v. WMurray, J (Heart of Midlothian), 1958 v. E
Murray, P (Edinburgh Hibernians), 1897 v. W; 1896 v. I
Mutch, G (Preston North End), 1938 v. E
Napier, C (Celtic), 1932 v. E; 1935 v. E & W; (Derby County), 1937 v. I
Narey, D (Dundee United), 1979 v. I
Neil, R. G (Hibernian), 1896 v. W; (Rangers), 1900 v. W
Neill, R. W (Queens Park), 1877-80 v. E; 1876-7-8 v. W
Neilles, P (Heart of Midlothian), 1914 v. W & I
Nelson, J (Cardiff City), 1922 v. W & I; 1928 v. E
Niblo, T (Aston Villa), 1904 v. E
Nibloe, J (Kilmarnock), 1929-31 v. E; 1930 v. W; 1931 v. I; 1932 v. E
Niven, F. B (Moffat), 1885 v. I
O'Donnell, F (Preston North End), 1937 v. E; (Blackpool), 1938 v. E & W
O'Hare, J (Derby County), 1970 v. I, W & E; 1971 v. W & I; 1972 v. I & W
Ormond, W (Hibernian), 1950-4 v. E
O'Rourke, J (Airdrieonians), 1907 v. I
Orr, J (Kilmarnock), 1892 v. W
Orr, R (Newcastle United), 1902-4 v. E
Orr. W (Celtic), 1904 v. W; 1905-8 v. I
Oswald, J (Third Lanark), 1889 v. E; (St. Bernard's), 1895 v. E
Parker, A (Falkirk), 1956 v. E, I & W; 1957 v. I & W; 1958 v. I, W & E
Parlane, D (Rangers), 1973 v. W; 1975 v. W, I & E; 1977 v. W
Parlane, R (Vale of Leven), 1879 v. E; 1878-9 v. W
Paterson, G (Celtic), 1939 v. I; 1946 v. W* & I*
Paterson, J (Leicester City), 1920 v. E
Paton, A (Motherwell), 1946 v. W* v. I*
Paton, D (St. Bernard's) 1896 v. W
Paton, M (Dumbarton), 1883-5-6 v. E; 1884-5 v. W
Paton, R (Vale of Leven), 1879 v. E & W
Patrick, J (St. Mirren, 1897 v. E & W
Paul, H McD (Queens Park), 1909 v. E, W & I
Paul, W (Partick Thistle), 1888-9-90 v. W
Paul, W (Dykebar), 1891 v. I
Pearson, T (Newcastle United), 1947 v. E
Pettigrew, W (Motherwell), 1976 v. W & I
Philips, J (Queen's Park), 1877 v. E; 1877-8 v.W

Plenderleith, J (Manchester City), 1961 v. I
Porteus, W (Heart of Midlothian), 1903 v. I
Provan, D (Rangers), 1964 v. I
Pringle, C (St. Mirren), 1921 v. W
Pryce, J (Edinburgh Hibernians), 1897 v. W
Pursell, P (Queens Park), 1914 v. W
Quinn, J (Celtic), 1908-9-10-12 v. E; 1906-10-12 v. W; 1905-6-8-10 v. I
Quinn, P (Motherwell), 1961 v. E
Rae, J (Third Lanark), 1889 v. W; 1890 v. I
Raeside, J. S (Third Lanark), 1906 v. W
Raisbeck, A. G (Liverpool), 1900-1-23-4-5-6-7 v. E; 1903 v. W
Rankin, G (Vale of Leven), 1890 v. E & I
Redpath, W (Motherwell), 1949 v. W & I; 1951 v. E; 1952 v. I & E
Reid, J. G (Airdrieonians), 1914-20 v. W; 1924 v. I
Reid, R (Brentford), 1938 v. I
Reid, W (Glasgow Rangers), 1911-13-14 v. E; 1911-13 v. W; 1911-12-13-14 v. I
Reilly, L (Hibernian), 1949 v. E & W; 1950 v. W & I; 1951 v. W & E; 1952-3 v. I, W & E; 1954 v. W; 1955 v. E; 1956 v. E, W & I; 1957 v. E, I & W
Rennie, H. G (Hearts), 1900 v. E & I; (Hibernian), 1901-2 v. E; 1902-3-5-8 v. W; 1902-3-4-6-8 v. I
Renny-Taylor, H. W (Royal Engineers), 1873 v. E
Rhind, A (Queens Park), 1872 v. E
Richmond, A (Queens Park), 1906 v. W
Richmond, J. T (Clydesdale), 1877 v. E; (Queens's Park), 1878 v. E; 1882 v. W
Ring, T (Clyde), 1955 v. W, I & E; 1957 v. E; 1958 v. I
Rioch, B (Derby County), 1975 v. W, I & E; 1976 v, W, I & E; (Everton), 1977 v. W, I & E; (Derby County), 1978 v. I & E
Ritchie, A (East Stirlingshire), 1891 v. W
Ritchie, H (Edinburgh Hibernians), 1923 v. W; 1928 v. I
Ritchie, J (Queens Park), 1897 v. W
Robb, D (Aberdeen), 1971 v. W & E
Robb, W (Rangers), 1926 v. W; (Hibernian), 1928 v. W
Robertson, G (Motherwell), 1910 v. W; (Sheffield Wednesday), 1912 v. W; 1913 v. E & I
Robertson, J (Nottingham Forest), 1978 v. I
Robertson, J (Tottenham Hotspur), 1965 v. W
Robertson, J. T (Everton), 1898 v. E; (Southampton), 1899 v. E; (Rangers), 1900-1-2-3-4 v. E; 1900-1-2-3-4-5 v. W; 1901-2-3 v. I
Robertson, P (Dundee), 1903 v. I
Robertson, T (Queens Park), 1890 v. E; 1889-92 v. I
Robertson, T (Heart of Midlothian), 1898 v. I
Robertson, W (Dumbarton), 1887 v. E & W
Robinson, R (Dundee), 1975 v. I
Robinson, W (Dumbarton), 1887 v. E & W
Rough, A (Partick Thistle), 1976 v. W, I & E; 1977 v. W, I & E; 1978 v. I & E; 1979 v. W
Rowan, A ()Caledonian), 1890 v. E; 1882 v. W
Russell, D (Heart of Midlothian), 1895 v. E; 1897-1901 v. W; 1895-8-1901 v. I
Russell, J (Cambuslang), 1890 v. I
Russell, W (Airdrieonians), 1925 v. E; 1924 v. W
St. John, I (Motherwell), 1960 v. E, I & W; 1961 v. E; (Liverpool), 1961 v. I, W & E; 1963 v. W, I & E; 1964 v. I; 1965 v. E
Sawers, W (Dundee), 1895 v. W
Scarff, P (Celtic), 1931 v. I
Scott, A (Rangers), 1957 v. I; 1958 v. W; 1962 v. I, W & E; (Everton), 1964 v. W
Scott, M (Airdrieonians), 1898 v. W

Scott, R (Airdrieonians), 1894 v. I
Scoular, J (Portsmouth), 1952 v. E; 1953 v. W & I
Sellar, W (Battlefield), 1885-6-7-8 v. E; 1887 v. W; (Queens Park), 1891-2-3 v. E; 1893 v. I
Semple, W (Cambuslang), 1886 v. W
Shankly, W (Preston North End), 1938 v. E; 1939 v. E, W & I
Sharp, J (Dundee), 1904 v. W; (Woolwich Arsenal), 1907-8 v. E; 1907 v. W; (Fulham), 1909 v. W
Shaw, D (Hibernian), 1946 v. E*; 1947 v. W & I; 1948 v. E; 1949 v. W & I
Shaw, F. W (Pollockshields Athletic), 1884 v. E & W
Shaw, J (Rangers), 1946 v. E*, W* & I*; 1947 v. E; 1948 v. I
Shearer, R (Rangers), 1961 v. E
Sillars, D. C (Queens Park), 1892-4 v. E; 1893-5 v. W; 1891 v. I
Simpson, J (Third Lanark), 1895 v. E, W & I
Simpson, J (Rangers), 1935-6-7 v. E, W & I; 1938 v. W & I
Simpson, R (Celtic), 1967 v. E; 1968 v. I & E
Sinclair, G, L (Heart of Midlothian), 1912 v. W; 1910-12 v. I
Skene, L. H (Queen's Park), 1904 v. W
Sloan, T (Third Lanark), 1904 v. W
Smellie, R (Queens Park), 1889-91-3 v. E; 1888 v. W; 1887-93 v. I
Smith, A (Rangers), 1898-1900-1-2-3-6-11 v. E; 1900-1-2-3-5-7 v. W; 1 v. I
Smith, G (Hibernian), 1946 v. W*; 1947 v. E & I; 1948 v. W; 1952 v. E; 1956 v. E, I & W
Smith, J (Rangers), 1935-8 v. I
Smith, J (Ayr United), 1924 v. E
Smith, J (Queens Park), 1872-3 v. E
Smith, J (Mauchline), 1877-9 v. E & W; (Edinburgh University), 1880-1 v. E; 1881 v. W; (Queens Park), 1883-4; 1883 v. W
Smith, N (Rangers), 1897-9-1900-2 v. E; 1898-9-1900-1 v. W; 1899-1900-1-2 v. I
Smith, R (Queens Park), 1872 v. E
Smith, T (Kilmarnock), 1934 v. E; (Preston North End), 1938 v. E
Somers, P (Celtic), 1905 v. E; 1900 v. W; 1905-7-? v. I
Somers, W. S (Third Lanark), 1879 v. E; 1879-80 v. W
Somerville, G (Queens Park), 1896 v. E
Souness, G (Liverpool), 1978 v. W & E; 1979 v. W, I, E
Speedie, F (Rangers), 1903 v. E, W & I
Spiers, J. H (Rangers), 1908 v. W
Stanton, P (Hibernian), 1969 v. I; 1972 v. W; 1973 v. W & I
Stark, J (Rangers), 1909 v. E & I
Steel, D (Huddersfield Town), 1923 v. E, W & I
Steel, W (Morton), 1947 v. E; (Derby County), 1948 v. E, W & I; 1949 v. E, W & I; 1950 v. E, W & I; (Dundee), 1951 v. W, I & E; 1952 v. W; 1953 v. W, I & E
Stein, C (Rangers), 1969 v. W, I & E; 1970 v. W & E; (Coventry City), 1973 v. I
Stephen, J (Bradford), 1947-8 v. W
Stevenson, G (Motherwell), 1928-31-2 v. W; 1929-30-2 v. I; 1930-1 v. E; 1933 v. I; 1934 v. E; 1935 v. I
Stewart, A (Queens Park), 1889 v. W; 1888 v. I
Stewart, A (Third Lanark), 1894 v. W
Stewart, D (Queens Park), 1893 v. W; 1894-7 v. I
Stewart, D (Dumbarton), 1888 v. I
Stewart, G (Hibernian), 1906 v. W; (Manchester City), 1906 v. E; 1907 v. E & W
Stewart, W (Queens Park), 1898-1900 v. I
Storrier, D (Celtic), 1899 v. E, W & I
Summers, W (St. Mirren), 1929 v. E
Tait, T. S (Sunderland), 1911 v. W
Taylor, J (Queens Park), 1872-3-4-5-6-? v. E; 1875 v. W

Taylor, J. D (Dumbarton), 1892-3 v. W; 1894 v. I; (St. Mirren), 1895 v. I
Taylor, W (Heart of Midlothian), 1892 v. E
Telfer, W (Motherwell), 1933-4 v. I
Telfer, W (St. Mirren), 1954 v. W
Templeton, R (Aston Villa), 1902 v. E; (Newcastle United), 1903-4 v. E; 1903 v. W; (Woolwidh Arsenal), 1905 v. W; (Kilmarnock), 1910-12 v. E; 1913 v. W; 1908-10-12 v. I
Thompson, A (Arthurlie), 1886 v. I
Thompson, J (Celtic), 1921 v. E, W & I
Thomson, A (Airdrieonians), 1909 v. I
Thomson, A (Celtic), 1926 v. E; 1923 v. W
Thomson, A (Third Lanark), 1889 v. W
Thomson, C (Hearts), 1905-7-8 v. E; 1905-6-7-8 v. W; 1904-5-6-7-8 v. I; (Sunderland), 1910-12-13-14 v. E; 1909-12-13 v. W; 1911-13 v. I
Thomson, D (Dundee), 1920 v. W
Thomson, J. J (Queens Park), 1872-3-4 v. E
Thomson, J (Everton), 1933 v. W
Thomson, R (Celtic), 1932 v. W
Thomson, R. W (Falkirk), 1927 v. W
Thomson, S (Lugar Boswell), 1884 v. W & I
Thomson, W (Dumbarton), 1892-3-8 v. W; 1898 v. I
Thomson, W (Dundee), 1896 v. W
Thornton, W (Rangers), 1947 v. W & I; 1948 v. E & I
Toner, W (Kilmarnock), 1959 v. W & I
Townsley, T (Falkirk), 1926 v. W
Troup, A (Dundee), 1920-5 v. E; 1921 v. W: 1921-2 v. I; (Everton), 1926 v. E
Turner, T (Arthurlie), 1884 v. W
Turner, W (Pollockshields Athletic), 1885-6 v. I
Ure, I (Dundee), 1962 v. W; 1963 v. W, I & E; (Arsenal), 1964-8 v. I
Urquhart, D (Hibernian), 1934 v. W
Vallance, T (Rangers), 1877-8-9-91 v. E; 1877-9-81 v. W
Veniners, A (Cowdenbeath), 1934 v. I; (Rangers), 1936 v. E; 1939 v. E
Waddell, T (Queens Park), 1892-3-5 v. E; 1891-3-5 v. I
Waddell, W (Rangers), 1946 v. E*, W* & I*; 1947 v. W; 1949 v. E, W & I; 1950 v. E & I; 1951 v. E; 1952 v. I & W; 1954 v. I; 1955 v. W & I
Wales, H (Motherwell), 1933 v. W
Walker, F (Third Lanark), 1922 v. W
Walker, G (St. Mirren), 1931 v. I
Walker, J (Heart of Midlothian), 1897 v. W; 1895-8 v. I; (Rangers), 1904 v. W & I
Walker, J (Swindon Town), 1911-12-13 v. E, W & I
Walker, R (Heart of Midlothian), 1900-1-2-3-4-5-7-8-9-12-13 v. E; 9-12-13 v. W; 1900-2-3-4-5-6-7-8-12 v. I
Walker, T (Heart of Midlothian), 1935 v. E & W; 1936-7-8-9 v. E, W & I
Walker, W (Clyde), 1909-10 v. I
Wallace, I (Coventry City), 1979 v. W
Wallace, W (Heart of Midlothian), 1965 v. I; 1966 v. E; (Celtic), 1967 v. E; 1968 v. I
Wardhaugh, J (Heart of Midlothian), 1957 v. L
Wark, J (Ipswich Town), 1979 v. W, I, E
Watson, A (Queens Park), 1881-2 v. E; 1881 v. W
Watson, J (Sunderland), 1903-4-5 v. E; 1903 v. W; (Middlesbrough), 1909 v. E & I
Watson, J (Rangers), 1878 v. W
Watson, J (Motherwell), 1948 v. I; (Huddersfield Town), 1954 v. I
Watson, W (Falkirk), 1898 v. W
Watt, F (Kilbirnie), 1891 v. E; 1889-90 v. W; 1889 v. I
Watt, W. W (Queens Park), 1887 v. I
Weir, A (Motherwell), 1960 v. E
Weir, J (Third Lanark), 1887 v. I

Weir, J. B (Queens Park), 1872-4-5 v. E; 1878 v. W
White, J (Albion Rovers), 1922 v. W; (Heart of Midlothian), 1923 v. I
White, J (Falkirk), 1960 v. I; (Tottenham Hotspur), 1960 v. W; 1961 v. W; 1962 v. I, W & E; 1963 v. W, I & E; 1964 v. I, W & E
White, W (Bolton Wanderers), 1907-8 v. E
Whitelaw, A (Vale of Leven), 1890 v. W; 1887 v. I
Wilson, A (Sheffield Wednesday), 1907-8-12-13 v. E; 1913 v. W; 1914 v. I
Wilson, A. N (Dunfermline), 1920-1 v. E, W & I; (Middlesbrough), 1922-3 v. E, W & I
Wilson, D (Queens Park), 1900 v. W
Wilson, D (Oldham Athletic), 1913 v. E
Wilson, D (Rangers), 1961 v. E, W & I; 1962 v. I, W & E; 1963 v. W & E; 1964 v. E; 1965 v. I & E
Wilson, G (Heart of Midlothian), 1905 v. E; 1905-6 v. W, 1905 v. I; (Everton), 1906 v. I; (Newcastle United), 1909 v. E
Wilson, H (Dumbarton), 1885 v. W
Wilson, H (Newmilns), 1890 v. W; (Sunderland), 1897 v. E; (Third Lanark), 1902 v. W; 1904 v. I
Wilson, J (Vale of Leven), 1889-90-1 v. E; 1888 v. W
Wilson, P (Celtic), 1926-31 v. I; 1933 v. E
Wiseman, W (Queens Park), 1927 v. W; 1930 v. I
Wood, G (Everton), 1979 v. I, E
Woodburn, W. A (Rangers), 1947 v. E; 1948 v. W & I; 1949 v. E; 1950-1-2 v. E, W & I
Wotherspoon, D (Queens Park), 1872-3 v. E
Wright, T (Sunderland), 1953 v. W, I & E
Wyllie, T (Rangers), 1890 v. I
Yeats, R (Liverpool), 1965 v. W
Young, A (Heart of Midlothian), 1960 v. E; 1961 v. W & I
Young, A (Everton), 1905 v. E; 1907 v. W
Young, G. L (Rangers), 1947 v. E & I; 1948 v. E & I; 1949 v. E, W & I; 1950-1-2-3 v. E, W & I; 1954 v. I & W; 1955 v. W & I; 1956 v. I, W & E, 1957 v. E, I & W
Young, J (Celtic), 1906 v. I
Younger, T (Hibernian), 1956 v. E, I & W; 1957 v. E, I & W; (Liverpool), 1958 v. I, W & E
Yorston, B (Aberdeen), 1931 v. I
Yorston, H (Aberdeen), 1955 v. W
*Victory International

WELSH INTERNATIONALS

Adams, H (Druids), 1883 v. E
Adams, J (Berwyn Rangers and Wrexham), 1882 vv. E & I
Allchurch, I (Swansea Town), 1951 v. E & I; 1952 v. E, S & I & Rest of UK; 1953 v. S, E & I; 1954 v. S, E & I; 19555 v. S, E & I; 1956 v. E, S & I; 1957 v. E & S; 1958 v. I; (Newcastle United), 1959 v. E, S & I; 1960 v. E & S; 1961 v. I; 196£262 v—E & S; (Cardiff City), 1963 v. S, E & I; 1964 v. E; 1965 v. S, E & I; (Swansea Town), 1968 v. E & S
Allchurch, L (Swana Town), 1955 v. I; 1958 v. S & I; 1959 v. S; (Sheffield United), 1962 v. S & I; 1964 v. E
Allen, B. W (Coventry City), 1951 i S & E
Arridge, S (Bootle), 1892 v. S & I; 1894 v. I; (Everton), 1895 v. I; 1896 v. E; (New Brighton), 1898 v. E & I; 1899 v. e E
Atbury T. A (Chester), 1846 v. E*
Astley, D. J (Charlton Athletic), 1931 v. I; (Aston Villa), 1932 v. E; 1933 v. E, S && I; 1932 v. E & S; 1935 v. S; 1936 v. E & I; (Derby County), 1939 v. E & S
Atherton, R (Hibernian), 1899 v. E & I; (Middlesbrough), 1903–4 v. E, S & I; 1905 v. I
Bailiff, W. E (Llanelly), 1913 v. E & S; 1913–20 v. I
Baker, C (Cardiff City), 1960 v. S S & I41961 v. S & E; 1962 v. S
Baker, W (Cardiff City), 1948 v. I
Bamford, T (Wrexham), 1931 v. E, S & I; 1932 v. I
Barness, W (Arsenal), 1943 v. E, S & I; 1949 v. E, S & I; 1950–1–2 v. E, S & I; 1952 v. Rest of UK; 1954 v. E & S; 1955 v. S
Bartlesyey, T (Glossop North End), 1898 v. E
Beadles, G. H (Cardiff City), 1925 v. E & S
Bell, J (Shrewsbury Engineers), 1881 v. E & S Bell, W. S (Crewe Alexandra), 1886 v. E, S & I
Bennion, S. R (Manchester United), 1926–7–8–9–30 v. S; 1928–9 v. E; 1928–9–32 2 v. IBlew, W. H (Wrexham), 1899–1903–4–6–8–9–10 v. E; 1899–1902–3–4–5–6–7–8–9 v. S; 1899–1902–4–5–6–8 v. I
Boden, T (Wrexexham) 1880 v. E
Bostock, A. M (Brecon of Shrewsbury), 1892 v. I
Boulter, L. M (Brentford), 1939 v. I
Bowdler, J. C. H (Shrrhrewsbury), 1890–2 v. I; 1891 v. S; (Wolverhampton Wanderers), 1893 v. S; 1894 v. E
Bowen, D. L (Arsenal), 1955 v. S; 1957 v. i; 1958–9 v. E, S & I
Bowen, E (Druids), 1880–3 v. S; 1883 v. I
Bowsher, S (Burnley), 1929 v. I
Britten, T. J (Parkgrove), 1—87878–80 v. S
Brookes, S. J (Llandudno), 1900 v. E & I
Brown, A. J (Aberdare Athletic), 1926 v. I
Bryan, T (Oswestry), 1886 v v. E I
Buckland, T (Bangor), 1899 v. E
Burgess, R (Tottenham Hotspur), 1946 v. E*, S* & I*; 1947 v. E, S & I; 1948 v. E & & S; 1949 v. E, S & I; 1950 v. E, S & I; 1951 v. S & I; 1952 v. E, S & I & Rest of UK; 1953–4 v. S, E & I
Burke, T (Wrexham anndnd Newton Heath), 1883–5–7 v. E; 1884–5–7–8 v. S; 1885 v. I
Burnett, T. B (Ruabon), 1877 v. S
Burton, A (Norwich City), 1963 . I; (Newcastle United), 1964 v. E; 1969 v. S, E & I
Burier, A (Druids), 1900 v. S & I
Butler, J (Chirk), 1893 v. E, S & I
Crtwright, L (Coventry City), 1974 v. S & I
Carty, T (Wrexham), 1889 v. I
Challen, J. B (Ruthin and Corinthians), 1887–8–90 cv v. E; 1887 v. S

Chapman, T (Newtown), 1894 v. E, S & I; 1895 v. S & I; (Manchester City), 1896–7 v. E
Charles, M (Swansea Town), 1955 v. I; 1956 v. E & S; 1957 v. E & I; 1958 v. E & S; 1959 v. E & S; (Arsenal), 1961 v. I, E & S; (Cardiff City), 1962 v. I; 1963 v. S
Charles, W. J (Leeds United), 1950–3 v. I; 1954 v. E, S & I; 1955 v. S, E & I; 1956 v. E, S & I; 1957 E, S & I; 1960 v. S; (Juventus), 1962 v. E; (Leeds United), 1963 v. S; (Cardiff City), 1964–5 v. S
Clark, R (Cardiff City), 1946 v. I*; (Manchester City), 1949 v. E; 1950 v. S & I; 1955 v. S & E; 1956 v. I
Collier, D (Grimsby Town), 1921 v. S
Collins, W (Llanelly), 1931 v. S
Conde, C (Chirk), 1884 v. E, S & I
Cook, F (Newport County), 1925 v. E & S; (Portsmouth), 1928 v. E & S; 1930 v. E, S & I; 1932 v. E & S
Crompton, W (Wrexham), 1932 v. E, S & I
Cross, K (Druids), 1881 v. E; 1879–81 v. S
Cross, E A (Wrexham), 1876–7 v. S
Crowe, V (Aston Villa), 1959 v. E & I; 1960 v. E & I; 1961 v. S, E & I; 1962 v. E & S
Cumner, R. H (Arsenal), 1939 v. E, S & I; 1946 v. S*
Curtis, A (Swansea City), 1976 v. S, E & I; 1978 v. E & S; 1979 v. S, E, I
Curtis, E. R (Cardiff City), 1928 v. S; (Birmingham City), 1932 v. S; 1934 v. I
Daniel, R. W (Arsenal), 1951 v. E & I; 1952 v. E, S & I & Rest of UK; 1953 v. S, E & I; (Sunderland), 1954 v. E, S & I; 1955 v. E & I; 1957 v. E, S & I
Darvell, S. L (Oxford University), 1897 v, S & I
Davies, A (Wrexham), 1876–7–8 v. S
Davies, A (Druids and Middlesbrough), 1904–5 v. S
Davies, A. O (Barmouth and Corinthians), 1886–7–8–90 v. E; 1885–7–9 v. S; 1885–8 v. I
Davies, C (Hereford), 1899–1900 v. I
Davies, D (Bolton Wanderers), 1908 v. E; 1904 v. S & I
Davies, D. W (Treharris), 1912 v. I; (Oldham Athletic), 1913 v. I
Davies, D (Everton), 1975 v. S, E & I; 1976 v. E & I; 1977 v. S, E & I; (Wrexham), 1978 v. E, S & I;1979 v. S, E, I
Davies, E. L (Stoke City), 1904 v. E; 1907 v. E, S & I; (Northampton Town), 1908 v. S; 1909–10–14 v. I; 1911–12–13–14 v. E & S
Davies, E. R (Newcastle United), 1953 v. S & E; 1954 v. E & S; 1958 v. E
Davies, G (Wrexham), 1978 v. E & I
Davies, Rev H (Corinthians and Wrexham), 1928 v. I
Davies, I (Liverpool Marine), 1923 v. S
Davies, J (Oswestry), 1885–6 v. E
Davies, J (Wrexham), 1879 v. S
Davies, J (Chirk, Everton, Millwall and Reading), 1891–5–6–7–1900 v. E; 1889–91–5 v. S & I
Davies, J. E (Druids, Newton Heath and Wolverhampton Wanderers), 1890–2–3 v. E; 1890 v. S
Davies, J. P (Corwen), 1883 v. E
Davies, L (Cardiff City), 1922–3–4–6–7–8–9–30 v. E; 1922–3–4–5–8–9–30 v. S; 1922–3–4–6–7–9 v. I
Davies, L. I (Wrexham), 1910–12–13 v. E; 1910–11–12–13 v. S; 1907–10–11–12–13–14 v. I
Davies, O (Wrexham), 1892 v. E; 1890 v. S; 1891–2 v. I
Davies, R (Norwich City), 1964 v. I; 1965 v. E; (Southampton), 1967 v. S, E & I; 1968 v. S & I; 1969 v. S, E & I; 1970 v. E, S & I; 1971 v. S, E & I; 1972 v. E, S & I; (Portsmouth), 1974 v. E
Davies, R (Wrexham Olympic), 1863–4–5 v. I
Davies, R (Druids), 1885–8 v. E; 1888 v. S & I
Davies, R. G (Nottingham Forest), 1946 v. E* & S*

Davies, S (Preston North End), 1920 v. E, S & I; (Everton), 1921 v. E, S & I; (West Bromwich Albion), 1922–6 v. E; 1922–5–6–7–8 v. S; 1922–5–6 v. I; (Rotherham United), 1930 v. I
Davies, T (Druids), 1902 v. E & I; 1903–4 v. S
Davies, W (Swansea Town), 1924 v. E, S & I; (Cardiff City), 1925–6 v. E; 1925–6–7 v. S; 1925–6–8 v. I; (Notts County), 1929–30 v. E, S & I
Davies, W (Bolton Wanderers), 1964 v. E; 1965 v. S, E & I; 1966 v. E, S & I; (Newcastle United), 1967 v. S & E; 1968 v. S & I; 1969 v. S, E & I; (Manchester City), 1972 v. E, S & I; (Manchester United), 1973 v. I
Davies, W (Wrexham), 1884 v. I
Davies, William (Wrexham), 1903–5 v. I; (Blackburn Rovers), 1908–9–11 v. E & S; 1909–11–12 v. I
Davies, W. C (Crystal Palace), 1908 v. S; (West Bromwich Albion), 1909–14 v. E; 1910 v. S
Davies, W. H (Oswestry), 1879–80 v. E; 1876–7 v. S
Davis, W (Millwall), 1913 v. E; 1913–14 v. S & I
Day, A (Tottenham Hotspur), 1934 v. I
Deacy, N (PSV Eindhoven), 1977 v. S, E & I; 1978 v. I
Dearson, D. J (Birmingham City), 1939 v. S & I; 1946 v. E* & S*
Derrett, S (Cardiff City), 1969 v. S
Dewey, F (Cardiff Corinthians), 1931 v. E & S
Doughty, J (Druids), 1888 v. E; 1886–7–8–9 v. S; 1887–8 v. I
Durban, A (Derby County), 1967 v. I; 1968 v. E, S & I; 1969 v. S, E & I; 1970 v. E, S & I; 1971 v. S, E & I; 1972 v. E, S & I
Dwyer, P (Cardiff City), 1978 v. E, S & I; 1979 v. S, E, I
Edwards, C (Llangollen), 1878 v. S
Edwards, G (Birmingham City), 1946 v. E* & S*; 1947 v. E, S & I; 1948 v. E; S & I
Edwards, H (Wrexham and Civil Service), 1880–2 v. E; 1878–80–2–3 v. S; 1884–7 v. I
Edwards, J (Oswestry), 1897 v. E; 1895–7 v. I
Edwards, J. H (The Wanderers), 1876 v. S
Edwards, T (Linfield), 1932 v. S
Edwards, T (Charlton Athletic), 1957 v. I
Egan, W (Chirk), 1892 v. S
Ellis, B (Motherwell), 1932 v. E; 1933 v. E & S; 1934 v. S; 1936 v. E; 1937 v. S
Ellis, W (Nunhead, Oswestry and Wrexham), 1931 v. E & S; 1932 v. I
England, M (Blackburn Rovers), 1962*3 v. I; 1964 v. E, S & I; 1965 v. E & I; 1966 v. E, S & I; (Tottenham Hotspur), 1967 v. S & E; 1968 v. E & I; 1970 v. E, S & I; 1972 v. E, S & I; 1973 v. S & I
Evans, B (Swansea City), 1973 v. S & E
Evans, D (Reading), 1926–7 v. I; 1927 v. E; (Huddersfield Town), 1929 v. S
Evans, J (Cardiff City), 1923 v. E; 1914–20 v. S; 1912–13–20–2–3 v. I
Evans, J (Oswestry), 1894 v. E; 1893–4 v. I
Evans, J. H (Southend United), 1922 v. E; 1922–3 v. S; 1922 v. I
Evans, H. P (Cardiff City), 1922–4 v. E, S & I
Evans, H. V (Wrexham), 1902 v. I
Evans, I (Crystal Palace), 1976 v. E & I; 1977 v. S, E & I
Evans, L (Cardiff City), 1931 v. E & S (Birmingham City), 1934 v. ?
Evans, L. H (Aberdare Athletic), 1927 v. I
Evans, M (Oswestry), 1884 v. E
Evans, R (Swansea Town), 1964 v. I
Evans, R (Clapton Orient), 1902 v. I
**Evans, R. E (Aston Villa), 1906–7–8 v. E; 1906–8 v. S; 1906 v. I; (Sheffield United), 1910 v. E; 1909–10 v. S; 1910 v. I
Evans, R. O (Wrexham), 1902 v. E, S & I; (Blackburn Rovers), 1908 v. I; (Coventry City), 1911–12 v. E; 1912 v. S; 1911–12 v. I
Evans, T. J (Clapton Orient), 1927 v. S; 1928 v. E & S; (Newcastle United), 1923 v. I

Evans, W (Tottenham Hotspur), 1933 v. I; 1934 v. E & S; 1935 v. E; 1936 v. E & I
Evans, W. A. W (Oxford University), 1876–7 v. S
Evans, W. G (Builth, Aston Villa and Bootle), 1890–1–2 v. E
Evelyn, E. C (Radnorshire), 1887 v. E
Eyton-Jones, J. A (Wrexham), 1884 v. E & S; 1893–4 v. I
Farmer, G (Oswestry), 1895 v. E & S
Finnigan, R (Wrexham), 1930 v. I
Flynn, B (Burnley), 1975 v. S, E & I; 1976 v. E & I; 1977 v. S, E & I; (Leeds United), 1978 v. E, S & I; 1979 v. S, E, I
Ford, T (Swansea Town), 1946 v. I*; 1947 v. S; (Aston Villa), 1947 v. I; 1948 v. S & I; 1949 v. E, S & I; 1950 v. E, S & I; 1951 v. S (Sunderland), 1951 v. E & I; 1952 v. E, S & I & Rest of UK; 1953 v. S, E & I; (Cardiff City), 1955 v. S, E & I; 1956 v. S, I & E; 1957 v. S
Foulkes, H. E (West Bromwich Albion), 1932 v. I
Foulkes, W. F (Newcastle United), 1952 v. E, S & I & Rest of UK; 1953 v. S & E; 1954 v. E, S & I
Fowler, J (Swansea Town), 1925–6–9 v. E; 1927–8 v. S; 1926 v. I
Garner, W (Aberystwyth), 1896 v. S
Gillam, S. G (Wrexham and Clapton Orient), 1890 v. E; 1895 v. S; 1899 v. I
Glascodine, G (Wrexham), 1879 v. ?
Glover, E. M (Grimsby Town), 1932 v. S; 1934 v. I; 1936 v. S; 1937 v. E, S & I; 1939 v. ?
Godding, G (Wrexham), 1923 v. S & I
Godfrey, B (Preston North End), 1964 v. I
Gough, R. T (Oswestry White Star), 1883 v. S & I
Gray, A (Oldham Athletic), 1924–5–6 v. E; 1924–5–6–7 v. S; 1924–5 v. I; (Manchester City), 1928–9 v. E; 1929 v. I; (Manchester Central), 1930 v. S; (Tranmere Rovers), 1932 v. E, S & I; (Chester), 1937–8 v. E, S & I
Gray, Dr W (Druids), 1876–8 v. S
Green, A. W (Aston Villa), 1901 v. I; 1903 v. E; (Notts County), 1904 v. S; 1904–6 v. I; 1906–7 v. E; (Nottingham Forest), 1908 v. S
Green, C (Birmingham City), 1966 v. E & S; 1967 v. E; 1968 v. E, S & I; 1969 v. S
Green, G. H (Charlton Athletic), 1938 v. I; 1939 v. E & I
Griffiths, A (Wrexham), 1975 v. E & I; 1976 v. S & I
Griffiths, F. J (Blackpool), 1900 v. E & S
Griffiths, G (Chirk), 1887 v. I
Griffiths, J. H (Swansea Town), 1953 v. I
Griffiths, M (Leicester City), 1947 v. I; 1950 v. E & S; 1951 v. E & I
Griffiths, P (Chirk), 1884–8 v. E; 1890 v. S; 1884–90–1 v. I
Griffiths, P (Everton), 1932 v. S
Griffiths, S (Wrexham), 1902 v. S
Griffiths, T. P (Everton), 1927–9–30–2 v. E; 1927–31–2 v. I; 1932 v. S; (Bolton Wanderers), 1933 v. E, S & I; (Middlesbrough), 1934 v. E & S; 1935 v. E & I; (Aston Villa), 1936 v. S & I; 1937 v. E, S & I
Hallam, J (Oswestry), 1889 v. E
Hanford, H (Swansea Town), 1934 v. I; 1935 v. S; 1936 v. E; (Sheffield Wednesday), 1936 v. I; 1938 v. E & S
Harrington, A (Cardiff City), 1956 v. I; 1957 v. E & S; 1958 v. S & I; 1961 v. S & E; 1962 v. E & S
Harrison, W. C (Wrexham), 1900 v. E & S; 1900–1 v. I
Harris, C (Leeds United), 1976 v. S; 1978 v. E, S & I
Harris, W (Middlesbrough), 1958 v. E & S
Hayes, A (Wrexham), 1890–4 v. I
Hennessey, W (Birmingham City), 1962 v. I; 1963 v. S & E; 1964 v. E & S; 1965 v. S & E; 1966 v. E; (Nottingham Forest), 1966 v. S & I; 1967 v. S & E; 1968 v. E, S & I; (Derby County), 1970 v. S & I; 1972 v. E & S
Hersee, M (Bangor), 1866 v. S & I
Hersee, R (Llandudno), 1886 v. I

Hewitt, R (Cardiff City), 1958 v. I
Hewitt, T. J (Wrexham), 1911 v. E, S & I; (Chelsea), 1913 v. E, S & I; (South Liverpool), 1914 v. E & S
Heywood, D (Druids), 1897 v. E
Hibbott, H (Newtown), 1880 v. E & S
Hibbott, R (Wrexham), 1885 v. S
Higham, G. G (Oswestry), 1879 v. E; 1878 v. S
Hockey, T (Norwich City), 1973 S, E & I
Hoddinott, F (Watford), 1921 v. E & S
Hodgkinson, A (Southampton), 1908 v. I
Hole, B (Cardiff City), 1963 v. I; 1964 v. I; 1965 v. S, E & I; 1966 v. E, S & I; (Blackburn Rovers), 1967 v. S, E & I; 1968 v. E, S & I
Hole, W (Swansea Town), 1922–3–8–9 v. E; 1921–3–8 v. I; 1928–9 v. S
Hollins, D (Newcastle United), 1963 v. I; 1964 v. E; 1965 v. I; 1966 v. S
Hopkins, J (Brentford), 1935 v. S & I; 1936 v. E & I; 1937 v. E, S & I; 1938 v. E & I; 1939 v. E, S & I
Hopkins, M (Tottenham Hotspur), 1956 v. I; 1957–8–9 v. E, S & I; 1960 v. E & S; 1961–2 v. I; 1963 v. S & I
Howell, G. G (Builth), 1890–1 v. E; 1888 v. I
Howells, R (Cardiff City), 1954 v. E & S
Hugh, A. R (Newport County), 1930 v. I
Hughes, A (Rhos), 1894 v. E & S
Hughes, A (Chirk), 1907 v. I
Hughes, E (Everton), 1899 v. E, S & I; (Tottenham Hotspur), 1901–4–5–6–7 v. E; 1901–4–5 v. S; 1902–4–5–6 v. I
Hughes, E (Wrexham), 1906 v. S; (Nottingham Forest), 1906–10–11–12 v. I; 1908–10–11–12 v. E; 1908–10–11–12 v. S; (Manchester City), 1913 v. E & S; 1914 v. I
Hughes, F. W (Norwich Victoria), 1882–3 v. E & I; 1883–4 v. S
Hughes, I (Luton Town), 1951 v. E & I
Hughes, J (Aberystwyth), 1879 v. S
Hughes, J (Cambridge University), 1877 v. S
Hughes, J (Everton), 1905 v. E, S & I
Hughes, J. I (Blackburn Rovers), 1935 v. I
Hughes, P. W (Bangor), 1889 v. E; 1887–9 v. I
Hughes, W (Caernarvon and Bottle), 1891 v. E; 1892 v. S & I
Hughes, W. A (Blackburn Rovers), 1949 v. E & I
Hughes, W. M (Birmingham City), 1938–9 v. E, S & I; 1946 v. E*, S*, & I*; 1947 v. E, S & I
Humphreys, J (Everton), 1947 v. I
Humphreys, R (Druids), 1888 v. I
Hunter, W. H (North End), 1887 v. I
Jackson, W (St. Helens), 1889 v. I
James, F (Chirk), 1893-4-8 v. E; 1894-4-9 v. I.
James, G (Blackpool), 1967 v. I; 1968 v. S; 1971 v. S, E & I
James, L (Burnley), 1973 v. S, E & I; 1974 v. E, S & I; 1975 v. S, E & I; (Derby County), 1976 v. S, E & I; 1977 v. S, E & I
James, R (Swansea City), 1979 v. S, E, I
James, W (West Ham United), 1931–2 v. I
Jarrett, R. H (Ruthin), 1880 v. S; 1889 v. I
Jarvis, A (Hull City), 1967 v. S, E & I
Jenkins, E (Lovell's Athletic), 1925 v. E
Jenkins, J (Brighton and Hove Albion), 1924–6 v. E; 1924–5–6–7 v. S; 1924–5 v. I
Jenkins, R. W (Rhyl), 1902 v. I
Jenkyns, C. A. L (Builth), 1892 v. E, S & I; (Small Heath), 1895 v. E; (Woolwich Arsenal), 1896–8 v. S; 1897 v. I; 1898 v. E
Jennings, W (Bolton Wanderers), 1914–23–4 v. E; 1914–20–4–7–9 v. S; 1932–4–7 v. I

John, R. F (Arsenal), 1926–7–8–30–2–7 v. E; 1923–30–6 v. S; 1923–5–8–33–5 v. I
John, W. R (Walsall), 1931 v. I; (Stoke City), 1933 v. E, S & I; 1934 v. E & S; (Preston North End), 1935 v. E & S; (Sheffield United), 1936 v. E, S & I; (Swansea Town), 1939 v. E & S
Johnson, M (Swansea Town), 1964 v. I
Jones, A (Druids), 1884 v. E & I; 1884–5 v. S
Jones, A. F (Oxford University), 1887 v. S
Jones, A. T (Nottingham Forest), 1905–6 v. E
Jones, B (Swansea Town), 1963 v. E, S & I; 1964 v. S & I; (Cardiff City), 1969 v. S, E & I
Jones, B (Wolverhampton Wanderers), 1935 v. I; 1936–7–8 v. E, S & I; (Arsenal), 1939 v. E, S & I; 1947 v. S & I; 1948 v. E; 1949 v. S
Jones, C (Nottingham Forest), 1926–8 v. E; 1927 v. S & I; (arsenal), 1930–2 v. E; 1930 v. S
Jones, C (Swansea Town), 1956 v. E, I & S; 1957 v. E, S & I; (Tottenham Hotspur), 1958 v. E, S & I; 1959 v. I; 1960 v. E, S & I; 1961 v. E, S & I; 1962 v. E, S & I; 1963 v. S & I; 1964 v. E, S & I; 1965 v. E, S & I; 1967 v. S & E; 1968 v. E & S
Jones, C. W (Birmingham City), 1935 v. I
Jones, D (Chirk), 1888 v. S & I; (Bolton Wanderers), 1889–90–3–4–5 v. E; 1889–91–8 v. S; 1889–90–2 v. I; (Manchester City), 1900 v. E & I
Jones, D (Norwich City), 1976 v. S; 1978 v. E
Jones, D. O (Leicester City), 1934 v. E & I; 1935 v. E & S; 1936 v. E & I; 1937 v. I
Jones, E (Chelsea), 1910 v. S & I; (Oldham Atheltic), 1911–12 v. E & S; 1914 v. I
Jones, F. W (Llandudno), 1893 v. S
Jones, G. P (Wrexham), 1907 v. S & I
Jones, H (Bangor and Queens Park), 1885–6–7–9–90 v. E; 1885–6–9–90–1 v. S; 1885–6–90 v. I
Jones, H (Aberavan), 1920 v. I
Jones, I (Swansea Town), 1920–2 v. S; 1921 v. E; 1920–1–2 v. I; (West Bromwich Albion), 1923 v. E; 1924 v. S; 1923–6 v. I
Jones, J (Liverpool), 1976 v. S; 1977 v. S, E & I; 1978 v. E, S & I; 1979 (Wrexham) v. S, E, I
Jones, J (Druids), 1876 v. S
Jones, J (Berwyn Rangers), 1883–4 v. S
Jones, J (Wrexham), 1925 v. I
Jones, J (Llandrindod Wells), 1910 v. S; 1908–9 v. I
Jones, J. L (Ryddlan), 1895 v. E, S & I; (Sheffield United), 1896–7 v. E, S & I; (Tottenham Hotspur), 1898–1902–4 v. E; 1898–9–1900–2–4 v. S; 1898–9–1902–4 v. I
Jones, J. L (Stoke City), 1906 v. S; (Middlesbrcugh), 1910 v. I
Jones, J. O (Bangor), 1901 v. S
Jones, J. T (Stoke City), 1912–13–20 v. E; 1912–14–20 v. S; 1912–13–14–20 v. I; (Crystal Palace), 1921–2 v. E & S; 1922 v. I
Jones, K (Aston Villa), 1950 v. S
Jones, L (Coventry City), 1935 v. I; 1936 v. S; 1937 v. E, S & I; (Arsenal), 1938 v. E, S & I; 1939 v. E & S
Jones, R (Bangor and Crewe Alexandra), 1889–90 v. E
Jones, R (Bangor), 1900 v. S & I
Jones, R (Druids), 1899 v. S; (Millwall), 1906 v. S & I
Jones, R. S (Wrexham), 1894 v. I; (Everton), 1898 v. S
Jones, S (Chester), 1887 v. I; 1890 v. S
Jones, S (Wrexham Olympic), 1896 v. E; 1893–5 v. S; 1893–6 v. I
Jones, T (Bangor), 1885 v. E & I; 1886 v. S
Jones, T (Manchester United), 1927 v. E; 1926–7–30 v. I
Jones, T. D (Aberdare), 1908 v. I

Jones, T. G (Everton), 1938 v. I; 1939 v. E, S & I; 1946 v. I*; 1947 v. E & S; 1948 v. E, S & I; 1949 v. E & I; 1950 v. E & S
Jones, T. J (Sheffield Wednesday), 1932 v. I
Jones, W (Druids), 1899 v. E
Jones, W. E. A (Swansea Town), 1946 v. S*; 1948 v. E & S; (Tottenham Hotspur), 1949 v. E & S
Jones, W. J (Aberdare), 1901 v. E & S; (West Ham United), 1902 v. E & S
Jones, W. L (Manchester City), 1905–6–7–9–10–11–13 v. E; 1906–7–8–9–13–14 v. S; 1905–6–7–9—14 v. I; (Southend United), 1920 v. E & I
Jones, W. P (Druids), 1889 v. E; 1890 v. S; 1889–90 v. I
Jones, W. R (Aberwstwyth), 1897 v. S
Keenor, F. C (Cardiff City), 1920–3–4–5–7–8—9—30–1 v. E; 1921–3–4–5–6—7–8–9—30–1 v. S; 1920–1–2–3—4–5–7–8–9–30–1 v. I; (Crewe Alexandra), 1933 v. S
Kelly, F. C (Wrexham), 1899 v. S; 1899–1902 v. I
Kelsey, A. J (Arsenal), 1954 v. E; 1955 v. S & I; 1956 v. E, I & S; 1957 v. E, I & S; 1958 v. E, S & I; 1959 v. E & S; 1960 v. E, I & S; 1961 v. S, E & I; 1962 v. E, S & I
Kenrick, L. I (Shropshire Wanderers and Druids), 1879–81 v. E; 1876–7–9 v S
Ketley, C. F (Druids), 1882 v. I
King, K (Swansea Town), 1955 v. E
Kinsey, N (Norwich City), 1951 v. I; 1952 v. E; (Birmingham City), 1954 v. I; 1956 v. E & S
Krzywicki, R (Huddersfield Town), 1970 v. E, S & I
Lambert, R (Liverpool), 1947 v. S; 1948 v. E
Lathom, G (Liverpool), 1905–7–8 v. E; 1905—6–7 v. S; 1907–9 v. I; (Southport Central), 1910 v. E; (Cardiff City), 1913 v. I
Lawrence, S (Swansea Town), 1932 v. I; 1934 v. E, S & I; 1935 v. E & S; 1936 v. S
Lawrence, E (Clapton Orient), 1930 v. I; (Notts County), 1932 v. S
Lea, C (Ipswich Town), 1965 v. I
Lea, W. A (Wrexham), 1889 v. E; 1891 v. S; 1891–3 v. I
Leary, P (Bangor), 1889 v. I
Leek, K (Leicester City), 1961 v. S, E & I; (Newcastle United), 1962 v. S; (Birmingham City), 1963 v. E; 1965 v. S
Lever, A. R (Leicester City), 1953 v. S
Lewis, B (Wrexham), 1892–3–4 v. E; 1892–3–4–5 v. S; 1894–4 v. I
Lewis, D (Arsenal), 1927–30 v. E; 1928 v. I
Lewis, D. J (Swansea Town), 1933 v. E & S
Lewis, J (Wrexham), 1881 v. E; 1884 v. S
Lewis, J (Bristol Rovers), 1906 v. E
Lewis, J (Cardiff City), 1926 v. S
Lewis, W (Swansea Town), 1927–8 v. E & I; 1929 v. S; (Huddersfield Town), 1930 v. E
Lewis, W (Bangor), 1885–6—7—8—9 v. E; 1886–7—9 v. S; 1889 v. I; (Crewe Alexandra), 1890–2 v. E; 1890–1–2—4 v. S; 1890–1–2–4 v. I; (Chester), 1895–6—7 v. E & S; 1895–6—8 v. I
Lloyd, B (Wrexham), 1976 v. S
Lloyd, J. W (Wrexham and Newtown), 1879–85 v. S
Lloyd, R. A (Ruthin), 1895 v. S; 1891 v. I
Lockley, A (Chirk), 1898 v. I
Lowrie, G (Coventry City), 1946 v. E* & S*; 1948 v. E, S & I
Lucas, M (Leyton Orient), 1962 v. I; 1963 v. S & E
Lucas, W. H (Swindon Town), 1946 v. E* & I*; (Swansea Town), 1949 v. S & I; 1950–1 v. E
Lumberg, A (Wrexham), 1929 v. I; 1930 v. E & S

Mahoney, J (Stoke City), 1968 v. E; 1973 v. E, S & I; 1974 v. E, S & I; 1975 v. S, E & I; 1976 v. E & I; 1977 v. E, S & I; (Middlesbrough), 1978 v. E, S & I; 1979 v. S, E, I
Martin, T (Newport County), 1930 v. I
Mates, J (Chirk), 1897 v. E & S; 1891 v. I
Mathias, J. F (Brymbo), 1897 v. E; 1896–7–9 v. S; 1896 v. I
Mathias, T. J (Wrexham), 1914–20—1–2 v. E; 1914–21–2–3 v. S; 1920–1—2 v. I
Matthews, R. W (Liverpool), 1921 v. I; (Bristol City), 1923 v. E; (Bradford), 1926 v. I
Matthews, W (Chester), 1908 v. E; 1905 v. I
Mays, A. W (Wrexham), 1929 v. I
McMillan, A (Shrewsbury Engineers), 1881 v. E & S
Medwin, T. C (Swansea Town), 1953 v. I; (Tottenham Hotspur), 1957 v. E, S & I; 1958 v. E, S & I;1959 v. E, S & I; 1960 v., E, S & I; 1961 v. S & E; 1963 v. E
Meredith, S (Chirk), 1900—1 v. S; 1901 v. E & I; (Stoke City), 1902–4 v. E; 1903 v. I; (Leyton Orient), 1907 v. E
Meredith, W. (Manchester City), 1895–6–7—8—9—1900—1—2—3–4—5 v. E; 1897—1902–3 v. S; 1895—6—7—8—1900—1—3 v. I; (Manchester United), 1907—8—9—10—12—13—14—20 v. E; 1907—9—10—11—12—13—14—20 v. S; 1907—8—9—10—11—12—13—14—20 v. I
Millership, (Rotherham County), 1920–1 v. E, S & I
Millington, A (West Bromwich Albion), 1963 v. S & E; (Crystal Palace), 1965 v. E; (Peterborough), 1967 v. E & I; 1968 v. I; (Swansea City), 1970 v. E, S & I
Mills, T. J (Clapton Orient), 1934 v. E & I; (Leicester City), 1935 v. E & S
Mills-Roberts, R. H (Bangor, Corinthians and Preston North End), 1885–6—7—8–92 v. E; 1885 v. S; 1885—8 v. I
Moore, G (Cardiff City), 1960 v. E, S & I; (Chelsea), 1963 v. I; (Manchester United), 1964 v. S & I; (Northampton Town), 1966 v. I; (Charlton Athletic), 1969 v. S, E & I; 1970 v. E, S & I
Morgan, J. R (Derby School and Swansea Town), 1880–1–2–3 v. E; 1879–80–1—2 v. S; 1882 v. I
Morgan, T (Wrexham), 1905 v. I
Morgan, T. R (Cambridge University), 1877 v. S
Morgan-Owen, H (Rhyl), 1901 v. E & S; (Oxford University), 1902 v. S; (Welshpool), 1906 v. E & I; (Corinthians), 1907 v. S
Morgan-Owen, M. M (Oxford University), 1898–1900 v. E; 1897–8–9 v. S; 1897 v. I; (Corinthians), 1904–6 v. S; 1906—7 v. E; 1906 v. I
Morley, E (Swansea Town), 1925 v. E; (Clapton Orient), 1929 v. E, S & I
Morris, A. G. (Aberystwyth), 1896-7 v. E; 1896 v. I & S; (Swindon Town), 1898 v. S; (Nottingham Forest), 1899-1903-5-7-8-10-11-12 v. E; 1899-1903-5-7-10-11 v. S; 1910-11 v. I
Morris, C (Chirk), 1900 v. E, S & I; (Derby County), 1901–2–3–4—8–9 v. E; v. S; 1901–3–4—6–9 v. I; (Huddersfield Town), 1910–11 v. E, S & I
Morris, H (Chirk and Manchester City), 1893 v. E, S & I; 1894 v. S; 1896–7 v. E & I
Morris, J (Oswestry), 1897 v. S
Morris, J (Chirk), 1898 v. I
Morris, R (Chirk). 1900–3 v. E; 1902 v. S; 1900—1—3 v. I
Morris, R (Newtown), 1902 v. E; 1902–3 v. S & I; (Liverpool), 1904 v. E; 1904—6 v. S; 1904—7–[v. I
Morris, S (Birmingham City), 1937—8 v. E & S
Morris, W (Burnley), 1946 v. I*; 1947 v. I; 1949 v. E; 1952 v. S, I & Rest of UK
Moulsdale, J. R. B (Corinthians), 1925 v. I
Murphy, J (West Bromwich Albion), 1933 v. E & I; 1934 v. E & S; 1935–6 v. E, S & I; 1937 v. S & I; 1938 v. E & S
Neal, J. E (Colwyn Bay), 1931 v. E & S

Newnes, J (Nelson), 1926 v. I

Newton, L. F (Cardiff Corinthians), 1925 v. I

Nicholas, D. S (Stoke City), 1923 v. S; (Swansea Town), 1927 v. E & I

Nichols, J (Newport County), 1924 v. E & I; (Cardiff City), 1925 v. E & S

Nicholas, P (Crystal Palace) 1979 v. S

Nock, W (Newtown), 1897 v. I

Nurse, M (Swansea Town), 1960 v. E & I; 1961 v. S, E & I; (Middlesbrough), 1963 v. E; 1964 v. E

O'Callaghan, E (Tottenham Hotspur), 1929 v. I; 1930–2 v. S; 1932 v. E; 1933—4 v. E, S & I; 1935 v. E

O'Sullivan, P (Brighton and Hove Albion), 1976 v. S

Oliver, A (Bangor), 1905 v. E & S

Owen, D (Newtown), 1879 v. E

Owen, E (Ruthin Grammar School), 1884 v. E, S & I

Owen, G (Chirk), 1892 v. E; 1889 v. S; 1889-91-3 v. I

Owen, J (Wrexham), 1902 v. I

Owen, T (Newtown), 1879 v. E

Owen, T (Crewe Alexandra), 1889 v. E & S

Owen, W (Chirk), 1884-7-8-9-91-2 v. E; 1888-9-90-1-2-3 v. S; 1885-9-90-3 v. I

Owen, W. P (Ruthin), 1880-1-2-3-4 v. E & S; 1882-4 v. I

Page, M (Birmingham City), 1972 v. S & I; 1973 v. E & I; 1974 v. S & I; 1975 v. S, E & I; 1976 v. E & I; 1978 v. E & S

Palmer, D (Swansea Town), 1958 v. E

Parris, J. E (Bradford), 1932 v. I

Parry, B. J (Swansea Town), 1951 v. S

Parry, C (Everton), 1891-3-4-5-6-8 v. E; 1891-5-6-8 v. S; 1896-7-8 v. I

Parry, E (Liverpool), 1923 v. E; 1922 v. S; 1923-5-6 v. I

Parry, H (Newtown), 1895 v. I

Parry, M (Liverpool), 1901-2-3-4-5-8-9 v. E; 1901-2-3-8-9 v. S; 1901-2-4-8 v. I

Parry, T. D (Oswestry), 1900-1-2 v. E; 1900-1 v. S & I

Paul, R (Swansea Town), 1949 v. E, S & I; 1950 v. E, S & I; (Manchester City), 1951-2 v. S, E & I; 1952 v. Rest of UK; 1953-4 v. S, E & I; 1955 v. S & E; 1956 v. E, I & S

Peake, E (Liverpool), 1909-12-13 v. E; 1909-10 v. S; 1908-9-$\frac{1}{4}$0-11-13-14 v. I

Peers, E. J (Wolverhampton Wanderers), 1914-20-1 v. E; 1914-20-1 v. S; 1914-21 v. I; (Port Vale), 1922-3 v. E; 1922 v. S & I

Perry, E (Doncaster Rovers), 1938 v. E, S & I

Phennah, F (Civil Service), 1878 v. S

Phennice, H (Wrexham), 1882 v. S

Phillips, C (Wolverhampton Wanderers), 1931 v. I; 1932 v. E; 1933 v. S; 1934-5 v. E, S & I; 1936 v. S; (Aston Villa), 1937 v. E & I; 1938 v. S; (Swansea City), 1979 v. S, E, I

Phillips, J (Chelsea), 1973-4 v. E

Phillips, L (Cardiff City), 1971 v. S, E & I; 1972 v. S & I; 1974 v. I; (Aston Villa), 1975 v. S, E & I; 1976 v. E & I; 1977 v. S & E; 1978 v. E & S

Poland, G (Wrexham), 1939 v. E

Powell, A (Leeds United), 1946 v. E* & I*; 1947 v. E & S; 1948 v. E, S & I; (Everton), 1949 v. E; (Birmingham City), 1951 v. S

Powell, D (Sheffield United), 1969 v. S, E & I; 1970 v. S, E & I

Powell, I (Queens Park Rangers), 1947 v. E; 1948 v. E, S & I; (Aston Villa), 1950-1 v. S

Powell, J (Druids and Newton Heath), 1880-2-3-4-7-8 v. E; 1879-80-2-3-7-8 v. S; 1882-3-8 v. I

Powell, S (Oswestry), 1886 v. E; 1885 v. S; 1886 v. I

Powell, S (Summerhill and West Bromwich Albion), 1891-2 v. E & S

Price, H (Aston Villa), 1909 v. E; 1907-9 v. S; 1908-9 v. I

Price, J (Druids and Wrexham), 1879-80-1-2 v. E; 1877-8-80-1-2-3 v. S; 1882-3 v. I
Pring, K (Rotherham United), 1967 v. I
Pryce-Jones, A. W (Newtown), 1895 v. E
Pryce-Jones, W. E (Newtown), 1888 v. E; 1887-8 v. S; 1888-90 v. I
Pugh, D. H (Wrexham), 1896-7 v. S & I; (Lincoln City), 1900-11 v. S; 1901 v. E
Pugley, J (Charlton Athletic), 1930 v. I
Pullen, W. K (Plymouth Argyle), 1926 v. E
Rea, J. C (Aberystwyth), 1894 v. E; 1894-5-6 v. S; 1894-6-7-8 v. I
Reece, G (Sheffield United), 1966 v. S, E & I; 1967 v. S; 1971 v. S, E & I; 1972 v. S & I; (Cardiff City), 1973 v. I; 1974 v. E, S & I; 1975 v. S & I
Reed, W. C (Ipswich Town), 1955 v. S
Reeds, W (Cardiff City), 1949 v. I; (Tottenham Hotspur), 1950 v. I
Rees, R (Coventry City), 1965 v. S, E & I; 1966 v. E, S & I; 1967 v. E & I; 1968 v. E, S & I; 1970 v. E, S & I
Richards, A (Barnsley), 1932 v. S
Richards, D (Wolverhampton Wanderers), 1931 v. I; 1933-4-5 v. E, S & I; 1936 v. S; (Brentford), 1936 v. E & I; 1937 v. S & E; (Birmingham City), 1937 v. I; 1938 v. E & I; 1939 v. E & S
Richards, G (Druids and Oswestry), 1899 v. E; 1899-1904 v. S; 1899-1902-5 v. I
Richards, R. W (Wolverhampton Wanderers), 1920-2 v. E; 1921 v. I; (West Ham United), 1924 v. E, S & I; (Mold), 1926 v. S
Richards, S (Cardiff City), 1947 v. E
Richards, W (Fulham), 1933 v. I
Roach J (Oswestry), 1885 v. I
Robbins, W (Cardiff City), 1931 v. E & S; 1932 v. I, S & E; (West Bromwich Albion), 1933 v. E, S & I; 1934-6 v. S
Roberts, D (Oxford United), 1973 v. I; 1974 v. E & S; (Hull City), 1975 v. I; 1976 v. S & I; 1977 v. I; 1978 v. S & I
Roberts, D (Druids), 1884-7-8-9 v. S; 1888-9 v. E; 1886 v. I; (Bolton Wanderers), 1890-2 v. S; 1891-2 v. I
Roberts, E (Wrexham Olympic), 1887 v. I
Roberts, J (Corwen), 1880-2-3 v. E; 1879-80-2
Roberts, J (Ruthin), 1881-2 v. S
Roberts, J (Bradford City), 1906-7 v. I
Roberts, J (Arsenal), 1971 v. S, E & I; 1972 v. E & I; (Birmingham City), 1973 v. S, E & I; 1974 v. E, S & I; 1975 v. S & E;; 1976 v. S
Roberts, J (Chirk), 1898 v. S
Roberts, P (Portsmouth), 1974 v. E
Roberts, R (Crewe Alexandra), 1893 v. E
Roberts, W (Llangollen and Berwyn Rangers), 1879-80-1-3 v. E & S
Roberts, W (Wrexham Olympic), 1886 v. E & S; 1886-7-91 v. I
Roberts, W. H (Ruthin), 1882-3-4 v. S; 1883 v. I
Rodrigues, P (Cardiff City), 1965 v. I; 1966 v. E & S; (Leicester City), 1966 v. I; 1967 v. S; 1968 v. E, S & I; 1969 v. E & I; 1970 v. E, S & I; (Sheffield Wednesday) 1971 v. S, E & I; 1972 v. E; 1973 v. S, E & I
Rogers, J. P (Wrexham), 1896 v. E, S & I
Rogers, W (Wrexham), 1931 v. E & S
Roose, L. R (Aberystwyth), 1900 v. I; (London Welsh), 1901 v. E, S & I; (Stoke City), 1902-4 v. E; 1902 v. S; (Everton), 1905 v. S & E; (Stoke City), 1906-7 v. E, S & I; (Sunderland), 1908-9-10 v. E; 1908-9-10-11 v. S; 1909-10 v. I
Rouse, V (Crystal Palace), 1959 v. I
Rowlands, A. S (Tranmere Rovers), 1914 v. E
Rowley, T (Tranmere Rovers), 1959 v. I
Russell, M (Merthyr Town), 1912 v. S & I; 1914 v. E; (Plymouth Argyle), 1920-1-2-3-4-5-6-9 v. E; 1920-1-3-4-5-6-8 v. S; 1920-1-2-3-4 v. I
Sabine, H. W (Oswestry), 1887 v. I

Savin, G (Oswestry), 1878 v. S
Sayer, P (Cardiff City), 1977 v. S, E & I
Sear, C (Manchester City), 1963 v. E
Scrine, F. H (Swansea Town), 1950 v. E & I
Shaw, E. G (Oswestry), 1884 v. S; 1882-4 v. I
Sherwood, A (Cardiff City), 1946 v. I*; 1947 v. E & I; 1948 v. S & I; 1949 v. E, S & I; 1950-1-2 v. E, S & I; 1952 v. Rest of UK; 1953 v. S, E & I; 1954 v. E, S & I; 1955 v. S, E & I; 1956 v. E, S & I; (Newport County), 1957 v. E & S
Shone, W (Oswestry), 1879 v. E
Shortt, W (Plymouth Argyle), 1946 v. I*; 1950 v. I; 1952 v. E, S, I & Rest of UK; 1953 v. S, E & I
Showers, D (Cardiff City), 1975 v. I
Sidlow, C (Wolverhampton Wanderers), 1946 v. E* & S*; (Liverpool), 1947 v. E & S; 1948 v. E, S & I; 1949 v. S; 1950 v. E
Sisson, H (Wrexham Olympic), 1886 v. S; 1885-6 v. I
Smallman, D (Wrexham), 1974 v. I; (Everton), 1975 v. E
Sprake, G (Leeds United), 1964 v. S & I; 1965 v. S; 1966 v. E & I; 1967 v. S; 1968 v. E & S; 1969-71 v. S, E & I; 1972 v. E, S & I; 1973-4 v. S & I
Squires, F (Swansea Town), 1946 v. S*
Stansfield, F (Cardiff City), 1949 v. S
Stevenson, B (Leeds United), 1978 v. I; 1979 v. S, E, I
Stitfall, A. F (Cardiff City), 1953 v. E
Sullivan, D (Cardiff City), 1953-4 v. I; 1955 v. E & I; 1957 v. E & S; 1958 v. I; 1959 v. S & I; 1960 v. E & S
Tapscott, D. R (Arsenal), 1955 v. S, E & I; 1956 v. E, I & S; 1957 v. I; (Cardiff City), 1959 v. E & I
Taylor, H (Wrexham), 1898 v. E
Taylor, O. D. S (Newtown), 1893-4 v. S & I
Thomas, C (Druids), 1900 v. S; 1899 v. I
Thomas, E (Cardiff Corinthians), 1925 v. E
Thomas, G (Wrexham Olympic), 1885 v. E & S
Thomas, H (Manchester United), 1927 v. E
Thomas, M (Wrexham), 1978 v. I
Thomas, R (Swindon Town), 1967 v. I; 1969 v. E & I; 1970 v. E, S & I; 1971 v. S, E & I; 1972 v. E, S & I; 1973 v. S, E & I; (Derby County), 1974 v. E, S & I; 1975 v. S, E & I; 1976 v. E; 1977 v. S, E & I
Thomas, S (Fulham), 1948 v. E, S & I; 1949 v. S
Thomas, T (Bangor), 1898 v. S & I
Thomas, W (Newport County), 1931 v. E & S
Thompson, D (Shropshire Wanderers), 1876 v. S
Thomson, G. F (Druids), 1876-7 v. S
Toshack, J (Cardiff City), 1969 v. S, E & I; (Liverpool), 1971 v. S, E & I; 1972 v. E; 1973 v. S & E; 1975 v. S & E; 1976 v. E; (Swansea City), 1979 v. S, E, I
Townsend, W (Newtown), 1887-93 v. I
Trainer, H (Wrexham),, 1895 v. E, S & I
Trainer, J (Wrexham), 1887-8 v. S; (Preston North End), 1889-93-4-5-7-8 v. E; 1889-90-1-2-6-7-8-9 v. S; 1892-4-5-7-9 v. I
Turner, H (Charlton Athletic), 1937-8 v. E, S & I; 1939 v. I
Turner, R E (Wrexham), 1891 v. E & I
Turner, W. H (Wrexham Olympic), 1887-91-2 v. E; 1890-1 v. S; 1887 v. 1
Vaughan, Jas (Druids), 1893-9 v. E; 1893 v. S & I
Vaughan, John (Druids), 1881-2-3-4 v. E; 1879-80-1-2-3 v. S; 1882-3 v. I
Vaughan, J. O (Rhyl), 1886 v. E & S; 1885-6 v. I
Vaughan, T (Rhyl), 1885 v. E
Vernon, T. R (Blackburn Rovers), 1957 v. I; 1958 v. E & S; 1959 v. S; 1960 v. I; 1961 v. S & E; (Everton), 1962 v. I; 1963 v. S & E; 1964 v. E & S; (Stoke City), 1965 v. I; 1966 v. E, S & I; 1967 v. I; 1968 v. E
Villars, A (Cardiff City), 1974 v. E & S

Vizard, E. T (Bolton Wanderers), 1911-12-14-20-1-2-3-4-6 v. E; 1911-12-13-21-2-4-6-7 v. S; 1911-14-21-3-4 v. I
Ward, D (Bristol Rovers), 1959 v. E; (Cardiff City), 1962 v. E
Warner, J (Swansea Town), 1937 v. E; (Manchester United), 1946 v. I*
Warren, F (Cardiff City), 1939 v. I; (Middlesbrough), 1931 v. I; 1933 v. E; (Heart of Midlothian), 1937-8 v. I
Watkins, A. E (Leicester Fosse and Millwall), 1898-1900 v. E & S; 1904 v. I
Watkins, W. M (Stoke City), 1902 v. E; 1908 v. I; (Aston Villa), 1903-4 v. I; (Sunderland), 1905 v. E, S, & I
Whatley, W (Tottenham Hotspur), 1939 v. E & S
Whitcomb, D (West Bromwich Albion), 1946 v. S*; 1947 v. E & S; (Sheffield Wednesday), 1947 v. I
White, P. F (Bangor and London Welsh), 1896 v. I
Wilcocks, A. R (Oswestry), 1890 v. I
Wilding, J (Wrexham Olympic and Bootle), 1885-6-7 v. E; 1885-8-92 v. S; 1885-6-8 v. I
Williams, B (Swansea Town), 1928 v. I; 1928-30 v. E; 1930 v. S; (Everton), 1931 v. I; 1932 v. E; 1933 v. E, S & I; 1935 v. I
Williams, E (Flint), 1893 v. E & S
Williams, E (Druids), 1901-2 v. E & I; 1901 v. S
Williams, G (Chirk), 1895 v. E; 1893-45 v. S; 1895-8 v. I
Williams, G (West Bromwich Albion), 1960 v. I; 1961 v. S & E; 1963 v. I; 1964 v. E, S & I; 1965 v. S, E & I; 1966 v. I; 1967 v. S, E & I; 1968 v. I
Williams, G (Swansea Town), 1961 v. I; 1962 v. E
Williams, G. O (Wrexham), 1907 v. I
Williams, H. J (Newport County), 1949 v. I; (Leeds United), 1950 v. I; 1951 v. S
Williams, J. H (Oswestry), 1884 v. E
Williams, J. T (Middlesbrough), 1925 v. I
Williams, J. W (Crystal Palace), 1912 v. S & I
Williams, R (Merthyr Town), 1921 v. E & S; (Sheffield Wednesday), 1923-6 v. S; 1927 v. E & I; (Manchester United), 1929 v. E & S
Williams, R (Newcastle United), 1935 v. S & E
Williams, R. P (Caernarvon), 1886 v. S
Williams, S. G (West Bromwich Albion), 1955 v. E & I; 1956 v. E & S; 1958-9-60 v. E, S & I; 1961 v. I; 1962 v. E, S & I; (Southampton), 1963 v. S & E; 1964 v. E & S; 1965 v. S & E
Williams, W (Druids), 1879-80-1-2 v. E; 1876-8-9-81-2 v. S; 1882-3 v. I
Williams, W (Northampton Town), 1925 v. S
Winter, D (Bolton Wanderers), 1946 v. E*
Woosnam, G (Newport County), 1879 v. S
Woosnam, P (West Ham United), 1959 v. E & S; 1960 v. E, S & I; 1961 v. S, E & I; 1962 v. E, S & I; (Aston Villa), 1963 v. I
Worthington, T (Newtown), 1894 v. S
Wynn, G (Chirk), 1903 v. I; (Wrexham), 1909 v. E, S & I; (Manchester City), 1910-12-13-14 v. E; 1912-13-14 v. S; 1911 v. I
Yorath, T (Leeds United), 1971 v. S, E & I; 1972 v. E, S & I; 1973 v. S; 1974 v. E, S & I; 1975 v. S; 1976 v. S, E & I; (Coventry City), 1977 v. S, E & I; 1978 v. E, S & I; 1979 v. S, E, I

* Victory International; ** See also List of Players for England; † Played in second half in place of L. R Roose, injured. **Note**-"C. R Smith" (Druids) who played v. England in 1881, was the assumed name of K Cross.

IRISH INTERNATIONALS

Aherne, T (Belfast Celtic), 1946 v. S* & W*; 1947 v. E; 1948 v. S; 1949 v. W; (Luton Town), 1950 v. W
Alexander, A (Cliftonville), 1895 v. S
Allen, C (Cliftonville), 1936 v. E
Allen, J (Limavady), 1887 v. E
Anderson, T (Manchester United), 1973 v. E, S & W; (Swindon Town), 1977 v. E, S & W; (Peterborough United), 1978 v. S, E & W
Anderson, W (Linfield), 1898 v. E & W; 1898-9 v. S
Andrews, W (Glentoran), 1908 v. S; (Grimsby Town), 1913 v. E & S
Armstrong, G (Tottenham Hotspur), 1977 v. E; 1978 v. S, E & W; 1979 v. E, S, W
Baird, G (Distillery), 1896 v. E, S & W
Baird, H (Huddersfield Town), 1935 v. E
Balfe, J (Shelbourne), 1909 v. E; 1910 v. W
Banbrick, J (Linfield), 1929-30 v. E, W & S; 1932 v. W; (Chelsea), 1935 v. W; 1936 v. E & S; 1940 v. W
Banks, S. J (Cliftonville), 1937 v. W
Barr, H. H (Linfield), 1962 v. E; (Coventry City), 1963 v. E
Barron, J (Cliftonville), 1894-7 v. E & W; 1894-5-6 v. S
Barry, J (Bohemians), 1900 v. S
Baxter, R (Distillery), 1887 v. S & W
Bennett, R (Dublin University), 1889 v. W
Berry, J (Cliftonville), 1888 v. S & W; 1889 v. E
Best, G (Manchester United), 1964 v. W; 1965 v. E & S; 1966 v. S & E; 1967 v. E; 1968 v. S; 1969 v. E, S & W; 1970 v. S, E & W; 1971 v. E, S & W
Bingham, W. L (Sunderland), 1952-3-4-5-6-7 v. E, S & W; 1958 v. S, E & W; (Luton Town), 1959 v. E, S & W; (Everton), 1961 v. E & S; 1962 v. E; 1963 v. E & S; (Port Vale), 1964 v. S & E
Black, J (Glentoran), 1901 v. E
Blair, J (Portadown), 1931-2 v. S; (Swansea), 1935 v. S
Blair, J (Cliftonville), 1907-8 v. E & S; 1907 v. W
Blair, R (Oldham Athletic), 1975 v. W
Blanchflower, J (Manchester United), 1954 v. W; 1955 v. E & S; 1956 v. S & W; 1957 v. E & S; 1958 v. S & E
Blanchflower, R. D (Barnsley), 1950 v. S & W; 1951 v. E & S; (Aston Villa), 1952 v. W; 1953 v. E, S & W; (Tottenham Hotspur), 1954-5-6-7-8-9-60-1-2 v. E, S & W; 1963 v. E & S
Bookman, L. O (Bradford City), 1914 v. W; (Luton Town), 1921 v. S & W; 1922 v. E
Bothwell, A (Ards), 1926-7 v. E & W; 1926 v. S
Boyle, P (Sheffield United), 1901-2-4 v. E; 1903 v. S & W
Bonner, P (Belfast Celtic), 1946 v. E* & S*
Bowler, G. C (Hull City), 1950 v. E, S & W
Braithwaite, R (Linfield), 1962 v. W; (Middlesbrough), 1964 v. W; 1965 v. E & S
Breen, T (Belfast Celtic), 1935 v. E & W; 1937 v. E & S; (Manchester United), 1937 v. W; 1938 v. E & S; 1939 v. W & S; 1946 v. E*, S* & W
Brennan, B (Bohemians), 1912 v. W
Brennan, R. A (Luton Town), 1949 v. W; (Birmingham City), 1950 v. E, S & W; (Fulham), 1951 v. E
Briggs, R (Manchester United), 1962 v. W
Brisby, D (Distillery), 1891 v. S
Brolly, T (Millwall), 1937-8 v. W; 1939 v. E & W
Brookes, E. A (Shelbourne), 1920 v. S
Brown, J (Glenavon), 1921 v. W; (Tranmere Rovers), 1924 v. E & W; 1926 v. W

Brown, J (Wolverhampton Wanderers), 1935 v. E & W; 1936 v. E; (Coventry City), 1937 v. E & W; 1938 v. S & W; (Birmingham City), 1939 v. E, S & W
Brown, W. M (Limavady), 1887 v. E
Browne, F (Cliftonville), 1887-8 v. E & S; 1887 v. W
Browne, R (Leeds United), 1936 v. E & W; 1938 v. E & W; 1939 v. E & S
Bruce, W (Glentoran), 1961 v. S; 1967 v. W
Buckle, H (Cliftonville), 1882 v. E
Buckle, R (Sunderland), 1904 v. E; (Bristol City), 1908 v. W
Burnett, J (Distillery), 1894-5 v. E & W; 1894 v. S
Burnison, J (Distillery), 1901 v. E & W
Burnison, S (Distillery), 1908-10 v. E; 1910 v. S; (Bradford), 1911-12 v. E; 1911 v. S; 1911-13 v. W
Burns, I (Glenavon), 1923 v. E
Butler, M. P (Blackpool), 1939 v. W
Campbell, J (Cliftonville), 1897-8-9-1900-3 v. E; 1897-8-1900-1-2-4 v. S; 1896-7-8-1901 v. W
Campbell, J (Crusaders), 1963 v. W; (Dundee), 1968 v. S & E
Campbell, J. P (Fulham), 1951 v. E & S
Campbell, W (Dundee), 1970 v. W & S
Carey, J (Manchester United), 1946 v. S* & W*; 1947 v. E, S & W; 1948 v. E; 1949 v. E, S & W
Carroll, F (Glenavon), 1925 v. S
Casey, T (Newcastle United), 1956 v. W; 1957 v. E, S & W; (Portsmouth), 1959 v. E
Cashin, M (Cliftonville), 1898 v. S
Caskey, W (Derby County), 1979 v. E
Cassidy, T (Newcastle United), 1974 v. S, E & W; 1976 v. S, E & W
Chambers, J (Distillery), 1921 v. W
Chambers, J (Bury), 1928-9 v. E; 1928-9-30 v. S & W; (Nottingham Forest), 1932 v. E, S & W
Chatton, H (Partick Thistle), 1925-6 v. E; 1925 v. S
Christian, J (Linfield), 1898 v. S
Clarke, R (Belfast Celtic), 1901 v. E & S
Clements, W (Coventry City), 1965 v. W; 1967 v. S & W; 1968 v. S & E; 1969 v. S & W; 1970 v. S, E & W; 1971 v. E, S & W; (Sheffield Wednesday), 1972 v. S, E & W; 1973 v. E, S & W; (Everton), 1974 v. S, E & W; 1975 v. E, S & W; (New York Cosmos), 1976 v. E & W
Clugston, J (Cliftonville), 1889-90-1-2-3 v. E; 1889-90-2-3 v. S; 1888-9-91-2-3 v. W
Cochrane, M (Distillery), 1898-9-1900 v. E; 1898-1900-1 v. S; 1898-1900 v. W
Cochrane, D (Leeds United), 1939 v. E & W; 1947 v. E, S & W; 1948 v. S, E & W; 1949 v. S & W; 1950 v. E & S
Cochrane, T (Burnley), 1978 v. E & W; (Middlesbrough), 1979 v. E
Collins, F (Glasgow Celtic), 1922 v. S
Condy, J (Distillery), 1886 v. E & S; 1892 v. W
Connor, J (Belfast Celtic), 1905-7-8-11 v. E & S; 1905-9-11 v. W
Connor, M. J (Glentoran), 1901 v. S & E; (Brentford), 1903 v. S & W; 1904 v. E
Cook, W (Celtic), 1933 v. E, W & S; 1935 v. E; (Everton), 1936 v. S & W; 1937-8-9 v. E, S & W
Cooke, S (Belfast YMCA), 1889-90 v. E; 1890 v. S
Coulter, J (Belfast Celtic), 1934 v. E, S & W; (Everton), 1935 v. E, S & W; 1937 v. S & W; (Grimsby Town), 1938 v. S & W; (Chelmsford City), 1939 v. S
Cowan, J (Queens Park), 1925 v. W
Coyle, R (Coleraine), 1956 v. E & S
Craig, A (Rangers), 1908 v. E; 1908-9 v. S; 1908 v. W; (Morton), 1914 v. E; 1912-14 v. S & W

Craig, D (Newcastle United), 1967 v. W; 1968 v. W; 1969 v. E, S & W; 1970 v. S, E & W; 1973 v. E, S & W
Crawford, S (Distillery), 1889-91-3 v. E & W; 1891 v. S
Croft, T (Queens Island), 1924 v. E
Crone, R (Distillery), 1890 v. E & W; 1889-90 v. S
Crone, W (Distillery), 1884-6-7-8 v. S; 1882-4-6-8-90 v. W
Crooks, W (Manchester United), 1922 v. W
Crossan, E (Blackburn Rovers), 1950 v. S; 1951 v. E; 1955 v. W
Crossan, J (Sparta-Rotterdam), 1960 v. E; (Sunderland), 1963 v. W; 1964 v. S, E & W; 1965 v. E & S; (Manchester City), ???? v. W; 1966 v. S & E; 1967 v. E & S; (Middlesbrough), 1968 v. S
Crothers, C (Distillery), 1907 v. W
Cumming, L (Huddersfield Town), 1929 v. W & S; (Oldham Athletic), 1930 v. E
Cunningham, R (Ulster), 1892-3 v. E; 1892 v. S & W
Cunningham, W (St Mirren), 1951 v. W; 1953 v. E; 1954-5 v. S; 1956-7 v. E, S & W; (Leicester City), 1958 v. S & W; 1959 v. E, S & W; 1960 v. S, E & W; (Dunferlime Atheltic), 1961 v. W; 1962 v. W
Curran, J. V (Glenavon), 1924 v. E; 1922 v. W; (Pontypridd), 1923 v. E & S
Curran, S (Belfast Celtic), 1926 v. W; 1926-8 v. S
Cush, W (Glenavon), 1951 v. E & S; 1954 v. S & E; 1957 v. W; (Leeds United), 1958 v. W; 1959-60 v. E, S & W
Dalton, W (YMCA), 1892-4 v. E; 1888-90-1-2-4 v. S; 1890-1-2-4 v. W
D'Arcy, S. D (Chelsea), 1952 v. W; 1953 v. E; (Brentford), 1953 v. S & W
Darling, J (Linfield), 1897-1902-3-5-6-9-10 v. E; 1897-1900-2-3-5-6-10-12 v. S; 1902-3-5-6-8-10 v. W
Davey, H (Reading), 1926-7-8 v. E; 1927 v. S; (Portsmouth), 1928 v. W
Davidson, J. R (Cliftonville), 1882-3-4-5 v. E; 1884 v. S; 1882-3-4 v. W
Davis, T (Oldham Athletic), 1937 v. E
Devine, W (Limavady), 1886 v. E & S; 1887-8 v. W
Dickson, D (Coleraine), 1970 v. W
Dickson, T (Linfield), 1957 v. S
Dickson, W (Chelsea), 1951 v. W; 1952-3 v. S, E & W; (Arsenal), 1954 v. E & W; 1955 v. E
Diffin, W (Belfast Celtic), 1931 v. W
Dill, A. H (Knock and Down Athletic), 1882-4-5 v. E; 1884-5 v. S; 1882-3-4 v. W
Doherty, I (Belfast Celtic), 1901 v. E
Doherty, J (Cliftonville), 1933 v. E & W
Doherty, J (Derry City), 1938 v. S
Doherty, P (Blackpool), 1935 v. E & W; 1936 v. E & S; (Manchester City), 1937 v. E & W; 1938 v. E & S; 1939 v. E & W; 1946 v. E*; (Derby County), 1946 v. W*; 1947 v. E; (Huddersfield Town), 1947 v. W; 1948 v. E & W; 1949 v. S; 1951 v. S
Donnelly, L (Distillery), 1913 v. W
Doran, J (Brighton and Hove Al;bion), 1921-2 v. E; 1922 v. W
Dougan, D (Blackburn Rovers), 1960 v. S; 1961 v. E & W; (Aston Villa), 1963 v. S; r02
Gorman, W (Brentford), 1947 v. E, S & W; 1948 v. W
Gowdy, J (Glenavon), 1920 v. E; (Queens Island), 1924 v. W; (Falkirk), 1926-7 v. E & S
Gowdy, W. A (Hull City), 1932 v. S; (Sheffield Wednesday), 1933 v. S; (Linfield), 1935 v. E, S & W; (Hibernian), 1936 v. W
Graham, L (Doncaster Rovers), 1951 v. W; 1952 v. E, S & W; 1953 v. S; 1954 v. E & W; 1955 v. S & W; 1956 v. E & S; 1959 v. E
Greer, W (Queens Park Rangers), 1909 v. E, S & W
Gregg, H (Doncaster Rovers), 1954 v. W; 1957 v. E, S & W; 1958 v. E & W; (Manchester United), 1959 v. E & W; 1960 v. S, E & W; 1961 v. E & S; 1962 v. S; 1964 v. S & E
Hall, G (Distillery), 1887 v. E

Halligan, W (Derby County), 1911 v. W; (Wolverhampton Wanderers), 1912 v. E
Hamill, M (Manchester United), 1912-14 v. E; 1914 v. S; (Belfast Celtic), 1920 v. E, S & W; (Manchester City), 1921 v. S
Hamilton, B (Linfield), 1971 v. E, S & W; (Ipswich), 1973 v. E, S & W; 1974 v. S, E & W; 1975 v. E; (Everton), 1976 v. S, E & W; 1977 v. E, S & W; (Millwall), 1978 v. S, E & W; (Swindon Town), 1979 v. E, S, W
Hamilton, J (Knock and Down Athletic), 1882 v. E & W
Hamilton, R (Distillery), 1908 v. W
Hamilton, R (Glasgow Rangers), 1928-30 v. S; 1929-30 v. E; 1932 v. S
Hamilton, W (Queens Park Rangers), 1978 v. S
Hamilton, W. D (Dublin Association), 1885 v. W
Hamilton, W. J (Dublin Association), 1885 v. W
Hampton, H (Bradford City), 1911-12-13-14 v. E; 1911-13 v. S; 1911-12-13 v. W
Hanna, D (Portsmouth R A), 1899 v. W
Hanna, J (Nottingham Forest), 1912 v. S & W
Hannon, D. J (Bohemians), 1908-11-13 v. E; 1908-11 v. S; 1912 v. W
Harkin, T (Southport), 1968 v. W
Harland, A (Linfield), 1923 v. E
Harvey, M (Sunderland), 1963 v. W; 1964 v. S, E & W; 1965 v. E, S & W; 1966 v. S, E & W; 1967 v. E & S; 1968 v. E & W; 1969 v. E
Harris, J (Cliftonville), 1921 v. W
Harris, V (Shelbourne), 1906-7-8 v. E; 1908 v. W; (Everton), 1909-10-11-12-13 v. E; 1909-10-11-12-14 v. S; 1909-10-11-14 v. W
Hastings, J (Knock and Down Athletic), 1882-4-6 v. E; 1884-6 v. S; 1882-3 v. W
Hatton, S (Linfield), 1963 v. S
Hayes, W. E (Huddersfield Town), 1938-9 v. E & S
Hegan, D (Wolverhampton Wanderers), 1972 v. S, E & W
Henderson, A. W (Ulster), 1885 v. E, S & W
Hewison, G (Moyola Park), 1885 v. E & S
Hill, J (Norwich City), 1959 v. W; 1962 v. W; 1963 v. S; (Everton), 1964 v. S & E
Hinton, E (Fulham), 1947 v. S & W; 1948 v. E, S & W; (Millwall), 1951 v. W
Hopkins, J (Brighton and Hove Albion), 1926 v. E
Houston, J (Linfield), 1912 v. S & W; (Everton), 1913 v. E, S & W; 1914 v. S
Houston, W (Linfield), 1933 v. W
Houston, W. G (Moyola Park), 1885 v. E & S
Hughes, W (Bolton Wanderers), 1951 v. W
Humphries, W (Ards), 1962 v. W; (Coventry City), 1963 v. E, S & W; 1964 v. S & E; 1965 v. S; (Swansea Town), 1965 v. W
Hunter, A (Blackburn Rovers), 1971 v. E, S & W; (Ipswich Town), 1972 v. S, E & W; 1973 v. E, S & W; 1974 v. S, E & W; 1975 v. E, S & W; 1976 v. S, E & W; 1977 v. E, S & W; 1979 v. S, W
Hunter, J (Distillery), 1905-6 v. W; 1906 v. E & S; (Belfast Celtic), 1908-9 v. W; 1909 v. E & S
Hunter, R. J (Cliftonville), 1884 c. E, S & W
Hunter, V (Coleraine), 1962 v. E
Irvine, R (Everton), 1923-4-5-6-7-8 v. E; 1922-4-8 v. S; 1923-7 v. W; (Portsmouth), 1929 v. E; 1930 v. S; (Connah's Quay), 1931 v. E; (Derry City), 1932 v. W
Irvine, R (Linfield), 1963 v. E, S & W; (Stoke City), 1965 v. W
Irvine, W (Burnley), 1963 v. W; 1965 v. S & W; 1966 v. S, E & W; 1967 v. E & S; 1968 v. E & W; (Preston North End), 1969 v. E; (Brighton and Hove Albion), 1972 v. S, E & W
Irving, S. J (Dundee), 1923-4-5-6 v. S; 1924-5 v. E; 1923-4-5-6 v. W; (Cardiff City), 1927-8 v. S, E & W; (Chelsea), 1929 v. E; 1931 v. W

Jackson, T (Everton), 1969 v. E, S & W; (Nottingham Forest), 1972 v. S, E & W; 1973 v. E, S & W; 1975 v. E, S & W; (Manchester United), 1977 v. E, S & W
Jennings, P (Watford), 1964 v. W; (Tottenham Hotspur), 1965 v. E & S; 1966 v. S, E & W; 1968 v. S, E & W; 1969 v. E, S & W; 1970 v. E & S; 1971 v. E, S & W; 1972 v. S, E & W; 1973 v. E, S & W; 1974 v. S, E & W; 1975 v. E, S & W; 1976 v. S, E & W; 1977 v. E, S & W; (Arsenal), 1979 v. E, S, W
Johnson, S (Belfast), 1890 v. W
Johnston, A (Distillery), 1884-6 E; 1886 v. S; 1882 v. W
Johnston, H (Portadown), 1927 v. W
Johnston, R (Old Park), 1885 v. S & W
Johnston, S (Linfield), 1893 v. S & W; 1894 v. E
Johnston, W (Glenavon), 1962 v. W
Johnstone, S (Distillery), 1905 v. W
Jones, J (Linfield), 1930-1-2 v. S; 1930-1 v. W; 1931-2 v. E; 1933-4-5 v. E, W & S; 1936 v. E & S; (Hibernian), 1936 v. W; 1937 v. E, W & S; (Glenavon), 1938 v. E
Jones, J (Glenavon), 1956 v. E & W
Jones, S (Distillery), 1934 v. E; (Blackpool), 1934 v. W; 1946 v. E*
Jordon, T (Linfield), 1895 v. E & W
Kavanagh, P (Glasgow Celtic), 1930 v. E
Keane, T. R (Swansea Town), 1949 v. S
Kearne, A (Distillery), 1900-2 v. E, S & W
Keith, D (Newcastle United), 1958 v. E & W; 1959 v. E, S & W; 1960 v. S & E; 1961 v. E, S & W; 1962 v. W
Kelly, H (Fulham), 1950 v. E & W; (Southampton), 1951 v. E & S
Kelly, J (Glentoran), 1896 v. E
Kelly, J (Derry City), 1932 v. E & W; 1933 v. E, W & S; 1934 v. W; 1936 v. E, S & W; 1937 v. E & S
Kelly, P (Manchester City), 1921 v. E
Kelly, P (Barnsley), 1950 v. S
Kennedy, J (Arsenal), 1925 v. E; 1923 v. W
Kernogham, N (Belfast Celtic), 1936 v. W; 1937 v. S; 1938 v. E
Kirkwood, H (Cliftonville), 1940 v. W
Kirwan, J (Tottenham Hotspur), 1902-3-4-5 v. E; 1903-4-5 v. S; 1900-2-3-4-5 v. W; (Chelsea), 1906 v. E; 1906-9 v. S; 1906-7 v. W
Lacey, W (Everton), 1909-10-11-12 v. E; 1909-10-11 v. S & W; (Liverpool), 1914-20-1-2 v. E & S; 1913-14-20-1 v. W; (New Brighton), 1925 v. E
Lawther, I (Sunderland), 1960 v. W; (Blackburn Rovers), 1962 v. S
Leatham, J (Belfast Celtic), 1939 v. W
Ledwidge, J. J (Shelbourne), 1906 v. S & W
Lemon, J (Glentoran), 1888 v. S; 1886-9 v. W
Leslie, W (YMCA), 1887 v. E
Lewis, J (Glentoran), 1899 v. E & W; 1899-1900 v. S
Little, J (Glentoran), 1898 v. W
Lockhart, H (Cliftonville), 1884 v. W
Lockhart, N (Linfield), 1947 v. E; (Coventry City), 1950-1-2 v. W; (Aston Villa), 1954 v. S & E; 1955-6 v. W
Lowther, R (Glentoran), 1888 v. E & S
Loyal, J (Clarence), 1891 v. S
Lutton, B (Wolverhampton Wanderers), 1970 v. S & E
Lyner, D (Glentoran), 1920 v. E; 1922 v. S; 1920-2 v. W; (Manchester United), 1923 v. E; (Kilmarnock), 1923 v. W
McAdams, W (Manchester City), 1954 v. W; 1955 v. S; 1957 v. E; 1958 v. S; (Bolton Wanderers), 1961 v. E, S & W; 1962 v. E
McAleny, J. M (Cliftonville), 1882 v. E & W
McAlinden, J (Belfast Celtic), 1938-9 v. S; (Portsmouth), 1947 v. E; (Southend United), 1949 v. E
McAllen, J (Linfield), 1898-9-1900 v. E; 1899-1900-2 v. S; 1899-1900-1 v. W

McAlpine, W. J (Cliftonville), 1901 v. S
McArthur, A (Distillery), 1886 v. W
McAuley, J (Huddersfield Town), 1911-12-13 v. E; 1912-13 v. S; 1911 v. W
McCabe, J. J (Leeds United), 1949 v. S & W; 1950 v. E; 1951 v. W; 1953 v. W; 1954 v. S
McCabe, W (Ulster), 1891 v. E
McCambridge, J (Ballymena), 1930 v. S & W; (Cardiff City), 1931 v. W; 1932 v. E
McCandless, J (Bradford), 1912-13-20 v. W; 1921 v. E; 1920 v. S
McCandless, W (Linfield), 1920 v. E & W; 1921 v. E; (Rangers), 1921-4-9 v. W; 1922-4-5 v. S
McCann, P (Belfast Celtic), 1910 v. E, S & W; (Glentoran), 1911-12 v. E; 1911 v. S; 1913 v. W
McCarthy, J (Belfast Celtic), 1946 v. E*
McCarthy, A (Ulster), 1903 v. S & W; (Linfield), 1904 v. S W; (Everton), 1905 v. E & S; (Belfast Celtic), 1907-8 v. E, S & W; (Glentoran), 1909 v. E, S & W
McCartney, J (Cliftonville), 1898 v. W
McCashin, J (Cliftonville), 1896 v. W; 1898-9 v. S
McCauley, P (Belfast Celtic), 1900 v. S
McCavana, T (Coleraine), 1955 v. S; 1956 v. E & S
McCaw, D (Distillery), 1882 v. E
McCaw, H (Linfield), 1931 v. E; 1930-1 v. S; 1927-31 v. W
McClatchey, J (Distillery), 1886 v. E, S & W
McClatchey, R (Distillery), 1895 v. S
McCleary, J. W (Cliftonville), 1955 v. W
McCleery, W (Linfield), 1930-1 v. E; 1930-1-2 v. W; 1931-2 v. S; 1938 v. E & W
McClelland, J (Arsenal), 1961 v. W
McCluggage, A (Bradford), 1924 v. E; (Burnley), 1928-9-31 v. E; 1927-8-9 v. S; 1927-8-9-30-1 v. W
McClure, G (Cliftonville), 1908-9 v. E; 1907 v. S & W
McConnelll, E (Cliftonville), 1904 v. S & W; (Glentoran), 1905 v. S; (Sunderland), 1906-7 v. E; 1908 v. S & W; (Sheffield Wednesday), 1909-10 v. S & W; 1910 v. E
McConnell, P (Doncaster Rovers), 1928 v. W; (Southport), 1932 v. E
McConnell, W. G (Bohemians), 1913-14 v. E & S; 1912-14 v. W
McConnell, W. H (Reading), 1926-7-8 v. E; 1925-6-7-8 v. W; 1927 v. S
McCourt, F. J (MAnchester City), 1952 v. E & W; 1953 v. E, S & W
McCoy, J (Distillery), 1896 v. W
McCracken, R (Crystal Palace), 1921-2 v. E; 1922 v. S & W
McCracken, W (Distillery), 1902-3-4 v. E; 1902-4 v. S; (Newcastle United), 1905-7-20-2 v. E; 1905-22-3 v. S; 1905-22-3 v. W
McCreery, D (Manchester United), 1976 v. E & W; 1977 v. E, S & W; 1978 v. S, E & W; 1979 v. W
McCrory, S (Southend United), 1958 v. E
McCullough, K (Belfast Celtic), 1935 v. W; 1936 v. E; (Manchester City), 1936 v. S; 1937 v. E & S
McCullough, W (Arsenal), 1964 v. S, E & W; 1965 v. E; (Millwall), 1967 v. E
McDonald, R (Glasgow Rangers), 1930 v. S; 1932 v. E
McDonnell, J (Bohemians), 1911 v. E & S; 1912-13 v. W
McFaul, I (Linfield), ???? sub v. E; (Newcastle United), 1970 v. W
McGarry, J. K (Cliftonville), 1951 v. W
McGee, G (Willington Park), 1885 v. E, S & W
McGregor, S (Glentoran), 1921 v. S
McGrath, C (Tottenham Hotspur), 1974 v. S, E & W; (Manchester United), 1977 v. E, S & W; 1978 v. S, E & W; 1979 v. E
McGrillen, J (Clyde), 1924 v. S; (Belfast Celtic), 1927 v. S
McGuire, E (Distillery), 1907 v. S
McIlroy, H (Cliftonville), 1906 v. E

Mcilroy, J (Burnley), 1952-3-4-5-6-7-8-9-60 v. E, S & W; 1961 v. E & W; 1962 v. E & S; 1963 v. E & S; (Stoke City), 1963 v. W; 1966 v. S & E
Mcilroy, S (Manchester United), 1974 v. S, E & W; 1975 v. E, S & W; 1976 v. S, E & W; 1977 v. E, S & W; 1978 v. S, E & W; 1979 v. E, S, W
Mcilvenny, J (Distillery), 1890-1 v. E
Mcilvenny, P (Distillery), 1924 v. W
McKeag, W (Glentoran), 1968 v. S & W
McKee, F. W (Cliftonville), 1906 v. S & W; (Belfast Celtic), 1914 v. E, S & W
McKelvie, H (Glentoran), 1901 v. W
McKenna, J (Linfield), 1946 v. E* & W; (Huddersfield Town), 1950 v. E, S & W; 1951 v. E & S; 1952 v. E
McKenzie, H (Distillery), 1923 v. S
McKenzie, R (Airdrie), 1967 v. W
McKeown, H (Linfield), 1892 v. E; 1892-3-4 v. S & W
Mackie, J. A (Arsenal), 1923 v. W; (Portsmouth), 1935 v. S & W
McKie, H (Cliftonville), 1895 v. E, S & W
McKinney, D (Hull City), 1921 v. S; (Bradford City), 1924 v. S
McKnight, J (Preston North End), 1912 v. S; (Glentoran), 1913 v. S
McLaughlin, J (Shrewsbury Town), 1962 v. E, S & W; 1963 v. W; (Swansea Town), 1964 v. W; 1965 v. E & W; 1966 v. W
McLean, T (Limavady), 1885 v. S
McMahon, J (Bohemians), 1934 v. S
McMaster, G (Glentoran), 1897 v. E, S & W
McMichael, A (Newcastle United), 1950-1 v. E & S; 1952-3-4-5 v. E, S & W; 1956 v. W; 1957-8 v. E, S & W; 1959 v. S & W; 1960 v. E, S & W
McMillan, G (Distillery), 1903 v. E; 1905 v. W
McMillan, S (Manchester United), 1963 v. E & S
McMillan, W (Belfast Celtic), 1946 v. E*, S* & W*
McMillen, W. S (Manchester United), 1934 v. E; 1935 v. S; 1937 v. S; (Chesterfield), 1938 v. S & W; 1939 v. E & S
McMordie, E (Middlesbrough), 1969 v. E, S & W; 1970 v. S, E & W; 1971 v. E, S & W; 1972 v. S, E & W
McMorran, E (Belfast Celtic), 1947 v. E; (Barnsley), 1951-2 v. E, S & W; 1953 v. E & S; (Doncaster Rovers), 1953 v. W; 1954 v. E; 1956 v. W
McNullan, D (Liverpool), 1926 v. E & W; 1927 v. S
McNinch, J (Ballymena), 1931-2 v. S; 1939 v. W
McParland, P (Aston Villa), 1954 v. W; 1955-6 v. E & S; 1957-8-9-60-1 v. E, S & W
McShane, J (Cliftonville), 1900 v. E & W; 1899-1900 v. S
McVickers, J (Glentoran), 1888 v. E; 1889 v. S
McWha, W. B. R (Cliftonville), 1882-3-4-5 v. E; 1882-3-5 v. W
Madden, O (Norwich City), 1938 v. E
Magill, J (Arsenal), 1962 v. E & S; 1963 v. E, S & W; 1964 v. S, E & W; 1965 v. E & S; 1966 v. S; (Brighton and Hove Albion), 1966 v. E & W
Maginnis, H (Linfield), 1900-4 v. E; 1900-3-4 v. S & W
Mahood, J (Belfast Celtic), 1926-8-9 v. S; 1928-9 v. E; 1928-9-30 v. W; (Ballymena), 1934 v. S
Manderson, B (Glasgow Rangers), 1925 v. E; 1920-5-6 v. S· 1920 v. W
Mansfield, J (Freebooters), 1901 v. E
Martin, C (Glentoran), 1947 v. S; (Leeds United), 1948 v. E, S & W· (Aston Villa), 1949 v. E; 1950 v. W
Martin, D (Belfast Celtic), 1934 v. E, S & W; 1935 v. S; (Wolverhampton Wanderers), 1935 v. E; 1936 v. W; (Nottingham Forest) 937 ، S· 1938 v. E & S; 1939 v. S
Martin, D. C (Cliftonville), 1882-3 v. E; 1882 v. W
Martin, P (Bo'ness), 1925 v. S
Mathieson, A (Luton Town), 1922 v. E; 1921 v. W
Maxwell, J (Linfield), 1903 v. E; 1905-7 v. S; 1902-3-5-6 W
Meek, W (Glentoran), 1925 v. W
Mehffy, J. A. C (Queens Island), 1922 v. W

Meldon, J (Freebooters), 1899 v. S & W
Mercer, H. V. A (Linfield), 1908 v. E
Mercer, J. T (Distillery and Derby County), 1898-9-1902-4 v. E; 1898-1903-5 v. S; 1898-1902-3- v. W
Miller, J (Middlesbrough), 1929 v. W & S; 1930 v. E
Miller, W (Barrow), 1932 v. W; 1933 v. S
Milligan, D (Chesterfield), 1939 v. W
Milne, R. G (Linfield Athletic), 1894-5-6-7-8-9-1902-3-4-6 v. E; 1894-6-7-8-1902-3-4-6 v. S; 1894-5-6-8-9-1901-2-4-6 v. W
Mitchell, C (Glentoran), 1934 v. W
Mitchell, E (Cliftonville), 1933 v. S
Mitchell, W (Distillery), 1932-3 v. E & W; (Chelsea), 1934 v. W & S; 1935-6 v. S & E; 1937 v. E, S & W; 1938 v. E & S
Molyneaux, T (Ligoniel), 1883-4-5-6 v. E & W; 1884-6-8 v. S
Montgomery, F (Coleraine), 1955 v. E
Moore, C (Glentoran), 1949 v. W
Moore, J (Aberdeen), 1933 v. E
Moore, J (Linfield Athletic), 1891 v. E, S & W
Moore, T (Ulster), ???? v. S & W
Moore, W. J (Falkirk), 1923 v. S
Moorehead, F. W (Dublin University), 1884 v. E
Moorehead, G (Linfield), 1923-8-9 v. S
Moran, J (Leeds City), 1912 v. S
Moreland, V (Derby County), 1979 v. E, S
Morgan, F. G (Linfield), 1923 v. E; (Nottingham Forest), 1927-8-9 v. E; 1924-8 v. S; 1928 v. W
Morgan, S (Port Vale), 1973 v. E, S & W; (Aston Villa), 1974 v. S & E; 1976 v. S
Morrison, J (Linfield Athletic), 1891 v. E & W
Morrison, T (Glentoran), 1895 v. E, S & W; (Burnley), 1899-1900 v. W; 1902 v. E & S
Morrogh, E (Dublin), 1896 v. S
Morrow, W. J (Moyola Park), 1883 v. E & W; 1884 v. S
Muir, R (Old Park), 1885 v. S & W
Mulholland, S (Celtic), 1906 v. E & S
Mulligan, J (Manchester City), 1921 v. S
Murphy, N (Queens Park Rangers), 1905 v. E, S & W
Murray, J. M (Motherwell), 1910 v. E & S; (Sheffield Wednesday), 1910 v. W
Neill, T (Arsenal), 1962 v. E, S & W; 1963 v. E & W; 1964 v. S, E & W; 1965 v. E, S & W; 1966 v. S, E & W; 1967 v. S & W; 1968 v. S & E; 1969 v. E, S & W; 1970 v. S, E & W; (Hull City), 1972 v. S, E & W; 1973 v. E, S & W
Nells, P (Nottingham Forest), 1923 v. E
Nelson, S (Arsenal), 1970 v. W; 1971 v. E, S & W; 1972 v. S, E & W; 1974 v. S & E; 1976 v. E; 1977 v. W; 1979 v. E, S, W
Nicholl, C (Aston Villa), 1975 v. E, S & W; 1976 v. S, E & W; 1977 v. W; (Southampton), 1978 v. S, E & W; 1979 v. E, W
Nicholl, H (Belfast Celtic), 1902-5 v. E; 1902 v. W
Nicholl, J (Manchester United), 1977 v. E, S & W; 1978 v. S, E & W; 1979 v. E, S, W
Nicholson, J (Manchester United), 1961 v. S & W; 1962 v. E & W; 1963 v. E & S; (Huddersfield Town), 1965 v. W; 1966 v. S, E & W; 1967 v. S & W; 1968 v. S, E & W; 1969 v. E, S & W; 1970 v. W, E & S; 1971 v. E, S & W
Nixon, R (Linfield), 1914 v. S
Nolan-Whelan, J. V (Dublin Freebooters and Corinthians), 1901 v. E; 1902 v. S; 1901-2 v. W
O'Brien, M. T (Queens Park Rangers), 1921-2 v. S; 1922 v. W; (Leicester City), 1924 v. S & W; (Hull City), 1925 v. S, E & W; 1926 v. W; (Derby County), 1927 v. W
O'Connell, P (Sheffield Wednesday), 1912 v. E & S; (Hull City), 1914 v. E, S & W

O'Driscoll, J. F (Swansea Town), 1949 v. E, S & W
O'Doherty, A (Coleraine), 1970 v. E
O'Flanagan, D. K (Arsenal), 1946 v. S* & W*
O'Hagan, C (Tottenham Hotspur), 1905-6 v. S & W; 1906 v. E; (Aberdeen), 1907-9 v. E; 1907 v. S & W
O'Hagen, W (Paisley St. Mirren), 1920 v. E & W
O'Hehir, J (Bohemians), 1910 v. W
O'Kane, L (Nottingham Forest), 1970 v. E & W; 1971 v. E, S & W; 1974 v. S, E & W; 1975 v. E & S
O'Mahoney, M (Bristol Rovers), 1939 v. S
O'Neill, J (Sunderland), 1962 v. W
O'Neill, M (Nottingham Forest), 1973 v. E, S & W; 1974 v. W; 1975 v. E & S; 1977 v. S; 1978 v. S, E & W
O'Reilly, H (Freebooters), 1901-4 v. S; 1901 v. W
Parke, J (Linfield), 1964 v. S; (Hibernian), 1964 v. E; (Sunderland), 1965 v. S & W; 1967 v. E & S; 1968 v. S & E
Peacock, R (Celtic), 1952 v. S; 1954 v. W; 1955-6 v. E & S; 1957 v. W; 1958 v. S, E & W; 1959 v. E, S & W; 1960 v. S & E; 1961 v. E & S; (Coleraine), 1962 v. S
Peden, J (Linfield Athletic and Distillery), 1888-9-91-2-3-6-8 v. E; 1887-8-90-3-6-7-8 v. S; 1887-8-90-1-2-3-6-7-8-9 v. W
Percy, J. C (Belfast YMCA), 1889 v. W
Platt, J (Middlesbrough), 1978 v. S, E & W
Ponsonby, J (Distillery), 1896-7-9 v. E; 1895-6-7 v. S; 1896-7 v. W.
Potts, R. H (Cliftonville), 1883 v. E & W
Priestley, T (Coleraine), 1933 v. S; (Chelsea), 1934 v. E
Pyper, Jas (Cliftonville), 1898-1900 v. E; 1897-8 v. S & W
Pyper, John (Cliftonville), 1897-9-1900 v. E & W; 1897-9-1900-2 v. S
Pyper, M (Linfield), 1932 v. W
Rankine, J (Limavady), 1883 v. E & W
Raper, E. O (Dublin University), 1886 v. W
Ratray, D (Avoniel), 1882-3 v. E; 1883 v. W
Rea, B (Glentoran), 1901 v. E
Redmond, J (Cliftonville), 1884 v. W
Reid, G (Cardiff City), 1923 v. S
Reid, J (Heart of Midlothian), 1931 v. E
Reid, J (Ulster), 1883 v. E; 1884 v. W; 1887 v. S; 1889 v. W; 1890 v. S & W
Reid, S. E (Derby County), 1934 v. E & W; 1936 v. E
Reilly, J (Portsmouth), 1900-2 v. E
Renneville, W. T (Leyton), 1910 v. E, S & W; (Aston Villa), 1911 v. W
**Reynolds, J (Distillery), 1890-1 v. E & W; 1891 v. S
Reynolds, R (Bohemians), 1905 v. W
Rice, P (Arsenal), 1971 v. E, S & W; 1972 v. S, E & W; 1973 v. E, S & W; 1974 v. S, E & W; 1975 v. E, S & W; 1976 v. S, E & W; 1977 v. E & S; 1979 v. E, S, W
Robens, F (Glentoran), 1931 v. S
Robinson, P (Distillery), 1920 v. S; (Blackburn Rovers), 1921 v. W
Rollo, D (Linfield), 1912-13-14 v. W; 1914 v. E; (Blackburn Rovers), 1921-2-3-6-7 v. E; 1920-1-4 v. S; 1920-1-2-3-5 v. W
Rosbottom, A (Cliftonville), 1887-8-9 v. E; 1887-8 v. S & W
Rowley, R. W. M (Southampton), 1929-30 v. W; 1929 v. S; 1930 v. E· (Tottenham Hotspur), 1931 v. W; 1932 v. S
Russell, A (Linfield), 1947 v. E
Russell, S (Bradford City), 1930 v. E & S; (Derry City), 1932 v. E
Ryan, R. A (West Bromwich Albion), 1950 v. W
Scott, E (Liverpool), 1921-2-6-7-8-9-30-1-3-4 v. E; 1920-1-6-7-8-9-33-4 v. S; 1921-5-6-7-8-9-32-3-4 v. W; (Belfast Celtic), 1936 v. E; 1935-6 v. S; 1936 v. W
Scott, J (Cliftonville), 1901 v. S
Scott, L. J (Dublin University), 1895 v. S & W

Scott, P (Everton), 1975 v. W; (York), 1976 v. S & W; 1978 v. S, E & W; 1979 v. S
Scott, T (Cliftonville), 1894-6-8 v. E; 1894-5-6-8 v. S; 1895-6-7-8-1900 v. W
Scott, W (Linfield), 1903-4 v. E, S & W; (Everton), 1905-7-8-9-10-11-12 v. E; 1905-7-8-9-10-11 v. S; 1908-9-11 v. W; (Leeds City), 1913 v. E, S & W
Scraggs, J (Glentoran), 1922 v. E; 1921 v. W
Seymour, H. C (Bohemians), 1914 v. W
Seymour, J (Cliftonville), 1907-9 v. W
Shanks, T (Woolwich Arsenal), 1903 v. S; 1904 v. W; 1905 v. E
Sharkey, P (Ipswich Town), 1976 v. S
Sheridan, J (Everton), 1903-4 v. E & S; 1903 v. W; (Stoke City), 1905 v. E
Sheehan, Dr G (Bohemians), 1900 v. E & W; 1899 v. S
Sherrard, J (Limavady), 1885 v. S; 1887-8 v. W
Sherry, J. J (Bohemians), 1906 v. E; 1907 v. W
Shields, J (Southampton), 1957 v. S
Silo, M (Belfast YMCA), 1888 v. E
Simpson, W (Glasgow Rangers), 1951 v. W; 1954 v. E & S; 1955 v. E; 1958 v. S, E & W; 1959 v. S
Sinclair, J (Knock and Down Athletic), 1882 v. E & W
Slemin, J (Bohemians), 1909 v. W
Sloan, A. S (London Caledonians), 1925 v. W
Sloan, H. A (Bohemians), 1903-5-7 v. E; 1904-9 v. S; 1906-7-8 v. W
Sloan, T (Cardiff City), 1926-8-9 v. E; 1926-7-8 v. W; 1926-7 v. S; (Linfield), 1930 v. W & S; 1931 v. S
Sloan, W (Tranmere Rovers), 1946 v. E* & W*; (Arsenal), 1947 v. W
Sloan, T (Manchester United), 1979 v. S, W
Small, J (Clarence), 1887 v. E
Small, J. M (Cliftonville), 1893 v. E, S & W
Smith, E. E (Cardiff City), 1923-4 v. E; 1921 v. S; 1923 v. W
Smith, J (Distillery), 1901 v. S & W
Smyth, R. H (Dublin University), 1886 v. W
Smyth, S (Wolverhampton Wanderers), 1948 v. E, S & W; 1949 v. S & W; 1950 v. E, S & W; (Stoke City), 1952 v. E
Smyth, W (Distillery), 1949 v. E & S; 1954 v. S & E
Snape, A (Airdrieonians), 1920 v. E
Spence, D (Bury), 1975 v. E, S & W; 1976 v. E & W; (Blackpool), 1979 v. E, S, W
Spencer, S (Distillery), 1890-2-3 v. E; 1890-2 v. S; 1892 v. W
Spiller, E. A (Cliftonville), 1883-4 v. E & W; 1884 v. S
Stanfield, O. M (Distillery), 1887-8-9-90-1-2-3-4-5-6-7 v. E; 1887-8-9-90-1-2-4-5-6-7 v. S; 1887-8-9-91-2-3-4-6-7 v. W
Steele, A (Charlton Athletic), 1926 v. W & S; (Fulham), 1929 v. W & S
Stevenson, A (Rangers), 1934 v. E, S & W; (Everton), 1935 v. E & S; 1936 v. S & W; 1937-8 v. E & W; 1946 v. S*; 1947 v. S & W; 1948 v. S
Stewart, A (Glentoran), 1967 v. W; 1968 v. S & E; (Derby County), ???? v. W
Stewart, R. H (Derry and Cliftonville), 1890-2-3-4 v. E & W; 1890-2-4 v. S
Stewart, T (Linfield), 1961 v. W
Swan, S (Linfield), 1899 v. S
Taggart, W (Walsall), 1899 v. W
Thompson, F. W (Cliftonville), 1910 v. E, S & W; (Bradford City), 1911-12-13 v. E; 1913 v. S; 19911-12-13 v. W; (Clyde), 1914 v. E & S
Thompson, J (Distillery), 1897 v. S
Thompson, J (Belfast Athletic), 1899 v. S
Thunder, P. J (Bohemians), 1911 v. W
Todd, J (Blackpool), 1946 v. E* & S*
Todd, S (Burnley), 1967 v. E; 1968 v. W; 1969 v. E, S & W; 1970 v. S
Toner, J (Arsenal), 1924-5 v. E; 1925 v. S; 1922-3-4 v. W; (St. Johnstone), 1927 v. E & S

Torrans, R (Linfield), 1893 v. S
Torrans, S (Linfield), 1892-3-4-5-6-7-8-9 v. E; 1889-90-1-2-3-4-5-6-7-8-1901 v. S; 1890-1-2-4-6-7-8-1901 v. W
Trainor, D (Crusaders), 1967 v. W
Tully, C (Celtic), 1949-50 v. E; 1952 v. S; 1953 v. E, S & W; 1954 v. S; 1956 v. E
Turner, E (Cliftonville), 1896 v. E & W
Turner, W (Cliftonville), 1886 v. E; 1886-8 v. S
Twoomey, J. F (Leeds United), 1938 v. W; 1939 v. E
Uprichard, N (Swindon Town), 1952 v. E, S & W; 1953 v. E & S; (Portsmouth), 1953 v. W; 1955-6 v. E, S & W; 1958-9 v. S
Vernon, J (Belfast Celtic), 1946 v. E*, S* & W; 1947 v. E & S; (West Bromwich Albion), 1947 v. W; 1948-9 v. E, S & W; 1950 v. E & S; 1951 v. E, S & W; 1952 v. S & E
Waddell, T (Cliftonville), 1906 v. S
Walker, J (Bury), 1911 v. S
Walker, R (Doncaster Rovers), 1955 v. W
Walsh, D (Linfield), 1946 v. S* & W*; (West Bromwich Albion), 1947 v. S & W; 1948-9 v. E, S & W; 1950 v. W
Walsh, W (Manchester City), 1948 v. E, S & W; 1949 v. E & S
Waring, R (Distillery), 1899 v. E
Warren, P (Shelbourne), 1913 v. E & S
Waters, J (Ulster), 1883-6-9 v. E; 1886-7 v. S; 1883-6-7-9 v. W
Waters, P (Glentoran), 1946 v. W*
Watson, T (Cardiff City), 1926 v. S
Wattle, J (Distillery), 1899 v. E
Webb, C. G (Brighton and Hove Albion), 1909-10 v. S; 1909 v. W
Weir, E (Clyde), 1928 v. W
Welsh, E (Carlisle United), 1966 v. W; 1967 v. W
Whiteside, T (Distillery), 1891 v. E
Whitfield, E. R (Dublin University), 1886 v. W
Will, A. H (Cliftonville), 1885 v. W
Williams, J (Cliftonville), 1890 v. E; 1892-3 v. S
Williams, J. R (Ulster), 1886 v. E & W
Willingham, T (Burnley), 1933 v. W; 1934 v. S
Willis, G (Linfield), 1906-7-12 v. S; 1906 v. W
Wilson, H (Linfield), 1925 v. W
Wilson, M (Distillery), 1884 v. E, S & W
Wilson, R (Cliftonville), 1888 v. S
Wilson, S (Glenavon), 1962 v. S; 1964 v. S; (Falkirk), 1964 v. E & W; 1965 v. E; (Dundee), 1966 v. W; 1967 v. S; 1968 v. E
Wilton, J. M (St Columbia Court), 1888-9-90 v. E; 1889-93 v. S; 1888-92 v. W
Wright, J (Cliftonville), 1906-7 v. E, S & W
Young, S (Linfield), 1907-8 v. E & S; (Airdrieonians), 1909-14 v. E; 1912-14 v. S; 1914 v. W

** See also List of Players for England   * Victory International

ENGLISH INTERNATIONALS

(AGAINST OVERSEAS AND COMMONWEALTH TEAMS)

Matches against Commonwealth countries are NOT regarded as FULL Internationals, as England's full strength has not been employed in these games.

A, represents Austria; Arg., Argentina; Aus., Australia; Bel., Belgium; B., Bohemia; Br., Brazil; Bul., Bulgaria; C., Canada; Ch., Chile; Col., Columbia; Cz., Czechoslovakia; Cyp., Cyprus; D., Denmark; Ec., Ecuador; Ei., Eire; E.G., East Germany; F., France; Fi., Finland; G., Germany; Gre., Greece; H., Hungary; Ho., Netherlands; I., Italy; L., Luxembourg; M., Mexico; Mal., Malta; N., Norway; P., Portugal; Pol., Poland; R., Rumania; R. of E., Rest of Europe; R. of W., Rest of World; R. of I., Republic of Ireland; S.A., South Africa; S., Sweden; Sp., Spain; Sw., Switzerland; U., Uruguay; U.S., U.S.A.; U.S.S.R., Soviet Union; W.G., West Germany; Y., Yugoslavia. European Championship match v. Northern Ireland in February 1979 is also included in this list of appearances.

A'Court, A (Liverpool), 1958 v. Br, A, USSR (World Cup)
Adcock, H (Leicester City), 1929 v. F, Bel, Sp
Ainsley, G. E (Leeds United), 1939 v. SA
Alderson, J. T (Crystal Palace), 1923 v. F
Allen, A (Stoke City), 1960 v. S
Allen, R (West Bromwich Albion), 1952 v. Sw; 1954 v. Y; 1955 v.
Anderson, S (Sunderland), 1962 v. A
Anderson, V (Nottingham Forest), 1979 v. Cz, S.
Angus, J (Burnley), 1961 v. A
Armfield, J (Blackpool), 1959 v. Br, Peru, M US; 1960 v. Y, Sp, H; 1961 (World Cup) v. L, P, Sp, M, I, A; 1962 v. A, Sw, Peru; (World Cup), v. L, P, H, Arg, Bul, Br; 1963 v. F(2), Br, EG, Sw; 1964 v. R of W; 1966 v. Y, Fi
Armitage, L (Stoke City), 1929 v. SA(2)
Ashmore, G. S. (West Bromwich Albion), 1926 v. Bel
Ashurst, W (Notts County), 1923 v. S(2); 1925 v. Bel
Astall, G (Birmingham City), 1956 v. Fi,
Astle, J (West Bromwich Albion), 1969 v. P; 1970 (World Cup) v. Cz
Aston, J (Manchester United), 1949 v. D, Sw, S, N, F; 1950 v. Ei, I, P, Bel; 1950 (World Cup) v. Ch, US
Atyeo, J (Bristol City), 1956 v. Br, S, Sp; 1967 v. D, R of I(2), H
Bacuzzi, J (Fulham), 1946 v. F†
Bailey, E. F (Tottenham Hotspur), 1950 (World Cup) v. Sp; 1951 v. Y; 1952 v. A(2), Sw
Bailey, H. P (Leicester Fosse), 1908 v. A(2), H, B
Bailey, M (Charlton Athletic), 1964 v. US
Baker, B. H (Everton), 1921 v. Bel
Baker, J (Hibernian), 1960 v. Y, Sp, H; (Arsenal), 1966 v. Sp, Pol
Ball, A (Blackpool), 1956 v. Y, WG, S; 1966 v. Sp, Pol, WG, Fi, D, Pol; (World Cup) v. U, Arg, P, WG; (Everton), 1967 v. Cz, Sp; 1968 v. WG, USSR, Sp, Y; 1969 v. R, P; 1970 v. Bel, Ec, Col; (World Cup), v. R, Br, WG; 1971 v. EG, Mal, Gre; (Arsenal), 1972 v. Sw, Gre, WG(2); 1973 v. W (World Cup), Y, W (World Cup), Sc (centenary match), Cz, Pol; 1975 v. WG, Cyp(2)
Bamber, J (Liverpool), 1920 v. SA(2)
Bamford, H (Bristol Rovers), 1952 v. Aus(5)
Banks, G (Leicester City), 1963 v. Br, Cz, EG; 1964 v. R of W, U, P(2), Arg; 1965 v. H, Y, WG, S; 1966 v. Sp, Pol(2), WG, Y, Fi (World Cup) v. U, M, F, Arg, P, WG; 1967 v. Cz; (Stoke City), 1968 v. USSR, WG, Sp, Y, USSR; 1969 v. R(2), F; 1970 v. H, Ec, Col (World Cup) v. R, Cz, Br; 1971 v. Mal, Gre, Mal; 1972 v. Sw, Gre, WG(2)
Banks, T (Bolton Wanderers), 1958 v. USSR(3), Br, A

Barkas, S (Manchester City), 1936 v. Bel; 1938 v. Cz
Barker, J (Derby County), 1935 v. I, Ho; 1936 v. G, A
Barnes, P (Manchester City), 1978 v. I, WG, Br, H; 1979 v. D, R of I, Cz, NI, Bul Bul, A
Barrett, A. F (Fulham), 1929 v. SA(2)
Barry, L (Leicester City), 1928 v. F, Bel; 1929 v. F, Bel, Sp
Barton, P. A (Birmingham City), 1921 v. Bell 1923 v. F; 1924 v. Bel
Bartram, S (Charlton Athletic), 1950 v. SA; 1952 v. Aus(2)
Bastin, C. S (Arsenal), 1933 v. I, Sw; 1934 v. H, Cz; 1935 v. I; 1936 v. G, A; 1938 v. G, Sw, F
Batten, H. G (Plymouth Argyle), 1952 v. Aus(5)
Baynham, R (Luton Town), 1956 v. D, Sp
Beasley, A (Huddersfield Town), 1939 v. SA(2)
Beattie, K (Ipswich Town), 1975 v. Cyp(2); 1976 v. Sw, P; 1977 v. Fi (World Cup), Ho; 1978 v. L
Bedford, H (Blackpool), 1923 v. S
Bell, C (Manchester City), 1968 v. S; 1969 v. Bul, F, P, Ho (World Cup) v. Cz; 1972 v. Gre, WG(2); 1973 v. W (World Cup), Y, W (World Cup), Sc (centenary match), Cz, Pol; 1974 v. A, Pol, I, Arg, E, G, Bul, Y; 1975 v. Cz, P, WG, Cyp(2); 1976 v. Sw, Cz
Benson, R. W (Sheffield United), 1910 v. SA(3)
Bentley, R. T. F (Chelsea), 1949 v. S; 1959 v. P, Bel (World Cup) v. Ch, US; 1953 v. Bel; 1955 v. G, Sp, P
Beresford, J (Aston Villa), 1934 v. Cz
Berry, A (Everton), 1910 v. SA
Berry, J. J (Manchester United), 1953 v. Arg, Ch, U; 1956 v. S
Betmead, H (Grimsby Town), 1937 v. Fi; 1939 v. SA(2)
Bishop, S. M (Leicester City), 1927 v. Bel, L, F
Blackburn, G. F (Aston Villa), 1924 v. F
Blackburn, W (Oxford University), 1901 v.
Blenkinsop, E (Sheffield Wednesday), 1928 v. F, Bel; 1929 v. F, Bel, Sp; 1930 v. G, A; 1931 v. F, Bel; 1932 v. Sp; 1933 v. A
Blockley, J (Arsenal), 1973 v. Y
Bloomer, S (Derby County), 1901 v.
Blunstone, F (Chelsea), 1955 v. F, P; 1957 v. Y
Bonetti, P (Chelsea), 1966 v. D; 1967 v. Sp, A; 1968 v. Sp; 1969 v. Ho, P (World Cup) v. W
Bowden, E. R (Arsenal), 1935 v. I; 1936 v. A; 1937 v. H
Bower, A. G (Corinthians), 1924-5 v. Bel
Bowles, S (Queens Park Rangers), 1974 v. P; 1977 v. I (World Cup) , Ho
Boyer, P (Norwich City), 1976 v. Wa (centenary)
Boyes, W (West Bromwich Albion), 1935 v. Ho (Everton), 1939 v. R of E
Brabrook, P (Chelsea), 1958 v. USSR; 1960 v. Sp
Bradford, G (Bristol Rovers), 1956 v. D
Bradford, J (Birmingham City), 1925 v. Bel; 1929 v. F, Sp; 1930 v. G, A
Bradley, W (Manchester United), 1959 v. I, US
Bradshaw, F (Sheffield Wednesday), 1908 v. A
Bray, J (Manchester City), 1936 v.
Bridges, B (Chelsea), 1965 v. H, Y; 1966 v. A
Bridgett, A (Sunderland), 1908 v. A(2), H, B; 1909 v. H(2), A
Britton, C. S (Everton), 1935 v. I; 1937 v. H, N, S; 1939 v. SA(3)
Broadbent, P (Wolverhampton Wanderers), 1958 v. USSR; 1959 v. I, Br
Broadis, I. A (Manchester City), 1952 v. A, I; 1953 v. Arg, Ch, U, US; (Newcastle United), 1954 v. H, Y; 1954 (World Cup) v. Bel, Sw, U
Brook, A. K (Corinthians), 1891 v. C
Brook, E. F (Manchester City), 1933 v. Sw; 1934 v. F, H Cz; 1935 v. I; 1937 v. H; 1939 v. SA
Brooking, T (West Ham United), 1974 v. P, Arg, EG, Bul, Y; 1976 v. P, W (centenary), Br, I, Fi (World Cup), I (World Cup), Ho; 1978 v. I, WG, H; 1979 v. D, R of I, NI, Bul S, A

Brooks, J (Tottenham Hotspur), 1975 v. Y, D
Bromilow, T. G (Liverpool), 1923 v. Bel
Broome, F. H (Aston Villa), 1938 v. G, Sw, F; 1939 v. N, I, R, Y; (Notts County), 1952 v. Aus(2)
Brown, A (Charlton Athletic), 1939 v. SA; 1946 v. Belt, Swt
Brown, G (Huddersfield Town), 1927 v. Bel, L, F
Brown, J. H (Sheffield Wednesday), 1927 v. Bel, L, F
Brown, W (West Ham United), 1924 v. Bel
Bruton, J (Burnley), 1928 v. F, Bel
Bryant, W (Clapton Orient), 1925 v. F
Buchan, C. M (Sunderland), 1921 v. Bel; 1923 v. F
Bulcock, J (Crystal Palace), 1910 v. SA(2)
Bullock, N (Bury), 1923 v. Bel
Burgess, H (Sheffield Wednesday), 1931 v. F, Bel
Burgin, E (Sheffield United), 1952 v. Aus(3)
Burrows, H (Sheffield Wednesday), 1934 v. H, Cz; 1935 v. Ho
Butler, J. D (Arsenal), 1925 v. Bel
Byrne, G (Liverpool), 1966 v. N
Byrne, J (West Ham United), 1963 v. Sw; 1964 v. U, P(2), R of I, Br, Arg
Byrne, R. W (Manchester United), 1954 v. H, Y; 1954 (World Cup), v. Bel, Sw, U; 1955 v. G, F, Sp, P; 1956 v. Br, S, Fi, G, D, Sp; 1957 v. Y, D(2), R of I(2); 1958 v. F
Ceasar, W. C (Dulwich Hamlet), 1925 v. Aus(1)
Callaghan, I (Liverpool), 1966 v. Fi (World Cup) v. F; 1978 v. Sw, L
Campbell, A. F (Huddersfield Town), 1932 v. Sp
Camsell, G. H (Middlesbrough), 1929 v. F, Bel; 1934 v. F; 1936 v. G, A, Bel
Carter, H (Sunderland), 1934 v. H; 1936 v. G; 1937 v. H; (Derby County), 1946 v. Swt, Ft; 1947 v. Ei, Ho, F, Sw
Carter, J. H (West Bromwich Albion), 1926 v. Bell; 1929 v. Bel, Sp
Catlin, A. E (Sheffield Wednesday), 1937 v. H, N, S
Chambers, H (Liverpool), 1921 v. Bel; 1923 v. Bel
Chandler, A (Leicester City), 1929 v. SA(3)
Channon, M (Southampton), 1973 v. Y, Sc (centenary), Cz, USSR, I; 1974 v. A, Pol, I, P, Arg, EG, Bul, Y; 1975 v. Cz, P, WG, Cyp(2); 1976 v. Sw, Cz, P, Br, I, Fi, W (centenary); 1977 v. Fi (World Cup), I (World Cup), L (World Cup), Arg, U; 1978 v. Sw
Charlton, J (Leeds United), 1965 v. H, Y, WG, S; 1966 v. A, Sp, Pol, WG, Y, Fi, D, Pol (World Cup) v. U, M, F Arg, P, WG; 1967 v. Cz; 1968 v. WG, Sp; 1969 v. R, F, Ho, P; 1970 v. Ho (World Cup) v. Cz
Charlton, R (Manchester United), 1958 v. P, Y; 1959 v. USSR, I, Br, Peru, M, US; 1960 v. S, Y, Sp, H; 1961 (World Cup) v. L, P, Sp, M, I, A; 1962 v. A, Sw, Peru (World Cup) v. L, P, H, Arg, Bul, Br; 1963 v. F, Br, Cz, EG, Sw; 1964 v. R of W, U, P, R of I, Br, Arg; 1965 v. Ho; 1966 v. A, Sp, Wg, Y, Fi, N, Pol (World Cup) v. U, M, F, Arg, P, WG; 1967 v. Cz; 1968 v. USSR(2), WG, Sp(2), S, Y; 1969 v. R(2), Bul, Ho, P; 1970 v. Ho, Ec, Col (World Cup) v. R, Cz, Br, W
Charlton, S (Exeter City), 1925 v. Aus(5)
Charnley, R (Blackpool), 1963 v. F
Cherry, T (Leeds United), 1976 v. W (centenary), Br, Fi; 1977 v. Ei, I (World Cup), L (World Cup), Br, Arg, U; 1978 v. Sw, L, I, Br; 1979 v. Cz, S
Chilton, A Manchester United), 1952 v. F
Chivers, M (Tottenham Hotspur), 1971 v. Mal, Gre, Mal; 1972 v. Sw, Gre, WG(2); 1973 v. W (World Cup), W (World Cup), Sc (centenary), Cz, Pol, USSR; 1974 v. A, Pol
Clamp, E (Wolverhampton Wanderers), 1958 v. USSR(2), Br, A
Clarke, A (Leeds United), 1970 (World Cup) v. Cz; 1971 v. EG, Mal; 1973 v. Sc (centenary), Cz, Pol, USSR, I; 1974 v. A, Pol, I; 1975 v. P; 1976 v. Cz
Clarke (Portsmouth), 1952 v. Aus(5)
Clayton, R (Blackburn Rovers), 1956 v. Br, S, Fi, G, Sp; 1957 v. Y, D(2), R of I(2); 1958 v. F, P, Y, USSR; 1959 v. USSR, I, Br, Peru, M, US; 1960 v. S, Y

Clemence, R (Liverpool), 1973 v. W (World Cup), W (World Cup); 1974 v. EG, Bul, Y; 1975 v. Cz, P, WG, Cyp; 1976 v. Sw, Cz, P, Br, Fi, W (centenary); 1977 v. Ei, Fi (World Cup), I (World Cup), Ho, L (World Cup), Br, Arg, U; 1978 v. Sw, L, I, WG; 1979 v. D, R of I, NI, Bul, A
Clement, D (Queens Park Rangers), 1976 v. I; 1977 v. I (World Cup), Ho
Clough, B (Middlesbrough), 1960 v. S
Coates, R (Tottenham Hotspur), 1971 v. Mal
Cockburn, H (Manchester United), 1947 v. Ei; 1948 v. I; 1949 v. D, Sw, S; 1951 v. Arg, P; 1952 v. F
Cohen, G (Fulham), 1964 v. U, P, R of I, US, Br; 1965 v. Bel, Ho, H, Y, WG, S; 1966 v. A, Sp, Pol, WG, N, D, Pol (World Cup) v. U, M, F, Arg, P, WG; 1967 v. Cz, Sp
Compton, L (Arsenal), 1951 v. Y

Connelly, J (Burnley), 1960 v. S; 1962 v. A, Sw; (World Cup) v. P; 1963 v. F; (Manchester United), 1965 v. H, Y, S; 1966 v. A, N, D (World Cup) v. U
Coopers, T (Derby County), 1929 v. F, Bel, Sp; 1931 v. F; 1932 v. Sp; 1934 v. H, Cz
Cooper, T (Leeds United), 1969 v. F; 1970 v. Ho, Ec, Col (World Cup) v. R, Cz, Br, WG; 1971 v. EG, Mal; 1972 v. Sw(2); 1975 v. P
Coppell, S (Manchester United), 1978 v. I, WG, Br, H; 1979 v. D, R of I, Cz, NI, Bul, A
Copping, W (Leeds United), 1933 v. I, Sw; 1934 v. F (Arsenal), 1935 v. I; 1936 v. A, Bel; 1937 v. N, S, Fi; 1938 v. Cz; 1939 v. R of E, R

Corbett, W. S (Birmingham), 1908 v. A, H, B
Corrigan, J (Manchester City),, 1978 v. Br
Cotterill, G. H (Old Brightonians), 1891 v. C
Cowan, S (Manchester City), 1926 v. Bel; 1930 v. A; 1931 v. Bel
Crawford, R (Ipswich Town), 1962 v. A
Crayston, W. J (Arsenal), 1936 v. G, A, Bel; 1938 v. Cz
Creek, F. N. S (Corinthians), 1923 v. F
Cresswell, W (Sunderland), 1923 v. F; 1924 v. Bel
Crompton, R (Blackburn Rovers), 1901 v. G; 1908 v. A(2), H, B; 1909 v. H(2), A

Crooks, S. D (Derby County), 1930 v. G, A; 1931 v. F, Bel; 1932 v. Sp, 1933 v. A; 1934 v. F, H, Cz; 1937 v. H
Crowe, C (Wolverhampton Wanderers), 1963 v. F
Cullis, S (Wolverhampton Wanderers), 1938 v. F, Cz; 1939 v. R of E, N, I, R, Y
Cunliff, J. N (Everton), 1936 v. Bel
Cunningham, L (West Bromwich Albion), 1979 v. S, A
Currie, A (Sheffield United), 1973 v. USSR, I; 1974 v. A, Pol, I; 1976 v. Sw; (Leeds United), 1978 v. Br, H; 1979 v. Cz, NI, S
Davies, A. S (Swindon Town), 1920 v. SA(3)
Davies, H. A (Stoke City), 1929 v. SA(2)
Davies, J (Birmingham St. George), 1891 v. C
Davison, J. E (Shefifield Wednesday), 1925 v. Au(3)
Dean, W. R (Everton), 1927 v. F, Bel, L; 1928 v. F, Bel; 1932 v. Sp
Deeley, N (Wolverhampton Wanderers), 1959 v. Br, Peru
Dickinson, J. W (Portsmouth), 1949 v. N, F; 1950 v. Ei, P, Bel (World Cup) v. Ch, US, Sp; 1951 v. Y; 1952 v. A(2), I, Sw; 1953 v. Bel, Arg, Ch, U; 1954 v. F, I, F, A, H(2), Y (World Cup) v. Bel, Sw, U; 1955 v. Sp, P; 1956 v. D, Sp; 1957 v. T, I

Dimmock, J. H (Tottenham Hotspur), 1926 v. Bel
Ditchburn, E. G (Tottenham Hotspur), 1949 v. Sw, S; 1953 v. US; 1957 v. Y, D

Dix, R. W (Derby County), 1939 v. N
Dobson, M (Burnley), 1974 v. P, EG, Bul, Y; 1975 v. Cz
Doggart, A. G (Corinthians), 1924 v. Bel
Dorrell, A. R (Aston Villa), 1925 v. Bel, F

Douglas, B (Blackburn Rovers), 1958 v. F, P, Y, USSR(2), Br, A; 1959 v. USSR; 1960 v. Y, H; 1961 (World Cup) v. L, P, Sp, M, I, A; 1962 v. Peru (World Cup) v. L, P, H, Arg, Bul, Br; 1963 v. Br, Sw
Doyle, M (Manchester City), 1976 v. W (centenary), Br, I; 1977 v. Ho
Drake, E. J (Arsenal), 1935 v. I; 1937 v. H; 1938 v. F
Duckworth, R (Manchester United), 1910 v. SA
Earle, S. G. J (Clapton Orient), 1924 v. F
Eastham, G (Arsenal), 1963 v. Br, Cz, EG; 1964 v. R of W, U, P, R of I, US, Br, Arg; 1965 v. H, WG, S; 1966 v. Sp, Pol, D
Eastham, G. R (Bolton Wanderers), 1935 v. Ho
Eckersley, W (Blackburn Rovers), 1950 (World Cup) v. Sp; 1951 v. Y, Arg, P; 1952 v. A(2), Sw; 1953 v. Arg, Ch, U, US; 1954 v. F(2), I, A, H
Edwards, D (Manchester United), 1955 v. F, Sp, P; 1956 v. Br, S, Fi, G; 1957 v. R of I(2), D(2); 1958 v. F
Edwards, W (Leeds United), 1927 v. F, Bel, L; 1928 v. F, Bel
Elkes, J. E (Tottenham Hotspur), 1925 v. Aus(5)
Ellerington, W (Southampton), 1949 v. N, F
Elliott, W (Burnley), 1952 v. U, A; 1953 v. Bel
Elvy, J. R (Luton Town), 1920 v. SA(3)
Ewer, F. H (Casuals), 1924 v. F; 1925 v. Bel
Fairhurst, D (Newcastle Unityed), 1934 v. F
Fantham, J (Sheffield Wednesday), 1962 (World Cup) v. L
Farnfield, A. S (Casuals), 1901 v.
Fazackerley, S (Sheffield United), 1920 v. SA(2)
Felton, W (Sheffield Wednesday), 1925 v. F
Fenton, E (West Ham United), 1939 v. SA(3)
Fenton, M (Middlesbrough), 1939 v. SA(3)
Finch, L. C (Barnet), 1939 v. SA(2)
Finney, T (Preston North End), 1947 v. Ei, Ho, F, P; 1948 v. Bel, S, I; 1949 v. S, N, F; 1950 v. Ei, I, P, Bel (World Cup) v. Ch, US, Sp; 1951 v. Arg, P; 1952 v. F, I, A, Sw; 1953 v. Bel, Arg, Ch, U, US; 1954 v. H, Y (World Cup) v. Bel, Sw, U; 1955 v. G; 1956 v. D, Sp; 1957 v. Y, D(2), R of I(2); 1958 v. F, P, Y, USSR(2); 1959 v. USSR
Fitchett, J (Bolton Wanderers), 1901 v.
Fleming, H. J (Swindon Town), 1909 v. H(2); 1910 v SA(2)
Flewin, R (Portsmouth), 1952 v. Aus(4)
Flowers, R (Wolverhampton Wanderers), 1955 v. F; 1959 v. I, Br, Peru, US; 1960 v. S, Y, Sp, H; 1961 (World Cup) v. L, P, Sp, M, I, A; 1962 v. A, Sw, Peru (World Cup) v. L, P, H, Arg, Bul, Br; 1963 v. F(2), Sw; 1964 v. R of I, US, P; 1965 v. Ho, WG, N
Fort, J (Millwall), 1921 v. Bel
Foster, R. E (Old Malvernians), 1901 v.
Fox, F. S (Gillingham), 1925 v. S
Francis, G (Queens Park Rangers), 1975 v. Sz, P; 1976 v. Sw, Cz, P, Br, Fi
Francis, T (Birmingham City), 1977 v. Ho, L (World Cup), Br; 1978 v. Sw, L, I, WG, Br, H; (Nottingham Forest), 1979 v. Bul, S, A
Franklin, N (Stoke City), 1946 v. Belt, Swt, Ft; 1947 v. Ei, Ho, F, Sw, P; 1948 v. Bel, S, I; 1949 v. D, Sw, N, F; 1950 v. Ei, I
Froggatt, J (Portsmouth), 1950 v. I; 1952 v. A(2), I, Sw; 1953 v. Bel, US
Froggatt, R (Sheffield Wednesday), 1953 v. Bel, US
Fry, C. B (Corinthians), 1891 v. C
Furness, W (Leeds United), 1933 v. I
Gadsby, K. J (Leeds United), 1939 v. SA
Galley, T (Wolverhampton Wanderers), 1939 v. N, S
Gardner, T (Aston Villa), 1934 v. Cz; 1935 v. Ho
Garrett, T (Blackpool), 1952 v. I
Gay, L. H (Corinthians), 1891 v. C
Gee, C. W (Everton), 1932 v. Sp
Geldard, A (Everton), 1933 v. I, Sw
George, C (Derby County), 1977 v. Ei

George, W (Aston Villa), 1901 v.
Gibbins, W. V. T (Clapton Orient), 1924-5 v. F
Gibbons, A. H (RAF), 1939 v. SA(2)
Gidman, J (Aston Villa), 1977 v. L (World Cup)
Gillard, I (Queens Park Rangers), 1975 v. WG; 1976 v. Cz
Goodall, F. R (Huddersfield Town), 1927 v. F, Bel, L; 1928 v. F, Bel; 1930 v. A; 1931 v. Bel; 1933 v. A, I Sw; 1934 v. F
Gough, H (Sheffield United), 1920 v. SA(2)
Goulden, L. A (West Ham United), 1937 v. N, S; 1938 v. Cz, G, Sw, F; 1939 v. R of E, I, R, Y
Graham, L (Millwall), 1925 v. Aus(5)
Graham, T (Nottingham Forest), 1931 v. F
Grainger, C (Sheffield United), 1956 v. Br, S, Fi,
Greaves, J (Chelsea), 1959 v. Peru, M, US; 1960 v. S, Y, Sp; 1961 (World Cup) v. L, P, S, I, A (Tottenham Hotspur), 1962 v. Sw, Peru; (World Cup) v. H, Arg, Bul, Br; 1963 v. F(2), Br, Cz, Sw; 1964 v. R of W, U, P(2), R of I, Br, Arg; 1965 v. Bel, Ho, H, Y; 1966 v. A, Y, N, D, Pol; (World Cup) v. U, M, F; 1967 v. Sp, A
Green, G. H. (Sheffield United), 1925 v. F; 1926 v. Bel; 1928 v. F, Bel
Greenhoff, B (Manchester United), 1977 v. E, Fi (World Cup), I (World Cup), Ho, Br, Arg, U; 1978 v. Br, H
Grosvenor, T (Birmingham), 1934 v. F
Hagan, J (Sheffield United), 1946 v. F†; 1949 v. D; 1952 v. Aus(3)
Haines, J. T. W. (West Bromwich Albion), 1949 v. Sw
Hales, L (Crewe Alexandra), 1901 v.
Hall, G. W (Tottenham Hotspur), 1934 v. F; 1938 v. Cz; 1939 v. R of I, Y
Hall, J (Birmingham City), 1956 v. Br, S, Fi, G, D, Sp; 1957 v. Y, D(2), R of I(2)
Halse, H. J (Manchester United), 1909 v. A
Hamilton, J (Crystal Palace), 1925 v. Aus(4)
Hampson, J (Blackpool), 1933 v. A
Hancocks, J (Wolverhampton Wanderers), 1949 v. Sw; 1951 v. Y
Hannaford, C (Clapton Orient), 1925 v. Aus(3)
Hannah, J (Norwich City), 1925 v. Aus(4)
Hapgood E (Arsenal), 1933 v. I, Sw; 1934 v. H, Cz; 1935 v. I, Ho; 1936 v. G, A, Bel; 1937 v. Fi; 1938 v. G, Sw, F; 1939 v. R of W, N, I, Y
Hardwick, G. F. M (Middlesbrough), 1946 v. Bel†, Sw†, F†; 1947 v. Ei, Ho, F, Sw, P; 1948 v. Bel, S
Hardy, H (Stockport County), 1924 v. Bel; 1925 v. Aus(2)
Hardy, S (Liverpool), 1909 v. H(2), A
Harris, G (Burnley), 1966 v. Pol
Harris, P. P (Portsmouth), 1950 v. Ei; 1954 v. H
Harrison, A (Nottingham Forest), 1929 v. SA(1)
Harrison, G (Everton), 1921 v. Bel
Harrow, J. H (Chelsea), 1923 v. S
Hart, E (Leeds United), 1929 v. SA(3); 1933 v. A; 1934 v. H, Cz
Hartley, F (Oxford City), 1923 v. F
Harvey, C (Everton), 1971 v. Mal
Hassall, H. W (Huddersfield Town), 1951 v. Arg, P; 1952 v. F
Hawkes, R. M (Luton), 1908 v. A(2), H, B
Haynes, J (Fulham), 1956 v. Br, S, Fi, G, Sp; 1957 v. Y, D, R of I(2); 1958 v. F, P, Y, USSR(3), Br, A; 1959 v. USSR, I, Br, Peru, M, US; 1960 v. Y, Sp, H; 1961 (World Cup) v. L, P, Sp, M, I, A; 1962 v. A, Sw, Peru (World Cup) v. P, H, Arg, Bul, Br
Hedley, G. A (Sheffield United), 1901 v.
Hegan, K. E (The Army), 1923 v. Bel, F; 1924 v. Bel
Hellawell, M (Birmingham City), 1963 v. F
Henry, R (Tottenham Hotspur), 1963 v. F
Henfrey, A. G (Corinthians), 1891 v. C
Hibbert, W (Bury), 1910 v. SA

Hibbs, H (Birmingham), 1929 v. SA(1); 1930 v. A, G; 1932 v. Sp; 1933 v. A Sw; 1934 v. F; 1935 v. Ho; 1936 v.
Hilditch, C. G (Manchester United), 1920 v. SA(3)
Hill, G (Manchester United). 1976 v. I; 1977 v. L (World Cup); 1978 v. Sw, L
Hill, J. H (Burnley and Newcastle United), 1927 v. Bel, F; 1929 v. F, Bel, Sp
Hill, R (Millwall Athletic), 1926 v. Bel
Hillsden, G. R (Chelsea), 1908 v. A, H, B
Hinton, A (Wolverhampton Wanderers), 1963 v. F; (Nottingham Forest), 1965 v. Bel
Hitchins, G (Aston Villa), 1961 v. M, I, A; (Inter Milan), 1962 v. Sw, Peru (World Cup) v. H, Br
Hobbs, H. H. F (Charlton Athletic), 1936 v. A, Bel
Hodkinson, A (Sheffield United), 1957 v. R of I(2), D
Holden, A (Bolton Wanderers), 1959 v. I, Br, Peru, M
Holley, G (Sunderland), 1909 v. H(2), A; 1910 v. SA(3)
Holliday, E (Middlesbrough), 1960 v. S
Hollins, J (Chelsea), 1967 v. Sp
Hopkinson, E (Bolton Wanderers), 1958 v. F, P, Y; 1959 v. I, Br, Peru, M, US
Houghton, W. E (Aston Villa), 1931 v. F, Bel; 1913 v. A
Howe, D (West Bromwich Albion), 1958 v. F, P, Y, USSR(3), Br, A; 1959 v. USSR, I, Br, Peru, M, US; 1960 v. S
Howe, J. R (Derby County), 1948 v. I
Hudson, A (Stoke City), 1975 v. WG, Cyp
Hutton, A. E (West Ham United), 1924 v. Bel; 1929 v. F, Bel, Sp
Hughes, E (Liverpool), 1969 v. Ho, P; 1971 v. EG, Mal, Gre, Mal; 1972 v. Sw, Gre, WG(2); 1973 v. W (World Cup), W (World Cup), Sc (centenary), Pol, USSR, I; 1974 v. A. Pol, I, Arg, EG, Bul, Y; 1975 v. Cz, P; 2977 v. I (World Cup), L (World Cup), Br, Arg, U; 1978 v. Sw, L, I, WG, H; 1979 v. D, R of I, NI, S
Hughes, L (Liverpool), 1950 (World Cup) v. Ch, US, Sp
Hulme, J. H. A (Arsenal), 1927 v. Bel, F
Hunt, G (Tottenham Hotspur), 1933 v. I, Sw
Hunt, R (Liverpool), 1962 v. A; 1963 v. EG; 1964 v. US, P; 1966 v. Sp, Pol, WG, Fi, N, Pol (World Cup) v. U, M, F, Arg, P, WG; 1967 v. Cz, Sp, A; 1968 v. USSR, WG, Sp(2), S, Y, USSR; 1969 v. R(2)
Hunter, N (Leeds United), 1966 v. WG, Y, Fi; 1967 v. A; 1968 v. Sp, S, Y, USSR; 1969 v. R; 1970 v. Ho; 1971 v. Mal; 1972 v. WG(2); 1973 v. W (World Cup), W (World Cup); 1974 v. A, Pol; 1975 v. Cz
Hurst, G (Charlton Athletic), 1952 v. Aus
Hurst, G (West Ham United), 1966 v. WG, Y, Fi, D (World Cup) v. Arg, P, WG; 1967 v. Cz, Sp, A; 1968 v. USSR; 1969 v. R(2), Bul, F, Ho; 1970 v. Bel, Ec, Col (World Cup) v. R, Br, WG; 1971 v. EG, Gre; 1972 v. Sw(2), Gre, W
Iremonger, J (Nottingham Forest), 1901 v.
Jack, D. B. N (Bolton Wanderers), 1928 v. F, Bel (Arsenal), 1930 v. G, A; 1931 v. A
Jackson, G (Everton), 1939 v. SA(3)
Jezzard, B. A. G (Fulham), 1954 v. H
Johnson, D (Ipswich Town), 1976 v. Sw
Johnson, J. A (Stoke City), 1937 v. N, S, Fi
Johnson, T. C. F (Manchester City), 1926 v. Bel (Everton), 1932 v. Sp
Johnson, W. H (Charlton Athletic), 1946 v. Swt, Ft
Johnston, H (Blackpool), 1947 v. Ho; 1953 v. Arg, Ch, US; 1954 v. H
Jones, H (Blackburn Rovers), 1927 v. Bel, L, F
Jones, H (Nottingham Forest), 1923 v. F
Jones, J. E (Everton), 1939 v. SA(2)
Jones, M (Sheffield United), 1965 v. WG, S (Leeds United), 1970 v. Ho
Jones, W. H (Liverpool), 1950 v. P, Bel
Joy, B (Casuals), 1936 v. Bel
Kail, E (Dulwich Hamlet), 1929 v. F, Bel, Sp
Kay, A (Everton), 1963 v. Sw

Kean, F. W (Sheffield Wednesday and Bolton Wanderers), 1923-6 v. Bel; 1927 v. L; 1929 v. F, Sp
Keegan, K (Liverpool), 1973 v. W (World Cup), W (World Cup); 1974 v. Arg, EG, Bul, Y; 1975 v. Cz, WG, Cyp(2); 1976 v. Sw, Cz, P, W (centenary), Br, Fi (World Cup); 1977 v. Ei, Fi (World Cup), I (World Cup), Ho, L (World Cup); (SV Hamburg), Br, Arg, U; 1978 v. Sw, I, WG, Br, H; 1979 v. D, R of I, Cz, NI, Bul, S, A
Keen, E (Derby County), 1933 v. A; 1937 v. H
Keeping, A. E (Southampton), 1929 v. SA(3)
Kelly, R (Huddersfield Town), 1927 v. L
Kennedy, R (Liverpool), 1976 v. W (centenary); 1977 v. L (World Cup); 1978 v. Sw, L
Kevan, D (West Bromwich Albion), 1958 v. P, Y, USSR(3), Br, A; 1959 v. M, US; 1961 v. M
Kieran, L (Tranmere Rovers), 1952 v. Aus
Kirchen, A. L (Arsenal), 1937 v. N, S, Fi
Knowles, C (Tottenham Hotspur), 1968 v. USSR, WG, Sp, S
Labone, B (Everton), 1963 v. F; 1967 v. Sp, A; 1968 v. Sp, S, Y, USSR; 1969 v. R, Bul; 1970 v. Bel, Ec, Col (World Cup) v. R, Br, W
Landels, J (Millwall), 1929 v. SA(1)
Langley, J (Fulham), 1958 v. P, Y
Langton, R (Blackburn Rovers), 1947 v. Ei, Ho, F, Sw (Preston North End), 1948 v. S; 1949 v. D, S (Bolton Wanderers), 1952 v. Aus(4)
Lampard, F (West Ham United), 1973 v. Y
Latchford, D (Everton), 1978 v. I, Br; 1979 v. D, R of I, Cz, NI, Bul, A
Lawler, C (Liverpool), 1971 v. Mal; 1972 v. Sw
Lawton, T (Everton), 1939 v. R of E, N, I, R, Y (Chelsea), 1946 v. Bel†, Sw†, F†; 1947 v. Ei, Ho, F, Sw, P; 1948 v. Bel (Notts County), 1948 v. S, I; 1949 v. D
Leade, A (Small Heath), 1901 v.
Lee, F (Manchester City), 1969 v. Bul, F, Ho, P; 1970 v. Ho, Bel, Ec, Col (World Cup) v. R, Br, WG; 1971 v. EG, Gre, Mal; 1972 v. Sw(2), Gre, W
Leaming, J (Brighton and Hove Albion), 1910 v. SA
Lewis, J. W (Walthamstow Avenue), 1930 v. SA(2)
Lievesley, J (Sheffield United), 1910 v. SA(3)
Lindsay, A (Liverpool), 1974 v. Arg, EG, Bul, Y
Lintott, E. H (Bradford City), 1909 v. H(2)
Lloyd, L (Liverpool), 1972 v. Sw
Lock, F (Charlton Athletic), 1952 v. Aus
Lofthouse, N (Bolton Wanderers), 1951 v. Y; 1952 v. A(2), I, Sw; 1953 v. Bel, Arg, Ch, U, US; 1954 v. F, I, F, A (World Cup) v. Bel, U; 1955 v. F, Sp, P; 1956 v. Sp, D, Fi; 1959 v. USSR
Longworth, E (Liverpool), 1920 v. SA(3); 1921 v. Bel; 1923 v. Bel
Lowe, E (Aston Villa), 1947 v. F, Sw, P
Lucas, T (Liverpool), 1924 v. F; 1926 v. Bel
McCue, J (Stoke City), 1952 v. Aus(4)
McDermott, T (Liverpool), 1978 v. Sw, L; 1979 v. S
Macdonald, M (Newcastle United), 1974 v. P; 1975 v. WG, Cyp(2); 1976 v. Cz, P
McDonald, C (Burnley), 19958 v. USSR(3), Br, A; 1959 v. USSR
McFarland, R (Derby County), 1971 v. Mal, Gre, Mal; 1972 v. Sw, Gre, WG; 1973 v. W (World Cup), W (World Cup), Cz, Pol, USSR, I; 1974 v. A, Pol, I; 1976 v. Cz; 1977 v. Ei, I (World Cup)
McGarry, W. H (Huddersfield Town), 1954 (World Cup) v. Sw, U; 1956 v. D
McGuinness, W (Manchester United), 1959 v. M
McNab, R (Arsenal), 1969 v. Bul, R
McNeil, M (Middlesbrough), 1961 (World Cup) v. L, P, Sp, M, I; 1962 (World Cup) v. L

Madeley, P (Leeds United), 1972 v. Sw(2), Gre, WG(2); 1974 v. Sc (centenary), Cz, Pol, USSR, I; 1974 v. A, Pol, I; 1975 v. Cz, P, Cyp; 1976 v. Cz, P, Fi (World Cup); 1977 v. Ei, Ho
Magee, T (West Bromwich Albion), 1923 v. S; 1925 v. Bel, F
Mahon, J (Huddersfield Town), 1939 v. SA(1)
Male, G. C (Arsenal), 1935 v. I, Ho; 1936 v. G, A, Bel; 1937 v. H, N, S, Fi; 1939 v. I, R, Y
Mannion, W (Middlesbrough), 1947 v. Ei, Ho, F, Sw, P; 1948 v. Bel, S, I; 1949 v. N, F; 1950 v, Ei, P, Bel (World Cup) v. Ch, US; 1951 v. Y; 1952 v. F
Mapson, J (Sunderland), 1930 v. SA(2)
Mariner, P (Ipswich Town), 1978 v. L
Marsden, W (Sheffield Wednesday), 1930 v.
Marsh, R (Manchester City), 1972 v. WG; 1973 v. W (World Cup), Y, W
Marshall, T (Bishop Auckland), 1901 v.
Matthews, R (Coventry City), 1956 v. Br, S,
Matthews, S (Stoke City), 1935 v. I; 1936 v. G; 1938 v. Cz, G, Sw, F; 1940 v. R of E, N, I, Y; (Blackpool), 1946 v. Bel†, Sw†, F†; 1947 v. Sw, P; 1948 v. Bel, I; 1949 v. D, Sw; 1950 (World Cup) v. Sp; 1954 v. F, I, F, A, H (World Cup) v. Bel, U; 1955 v. G, F, .Sp, P; 1956 v. Br; 1957 v. Y, D(2), R of I
Matthews, V (Sheffield United), 1928 v. F, Bel
Medley, L. D (Tottenham Hotspur), 1951 v. Y; 1952 v. F, A
Melia, J (Liverpool), 1963 v. Sw
Mercer, D. W (Hull City and Sheffield United), 1920 v. S, A; 1923 v. Bel
Mercer, J (Everton), 1939 v. I, R, Y; 1946 v. Bel†
Merrick, G (Birmingham City), 1952 v. A(2), I, Sw; 1953 v. Bel, Arg, Ch, U; 1954 v. F, I, F, A, H(2), Y (World Cup) v. Bel, Sw, U
Metcalfe, V (Huddersfield Town), 1951 v. Arg, P
Milburn, J. E. T (Newcastle United), 1949 v. Sw; 1950 v. P, Bel (World Cup) v. Sp; 1951 v. Arg, P; 1952 v. F; 1956 v. D
Milne, G (Liverpool), 1963 v. Br, Cz, EG; 1964 v. R of W,, U, P, R of I, Br, Arg; 1965 v. Bel
Miller, B (Burnley), 1961 v. A
Miller, J. E (Charlton Athletic), 1923 v. S
Mills, G (Chelsea), 1938 v. Cz
Mills, M (Ipswich Town), 1973 v. Y; 1976 v. W (centenary), Br, Fi (World Cup); 1977 v. I (World Cup); 1978 v. WG, Br, H; 1979 v. D, R of I, NI, Bul, A
Milton, C. A (Arsenal), 1952 v. A
Moore, R (West Ham United), 1962 v. Peru (World Cup) v. H, Arg, Bul, Br; 1963 v. F(2), Br, Cz, EG, Sw; 1964 v. R of W, U, P(2), R of I, Br, Arg; 1965 v. Bel, H, Y, WG, S; 1966 v. A, Sp, Pol, WG, N, D, Pol; (World Cup) v. U, M, F, Arg, P, WG; 1967 v. Cz, Sp, A; 1968 v. USSR(2), WG, Sp(2), S, Y; 1969 v. R, Bul, F, Ho, P; 1970 v. Bel, Ec, Col (World Cup) v. R, Cz, Br, WG; 1971 v. EG, Gre, Mal; 1972 v. Sw(2), Gre, WG(2); 1973 v. W (World Cup), Y, W (World Cup), Sc (centenary), Cz, Pol, USSR, I; 1974 v. I
Moore, J (Derby County), 1923 v. S
Moore, W. G. B (West Ham United), 1923 v. S
Morris, J (Derby County), 1949 v. N, F; 1950 v. Ei
Morris, W (Wolverhampton Wanderers), 1939 v. R
Mort, T (Aston Villa), 1924 v. F
Mortensen, S. H (Blackpool), 1947 v. P; 1948 v. Bel, S, I; 1949 v. S, N; 1950 v. I, P, Bel (World Cup) v. Ch, US, Sp; 1951 v. Arg; 1954 v. F, I, F, A, H
Morton, J (West Ham United), 1938 v. Cz
Moss, F (Aston Villa), 1924 v. Bel
Moss, F (Arsenal), 1934 v. H, Cz; 1935 v. ??????
Mozley, B (Derby County), 1950 v. Ei
Mullen, J (Wolverhampton Wanderers), 1946 v. Bel†; 1949 v. N, F; 1950* v. Bel (World Cup) v. Ch, US; 1954 v. F, I, F, A, Y; 1954 (World Cup) v. Sw
Mullery, A (Tottenham Hotspur), 1963 v. Ho; 1967 v. Sp, A; 1968 v. USSR, WG, Sp(2), S, Y; 1969 v. R, Bul, F, Ho, P; 1970 v. Ec, Col (World Cup) v. R, Cz, Br, WG; 1971 v. EG, Mal, Gre; 1972 v. Sw

'6

Neal, P (Liverpool), 1976 v. W (centenary), I; 1977 v. Br, Arg, U; 1978 v. Sw, I, WG, H; 1979 v. D, R of I, NI, Bul, A
Newton, K (Blackburn Rovers), 1966 v. WG; 1967 v. Sp, A; 1968 v. Sp, S, Y; 1969 v. R, Bul, F; (Everton), 1970 v. Ho, Ec, Col (World Cup) v. R, Cz, W
Nicholls, J (West Bromwich Albion), 1954 v. Y
Nicholson, W. E (Tottenham Hotspur), 1951 v P
Nish, D (Derby County), 1974 v. P
Norman, M (Tottenham Hotspur), 1962 v. Peru (World Cup) v. H, Arg, Bul, Br; 1963 v. F, Br, Cz, EG; 1964 v. R of W, U, P(2), US, Br, Arg; 1965 v. Bel, H
Oakes, J (Charlton Athletic), 1939 v. SA
O'Dowd, P (Chelsea), 1963 v. Sw
O'Grady, M (Leeds United), 1969 v. F
Oliver, L (Fulham), 1929 v. Bel
Oldney, B (Aston Villa), 1928 v. F, Bel; 1929 v. SA(2)
Osborne, F. R (Fulham and Tottenham Hotspur), 1923 v. F; 1925–6 v. Bel
Osgood, P (Chelsea), 1970 v. Bel; 1974 v. I
Owen, S (Luton Town), 1952 v. Aus(2); 1954 v. H, Y (World Cup) v. Bel
Page, L. A. A (Burnley), 1927 v. Bel, L, F
Parker, D (West Ham United), 1952 v. Aus(3)
Parker, T. R (Southampton), 1925 v. F
Parkes, P (Queens Park Rangers), 1974 v. P
Parsons, A. W (Clapton Orient), 1901 v.
Patchitt, B. A. C (Corinthians), 1933 v. S(2)
Paine, T (Southampton), 1963 v. Cz, EG; 1964 v. R of W, U, US, P; 1965 v. H, Y, WG, S; 1966 v. A, Y, N (World Cup) v. M
Payne, J (Luton Town), 1937 v. Fi
Peacock, A (Middlesbrough), 1962 (World Cup) v. Arg, Bul
Peacock, J (Middlesbrough), 1929 v. F, Bel, Sp
Pearson, S (Manchester United), 1976 v. Br, Fi (World Cup); 1977 v. Ei, Br, Arg, U; 1978 v. I, W
Pearson, S. G (Manchester United), 1950 v. I; 1951 v. P; 1952 v. I
Pease, W. H (Middlesbrough), 1929 v. SA(2)
Pegg, D (Manchester United), 1957 v. R of I
Pelly, F. R (Old Forester), 1891 v. C
Pejic, M (Stoke City), 1974 v. P
Pennington, J (West Bromwich Albion), 1903 v. A; 1909 v. H(2), A
Pentland, F. B (Middlesbrough), 1909 v. H(2), A
Perry, W (Blackpool), 1956 v. Sp
Peters, M (West Ham United), 1966 v. Y, Fi, Pol (World Cup) v. M, F, Arg, P, WG; 1967 v. Cz; 1968 v. USSR(2), WG, Sp(2), S, Y; 1969 v. R, Bul, F, Ho; 1970 v. Ho, Bel (Tottenham Hotspur), Ec, Col (World Cup) v. R, Cz, Br, WG; 1971 v. EG, Mal, Gre, Mal; 1972 v. Sw, Gre, WG; 1973 v. Sc (centenary), Cz, Pol, USSR, I; 1974 v. A, Pol, I, P
Phillips, L. H (Portsmouth), 1955 v.
Pickering, F (Everton), 1964 v. US; 1965 v. Bel
Plum, S. L (Charlton Athletic), 1923 v. F
Pointer, R (Burnley), 1962 (World Cup) v. L, P
Poynton, C (Tottenham Hotspur), 1925 v. Aus
Price, W. G (Fulham), 1929 v. SA(1)
Pye, J (Notts County), 1946 v. Belt (Wolverhampton Wanderers), 1950 v. Ei
Quixall, A (Sheffield Wednesday), 1954 v. F, I, F, A; 1955 v. Sp, P
Radford, J (Arsenal), 1969 v. R
Raine, J. E (Glossop), 1910 v. SA(2)
Ramsey, A. E (Southampton), 1949 v. Sw (Tottenham Hotspur), 1950 v. I, P, Bel (World Cup) v. Ch, US, Sp; 1951 v. Y, Arg, P; 1952 v. F, A(2), I, Sw; 1953 v. Bel, Arg, Ch, U, US; 1954 v. F, I, F, A, H
Rawlings, A (Preston North End), 1921 v. Bel
Read, A (Tuffnell Park), 1921 v. Bel
Reaney, P (Leeds United), 1971 v. Mal
Revie, D (Manchester City), 1955 v. F; 1956 v. D

Richards, G (Derby County), 1909 v. A; 1910 v. SA(2)
Richardson, J. R (Newcastle United), 1933 v. I, Sw
Richardson, W. G (West Bromwich Albion), 1935 v. Ho
Rigby, A (Blackburn Rovers), 1927 v. Bel, L, F
Rimmer, E. J (Sheffield Wednesday), 1930 v. G, A; 1932 v. Sp
Robb, G (Tottenham Hotspur), 1954 v. H
Roberts, F (Manchester City), 1925 v. Bel, F
Roberts, H (Millwall), 1931 v. Bel
Roberts, W. T (Preston North End), 1924 v. Bel
Robinson, J (Sheffield Wednesday), 1937 v. Fi; 1938 v. G, Sw
Robson, R (West Bromwich Albion), 1958 v. F, USSR(2), Br, A; 1960 v. Sp, H; 1961 (World Cup) v. L, P, Sp, M, I; 1962 v. Sw (World Cup) v. L, P

Rogers, D (Swindon Town), 1920 v. SA
Rowe, A (Tottenham Hotspur), 1934 v. F
Rowley, J. F (Manchester United), 1949 v. Sw, S, F; 1950 v. Ei
Royle, J (Everton), 1971 v. Mal; 1973 v. Y (Manchester City), 1976 v. I; 1977 v. Fi (World Cup), L (World Cup)

Rutherford, J (Newcastle United), 1908 v. A(2), H, B
Ryder, C. F (Old Carthusians), 1901 v.
Sadler, D (Manchester United), 1968 v. USSR; 1971 v. E
Sagar, E (Everton), 1936 v. A, Bel
Scott, L (Arsenal), 1945 v. Belt, Swt; 1947 v. Ei, Ho, F, Sw, P; 1948 v. Bel, S, I; 1949 v. D
Seddon, J (Bolton Wanderers), 1923 v. F, S(2); 1924 v. Bel
Seed, J (Tottenham Hotspur), 1921 v. Bel; 1923 v. Bel; (Sheffield Wednesday), 1929 v. SA(2)

Sewell, J (Sheffield Wednesday), 1952 v. Aus(5), A, Sw; 1954 v. H(2)
Seymour, G. S (Newcastle United), 1925 v. Aus(2)
Shackleton, L. F (Sunderland), 1949 v. D; 1955 v.
Shaw, G (Sheffield United), 1959 v. USSR, I
Shaw, J (Sheffield United), 1952 v. Aus(5)
Shelley, F. A (Southampton), 1929 v. SA(3)
Shellito, K (Chelsea), 1963 v. Cz
Shilton, P (Leicester City), 1971 v. EG; 1972 v. Sw; 1973 v. Y, Sc (centenary), Cz, Pol, USSR, I; 1974 v. A, Pol, I, Arg; 1975 v. Cyp; 1978 v. H; 1979 v. Cz, S, A
Shimwell, E (Blackpool), 1949 v. S
Silcock, J (Manchester United), 1923 v. S
Silett, R. P (Chelsea), 1955 v. F, Sp, P
Silto, W. A (Swindon Town), 1910 v. SA
Simms, E (Stockport County), 1925 v. Aus(5)
Slater, W (Wolverhampton Wanderers), 1955 v. G; 1958 v. P, Y, USSR(3), Br, A; 1959 v. USSR

Smith, G. O (Corinthians), 1901 v.
Smith, J (Bolton Wanderers), 1920 v. SA(3)
Smith, J (Portsmouth), 1932 v. Sp
Smith, J. R (Millwall), 1939 v. N
Smith, L (Brentford), 1939 v. R; (Aston Villa), 1946 v. Swt, Ft
Smith, L (Arsenal), 1953 v. Bel
Smith, R (Tottenham Hotspur), 1961 (World Cup) v. L, P, Sp; 1963 v. F, Br, Cz, EG; 1964 v. R of W

Smith, T (Birmingham City), 1960 v. S
Smith, W (Nottingham Forest), 1891 v. C
Smith, W (Manchester City), 1901 v.
Smith, W (Birmingham City), 1952 v. Aus
Spence, J (Manchester United), 1926 v. Bel
Spencer, C. W (Newcastle United), 1925 v. Aus(5)
Spencer, R (Chelsea), 1936 v. A, Bel

Springett, R (Sheffield Wednesday), 1960 v. Y, Sp, H; 1961 (World Cup) v. L, P, Sp, M, I, A; 1962 v. A, Sw, Peru (World Cup) v. L, P, H, Arg, Bul, Br; 1963 v. F(2), Sw; 1966 v. A, N
Sproston, B (Leeds United), 1938 v. Cz, G, Sw, P (Tottenham Hotspur), 1939 v. R of E; (Manchester City), 1939 v. N
Stainforth, R (Huddersfield Town), 1954 v. H, Y; 1954 (World Cup) v. Bel, Sw, U; 1965 v.
Standborough, M. H (Old Carthusians), 1891 v. C
Steele, F. C (Stoke City), 1937 v. N, S, Fi
Stephenson, G (Derby County), 1928 v. F, Bel (Sheffield Wednesday), 1931 v. F
Stephney, A (Manchester United), 1968 v. S
Stiles, N (Manchester United), 1965 v. H, Y, S; 1966 v. A, Sp, Pol, WG, N, D, Pol; (World Cup) v. U, M, F, Arg, P, WG; 1967 v. Cz; 1968 v. USSR; 1969 v. R
Stoker, L (Birmingham City), 1934 v. H
Storer, H (Derby County), 1924 v. F
Storey, P (Arsenal), 1971 v. Gre; 1972 v. Sw, WG; 1973 v. W (World Cup), Y, W (World Cup), Sc (centenary), Cz, Pol, USSR, I
Storey-Moore, I (Nottingham Forest), 1970 v. Ho
Strange, A. H (Sheffield Wednesday), 1930 v. A, G; 1931 v. F, Bel; 1932 v. Sp; 1933 v. A, I, Sw; 1934 v. F
Sturgess, A (Sheffield United), 1910 v. SA(2)
Summerbee, M (Manchester City), 1968 v. WG, Sp; 1972 v. Sw
Swan, P (Sheffield Wednesday), 1960 v. Y, Sp, H; 1961 (World Cup) v. L, P, Sp, M, I, A; 1962 v. A, Sw (World Cup) v. L, P
Swift, F. V (Manchester City), 1946 v. Swt, Belt; 1947 v. Ei, Ho, F, Sw, P; 1948 v. Bel, S, I; 1949 v. D, N
Talbot, B (Ipswich Town), 1977 v. Br, Arg, U
Tambling, R (Chelsea), 1963 v. F; 1966 v. Y
Tate, J. T (Aston Villa), 1931 v. F, Bel
Taylor, E (Huddersfield Town), 1923 v. Bel; 1924 v. F
Taylor, E (Blackpool), 1954 v. H
Taylor, J. G (Fulham), 1951 v. Arg, P
Taylor, P (Liverpool), 1948 v. S
Taylor, T (Manchester United), 1953 v. Arg, Ch, U; 1954 (World Cup) v. Bel, Sw; 1956 v. Br, S, Fi, G; 1957 v. Y, D($\frac{1}{2}$), R of I(2); 1958 v. F
Temple, D (Everton), 1965 v. W
Thomas, D (Queens Park Rangers), 1975 v. P, Cyp
Thompson, F (Nottingham Forest), 1891 v. C
Thompson, P (Liverpool), 1964 v. P(2), R of I, US, Br, Arg; 1965 v. Bel, Ho
Thompson, P (Liverpool), 1976 v. W (centenary), Br, I, Fi; 1977 v. Fi (World Cup); 1979 v. R of I, Cz, Bul, S, A
Thompson, R (Wolverhampton Wanderers), 1964 v. Us, P, Arg; 1965 v. Bel, Ho
Thompson, W. P (Nottingham Forest), 1929 v. SA(2)
Thornewell, G (Derby County), 1923 v. S(2); 1924–5 v. F
Thwaites, H (Corinthians), 1901 v.
Tilson, C. F (Manchester City), 1934 v. H, Cz
Todd, C (Derby County), 1974 v. P, Arg, EG, Bul, Y; 1975 v. WG, Cyp(2); 1976 v. Sw, Cz, P, Br, Fi (World Cup); 1977 v. Ei, Fi (World Cup)
Topham, A. G (Casuals), 1891 v. C
Towers, T (Sunderland), 1976 v. I
Tresadern, J (West Ham United), 1923 v. S
Tueart, D (Manchester City), 1977 v. Fi (World Cup)
Tunstall, F (Sheffield United), 1924 v. F
Turnbull, R (Bradford), 1920 v. SA(3); (Leeds United), 1920 v. SA(2)
Turner, H (Huddersfield Town), 1931 v. F, Bel
Tweedy, G. J (Grimsby Town), 1937 v. H
Ufton, D. G (Charlton Athletic), 1954 v. F, I, F, A

Urwin, T (Middlesbrough), 1923 v. S(2); 1924 v. Bel
Venables, T (Chelsea), 1965 v. Bel, Ho
Vickers, H (Casuals), 1901 v.
Viollet, D (Manchester United), 1960 v. H; 1962 (World Cup) v. L
Volsey, W (Millwall), 1920 v. SA(3)
Wadsworth, S. J (Huddersfield Town), 1923 v. Bel
Waiters, A (Blackpool), 1964 v. R of I, Br; 1965 v. Bel, Ho
Walker, W. H (Aston Villa), 1923 v. S(2); 1925 v. Bel, F; 1933 v. A
Wall, G (Manchester United), 1910 v. SA(3)
Waller, W. H (Richmond Association), 1901 v.
Walsh, J (Liverpool), 1925 v. Aus(3)
Ward, T. V (Derby County), 1948 v. Bel
Warren, B (Derby County), 1908 v. A(2), H, B; 1909 v. H(2), A
Waring, T (Aston Villa), 1931 v. F, Bel
Watson, D (Sunderland), 1974 v. P, Arg, EG, Bul, Y; 1975 v. Cz, P, WG, Cyp(2); (Manchester City), 1976 v. Sw, P; 1977 v. Ho, L (World Cup), Br, Arg, U; 1978 v. Sw, L, I, WG, Br, H; 1979 v. D, R of I, Cz, NI, Bul, S, A
Watson, V. M (West Ham United), 1930 v. G, A
‡Webster, H (Bolton Wanderers), 1952 v. Aus
Webster, M (Middlesbrough), 1930 v. A,
Wedlock, W (Bristol City), 1903 v. A(2), H, B; 19909 v. H(2), A; 1910 v. SA(3)
Welsh, D (Charlton Athletic), 1933 v. G, Sw; 1939 v. R
West, G (Everton), 1969 v. Bul
Westwood, R. W (Bolton Wanderers), 1935 v. Ho; 1936 v.
Wharton, S. E (Small Heath), 1901 v.
White, T. A (Everton), 1933 v. I
Whitworth, S (Leicester City), 1975 v. WG, Cyp; 1976 v. Sw, P
Whittaker, A (Blackburn Rovers), 1901 v.
Whymark, T (Ipswich Town), 1978 v. L
Wignall, F (Nottingham Forest), 1965 v. Ho
Wilkins, R (Chelsea), 1976 v. I; 1977 v. Ei, Fi (World Cup), Br, Arg, U; 1978 v. Sw, L, I, WG, H; 1979 v. D, R of I, Cz, Bul, S, A
Williamson, E. C (Arsenal), 1923 v. S(2)
Williams, B. F (Wolverhampton Wanderers), 1946 v. Ft; 1949 v. F; 1950 v. Ei, I, P, Bel; 1951 v. Y, Arg, P; 1951 v. Y, Arg, P; 1950 (World Cup) v. Ch, US, Sp; 1952 v. F; 1955 v. G, F, Sp, P
Williams, J. J (Stoke City), 1929 v. SA(2)
Williams, W (West Ham United), 1925 v. Aus(2)
Willingham, C. K (Huddersfield Town), 1937 v. Fi; 1938 v. G, Sw, Fi; 1939 v. R of E, N, I, Y
Willis, A (Tottenham Hotspur), 1952 v. F
Wilshaw, D (Wolverhampton Wanderers), 1954 (World Cup) v. Sw, U; 1955 v. F, Sp, P; 1956 v. Fi,
Wilson, G (Sheffield Wednesday), 1921 v. Bel; 1923 v. Bel; 1924 v. F
Wilson, R (Huddersfield Town), 1960 v. Y, Sp, H; 1962 v. A, Sw, Peru (World Cup) v. P, H, Arg, Bul, Br; 1963 v. F, Br, Cz, EG, Sw; 1964 v. R of W, U, P(2), R of I, Br, Arg (Everton), 1965 v. H, Y, WG, S; 1966 v. A, Sp, Pol(2), Y, Fi, D (World Cup) v. U, M, F, Arg, P, WG; 1967 v. Cz, A; 1968 v. USSR(2), WG, Sp(2), Y
Windridge, J. E (Chelsea), 1908 v. A(2), H, B
Wood, R (Manchester United), 1956 v. Fi
Woodcock, T (Nottingham Forest), 1979 v. R of I, Cz, Bul, S, A
Woodcock, W (Manchester United), 1920 v. SA(2)
Woodhouse, J (Brighton and Hove Albion), 1920 v. SA
Woodley, V (Chelsea), 1937 v. N, S, Fi; 1938 v. Cz, G, Sw, F; 1939 v. R of E, N, I, R, Y
Woodward, V. J (Tottenham Hotspur), 1908 v. A(2), H, B; 1909 v. H(2), A; 1910 v. SA(3)
Wooldridge, W (Wolverhampton Wanderers), 1901 v.
Worthington, F (Leicester City), 1974 v. Arg, EG, Bul, Y; 1975 v. Cz

Worrall, F (Portsmouth), 1935 v. Ho
Wright, D (Newcastle United), 1939 v. N
Wright, T (Everton), 1968 v. USSR; 1969 v. R(2), Ho; 1970 v. Bel (World Cup) v. Br
Wright, W. A (Wolverhampton Wanderers), 1946 v. Bel†, Sw†, F†; 1947 v. Ei, H, F, Sw, P; 1948 v. Bel, S, I; 1949 v. D, Sw, S, N, F; 1950 v. Ei, I, P, Bel (World Cup) v. Ch, US, Sp; 1951 v. Arg; 1952 v. F, A(2), I, Sw; 1953 v. Bel, Arg, Ch, U, US; 1954 v. F, I, F, A, H(2), Y (World Cup) v. Bel, Sw, U; 1955 v. G, F, Sp, P; 1956 v. Br, S, Fi, G, D, Sp; 1957 v. T, D(2), R of I(2); 1958 v. USSR(3), Br, A, F; 1959 v. USSR, I, Br, Peru, M, US
Young, A (Huddersfield Town), 1937 v. H, N, S; 1938 v. G, Sw, F

* Substitute. † Victory International. ‡ Webster acted as substitute for Broome.

EUROPEAN CHAMPIONS' CUP
1978 – 79

LINFIELD 0 LILLESTROM 0
First Round, First Leg in Linfield (6,000), September 13, 1978

Linfield.—Barclay; Fraser, Garrett, Coyle, Rafferty, Dornan, Nixon, Jameson, Martin, Kirk, Murray.

Lillestrom.—Amundsen; Hammer, Birkelund, Kordahl, Berg, Gronlund, Hansen (L), Lonstad, Hansen (V), Lund, Tomteberget.

LILLESTROM 1 LINFIELD 0
First Round, Second Leg in Norway (5,600), September 27, 1978

Lillestrom.—Amundsen; Hammer, Birkelund, Berg, Gronlund, Hansen (Dokken), Lonstad, Hansen (V), Lund, Tomteberget.

Linfield.—Barclay; Fraser, Garrett, Kirk, Rafferty, Dornan, Nixon, Jameson, Martin, Hewitt (Dunlop), Murray.

Scorer: Lillestrom—Lonstad.

Aggregate: Lillestrom 1 Linfield 0

OMONIA 2 BOHEMIANS 1
First Round, Second Leg in Dublin (6,000), September 27, 1978

Scorers: Omonia—Kaharis, Gootokritou. Bohemians—O'Connor (P).

BOHEMIANS 1 OMONIA 0
First Round, Second Leg in Dublin (600), September 27, 1978

Scorer: Bohemians—Joyce.

Aggregate: Omonia 2 Bohemians 2 (Bohemians won on away goals.)

BOHEMIANS 0 DRESDEN 0
Second Round, First Leg in Dublin (6,000), October 18, 1978

DRESDEN 6 BOHEMIANS 0
Second Round, Second Leg in Dresden (33,000), November 1, 1978

Scorers: Dresden—Trautmann 2, Doerner, Schmuck, Riedel (pen), Kotte (pen).

Aggregate: Dresden 6 Bohemians 0

JUVENTUS 1 RANGERS 0
First Round, First Leg in Turin (70,000), September 13, 1978

Juventus. Zoff; Cuccureddu, Cabrini, Furino, Morini, Scirea, Causio, Tardelli, Virdis, Benetti (Fanna), Bettega.

Rangers.—McCloy; Jardine, Forsyth (A), Forsyth (T), Jackson, MacDonald, Miller, Russell, Parlane, Smith, Watson.

Scorer: Juventus—Virdis.

RANGERS 2 JUVENTUS 0
First Round, Second Leg at Ibrox Park (44,000), September 27, 1978

Rangers.—McCloy; Jardine, Forsyth (A), Forsyth (T), Jackson, MacDonald, McLean, Russell, Parlane, Johnstone, Smith.

Juventus.—Zoff; Cuccureddu, Cabrini, Furino (Benetti), Morini, Scirea, Causio, Tardelli (Fanna), Virdis, Gentile, Bettega.

Scorers: Rangers—MacDonald, Smith.

Aggregate: Rangers 2 Juventus 1

RANGERS 0 PSV EINDHOVEN 0
Second Round, First Leg at Ibrox Park (44,000), October 18, 1978

Rangers.—McCloy; Jardine, Forsyth (A), Forsyth (T), Jackson (Miller), MacDonald, McLean, Russell, Parlane (Cooper), Johnstone, Smith.

PSV.—Van Engelen; Deijkers, Stevens, Brandts, Poortvliet, Lubse, Postuma, Willy Van der Kerkhof (Hooyer), Van Kraay, Krigh, Van der Kuylen (Jansen).

PSV EINDHOVEN 2 RANGERS 3
Second Round, Second Leg in Eindhoven (28,000), November 1, 1978

PSV.—Van Engelen; Krijgh (Smits), Stevens, Van Kraay, Brandts, Willy Van der Kerkhof, Jansen, Poortvliet, Rene Van der Kerkhof, Lubse, Deykers.

Rangers.—McCloy; Jardine, Forsyth (A), Forsyth (T), Johnstone, MacDonald, McLean, Russell, Parlane, Smith, Watson.

Scorers: PSV—Lubse, Deykers. Rangers—MacDonald, Johnstone, Russell.

Aggregate: Rangers 3 PSV Eindhoven 2

F.C. COLOGNE 1 RANGERS 0
Quarter-Final, First Leg in Cologne (40,000), March 6, 1979

Cologne.—Schumacher; Konopka, Zimmermann, Schuster, Gerber, Cullmann, Glowacz (Prestin), Elohe, Muller, Neumann, Littbarski.

Rangers.—McCloy; Jardine, Dawson, Forsyth, Jackson, MacDonald, McLean, Russell, Parlane (Urquhart), Smith, Denny (Miller).

Scorer: Cologne—Muller.

RANGERS 1 F.C. COLOGNE 1
Quarter-Final, Second Leg at Ibrox Park (44,000), March 22, 1979

Rangers.—McCloy; Jardine, Dawson (Johnstone), Forsyth, Jackson, MacDonald, McLean, Russell, Urquhart (Parlane), Smith, Cooper.

Cologne.—Schumacher; Konopka, Zimmermann, Strack (Prestin), Gerber, Cullmann, Schuster, Flohe, Muller, Neumann, Van Gool (Glowacz).

Scorers: Rangers—McLean. F.C. Cologne—Muller.

Aggregate: F.C. Cologne 2 Rangers 1

NOTTINGHAM FOREST 2 LIVERPOOL 0
First Round, First Leg in Nottingham (38,316), September 13, 1978

Nottm. For.—Shilton, Anderson, Barrett, McGovern, Lloyd, Burns, Gemmill, Bowyer, Birtles, Woodcock, Robertson.

Liverpool.–Clemence; Neal Kennedy (A), Thompson, Kennedy (R), Hughes, Dalglish, Case, Heighway, McDermott (Johnson), Souness.

Scorers: Nottingham Forest—Birtles, Barrett.

LIVERPOOL 0 NOTTINGHAM FOREST 0
First Round, Second Leg at Anfield (51,679), September 27, 1978

Liverpool.—Clemence; Neal, Kennedy (A), Thompson, Kennedy (R), Hughes, Dalglish, Case (Fairclough), Heighway, McDermott (Johnson), Souness.

Nottm. For.—Shilton; Anderson, Clark, McGovern, Lloyd, Burns, Gemmill, Bowyer, Birtles, Woodcock, Robertson.

Aggregate: Nottingham Forest 2 Liverpool 0

AEK ATHENS 1 NOTTINGHAM FOREST 2
Second Round, First Leg in Athens (35,000), October 18, 1978

AEK.—Stergioudas; Moussouris, Idzoglou (Damlanidas), Ravousis, Nikolaou, Viera, Tassos (Tsamis), Nikoloudis, Vajevic, Ardizoglou, Mavros.

Nottm. For.—Shilton; Anderson, Clark, McGovern, Lloyd, Burns, Bowyer, Gemmill, Birtles, Woodcock, Robertson.

Scorers: AEK—Tassos (pen). Nottingham Forest—McGovern, Birtles.

NOTTINGHAM FOREST 5 AEK ATHENS 1
Second Round, Second Leg in Nottingham (38,069), November 1, 1978

Nottm. For.—Shilton, Anderson, Clark (Mills), O'Hare, Lloyd, Needham, Gemmill, Bowyer, Birtles, Woodcock, Robertson.

AEK.—Christidis; Moussouris, Idzoglou, Ravousis, Nikolaou, Domazos, Tassos, Nikoloudis, Bajevic, Ardizoglou, Mavros.

Scorers: Nottingham Forest—Needham, Woodcock, Anderson, Birtles 2. AEK—Bajevic.

Aggregate: Nottingham Forest 7 AEK Athens 2

NOTTINGHAM FOREST 4 GRASSHOPPERS 1
Quarter-Finals, First Leg in Nottingham (31,949), March 7, 1979

Nottm. For.—Shilton; Anderson, Clark, McGovern, Lloyd, Needham, O'Neill, Gemmill, Birtles, Woodcock, Robertson.

Grasshoppers.—Berbig; Wehrli, Heinz Hermann, Montandon, Hey, Bauer, Meyer, Eigl, Sulser, Ponte, Herbert Hermann.

Scorers: Nottingham Forest—Birtles, Robertson (pen), Gemmill, Lloyd. Grasshoppers—Sulser.

GRASSHOPPERS 1 NOTTINGHAM FOREST 1
Quarter-Finals, Second Leg in Zurich (17,800), March 21, 1979

Grasshoppers.—Berbig; Wehrli, Heinz Hermann, Montandon, Hey, Bauer, Traber, Egli, Sulser, Ponte, Herbert Hermann.

Nottm. For.—Shilton; Anderson, Barrett, McGovern, Lloyd, Needham, O'Neill, Gemmill, Birtles, Woodcock, Robertson.

Scorers: Grasshoppers—Sulser. Nottingham Forest—O'Neill.

Aggregate: Nottingham Forest 5 Grasshoppers 2

NOTTINGHAM FOREST 3 F. C. COLOGNE 3
Semi-Final, First Leg in Nottingham (40,804), April 11, 1979

Nottm. For.—Shilton, Barrett, Bowyer, McGovern, Lloyd, Needham, O'Neill, Gemmill (Clark), Birtles, Woodcock, Robertson.

F. C. Cologne.—Schumacher, Konopka, Zimmermann, Schuster, Gerber Cullmann, Van Gool, Glowacz (Okudera), Muller, Neumann, Prestin.

Scorers: Nottingham Forest—Birtles, Bowyer, Robertson, F. C. Cologne—Van Gool, Muller, Okudera.

F. C. COLOGNE 0 NOTTINGHAM FOREST 1
Semi-Final, Second Leg in Cologne (60,000), April 25, 1979

F. C. Cologne.—Schumacher, Konopka, Zimmermann, Strack, Schuster, Cullmann, Van Gool, Glowacz (Okudera), Muller (Flohe), Neumann, Prestin.

Nottm. For.—Shilton, Anderson, Clark, McGovern, Lloyd, Burns, O'Neill, Bowyer, Birtles, Woodcock, Robertson.

Scorer: Nottingham Forest—Bowyer.

Aggregate: Nottingham Forest 4 F. C. Cologne 3

FINAL

NOTTINGHAM FOREST 1 MALMO 0
In Munich (60,000), May 30, 1979

Nottm. For.—Shilton, Anderson, Clark, McGovern, Lloyd, Burns, Francis, Bowyer, Birtles, Woodcock, Robertson.

Malmo.—Moller, Andersson (R), Erlandsson, Johsson, Andersonn (M), Tapper (Malmberg), Ljungberg, Prytz, Hansson, Cervin, Kindvall.

Scorer: Nottingham Forest—Francis.

EUROPEAN CUP FINALS

1978–79	NOTTINGHAM FOREST 1, MALMO 0 (Munich, 60,000).
1977–78	LIVERPOOL 1, BRUGES 0 (Wembley, 92,000).
1976–77	LIVERPOOL 3, BORUSSIA MOENCHENGLADBACK 1 (Rome, 57,000).
1975–76	BAYERN MUNICH 1, ST. ETIENNE 0 (Glasgow, 54,864).
1974–75	BAYERN MUNICH 2, LEEDS UNITED 0 (Paris, 50,000).
1973–74	BAYERN MUNICH 4, ATLETICO MADRID 0 (after replay) (Brussels, 65,000).
1972–73	AJAX 1, JUVENTUS 0 (Belgrade, 100,000).
1971–72	AJAX 2, INTER MILAN 0 (Rotterdam, 67,000).
1970–71	AJAX 2, PANATHINAIKOS 0 (Wembley, 90,000).
1969–70	FEYENOORD 2, GLASGOW CELTIC 1 (Milan, 50,000).
1968–69	A.C. MILAN 4, AJAX 1 (50,000).
1967–68	MANCHESTER UNITED 4, BENFICA 1 (Wembley, 100,000).
1966–67	GLASGOW CELTIC 2, INTER MILAN 1 (Lisbon, 56,000).
1965–66	REAL MADRID 2, PARTIZAN BELGRADE 1 (Brussels, 55,000).
1964–65	INTER MILAN 1, BENFICA 0 (Milan, 80,000).
1963–64	INTER MILAN 3, REAL MADRID 1 (Vienna, 74,000).
1962–63	A.C. MILAN 2, BENFICA 1 (Wembley, 45,000).
1961–62	BENFICA 5, REAL MADRID 3 (Amsterdam, 65,000).
1960–61	BENFICA 3, BARCELONA 2 (Berne, 28,000).
1959–60	REAL MADRID 7, EINTRACHT FRANKFURT 3 (Glasgow, 135,000).
1958–59	REAL MADRID 2, RHEIMS 0 (Stuttgart, 80,000).
1957–58	REAL MADRID 3, MILAN 2 (after extra time) (Brussels, 67,000).
1956–57	REAL MADRID 2, FIORENTINA 0 (Madrid, 124,000).
1955–56	REAL MADRID 4, RHEIMS 3 (Paris, 38,000).

EUROPEAN CUP-WINNERS CUP 1978 – 79

BEVEREN 3 BALLYMENA 0
First Round, First Leg in Beveren (17,000), September 13, 1978

Beveren.—Pfaff; Jaspers, Buyl, Van Genechten, Baecke, Schoenberger, Hofkens, Cluytens, Stevens, Albert, Janssens.

Ballymena.—Brown; Donald, McCulloch, Jackson, Butcher, Sloan, Simpson, McQuiston, Mullan, McLean, Shaw.

Scorers: Beveren—Albert, Stevens, Schoenberger (pen).

BALLYMENA 0 BEVEREN 3
First Round, Second Leg in Ballymena (4,000), September 27, 1978

Ballymena.—Brown; Donald, Butcher, McCullough, Jackson, Shaw (Spence) McQuiston, McAvoy, Mullan, Simpson, McClean.

Beveren.—Pfaff; Jaspers, Van Genechten, Buyl, Baecke, Hofkens, Schoenberger, Albert (Truyens), Stevens (Wissman), Cluytens, Janssens.

Scorers: Beveren—Janssens 2, Wissman.

Aggregate: Beveren 6 Ballymena 0

RIJEKA 3 WREXHAM 0
First Round, First Leg in Yugoslavia (9,000), September 13, 1978

Rijeka.—Auramovic (Ravnic); Makin, Hrstic, Cukrov, Radin, Juricic, Durkalic, Fegic (Bursdc), Tomic, Ruzik, Desnica.

Wrexham.—Davies; Hill, Whittle, Davis, Roberts, Thomas, Shinton, Sutton, McNeil (Williams), Lyons, Cartwright.

Scorers: Rijeka—Tomic, Durkalic, Cukrov.

WREXHAM 2 RIJEKA 0
First Round, Second Leg at Wrexham (10,469), September 27, 1978

Wrexham.—Davies; Hill, Whittle, Davis, Cegielski, Thomas, Shinton, Sutton, McNeil, Williams, Cartwright.

Rijeka.—Avramovic; Makin, Hristic, Cukrov, Radin, Juricic, Durkalic, Desnica, Fegic, Tomic, Ruzic.

Scorers: Wrexham—McNeil, Cartwright.

Aggregate: Rijeka 3 Wrexham 2

SHAMROCK ROVERS 2 APOEL 0
First Round, First Leg in Dublin (5,000), September 13, 1978

Scorers: Shamrock Rovers—Giles, Lynex.

APOEL 0 SHAMROCK ROVERS 1
First Round, Second Leg in Cyprus (15,000), September 27, 1978

Aggregate: Shamrock Rovers 3 Apoel 0

BANIK 3 SHAMROCK ROVERS 0
Second Round, First Leg in Czechoslovakia (12,000), October 18, 1978

Scorers: Banik—Knapp, Radimec, Rygel.

SHAMROCK ROVERS 1 BANIK 3
Second Round, Second Leg in Dublin (5,000), November 1, 1978

Scorers: Shamrock Rovers—Giles. Banik—Licka 2, Albrecht.

Aggregate: Banik 6 Shamrock Rovers 1

MAREK STANKE DIMITROV 3 ABERDEEN 2
First Round, First Leg in Bulgaria (20,000), September 13, 1978

Marek.—Stoyanov; Sevdin, Kolev, Karakolev, Palev, Rainov, Pargov, Tomov, Petrov (I), Ventislav, Petrov (V).

Aberdeen.—Leighton; Kennedy, McLelland, McMaster, Garner (Rouvvie), Miller, Sullivan, Jarvie, Harper, Archibald, Scanlon.

Scorers: Marek—Petrov (V), Petrov (I) 2. Aberdeen—Jarvie, Harper.

ABERDEEN 3 MAREK STANKE DIMITROV 0
First Round, Second Leg at Pittodrie Park (25,000), September 27, 1978

Aberdeen.—Leighton; Kennedy, McLelland, McMaster, McLeish, Miller, Sullivan (Strachan), Archibald, Harper, Jarvie, Scanlon.

Marek.—Stoinov; Sevdin, Kolev, Karakolev, Palev, Rainov, Pargov (Brankov), Tomov, Petrov (I), Petrov (V), Dimitrov.

Scorers: Aberdeen—Strachan, Jarvie, Harper.

Aggregate: Aberdeen 5 Marek Stanke Dimitrov 3

FORTUNA DUSSELDORF 3 ABERDEEN 0
Second Round, First Leg in Dusseldorf (10,500), October 18, 1978

Fortuna.—Woyke; Brei, Zewe, Zimmermann, Baltes, Kohnen, Gunther, Schmitz, Weikl, Allofs, Seel.

Aberdeen.—Leighton; Kennedy, McLeish, Miller, McLelland, Rougvie, McMaster (Scanlon), Jarvie (Strachan), Sullivan, Archibald, Harper.

Scorers: Fortuna Dusseldorf—Gunther 2, Zimmermann.

ABERDEEN 2 FORTUNA DUSSELDORF 0
Second Round, Second Leg at Pittodrie Park (16,800), November 1, 1978

Aberdeen.—Clark; Rougvie, McLelland, McMaster, McLeish, Miller, Sullivan, Archibald, Harper, Jarvie, Strachan.

Fortuna.—Woyke; Brei, Zewe, Zimmermann, Baltes, Kohnen, Wael, Lund, Gunther, Allofs, Seel.

Scorers: Aberdeen—McLelland, Jarvie.

Aggregate: Fortuna Dusseldorf 3 Aberdeen 2

AZ 67 0 IPSWICH TOWN 0
First Round, First Leg in Holland (18,000), September 13, 1978

AZ 67.—Meskovic; Arntz, Spelbos, Metgod, Van Rijnsoever (Tol), Peters, Ressel, Van Hanegem, Kist, Nygaard (HovenKamp), De Graaf.

Ipswich.—Cooper; Burley, Osman, Beattie, Tibbott, Talbot, Wark, Mills, Mariner, Whymark (Geddis), Woods.

IPSWICH TOWN 2 AZ 67 0
First Round, Second Leg at Portman Road (23,814), September 27, 1978

Ipswich.—Cooper; Burley, Tibbott, Talbot, Osman, Beattie, Mills, Wark, Mariner, Whymark, Woods.

AZ 67.—Vooys; Van Rijnsoever, Spelbos, Metgod, Hovenkamp, Peters, Ressel, Van Hanegam, Kist, Arntz, De Graaf (Nygaard).

Scorers: Ipswich Town—Mariner, Wark (pen).

Aggregate: Ipswich Town 2 AZ 67 0

IPSWICH TOWN 1 SW INNSBRUCK 0
Second Round, First Leg at Portman Road (20,394), October 18, 1978

Ipswich.—Cooper, Burley, Tibbott, Talbot, Hunter, Osman, Mills, Wark, Mariner (Geddis), Whymark, Woods.

SW Innsbruck.—Freidl Koncilia; Zanon, Auer, Silkio, Werner Schwarz (Gartner), Hanschitz, Scharman, Peter Koncilia, Oberacher, Hickersberger, Braschler (Wolfgang Schwarz).

Scorer: Ipswich Town—Wark (pen).

SW INNSBRUCK 1 IPSWICH TOWN 1
Second Round, Second Leg in Innsbruck (18,000), November 1, 1978

SW Innsbruck.—Freidl Koncilia; Zanon, Forstinger, Auer, Sikic (Muller), Hanschitz, Scharmann, Peter Koncilia, Hickersberger, Oberacher (Wolfgang Schwarz), Braschler.

Ipswich.—Cooper; Burley, Tibbott, Talbot, Hunter, Osman, Mills, Wark, Mariner, Geddis (Whymark), Woods (Gates).

Scorers: SW Innsbruck—Oberacher. Ipswich Town—Burley.

Aggregate: Ipswich Town 2 SW Innsbruck 1

IPSWICH TOWN 2 BARCELONA 1
Quarter-Final, First Leg at Portman Road (28,000), March 7, 1979

Ipswich.—Cooper; Burley, Tibbott, Mills, Osman, Butcher, Wark, Muhren, Brazil, Gates, Geddis (Hunter).

Barcelona.—Artola; Zuviria, Migueli, Olmo, De la Cruz, Neeskens (Costas), Vigo, Heredia, Krankl, Asensi, Martinez.

Scorers: Ipswich Town—Gates 2. Barcelona—Vigo.

BARCELONA 1 IPSWICH TOWN 0
Quarter-Final, Second Leg in Barcelona (110,000), March 21, 1979

Barcelona.—Artola; Zuviria, Migueli, Olmo, Albaladejo, Asensi, Neeskens, Martinez, Rexach, Krankl, Heredia.

Ipswich.—Cooper; Burley, Osman, Butcher, Beattie, Wark (Parkin), Muhren, Mills, Gates (Geddis), Brazil, Woods.

Scorer: Barcelona—Migueli.

Aggregate: Barcelona 2 Ipswich Town 2 (Barcelona win on away goal.)

FINAL

BARCELONA 4 FORTUNA DUSSELDORF 3
In Berne, May 16, 1979, (after extra-time)

EUROPEAN CUP–WINNERS' CUP FINALS

1979—BARCELONA BEAT FORTUNA DUSSELDORF (4–3)
1978—ANDERLECHT BEAT FK AUSTRIA (4–0)
1977—SV HAMBURG BEAT ANDERLECHT (2–0)
1976—ANDERLECHT BEAT WEST HAM UNITED (4–2)
1975—DINAMO KIEV BEAT FERENCVAROS (3–0)

1974—MAGDEBORG BEAR A.C. MILAN (2–0)
1973—A.C. MILAN BEAT LEEDS UNITED (1–0)
1972—GLASGOW RANGERS BEAT MOSCOW DYNAMO (3–2)
1971—CHELSEA BEAT REAL MADRID (2–1 after 1–1)
1970—MANCHESTER CITY BEAT GORNIK ZABRZE (2–1)
1969—SLOVAN BRATISLAVA BEAT BARCELONA (3–2)
1968—A.C. MILAN BEAT S.V. HAMBURG (2–0)
1967—BAYERN MUNICH BEAT GLASGOW RANGERS (1–0)
1966—BORUSSIA DORTMUND BEAT LIVERPOOL (2–1)
1965—WEST HAM UNITED BEAT MUNICH (2–0)
1964—SPORTING LISBON BEAT MTK BUDAPEST (1–0 after 3–3)
1963—TOTTENHAM HOTSPUR BEAT ATLETICO MADRID (5–1)
1962—ATLETICO MADRID BEAT FLORENTINA (3–0 after 1–1)
1961—FLORENTINA BEAT GLASGOW RANGERS (4–1 on agg.)

UEFA CUP 1978–79

STANDARD LIEGE 1 DUNDEE UNITED 0
First Round, First Leg in Ghent (18,000), September 12, 1978

Liege.—Preud'homme; Gerets, Plessers, Garot, Poel, Labarbe, Denier, Graf, Wellens, Sigurvinsson, Marechal (Onal).

Dundee U.—McAlpine; Kirkwood, Kopel, Robinson, Hegarty, Narey, Smith, Addison, Sturrock (Dodds), Holt, Payne (Frye).

Scorer: Standard Liege—Denier.

DUNDEE UNITED 0 STANDARD LIEGE 0
First Round, Second Leg at Tannadice Park (9,500), September 27, 1978

Dundee U.—McAlpine; Stewart, Kopel, Holt, Hegarty, Narey, Smith, Addison (Fleming), Payne, Sturrock, Dodds.

Liege.—Preud'homme; Gerets, Renquin, Garot, Poel, Labarbe, Denier, Graf, Wellens, Sigurvinsson, De Matos.

Aggregate: Standard Liege 1 Dundee United 0

IBV VESTMANN 0 GLENTORAN 0
First Round, First Leg in Iceland (1,000), September 5, 1978

IBV.—Sveinsson (A); Oskarsson, Fropjofsson, Hallgrimsson, Finnbogasson, Sveinsson (S), Sigporsson, Valrysson, Porleifsson, Palsson, Baldvinsson.

Glentoran.—Matthews; Dougan, McFall (R), Porter, Cranston, Moreland, Caskey (J), Jamison, Caskey (W), McFall (G), O'Neill.

GLENTORAN 1 IBV VESTMANN 1
First Round, Second Leg in Glentoran (5,000), September 14, 1978

Glentoran.—Matthews; Dougan, McFall (R), Porter, Cranston, Moreland, Caskey (J), Jamison, Caskey (W), McFall (G), O'Neill.

IBV.—Sveinsson (A); Oskarsson, Fropjofsson, Hallgrimsson, Finnbogasson, Sviensson (S), Sigporsson, Valrysson, Porleifsson (Earlingsson), Palsson (Porsteinsson), Baldvinsson.

Scorers: Glentoran—Caskey (W). IBV Vestmann—Oskarsson.

Aggregate: IBV Vestmann 1 Glentoran 1 (IBV Vestmann win on away goal.)

FINN HARPS 0 EVERTON 5
First Round, First Leg in Eire (5,000), September 12, 1978

Finn.—Mahon (Harper); McDowell, Hutton, O'Docherty, Sheridan, Healy Logan, Minnock, McGuinness (Stephenson), Duffy, Ferry.

Everton.—Wood; Darracott, Pejic, Lyons (Higgins), Wright, Nulty, King, Ross, Latchford, Walsh, Thomas.

Scorers: Everton—Thomas, King 2, Latchford, Walsh.

EVERTON 5 FINN HARPS 0
First Round, Second Leg at Goodison Park (21,611), September 26, 1978

Everton.—Wood; Darracott, Pejic, Lyons (Higgins), Wright, Ross, King, Dobson, Latchford, Walsh, Thomas (Robinson).

Finn.—Harper (Mahon); McDowell, Hutton, O'Doherty (T), Sheridan, McGuiness (P), Logan, Healy (F), McGuiness (T), Ferry, Minnock.

Scorers: Everton—King, Latchford, Walsh, Ross, Dobson.

Aggregate: Everton 10 Finn Harps 0

EVERTON 2 DUKLA PRAGUE 1
Second Round, First Leg at Goodison Park (32,857), October 18, 1978

Everton.—Wood; Darracott (Robinson), Pejic, Lyons, Wright, Ross, King, Dobson, Latchford, Walsh, Thomas.

Dukla.—Stromsik; Barmos, Macela, Samek, Fiala, Rott, Peic (Bilsky), Novac, Stambacher, Nethoda, Gajdusek.

Scorers: Everton—Latchford, King. Dukla—Macela.

DUKLA PRAGUE 1 EVERTON 0
Second Round, Second Leg in Prague (35,000), November 1, 1978

Dukla.—Stromsik; Macela, Samek, Novak, Barmos, Peic (Berger), Vizek, Bilsky, Nehoda, Gajdusek, Stambacher.

Everton.—Wood; Darracott, Pejic, Kenyon, Wright, Nulty (King), Ross, Dobson, Latchford, Walsh, Thomas.

Scorer: Dukla Prague—Gajdusek.

Aggregate: Dukla Prague 2 Everton 2 (Dukla Prague win on away goal.)

HIBERNIAN 3 NORRKOPING 2
First Round, First Leg at Easter Road (10,000), September 13, 1978

Hibs.—McDonald; Duncan, Smith, Rae, Fleming, McNamara, Murray, McLeod, Higgins, Carroll (Hutchinson), Temperley.

Norrkoping.—Jonsson; Eek, Andersson, Fredriksson, Ohlsson, Bernsten, Eriksson, Lundqvist, Liljedahl, Svensson (Helberg), Larsson.

Scorers: Hibernian—Higgins 2, Temperley. Norrkoping—Ohisson, Andersson.

NORRKOPING 0 HIBERNIAN 0
First Round, Second Leg in Sweden (1,300), September 27, 1978

Norrkoping.—Johnson; Eek, Andersson, Fredriksson, Bernsten, Eriksson, Lundqvist, Liljedahl, Ohlsson, Svensson, Larsson.

Hibs.—McDonald; Duncan, Smith, Rae, Fleming, McNamara, McLeod, Higgins, Stewart, Hutchinson, Bremner.

Aggregate: Hibernian 3 Norrkoping 2

STRASBOURG 2 HIBERNIAN 0
Second Round, First Leg in France (25,000), October 18, 1978

Strasbourg.—Dropsy; Marx (Deutschmann), Specht, Novi, Domenech, Jouve (Ehrlacher), Dugueperoux, Piasecki, Wagner, Tanter, Gemmrich.

Hibs.—McDonald; Duncan, Stewart, McNamara, Smith, Bremner, McLeod, Campbell, Rae, Hutchinson, Higgins.

Scorers: Strasbourg—Gemmrich, Piasecki (pen).

HIBERNIAN 1 STRASBOURG 0
Second Round, Second Leg at Easter Road (14,662), November 1, 1978

Hibs.—McDonald; Duncan, Smith, Bremner, Stewart, McNamara, Rae, McLeod, Hutchinson, Higgins, Murray.

Strasbourg.—Dropsy; Marx, Domenech, Specht, Novi, Dugueperoux, Tanter, Piasecki, Wagner, Gemmrich, Deutschmann.

Scorer: **Hibernian—McLeod (pen).**

Aggregate: Strasbourg 2 Hibernian 1

ARSENAL 3 LOKOMOTIVE LEIPZIG 0
First Round, First Leg at Highbury (34,233), September 13, 1978

Arsenal.—Jennings; Rice, Nelson, Price, Walford, Young, Brady (Gatting), Sunderland, Stapleton, Harvey (Heeley), Rix.

Leipzig.—Stotzner; Sekora (Roth), Hammer, Grobner, Fritsche, Altmann, Moldt, Liebers, Kinne, Lowe (Eichhorn), Kuhn.

Scorers: Arsenal—Stapleton 2, Sunderland.

LOKOMOTIVE LEIPZIG 1 ARSENAL 4
First Round, Second Leg in Leipzig (22,000), September 27, 1978

Leipzig.—Stotzner; Hammer, Grobner, Fritsche, Moldt, Kinne, Kuhn, Dennstedt, Baum (Altmann), Eichhorn, Liebers.

Arsenal. Jennings; Rice, Nelson, Price (Vaessen), O'Leary, Young (Walford), Brady, Sunderland, Stapleton, Devine, Rix.

Scorers: Leipzig—Stapleton (o.g.). Arsenal—Brady, Stapleton 2, Sunderland.

Aggregate: Arsenal 7 Lokomotive Leipzig 1

HAJDUK SPLIT 2 ARSENAL 1
Second Round, First Leg in Yugoslavia (30,000), October 18, 1978

Hajduk.—Cosic; Primorac, Krsticeaic (Maricic), Jovanic, Peruzociv, Rozic, Zungul, Musinic, Cop (Vujovic), Djordjevic, Surjak.

Arsenal.—Jennings; Rice, Nelson, Price, O'Leary, Young, Brady, Kosmina, Stapleton, Heeley, Rix.

Scorers: Hajduk Split—Cop, Djordjevic. Arsenal—Brady.

ARSENAL 1 HAJDUK SPLIT 0
Second Round, Second Leg at Highbury (41,787), November 1, 1978

Arsenal.—Jennings; Rice, Nelson, Price, O'Leary, Young, Brady, Gatting, Stapleton, Heeley (Kosmina), Rix.

Hajduk.—Budincevic; Primorac, Krsticevic, Luketin (Cop), Pruzovic, Rozic, Zungul, Muzinic, Jovanic, Djordjevic, Surjak.

Scorer: Arsenal—Young.

Aggregate: Arsenal 2 Hajduk Split 2 (Arsenal win on away goal.)

RED STAR BELGRADE 1 ARSENAL 0
Third Round, First Leg in Yugoslavia (50,000), November 22, 1978

Red Star.—Stojanovic; Jovanovic, Jovin, Muslin, Keri, Jurisic, Petrovic, Blagojevic (Milosajlievic), Savic, Sestic, Lukic (Simic).

Arsenal.—Jennings; Rice, Nelson, Price, O'Leary, Young, Heeley, Sunderland, Stapleton, Walford, Rix.

Scorer: Red Star—Blagojevic.

ARSENAL 1 RED STAR BELGRADE 1
Third Round, Second Leg at Highbury (41,566), December 6, 1978

Arsenal.—Jennings; Rice, Nelson, Price, O'Leary, Young, Heeley (Kosmina), Gatting, Stapleton, Sunderland, Rix (Macdonald).

Red Star.—Stoyanovic; Jovanovic, Krmpotic, Muslin, Keri, Jurisic, Petrovic, Blagojevic, Savic, Milosavljevic, Boronika.

Scorers: Arsenal—Sunderland. Red Star—Savic.

Aggregate: Red Star Belgrade 2 Arsenal 1

GALATASARAY 1 W.B.A. 3
First Round, First Leg in Turkey (50,000), September 13, 1978

Galatasaray.—Eser; Mufit, Erdogan, Gungor, Fatih, Mehmet, Oner, Ali, Cuneyt, Gokmen, Tuncay.

W.B.A.—Godden; Batson, Statham, Cunningham, Wile, Robertson, Robson, Brown (A), Regis, Trewick, Cantello.

Scorers: Galatasaray—Fatih (pen). W.B.A.—Robson, Regis, Cunningham.

W.B.A. 3 GALATASARAY 1
First Round, Second Leg at The Hawthorns (22,380), September 27, 1978

W.B.A.—Godden (Grew); Batson, Statham, Trewick (Brown, T), Wile, Robertson, Robson, Brown (A), Regis, Cantello, Cunningham.

Galatasaray.—Bahatin, Mufit, Erdogan, Gungor, Tuncay, Fatih, Oner, Gurcan, Cuneyt, Tacettin, Turgay.

Scorers: W.B.A.—Robson, Cunningham (pen), Trewick. Galatasaray—Turgay.

Aggregate: W.B.A. 6 Galatasaray 2

SPORTING BRAGA 0 W.B.A. 2
Second Round, First Leg in Portugal (20,000), October 18, 1978

Braga.—Conhe Artur; Fernando, Serra, Cardoso,, Paulo, Rocha, Jose Artur, Rodrigo, Chico Faria, Lito, Nelinho.

W.B.A.—Godden; Batson, Statham, Cunningham, Wile, Robertson, Robson, Brown (A), Regis, Cantello, Brown (T).

Scorer: W.B.A.—Regis 2.

W.B.A. 1 SPORTING BRAGA 0
Second Round, Second Leg at The Hawthorns (26,019), November 1, 1978

W.B.A.—Godden; Batson, Statham, Cunningham, Wile, Robertson, Robson (Trewick), Brown (A), Regis, Cantello (Martin), Brown (T).

Braga.—Cohne; Correira, Serra, Cardoso, Bilala (Mendes), Paulo Rocha, Jose Artur, Garcia (Fontes), Chico Faria, Lito, Nelinho.

Scorer: W.B.A.—Brown (A).

Aggregate: W.B.A. 3 Sporting Braga 0

VALENCIA 1 W.B.A. 1
Third Round, First Leg in Spain (50,000), November 22, 1978

Valencia.—Pereira; Cervero, Castellano, Arias, Botubot, Cabral, Saura, Bonhof, Felman, Solsona, Kempes.

W.B.A.—Godden; Batson, Statham, Trewick, Wile, Robertson, Robson, Brown (A), Regis, Cantello, Cunningham.

Scorers: Valencia—Felman. W.B.A.—Cunningham.

W.B.A 2 VALENCIA 0
Third Round, Second Leg at The Hawthorns (38,000), December 6, 1978

W.B.A.—Godden; Batson, Statham, Brown (T), Wile, Robertson, Robson, Brown (A), Regis, Cantello (Trewick), Cunningham.

Valencia.—Manzadedo; Carrette, Cordero, Arias, Botubot, Bonhof, Saura, Cabral, Kempes, Solsona, Felman (Diarte).

Scorers: W.B.A—Brown (T), 2 (1 pen).

Aggregate: W.B.A. 3 Valencia 1

RED STAR BELGRADE 1 W.B.A. 0
Quarter-Final, First Leg in Yugoslavia (95,000), March 7, 1979

Red Star.—Stojanovic; Jovanovic, Krmpotic, Muslin, miletovic, Jurisic, Petrovic (Milosauljevic), Blagojevic, Savic, Milovanovic, Sestic (Simic).

W.B.A.—Godden; Batson, Statham, Trewick, Wile, Robertson, Robson, Brown (A), Regis, Brown (T), Cunningham.

Scorer: Red Star Belgrade—Savic.

W.B.A. 1 RED STAR BELGRADE 1
Quarter-Final, Second Leg at The Hawthorns (31,110), March 21, 1979

W.B.A.—Godden; Batson, Statham, Brown (T), Wile, Robertson, Robson, Brown (A), Regis, Cantello, Cunningham.

Red Star.—Stojanovic; Jovanovic, Krmpotic, Muslin, Jurisic, Jelikic, Sestic, Blagojevic, Savic, Borovnica, Milosavljevic.

Scorers: W.B.A.—Regis. Red Star Belgrade—Sestic.

Aggregate: Red Star Belgrade 2 W.B.A. 1

TWENTE ENSCHEDE 1 MANCHESTER CITY 1
First Round, First Leg in Holland (12,000), September 13, 1978

Twente.—Pasveer; Van Ierssel, Drost, Overweg, Wildschut, Thijssen, Van der Vall, Otto, Bos (Smard), Gritter, Thoresen.

Man. C.—Corrigan; Clements, Power, Viljoen, Watson, Futcher (P), Channon, Owen, Palmer, Hartford, Barnes.

Scorers: Twente—Thoresen. Manchester City—Watson.

MANCHESTER CITY 3 TWENTE ENSCHEDE 2
First Round, Second Leg at Maine Road (29,330), September 27, 1978

Man. C.—Corrigan; Clements, Power, Viljoen (Bell), Watson, Futcher (P), Channon, Owen, Kidd, Hartford, Barnes.

Twente.—Pasveer; Van Ierssel, Overweg, Drost, Wildschut, Thijssen, Van der Vall, Pahlplatz, Gritter, Bos (Bruggnink), Thoresen.

Scorers: Manchester City—Wildschut (o.g.), Kidd, Bell. Twente—Overweg, Gritter.

Aggregate: Manchester City 4 Twente Enschede 3

MANCHESTER CITY 4 STANDARD LIEGE 0
Second Round, First Leg at Maine Road (27,498), October 18, 1978

Man. C.—Corrigan; Clements, Donachie, Booth, Watson, Viljoen (Keegan), Palmer, Bell, Kidd, Hartford, Barnes.

Liege.—Preud'homme; Gerets, Renquin, Garot, Poel, Onal, Denier, Graf, Wellens, Sigurvinsson, de Matos.

Scorers: Manchester City—Hartford, Kidd 2 (1 pen), Palmer.

STANDARD LIEGE 2 MANCHESTER CITY 0
Second Round, Second Leg in Liege (30,000), November 1, 1978

Liege.—Preud'homme; Gerets, Renquin, Garot, Poel, Labarbe, Onal, Graf, Wellens (Denier), Sigurvinsson, De Matos (Plessers).

Man. C.—Corrigan; Clements, Conachie, Booth, Watson, Owen, Channon, Bell, Kidd, Hartford, Palmer.

Scorers: Standard Liege—Sigurvinsson 2 (1 pen).

Aggregate: Manchester City 4 Standard Liege 2

AC MILAN 2 MANCHESTER CITY 2
Third Round, First Leg in Milan (40,000), November 23, 1978

AC Milan.—Albertosi; Collovati, Maldera, De Vecchi, Bet, Baresi, Buriani, Bigon, Novellino, Rivera, Chiodi.

Man. C.—Corrigan; Clements, Donachie, Booth, Watson, Power, Viljoen (Keegan), Bell, Kidd, Hartford, Palmer.

Scorers: AC Milan—Bigon 2. Manchester City—Kidd, Power.

MANCHESTER CITY 3 AC MILAN 0
Third Round, Second Leg at Maine Road (38,026), December 6, 1978

Man. C.—Corrigan; Keegan, Donachie, Booth, Watson, Power, Channon, Viljoen, Kidd, Hartford, Barnes.

AC Milan.—Albertosi; Collovati, Maldera, De Vecchi, Bet, Baresi, Buriani, Antonelli, Novellino, Rivera (Boldini), Sartori.

Scorers: Manchester City—Booth, Hartford, Kidd.

Aggregate: Manchester City 5 AC Milan 2

MANCHESTER CITY 1 BORUSSIA MONCHENGLADBACH 1
Quarter-Final, First Leg at Maine Road (39,005), March 7, 1979

Man. C.—Corrigan; Donachie, Power, Reid, Watson, Booth, Channon, Viljoen, Kidd, Hartford, Barnes.

Monchengladbach.—Kneib; Schaffer, Hannes, Schafer, Klinkhammer, Bruns, Simonsen, Kulik, Del Haye, Nielsen, Lienen.

Scorers: Manchester City—Channon. Borussia—Lienen.

BORUSSIA MONCHENGLADBACH 3 MANCHESTER CITY 1
Quarter-Final, Second Leg in West Germany (35,000), March 20, 1979

Monchengladbach.—Kneib; Schaffer, Hannes, Schafer, Ringels, Bruns, Simonsen, Kulik, Del Haye (Amrath), Wohlers, Lienen.

Man. C.—Corrigan; Donachie, Power, Reid (Deyna), Watson, Booth, Channon, Viljoen, Henry, Hartford, Barnes.

Scorers: Borussia—Kulik, Bruns, Del Haye. Manchester City—Deyna.

Aggregate: Borussia Monchengladbach 4 Manchester City 2

FINAL

RED STAR BELGRADE 1 BORUSSIA MOENCHENGLADBACK 1
First Leg in Belgrade, May 9, 1979

BORUSSIA MOENCHENGLADBACK 2 RED STAR BELGRADE 1
Second Leg in Moenchengladback, May 23, 1979

Borussia Moenchengladback won 3-2 on aggregate

UEFA CUP WINNERS

1979—BORUSSIA MOENCHENGLADBACH
1978—PSV EINDHOVEN
1977—JUVENTUS
1976—LIVERPOOL
1975—BORUSSIA MOENCHENGLADBACH
1974—FEYENOORD
1973—LIVERPOOL
1972—TOTTENHAM HOTSPUR
1971—LEEDS UNITED
1970—ARSENAL
1969—NEWCASTLE UNITED
1968—LEEDS UNITED
1967—DYNAMO ZAGREB
1966—BARCELONA
1965—FERENCVAROS
1964—REAL ZARAGOSSA
1963—VALENCIA
1962—VALENCIA
1961—A.S. ROMA
1960—BARCELONA
1959—
1958—BARCELONA

LEAGUE HONOURS LIST

FOOTBALL LEAGUE

	First	Pts.	Second	Pts.	Third	Pts.
1888-9*a*	Preston N. E.	40	Aston Villa	29	W'hampton W.	27
1889-90*a*	Preston N. E.	33	Everton	31	Blackburn R.	28
1890-1*a*	Everton	29	Preston N. E.	27	Notts C.	26
1891-2*b*	Sunderland	42	Preston N. E.	37	Bolton W.	36

FIRST DIVISION

1892-3*c*	Sunderland	48	Preston N. E.	47	Everton	38
1893-4*c*	Aston Villa	44	Sunderland	38	Derby C.	36
1894-5*c*	Sunderland	47	Everton	42	Aston Villa	39
1895-6*c*	Aston Villa	45	Derby C.	41	Everton	39
1896-7*c*	Aston Villa	47	Sheffield U.	36	Derby C.	35
1897-8*c*	Sheffield U.	42	Sunderland	37	W'hampton W.	35
1898-9*d*	Aston Villa	45	Liverpool	43	Burnley	39
1899-1900*d*	Aston Villa	50	Sheffield U.	48	Sunderland	41
1900-1*d*	Liverpool	45	Sunderland	43	Notts C.	40
1901-2*d*	Sunderland	44	Everton	41	Newcastle U.	37
1902-3*d*	The Wednesday	42	*Aston Villa	41	Sunderland	41
1903-4*d*	The Wednesday	47	Manchester C.	44	Everton	43
1904-5*d*	Newcastle U.	48	Everton	47	Manchester C.	43
1905-6*e*	Liverpool	51	Preston N. E.	47	The Wednesday	44
1906-7*e*	Newcastle U.	51	Bristol City	48	Everton	45
1907-8*e*	Manchester U.	52	*Aston Villa	43	Manchester C.	43
1908-9*e*	Newcastle U.	53	Everton	46	Sunderland	44
1909-10*e*	Aston Villa	53	Liverpool	48	Blackburn R.	45
1910-11*e*	Manchester U.	52	Aston Villa	51	Sunderland	45
1911-12*e*	Blackburn R.	49	Everton	46	Newcastle U.	44
1912-13*e*	Sunderland	54	Aston Villa	50	Sheffield W.	49
1913-14*e*	Blackburn R.	51	Aston Villa	44	Middlesbrough	43
1914-15*e*	Everton	46	Oldham A.	45	Blackburn R.	43
1919-20*f*	West Brom. A.	60	Burnley	51	Chelsea	49
1920-1*f*	Burnley	59	Manchester C.	54	Bolton W.	52
1921-2*f*	Liverpool	57	Tottenham H.	51	Burnley	49
1922-3*f*	Liverpool	60	Sunderland	54	Huddersfield T.	53
1923-4*f*	*Huddersfield T.	57	Cardiff C.	57	Sunderland	53
1924-5*f*	Huddersfield T.	58	West Brom. A.	56	Bolton W.	55
1925-6*f*	Huddersfield T.	57	Arsenal	52	Sunderland	48
1926-7*f*	Newcastle U.	56	Huddersfield T.	51	Sunderland	49
1927-8*f*	Everton	53	Huddersfield T.	51	Leicecester C.	48
1928-9*f*	Sheffield W.	52	Leicester C.	51	Aston Villa	50
1929-30	Sheffield W.	60	Derby C.	50	Manchester C.	47
1930-1*f*	Arsenal	66	Aston Villa	59	Sheffield W.	52
1931-2*f*	Everton	56	Arsenal	54	Sheffield W.	50
1932-3*f*	Arsenal	58	Aston Villa	54	Sheffield W.	51
1933-4*f*	Arsenal	59	Huddersfield T.	56	Tottenham H.	49
1934-5*f*	Arsenal	58	Sunderland	54	Sheffield W.	49
1935-6*f*	Sunderland	56	Derby C.	48	Huddersfield T.	43
1936-7*f*	Manchester C.	57	Charlton A.	54	Arsenal	52
1937-8*f*	Arsenal	52	W'hampton W.	51	Preston N. E.	49
1938-9*f*	Everton	59	W'hampton W.	55	Charlton A.	50
1946-7*f*	Liverpool	57	*Manchester U.	56	W'hampton W.	56
1947-8*f*	Arsenal	59	*Manchester U.	52	Burnley	52
1948-9*f*	Portsmouth	58	*Manchester U.	53	Derby C	53
1949-50*f*	*Portsmouth	53	W'hampton	53	Sunderland	52

1950-1*f*	Tottenham H. .. 50	Manchester U. . 56	Blackpool 50
1951-2*f*	Manchester U. . 57	*Tottenham H. . 53	Arsenal 53
1952-3*f*	*Arsenal 54	Preston N. E. ... 54	W'hampton W. 51
1953-4*f*	W'hampton W. 57	West Brom. A. . 53	Huddersfield T. 51
1954-5*f*	Chelsea 52	*W'hampton W. 48	Portsmouth 48
1955-6*f*	Manchester U. . 60	*Blackpool 49	W'hampton W. 49
1956-7*f*	Manchester U. . 64	*Tottenham H. . 56	Preston N. E. ... 56
1957-8*f*	W'hampton W. 64	Preston N. E. ... 59	Tottenham H. .. 51
1958-9*f*	W'hampton W. 61	Manchester U. . 55	Arsenal 50
1959-60*f*	Burnley 55	W'hampton W. 54	Tottenham H. .. 53
1960-1*f*	Tottenham H. .. 66	Sheffield W. ... 58	W'hampton W. 57
1961-2*f*	Ipswich T. 56	Burnley 53	Tottenham H. .. 52
1962-3*f*	Everton 61	Tottenham H. .. 55	Burnley 54
1963-4*f*	Liverpool 57	Manchester U. . 53	Everton 52
1964-5*f*	*Manchester U. . 61	Leeds U. 61	Chelsea 56
1965-6*f*	Liverpool 61	*Leeds U. 55	Burnley 55
1966-7*f*	Manchester U. . 60	*Notts F. 56	Tottenham H. .. 56
1967-8*f*	Manchester C. . 58	Manchester U. . 56	Liverpool 55
1968-9*f*	Leeds U. 67	Liverpool 61	Everton 57
1969-70*f*	Everton 66	Leeds United .. 57	Chelsea 55
1970-1*f*	Arsenal 65	Leeds United .. 64	Tottenham H. .. 52
1971-2*f*	Derby C. 58	*Leeds U. 57	Liverpool 57
1972-3*f*	Liverpool 60	Arsenal 57	Leeds U. 53
1973-4*f*	Leeds U. 62	Liverpool 57	Derby C. 48
1974-5*f*	Derby C. 53	*Liverpool 51	Ipswich T. 51
1975-6*f*	Liverpool 60	Queens Park R. 59	Manchester U. . 56
1976-7*f*	Liverpool 57	Manchester C. . 56	Ipswich T. 52
1977-8*f*	Nottm F. 64	Liverpool 57	Everton 55
1978-9*f*	Liverpool 68	Nottm F. 60	West Brom. A. . 59

Maximum points: *a*, 44; *b*, 52; *c*, 60; *d*, 68; *e*, 76; *f*, 84

* Won goal average. No competition during 1915-19 and 1939-45

SECOND DIVISION

	First Pts.	Second Pts.	Third Pts.
1892-3*a*	Small Heath ... 36	Sheffield U. 35	Darwen 30
1893-4*b*	Liverpool 50	Small Heath ... 42	Notts C. 39
1894-5*c*	Bury 48	Notts C. 39	Newton Heath . 38
1895-6*c*	*Liverpool 46	Manchester C. . 46	Grimsby T. 42
1896-7*c*	Notts C. 42	Newton Heath . 39	Grimsby T. 38
1897-8*c*	Burnley 48	Newcastle U. .. 45	Manchester C. . 39
1898-9*d*	Manchester C. . 52	Glossop N. E. .. 46	Leicester F. 45
1899-1900*d*	The Wednesday 54	Bolton W. 52	Small Heath ... 46
1900-1*d*	Grimsby T. 49	Small Heath ... 48	Burnley 44
1901-2*d*	West Brom. A. . 55	Middlesbrough 51	Preston N. E. ... 42
1902-3*d*	Manchester C. . 54	Small Heath ... 51	Woolwich A. ... 42
1903-4*d*	Preston N. E. ... 50	Woolwich A. ... 49	Manchester U. . 43
1904-5*d*	Liverpool 58	Bolton W. 56	Manchester U. . 53
1905-6*e*	Bristol C. 66	Manchester U. . 62	Chelsea 53
1906-7*e*	Notts F. 60	Chelsea 57	Leicester F. 48
1907-8*e*	Bradford C. 54	Leicester F. 52	Oldham A. 50
1908-9*e*	Bolton W. 52	*Tottenham H. . 51	West Brom. A. . 51
1909-10*e*	Manchester C. . 54	*Oldham A. 53	Hull City 53
1910-11*e*	West Brom. A. . 53	Bolton W. 51	Chelsea 49
1911-12*e*	Derby C. 54	Chelsea 54	Burnley 52
1912-13*e*	Preston N. E. ... 53	Burnley 50	Birmingham C. 46
1913-14*e*	Notts C. 53	*Bradford 49	Woolwich A. ... 49
1914-15*e*	Derby C. 53	Preston N. E. ... 50	Barnsley 47
1919-20*f*	Tottenham H. .. 70	Huddersfield T. 64	Birmingham C. 56

1920-1*f*	*Birmingham C. 58	Cardiff C. 58	Bristol C. 51
1921-2*f*	Nottm. F. 56	*Stoke C. 52	Barnsley 52
1922-3*f*	Notts. C. 53	*West Ham U. .. 51	Leicester C. 51
1923-4*f*	Leeds U. 54	*Bury 51	Derby C. 51
1924-5*f*	Leicester C. 59	Manchester U. . 57	Derby C. 55
1925-6*f*	Sheffield W. ... 60	Derby C. 57	Chelsea 52
1926-7*f*	Middlesbrough 62	*Portsmouth ... 54	Manchester C. . 54
1927-8*f*	Manchester C. . 59	Leeds U. 57	Chelsea 54
1928-9*f*	Middlesbrough 55	Grimsby T. 53	Bradford 48
1929-30*f*	Blackpool 58	Chelsea 55	Oldham A. 53
1930-1*f*	Everton 61	West Brom. A. . 54	Tottenham H. .. 51
1931-2*f*	W'hampton W. 56	Leeds U. 54	Stoke C. 52
1932-3*f*	Stoke C. 56	Tottenham H. .. 55	Fulham 50
1933-4f	Grimsby T. 59	Preston N. E. ... 52	Bolton W. 51
1934-5*f*	Brentford 61	*Bolton W. 56	West Ham U. .. 56
1935-6*f*	Manchester U. . 56	Charlton A. 55	Sheffield U. ... 52
1936-7*f*	Leicester C. 56	Blackpool 55	Bury 52
1937-8*f*	Aston Villa 57	*Manchester U. 53	Sheffield U. 53
1938-9*f*	Blackburn R. ... 55	Sheffield U. 54	Sheffield W. ... 53
1939-45	*Competition cancelled owing to war*		
1946-7*f*	Manchester C. . 62	Burnley 58	Birmingham C. 55
1947-8*f*	Birmingham C. 59	Newcastle U. .. 56	Southampton .. 52
1948-9*f*	Fulham 57	West Brom. A. 56	Southampton 52
1949-50*f*	Tottenham H. .. 61	*Sheffield W. ... 52	Sheffield U. 52
1950-1*f*	Preston N. E. ... 57	Manchester C. 52	Cardiff C. ... 50
1951-2*f*	Sheffield W. ... 52	*Cardiff C. 51	Birmingham C. 51
1952-3*f*	Sheffield U. 60	Huddersfield T. 58	Luton T. 52
1953-4*f*	*Leicester C. 56	Everton 56	Blackburn R. ... 55
1954-5*f*	*Birmingham C. 54	*Luton T 54	Rotherham U. .. 54
1955-6*f*	Sheffield W. ... 55	Leeds U. 52	Liverpool 48
1956-7*f*	Leicester C. 61	Notts. F. 54	Liverpool 53
1957-8*f*	West Ham U. .. 57	Blackburn R. ... 56	Charlton A. 55
1958-9*f*	Sheffield W. ... 62	Fulham 60	Sheffield U. 53
1959-60*f*	Aston Villa 59	Cardiff C. 58	Liverpool 50
1960-1*f*	Ipswich T. 59	Sheffield U. 58	Liverpool 52
1961-2*f*	Liverpool 62	Leyton O. 54	Sunderland 53
1962-3*f*	Stoke C. 53	*Chelsea 52	Sunderland 52
1963-4*f*	Leeds U. 63	Sunderland 61	Preston N. E. ... 56
1964-5*f*	Newcastle U. .. 57	Northampton T. 56	Bolton W. 50
1965-6*f*	Manchester C. . 59	Southampton .. 54	Coventry C. 53
1966-7*f*	Coventry C. 59	W'hampton W. 58	Carlisle U. 52
1967-8*f*	Ipswich T. 59	*Queens Park R. 58	Blackpool 58
1968-9*f*	Derby C. 63	Crystal Palace . 56	Charlton A. 50
1969-70*f*	Huddersfield T. 60	Blackpool 53	Leicester C. 51
1970-1*f*	Leicester C. 59	Sheffield U. 56	Cardiff C. 53
1971-2f	Norwich 57	Birmingham C. 56	Millwall 55
1972-3*f*	Burnley 62	Queens Park R. 61	Aston Villa 60
1973-4*f*	Middlesbrough 65	Luton T. 50	Carlisle 49
1974-5*f*	Manchester U. . 61	Aston Villa 58	Norwich 53
1975-6*f*	Sunderland 56	Bristol C. 53	West Brom. A. . 53
1976-7*f*	W'hampton W. 57	Chelsea 55	Nottm F. 52
1977-8*f*	Bolton W. 58	Southampton .. 57	Tottenham H. .. 56
1978 9*f*	C. Palace 57	Brighton & H. A. 56	Stoke C. 56

Maximum points: *a*, 44; *b*, 56; *c*, 60; *d*, 68; *e*, 76; *f*, 84 *Won goal average

THIRD DIVISION

	First Pts.	Second Pts.	Third Pts.
1958-9	Plymouth A. ... 62	Hull C. 61	Brentford 57
1959-60	Southampton .. 61	Norwich C. 59	Shrewsbury T. . 52

1960-1	Bury 68	Walsall 62	Queens Park R. 60
1961-2	Portsmouth 65	Grimsby T. 62	Bournemouth .. 59
1962-3	Northampton T. 62	Swindon T. 58	Port Vale 54
1963-4	*Coventry C. 60	Crystal Palace . 60	Watford 58
1964-5	Carlisle U. 60	*Bristol C. 59	Mansfield T. ... 59
1965-6	Hull C. 69	Millwall 65	Queens Park R. 57
1966-7	Queens Park R. 67	Middlesbrough 55	Watford 54
1967-8	Oxford U. 57	Bury 56	Shrewsbury T. . 55
1968-9	*Watford 64	Swindon T. 64	Luton T. 61
1969-70	Orient 62	Luton T. 60	Bristol R. 56
1970-1	Preston N. E. ... 61	Fulham 60	Halifax T. 56
1971-2	Aston Villa 70	Brighton 65	Bournemouth .. 62
1972-3	Bolton W. 61	Notts C. 57	Blackburn R. ... 55
1973-4	Oldham A. 62	*Bristol R. 62	York C. 61
1974-5	Blackburn R. ... 60	Plymouth A. ... 59	Charlton A. 55
1975-6	Hereford U. 63	Cardiff C. 57	Millwall 56
1976-7	Mansfield T. ... 64	Brighton & H. A. 61	Crystal Palace . 59
1977-8	Wrexham 61	Cambridge U. .. 58	Preston N. E. ... 56
1978-9	Shrewsbury T. . 61	Watford 60	Swansea C. 60

Maximum points 92 *Won on goal average

FOURTH DIVISION

	First Pts.	Second Pts.	Third Pts.
1958-9	Port Vale 64	*Coventry C. 60	York C. 60
1959-60	Walsall 65	*Notts C. 60	Torquay U. 60
1960-1	P'borough U. .. 66	Crystal Palace . 64	Northampton T. 60
1961-2	Millwall 56	Colchester U. .. 55	Wrexham 53
1962-3	Brentford 62	*Oldham A. 59	Crew A. 59
1963-4	*Gillingham 60	Carlisle U. 60	Workington T. . 59
1964-5	Brighton & H. A. 63	*Millwall 62	York C. 62
1965-6	*Doncaster R. ... 59	Darlington 59	Torquay U. 58
1966-7	Stockport C. ... 64	*Southport 59	Barrow 59
1967-8	Luton T. 66	Barnsley 61	Hartlepools 60
1968-9	Doncaster R. ... 59	Halifax T. 57	Rochdale 56
1969-70	Chesterfield 64	Wrexham 61	Swansea T. 60
1970-1	Notts C. 69	Bournemouth .. 60	Oldham A. 59
1971-2	Grimsby T. 63	Southend U. ... 60	Brentford 59
1972-3	Southport 62	Hereford 58	Cambridge 57
1973-4	P'borough U. .. 65	Gillingham 62	Colchester U. .. 60
1974-5	Mansfield T. ... 68	Shrewsbury T. . 62	Rotherham U. .. 58
1975-6	Lincoln C. 74	Northampton T. 68	Reading 60
1976-7	Cambridge U. .. 65	Exeter C. 62	Colchester U. .. 59
1977-8	Watford 71	Southend U. ... 60	Swansea C. 56
1978-9	Reading 65	Grimsby T. 61	Wimbledon 61

THIRD DIVISION—Southern Section to 1957-8

	First Pts.	Second Pts.	Third Pts.
1920-1*a*	Crystal Palace .. 59	Southampton .. 54	Queens Park R. 53
1921-2*a*	*Southampton ..61	Plymouth A. ... 61	Portsmouth 53
1922-3*a*	Bristol C. 59	*Plymouth A. ... 53	Swansea T. 53
1923-4*a*	Portsmouth 59	Plymouth A. ... 55	Millwall 54
1924-5*a*	Swansea T. 57	Plymouth A. ... 56	Bristol C. 53
1925-6*a*	Reading 57	Plymouth A. ... 56	Millwall 53
1926-7*a*	Bristol C. 62	Plymouth A. ... 60	Millwall 56
1927-8*a*	Millwall 65	Northampton T. 55	Plymouth A. ... 53
1928-9*a*	*Charlton A. 54	Crystal Palace . 54	Northampton T. 52
1929-30*a*	Plymouth A. 68	Brentford 61	Queens Park R. 51

1930-1*a*	Notts C.	59	Crystal Palace	51	Brentford	50
1931-2*a*	Fulham	57	Reading	55	Southend U.	53
1932-3*a*	Brentford	62	Exeter C.	58	Norwich C.	57
1933-4*a*	Norwich C.	61	*Coventry C.	54	Reading	54
1934-5*a*	Charlton A.	61	Reading	53	Coventry C.	51
1935-6*a*	Coventry C.	57	Luton T.	56	Reading	54
1936-7*a*	Luton T.	58	Notts C.	56	Brighton & H. A.	53
1937-8*a*	Millwall	56	Bristol C.	55	Queens Park R.	53
1938-9*a*	Newport C.	55	Crystal Palace	52	Brighton & H. A.	49
1939-45	*Competition cancelled owing to war*					
1946-7*a*	Cardiff C.	66	Queens Park R.	57	Bristol C.	51
1947-8*a*	Queens Park R.	61	Bournemouth	57	Walsall	51
1948-9*a*	Swansea T.	62	Reading	55	Bournemouth	52
1949-50*a*	Notts C.	58	*Northampton T.	51	Southend U.	51
1950-1*d*	Nottm F.	70	Norwich C.	64	Reading	57
1951-2*d*	Plymouth A.	66	*Reading	61	Norwich C.	61
1952-3*d*	Bristol R.	64	*Millwall	62	Northampton T.	62
1953-4*d*	Ipswich T.	64	Brighton & H. A.	61	Bristol C.	56
1954-5*d*	Bristol C.	70	Leyton O.	61	Southampton	59
1955-6*d*	Leyton O.	66	Brighton & H. A.	65	Ipswich T.	64
1956-7*d*	*Ipswich T.	59	Torquay U.	59	Colchester U.	58
1957-8*d*	Brighton & H. A.	60	*Brentford	58	Plymouth A.	58

THIRD DIVISION—Northern Section to 1957-8

	First	Pts.	Second	Pts.	Third	Pts.
1921-2*b*	Stockport C.	56	*Darlington	50	Grimsby T.	50
1922-3*b*	Nelson	51	Bradford C	47	Walsall	56
1923-4*a*	W'hampton W.	63	Rochdale	62	Chesterfield	54
1924-5*a*	Darlington	58	Nelson	53	New Brighton	53
1925-6*a*	Grimsby T.	61	Bradford	60	Rochdale	55
1926-7*a*	Stoke C.	63	Rochdale	58	Bradford	57
1927-8*a*	Bradford	63	Lincoln C.	55	Stockport C.	54
1928-9*a*	Bradford c.	63	Stockport C.	62	Wrexham	52
1929-30*a*	Port Vale	67	Stockport C.	63	Darlington	50
1930-1*a*	Chesterfield	58	Lincoln C.	57	Wrexham	54
1931-2*c*	*Lincoln C.	57	Gateshead	57	Chester	50
1932-3*a*	Hull C.	59	Wrexham	57	Stockport C.	54
1933-4*a*	Barnsley	62	Chesterfield	61	Stockport C.	59
1934-5*a*	Doncaster R.	57	Halifax T.	55	Chester	54
1935-6*a*	Chesterfield	60	Chester	55	Tranmere R.	55
1936-7*a*	Stockport C.	60	Lincoln C.	57	Chester	53
1937-8*a*	Tranmere R.	56	Doncaster R.	54	Hull C.	53
1938-9*a*	Barnsley	67	Doncaster R.	56	Bradford C.	52
1939-45	*Competition cancelled owing to war*					
1946-7*a*	Doncaster R.	72	Rotherham U.	64	Chester	56
1947-8*a*	Lincoln C.	60	Rotherham U.	59	Wrexham	50
1948-9*a*	Hull C.	65	Rotherham U.	62	Doncaster R.	50
1949-50*a*	Doncaster R.	55	Gateshead	53	Rochdale	51
1950-1*d*	Rotherham U.	71	Mansfield T.	64	Carlisle U.	62
1951-2*d*	Lincoln C.	69	Grimsby T.	66	Stockport C.	59
1952-3*d*	Oldham A.	59	Port Vale	58	Wrexham	56
1953-4*d*	Port Vale	69	Barnsley	58	Scunthorpe U.	57
1954-5*d*	Barnsley	65	Accrington S.	61	Scunthorpe U.	58
1955-6*d*	Grimsby T.	68	Derby C.	63	Accrington S.	59
1956-7*d*	Derby C.	63	Hartlepool U.	59	Accrington S.	58
1957-8*d*	Scunthorpe U.	66	Accrington S.	59	Bradford C.	57

Maximum points: *a,* 84, *b,* 76; *c,* 80; *d,* 92 *Won on goal average

LEAGUE TITLE WINS

LEAGUE DIV. 1

Liverpool	11
Arsenal	8
Everton	7
Manchester United	7
Aston Villa	6
Sunderland	6
Newcastle United	4
Sheffield Wed.	4
Huddersfield Town	3
Wolverhampton W.	3
Blackburn Rovers	2
Burnley	2
Derby County	2
Leeds United	2
Manchester City	2
Portsmouth	2
Preston North End	2
Tottenham Hotspur	2
Chelsea	1
Derby County	1
Ipswich Town	1
Nottingham Forest	1
Sheffield United	1
West Bromwich A.	1

LEAGUE DIV. 2

Manchester City	6
Leicester City	5
Sheffield W.	5
*Birmingham City	4
Liverpool	4
Derby County	3
Middlesbrough	3
Notts County	3
Preston North End	3
Aston Villa	2
Bolton Wanderers	2
Burnley	2
Grimsby Town	2
Ipswich Town	2
Leeds United	2
Manchester United	2
Nottingham Forest	2
Stoke City	2
Tottenham Hotspur	2
West Bromwich A.	2
Wolverhampton W.	2
Blackburn Rovers	1
Blackpool	1
Bradford City	1
Brentford	1
Bristol City	1
Bury	1
Coventry City	1
Crystal Palace	1
Everton	1
Fulham	1
Huddersfield Town	1
Newcastle United	
Norwich City	1
Sheffield United	1
Sunderland	1
West Ham United	1

* Once as Small Heatl

LEAGUE DIVISION 3—Aston Villa, Blackburn Rovers, Bolton Wanderers, Bury, Carlisle United, Coventry City, Hereford, Hull City, Leyton Orient, Mansfield Town, Northampton Town, Oldham, Oxford United, Plymouth Argyle, Portsmouth, Preston North End, Queens Park Rangers, Shrewsbury Town Southampton, Watford, Wrexham.

LEAGUE DIVISION 4—Doncaster Rovers and Petererborough United, twice; Brentford, Brighton & Hove Albion, Cambridge United, Chesterfield, Gillingham, Grimsby Town, Lincoln, Luton Town, Mansfield Town, Millwall, Notts County, Port Vale, Reading, Southport, Stockport County, Walsall, Watford.

To 1957–58

DIVISION III (South)—Bristol City, three times; Charlton Athletic, Ipswich Town, Millwall Athletic, Notts County, Plymouth Argyle, Swansea Town, twice; Brentford, Brighton & Hove Albion, Bristol Rovers, Cardiff City, Crystal Palace, Coventry City, Fulham, Leyton Orient, Luton Town, Newport County, Norwich City, Nottingham Forest, Norwich City, Portsmouth, Queen's Park Rangers, Reading, Southampton.

DIVISION III (North)—Barnsley, Doncaster Rovers, Lincoln City, three times; Chesterfield, Grimsby Town, Hull City, Port Vale, Stockport County, twice; Bradford, Bradford City, Darlington, Derby County, Nelson, Oldham Athletic, Rotherham United, Stoke City, Tranmere Rovers, Wolverhampton Wanderers, Scunthorpe United.

APPLICATIONS FOR RE-ELECTION

DIVISION 4—NINE: Hartlepools United. **SIX**: Barrow. **FIVE**: Lincoln City, Southport. **FOUR**: Bradford, Chester, Crewe, Darlington, Stockport County, Workington, York City. **THREE**: Doncaster, Halifax, Rochdale. **TWO**: Bradford City, Newport, Northampton. **ONE**: Aldershot, Exeter City, Gateshead, Grimsby, Port Vale, Scunthorpe, Swansea, Wrexham, York City. (Accrington Stanley resigned and Oxford United were elected. Barrow were not re-elected and were replaced by Hereford. Bradford were not re-elected and were replaced by Cambridge United. Gateshead were not re-elected and were replaced by Peterborough United. Port Vale were forced to re-apply following expulsion.

DIVISION 3 (to 1957–58)—SEVEN: Newport, Walsall, **SIX**: Exeter City, Halifax Town, Southport. **FIVE**: Accrington Stanley, Barrow, Gillingham, New Brighton. **FOUR**: Norwich City, Rochdale. **THREE**: Crewe Alexandra, Crystal Palace, Darlington, Hartlepools United, Merthyr Town, Swindon Town, Workington. **TWO**: Aberdare Athletic, Aldershot, Ashington, Bournemouth, Brentford, Chester, Colchester United, Durham City, Millwall, Nelson, Queen's Park Rangers, Rotherham United, Southend United, Tranmere Rovers, Watford. **ONE**: Bradford City, Brighton & Hove Albion, Bristol Rovers, Cardiff City, Carlisle United, Charlton Athletic, Gateshead, Grimsby Town, Mansfield Town, Shrewsbury Town, Stockport County, Thames, Torquay United, York City.

RELEGATED CLUBS

1891–2—League extended, Newton Heath, Nottingham Forest and Sheffield Wednesday admitted. *Second Division formed* including Darwen.
1892–3—In Test matches, Darwen and Sheffield United won promotion in place of Accrington and Notts County.
1893–4—In Tests, Liverpool and Small Heath won promotion. Darwen and Newton Heath relegated.
1894–5—After Tests, Bury promoted, Liverpool relegated.
1895–6—After Tests, Liverpool promoted, Small Heath relegated.
1896–7—After Tests, Notts County promoted, Burnley relegated.
1897–8—Test system abolished after success of Burnley and Stoke, League extended. Blackburn Rovers and Newcastle United elected to First Division. *Automatic promotion and relegation introduced.*

Division 1 to Division 2

1898–9—Bolton Wanderers and Sheffield Wednesday
1899–1900—Burnley and Glossop
1900–1—Preston North End and West Bromwich Albion
1901–2—Small Heath and Manchester City
1902–3—Grimsby Town and Bolton Wanderers
1903–4—Liverpool and West Bromwich Albion
1904–5—League extended. Bury and Notts County, two bottom clubs in First Division, re-elected
1905–6—Nottingham Forest and Wolverhampton Wanderers
1906–7—Derby County and Stoke
1907–8—Bolton Wanderers and Birmingham
1908–9—Manchester City and Leicester Fosse
1909–10–Bolton Wanderers and Chelsea
1910–11–Bristol City and Nottingham Forest
1911–12–Preston North End and Bury
1912–13–Notts County and Woolwich Arsenal
1913–14–Preston North End and Derby County
1914–15–Tottenham Hotspur and *Chelsea

1919–20–Notts C. and Sheffield W. ....
1920–1—Derby C. and Bradford ....
1921–2—Bradford C. and Manchester U. .
1922–3—Stoke and Oldham A. ....
1923–4—Chelsea and Middlesbrough ....
1924–5—Preston N. E. and Notts F. ....
1925–6—Manchester C. and Notts C. .....
1926–7—Leeds U. and West Brom. A .....
1927–8—Tottenham H. & Middlesbrough
1928–9—Bury and Cardiff C. ....
1929–30–Burnley and Everton ....
1930–1—Leeds U. and Manchester U. ....
1931–2—Grimsby T. and West Ham U. ....
1932–3—Bolton W. and Blackpool ....
1933–4—Newcastle U. and Sheffield U. ..
1934–5—Leicester C. and Tottenham H. .
1935–6—Aston Villa and Blackburn R. ....
1936–7—Manchester U. & Sheffield W. ..
1937–8—Manchester C. and W.B.A. ......
1938–9—Birmingham and Leicester C. ...
1946–7—Brentford and Leeds U. ....
1947–8—Blackburn R. and Grimsby T. ...
1948–9—Preston N. E. and Sheffield U. ..
1949–50–Manchester C. & Birmingham ..
1950–1—Sheffield W. and Everton ....
1951–2—Huddersfield T. and Fulham .....
1952–3—Stoke C. and Derby C. ....
1953–4—Middlesbrough and Liverpool ...
1954–5—Leicester C. and Sheffield W. ...
1955–6—Huddersfield T. and Sheff. U. ...
1956–7—Charlton A. and Cardiff C. ....
1957–8—Sheffield W. and Sunderland ...
1958–9—Portsmouth and Aston Villa ....
1959–60–Luton T. and Leeds U. ....
1960–1—Preston N. E. and Newcastle U.
1961–2—Chelsea and Cardiff C. ....
1962–3—Manchester C. and Leyton O. ...
1963–4—Bolton W. and Ipswich T. ....
1964–5—W'hampton W. & B'ham C. .....
1965–6—Northampton T. & Blackburn R.
1966–7—Aston Villa and Blackpool ....
1967–8—Fulham and Sheffield U. ....
1968–9—Leicester C. and Q.P.R. ....
1969–70–Sheffield W. and Sunderland ...
1970–1—Burnley and Blackpool ....
1971–2—Notts F. and Huddersfield ....
1972–3—W.B.A. and Crystal Palace ......
1973–4—Norwich, Man. U. & S'hampton
1974–5—Chelsea, Luton and Carlisle .....
1975–6—Sheff. U. Burnley and Wolves ...
1976–7—Tottenham, Stoke, Sunderland .
1977–8—Leicester, West Ham, Newcastle
1978–9—Q.P.R., Birmingham, Chelsea ..

Division 2 to Division 3
Stockport County
Bradford and Bristol C.
Rotherham C., W'hampton W.
Nelson and Bristol C.
Crystal Palace, Coventry C.
Stoke C. and Stockport C.
Darlington and Bradford C.
Fulham and South Shields
Port Vale and Clapton Orient
Hull C. and Notts C.
Reading and Cardiff C.
Barnsley and Bristol C.
Chesterfield and Charlton A.
Millwall and Lincoln C.
Oldham A. and Notts C.
Port Vale and Hull City
Doncaster R. and Bradford C.
Barnsley and Stockport C.
Norwich C. and Tranmere R.
Swansea T. and Newport C.
Doncaster R. and Millwall
Nottingham F. and Lincoln C.
Plymouth A. and Bradford
Grimsby T. and Chesterfield
Coventry C. and Q.P.R.
Southampton and Barnsley
Brentford and Oldham A.
Ipswich T. and Derby C.
Plymouth A. and Hull C.
Port Vale and Bury
Doncaster R. and Notts C.
Barnsley and Grimsby T.
Bristol C. and Hull C.
Lincoln C. and Portsmouth
Brighton and Bristol R.
Walsall and Luton T.
Grimsby T. and Scunthorpe U.
Swindon T. and Swansea T.
Middlesbrough and Leyton O.
Northampton T. and Bury
Plymouth A., Rotherham U.
Fulham and Bury
Aston Villa and Preston N. E.
Bolton W. and Blackburn R.
Charlton and Watford
Brighton and Huddersfield
Swindon, Preston, C. Palace
Millwall, Cardiff, Sheff. W.
Portsmouth, Oxford, York
Carlisle, Plymouth, Hereford
Hull, Mansfield, Blackpool
Sheff. Utd., Millwall, Blackburn

** Subsequently re-elected to Division when League was extended after the war.*

Division 3 to Division 4

1958–9—Rochdale, Notts County, Doncaster Rovers and Stockport County
1959–60–Accrington Stanley, Wrexham, Mansfield Town and York City
1960–1—Chesterfield, Colchester United, Bradford City and Tranmere Rovers

1961–2—Newport County, Brentford, Lincoln City and Torquay United
1962–3—Bradford, Bright & Hove A., Carlisle United and Halifax Town
1963–4—Millwall, Crewe Alexandra, Wrexham and Notts County
1964–5—Luton Town, Port Vale, Colchester United and Barnsley
1965–6—Southend United, Exeter City, Brentford and York City
1966–7—Doncaster Rovers, Workington, Darlington and Swansea Town
1967–8—Scunthorpe United, Colchester United, Grimsby Town and Peterborough United (demoted)
1968–9—Oldham Athletic, Crewe Alexandra, Hartlepool and Northampton Town
1969–70–Bournemouth, Southport, Barrow and Stockport County
1970–1—Gillingham, Doncaster Rovers, Bury and Reading
1971–2—Mansfield Town, Barnsley, Torquay United and Bradford City
1972–3—Scunthorpe United, Swansea Town, Brentford and Rotherham United
1973–4—Cambridge United, Shrewsbury Town, Rochdale and Southport
1974–5—Bournemouth, Watford, Tranmere Rovers and Huddersfield
1975–6—Halifax, Southend, Colchester United and Aldershot
1976–7—Reading, Northampton Town, Grimsby Town and York City
1977–8—Portsmouth, Hereford United, Bradford City and Port Vale
1978–9—Peterborough, Walsall, Tranmere, Lincoln

THE WAY TO WEMBLEY

ARSENAL

THIRD ROUND: Sheffield Wednesday 1–1 A (Sunderland)

Replay: Sheffield Wednesday 1–1 H (Brady)

2nd Replay, at Leicester: Sheffield Wednesday 2–2 A (Brady, Sunderland)

3rd Replay, at Leicester: Sheffield Wednesday 3–3 A (Stapleton 2, Young)

4th Replay, at Leicester: Sheffield Wednesday 2–0 A (Gatting, Stapleton)

FOURTH ROUND: Notts County 2–0 H (Young, Talbot)

FIFTH ROUND: Nott'm Forest 1–0 A (Stapleton)

SIXTH ROUND: Southampton 1–1 A (Price)

Replay: Southampton 2–0 H (Sunderland 2)

SEMI–FINAL at Villa Park: Wolverhampton W. 2–0 (Stapleton, Sunderland)

F.A. CUP SCORERS: Stapleton 5, Sunderland 5, Brady 2, Young 2, Gatting 1, Price 1, Talbot 1, Total: 17

MANCHESTER UNITED

THIRD ROUND: Chelsea 3–0 H (Coppell, Grimes, Greenhoff J.)

FOURTH ROUND: Fulham 1–1 H (Greenhoff J.)

Replay: Fulham 1–0 A (Greenhoff J.)

FIFTH ROUND: Colchester Utd. 1–0 A (Greenhoff J.)

SIXTH ROUND: Tottenham Hotspur 1–1 A (Thomas)

Replay: Tottenham Hotspur 2–0 H (Jordan, McIlroy)

SEMI–FINAL, at Maine Road: Liverpool 2–2 (Greenhoff B., Jordan)
Replay, at Goodison Park: Liverpool 1–0 A (Greenhoff J.)

F.A. CUP SCORERS: Greenhoff J. 5, Jordan 2, Coppel 1, Greenhoff B. 1, McIlroy 1, Grimes 1, Thomas 1, Total: 12

F.A. CUP WINS AT A GLANCE

Aston Villa ... 7
Blackburn Rovers ... 6
Newcastle United ... 6
The Wanderers ... 5
Tottenham Hotspur ... 5
West Brom. Albion ... 5
Arsenal ... 5
Bolton Wanderers ... 4
Manchester City ... 4
Manchester United ... 4
Sheffield United ... 4
Wolverhampton Wanderers ... 4
Everton ... 3
Sheffield Wednesday 3
Bury ... 2
Liverpool ... 2
Nottingham Forest ... 2
Old Etonians ... 2
Preston North End ... 2
Sunderland ... 2
West Ham United ... 2
Barnsley ... 1
Blackburn Olympic ... 1
Blackpool ... 1
Bradford City ... 1
Burnley ... 1
Cardiff City ... 1
Charlton Athletic ... 1
Chelsea ... 1
Clapham Rovers ... 1
Derby County ... 1
Huddersfield Town ... 1
Ipswich Town ... 1
Leeds United ... 1
Notts County ... 1
Old Carthusians ... 1
Oxford University ... 1
Portsmouth ... 1
Royal Engineers ... 1
Southampton ... 1

APPEARANCES IN FINALS

Newcastle ... 11
West Brom. Albion . 10
Arsenal ... 10
Aston Villa ... 9
Blackburn Rovers ... 8
Wolverhampton W. .. 8
Bolton Wanderers ... 7
Everton ... 7
Manchester City ... 7
Manchester United . 8
Preston North End ... 7
Liverpool ... 6
Old Etonians ... 6
Sheffield United ... 6
Huddersfield Town ... 5
Sheffield Wednesday 5
*The Wanderers ... 5
*Tottenham Hotspur 5
Derby County ... 4
Leeds United ... 4
Leicester City ... 4
Oxford University ... 4
Royal Engineers ... 4
Blackpool ... 3
Burnley ... 3
Chelsea ... 3
Portsmouth ... 3
Southampton ... 3
Sunderland ... 3
West Ham United ... 3
Barnsley ... 2
Birmingham City ... 2
*Bury ... 2
Cardiff City ... 2
Charlton Athletic ... 2
Clapham Rovers ... 2
*Nottingham Forest 2
Notts County ... 2
Queens Park (Glas.) 2
*Blackburn Olympic . 1
*Bradford City ... 1
Bristol City ... 1
Fulham ... 1
*Ipswich Town ... 1
Luton Town ... 1
*Old Carttrttrttththusians 1

* Denotes undefeated

APPEARANCES IN SEMI-FINALS

West Brom. Albion . 18
Aston Villa ... 17
Everton ... 17
Blackburn Rovers .. 16
Manchester United 15
Arsenal ... 14
Derby County ... 13
Newcastle ... 13
Sheffield W. ... 13
Bolton Wanderers . 12
Wolverhampton W. 12
Liverpool ... 12
Chelsea ... 10
Nottingham Forest 10
Preston North End . 10
Sheffield United ... 10
Sunderland ... 10
Manchester City ... 9
Tottenham Hotspur .. 9
Birmingham City ... 9
Burnley ... 8
Southampton ... 8
Huddersfield Town ... 7
Leeds United ... 7
Leicester City ... 6
Old Etonians ... 6
Oxford University ... 6
Fulham ... 5
The Wanderers ... 5
Notts County ... 4
Portsmouth ... 4
Queens Park (Glas) .. 4
Royal Engineers ... 4
West Ham United ... 4
Blackpool ... 3
Cardiff City ... 3
Clapham Rovers ... 3
Millwall ... 3
Old Carthusians ... 3
Stoke City ... 3
The Swifts ... 3
Barnsley ... 2
Blackburn Olympic ... 2
Bristol City ... 2
Bury ... 2
Charlton Athletic ... 2
Crystal Palace ... 2
Darwen ... 2
Grimsby Town ... 2
Ipswich Town ... 2
Swansea Town ... 2
Swindon Town ... 2
Bradford City ... 1
Cambridge Univ. ... 1
Crewe Alexandra ... 1
Derby Junction ... 1
Glasgow Rangers ... 1
Hull City ... 1
Luton Town ... 1
Marlow ... 1
Norwich City ... 1
Oldham Athletic ... 1
Old Harrovians ... 1
Orient ... 1
Port Vale ... 1
Reading ... 1
Shropshire Wandrs. 1
York City ... 1
Watford ... 1

1930 World Cup Top Four 1978

1930 (in Uruguay)	Champions:	URUGUAY
	2:	Argentina
	3:	United States
	4:	Yugoslavia
1934 (in Italy)	Champions:	ITALY
	2:	Czechoslovakia
	3:	Germany
	4:	Austria
1938 (in France)	Champions:	ITALY
	2:	Hungary
	3:	Brazil
	4:	Sweden
1950 (in Brazil):	Champions:	URUGUAY
	2:	Brazil
	3:	Sweden
	4:	Spain
1954 (in Switzerland)	Champions:	WEST GERMANY
	2:	Hungary
	3:	Austria
	4:	Uruguay
1958 (in Sweden)	Champions:	BRAZIL
	2:	Sweden
	3:	France
	4:	West Germany
1962 (in Chile)	Champions:	BRAZIL
	2:	Czechoslovakia
	3:	Chile
	4:	Yugoslavia
1966 (in England)	Champions:	ENGLAND
	2:	West Germany
	3:	Portugal
	4:	Soviet Union
1970 (in Mexico)	Champions:	BRAZIL
	2:	Italy
	3:	West Germany
	4:	Uruguay

1974 (in West Germany)	Champions:	WEST GERMANY
	2:	Netherlands
	3:	Poland
	4:	Brazil
1978 (in Argentina)	Champions:	ARGENTINA
	2:	Netherlands
	3:	Brazil
	4:	Italy

HOW ARSENAL WON THE F.A. CUP

3rd Round	4th Round	5th Round	6th Round	Semi-Finals	
*Hartlepool .... 2 Leeds U. 6	Leeds** 3-0	*W.B.A. 1-1	*Southampton 1-0	Arsenal 2	ARSENAL 3
*Coventry C. ... 2-0 W.B.A. 2-4	W.B.A. 3-2				
*Preston .... 3 Derby Cnty. 0	*Preston N.E. 0	Southampton 1-2			
*Wimbledon ...... 0 Southampton ... 2	Southampton ... 1				
*Nottm. F. .... 2 Aston Villa 0	*Nottm. F. 3	*Nottm. F. 0	Arsenal 1-2		
*York City .... 2 Luton Town 0	York City 1				
*Sheffield W. †1-1-2-3-0 Arsenal 1-1-2-3-2	*Arsenal 2	Arsenal 1		(at Villa Park)	
*Notts. County ... 4 Reading 2	Notts County ... 0				
*Middlesbro. .. 1-0 Crystal Palace 1-1	*Crystal Palace .. 3	*Crystal Palace .. 0	*Wolves 1-3	Wolves. 0	
*Bristol City ...... 3 Bolton W. 1	Bristol City 0				
*Newcastle U. .... 3 Torquay U. 1	*Newcastle U. . 1-0	Wolves 1			
*Brighton .... 2 Wolves. 3	Wolves 1-1				
*Sheffield U. ... 0-0 Aldershot 0-1	*Aldershot 2	*Aldershot 2-1	Shrewsbury T. 1-1		
*Swindon Town . 3 Cardiff City 0	Swindon Town . 1				
*Shrewsbury T. .. 3 Cambridge U. ... 1	*Shrewsbury T. .. 2	Shrewsbury T. 2-3			
*Manchester C. 0-4 Rotherham ... 0-2	Manchester C. .. 0				

*Stoke City 0
Oldham A. 1
*Leicester C. 3
Norwich City....0
*Tottenham ... 1-3
Altrincham ... 1-0
*Wrexham 6
Stockport 2
*Newport C. 2
West Ham 1
*Darlington 0
Colchester U. ... 1
*Fulham 2
Q.P.R. 0
***Man U.** 3
Chelsea 0
*Ipswich T. 3
Carlisle U. 2
*Orient 3
Bury 2
*Swansea City ...0
Bristol Rovers... 1
*Charlton 1-2
Maidstone ... 1-1
*Southend U... 0-0
Liverpool 0-3
Millwall†† 1
Blackburn R. 2
*Birmingham C...0
Burnley 2
*Sunderland......2
Everton 1

*Oldham A. 3
Leicester C. 1
*Tottenham ... 3-3
Wrexham 3-2
*Newport C. ... 0-0
Colchester U. 0-1
*Fulham 1-0
Man. U. 1-1
*Ipswich Town 0-2
Orient......... 0-0
*Bristol Rovers ... 1
Charlton 0
*Liverpool 1
Blackburn R. 0
*Burnley 1-3
Sunderland .. 1-0

*Oldham A. 0
Tottenham 1
*Colchester U. ...0
Man. U. 1
*Ipswich Town ...6
Bristol Rovers...1
*Liverpool 3
Burnley 0

*Tottenham ... 1-0
Man. U. 1-2
*Ipswich Town ...0
Liverpool 1

Man. U. 2-1
(at Maine Road:
Replay at Goodison Park
Liverpool 2-0

MANCHESTER UNITED 2

*Denotes home team † (3rd round replays played at Leicester) **Both games at West Bromwich ††Played at Blackburn.

F.A. CUP FINALS 1896-1979

1895-6 **SHEFFIELD WEDNESDAY**—Massey; Earp, Langley; H. Brandon, Crawshaw, Petrie; Brash, Brady, L. Bell, Calvis, Spiksley.
WOLVERHAMPTON WANDERERS—Tennant; Baugh, Dunn; Owen, Malpass, Griffiths; Tonks, Henderson, Beats, Wood, Black.
Scorers: Sheffield Wednesday—Spiksley 2, Wolverhampton—Black.

1896-7 **ASTON VILLA**—Whitehouse; Spencer, Evans; Reynolds, Cowan (Jas.), Crabtree; Athersmith, Devey (J.), Campbell, Weldon, Cowan (John).
EVERTON—Menham; Meecham, Storrier; Boyle, Holt, Stewart; Taylor, Bell, Hartly, Chadwick, Milward.
Scorers: Aston Villa—Campbell, Wheldon, Crabtree, Everton—Bell, Boyle.

1897-8 **NOTTINGHAM FOREST**—Allsop; Ritchie, Scott; Forman (Frank), McPherson, Wragg; McInnes, Richards, Benbow, Capes, Spoucer.
DERBY COUNTY—Fryer; Methven, Leiper; Cox, Goodall (A.), Turner; Goodall (J), Bloomer, Boag, Stevenson, McQueen.
Scorers: Nottingham Forest—Capes 2, McPherson, Derby County—Bloomer.

1898-9 **SHEFFIELD UNITED**—Foulke; Thickett, Boyle; Johnson, Morren, Needham; Bennett, Beers, Hedley, Almond, Priest.
DERBY COUNTY—Fryer; Methven, Staley; Cox, Peterson, May; Arksden, Bloomer, Boag, McDonald, Allen.
Scorers: Sheffield United—Bennett, Beers, Almond, Priest, Derby County—Boag.

1899-1900 **BURY** — Thompson; Darrock, Davidson; Pray, Leeming, Ross, Richards, Wood, McLuckie, Sagar, Plant.
SOUTHAMPTON — Robinson, Meehan, Durber, Meston, Chadwick, Petrie, Turner, Yates, Farrell, Wood, Milward.

1900-1 **TOTTENHAM HOTSPUR**—Clawley; Erentz, Tait; Morris, Hughes, Jones; Smith, Cameron, Brown, Copeland, Kirwan.
SHEFFIELD UNITED—Foulke; Thickett, Boyle; Johnson, Morren, Needham; Bennett, Field, Hedley, Priest, Lipsham.
Scorers: (first match) Tottenham Hotspur—Brown 2, Sheffield United—Bennett, Priest.
Scorers: (second match) Tottenham Hotspur—Cameron, Smith, Brown, Sheffield United—Priest.

1901-2 **SHEFFIELD UNITED**—Foulke; Thickett, Boyle; Needham, Wilkinson, Johnson; Barnes, Common, Hedley, Priest, Lipsam. (Bennett was injured in the first match and Barnes took his place in the re-play.)
SOUTHAMPTON—Robinson; C. B. Fry, Molyneux; Metson, Bowman, Lee; A. Turner, Wood, Brown, Chadwick, J. Turner.
Scorers: (first match) Sheffield United—Common, Southampton—Wood. **Scorers:** (second match) Sheffield United—Hedley, Barnes, Southampton—Brown.

1902-3 **BURY**—Monteith; Lensey, McEwan; Johnson, Thorpe, Ross; Richards, Wood, Sagar, Leeming, Plant.
DERBY COUNTY—Fryer; Methven, Merris; Warrent, Goodall (A.), May; Warrington, York, Boag, Richards, Davis.
Scorers: Bury—Ross, Sagar, Leeming 2, Wood, Plant.

1903-4 **MANCHESTER CITY**—Hillman; McMahon, Burgess; Frost, Hynde, S. B. Ashworth; Meredith, Livingstone, Gillespie, Turnbull (A.), Booth.
BOLTON WANDERERS—D. Davies; Brown, Struthers; Clifford, Greenhaigh, Freebairn; Stokes, Marsh, Yenson, White, Taylor.
Scorer: Manchester City—Meredith.

1904-5 **ASTON VILLA**—George; Spencer, Miles; Pearson, Leake, Windmill; Brawn, Garratty, Hampton, Bache, Hall.
NEWCASTLE UNITED—Lawrence; McCombie, Carr; Gardner, Aitken, McWilliam; Rutherford, Howie, Appleyard, Veitch, Gosnell.
Scorer: Aston Villa—Hampton 2.

1905-6 **EVERTON**—Scott; Balmer (W.), Crelly; Makepeace, Taylor, Abbott; Sharp, Bolton, Young, Settle, H. P. Hardman.
NEWCASTLE UNITED—Lawrence; McCombie, Carr, Gardner, Aitken, McWilliam; Rutherford, Howie, Veitch, Orr, Gosnell.
Scorer: Everton—Young.

1906-7 **SHEFFIELD WEDNESDAY**—Lyall; Layton, Burton; Brittleton, Crawshaw, Bartlett; Chapman, Bradshaw, Wilson, Stewart, Simpson.
EVERTON—Scott, Balmer (W.), Balmer (R.), Makepeace, Taylor, Abbott; Sharp, Bolton, Young, Settle, H. P. Hardman.
Scorers: Sheffield Wednesday—Stewart, Simpson, Everton—Sharp.

1907-8 **WOLVERHAMPTON WANDERERS**—Lunn; Jones, Collins, K. R. G. Hunt, Wooldridge, Bishop; Harrison, Shelton, Hedley, Radford, Pedley.
NEWCASTLE UNITED—Lawrence; McCracken, Pudan; Gardner, Veitch, McWilliam; Rutherford, Howie, Appleyard, Speedie, Wilson.
Scorers: Wolverhampton Wanderers—Rsv. K. R. G. Hunt, Hedley, Harrison, Newcastle United—Howie.

1908-9 **MANCHESTER UNITED**—Moger; Stacey, Hayes; Duckworth, Roberts, Bell; Meredith, Halse, Turnbull (J.), Turnbull (A.), Wall.
BRISTOL CITY—Clay; Annan, Cottle; Hanlin, Wedlock, Sspear; Staniforth, Hardy, Gilligan, Burton, Hilton.
Scorer: Manchester United—Turnbull (A.).

1909-10 **NEWCASTLE UNITED**—Lawrence; McCracken, Carr; Veitch, Low, McWilliam; Rutherford, Howie, Shepherd, Higgins, Wilson, (Whitson was injured in first match and Carr took his place in the replay.).
BARNSLEY—Mearns; Downs, Ness; Glendenning, Boyle, Utley; Bartrop, Gadsby, Lillycrop, Tuffnell, Forman.
Scorers: (first match) Newcastle United—Rutherford. Barnsley—Tuffnell.
Scorers: (second match) Newcastle United—Shepherd 2 (1 penalty).

1910-11 **BRADFORD CITY**—Mellors; Campbell, Taylor; Robinson, Torrance, McDonald; Logan, Spiers, O'Rourke, Devine, Thompson. (Gildea played centre half in the first match).
NEWCASTLE UNITED—Lawrence; McCracken, Whitson; Veitch, Low, Willis; Rutherford, Jobey, Stewart, Higgins, Wilson.
Scorer: Bradford City—Spiers.

1911-12 **BARNSLEY**—Cooper; Downs, Taylor; Glendinning, Bratley, Utley; Bartrop, Tuffnell, Lillycrop, Travers, Moore.
WEST BROMWICH ALBION—Pearson; Cook, Pennington; Badeley, Buck, McNeal; Jephcott, Wright, Pailor, Bowser, Shearman.
Scorer: Barnsley—Tuffnell.

1912-13 **ASTON VILLA**—Hardy; Lyons, Weston; Barber, Harrop, Leach; Wallace, Hasle, Hampton, Stephenson (C.), Bache.
SUNDERLAND—Butler; Gladwin, Ness; Cuggy, Thompson, Low; Mordue, Buchan, Richardson, Holley, Martin.
Scorer: Aston Villa—Barber.

1913-14 **BURNLEY**—Sewell; Bamford, Taylor; Halley, Boyle, Watson; Nesbit, Lindley, Freeman, Hodgson, Mosscrop.
LIVERPOOL—Campbell; Longworth, Pursell; Fairfoul, Ferguson,

McKinlay, Sheldon, Metcalf, Miller, Lacey, Nicholl.
Scorer: Burnley—Freeman.

1914-15 **SHEFFIELD UNITED**—Gough; Cook, English; Sturgess, Brelsford, Utley; Simmons, Fazakerley, Kitchen, Masterman, Evans.
CHELSEA—Molyneux; Bettridge, Harrow; Taylor, Logan, Walker; Ford, Halse, Thompson, Croal, McNeil.
Scorers: Sheffield United—Simmons, Fazakerley, Kitchen.

1919-20 **ASTON VILLA**—Hardy; Smart, Weston; Ducat, Barson, Moss; Wallace, Kirton, Walker, Stephenson (C.), Dorrell.
HUDDERSFIELD TOWN—Mutch; Wood, Bullock; Slade, Wilson, Watson; Richardson, Mann, Taylor, Swan, Islip.
Scorer: Aston Villa—Kirton.

1920-1 **TOTTENHAM HOTSPUR**—Hunter; Clay, M'Donald; Smith, Walters, Grimsdell; Banks, Seed, Cantrell, Bliss, Dimmock.
WOLVERHAMPTON WANDERERS—George; Woodward, Marshall; Gregory, Hodnett, Riley; Lea, Burrill, Edmonds, Potts, Brooks.
Scorer: Tottenham Hotspur—Dimmock.

1921-2 **HUDDERSFIELD TOWN**—Mutch; Wood, Wadsworth; Slade, Wilson, Watson; Richardson, Mann, Islip, Stephenson, Smith (W. H.).
PRESTON NORTH END—J. F. Mitchell; Hamilton, Doolan, Duxbury, McCall, Williamson; Rawlings, Jefferis, Roberts, Woodhouse, Quinn.
Scorer: Huddersfield Town—Smith (W. H.) pen.

1922-3 **BOLTON WANDERERS**—Pym; Howarth, Finney; Nuttall, Seddon, Jennings; Butler, Jack, Smith (J. R.), Smith (J.), Vizard.
WEST HAM UNITED—Hufton; Henderson, Young; Bishop, Kay, Tresadern; Richards, Brown, Watson (V.), Moore, Ruffell.
Scorers: Bolton Wanderers—Jack, Smith (J. R.)

1923-4 **NEWCASTLE UNITED**—Bradley; Hampson, Hudspeth, Mooney, Spencer, Gibson; Low, Cowan, Harris, M'Donald, Seymour.
ASTON VILLA—Jackson; Smart, Mort; Moss, Dr. V. E. Milne, Blackburn; York, Kirton, Capewell, Walker, Dorrell.
Scorers: Newcastle United—Harris, Seymour.

1924-5 **SHEFFIELD UNITED**—Sutcliffe; Cook, Milton; Pantling, King, Green; Mercer, Boyle, Johnson, Gillespie, Tunstall.
CARDIFF CITY—Farquharson; Nelson, Blair, Wake, Keenor, Hardy; Davies (W.). Gill, Nicholson, Beadles, Evans (J.).
Scorer: Sheffield United—Tunstall.

1925-6 **BOLTON WANDERERS**—Pym; Haworth, Greenhaigh; Nuttall, Seddon, Jennings; Butler, Jack, Smith (J. R.), Smith (J.), Vizard.
MANCHESTER CITY—Goodchild; Cookson, McCloy; Prindle, Cowan, McMullan; Austin, Browell, Roberts, Johnson, Hicks.
Scorer: Bolton Wanderers—Jack.

1926-7 **CARDIFF CITY**—Farquharson; Nelson, Watson; Keenor, Sloan, Hardy; Curtis, Irving, Ferguson, Davies (L.), M'Lachlan.
ARSENAL—Lewis; Parker, Kennedy; Baker, Butler, John; Hulme, Buchan, Brain, Blyth, Hoar.
Scorer: Cardiff City—Ferguson.

1927-8 **BLACKBURN ROVERS**—Crawford; Hutton, Jones; Healless, Rankin, Campbell; Thornewell, Puddefoot, Roscamp, M'Lean, Rigby.
HUDDERSFIELD TOWN—Mercer; Goodall, Barkas; Redfern, Wilson, Steele; Jackson (A.), Kelly, Brown, Stephenson, Smith (W. H.).
Scorers: Blackburn Rovers—Rosecamp 2, M'Lean, Huddersfield Town—Jackson.

1928-9 **BOLTON WANDERERS**—Pym; Howarth, Finney; Kean, Seddon, Nuttall; Butler, M'Clelland, Blackmore, Gibson, Cook (W.).
PORTSMOUTH—Gilfillan; Mackie, Bell; Nichol, McIlwaine, Thackeray; Forward, Smith (J.)., Weedle, Watson, Cook (F.).
Scorers: Bolton Wanderers—Butler, Blackmore.

1929-30 **ARSENAL**—Preedy; Parker, Hapgood; Baker, Seddon, John; Hulme, Jack, Lambert, James, Bastin.
HUDDERSFIELD TOWN—Turner; Goodall, Spence; Naylor, Wilson, Campbell; Jackson (A.), Kelly, Davies, Raw, Smith (W. H.).
Scorers: Arsenal—James, Lambert.

1930-1 **WEST BROMWICH ALBION**—Pearson; Shaw, Trentham; Magee, Richardson (W.), Edwards; Glidden, Carter, Richardson (W. G.), Sandford, Wood.
BIRMINGHAM CITY—Hibbs; Liddell, Barkas; Cringan, Morrall, Leslie, Briggs, Crosbie, Bradford, Gregg, Curtis.
Scorers: West Bromwich Albion—Richardson (W. G.) 2, Birmingham—Bradford.

1931-2 **NEWCASTLE UNITED**—McInroy; Nelson, Fairhurst, McKenzie, Davidson, Weaver; Boyd, Richardson, Allen, McMenemy, Lang.
ARSENAL—Moss; Parker, Hapgood; Jones (C.), Roberts, Male; Hulme, Jack, Lambert, Bastin, John.
Scorers: Newcastle United—Allen 2. Arsenal—John.

1932-3 **EVERTON**—Sagar; Cook, Cresswell; Britton, White, Thompson; Geldard, Dunn, Dean, Johnson, Stein.
MANCHESTER CITY—Langford; Cann, Dale; Busby, Cowan, Bray; Toseland, Marshall, Herd, McMullan, Brook.
Scorers: Everton—Stein, Dean, Dunn.

1933-4 **MANCHESTER CITY**—Swift; Barnett, Dale; Busby, Cowan, Bray; Toseland, Marshall, Tilson, Herd, Brook.
PORTSMOUTH—Gilfillan; Mackie, Smith (W.); Nichol, Allen, Thackeray; Worrall, Smith (J.), Weddle, Easson, Rutherford.
Scorers: Manchester City—Tilson 2, Portsmouth—Rutherford.

1934-5 **SHEFFIELD WEDNESDAY**—Brown; Nibloe, Catlin; Sharp, Millership, Burrows; Hooper, Surtees, Palethorpe, Starling, Rimmer.
WEST BROMWICH ALBION—Pearson; Shaw, Trentham, Murphy, Richardson (W.), Edwards; Glidden, Carter, Richardson (W. G.), Sandford, Boyes.
Scorers: Sheffield Wednesday—Rimmer 2, Palethorpe, Hooper, West Bromwich Albion—Boyes, Sandford.

1935-6 **ARSENAL**—Smith; Male, Hapgood; Crayston, Roberts, Copping; Hulme; Bowden, Drake, James, Bastin.
SHEFFIELD UNITED—Smith; Hooper, Wilkinson; Jackson, Johnson, McPherson; Barton, Barclay, Dodds, Pickering, Williams.
Scorer: Arsenal—Drake.

1936-7 **SUNDERLAND**—Mapson; Gorman, Hall; Thomson, Johnson, McNab; Duns, Carter, Gurney, Gallacher, Burbanks.
PRESTON NORTH END—Burns; Gallimore, Beattie (A.); Shankly, Tremelling, Milne; Dougal, Beresford, O'Donnell (F.), Fagan, O'Donnell (H.).
Scorers: Sunderland—Gurney, Carter, Burbanks, Preston North End—O'Donnell (F.).

1937-8 **PRESTON NORTH END**—Holdcroft; Gallimore, Beattie (A.); Shankly, Smith, Batley; Watmough, Mutch, Maxwell, Beattie (R.), O'Donnell (H.).
HUDDERSFIELD TOWN—Hesford; Craig, Mountford; Willingham, Young, Boot; Hulme, Isaac, McFayden, Barclay, Beasley.
Scorer: Preston North End—Mutch (pen.).

1938-9 **PORTSMOUTH**—Walker; Morgan, Rochford; Guthrie, Rowe, Wharton; Worrall, McAlinden, Anderson, Barlow, Parker.

WOLVERHAMPTON WANDERERS—Scott; Morris, Taylor; Galley, Cullis, Gardiner; Burton, McIntosh, Westcott, Dorsett, Maguire.
Scorers: Portsmouth—Parker 2, Barlow, Anderson. Wolverhampton Wanderers—Dorsett.

1945-6 **DERBY COUNTY**—Woodley; Nicholas, Howe; Bullions, Leuty, Musson; Harrison, Carter, Stamps, Doherty, Duncan.
CHARLTON ATHLETIC—Bartram; Phipps, Shreeve; Turner (H.), Oakes, Johnson; Fell, Brown, Turner (A. A.), Welsh, Duffy.
Scorers: Derby County—Turner (H.) (o.g.), Doherty, Stamps 2. Charlton Athletic—Turner (H.).

1946-7 **CHARLTON ATHLETIC**—Bartram; Croker, Shreeve, Johnson, Phipps, Whittaker; Hurst, Dawson, Robinson (W.), Welsh, Duffy.
BURNLEY—Strong; Woodruff, Mather; Atwell, Brown, Bray, Chew, Morris, Harrison, Potts, F. P. Kippax.
Scorer: Charlton Athletic—Duffy.

1947-8 **MANCHESTER UNITED**—Crompton; Carey, Aston; Anderson, Chilton, Cockburn; Delaney, Morris, Rowley, Pearson, Mitten.
BLACKPOOL—Robinson; Shimwell, Crosland; Johnston, Hayward, Kelly; Matthews, Munro, Mortenson, Dick, Rickett.
Scorers: Manchester United—Rowley 2, Pearson, Anderson. Blackpool—Shimwell (pen.), Mortensen.

1948-9 **WOLVERHAMPTON WANDERERS**—Williams; Pritchard, Springthorpe; Crook (W.), Shorthouse, Wright; Hancocks, Smyth, Pye, Dunn, Mullen.
LEICESTER CITY—Bradley; Jelly, Scott; Harrison (W.)., Plummer, King, Griffiths, Lee, Harrison (J.), Chisholm, Adam.
Scorers: Wolverhampton Wanderers—Pye 2, Smyth. Leicester City—Griffiths.

1949-50 **ARSENAL**—Swindin; Scott, Barnes; Forbes, Crompton (L.), Mercer; Cox, Logie, Goring, Lewis, Crompton (D.).
LIVERPOOL—Sidlow; Lambert, Spicer; Taylor, Hughes, Jones; Payne, Baron, Stubbins, Fagan, Liddell.
Scorer: Arsenal—Lewis 2.

1950-1 **NEWCASTLE UNITED**—Fairbrother, Cowell; Corbett; Harvey, Brennan, Crowe; Walker, Taylor, Milburn, Robledo (G.), Mitchell.
BLACKPOOL—Farm; Shimwell, Garrett; Johnston, Hayward, Kelly; Matthews, Mudie, Mortensen, W. J. Slater, Perry.
Scorer: Newcastle United—Milburn 2.

1951-2 **NEWCASTLE UNITED**—Simpson; Cowell, McMichael; Harvey, Brennan, Robledo (E.); Walker, Foulkes, Milburn, Robledo (G.), Mitchell.
ARSENAL—Swindon; Barnes, Smith (L.); Forbes, Daniel, Mercer; Cox, Logie, Holton, Lishman, Roper.
Scorer: Newcastle United—Robledo (G.).

1952-3 **BLACKPOOL**—Farm; Shimwell, Garrett; Fenton, Johnston, Robinson; Matthews, Taylor, Mortensen, Mudie, Perry.
BOLTON WANDERERS—Hanson; Ball, Banks (R.), Wheeler, Barrass, Bell; Holden, Moir, Lofthouse, Hassall, Langton.
Scorers: Blackpool—Mortensen 3, Perry. Bolton Wanderers—Lofthouse, Moir, Bell.

1953-4 **WEST BROMWICH ALBION**—Sanders; Kennedy, Milward; Dudley, Dugdale, Barlow; Griffin, Ryan, Allen, Nichols, Lee.
PRESTON NORTH END—Thompson; Cunningham, Walton; Doherty, Marston, Forbes; Finney, Foster, Wayman, Baxter, Morrison.
Scorers: West Bromwich Albion—Allen 2, Griffin. Preston North End—Morrison, Wayman.

1954-5 **NEWCASTLE UNITED**—Simpson, Cowell, Batty; Scoular, Stokoe, Casey; White, Milburn, Keeble, Hannah, Mitchell.
MANCHESTER CITY—Trautmann; Meadows, Little; Barnes, Ewing, Paul; Spurdle, Hayes, Revie, Johnstone, Fagan.
Scorers: Newcastle United—Milburn, Mitchell, Hannah. Manchester City—Johnstone.

1955-6 **MANCHESTER CITY**—Trautmann; Leivers, Little; Barnes, Ewing, Paul; Johnstone, Hayes, Revie, Dyson, Clarke.
BIRMINGHAM CITY—Merrick; Hall, Green; Norman, Smith, Boyd; Astall, Kinsey, Brown, Murphy, Govan.
Scorers: Manchester City—Hayes, Dyson, Johnstone. Birmingham City—Kinsey.

1956-7 **ASTON VILLA**—Sims; Lynn, Aldis; Crowther, Dugdale, Saward; Smith, Sewell, Myerscough, Dixon, McParland.
MANCHESTER UNITED—Wood; Foulkes, Byrne; Colman, Blanchflower, Edwards; Berry, Whelan, Taylor (T.), Charlton, Pegg.
Scorers: Aston Villa—McParland 2. Manchester United—Taylor.

1957-8 **BOLTON WANDERERS**—Hopkinson; Hartle, Banks; Hennin, Higgins, Edwards; Birch, Stevens, Lofthouse, Perry, Holden.
MANCHESTER UNITED—Gregg; Foulkes, Greaves; Goodwin, Cope, Crowther; Dawson, Taylor (E.), Charlton, Viollet, Webster.
Scorer: Bolton Wanderers—Lofthouse 2.

1958-9 **NOTTINGHAM FOREST**—Thompson; Whare, McDonald; Whitefoot, McKinley, Burkett; Dwight, Quigley, Wilson, Gray, Imlach.
LUTON TOWN—Baynham; McNally, Hawkes; Groves, Owen, Pacey; Bingham, Brown, Morton, Cummings, Gregory.
Scorers: Nottingham Forest—Dwight, Wilson. Luton Town—Pacey.

1959-60 **WOLVERHAMPTON WANDERERS**—Finlayson; Showell, Harris; Clamp, Slater, Flowers; Deeley, Stobart, Murray, Broadbent, Horne.
BLACKBURN ROVERS—Leyland; Bray, Whelan; Clayton, Woods, McGrath, Bimpson, Dobin, Dougan, Douglas, McLeod.
Scorers: Wolverhampton Wanderers—McGrath (o.g.). Deeley 2.

1960-1 **TOTTENHAM HOTSPUR**—Brown, Baker, Henry; Blanchflower Norman, Mackay; Jones, White, Smith, Allen, Dyson.
LEICESTER CITY—Banks; Chalmers, Norman; McLintock, King, Appleton; Riley, Walsh, McIlmoyle, Keyworth, Cheesbrough.
Scorers: Tottenham Hotspur– Smith, Dyson.

1961-2 **TOTTENHAM HOTSPUR**—Brown; Baker, Henry; Blanchflower. Norman, Mackay; Medwin, White, Smith, Greaves, Jones.
BURNLEY—Blacklaw; Angus, Elder; Adamson, Cummings, Miller, Connelly, McIlroy, Pointer, Robson, Harris.
Scorers: Tottenham Hotspur—Greaves, Smith, Blanchflower (pen.). Burnley—Robson.

1962-3 **MANCHESTER UNITED**—Gaskell; Dunne, Cantwell; Crerand, Foulkes, Setters; Giles, Quixall, Herd, Law, Charlton.
LEICESTER CITY—Banks; Sjoberg, Norman; McLintock, King, Appleton; Riley, Cross, Keyworth, Gibson, Stringfellow.
Scorers: Manchester United—Law, Herd 2. Leicester City Keyworth.

1963-4 **WEST HAM UNITED**—Standen; Bond, Burkett; Bovington, Brown, Moore; Brabrook, Boyce, Byrne, Hurst, Sissons.
PRESTON NORTH END—Kelly; Ross, Smith; Lawton, Singleton, Kendall; Wilson, Ashworth, Dawson, Spavin, Holden.
Scorers: West Ham United—Sissons, Hurst, Boyce. Preston North End—Holden, Dawson.

1964-5 **LIVERPOOL**—Lawrence; Lawler, Byrne; Strong, Yeats, Stevenson; Callaghan, Hunt, St. John, Smith, Thompson.
LEEDS UNITED—Sprake; Reaney, Bell; Bremner, Charlton, Hunter;

Giles, Storrie, Peacock, Collins, Johanneson.
Scorers: Liverpool—Hunt, St. John. Leeds United—Bremner.

1965-6 **EVERTON**—West; Wright, Wilson; Gabriel, Labone, Harris; Scott, Trebilcock, Young, Harvey, Temple.
SHEFFIELD WEDNESDAY—Springett; Smith, Megson; Eustace, Ellis, Young, Pugh, Fantham, McCalliog, Ford, Quinn.
Scorers: Everton—Trebilcock 2, Temple. Sheffield Wednesday—McCalliog, Ford.

1966-7 **TOTTENHAM HOTSPUR**—Jennings; Kinnear, Knowles; Mullery, England, Mackay; Robertson, Greaves, Gilzean, Venables, Saul. Sub: Jones.
CHELSEA—Bonetti; Harris (A.), McCreadie; Hollins, Hinton, Harris (R.); Cooke, Baldwin, Hately, Tambling, Boyle. Sub: Kirkup.
Scorers: Tottenham Hotspur—Robertson, Saul. Chelsea—Tambling.

1967-8 **WEST BROMWICH ALBION**—Osborne; Fraser, Williams; Brown, Talbut, Kaye; Lovett, Collard, Astle, Hope, Clark. Sub: Clarke.
EVERTON—West; Wright, Wilson; Kendall, Labone, Harvey; Husband, Ball, Royle, Hurst, Morrissey. Sub: Kenyon.
Scorer: West Bromwich Albion—Astle.

1968-9 **MANCHESTER CITY**—Dowd; Book, Pardoe; Doyle, Booth, Oakes, Summerbee, Bell, Lee, Young, Coleman. Sub: Connor.
LEICESTER CITY—Shilton; Rodrigues, Nish, Roberts, Woollett, Cross; Fern, Gibson, Lockhead, Clarke, Glover. Sub: Manley.
Scorer: Manchester City—Young.

1969-70 **CHELSEA**—Bonetti; Webb, McCreadie; Hollins, Dempsey, Harris; Baldwin, Houseman, Osgood, Hutchinson, Cooke. Sub: Hinton.
LEEDS UNITED—Sprake; Madeley, Cooper; Bremner, Charlton, Hunter; Lorimer, Clarke, Jones, Giles, Gray. Sub: Bates.
Scorers: Chelsea—Houseman, Hutchinson. Leeds—Charlton, Jones.
Replay: Chelsea unchanged. Leeds: Harvey for Sprake.
Scorers: Chelsea—Osgood, Webb, Leeds—Jones.

1970-1 **ARSENAL**—Wilson; Rice, McNab; Storey, McLintock, Simpson; Armstrong, Graham, Radford, Kennedy, George. Sub: Kelly.
LIVERPOOL—Clemence; Lawler, Lindsay; Smith, Lloyd, Hughes, Callaghan, Evans, Heighway, Toshack, Hall. Sub: Thompson.
Scorers: Arsenal—Graham, George. Liverpool—Heighway.

1971-2 **LEEDS UNITED**—Harvey; Reaney, Madeley; Bremner, Charlton, Hunter; Lorimer, Clarke, Jones, Giles, Gray. Sub: Bates.
ARSENAL—Barnett; Rice, McNab; Storey, McLintock, Simpson; Armstrong, Radford, George, Ball, Graham. Sub: Kennedy.
Scorer: Leeds United—Clarke.

1972-3 **SUNDERLAND**—Montgomery; Malone, Guthrie; Horswill, Watson, Pitt; Kerr, Hughes, Halom, Porterfield, Tuart. Sub: Young.
LEEDS UNITED—Harvey; Reaney, Cherry; Bremner, Madeley, Hunter; Lorimer, Clarke, Jones, Giles, Gray. Sub: Yorath.
Scorer: Sunderland—Porterfield.

1973-4 **LIVERPOOL**—Clemence; Smith, Lindsay; Thompson, Cormack, Hughes; Keegan, Hall, Heighway, Toshack, Callaghan. Sub: Lawler.
NEWCASTLE UNITED—McFaul; Clarke, Kennedy; McDermott, Howard, Moncur; Smith, Cassidy, Macdonald, Tudor, Hibbitt. Sub: Gibb.
Scorers: Liverpool—Keegan (2). Heighway.

1974-5 **WEST HAM UNITED**—Day; McDowell, Lampard; Bonds, Taylor (T.), Lock; Jennings, Paddon, Taylor (A.), Brooking, Holland, Sub: Gould.
FULHAM—Mellor; Cutbush, Fraser; Mullery, Lacy, Moore; Mitchell, Conway, Busby, Slough, Barrett. Sub: Lloyd.
Scorer: West Ham United—Taylor (A.) 2.

1975-6 **SOUTHAMPTON**—Turner; Rodrigues, Peach; Holmes, Blyth, Gilchrist; Steele, Channon, Osgood, Stokes, McCalliog. Sub: Fisher.
MANCHESTER UNITED—Stepney; Forsyth, Houston; Daly, Greenhoff, Buchan; Coppell, McIlroy, Pearson, Macari, Hill. Sub: McCreary.
Scorer: Southampton—Stokes.

1976-7 **MANCHESTER UNITED**—Stepney; Nichol, Albiston; McIlroy, Greenhoff (B.), Buchan; Coppell, Greenhoff (J.), Pearson, Macari, Hill. Sub: McCreery.
LIVERPOOL—Clemence; Neal, Jones; Smith, Hughes, Kennedy· McDermott, Case, Keegan, Heighway, Johson. Sub: Callaghan.
Scorers: Manchester United—Pearson, Greenhoff (J.). Liverpool—Case.

1977-8 **IPSWICH TOWN**—Cooper; Burley, Mills; Talbot, Hunter, Beattie; Osborne, Wark, Marriner, Geddis, Woods. Sub: Lambert.
ARSENAL—Jennings; Rice, Nelson; Price, O'Leary, Young; Brady, Sunderland, Macdonald, Stapleton, Hudson. Sub: Rix.
Scorer: Ipswich Town—Osborne.

1978-9 **ARSENAL**—Jennings, Rice, Nelson, Talbot, O'Leary, Young, Brady, Sunderland, Stapleton, Price, Rix. Sub: Walford.
MANCHESTER UNITED—Bailey, Nicholl, Albiston, McIlroy, McQueen, Buchan, Coppel, Greenhoff (J.), Jordan, Macari, Thomas. Sub: Greenhoff (B.).
Scorers: Arsenal—Talbot, Stapleton, Sunderland. Manchester United—McQueen, McIlroy.

F.A. CUP WINNERS

From Kennington Oval to Wembley Stadium

AT KENNINGTON OVAL

1871-2—Wanderers beat Royal Engineers (1-0)

AT LILLIE BRIDGE

1872-3—Wanderers beat Oxford University (2-0)

AT KENNINGTON OVAL

1873-4—Oxford University beat Royal Engineers (2-0)
1874-5—Royal Engineers beat Old Etonians (2-0, after a draw 1-1)
1875-6—Wanderers beat Old Etonians (3-0, after a draw 0-0)
1876-7—Wanderers beat Oxford University (2-0 after extra half-hour)
1877-8—*Wanderers beat Royal Engineers (3-1)
1878-9—Old Etonians beat Clapham Rovers (1-0)
1879-80—Clapham Rovers beat Oxford University (1-0)
1880-1—Old Carthusians beat Old Etonians (3-0)
1881-2—Old Etonians beat Blackburn Rovers (1-0)
1882-3—Blackburn Olym. beat Old Etonians (2-1, after extra half-hour)
1883-4—Blackburn Rovers beat Queens Park (Glasgow) (2-1)
1884-5—Blackburn Rovers beat Queens Park (Glasgow) (2-0)
1885-6—†‡Blackburn R. beat W. Brom. A. (2-0, after a draw 0-0)
1886-7—Aston Villa beat West Bromwich Albion (2-0)
1887-8—West Bromwich Albion beat Preston North End (2-1)
1888-9—Preston North End beat Wolverhampton Wanderers (3-0)
1889-90—Blackburn Rovers beat Sheffield Wednesday (6-1)
1890-1—Blackburn Rovers beat Notts County (3-1)
1891-2—West Bromwich Albion beat Aston Villa (3-0)

AT FALLOWFIELD, MANCHESTER

1892–3—Wolverhampton Wanderers beat Everton (1–0)

AT EVERTON

1893–4—Notts County beat Bolton Wanderers (4–1)

AT CRYSTAL PALACE

1894–5—Aston Villa beat West Bromwich Albion (1–0)
1895–6—Sheffield Wednesday beat Wolverhampton Wanderers (2–1)
1896–7—Aston Villa beat Everton (3–2)
1897–8—Nottingham Forest beat Derby County (3–1)
1898–9—Sheffield United beat Derby County (4–1)
1899–1900—Bury beat Southampton (4–0)
1900–1—††Tottenham H. beat Sheffield U. (3–1, after a draw 2–2)
1901–2—Sheffield United beat Southampton (2–1, after a draw 1–1)
1902–3—Bury beat Derby County (6–0)
1903–4—Manchester City beat Bolton Wanderers (1–0)
1904–5—Aston Villa beat Newcastle United (2–0)
1905–6—Everton beat Newcastle United (1–0)
1906–7—Sheffield Wednesday beat Everton (2–1)
1907–8—Wolverhampton Wanderers beat Newcastle United (3–1)
1908–9—Manchester United beat Bristol City (1–0)
1909–10—**Newcastle United beat Barnsley (2–0, after 1–1)
1910–11—*a*Bradford City beat Newcastle United (1–0, after a draw 0–0)
1911–12—*b*Barnsley beat West Bromwich Albion (1–0, after a draw 0–0)
1912–13—Aston Villa beat Sunderland (1–0)
1913–14—Burnley beat Liverpool (1–0)
1914–15—Sheffield United beat Chelsea (3–0) (at Old Trafford)

AT STAMFORD BRIDGE

1919–20—††Aston Villa beat Huddersfield Town (1–0)
1920–1—Tottenham Hotspur beat Wolverhampton Wanderers (1–0)
1921–2—Huddersfield Town beat Preston North End (1–0)

AT WEMBLEY STADIUM

1922–3—Bolton Wanderers beat West Ham (2–0)
1923–4—Newcastle United beat Aston Villa (2–0)
1924–5—Sheffield United beat Cardiff City (1–0)
1925–6—Bolton Wanderers beat Manchester City (1–0)
1926–7—Cardiff City beat Arsenal (1–0)
1927–8—Blackburn Rovers beat Huddersfield Town (3–1)
1928–9—Bolton Wanderers beat Portsmouth (2–0)
1929–30—Arsenal beat Huddersfield Town (2–0)
1930–1—West Bromwich Albion beat Birmingham (2–1)
1931–2—Newcastle United beat Arsenal (2–1)
1932–3—Everton beat Manchester City (3–0)
1933–4—Manchester City beat Portsmouth (2–1)
1934–5—Sheffield Wednesday beat West Bromwich Albion (4–2)
1935–6—Arsenal beat Sheffield United (1–0)
1936–7—Sunderland beat Preston North End (3–1)
1937–8—††Preston North End beat Huddersfield Town (1–0)
1938–9—Portsmouth beat Wolverhampton Wanderers (4–1)
1945–6—††Derby County beat Charlton (4–1)
1946–7—††Charlton Athletic beat Burnley (1–0)
1947–8—Manchester United beat Blackpool (4–2)
1948–9—Wolverhampton Wanderers beat Leicester City (3–1)
1949–50—Arsenal beat Liverpool (2–0)

1950–1—Newcastle United beat Blackpool (2–0)
1951–2—Newcastle United beat Arsenal (1–0)
1952–3—Blackpool beat Bolton Wanderers (4–3)
1953–4—West Bromwich Albion beat Preston North End (3 2)
1954–5—Newcastle United beat Manchester City (3–1)
1955–6—Manchester City beat Birmingham City (3–1)
1956–7—Aston Villa beat Manchester United (2–1)
1957–8—Bolton Wanderers beat Manchester United (2–0)
1958–9—Nottingham Forest beat Luton Town (2–1)
1959–60—Wolverhampton Wanderers beat Blackburn Rovers (3 0)
1960–1—Tottenham Hotspur beat Leicester City (2–0)
1961–2—Tottenham Hotspur beat Burnley (3–1)
1962–3—Manchester United beat Leicester City (3–1)
1963–4—West Ham United beat Preston North End (3–2)
1964–5—††Liverpool beat Leeds United (2–1)
1965–6—Everton beat Sheffield Wednesday (3–2)
1966–7—Tottenham Hotspur beat Chelsea (2–1)
1967–8—††West Bromwich Albion beat Everton (1–0)
1968–9—Manchester City beat Leicester City (1–0)
1969–70—††Chelsea beat Leeds (2–1, after a draw 2–2
1970–1—††Arsenal beat Liverpool (2–1)
1971–2—Leeds beat Arsenal (1–0)
1972–3—Sunderland beat Leeds (1–0)
1973–4—Liverpool beat Newcastle (3–0)
1974–5—West Ham beat Fulham (2–0)
1975–6—Southampton beat Manchester United (1–0)
1976–7—Manchester United beat Liverpool (2–1)
1977–8—Ipswich Town beat Arsenal (1–0)
1978–9—Arsenal beat Manchester United (3–2)

*Won outright, but restored to the. Association. †A special trophy was awarded for the third consecutive win. ‡First time final tie played in the provinces—replay at Derby. ‡‡Replayed at Bolton. **Replayed at Everton. *a* Replayed at Old Trafford, new trophy provided. *b* Replayed at Bramall Lane. Sheffield. ††After extra time.

FOOTBALL LEAGUE TABLES

DIVISION ONE

Champions: Liverpool. **Runners-up**: Nottingham Forest

		Home			Goals		Away			Goals		
	P.	W.	D.	L.	F.	A.	W.	D.	L.	F.	A.	Pts.
Liverpool	42	19	2	0	51	4	11	6	4	34	12	68
Notts. For.	42	11	10	0	34	10	10	8	3	27	16	60
WBA	42	13	5	3	38	15	11	6	4	34	20	59
Everton	42	12	7	2	32	17	5	10	6	20	23	51
Leeds U.	42	11	4	6	41	25	7	10	4	29	27	50
Ipswich	42	11	4	6	34	21	9	5	7	29	28	49
Arsenal	42	11	8	2	37	18	6	6	9	24	30	48
Aston V.	42	8	9	4	37	26	7	7	7	22	23	46
Man Utd.	42	9	7	5	29	25	6	8	7	31	38	45
Coventry	42	11	7	3	41	29	3	9	9	17	39	44
Tottenham ..	42	7	8	6	19	25	6	7	8	29	36	41
Middlesbro ...	42	10	5	6	33	21	5	5	11	24	29	40
Bristol C.	42	11	6	4	34	19	4	4	13	13	32	40
Southampton .	42	9	10	2	35	20	3	6	12	12	33	40
Man C.	42	9	5	7	34	28	4	8	9	24	28	39
Norwich	42	7	10	4	29	19	0	13	8	22	38	37
Bolton	42	10	5	6	36	28	2	6	13	18	47	35
Wolves	42	10	4	7	26	26	3	4	14	18	42	34
Derby Co.	42	8	5	8	25	25	2	6	13	19	46	31
QPR	42	4	9	8	24	33	2	4	15	21	40	25
Birmingham	42	5	9	7	24	25	1	1	19	13	39	22
Chelsea	42	3	5	13	23	42	2	5	14	21	50	20

Relegated: Queens Park Rangers, Birmingham City, Chelsea

DIVISION TWO

Promoted: Crystal Palace (Champions), Brighton, Stoke City

		Home			Goals		Away			Goals		
	P.	W.	D.	L.	F.	A.	W.	D.	L.	F.	A.	Pts.
Crystal P.	42	12	7	2	30	11	7	12	2	21	13	57
Brighton	42	16	3	2	44	11	7	7	7	28	28	56
Stoke	42	11	7	3	35	15	9	9	3	23	16	56
Sunderland ...	42	13	3	5	39	19	9	8	4	31	25	55
West Ham	42	12	7	2	46	15	6	7	8	24	24	50
Notts C.	42	8	10	3	23	15	6	6	9	25	45	44
Preston	42	7	11	3	36	23	5	7	9	23	34	42
Newcastle	42	13	3	5	35	24	4	5	12	16	31	42
Cardiff	42	12	5	4	34	23	4	5	12	22	47	42
Fulham	42	10	7	4	35	19	3	8	10	15	28	41
Orient	42	11	5	5	32	18	4	5	12	19	33	40
Cambridge	42	7	10	4	22	15	5	6	10	22	37	40
Burnley	42	11	6	4	31	22	3	6	12	20	40	40
Oldham	42	10	7	4	36	23	3	6	12	16	38	39
Wrexham	42	10	6	5	31	16	2	8	11	14	26	38
Bristol R.	42	10	6	5	34	23	4	4	13	14	37	38
Leicester	42	7	8	6	28	23	3	9	9	15	29	37
Luton	42	11	5	5	46	24	2	5	14	14	33	36
Charlton	42	6	8	7	28	28	5	5	11	32	41	35
Sheff. U	42	9	6	6	34	24	2	6	13	18	45	34
Millwall	42	7	4	10	22	29	4	6	11	20	32	32
Blackburn	42	5	8	8	24	29	5	2	14	17	43	30

Relegated: Sheffield United, Millwall, Blackburn Rovers

DIVISION THREE

Promoted: Shrewsbury Town (Champions), Watford, Swansea City

		Home			Goals		Away			Goals		
	P.	W.	D.	L.	F.	A.	W.	D.	L.	F.	A.	Pts.
Shrewsbury	46	14	9	0	36	11	7	10	6	25	30	61
Watford	46	15	5	3	47	22	9	7	7	36	30	60
Swansea	46	16	6	1	57	32	8	6	9	26	29	60
Gillingham	46	15	7	1	39	15	6	10	7	26	27	59
Swindon	46	17	2	4	44	14	8	5	10	30	38	57
Carlisle	46	11	10	2	31	13	4	12	7	22	29	52
Colchester	46	13	9	1	35	19	4	8	11	25	36	51
Hull	46	12	9	2	36	14	7	2	14	30	47	49
Exeter	46	14	6	3	38	18	3	9	11	23	38	49
Brentford	46	14	4	5	35	19	5	5	13	18	30	47
Oxford	46	10	8	5	27	20	4	10	9	17	30	46
Blackpool	46	12	5	6	38	19	6	4	13	23	40	45
Southend	46	11	6	6	30	17	4	9	10	21	32	45
Sheff. W.	46	9	8	6	30	22	4	11	8	23	31	45
Plymouth	46	11	9	3	40	27	4	5	14	27	41	44
Chester	46	11	9	3	42	21	3	7	13	15	40	44
Rotherham	46	13	3	7	30	23	4	7	12	19	32	44
Mansfield	46	7	11	5	30	24	5	8	10	21	28	43
Bury	46	6	11	6	35	32	5	9	9	24	33	42
Chesterfield	46	10	5	8	35	34	3	9	11	16	31	40
Peterboro	46	8	7	8	26	24	3	7	13	18	39	36
Walsall	46	7	6	10	34	32	3	6	14	22	39	32
Tranmere	46	4	12	7	26	31	2	4	17	19	47	28
Lincoln	46	5	7	11	26	38	2	4	17	15	50	25

Relegated: Peterborough United, Walsall, Tranmere Rovers, Lincoln City

DIVISION FOUR

Promoted: Reading (Champions), Grimsby Town, Wimbledon, Barnsley

		Home			Goals		Away			Goals		
	P.	W.	D.	L.	F.	A.	W.	D.	L.	F.	A.	Pts.
Reading	46	19	3	1	49	8	7	10	6	27	27	65
Grimsby	46	15	5	3	51	23	11	4	8	31	26	61
Wimbldn	46	18	3	2	50	20	7	8	8	28	26	61
Barnsley	46	15	5	3	47	23	9	8	6	26	19	61
Aldershot	46	16	5	2	38	14	4	12	7	25	33	57
Wigan	46	14	5	4	40	24	7	8	8	23	24	55
Portsmth	46	13	7	3	35	12	7	5	11	27	36	52
Newport	46	12	5	6	39	28	9	5	9	27	27	52
Huddrsfld	46	13	8	2	32	15	5	3	15	25	38	47
York	46	11	6	6	33	24	7	5	11	18	31	47
Torquay	46	14	4	5	38	24	5	4	14	20	41	46
Scunthrp	46	12	3	8	33	30	5	8	10	21	30	45
Hartlpool	46	7	12	4	35	28	6	6	11	22	38	44
Hereford	46	12	8	3	35	18	3	5	15	18	35	43
Bradford	46	11	5	7	38	26	6	4	13	24	42	43
Port Vale	46	8	10	5	29	28	6	4	13	28	42	42
Stockport	46	11	5	7	33	21	3	7	13	25	39	40
Bournmth	46	11	6	6	34	19	3	5	15	13	29	39
Nrthmptn	46	12	4	7	40	30	3	5	15	24	46	39
Rochdale	46	11	4	8	25	26	4	5	14	22	38	39
Darlington	46	8	8	7	25	21	3	7	13	24	45	37
Doncaster	46	8	8	7	25	22	5	3	15	25	51	37
Halifax	46	7	5	11	24	32	2	3	18	15	40	26
Crewe	46	3	7	13	24	41	3	7	13	19	49	26

Re-elected: Darlington, Doncaster Rovers, Halifax Town, Crewe Alexandra

SCOTTISH LEAGUE TABLES

PREMIER DIVISION

Champions: Celtic **Runners-up**: Rangers

		Home			Goals		Away			Goals		
	P.	W.	D.	L.	F.	A.	W.	D.	L.	F.	A.	Pts.
Celtic	36	13	3	2	32	12	8	3	7	29	25	48
Rangers	36	12	5	1	32	10	6	4	8	20	25	45
Dundee U.	36	12	4	2	33	16	6	4	8	23	21	44
Aberdeen	36	9	5	4	39	16	4	9	5	20	20	40
Hibernian	36	7	9	2	23	16	5	4	9	21	32	37
St. Mirren	36	8	3	7	23	20	7	3	8	22	21	36
Morton	36	9	4	5	34	23	3	8	7	18	30	36
Partick	36	10	2	6	31	21	3	6	9	11	18	34
Hearts	36	5	5	8	19	25	3	2	13	20	46	23
Motherwell	36	2	5	11	20	38	3	2	13	13	48	17

Relegated: Hearts, Motherwell

DIVISION ONE

Promoted: Dundee (Champions), Kilmarnock

		Home			Goals		Away			Goals		
	P.	W.	D.	L.	F.	A.	W.	D.	L.	F.	A.	Pts.
Dundee	39	13	5	1	36	12	11	2	7	32	24	55
Kilmarnock	39	13	5	1	41	14	9	5	6	31	21	54
Clydebank	39	15	2	3	48	23	9	4	6	30	27	54
Ayr	39	12	3	5	39	19	9	2	8	32	33	47
Hamilton	39	13	4	2	39	17	4	5	11	23	43	43
Airdrie	39	9	4	7	44	33	7	4	8	28	28	40
Dumbarton	39	9	3	8	30	21	5	8	6	28	28	39
Stirling A.	39	6	4	9	23	29	7	5	8	20	26	35
Clyde	39	8	3	8	30	29	5	5	10	24	36	24
Arbroath	39	8	6	6	33	26	3	5	11	17	35	33
Raith	39	8	3	8	29	21	4	5	11	18	34	22
St. Johnstone .	39	6	8	6	32	28	4	3	12	25	38	31
Montrose	39	4	6	9	31	37	4	3	13	24	55	25
Queen of S.	39	8	4	8	31	35	0	4	15	12	58	24

Relegated: Montrose, Queen of the South

DIVISION TWO

Promoted: Berwick Rangers (Champions), Dunfermline

		Home			Goals		Away			Goals		
	P.	W.	D.	L.	F.	A.	W.	D.	L.	F.	A.	Pts.
Berwick	39	11	6	3	45	22	11	4	4	37	22	54
Dunfermline ...	39	13	6	1	41	19	6	8	5	25	21	52
Falkirk	39	13	4	3	39	16	6	8	5	27	21	50
East Fife	39	10	2	7	33	22	7	7	6	31	31	43
Cowdenbeath .	39	10	5	4	37	22	6	5	9	26	36	42
Alloa	39	10	7	3	36	26	6	2	11	21	36	41
Albion R.	39	9	6	4	28	17	6	4	10	29	39	40
Forfar	39	9	7	4	35	25	4	5	10	20	27	38
Stranraer	39	11	1	7	32	27	7	1	12	20	39	38
Stenh'smuir ...	39	6	4	10	34	30	6	4	9	20	28	32
Brechin	39	8	7	5	31	33	1	7	11	18	32	32
E. Stirling	39	10	4	5	42	31	2	4	14	19	56	32
Queens Pk.	39	4	7	8	19	19	4	5	11	27	38	28
Meadowbank ..	39	5	3	11	17	31	3	5	12	20	43	24

SCOTTISH LEAGUE DIV. 1

	First	Pts.	Second	Pts.	Third	Pts.
1896–7*a*	Hearts	28	Hibernian	26	Rangers	25
1897–8*a*	Celtic	33	Rangers	29	Hibernian	22
1898–9*a*	Rangers	36	Hearts	26	Celtic	24
1899-1900*a*	Rangers	32	Celtic	25	Hibernian	24
1900–1*c*	Rangers	35	Celtic	29	Hibernian	25
1901–2*a*	Rangers	28	Celtic	26	Hearts	22
1902–3*b*	Hibernian	37	Dundee	31	Rangers	29
1903–4*d*	Third Lanark ...	43	Hearts	39	Rangers	38
1904–5*a*	†Celtic	41	Rangers	41	Third Lanark ...	35
1905–6*e*	Celtic	49	Hearts	39	Rangers	38
1906–7*f*	Celtic	55	Dundee	48	Rangers	45
1907–8*f*	Celtic	55	Falkirk	51	Rangers	50
1908–9*f*	Celtic	51	Dundee	50	Clyde	48
1909–10*f*	Celtic	54	Falkirk	52	Rangers	49
1910–11*f*	Rangers	52	Aberdeen	48	Falkirk	44
1911–12*f*	Rangers	51	Celtic	45	Clyde	42
1912–13*f*	Rangers	53	Celtic	49	*Hearts	41
1913–14*g*	Celtic	65	Rangers	59	*Hearts	54
1914–15*g*	Celtic	65	Hearts	61	Rangers	50
1915–16*g*	Celtic	67	Rangers	56	Morton	51
1916–17*g*	Celtic	64	Morton	54	Rangers	53
1917–18*f*	Rangers	56	Celtic	55	*Kilmarnock	43
1918–19*f*	Celtic	58	Rangers	57	Morton	47
1919–20*h*	Rangers	71	Celtic	68	Motherwell	57
1920–1*h*	Rangers	76	Celtic	66	Hearts	56
1921–2*h*	Celtic	67	Rangers	66	Raith Rovers ...	56
1923–3*g*	Rangers	55	Airdrieonians ..	50	Celtic	40
1923–4*g*	Rangers	59	Airdrieonians ..	50	Celtic	41
1924–5*g*	Rangers	60	Airdrieonians ..	57	Hibernians	52
1925–6*g*	Celtic	58	*Airdrieonians ..	50	Hearts	50
1926–7*g*	Rangers	56	Motherwell	51	Celtic	49
1927–8*g*	Rangers	60	*Celtic	55	Motherwell	55
1928–9*g*	Rangers	67	Celtic	51	Motherwell	50
1929–30*g*	Rangers	60	Motherwell	55	Aberdeen	53
1930–1*g*	Rangers	60	Celtic	58	Motherwell	56

1931–2*g*	Motherwell 66	Rangers 61	Celtic 48
1932–3*g*	Rangers 62	Motherwell 59	Hearts 50
1933–4*g*	Rangers 66	Motherwell 62	Celtic 47
1934–5*g*	Rangers 55	Celtic 52	Hearts 50
1935–6*g*	Celtic 68	*Rangers 61	Aberdeen 61
1936–7*g*	Rangers 61	Hearts 58	Rangers 49
1937–8*g*	Celtic 61	Hearts 58	Rangers 49
1938–9*g*	Rangers 59	Celtic 48	Aberdeen 46
1946–7*f*	Rangers 46	Hibernian 44	Aberdeen 39
1947–8*f*	Hibernian 48	Rangers 46	Partick Thistle . 36
1948–9*i*	Rangers 46	Dundee 45	Hibernian 39
1949–50*i*	Rangers 50	Hibernian 49	Hearts 43
1950–1*i*	Hibernian 48	*Rangers 38	Dundee 38
1951–2*i*	Hibernian 45	Rangers 41	East Fife 37
1952–3*i*	*Rangers 43	Hibernian 43	East Fife 39
1953–4*i*	Celtic 43	Hearts 38	Partick Thistle . 35
1954–5*f*	Aberdeen 49	Celtic 46	Rangers 41
1955–6*f*	Rangers 52	Aberdeen 46	Hearts 45
1956–7*f*	Rangers 55	Hearts 53	Kilmarnock 42
1957–8*f*	Hearts 62	Rangers 49	Celtic 46
1958–9*f*	Rangers 50	Hearts 48	Motherwell 44
1959–60*f*	Hearts 54	Kilmarnock 50	Rangers 42
1960–1*f*	Rangers 51	Kilmarnock 50	Third Lanark ... 42
1961–2*f*	Dundee 54	Rangers 51	Celtic 46
1962–3*f*	Rangers 57	Kilmarnock 48	Partick Thistle . 46
1963–4*f*	Rangers 55	Kilmarnock 49	Celtic 47
1964–5*f*	*Kilmarnock 50	Hearts 50	Dunfermline ... 49
1965–6*f*	Celtic 57	Rangers 55	Kilmarnock 45
1966–7*f*	Celtic 58	Rangers 55	Clyde 46
1967–8*f*	Celtic 63	Rangers 61	Hibernian 45
1968–9*f*	Celtic 54	Rangers 49	Dunfermline ... 45
1969–70*f*	Celtic 57	Rangers 45	Hibernian 44
1970–1*f*	Celtic 56	Aberdeen 54	St. Johnstone . 44
1971–2*f*	Celtic 60	Aberdeen 50	Rangers 44
1972–3*f*	Celtic 57	Rangers 56	Hibernian 45
1973–4*f*	Celtic 53	Hibernian 49	Rangers 48
1974–5*f*	Rangers 56	Hibernian 49	Celtic 45

Maximum points: *a*, 36; *b*, 44; *c*, 40; *d*, 52; *e*, 60; *f*, 68; *g*, 76; *h*, 84; *i*, 60
* Won on goal average † Won on deciding match
Competition suspended 1940–5 during war

SCOTTISH PREMIER DIVISION

	First Pts.	Second Pts.	Third Pts.
1975–6	Rangers 54	Celtic 48	Hibernian 43
1976–7	Celtic 55	Rangers 46	Aberdeen 43
1977–8	Rangers 55	Aberdeen 53	Dundee U. 40
1978–9*a*	Celtic 48	Rangers 45	Dundee U. 44

Maximum points: 72

Relegated from Division One

1921–2	†Queens P., Dum'ton Clydebank	1925–6	Raith R., Clydebank
1922–3	Albion R., Alloa	1926–7	Morton, Dundee U.
1923–4	Clyde, Clydebank	1927–8	Dun'line A., Bo'ness
1924–5	Third L., Ayr U.	1928–9	Third L., Raith R.
		1929–30	St. J'stone, Dundee U.

1930–1	Hibernian, East F.	1956–7	Dunfermline A., Ayr U.
1931–2	Dundee U., Leith A.	1957–8	East F., Queens P.
1932–3	Morton, East S.	1958–9	Queen of South, Falkirk
1933–4	Third L., Cowdenbeath	1959–60	Arbroath, Stirling A.
1934–5	St. Mirren, Falkirk	1960–1	Ayr U., Clyde
1935–6	Airdrie, Ayr U.	1961–2	St. J'stone, Stirling A.
1936/7	D'line A., Albion R.	1962–3	Clyde, Raith R.
1937–8	Dundee, Morton	1963–4	Queen of South, East S.
1938–9	Queens Park, Raith R.	1964–5	Aidrieonians, Third L.
1946–47	Kil'nock, Hamilton A.	1965–6	Morton, Hamilton A.
1947–8	Airdrie, Queens Park	1966–7	St. Mirren, Ayr U.
1948–9	Morton, Albion R.	1967–8	Motherwell, Stirling A.
1949–50	Q'n of South, Stirling A.	1968–9	Falkirk, Arbroath
1950–1	Clyde, Falkirk	1969–70	Patrick T., Raith R.
1951–2	Morton, Stirling A.	1970–1	Cow'beath, St. Mirren
1952–3	Motherwell, Third L.	1971–2	Clyde, Dunfermline
1953–4	Airdrie, Hamilton A.	1972–3	Airdrie, Kilmarnock
1954–5	No clubs relegated	1973–4	East F., Falkirk
1955–6	Stirling A., Clyde		

† *Won on deciding match* *Competition suspended 1940–45 during war*

Relegated from Premier Division

1975–6	Dundee, St. Johnstone	1977–8	Ayr U., Clydebank
1976–7	Kilmarnock, Hearts	1978–9	Hearts, Motherwell

SCOTTISH LEAGUE DIV. 2

	First	Pts.	Second	Pts.	Third	Pts.
1921–2*a*	†Alloa	60	Cowdenbeath	47	Armadale	45
1922–3*a*	Queens Park	57	Clydebank	52	St. Johnstone	50
1923–4*a*	St. Johnstone	56	Cowdenbeath	55	*Bathgate	44
1924–5*a*	Dundee U.	50	Clydebank	48	Clyde	47
1925–6*a*	Dunfermline A.	59	Clyde	53	Ayr U.	52
1926–7*a*	Bo'ness	56	Raith R.	49	Clydebank	45
1927–8*a*	Ayr U.	54	Third Lanark	45	*Kings Park	44
1928–9*b*	Dundee U.	51	Morton	50	Arbroath	47
1929–30*a*	*Leith Athletic	57	East Fife	57	Albion R.	54
1930–1*a*	Third Lanark	61	Dundee U.	50	Dunfermline A.	47
1931–2*a*	*East Stirling	55	St. Johnstone	55	Stenhousemuir	46
1932–3*c*	Hibernian	55	Queen of South	49	Dunfermline A.	47
1933–4*c*	Albion R.	45	*Dunfermline A.	44	Arbroath	44
1934–5*c*	Third Lanark	52	Arbroath	50	St. Bernard's	47
1935–6*c*	Falkirk	59	St. Mirren	52	Morton	48
1936–7*c*	Ayr U.	54	Morton	51	St. Bernard's	48
1937–8*c*	Raith R.	59	Albion R.	48	Airdrie	47
1938–8*c*	Cowdenbeath	60	*Alloa	48	East Fife	48
1946–7*d*	Dundee U.	45	Airdrie	42	East Fife	31
1947–8*e*	East Fife	53	Albion R.	42	Hamilton A.	40
1948–9*e*	Raith R.	42	Stirling A.	42	*Airdrie	41
1949–50*e*	Morton	47	Airdrie	44	St. Johnstone	36
1950–1*e*	*Queen of South	45	Stirling A.	45	*Ayr U.	36
1951–2*e*	Clyde	44	Falkirk	43	Ayr U.	39
1952–3*e*	Stirling A.	44	Hamilton A.	43	Queens Park	37
1953–4*e*	Motherwell	45	Kilmarnock	42	*Third Lanark	36
1954–5*e*	Airdrieonians	46	Dunfermline A.	42	Hamilton A.	39
1955–6*b*	Queens Park	54	Ayr U.	51	St. Johnstone	49
1956–7*b*	Clyde	64	Third Lanark	51	Cowdenbeath	45
1957–8*b*	Stirling A.	55	Dunfermline A.	42	Arbroath	47

1958–9*b*	Ayr U.	60	Arbroath	51	Stenhousemuir	46
1959–60*b*	St. Johnstone	53	Dundee U.	50	Queen of South	49
1960–1*b*	Stirling A.	55	Falkirk	54	Stenhousemuir	50
1961–2*b*	Clyde	54	Queen of South	53	Morton	44
1962–3*b*	St. Johnstone	55	East Stirling	49	Morton	48
1963–4*b*	Morton	67	Clyde	53	Arbroath	46
1964–5*b*	Stirling A.	59	Hamilton A.	50	Queen of South	45
1965–6*b*	Ayr U.	53	Airdrieonians	50	Queen of South	47
1966–7*b*	Morton	69	Raith R.	58	Arbroath	57
1967–8*b*	St. Mirren	62	Arbroath	53	East Fife	49
1968–9*b*	Motherwell	64	Ayr U.	53	East Fife	48
1969–70*b*	Falkirk	56	Cowdenbeath	55	Queen of South	50
1970–1*b*	Partick T.	56	East Fife	51	Arbroath	46
1971–2*b*	*Dumbarton	52	Arbroath	52	Stirling A.	50
1972–3*b*	Clyde	56	Dunfermline A.	52	Raith R.	47
1973–4*b*	Airdrieonians	60	Kilmarnock	58	Hamilton A.	55
1974–5*b*	Falkirk	54	*Queen of South	53	Montrose	53
1975–6*d*	*Clydebank	40	Raith R.	40	Alloa	35
1976–7*f*	Stirling A.	55	Alloa	51	Dunfermline A.	50
1977–8*f*	*Clyde	53	Raith R.	53	Dunfermline A.	48
1978–9	Berwick	54	Dunfermline	52	Falkirk	50

Maximum points: a, 76; *b,* 72; *c,* 68; *d,* 52; *e,* 60; *f,* 78

T Season 1921–2—Only 1 club promoted, 3 clubs relegated

* On goal average

SCOTTISH CUP FINAL

RANGERS 0 HIBERNIAN 0

At Hampden Park (50,610), May 12, 1979

Rangers.—McCloy, Jardine, Dawson, Johnstone, Jackson, MacDonald, (Miller), McLean, Russell, Parlane, Smith, Cooper.

Hibernian.—McArthur, Brazil, Duncan, Bremner, Stewart, McNamara, Hutchinson, (Rae), MacLeod, Campbell, Callachan, Higgins.

First Replay

RANGERS 0 HIBERNIAN 0

At Hampden Park (33,504), May 16, 1979

Rangers.—McCloy, Jardine, Dawson, Johnstone, Jackson, Macdonald, McLean, (Miller), Russell, Parlane, Smith, Cooper.

Hibernian.—McArthur, Brazil, Duncan, Brenmer, Stewart, McNamara, Rae, MacLeod, Campbell, Callachan, Higgins.

Second Replay

RANGERS 3 HIBERNIAN 2

(After extra-time. Score 2–2 at 90 mins)

At Hampden Park (30,602), May 28, 1979

Rangers.—McCloy, Jardine, Dawson, Johnstone, Jackson, Watson, (Miller), McLean, (Smith), Russell, Parlane, MacDonald, Cooper.

Hibernian.—McArthur, Brazil, Duncan, Bremner, Stewart, McNamara, Rae, MacLeod, Campbell, Callachan, (Brown), Higgins, (Hutchinson).

Scorers: Rangers—Johnstone 2, Duncan (own goal). Hibernian—Higgins, MacLeod (pen).

FOOTBALL LEAGUE CUP FINALS

1960–61 Rotherham United 2 Aston Villa 0
Aston Villa 3 Rotherham United 0
(Aston Villa won 3–2 on aggregate)
1961–62 Rochdale 0 Norwich City 3
Norwich City 1 Rochdale 0
(Norwich City won 4–0 on aggregate)
1962–63 Birmingham City 3 Aston Villa 1
Aston Villa 0 Birmingham City 0
(Birmingham City won 3–1 on aggregate)
1963–64 Stoke City 1 Leicester City 1
Leicester City 3 Stoke City 2
(Leicester won 4–3 on aggregate)
1964–65 Chelsea 3 Leicester City 2
Leicester City 0 Chelsea 0
(Chelsea won 3–2 on aggregate)
1965–66 West Ham United 2 W.B.A. 1
W.B.A. 4 West Ham United 1
(W.B.A. won 5–3 on aggregate)
1966–67* Q.P.R. 3 W.B.A. 2
1967–68 Leeds United 1 Arsenal 0
1968–69 Swindon Town 3 Arsenal 1
1969–70 Manchester City 2 W.B.A. 1
1970–71 Tottenham Hotspur 2 Aston Villa 0
1971–72 Stoke City 2 Chelsea 1
1972–73 Tottenham Hotspur 1 Norwich City 0
1973–74 Wolverhampton W. 2 Manchester City 1
1974–75 Aston Villa 1 Norwich City 0
1975–76 Manchester City 2 Newcastle United 1
1976–77 Aston Villa 3 Everton 2
(After 0–0 and 1–1 draws)
1977–78 Nottingham Forest 1 Liverpool 0
(After 0–0 draw)
1978–79 Nottingham Forest 3 Southampton 2

* The 1966-67 game between Q.P.R. and W.B.A. was the first League Cup Final played at Wembley.

1978–79 Final Teams
Wembley (100,000), March 17, 1979

Nottm. For.—Shilton, Barrett, Clark, McGovern, Lloyd, Needham, O'Neill, Gemmill, Birtles, Woodcock, Robertson.

Southampton.—Gennoe, Golac, Peach, Williams, Nicholl, Waldron, Ball, Boyer, Hayes (Sealy), Holmes, Curran.

Scorers: Nottm. For.—Birtles 2, Woodcock. Southampton.—Peach, Holmes.

HOW FOREST WON THE FOOTBALL LEAGUE CUP

2nd Round	3rd Round	4th Round	5th Round	Semi-finals (2 legs)	FINAL WEMBLEY STADIUM
Oldham A. 0–2	NOTTM. F. 5	NOTTM. F. 3	NOTTM. F. 3	NOTTM. F. 3–0	NOTTINGHAM FOREST 3
NOTTM. F. 0–4					
Oxford U. 1–2	Oxford U. 0				
Plymouth A. 1–1					
Everton 8	Everton 1	Everton 2			
Wimbledon 0					
Fulham 2–0	Darlington 0				
Darlington 2–1					
Burnley 1–3	Burnley 1	Brighton & Hove . 1	Brighton & Hove . 1		
Bradford City . . 1–2					
Brighton & Hove . 1	Brighton & Hove . 3				
Millwall 0					
Mid'brough 0–0	P'borough U. . . 1–2	P'borough U. 0			
P'borough U. . . 0–1					
West Ham U. . . 0–1	Swindon Town 1–0				
Swindon Town 0–2					
Orient 1	Chesterfield 4	Charlton A. 2	Stoke City 0–1	Watford 1–0	
Chesterfield 2					
Walsall 1	Charlton A. 5				
Charlton A. 2					
North'ton T. ...0–1	Northampton T. . . 1	Stoke City 3			
Hereford U. 0–0					
Sunderland 0	Stoke City 3				
Stoke City 2					
Exeter City 2	Exeter City 2	Exeter City 0	Watford 0–3		
Blackburn R. 1					
Bolton W. 2	Bolton W. 1				
Chelsea 1					
Stockport C. 2	Manchester U. ..1	Watford 2			
Manchester U. ...3					
Watford 2	Watford 2				
Newcastle U. 1					

Preston N.E. 1	Q.P.R. 2	Q.P.R. 0	Leeds U. 4	Leeds U. 2–0	**SOUTHAMPTON 2**
Q.P.R. 3					
Swansea City . 2–3	Swansea City 0				
Tottenham H. . 2–1					
Sheffield U. 1	Sheffield U. 1	Leeds U. 2			
Liverpool 0					
W.B.A. 0–0–0	Leeds U. 4				
Leeds U. 0–0–1					
Aston Villa 1	Aston Villa .. 1–0–3	Aston Villa 0	Luton Town 1		
Sheffield W. 0					
Bristol City 1	Crystal Pal. . 1–0–0				
Crystal Palace 2					
Luton Town 2	Luton Town 2	Luton Town 2			
Wigan Athletic ... 0					
Crewe Alexandra 2	Crewe Alexandra 0				
Notts. County 0					
Chester 2	Chester 0	Norwich City 1	Manchester C. ... 1	**SOUTH'TON** .. 2–1	
Coventry City 1					
Wrexham 1	Norwich City 2				
Norwich City 3					
Blackpool 2	Blackpool 1–0	Manchester C. ... 3			
Ipswich Town 0					
Manchester C. ... 2	Manchester C. 1–3				
Girmsby Town ... 0					
Rotherham U. 3	Rotherham U. . 2–0	Reading 0–0	**SOUTH'TON** 2		
Arsenal 1					
Reading 1	Reading 2–1				
Wolves 0					
Leicester C. 0	Derby County 0	**SOUTH'TON** .. 0–2			
Derby County 1					
Birmingham C. ... 2	**SOUTH'TON** 1				
South'ton 5					

CHIEF RECORDS

TOP SCORES AND SCORERS

(* denotes home team)

Highest: Arbroath 36, Bon Accord 0, in Scottish Cup, 1885.

In Internationals: England 17, *Australia 0, at Sydney, 1951; England 15, *France 0, at Paris, 1906 (amateur); England 13, *Ireland 0, at Belfast, 1882 (record in U.K.); *England 9, Scotland 3, at Wembley, 1961.

In F.A. Cup: *Preston North End, 26, Hyde 0, 1887.

In Football League (First Division): *Aston Villa 12, Accrington 2, 1892; *Spurs 10, Everton 4, 1958; *West Bromwich Albion 12, Darwen 0, 1892; Nottingham Forest 12, Leicester Fosse 0, 1909. Record Away win: Sunderland 9, *Newcastle United 1, 1908; Wolves 9, *Cardiff City 1, 1955.

Second Division: *Manchester City 11, Lincoln City 3, 1895; *Newcastle United 13, Newport County 0, 1946; *Small Heath 12, Walsall Town Swifts 0, Dec. 17, 1892; *Darwen 12, Walsall 0, Dec. 26, 1896; *Small Heath 12, Doncaster Rovers 0, April 11, 1903. Record Away win: Sheffield United 10, *Burslem Port Vale 0, 1892.

Third Division: *Tranmere R. 9, Accrington Stanley 0, 1958–9; *Brighton 9, Southend 1, Nov. 27, 1965; *Brentford 9, Wrexham 0, 1963–4.

Third Division (North): *Stockport County 13, Halifax Town 0, 1934; *Tranmere Rovers 13, Oldham Athletic 4, Dec. 26, 1935. *(17 is highest Football League aggregate score.)* Record Away in: Barnsley 9, *Accrington Stanley 0, 1934.

Third Division (South): *Luton Town 12, Bristol Rovers 0, April 13, 1936; *Gillingham 9, Exeter City 4, Jan. 7, 1951. Record Away win: Walsall 8, *Northampton 0, 1946–7.

Fourth Division: *Oldham Ath. 11, Southport 0, Dec. 26, 1962; *Hartlepools U. 10, Barrow 1, 1958–9; *Wrexham 10, Hartlepools U. 1, 1961–2.

In Scottish League: *Celtic 11, Dundee 0, 1895. Record Away win: Hibs. 11, *Airdrie 1, Oct. 24, 1959.

Div.	English League	Goals	Games
I —	W. R. Dean, Everton, 1927–8	60	— 39
II —	G. Camsell, Middlesbrough, 1926–7	59	— 37
III (S)	J. Payne, Luton Town, 1936–7	55	— 39
III (N)	E. Hartson, Mansfield Town, 1936–7	55	— 41
III —	D. Reeves, Southampton, 1959/60	39	— 46
IV —	T. Bly, Peterborough U., 1960–1	52	— 46

IN INTERNATIONALS

	Goals	Matches
R. Charlton, Manchester United	49	— 106
J. Greaves, Tottenham Hotspur	44	— 58
T. Finney, Preston North End........................	30	— 76
N. Lofthouse, Bolton Wanderers	30	— 32
S. Bloomer, Derby County............................	28	— 23

IN FOOTBALL LEAGUE

Div.		Goals
I	E. Drake (Arsenal), v. Aston Villa, Dec, 14, 1935	
	J.Ross (Preston N.E.), v. Stoke, Oct. 6, 1888	7
II	*N.Coleman (Stoke), v. Lincoln, Feb. 23, 1957	7
	T. Briggs (Blackburn Rovers), v. Bristol Rovers, Feb. 5, 1955	7
III (S)	J. Payne (Luton Town), v. Bristol Rovers, April 13, 1936	10
III (N)	R. Bell (Tranmere Rovers), v. Oldham Athletic, Dec. 26, 1935	9

*** Scored from the wing**

SCOTLAND

Div.		Goals
I	J. McGrory (Celtic), v. Dumfermline Athletic, Jan. 14, 1928	8
II	J. Calder (Morton), v. Raith Rovers, April 18, 1936 at Greenock	8
	O. McNally (Arthurlie), v. Armdale, Oct. 1, 1927	8
	J. Dyet (Kings Park), v. Forfar Athletic, Jan. 2, on his debut for the club	8

IN CUP FOOTBALL

In Scottish Cup: J. Petrie Arbroath), v. Bon Accord, at Arbroath, Sept. 14, 1928 .... **13**

In F.A. Cup: Ted MacDougall (Bournemouth), v. Margate, Nov. 20, 1971 .... **9**

In F.A. Cup Final: Wm. Townley (Blackburn Rovers), v. Sheffield Wednesday, at Kennington Oval, 1890; J. Logan (Notts County), v. Bolton Wanderers, at Everton, 1894; S. Mortensen (Blackpool), v. Bolton Wanderers, at Wembley, 1953 .... **3**

Record F.A. Cup Final win: Bury 6, Derby County 0, 1903

AGGREGATE LEAGUE SCORING RECORDS

	Goals
†Arthur Rowley (Shrewsbury, Leicester, etc.)	**434**
James McGrory (Glasgow Celtic)	**410**
Hugh Gallacher (Airdrie, Newcastle United, etc.)	**386**
W. R. Dean (Everton, etc.)	**379**
Hugh Ferguson (Motherwell, Cardiff City, etc.)	**362**
Jimmy Greaves (Chelsea, Spurs, West Ham)	**357**
Stephen Bloomer (Derby County, etc.)	**352**
George Camsell (Middlesbrough)	**348**
John Atyeo (Bristol City)	**315**
Joe Smith (Bolton, Stockport)	**315**
Victor Watson (West Ham, Southampton)	**312**

†**Rowley,** who retired in 1965, achieved his record with West Bromwich (4 goals), Fulham (27), Leicester (251) and Shrewsbury (152).

Over 500 Goals: J. McGrory (Glasgow Celtic) scored 550 goals in first class football (1922–3 to 1937–8).

GREATEST WORLD CROWDS

World Cup, Rio de Janeiro, 1950. Final match (Brazil v. Uruguay) attendance 200,000; receipts £125,000.

Total attendance in three matches (including play-off) between Santos (Brazil) and Milan for the Inter-Continental Cup (unofficial world club championship) 1963, exceeded 375,000.

BRITISH RECORD CROWDS

Most to Pay: 149,547, Scotland v. England, at Hampden Park, Glasgow, 1937.

At Scottish F.A. Cup Final: 146,433, Celtic v. Aberdeen, at Hampden Park, 1937.

For British Club Match (apart from a Cup Final): 143,470 Rangers v. Hibernian, at Hampden Park, March 27, 1948.

At F.A. Cup Final: 126,047, Bolton Wanderers v. West Ham United, at Wembley Stadium, 1923. 100,000 Chelsea v. Leeds, at Wembley; 62,000, replay at Old Trafford, 1970.

World Cup Qualifying Tie: 107,580, Scotland v. Poland Hampden Park, October 13, 1965 (British floodlight record).

At European Cup Final: 127,621, Real Madrid v. Eintracht, West Germany, at Hampden Park, Glasgow, 1960.

European Cup-Winners' Cup Final: 100,000 West Ham v. Munich, at Wembley, May 19, 1965.

Scottish League: 118,567, Rangers v. Celtic, January 2, 1939.

Scottish League Cup Final: 107,609, Celtic v. Rangers, at Hampden Park, October 23, 1965.

English League: 82,950, Manchester United v. Arsenal, January 17, 1948 (at Maine Road).

In English Provinces: 84,569, Manchester City v. Stoke City (F.A. Cup), March 3, 1934.

Record Aggregate: 265,199 at two matches between Rangers and Morton, in the Scottish Cup Final, 1947–8.

CUP AND LEAGUE DOUBLES

F.A. Cup and League Championship: Preston North End, 1889; Aston Villa, 1887; Tottenham Hotspur, 1961; Arsenal, 1971.

F.A. Cup and Promotion: West Bromwich Albion, 1931.

Football League Cup and League Championship: Nottingham Forest, 1978.

Scottish Cup and League Championship:
Celtic, 71–72–74–77;
Rangers, 1928–30–34–35–49–50–53–63–64–76–78.

MOST INTERNATIONALS

W. A. (Billy) Wright, of the Wolves, overhauled Bob Crompton's record of 42 appearances for England in full Internationals in May 1952, and acted as captain for the 50th time in April 1955, at Wembley against Scotland. He retired in 1959. Total: 105 appearances.

Bobby Charlton, of Manchester United beat Wright's record in the World Cup match against West Germany in Leon, Mexico, in June 1970 and **Bobby Moore** of West Ham overtook Charlton's figure when he won his 107th cap against Italy in Turin, in June 1973.

INTERNATIONAL CHAMPIONSHIP

England: W. A. Wright (Wolves), 38; R. Crompton (Blackburn Rovers), 34.

Scotland: A. Morton (Rangers), 30.

Ireland: D. Blanchflower (Aston Villa and Spurs), 37.

Full and Amateur Internationals: V. J. Woodward, 60. Sir Stanley Mathews of Stoke City and Blackpool played 84 times for England and twice for the United Kingdom. These include war-time games, which are not full internationals.

NATIONAL ASSOCIATIONS FORMED

F.A. on Oct. 26	**1863**	**F.A. of Wales.....**	**1876**
Scottish F.A.	**1873**	Irish F.A.	**1904**
Federation of International Football Associations			**1904**

NATIONAL COMPETITIONS LAUNCHED

F.A. Cup	**1871**	Welsh Cup	**1877**
Scottish Cup	**1873**	Irish Cup	**1880**
World (Jules Rimet) Cup, at Montevideo			**1930**
International Championship..................................			**1883–4**
Youth Internationals (16–18)			**1946–7**
Olympic Games Tournament, at Shepherd's Bush			**1908**

OLDEST CLUB

Oldest Association Football Club is Sheffield F. C. (formed in 1855). The minute book for 1857 is still in existence.

INNOVATIONS

Size of Ball: Fixed in **1872.**

Shinguards: Introduced and registered by Sam Weller Widdowson, Nottingham Forest International in **1874.**

Referee's Whistle: First used on Nottingham Forest's ground in **1978.**

Three Half-backs: Turton, Wrexham and Nottingham Forest all claim to have been pioneers of this system of play.

Professionalism: Legalised in England in the summer of **1885** as a result of an agitation by Lancashire clubs.

Goal-nets: Invented and patented in **1890** by Mr. Brodie of Liverpool. They were first used in the North v. South match in January, **1891.**

Referees and Linesman: Replaced umpires and referees in January, **1891.**

Penalty-kick: Introduced at Irish F.A.'s request in the season **1891–2.** The penalty law ordering the goalkeeper to remain on the goal-line came into force in September, **1905,** and the order to stand on his goal-line until the ball is kicked arrived in **1929–30.**

White ball: First came into official use in **1951.**

Floodlighting: First F.A. Cup-tie (replay), Kidderminster Harriers v. Brierley Hill Alliance, **1955.**

Electrified pitch to beat frost tried by Everton at Goodison Park in **1958.**

First Soccer Closed-circuit TV: At Coventry City ground in 1965 some 10,000 fans saw their team win at Cardiff, 120 miles away.

PLAYERS WITH MOST CAPS

Full Internationals including the International Championship and matches against foreign countries in normal times.

War-time matches, Victory International and the like, and matches against Commonwealth countries are **not** regarded as **full** International. Leaders therefore include:

England	Total
R. Moore	108
R. Charlton	106
W. A. Wright	105
T. Finney	76
G. Banks	73

Scotland

K. Dalglish	67
D. Law	54
G. Young	50
R. Evans	48

Wales

Ivor Allchurch	67
Cliff Jones	57
W. Meredith	48

Ireland

P. Jennings	79
T. Neill	59
D. Blanchflower	56
W. L. Bingham	56

Bjorn Nordqvist, of Sweden, broke the world record for international appearances, passing Bobby Moore's figure of 108, when he gained his 109th cap against Brazil in the World Cup Final series in Argentina. He played two more games in the series, taking his total to 111.

YOUNGEST CAPS

	Age
N. Kernoghan (Ireland, Belfast C.)	**17** years, **80** days
J. Nicholson (Ireland, Man. U.)	**17** years, **256** days
G. Best (Ireland, Man U.)	**17** years, **328** days
J. Charles (Wales, Leeds U.)	**18** years, **71** days
D. Edwards (England, Man. U.)	**18** years, **183** days
G. Moore (Wales, Cardiff C.)	**18** years, **224** days
G. Sprake (Wales, Leeds U.)	**18** years, **231** days
D. Law (Scotland, Huds'field T.)	**18** years, **236** days
A. Elder (Ireland, Burnely)	**18** years, **343** days
J. Giles (Eire, Man. U.)	**18** years, **361** days

OFF/SIDE LAW ALTERATION

Off-side: The law was amended to its present form in **1925–6.** At a meeting of the International Board, in Paris, on June 13, 1925, it was decided, on the proposal of the Scottish F.A., that (in brief) a player shall not be off-side if two (instead of three) opponents are nearer their own goal-line.

PLAYED FOR TWO COUNTRIES

John Reynolds (West Bromwich Albion) played for both England and Ireland in the 1890s.

R. E. Evans (Sheffield United) had played 10 times for Wales when capped by England, in 1910–11.

R. H. Birkett (Clapham Rovers), **C. S. Wilson** (Cambridge University) and **J. W. Sutcliffe** (Bolton Wanderers) gained Association and Rugby International caps for England. **H. W. Renny-Tailyour** played for Scotland v. England at Rugby football (1872) and Soccer (1873).

Queens Park provided **all eleven** Scottish players for the first international match against England in 1872.

The Corinthians supplied **all eleven** England players versus Wales at Wrexham in 1894 and won 5–1. They again supplied **all eleven** players against Wales, at Queen's Club, in 1895, and drew 1–1.

Arsenal contributed **seven** of England's XI versus Italy at Arsenal Stadium in 1934, England won 3–2.

YOUNGEST PLAYERS

Albert Geldard played for Bradford in September, 1929, at the age of 15 years and 156 days.

Clifford Bastin, of Arsenal, won Football League Championship and F.A. Cup medals, and also his first International cap before he turned 20.

Terry Venables (Chelsea, now manager of Crystal Palace), at 21, became in 1964 the first player to hold England caps at five levels — school, youth, amateur, under-23 and full international.

Youngest Centurion: Jimmy Greaves (Chelsea) scored his 100th Football League goal at the age of 20 years 9 months. With Spurs he scored his 200th League goal in December, 1963, at precisely the same age as "Dixie" Dean — 23 years 290 days.

Youngest Cup Finalist: Howard Kendall (Preston North End, now Birmingham) who played at left-half against West Ham United at Wembley, 1964, 20 days before his 18th birthday.

Youngest 1st Division Player: Derek Forster (Sunderland) who, in 1964, at 15 and 185 days, also became the youngest goalkeeper in Football League history.

GOALS IN INTERNATIONAL FOOTBALL

SIX by

N. Lofthouse for Football League v. Irish League, at Wolverhampton, September 24, 1952. Result: 7–1.

J. Bambrick, Linfield centre forward, including double hat-trick, for Ireland against Wales, at Belfast, February 1, 1930. Result: 7–0.

W. C. Jordan (Oxford University and West Bromwich Albion) in Amateur International for England v. France, at Park Royal, March 23, 1908. Result: 12–0.

V. J. Woodward (Tottenham Hotspur) for England v. Holland in Amateur International, at Stamford Bridge, December 11, 1909. Result: 9–1.

FIVE by

S. Bloomer for England v. Wales, at Cardiff, March 16, 1896.

H. Gallacher for Scotland against Ireland, at Belfast, February 23, 1929. Result: 7–3.

G. W. Hall for England v. Ireland, at Manchester United's ground, November 16, 1938. Five in succession (first three in three-and-a-half minutes). Result: 7–0.

M. Macdonald for England v. Cyprus, at Wembley, April 16, 1975. Result: 5—0.

H. Gallacher for Scottish League against Irish League, at Belfast, November 11, 1925. Result: 7–3.

B. Battles — four in succession — for Scottish League against Irish League, at Firhill Park, Glasgow, October 31, 1928. Result: 8–2.

R. Flavell for Scottish League against Irish League, at Belfast, April 30, 1947. Result: 7–4.

J. Bradford for Football League v. Irish League, at Everton, September 25, 1929. Result: 7–2.

A Stubbins for Football League v. Irish League, at Blackpool, October 18, 1950. Result: 6–3.

B. Clough for Football League v. Irish League, at Belfast, September 23, 1959. Result: 5–0.

FOUR by

D. Wilshaw for England v. Scotland, at Wembley, April 2, 1955. Result: 7–2.

GOALS IN A SEASON: DEAN'S 60

W. R. Dean, Everton forward, created a League scoring record in 1927–8 with an aggregate of 60 in 39 matches. He also scored three goals in F.A. Cup-ties, and 19 in representative games (total 82).

G. Camsell, of Middlesbrough, previously held the record with 59 goals in 37 League matches, his total for the season (1926–7) being 75.

MOST GOALS IN A MATCH

TOP SCORE by a player in a match is **13** in Scottish Cup and **10** in Football League.

December 14, 1935: E. Drake for Arsenal v. Aston Villa (Div. I). Scored six goals with his first six shots and in all equalled the Football League record by scoring **7**

February 5, 1955: T. Briggs for Blackburn Rovers v. Bristol Rovers set new Second Division record during 8–3 win by scoring **7**

February 23, 1957: N. J. Coleman for Stoke City v. Lincoln City in Second Division broke new ground as a winger by scoring **7**

December 26, 1935: R. Bell or Tranmere Rovers v. Oldham Athletic (Div. III North) beat record in a 13–4 win by scoring **9**

April 13, 1936: J. Payne set the new record on his debut as a centre-forward for Luton Town v. Bristol Rovers (Div. III South). To a 12–0 win he contributed **10**

OTHER BIG HAULS

G. Baker for St. Mirren v. Glasgow University in Scottish Cup, January 30, 1960–1.

J. Simpson (Partick Thistle), **J. Fleming** (Glasgow Rangers) and **J. Baker** (Hibs.) each scored nine against minor clubs in the Scottish Cup.

E. Gemmell for Oldham Athletic v. Chester in Third Division North (11–2) 1952, and **A. J. Whitehurst,** for Bradford City v. Tranmere Rovers (Third Division North) 1929; both scored seven.

W. H. Minter scored seven goals for St. Albans City in a replayed F.A. Cup-tie against Dulwich Hamlet, November 22, 1922, and was on the losing side. Dulwich Hamlet won 8–7.

D. Law scored all six for Manchester City at Luton (6–2) in abandoned F.A. Cup-tie, January, 1961.

L. Page, Burnley outside-left, when tried for the first time as centre-forward, accomplished the double hat-trick for Burnley in a vital League match against Birmingham, at St. Andrews, April 10, 1926. Burnely won 7–1.

D. Wilson, Glasgow Rangers outside-left, scored six goals from centre-forward at Falkirk in Scottish League, March 17, 1962. Result: 7–1.

J. Astle, West Bromwich Albion striker, scored three hat-tricks in eight days in September, 1965.

F.A. CUP FINAL RECORD

Three Goals: by **W. Townley** for Blackburn Rovers, 1890; by **J. Logan** for Notts County, 1894; and **S. Mortensen** for Blackpool, 1953.

Headed Four Goals: In the 1963 F.A. Amateur Cup Final at Wembley **E. Reynolds** headed all four of Wimbledon's goals (4–2) against Sutton United.

D. Hyde (Hendon) in his first amateur international scored four goals for England v. Wales at Shrewsbury, 1965, equalling 1922 record of Norman Creek.

GOALS BY WINGERS: First Division

	Season	Matches	Goals
C. Bastin (Arsenal)	1932–3	42	33
Scottish League (Div. I)			
R. Ferrier (Motherwell)	1929–30	27	32
Scottish League (Div. II)			
K. Dawson (Falkirk)	1935–6	34	39

Thirteen in a Match: by **J. Petrie,** outside-right for Arbroath v. Bon Accord, Scottish Cup, 1885. Result: 36–0.

Seven from the wing: by **N. J. Coleman,** outside-right for Stoke City v. Lincoln City (8–0), February 23, 1957.

Six from the wing: by **H. Melrose** for Dunfermline v. Partick Thistle, 1959.

Five from the wing: by **A. McGuigan** for Liverpool v. Stoke, 1902; **W. Robbins,** outside-left, for Cardiff City v. Thames, February 6, 1932; **A. Turner** for Doncaster Rovers v. New Brighton, February 16, 1935; **G. Smith** for Hibs. v. Third Lanark, November 8, 1947; **T. J. Eglington** for Everton v. Doncaster, September 27, 1952; **P. Harris** for Portsmouth v. Aston Villa, September 3, 1958 (including a penalty kick); **J. Summers** (twice) for Charlton v. Huddersfield (1957) and Portsmouth (1960); **H. Melrose** for Dunfermline v. Falkirk, 1964; **R. Auld** for Celtic v. Airdrie, 1965; **R. Tambling** for Chelsea v. Aston Villa, 1966.

In March, 1964, **J. Brownsword** (Scunthorpe United) became the first full-back to score 50 Leauge goals. **S. Lynn** (Birmingham and formerly Aston Villa) achieved this figure in 1965.

QUICKEST GOALS AND RAPID SCORING

Six Seconds after Kick-off: by **A. Mundy** for Aldershot v. Hartlepools, October 25, 1958; **K. Smith** for Crystal Palace v. Derby County, December 12, 1964.

(A goal in four seconds was claimed by Jim Fryatt, Bradford centre-forward against Tranmere Rovers, April 25, 1965.)

Scored First Kick: W. F. Foulkes (Newcastle United) for Wales v. England, at Cardiff, October, 1951, in his first International match.

Five Goals in 20 minutes: F. Keetley in Lincoln's 9 1 win over Halifax in Div. III (North), January 16, 1932; **B. Dear** for West Ham United v. West Bromwich Albion (6- 1) April 16, 1965.

Four Goals in five minutes: by **J. McIntyre** for Blackburn Rovers v. Everton (League), September 16, 1922; **W. G. Richardson** for West Bromwich Albion v. West Ham United (League), November 7, 1931.

Three in three Minutes: B. Lane for Watford v. Clapton Orient, December 20, 1933.

Three in two minutes: J. Scarth for Gillingham v. Leyton Orient, November 1, 1952.

Sunderland scored eight goals in 28 minutes at Newcastle (9–1), December, 1908.

SCOTTISH PREMIER LEAGUE

The top ten teams in the Scottish First Division at the end of the 1974–5 season formed the Scottish Premier League for 1975–6.

The bottom eight in the First Division, with the top six of Division Two, became the new First Division and the rest became Division Two.

CUP SENSATIONS

Four months before the 1966 World Cup finals in England the World Cup itself, the gold Jules Rimet Trophy, insured for £30,000, was stolen while on exhibition in London. One week later, March 27, the Cup, undamaged and wrapped in a copy of the News of the World, was found inthe front garden of his home at Norwood, London; by a man and his dog. The finder obtained rewards exceeding £5,000; the dog, Pickles became famous overnight.

The original F.A. Cup was stolen from a shop window in Birmingham, 1895, while Aston Villa were the holders. A new trophy was provided and this was withdrawn and presented to Lork Kinnaird, the president of the F.A., February 6, 1911, in appreciation of his services to the game.

The Scottish F.A. withheld their Cup and medals in 1908–9 after Rangers and Celtic had played two drawn games at Hampden Park. Spectators rioted.

CHIEF F.A. CUP WINNERS

Seven Times: Aston Villa.

Six Times: Newcastle United and Blackburn Rovers.

Five Times: The Wanderers, Tottenham Hotspur and West Bromwich Albion, Arsenal.

Three Times in Succession: The Wanderers (1876–7–8) and Blackburn Rovers (1884–5–6).

Trophy Handed Back: The trophy became the Wanderers' absolute property in 1878, but they handed it back to the Association on condition that it was not to be won outright by any club. Hence Blackburn Rovers, after 1896, were presented with a commemoration shield.

In Successive Years of Professional Play: Blackburn Rovers (in 1890 and 1891), Newcastle United (in 1951 and 1952) and Tottenham Hotspur (in 1961 and 1962) won the Cup in successive years.

Record Final-tie score: Bury 6, Derby County 0 (1903).

Most Wins at Wembley: Newcastle United 5, Bolton Wanderers 4, Arsenal 5.

CUP "FIRSTS"

Out of Country: Cardiff City, by defeating Arsenal 1–0 in the 1927 Final-tie at Wembley, became the first and only club to take the F.A. Cup out of England.

All-English Winning XI: First club to win the F.A. Cup with an all-English XI was West Bromwich Albion, in 1887–8.

Wolves' Honours: Wolverhampton Wanderers were the first team to win the Cup on a ground originally chosen out of London. They beat Everton 1–0 at Fellowfield, Manchester, in 1893. Wolves again won the Cup in 1908.

Won Both Cups: Old Carthusians won the F.A. Cup in 1881 and the F.A. Amateur Cup in 1894 and 1897.

CUP GIANT KILLING—IN F.A. CUP

1979	Charlton	1	Maidstone	1
(Replay: Charlton won 2–1)				
1979	Newport	2	West Ham	1
1979	Tottenham	1	Altrincham	1
(Replay: Tottenham won 3–0)				
1978*	Newcastle	2	Wrexham	2
(Replay: Wrexham won 4–1)				
1978*	Walsall	1	Leicester	0
1978*	Stoke	2	Blyth S.	3
1976*	Leeds U.	0	C. Palace	1
1975*	Burnley	0	Wimbledon	1
1973	Leeds U.	0	Bristol C.	1
(Replay after 1 1 draw)				
1972*	Hereford	2	Newcastle	1
(Replay after 1–1 draw)				
1971*	Colchester	3	Leeds U.	2
1969*	Mansfield	3	West Ham	0
1968*	Tranmere	2	Coventry	0
(Replay after 1–1 draw)				
1967*	Swindon	3	West Ham	0
(Replay after 3–3 draw)				
1967*	Man. U.	1	Norwich C.	2
1968*	Southport	2	Cardiff C.	0
1966*	Ipswich T.	2	Southport	3
(Replay after 0–0 draw)				
1966*	Stoke C.	0	Walsall	2
1965*	Peterboro'	2	Arsenal	1
1964*	Newcastle	1	Bedford T.	2
1964*	Aston V.	0	Aldershot	0
(Replay: Aldershot won 2–1)				
1964*	Oxford U.	3	Blackburn R.	1
1961*	Chelsea	1	Crewe A.	2

1960*Man. C. ... 1 South'ton .. 5
1959*Norwich C. 3 Man. U. 0
1959*Spurs ..... 1 Norwich C. 1
(Replay: Norwich won 1–0)
1959*Worcester 2 Liverpool ... 1
1959*Tooting ... 3 Bournem'th 1
1959*Tooting ... 2 North'ton .. 1
1958*Newcastle 1 Scunthorpe 3
1957*Wolves ... 0 Bournem'th 1
1957*B'mouth .. 3 Spurs 1
1956*Arsenal ... 2 Bedford T. . 2
(Replay: Arsenal won 2–1)
1956*Derby C. .. 1 Boston U. .. 6
1955*York C. ... 2 Spurs 1
1955*Blackpool 0 York C. 2
1954*Arsenal ... 1 Norwich C. 2
1954*Port Vale . 2 Blackpool .. 0

1953*Halifax T. . 3 Cardiff 1
1952*Everton ... 1 Leyton O. .. 3
1949*Yeovil T. .. 2 Sunderland 1
1948*Colchester 1 Hud'field ... 0
1948*Arsenal ... 0 Bradford ... 1
1939*Ch'lmsf'd C 4 South'ton .. 1
1933*Walsall ... 2 Arsenal 0
1923*Spurs ..... 0 Worksop T. 0
(Replay: Spurs won 9–0 at home)
1923*Man. C. ... 1 Charlton A. 2
1923*Charlton .. 2 Preston N. E. 0
1923*Charlton .. 1 West Brom 0
1923*Newcastle 0 South'ton .. 0
(Southampton won replay 3–1)
1922*Everton ... 0 Crystal P. .. 6
1921*Hull C. .... 3 Burnley 0
1920*Newcastle 0 Hud'field ... 1

IN SCOTTISH CUP

1967*Berwick R. 1 Rangers 0
1966*Alloa A. ... 3 Ross C. 5
1962*East S. .... 1 Motherwell 0
1959*Fraserb'gh 1 Dundee 0
1957*M'well .... 1 Dunbarton . 3
1954*Berwick R. 3 Dundee 0
1952*Berwick R. 4 Alloa A. 1
1938*East F. .... 1 Aberdeen .. 1
(East Fife went on to win Cup)

1938*Hibernian . 2 Edinburgh C. 3
1937*Kil'nock ... 1 Brechin C. 2
1937*Duns ...... 2 Dumbarton 0
1959*B'burn U. . 2 Falkirk 1
1922*Bathgate . 1 Falkirk ... 0
1920*Armadale 1 Hibernian . 0
1920*Armadale 1 Clyde .. 0
1913*Rangers .. 1 Falkirk 3
*Home team

FIRST F.A. CUP ENTRANTS (1871–2)

Barnes, Civil Service, Crystal Palace, Clapham Rovers, Donnington School (Spalding), Hampstead Heathens, Harrow Chequers, Hitchin, Maidenhead, Marlow, Queen's Park (Glasgow), Reigate Priory, Royal Engineers, Upton Park and Wanderers. Total 15. Three scratched. Maidenhead and Marlow claim to be the only clubs who have never missed any entry since the F.A. Cup's inception.
Record F.A. Cup Entry .... 674 in 1921

SECOND DIVISION CUP WINNERS

Notts County (1894), Wolves (1908), Barnsley (1912), West Bromwich Albion (1931), Sunderland (1973), Southampton (1976). When the Spurs won the Cup in 1901 they were a Southern League club.

THIRD DIVISION SEMI-FINALISTS

Millwall (1937), Port Vale (1954), York City (1955), Norwich City (1959), Crystal Palace (1976).

FIVE WINNING MEDALS

Lord Kinnaird (The Wanderers and Old Etonians), **C. H. R. Wollaston** (The Wanderers) and **James Forrest** (Blackburn Rovers) each secured five F.A. Cup winners' medals.

AMATEUR CUP RECORD

Bishop Auckland hold the F.A. Amateur Cup record with 10 wins, and in 1957 became the only club to carry off the trophy in three successive seasons. Five wins: Clapton and Crook Town.

LONGEST TIES

Only one tie in the history of the F.A. Cup has gone to six matches **Alvechurch v. Oxford City** in the fourth qualifying round, 1971–2. The total playing time was eleven hours. This beats the nine hours twenty-two minutes between **Stoke City and Bury,** January 1955.

In the last qualifying round of the Cup, December, 1924, **Barrow beat Gillingham** in the fifth meeting and after playing for nine hours.

In the third qualifying round of the Cup, November, 1924, **Leyton beat Ilford** in the fifth meeting after nine hours.

In the fourth round proper, 1955–6, **Chelsea beat Burnley** after five games lasting nine hours.

Hull City and Darlington had a marathon second-round tie in 1960 before Hull won 3–0 at the fifth attempt.

Arsenal beat Sheffield Wednesday in their fifth meeting in the third round of the F.A. Cup in January, 1979.

In the qualifying competition of the Cup, October/November, 1899, **New Brompton beat Woolwich Arsenal** in the fifth meeting after playing for eight hours. Extra time was sometimes impossible owning to weather conditions.

WAR-TIME MARATHON

Match of 203 minutes: Stockport County's Second-leg tie with Doncaster Rovers in the Third Division North Cup, March 30, 1946, lasted 203 minutes and a replay was still necessary.

TEN PLAYERS SENTENCED

Ten professional and former professional footballers, found guilty of conspiracy to defraud by "fixing" matches, were all sent to prison at Nottingham Assizes, January 26, 1965.

RECORD LEAGUE FINES

Sunderland were fined £5,000, accompanied by suspensions, late in season 1956–7, following allegations of "making illegal payments contrary to the regulations of the Football League".

Everton (Cup-winners) were fined £2,000 in April, 1966, after playing 11 reserves in a League match against Leeds one week before their F.A. Cup Semi-final with Manchester United.

In March, 1958, **Port Vale** were fined £2,000 and expelled from the Football League for illegal payments to players. They had already been fined £2,000 by the F.A. for the same offence.

In March, 1961, **Burnley** were fined £1,000 for playing nine reserves against Chelsea on the Saturday preceding their European Cup tie and F.A. Cup semi-final.

In November, 1967, **Millwall** were fined £1,000 by the F.A. following an attack on a referee at The Den.

In the same month Peterborough were fined £500 for illegal payments to players. They were later demoted from the Third to Fourth Division.

Manchester United were fined £7,000 for irregularities in the club's administration in 1969, while **Derby** were fined £10,000, also for administrative irregularities in April, 1970.

Leeds United were fined £5,000 for fielding virtually an all-reserve side in the First Division in April, 1970.

Exeter City were fined £5,000 in 1974 for refusing to play their League match with Scunthorpe as they had only nine fit players.

Millwall were fined £1,500 and the ground was closed for two weeks following crowd disturbances at the F.A. Cup quarter-final against Ipswich Town on March 11, 1978. They were barred from playing home F.A. Cup-ties for the next two seasons, and the sale of alcoholic drinks at The Den was prohibited until further notice. It was the fourth time the ground had been closed, the previous occasions being 1934, 1947 and 1950.

EXTENSIONS

Clubs	*Season*	*Clubs*	*Season*
12 to 14	1891–2	40 to 44	1919–20
*14 to 28	1892–3	†44 to 66	1920–1
28 to 31	1893–4	‡66 to 86	1921–2
31 to 32	1894–5	86 to 88	1923–4
32 to 36	1898–9	88 to 92	1950–1
36 to 40	1905–6		

*Second Division formed. ‡Third Division (North) formed. †Third Division (South) formed from Southern League clubs.

FOUR DIVISIONS

In May, 1957, the Football League decided to re-group the two Sections of the Third Division into Third and Fourth Division in season 1958–9.

OLDEST LEAGUE CLUBS

The oldest Football League clubs are: Notts County, 1862; Nottingham Forest, 1865; and Sheffield Wednesday, 1866. The first Stoke club was formed in 1863.

Down Together: In 1936 the Blackburn and Aston Villa clubs were relegated to the Second Division together.

Sunderland: Relegated in 1958 after maintaining First Division status since their election in 1890.

Aston Villa: Relegated with **Preston North End**, to the Third Division in 1970.

Arsenal Up: When the League was extended in 1919–20 Woolwich Arsenal (sixth in Division Two in 1914–15, last season before the war) were elected to Division One.

Spurs Down: At the same meeting Chelsea (due for relegation) retained their place in Division One but the bottom club (Tottenham Hotspur had to go down to Division Two.

LEAGUE HAT-TRICKS

Huddersfield Town created a record in 1925–6 by winning the League Championship for the third year in succession. They finished second in 1926–7 and 1927–8 when they were also F.A. Cup runners-up.

Arsenal equalled this League hat-trick in 1934–5. Their League positions, from 1930–1 onwards, had been 1, 2, 1, 1, 1, while in 1929–30 they won the F.A. Cup and in 1931–2 were runners-up.

Champions in Successive Seasons

Preston North End (1888–9, 1889–90).
Sunderland (1891–2, 1892–3).
Aston Villa (1895–6, 1896–7, 1898–9, 1899–1900).
Sheffield Wednesday (1902–3, 1903–4, 1928–9, 1929–30).
Liverpool (1921–2, 1922–3, 1975–6, 1976–7).
Portsmouth (1948–9, 1949–50).
Manchester United (1955–6, 1956–7).
Wolverhampton Wanderers (1957–8, 1958–9).

Tottenham Hotspur won the Second Division Championship in 1949–50 and the First Division Championship 1950–1, a double also achieved by Ipswich Town in 1960–1 and 1961–2.

MOST POINTS IN A SEASON

In Football League: Lincoln City set a Football League points record in the 1975–6 season with 74 from 46 games, including 32 victories.

First Division: Liverpool (1978–79), 68 points from 42 matches.

Second Division: Tottenham Hotspur (1919–20), 70 points from 42 matches.

Fewest Points: Doncaster Rovers, 8 points (of possible 68) in Second Division, 1904–5. Stirling Albion 6 points (of possible 60) in Scottish League Division A, 1954–5.

MOST CHAMPIONSHIP WINS

Liverpool, by winning the League championship in 1976–77, established a new record of 10 championship victories. They also won the European Cup in the same season and were the beaten finalists in the F.A. Cup. Liverpool increased the record with their 11th championship in the 1978–79 season.

Undefeated in League season: In 1893–4 **Liverpool** won 22 and drew 6 of their 28 Second Division games, and then won their Test Match for promotion.

Home Runs: Sunderland were undefeated at home in Football League (Div. 1) in seasons 1891–1, 2–3, 4–5 and 5–6, losing only one home match in 1893–4. **Brentford** won all 21 home games in 1929–30 in the Third Division (South). Others have won all home games in a smaller programme.

Record Home Run: Millwall set up a new unbeaten home League record of 59 games during the 1966–7 season. The run began on August 24, 1964 when Millwall were in the Fourth Division and it ended when Plymouth Argyle beat them in a Second Division match on January 14, 1967.

Third to First: Charlton Athletic, in 1936, completed an advance from the Third to the First division in successive seasons. **Queen's Park Rangers** became the second club to achieve the feat in 1968.

Fourth to first: Northampton Town, in 1965, became the first club to climb from the Fourth to the First Division. They returned to the Fourth Division in 1969

FAMOUS CLUB FEATS

Tottenham Hotspur, in 1960–1, not only carried off the First Division Championship and the F.A. Cup for the first time this century but set up other records by opening with 11 successive wins, registering most First Division wins (31), most away wins in the League's history (16), and equalling Arsenal's First Division record of 66 points. They already held the Second Division record of 70 points (1919–20).

Arsenal repeated Tottenham's double feat by winning the F.A. Cup and the Football League Championship in 1970–1.

Preston North End, in season 1888–9, won the League Championship without losing a match and the F.A. Cup without having a goal scored against them throughout the competition.

Bury, in 1903, also won the F.A. Cup without conceding a goal.

Three Years — Three Honours: Everton won the Second and First Division Championships and the F.A. Cup in successive seasons, 1930–1, 1–2, 2–3. The **Wolves** won the League in 1958 and 1959, and the F.A. Cup in 1960.

Liverpool won the League Championship in 1964, the F.A. Cup in 1965 and the Championship again in 1966. In 1978 they became the first British club to win the European Cup in successive seasons.

Liverpool created two new First Division records in the 1978–79 season. They won the League Championship with a record 68 points and only conceded 16 League goals in a 42 match programme.

Triple Bids: Manchester United, in 1956–7, were in the running for a triple triumph — capture of Football League, F.A. Cup and European Cup Honours — until the closing days of the season when they fell to Real Madrid in the European semi-finals and then lost the English Final after early injury to their goalkeeper. **Wolves** missed the triple honour and three successive League Championships by a goal in 1960, when they also won the F.A. Cup. **Liverpool** won the League Championship and the European Cup in 1976–7 and were beaten by Manchester United in the F.A. Cup Final.

RECORD LEAGUE RUN

Leeds United hold the record unbeaten sequence in the Football League — 34 matches spanning seasons 1968–9—1969–70. The run ended on August 30, 1969 when Leeds lost 2–3 at Everton. Their sequence comprised 19 wins and 15 draws. In the 1973–4 season, going 29 games without defeat. Their sequence ended at Stoke city.

Best Debut: Ipswich Town won the First Division at their first attempt in 1961–2. **Peterborough United** in their first season in the Football League (1960–1) not only won the Fourth Division but set up a new scoring record for the League of 134 goals. **Hereford United** were promoted from the Fourth Division in their first League season, 1972–3.

LEAGUE RECORDS

The original 12 members of the Football League (formed in 1888) were: Accrington, Aston Villa, Blackburn Rovers, Bolton Wanderers, Burnley, Derby County, Everton, Notts County, Preston North End, Stoke, West Bromwich Albion, and Wolverhampton Wanderers.

LEAGUE'S TOP SCORERS

Season	Player	Goals
1978–79 ...	R. Jenkins (Watford)	29
1977–8	S. Phillips (Brentford)	32
1976–7	P. Ward (Brighton)	32
1975–6	R. McNeil (Hereford)	35
1974–5	R. McNeil (Hereford)	30
1973–4	B. Yeo (Gillingham)	31
1972–3	B. Robson (West Ham United)	28
1971–2	T. MacDougall (Bournemouth).........	35
1970–1	T. MacDougall (Bournemouth).........	42
1969–70 ...	A. Kinsey (Wrexham)	27
1968–9 . ..	J. Greaves (Tottenham Hotspur)	27
1967–8	G. Best (Manchester United) and R. Davies (Southampton)...............	28
1966–7	R. Davies (Southampton)...............	37
1965–6	K. Hector (Bradford).....................	44
1964–5 ...	A. Jeffrey (Doncaster Rovers)..........	36
1963–4	H. McIlmoyle (Carlisle United)	39
1962–3	J. Greaves (Tottenham Hotspur)	37
1961–2 . ..	R. Hunt (Liverpool)	41
1960–1 ...	T. Bly (Peterborough United)...........	52
1959–60 ..	C. Holton (Watford)	48
1958–9	B. Clough (Middlesbrough).............	42
1957–8	T. Johnston (Blackburn, Leyton).......	44

LEAGUE GOAL RECORDS

The highest goal-scoring aggregate in the Football League and Scottish League are as follows:

FOR

	Goals	*Games*	*Club*	*Season*
Div. 1	128	42	Aston Villa	1930–1
Div. 2	122	42	Middlesbrough	1926–7
Div 3(S)	127	42	Millwall	1927–8
Div. 3(N)	128	42	Bradford City	1928–9
Div. 3	111	46	Q.P.R	1961–2
Scot. L. 1	132	34	Hearts	1957–8
Scot. L. 2	142	34	Raith Rovers	1937–8

AGAINST

	Goals	*Games*	*Club*	*Season*
Div. 1	125	42	Blackpool	1930–1
Div. 2	141	34	Darwen	1898–9
Div. 3(S)	135	42	Merthyr T.	1929–30
Div. 3(N)	136	42	Nelson	1927–8
Div. 3	123	46	Accrington S.	1959–60
Div. 4	109	46	Hartlepools	1959–60
Scot. L. 1	137	30	Leith A.	1931–2
Scot. L. 2	146	30	Edinburgh C.	1931–2

BEST DEFENSIVE RECORDS
*** Denotes under old off-side law**

Div.	Goals Agst.	Games	Club	Season
1	16	42	Liverpool	1978–9
1	*15	22	Preston N. E.	1888–9
1	24	42	Liverpool	1968–9
1	24	42	Liverpool	1970–1
1	*28	42	Huddersfield T.	1924–5
1	*28	34	Sheffield W.	1903–4
1	*18	28	Liverpool	1893–4
2	*22	34	Sheffield W.	1899–1900
2	*22	34	W. Arsenal	1903–4
2	*23	42	Manchester U.	1924–4
2	24	42	Birmingham C.	1947–8
3(S)	*21	42	Southampton	1921–2
3(S)	30	42	Cardiff City	1946–7
3(N)	*21	38	Stockport C.	1921–2
3(N)	*26	42	Rochdale	1923–4
3(N)	21	46	Port Vale	1953–4
3	34	46	Watford	1968–9
4	30	46	Gillingham	1963–4

Scottish League

Div.	Goals Agst.	Games	Club	Season
1	*12	22	Dundee	1902–3
1	*14	38	Celtic	1913–14
1	22	38	Rangers	1923–4
1	26	30	Rangers	1946–7
1	26	30	Rangers	1949–50
1	26	30	Hibernian	1950–1
1	26	30	Aberdeen	1954–5
1	27	34	Rangers	1955–6
1	24	34	Celtic	1967–8
1	28	22	Celtic	1972–3
1	*16	22	Abercorn	1908–9
2	23	36	St. Mirren	1967–8
2	*29	38	Clydebank	1922–3
2	29	34	Hibernian	1932–3
2	28	36	Queens Park	1955–6
2	38	36	Clyde	1972–3
2	20	38	Morton	1966–7

CELTIC'S GRAND SLAM

Glasgow Celtic's record in the 1966–7 season was the most successful in British club history. They won the **Scottish League**, the **Scottish Cup**, the **Scottish League Cup**, the **Glasgow Cup** and became the first British club to win the **European Cup**.

In 1968–9 they again triumphed in the **Scottish League**, the **Scottish Cup** and the **Scottish League Cup.**

SCOTTISH TOP SCORERS

Div.		*Goals*	*Games*
I	W. Macfadyen, Motherwell, 1931–2	**52** –	**34**
II	J. Smith, Ayr United, 1927–8	**66** –	**38**

RANGERS' MANY RECORDS

Rangers (Glasgow) have achieved a number of record-breaking feats chief of which may be tabulated as follows:

League Champions: 36 times (and once joint holders).

Winning every match in Scottish League (1898–9 season).

Winning everything played for: 1929–30, 1933–4 and 1977–8 seasons. Celtic performed the same feat twice – 1908 and 1967.

Major hat-trick: League Cup, League Championship, Scottish F.A. Cup (1948–9, 1963–4, 1975–6, 1977–8).

Scottish Cup Wins: Rangers 22; Celtic 25.

In the Rangers v. Celtic Scottish League Match in September, 1931, John Thompson, the Celtic and Scottish International goalkeeper, sustained a fractured skull and died the same evening.

John White (27), Tottenham Hotspur Scottish International forward was killed by lightning on a London golf course in July, 1964.

Two players were killed by lightning during the Army Cup Final replay at Aldershot in April, 1948.

Tommy Allden (23), Highgate United centre-half was struck by lightning during Highgate's Amateur Cup quarter-final with Enfield Town on February 25, 1967. Four other players were also struck but recovered – Allden died in hospital the following day

Derek Dooley, Sheffield Wednesday centre-forward and top scorer in 1951–2 in the Football League with 46 goals in 30 matches, broke a leg in the League match at Preston on February 14, 1953, and, complications setting in, had to lose the limb by amputation

CELTIC'S RECORD 63

Celtic hold the Scottish League record run of success with 63 matches undefeated, from November 13, 1915 to April 21, 1917, when Kilmarnock won 2–0 at Parkhead.

Greenock Morton in 1963–4 were undefeated in home League matches, obtained a record 67 points out of 72 and scored 135 goals, clinching promotion as early as February 29.

Queens Park (Glasgow) did not have a goal scored against them during the first seven years of their existence.

UP FIRST TIME

The following clubs have won promotion the season after losing their position in the First Division of the League:

Sheffield Wednesday, *1899–1900, *1951–2, *1955–6, *1958–9
Bolton Wanderers, 1899–1900, *1908–9, 1910–11
West Bromwich Albion, *1901–2
Manchester City, *1902–3, *1909–10, 1950–1
Burnley, *1897–8
Small Heath, 1902–3
Liverpool, *1904–5
Nottingham Forest, *1906–7
Preston North End, *1912–13, 1914–15
Notts County, *1913–14
Derby County, *1914–15
Tottenham Hotspur, *1919–20, 1977–8
Leeds United, 1927–8, 1931–2
Middlesbrough, *1928–9
Everton, *1930–1
Manchester United, 1937–8, *1974–5
Huddersfield Town, 1952–3
Aston Villa, *1959–60
Chelsea, 1962–3
Norwich City, 1974–5
Wolverhampton Wanderers, 1976–7

** Here denotes Champions*

WEMBLEY'S RECORD RECEIPTS

Wembley Stadium underwent considerable alteration during 1962–3 period in preparation for the World Cup in 1966. The enclosure is now completely covered and is one of the most imposing in the world. Higher admission fees at the 1963 F.A. Cup Final resulted in 100,000 spectators paying a record £89,000.

In 1968 this rose to a new peak of £110,000, for the F.A. Cup Final between W.B.A. and Everton and the record was broken later in the same month when receipts reached £120,000 for the European Cup Final between Manchester United and Benfica.

Receipts figures rose dramatically and for the 1976 F.A. Cup Final between Southampton and Manchester United, 100,000 people paid £420,000.

The £500,000 mark was reached for the 1978 F.A. Cup Final between Ipswich and Arsenal.

EARLIER CUP FINAL CROWDS

At Crystal Palace

1895 ..	42,560	1902 ..	48,036	1908 ..	74,967
1896 ..	48,036	replay .	33,050	1909 ..	67,651
1897 ..	65,891	1903 ..	64,000	1910 ..	76,980
1898 ..	62,017	1904 ..	61,734	1911 ..	69,098
1899 ..	73,833	1905 ..	101,117	1912 ..	54,434
1900 ..	68,945	1906 ..	75,609	1913 ..	120,028
1901 ..	110,802	1907 ..	84,584	1914 ..	72,778

British Record Mid-Week Attendance: Celtic v. Leeds, second leg of European Cup semi-final, April 15, 1970 at Hampden Park **134,000**

F.A. Cup Semi-Final Record Receipts: aggregate takings for the 1974 semi-final at Old Trafford and the replay at Villa Park, Liverpool v. Leicester **£184,000**

Amateur Record: F.A. Amateur Cup Final, Pegasus v. Harwich at Wembley, 1953 .... **100,000**

DOUBLE SCOTTISH FINAL

Rangers v. Celtic drew 129,643 and 120,273 people to the Scottish Cup Final and replay at Hampden Park, Glasgow, in 1963, but the aggregate was not a record. The 1963 total of receipts was £50,500.

WEMBLEY INVASION DAY

Memorable scenes were witnessed at the first F.A. Cup Final at Wembley, April 28, 1923, between Bolton Wanderers and West Ham United. An accurate return of the attendance could not be made owing to the crowd breaking in, but there were probably 150,000 spectators present. The start of the match was delayed for 40 minutes owing to the crowd invading the playing pitch.

The gross gate receipt was £27,776. The two clubs and the Football Association each received £6,365 and the F.A. refunded £2,797 to ticket-holders who were unable to get to their seats.

At subsequent Finals, admission has been by ticket only.

SIR STANLEY MATTHEWS

"For services to Association Football", Stanley Matthews (Stoke City, Blackpool and England), already a C.B.E., became the first professional footballer to receive a knighthood. This was bestowed in 1965, his last season.

Before he retired and five days after his 50th birthday, he played for Stoke to set a final record as the oldest First Division footballer.

Over a brilliant span of 33 years, he played in 886 matches, including 54 full-internationals, 701 League games and 86 F.A. Cup-ties, and scored 95 goals.

CHANGES IN LAWS

Goalkeeper's use of hands restricted to penalty area, **1912.**

Ten Yards: The distance from the ball at which opponents may stand during the taking of a free-kick, was altered from six to ten yards in **1913.**

Throw-in: A player cannot be off-side when a throw-in is taken **June, 1920**

Goalkeeper's Jersey: Goalkeepers in International games to wear jerseys of deep yellow .... **June, 1921**

Colour-clash: Where the colours of teams clash in the Football League, the visitors must change .... **June, 1924**

Goal from corner: Scotland carried proposal that a goal can be scored 'direct' from a corner kick .... **June, 1924**

TRANSFER TRAIL

Almost £20 million changed hands between British clubs in transfer deals in the 1978–79 season. This table shows how the fees have mounted since the first £1,000 transfer in 1905.

Player	*From*	*To*	*Date*	*£*
**T. Francis	Birmingham .	Nottm. Forest	Feb. 1979	1.150,500
***P. Parkes ...	Q.P.R.	West Ham ...	Feb. 1979	.565,000
D. Mills	Middlesboro	W.B.A.	Jan. 1979	.516,000
G. McQueen ...	Leeds U.	Man. U.	Mar. 1978	.500,000
K. Keegan	Liverpool	Hamburg	June 1976	.500,000
B. Talbot	Ipswich	Arsenal	Jan. 1979	.450,000
K. Dalglish	Celtic	Liverpool	Aug. 1977	.440,000
C. George	Derby	Southampton	Dec. 1978	.400,000
K. Hird	Blackburn	Leeds	Mar. 1979	.354,000
J. Jordan	Leeds U.	Man. U.	Nov. 1977	.350,000
‡R. Latchford ..	Birmingham .	Everton	Feb. 1974	.350,000
P. Shilton	Leicester	Stoke	Nov. 1974	.340,000
M. Macdonald .	Newcastle ...	Arsenal	July 1976	.333,000
P. Hart	Blackpool	Leeds U.	Mar. 1978	.330,000
L. James	Burnley	Derby	Nov. 1975	.310,000
M. Dobson	Burnley	Everton	Aug. 1974	.300,000
D. Hales	Charlton	Derby	Dec. 1976	.300,000
D. Tueart	Sunderland ..	Man. C.	Mar. 1974	.275,000
P. Osgood	Chelsea	Southampton	Mar. 1974	.275,000
D. Watson	Sunderland ..	Man. C.	June 1975	.275,000
A. Hartford	W.B.A.	Man. C.	Aug. 1974	.275,000
D. Nish	Leicester	Derby	Aug. 1972	.250,000
D. McKenzie ...	Nottm. F.	Leeds U.	Aug. 1974	.250,000
A. Hudson	Chelsea	Stoke	Jan. 1974	.240,000
L. Lloyd	Liverpool	Coventry	Aug. 1974	.240,000
T. Currie	Sheffield U. ..	Leeds U.	July 1976	.240,000
D. Hay	Celtic	Chelsea	July 1974	.225,000
T. MacDougall .	Bournemouth	Man. U.	Sept. 1972	.220,000
A. Ball	Everton	Arsenal	Dec. 1971	.220,000
B. Rioch	A. Villa	Derby	Feb. 1974	.200,000
R. Kennedy	Arsenal	Liverpool	July 1974	.200,000
J. Royle	Everton	Man. C.	Dec. 1974	.200,000
J. Blockley	Coventry	Arsenal	Oct. 1972	.200,000
L. Macari	Celtic	Man. U.	Jan. 1973	.200,000
I. Moore	Nottm. F.	Man. U.	Mar. 1972	.200,000
R. Marsh	Q.P.R.	Man. C.	Mar. 1972	.200,000
‡M. Peters	West Ham ...	Tottenham H.	Mar. 1970	.200,000
S. Pearson	Hull C.	Man. U.	May 1974	.200,000
R. Hankin	Burnley	Leeds U.	Sept. 1976	.200,000
A. Hudson	Stoke C.	Arsenal	Dec. 1976	.200,000
D. Johnson	Ipswich	Liverpool	Aug. 1976	.200,000
R. Lee	Leicester	Sunderland ..	Sept. 1976	.200,000
D. McKenzie ...	Leeds U.	Anderlecht ...	June 1976	.200,000
D. McKenzie ...	Anderlecht ...	Everton	Dec. 1976	.200,000
P. Taylor	C. Palace	Tottenham H.	Sept. 1976	.200,000
R. Coates	Burnley	Tottenham H.	May 1971	.190,000
J. Harper	Aberdeen	Everton	Dec. 1972	.180,000
‡H. Kendall	Everton	Birmingham	Feb. 1974	.180,000
B. Rioch	Derby	Everton	Dec. 1976	.180,000
M. Burns	Blackpool	Newcastle ...	June 1974	.175,000

M. Macdonald .	Luton	Newcastle ...	May 1971	.175,000
C. Todd	Sunderland ..	Derby	Feb. 1971	.175,000
G. Daly	Man. U.	Derby	Mar. 1977	.175,000
T. MacDougall .	Man. U.	West Ham ...	Feb. 1973	.170,000
S. Kember	C. Palace	Chelsea	Sept. 1971	.170,000
‡G. Paddon	Norwich	West Ham ...	Dec. 1973	.170,000
D. Thomas	Burnley	Q.P.R.	Oct. 1972	.165,000
A. Clarke	Leicester	Leeds U.	June 1969	.165,000
T. McDermott .	Newcastle ...	Liverpool	Nov. 1974	.160,000
P. Went	Fulham	Portsmouth ..	Dec. 1973	.154,000
A. Conn	Rangers	Tottenham H.	July 1974	.150,000
J. Duncan	Dundee	Tottenham H.	Oct. 1974	.150,000
‡H. Newton	Nottm. F.	Everton	Oct. 1970	.150,000
D. Rogers	Swindon	C. Palace	Nov. 1972	.150,000
‡A. Clarke	Fulham	Leicester	June 1968	.150,000
T. Green	Blackpool	Newcastle U.	Oct. 1971	.150,000
M. Buchan	Aberdeen	Man. U.	Mar. 1972	.130,000
C. Stein	Rangers	Coventry	Oct. 1972	.130,000
M. Chivers	Southampton	Tottenham H.	Jan. 1968	.125,000
W. Rafferty	Carlisle	Wolves	Mar. 1978	.125,000
A. Gowling	Newcastle U.	Bolton W. .	Mar. 1978	.120,000
B. Butlin	Luton	Nottm. F.	Sept. 1974	.120,000
M. Holden	Preston N.E. .	Sunderland ..	May 1975	.120,000
G. Graham	Arsenal	Man. U.	Oct. 1972	.120,000
P. Taylor	Southend	C. Palace	Oct. 1973	.120,000
D. Law	Turin	Man. U.	July 1962	.116,000
S. Bowles	Carlisle	Q.P.R.	Sept. 1972	.110,000
T. Hateley	A. Villa	Chelsea	Oct. 1966	.100,000
M. Jones	Sheffield U. ...	Leeds U.	Sept. 1967	.100,000
J. Baxter	Sunderland ..	Nottm. F.	Dec. 1967	.100,000
A. Evans	Wolves	Liverpool	Sept. 1968	.100,000
R. Morgan	Q.P.R.	Tottenham H.	Feb. 1969	.100,000
‡‡C. Stein	Hibernian	Rangers	Oct. 1968	.100,000
D. Watson	Rotherham ...	Sunderland ..	Dec. 1970	100,000
J. Greaves	Milan	Tottenham H.	Nov. 1961	. 98,000
T. Hateley	Chelsea	Liverpool	June 1967	. 96,000
C. Chilton	Hull C.	Coventry	Sept. 1971	. 92,000
‡‡D. Kemp	Portsmouth ..	Carlisle U.	Mar. 1978	. 75,000
A. Gilzean	Dundee	Tottenham H.	Dec. 1964	. 72,500
J. Baker	Turin	Arsenal	July 1962	. 70,000
J. Baxter	Rangers	Sunderland ..	May 1965	. 70,000
J. Charles	Leeds U.	Juventus	Apr. 1957	. 65,000
F. Lee	Bolton W.	Man. C.	Oct. 1967	. 60,000
J. Greaves	Tottenham H.	West Ham ...	Mar. 1970	. 60,000
P. Crerand	Celtic	Man. U.	Feb. 1963	. 56,000
D. Law	Huddersfield T.	Man. C.	Mar. 1960	. 55,000
A. Kay	Sheffield W. .	Everton	Dec. 1962	. 55,000
J. Charles	Juventus	Leeds U.	Aug. 1962	. 53,000
G. Banks	Leicester C. ..	Stoke C.	Apr. 1967	. 52,000
T. Hennessey ..	Birmingham .	Nottm. F.	Nov. 1965	. 50,000
G. Eastham	Newcastle U.	Arsenal	Nov. 1960	. 47,500
A. Quixall	Sheffield W. .	Man. U.	Sept. 1958	. 45,000
Mel Charles	Swansea T. ..	Arsenal	Mar. 1959	. 40,000
R. Wilson	Huddersfield T.	Everton	July 1964	. 40,000
C. Jones	Swansea T. ..	Tottenham H.	Feb. 1958	. 35,000
J. Sewell	Notts County	Sheffield W.	Mar. 1951	. 34,000
T. Ford	Sunderland ..	Cardiff C.	Nov. 1953	. 30,000
D. Blanchflower	A. Villa	Tottenham H.	Dec. 1954	. 30,000
D. Mackay	Hearts	Tottenham H.	Mar. 1959	. 30,000
T. Taylor	Barnsley	Man. U.	Mar. 1953	. 29,999

T. Docherty ..	Preston N.E. .	Arsenal	Aug. 1958	. 29,500
D. Revie	Man. C.	Sunderland ..	Nov. 1956	. 24,000
A. Ramsey	Southampton	Tottenham H.	May 1949	. 21,000
L. Shackleton .	Newcastle U.	Sunderland ..	Feb. 1948	. 20,000
T. Lawton	Chelsea	Notts County	Nov. 1947	. 20,000
Ivor Allchurch .	Swansea T. ..	Newcastle U.	Oct. 1958	. 20,000
W. Steel	Derby	Dundee	Sept. 1950	. 17,500
Bryn Jones ...	Wolves	Arsenal	Aug. 1938	. 14,000
A. Stubbins	Newcastle U.	Liverpool	Sept. 1946	. 13,000
L. Shackleton .	Bradford	Newcastle U.	Oct. 1946	. 13,000
T. Lawton	Everton	Chelsea	Nov. 1945	. 11,500
S. Matthews ...	Stoke City	Blackpool	May 1947	. 11,500
R. Allen	Q.P.R.	Man. U.	Jan. 1950	. 11,000
D. B. N. Jack ...	Bolton W.	Arsenal	Oct. 1920	. 10,950
H. Gallacher ...	Newcastle U.	Chelsea	May 1930	. 11,000
P. Doherty	Blackpool	Man. C.	Feb. 1936	. 10,000
L. Johnstone ...	Clyde	Hibernian	Jan. 1947	. 10,000
A. James	Preston N.E. .	Arsenal	June 1929	. 9,000
A. Jackson	Huddersfield T.	Chelsea	Sept. 1930	. 8,500
J. H. Hill	Burnley	Newcastle U.	Oct. 1928	. 8,000
R. Kelly	Burnley	Sunderland ..	Dec. 1925	. 6,550
H. Gallacher ...	Airdrieonians	Newcastle U.	Dec. 1925	. 6,500
*T. Lawton	Burnley	Everton	Dec. 1936	. 6,500
W. Cresswell ..	South S.	Sunderland ..	Mar. 1922	. 5,500
S. C. Puddefoot	West Ham ...	Falkirk	Feb. 1922	. 5,500
S. Matthews ...	Blackpool	Stoke City	Oct. 1961	. 2,800
A. Common	Sunderland ..	Middlesbrough	Feb. 1905	. 1,000

*At the age of seventeen. ‡‡The first £100,000 deal between Scottish clubs.
**A record fee between British clubs. ‡Including one or more players.
***World record transfer for goalkeeper

UNCHANGED

All four clubs seeking re-election at the end of the 1978–79 season, Darlington, Doncaster Rovers, Halifax Town and Crewe Alexandra were voted back in at The Football League Annual General Meeting.

The following are the arrivals and departures since 1923:

Year	In	Out
1923	Doncaster Rovers	Stalybridge Celtic
	New Brighton	
1927	Torquay Athletic	Aberdare Athletic
1928	Carlisle United	Durham City
1929	York City	Ashington
1930	Thames	Merthyr Tydfil
1931	Mansfield Town	Newport County
	Chester	Nelson
1932	Aldershot	Thames
	Newport County	Wigan Borough
1938	Ipswich Town	Gillingham
1950	Colchester United	
	Gillingham	
	Scunthorpe United	
	Shrewsbury Town	
1951	Workington	New Brighton
1960	Peterborough United	Gateshead
1962	Oxford United	Accrington Stanley
1970	Cambridge United	Bradford
1972	Hereford United	Barrow
1977	Wimbledon	Workington
1978	Wigan Athletic	Southport

GREAT SERVICE

Jimmy Dickinson, holder of 48 English caps, played his 764th – and last – League match for Portsmouth at Northampton on his 40th birthday, April, 1965.

Harold Bell, of Tranmere Rovers, never absent for nine seasons (1946–55), had an unbroken run of 401 League appearances.

Ronald Ashman, of Norwich City (later manager), played in 662 matches for that club.

John Atyeo, 15 years with Bristol City, made 635 appearances and scored 350 League and Cup goals.

Sam Bartram's appearances in goal for Charlton Athletic totalled 613 (Football League 582, F.A. Cup 31).

The **entire defence** of Huddersfield Town played in all 42 Second Division matches in season 1952–3, namely, Wm. Wheeler (goal), Ronald Staniforth and Laurence Kelly (full-backs), Wm. H. McGarry, D. W. McEvoy and W. L. Quested (half-backs), in addition, Victor Metcalfe played in all 42 League matches at outside-left.

HIGH FOREIGN FEES FOR BRITISH PLAYERS

In April, 1957, Juventus F.C. of Turin paid the then record transfer-fee for a British player for **John Charles**, Welsh International and Leeds United, who received a £10,000 share of **£65,000**

In May, 1961, Turin paid the equivalent of £8,000 to **Joe Baker**, Hibernian and English International centre-forward, the actual transfer-fee being about **£73,000**

In June, 1961, **Gerry Hitchens** (England and Aston Villa) was guaranteed £25,000 earnings in three years by Internationale (Milan), the transfer-fee being approx. **£80,000**

In June, 1961, Milan offered Chelsea £83,000 for **Jimmy Greaves**, English International inside-forward, who was guaranteed earnings of £40,000 in three years including £10,000 for signing-on, a transfer-fee of **£83,000**

In June, 1961, Turin reported signing **Denis Law** (Scottish International of Manchester City) who received about £40,000 the transfer-fee being around **£100,000**

In June, 1977, S. V. Hamburg paid £500,000 to Liverpool for England striker Kevin Keegan **£500,000**

FOOTBALLER OF THE YEAR

Winners of Football Writers' Association statuette:

1947–8–**S. Matthews** (Blackpool), 1948–9–**J. Carey** (Manchester United), 1949–50–**J. Mercer** (Arsenal), 1950–1–**H. Johnston** (Blackpool), 1951–2–**W. A. Wright** (Wolverhampton Wanderers), 1952–3–**N. Lofthouse** (Bolton Wanderers), 1953–4–**T. Finney** (Preston North End), 1954–5–**D. Revie** (Manchester City), 1955–6–**B. Trautmann** (Manchester City), 1956–7–**T. Finney** (Preston North End), for second time, 1957–8–**D. Blanchflower** (Tottenham Hotspsur), 1958–9–**S. Owen** (Luton Town), 1959–60–**W. J. Slater** (Wolverhampton Wanderers), 1960–1–**D. Blanchflower** (Tottenham Hotspur), for second time, 1961–2–**J. Adamson** (Burnley), 1962–3–**S. Matthews** (Stoke City), for second time, 1963–4–**R. Moore** (West Ham United), 1964–5–**R. Collins** (Leeds United), 1965–6–**R. Charlton** (Manchester United), 1966–7–**J. Charlton** (Leeds United), 1967–8–**G. Best** (Manchester United), 1968–9–**T. Book** (Manchester City) tied with **D. Mackay** (Derby County), 1969–70–**B. Bremner** (Leeds United), 1970–1–**F. McLintock** (Arsenal), 1971–2–**G. Banks** (Stoke City), 1972–3–**P. Jennings** (Tottenham Hotspur), 1973–4–**I. Callaghan** (Liverpool), 1974–5–**A. Mullery** (Fulham), 1975–6–**K. Keegan** (Liverpool), 1976–7–**E. Hughes** (Liverpool), 1977–8–**K. Burns** (Nottingham Forest), 1978–9–**K. Dalglish** (Liverpool).

OVERSEAS TESTS

England first competed in the World Cup in 1950 in Brazil, failing to reach the concluding stages after a staggering defeat by United States.

Three Draws Abroad: In June, 1977 for England in Brazil, Argentina and Uruguay.

First Defeat Abroad sustained by England's full (professional) international team was by Spain (4–3) at Madrid in May, 1929. By Scotland v. Austria (5–0) in 1931.

Four Wins Abroad: in June and July 1966 for England in Finland, Norway, Denmark and Poland.

Three Defeats Abroad: In May, 1959 for England in Brazil, Peru and Mexico.

ENGLAND'S HOME RECORD

England's defeat by Hungary at Wembley in November 1953, was her first home fall to a Continental Country, although Eire had won at Everton in 1949. Full list of results in visits from countries outside our International Championship is appended.

Mar., 1923	Belgium	6–1
Dec. 1924*a*	Belgium	4–0
Dec., 1931	Spain	7–1
Dec. 1931	Austria	4–3
Dec. 1933	France	4–1
Nov., 1934	Italy	3–2
Dec., 1935	Germany	3–0
Dec., 1936	Hungary	6–2
Dec., 1937	Czechoslovakia	5–4
Oct., 1938	Rest of Europe	3–0
Nov., 1938*b*	Norway	4–0
Nov., 1946*c*	Holland	8–2
May, 1947	France	3–0
Nov., 1947	Sweden	4–2
Dec., 1948	Switzerland	6–0
Sept., 1949*d*	Eire	0–2
Dec., 1949	Italy	2–0
Nov., 1950	Yugoslavia	2–0
May, 1951	Argentina	2–1
May, 1951*d*	Portugal	5–2
Oct., 1951	France	2–2
Nov. 1951	Austria	2–2
Nov., 1952	Belgium	5–0
Oct., 1953	Rest of World	4–4
Nov., 1953	Hungary	3–6
Dec., 1954	Germany	3–1
Nov., 1955	Spain	4–1
May, 1956	Brazil	4–2
Nov., 1956	Yugoslavia	3–0
Dec., 1956*e*	Denmark	5–2
May, 1957	R. of Ireland	5–1
Nov., 1957	France	4–0
May, 1958	Portugal	2–1
Oct., 1958	Russia	5–0
May, 1959	Italy	2–2
Oct., 1959	Sweden	2–3
May, 1960	Yugoslavia	3–3
Oct., 1960	Spain	4–2
May, 1961	Mexico	8–0
Sept., 1961	Luxembourg	4–1
Oct., 1961	Portugal	2–0
April, 1962	Austria	3–1
May, 1962	Switzerland	3–1
Oct., 1962*f*	France	1–1
May, 1963	Brazil	1–1
Oct., 1963	Rest of World	2–1
May, 1964	Uruguay	2–1
Oct., 1964	Belgium	2–1
May, 1965	Hungary	1–0
Oct., 1965	Austria	2–3
Jan., 1966*d*	Poland	1–1
Feb., 1966	West Germany	1–0
May, 1966	Yugoslavia	2–0
July, 1966*w*	Uruguay	0–0
July, 1966*w*	Mexico	2–0
July, 1966*w*	France	2–0
July, 1966*w*	Argentina	1–0
July, 1966*w*	Portugal	2–1
July, 1966*w*	West Germany	4–2
Nov., 1966	Czechoslovakia	0–0
May, 1967	Spain	2–0
Dec., 1967	Russia	2–2
April, 1968	Spain	1–0
May, 1968	Sweden	3–1
Dec., 1968	Bulgaria	1–1
Jan., 1969	Rumania	1–1
Mar., 1969	France	5–0
Dec., 1969	Portugal	1–0
Jan., 1970	Holland	0–0
Nov., 1970	East Germany	3–1
April, 1971	Greece	3–0
May, 1971	Malta	5–0
Nov., 1971	Switzerland	1–1
April, 1972	West Germany	1–3
Oct., 1972	Yugoslavia	1–1
Sept., 1973	Austria	7–0
Oct., 1973*w*	Poland	1–1
Nov., 1973	Italy	0–1
May, 1974	Argentina	2–2
Oct., 1974	Czechoslovakia	3–0
Nov., 1974	Portugal	0–0
Mar., 1975	West Germany	2–0
April, 1975	Cyprus	5–0
Sept., 1976	R. of Ireland	1–1
Oct., 1976*w*	Finland	2–1
Feb., 1977	Holland	0–2
Mar., 1977*w*	Luxembourg	5–0
Sept., 1977	Switzerland	0–0
Nov., 1977*w*	Italy	2–0
April, 1978	Brazil	1–1
May, 1978	Hungary	4–1
Nov., 1978	Czechoslovakia	1–0

All matches played in London except (*a*) at West Bromwich, (*b*) Newcastle, (*c*) Huddersfield, (*d*) Everton, (*e*) Wolverhampton and (*f*) Hillsborough, (*w*) World Cup.

DAYS OF TRAGEDY

Some 300 people were killed and at least 500 injured when the crowd rioted over a disallowed goal at the National Stadium in Lima, Peru, May 24, 1964. The teams, from Argentina and Peru, were competing to play in the Olympic Games in Tokyo. The maddened mob surged out of their seats, smashed windows and set buildings on fire. Most of those killed were trampled to death.

The worst disaster in the history of British football occurred at Glasgow Rangers' ground at **Ibrox Park**, January 2, 1971.

Sixty-five people were trampled to death as they tumbled down a stairway at the ground after the Rangers v. Celtic New Year's Day match.

The tragedy eclipsed even the **Bolton** disaster when 33 people were killed and about 500 injured at the Bolton v. Stoke Cup-tie, March 9, 1946.

There was another crowd disaster at **Ibrox** in 1902 when part of the terracing collapsed during the Scotland v. England international. Twenty-five people were killed.

Eight leading players and three officials of **Manchester United** and eight newspaper representatives, were among those who perished in an aeroplane disaster at Munich, February 6, 1958, during take-off following a European Cup-tie in Belgrade. The players were Roger Byrne, Geoffrey Bent, Eddie Colman, Duncan Edwards, Mark Jones, David Pegg, Tommy Taylor and Liam Whelan, and the officials were Walter Crickmer (secretary), Tom Curry (trainer) and Herbert Whalley (coach). The newspaper representatives were Alf Clarke, Don Davies, George Follows, Tom Jackson, Archie Ledbrooke, Henry Rose, Eric Thompson and Frank Swift (former International goalkeeper of Manchester City).

THREE UP–THREE DOWN

The Football League Annual General Meeting of June 1973 agreed to adopt the promotion and relegation system of three up and three down.

The new system came into force in the 1973–4 season and applied only to the first three divisions; four were still relegated from the Third and four promoted from the Fourth.

It was the first change in the promotion and relegation system for the top two divisions in 81 years.

OFF-SIDE LAW ALTERATION

Off-side Experiments: In the 1949 practice matches an experiment was tried in Scotland limiting off-side to one-third of the field at each end and adopting in those areas the old off-side law governed by three (instead of two) defenders.

Foul Throw: In the case of a foul throw, the throw reverts to the other side .... **June, 1931**

Goalkeeper's Steps: In possession of the ball a goalkeeper is permitted to take four instead of two step **1931**

The goalkeeper must release the ball after taking four steps **1967**

Foreign Players: A professional player who is not a British-born subject is not eligible to take part in any competition under British jurisdiction unless he has a two years' qualification **June, 1931**

Two Referees: F.A. proposal that trials be held of the two referees' system in the season's practice games and in three selected League matches, with the consent of the clubs concerned, was defeated at the Association's Annual Meeting **1937**

Laws of Play Re-written **1938**

END OF WAGE LIMIT

Freedom from the maximum wage system–in force since the formation of the Football League in 1888–was secured by the Professional Footballers' Association in 1961. About this time Italian clubs renewed overtures for transfer of British stars (the first to depart having been **John Charles**, Welsh International of Leeds United, 1957). Fulham's **Johnny Haynes** became the first British player to earn a wage of around £100 a week.

Watering the pitch has been officially recognised and regulated in the Football League since the season of **1939–40**. It is permissible except during November, December, January and February.

Numbering players in Football League matches was made compulsory in 1939–40.

SUBSTITUTES

In 1965, the Football League, by 39 votes to 10, agreed that one substitute be allowed for an injured player at any time during a League match.

In 1957 a F.I.F.A proposal to allow substitution of an injured goalkeeper in competitive football was defeated.

When L. R. Roose, the Welsh goalkeeper, retired hurt in the England match at Wrexham, March 10, 1903, D. Davies (Bolton Wanderers) was allowed to take his place as substitute. Thus Wales used 12 players.

Four Forward Positions: Jack Rowley and **Bobby Charlton** (Manchester United) played for England in four of the five forward positions–all except outside right. **Frank Broome** (Aston Villa and Notts County) played in four forward positions in seven internationals. **Tom Finney** (Preston North End), was chosen to play in three positions–on both wings and at centre-forward.

SOCCER SECRETARIES

Football Association: E. A. Croker, 16 Lancaster Gate, London W.2.
Scottish F.A.: E. Walker, 6 Park Gardens, Glasgow C.3.
Irish F.A.: W. Drennan, 20 Windsor Avenue, Belfast 9.
Football Association of Wales: T. Morris, 3 Fairy Road, Wrexham.
Football Association of Ireland (Eire): P. O'Driscoll, 80 Merrion Square, Dublin 2.
League of Ireland: E. J. Dowling, 80 Merrion Square, Dublin 2.
Federation Internationale de Football Association (F.I.F.A.): Dr. H. Kaiser, Hitzigweg 11, Zurich 8032, Switzerland.
Union of European Football Association (U.E.F.A.): H. Bangerter, Case Postale 16, Laubeggstrasse 70, Berne 15, Switzerland.
Football League: A. Hardaker, Lytham St. Anne's, Lancs.
Scottish League: T. Maule, 170 Hope Street, Glasgow.
Football Combination: T. P. R. Kirkup, 59 Poplar Road, Merton Park, London SW19 3JS.
Northern League: G. Nicholson, 99 Watling Road, Bishop Auckland, Co. Durham.
North Regional League: J. E. Bennison, 35 West Quadrant, Firth Park, Sheffield 5.
Southern League: W. Dellow, 1 Cartmel Close, Great Tylers, Wray Common, Reigate, Surrey.
West Midlands (Regional) League: C. G. Davis, 34 Charles Way, Malvern Link, Malvern, Worcs.
Professional Footballers' Association: C. Lloyd, 105 Corn Exchange Buildings, Hanging Ditch, Manchester 4.
Northern Premier League: G. Graham, 36 Foregate, Highgate Park, Fulwood, Preston.

MILESTONES OF SOCCER

1855 Sheffield club formed
1862 Notts County (oldest League club) formed
1863 F.A. came into being
1867 Queen's Park club formed

1871 F.A. Cup introduced
1872 Official Internationals began
1873 Scottish F.A. formed
1873 Scottish Cup introduced
1874 Oxford first met Cambridge
1874 Shinguards introduced
1875 Crossbar introduced
1876 Scotland first played Wales
1876 F.A. of Wales formed
1877 Welsh Cup introduced
1878 Referee's whistle used
1879 England first played Wales
1880 Cliftonville, first Irish club formed
1880 Irish F.A. founded
1880 Irish Cup introduced
1882 International Board formed
1882 England first played Ireland
1882 Wales first played Ireland
1883 Two-handed throw arrived
1885 Cup went to provinces
1885 Record Scottish Cup score (36–0)
1885 Professionalism legalised
1886 Law governing International Board formed by England, Scotland, Wales and Ireland
1886 Blackburn Rovers won F.A. Cup for third successive season
1887 Record F.A. Cup score (26–0)
1888 First all-English team to win F.A. Cup (West Bromwich Albion)
1888 Football League founded by Mr. Wm. McGregor
1889 Preston won Cup and League
1890 Irish League formed
1890 Mr. J. C. Clegg elected Chairman F.A.
1891 Scottish League formed
1891 Goal-nets arrived
1891 Penalty-kick introduced
1892 Inter-League games began
1892 Second Division formed
1893 F.A. Amateur Cup launched
1894 Southern League formed
1895 F.A. Cup stolen
1897 Aston Villa won Cup and League
1898 Promotion and relegation introduced
1901 Maximum wage rule in force
1901 Spurs first professional club to take F.A. Cup south
1901 First 100,000 attendance (110,802) at F.A. Cup Final
1902 Welsh League formed
1902 Ibrox Park disaster
1903 Record Cup Final win (6–0) by Bury over Derby County
1904 F.I.F.A. founded
1905 First £1,000 transfer
1907 A.F.A founded
1907 Wales first won International Championship
1907 Players' Union revived
1908 Transfer fee limit (£350) fixed in January
1908 Limit withdrawn in April
1908 U.K. won Olympic Games title at Shepherd's Bush
1908 F.A. Charity Shield introduced
1908 England won International Champtionship without conceding a goal
1909 Scottish Cup withheld owing to riot at Final Tie
1909 Football League "majority"
1911 Central League formed

1912 Transfer System Test Case
1912 U.K. last won Olympic title (Stockholm)
1913 F.A. Jubilee banquet
1914 King George V at Cup Final
1914 Amateur "split" ended
1914 Ireland first won International Championship
1916 Entertainment Tax began
1919 League extended to 44 clubs
1919 Season extended
1920 Third Division (South) formed
1921 Third Division (North) formed
1922 Scottish League (Div. II)
1922 Corinthians entered F.A. Cup
1923 First Wembley Cup Final
1924 Wales won all Internationals
1925 New off-side law
1925 Huddersfield Town won Div. I for third successive season
1927 Cup taken out of England (Cardiff City)
1928 Britain left F.I.F.A.
1928 First £10,000 transfer
1928 Dean (Everton) created League scoring record
1930 World Cup inaugurated, won by Uruguay
1931 West Bromwich Albion won Cup and promotion
1933 Everton hat-trick, Won Div. II, Div. I and Cup in successive seasons
1933 Scottish F.A. Diamond Jubilee
1934 Death of Mr. H. Chapman
1934 Sir Frederick Wall retired
1934 Mr. S. F. Rous apointed F.A. Secretary
1934 England lost first two matches on Continental tour
1935 Arsenal equalled Huddersfield Town's League hat-trick record
1935 Rangers won Scottish League and Cup for second successive season
1935 Official two-referee trials
1935 Payne's 10 goal League record
1936 McGrory (Celtic) set up British aggregate League scoring record
1936 Dean passed Bloomer's English aggregate League scoring record
1937 King George VI and Queen Elizabeth at F.A. Cup Final
1937 British record of 140,547 attendance at Scotland v. England match at Hampden Park, Glasgow
1937 Mr. W. Pickford appointed President of F.A.
1938 Death of S. Bloomer
1938 East Fife, first Second Division club to win Scottish Cup
1938 Football League Jubilee
1938 F.A.'s 75th anniversary
1938 Laws of play re-written
1938 Arsenal paid record £14,000 fee for B. Jones (Wolverhampton Wanderers)
1939 First six-figure attendance at League match (Rangers v. Celtic)
1939 Mr. W. C. Cuff, President Football League
1939 Numbering of players in Football League
1939 All normal Competitions suspended for duration of Second World War
1945 F.A. Cup resumed
1946 British associations rejoined F.I.F.A.
1946 Derby County won first post-war Cup Final
1946 Bolton disaster (33 killed) during F.A. Cup tie with Stoke City
1947 Great Britain beat Rest of Europe 6–1 at Glasgow
1947 Doncaster Rovers (Third N. Champions) set new Football League record of 72 points
1949 Mr. S. F. Rous, Secretary F.A. knighted
1949 Death of Mr. W. C. Cuff (Football League President)
1950 Third Division extended to 48 clubs

1950 World record gate (200,000) at World Cup at Rio
1950 Scotland first beaten at home by foreign team (Austria)
1952 Newcastle United equalled Blackburn Rovers' record of 1890 and 1891 by winning F.A. Cup in successive seasons
1953 The "Stanley Matthews" Cup Final
1953 F.A.'s 90th anniversary
1953 Hungary beat England at Wembley
1954 Death of V. Woodward
1954 Germany won World Cup
1954 England beat Germany at Wembley
1954 Hungary beat England 7—1 at Budapest
1954 Wolves beat Russian champions and Honved (including six Hungarian Internationals)
1955 Wolves beat Moscow Dynamo, Russian Champions
1957 Mr. Alan Hardaker, Secretary Football League
1957 S. Matthews awarded C.B.E.
1957 Entertainment Tax withdrawn
1957 Manchester United (League Champions) missed Double by losing Cup Final after injury to goalkeeper
1958 Manchester United air crash
1958 B. Meredith died
1958 Four Divisions introduced
1958 England first played U.S.S.R (Moscow)
1958 Brazil won World Cup (Stockholm)
1958 Wolves won everything for which they competed except F.A. Cup
1959 England lost on tour to Brazil, Peru and Mexico
1959 B. Wright retired (105 caps)
1959 Football League established fixtures copyright and for use thereof pools promoters agreed to pay approximately £300,000 a year (to include Scottish League) for 10 years
1960 Record transfer fee of £55,000 paid by Manchester City for Denis Law (Huddersfield Town)
1960 Wolves (Cup winners) missed Double and League Championship hat-trick by one goal
1960 For fifth time in 10 seasons F.A Cup Final team reduced to 10 men by serious injury
1960 F.A. Recognised English Sunday football
1961 Maximum wage removed
1961 Spurs won League and Cup
1961 First British £100-a-week wage paid (by Fulham to J. Haynes)
1961 Transfers of British stars to Italy raised sums involved to six figures
1961 Mr. G. H. Doggart, Chairman of F.A.
1961 Spurs paid £98,000 for J. Greaves
1961 Sir Stanley Rous became President of F.I.F.A.
1962 Spurs joined Blackburn Rovers and Newcastle in winning Cup in successive seasons
1962 Manchester United raised record British transfer-fee to £116,000 fo Denis Law
1963 Football League's 75th Jubilee
1963 F.A. Centenary
1963 Season extended to end of May owing to severe winter
1963 Mr. G. Doggart (Chairman) died during F.A. annual meeting
1963 English "retain and transfer" system ruled illegal in High Court test case
1964 Rangers' secona great hat-trick – Scottish Cup, League Cup and League Championship
1964 Football League and Scottish League guaranteed £500,000 a year ir new fixtures copyright agreement with pools promoters
1965 Stanley Matthews knighted in farewell season

1965 A. Rowley (Shrewsbury Town) retired with all-time record of 434 League goals
1966 Substitutes allowed for injured players in Football League matches
1966 England won World Cup
1967 Alf Ramsey, England team manager, knighted; B. Moore, England World Cup captain, is awarded the O.B.E.
1967 Celtic become first British team to win European Cup – also take all three major Scottish titles
1968 Manchester United succeed Celtic as European Champions by beating Benfica 4–1 at Wembley
1970 Brazil regain the World Cup
1971 Arsenal emulate Spurs double achievement by winning the League and Cup
1974 West Germany win the World Cup
1977 Liverpool achieve the double of League Championship and European Cup. They are also beaten finalists in the F.A. Cup
1978 Nottingham Forest win the League Championship, for the first time in the clubs' 113-year existence, a year after being promoted from the Second Division
1978 Liverpool became the first British club to win the European Championships' Cup in successive seasons
1978 Argentina win the World Cup
1978 Viv Anderson (Nottingham Forest) the first black player to win a full England cap
1979 Trevor Francis becomes the first British million pound footballer when he joins Nottingham Forest from Birmingham City.
1979 Nottingham Forest win the European Cup to keep the trophy in England for the third successive season. Trevor Francis scoring the goat that beat Malmo (Sweden) 1–0.

REPUBLIC OF IRELAND RECORDS

YOUNGEST CAPS: Jimmy Holmes. 17 years, 200 days, v. Austria, May 1971.
MOST CAPS: Johnny Giles 57, (After game v. Denmark, May 2nd), Allan Kelly 47.
GOALS IN INTERNATIONAL FOOTBALL:
4. Paddy Moore for Eire v. Belgium, February 25, 1934. Result 4–4.
4. Don Givens for Eire v. Turkey, October 29, 1975. Result 4–0.
LEAGUE AND CUP DOUBLE:
Shamrock Rovers, 1924–25, 1931–32, 1963–64.
Bohemians, 1927–28.
Cork Athletic, 1950–51.
Cork United, 1940–41.
Dundalk, 1978–79.
St. James' Gate, 1921–22.
LEAGUE OF IRELAND, TOP SCORERS

		Goals
1969–70	D. Wiggington (Cork Hibernians)	21
1970–71	B. Bradley (Finn Harps)	20
1971–72	T. Marsden (Cork Hibernians)	24
1972–73	T. Harkin (Finn Harps)	20
1973–74	T. O'Connor and T. Flanagan (Bohemians)	18
1974–75	B. Bradley (Finn Harps)	21
1975–76	B. Bradley (Finn Harps)	29
1976–77	S. Wallace (Waterford)	16
1977–78	T. O'Connor (Bohemians)	24
1978–79	J. Delamere (Shelbourne)	17

HOME CHAMPIONSHIP

NORTHERN IRELAND 0 ENGLAND 2

In Belfast (35,000), May 19, 1979

Northern Ireland: Jennings (Arsenal); Rice (Arsenal); Nichol (J) (Manchester United); Nicholl (C) (Southampton); Nelson (Arsenal); Moreland (Derby); sub. McGrath (Manchester United); Hamilton (Swindon); McIlroy (Manchester United); Armstrong (Tottenham); Caskey (Derby); Cochrane (Middlesbrough); sub. Spence (Blackpool).

England: Clemance (Liverpool); Neal (Liverpool); Thompson (Liverpool); Watson (Manchester City); Mills (Ipswich); Wilkins (R) (Chelsea); McDermott (Liverpool); Currie (Leeds); Coppell (Manchester United); Latchford (Everton); Barnes (Manchester City).

Scorers: England—Watson, Coppell.

WALES 3 SCOTLAND 0

At Ninian Park (20,371), May 19, 1979

Wales: Davies (Wrexham); Stevenson (Leeds); Jones (Wrexham); Mahoney (Middlesbrough); Dwyer (Cardiff); Phillips (Swansea); Yorath (Coventry); subs. Nicholls (Crystal Palace); Flynn (Leeds); James (Swansea); Toshack (Swansea); Curtis (Leeds).

Scotland: Rough (Partick); Burley (Ipswich); Gray (F) (Leeds); Wark (Ipswich); Hegarty (Dundee United); Hansen (Liverpool); Dalglish (Liverpool); Souness (Liverpool); Wallace (Coventry); sub. Jordan (Manchester United); Hartford (Manchester City); Graham (Leeds).

Scorer: Wales—Toshack 3.

SCOTLAND 1 NORTHERN IRELAND 0

At Hampden Park (28,529), May 22, 1979

Scotland: Wood (Everton); Burley (Ipswich Town); McQueen (Manchester United); Hegarty (Dundee United); Gray F. (Leeds United); Wark (Ipswich Town); sub. Narey (Dundee United); Souness (Liverpool), Hartford (Manchester City); Dalglish (Liverpool); Jordan (Manchester United); Graham (Leeds United).

Northern Ireland: Jennings (Arsenal); Rice (Arsenal); Nichol (Manchester United); Hunter (Ipswich Town); Nelson (Arsenal); Hamilton (Swindon Town), McIlroy (Manchester United); sub. Scott (Aldershot); Moreland (Derby County); Sloan (Manchester United); Armstrong (Tottenham Hotspur), Spence (Blackpool).

Scorer: Scotland—Graham.

ENGLAND 0 WALES 0

At Wembley (74,220), May 23, 1979

England: Corrigan (Manchester City); Cherry (Leeds United); Hughes (Liverpool); Watson (Manchester City); Sansom (Crystal Palace); McDermott (Liverpool); Wilkins (Chelsea); SUB. Brooking (West Ham); Currie (Leeds United); Keegan (S. V. Hamburg); sub. Coppell (Manchester United); Latchford (Everton); Cunningham (West Bromwich Albion).

Wales: Davies (Wrexham); Stevenson (Leeds United); Dwyer (Cardiff City); Phillips (Swansea City); Jones J. (Wrexham); Mahoney (Middlesbrough); Yorath (Coventry City); Flynn (Leeds United); James (Swansea City); Toshack (Swansea City); Curtis (Leeds United).

NORTHERN IRELAND 1 WALES 1

At Windsor Park, Belfast, (6,500), May 25, 1979

Northern Ireland: Jennings (Arsenal); Rice (Arsenal); Nicholl C. (Southampton); Hunter (Ipswich Town); Nelson (Arsenal); Nicholl J. (Manchester United); McCreery (Manchester United); McIlroy (Manchester United); Hamilton (Swindon Town); Armstrong (Tottenham Hotspur); Spence (Blackpool); Sub. Sloan.

Wales: Davies (Wrexham); Stevenson (Leeds United); Dwyer (Cardiff City); Phillips (Swansea City); Jones J. (Wrexham); Mahoney (Middlesbrough); Yorath (Coventry City); Flynn (Leeds United); James (Swansea City); Toshack (Swansea City); Curtis (Leeds United); Sub. Nicholas (Crystal Palace).

Scorers: Northern Ireland—Spence; Wales—James.

ENGLAND 3 SCOTLAND 1

At Wembley (100,000), May 26, 1979

England: Clemence (Liverpool); Neal (Liverpool); Thompson (Liverpool); Watson (Manchester City); Mills (Ipswich Town); Coppell (Manchester United); Wilkins (Chelsea); Brooking (West Ham United), Barnes (Manchester City); Keegan (S. V. Hamburg), Latchford (Everton).

Scotland: Wood (Everton); Burley (Ipswich Town); McQueen (Manchester United); Hegarty (Dundee United); Gray F. (Leeds United); Wark (Ipswich Town); Souness (Liverpool); Hartford (Manchester City); Dalglish (Liverpool); Jordan (Manchester United); Graham (Leeds United).

Scorers: England—Barnes, Coppel, Keegan. Scotland—Wark

CHAMPIONSHIP GOALSCORERS

England	Coppel (2), Watson, Barnes, Keegan.
Wales	Toshack (3), James.
Scotland	Graham, Wark.
Northern Ireland	Spence.

	P.	W	D.	L.	F.	A.	Pts.
England	3	2	1	0	5	1	5
Wales	3	1	2	0	4	1	4
Scotland	3	1	0	2	2	6	2
Northern Ireland	3	0	1	2	1	4	1

INTERNATIONAL TOURNAMENT

WINNERS OF THE TITLE SINCE FULL SERIES OF GAMES BEGAN

Season	Winner	Pts.
1883–84	Scotland	6
1884–85	Scotland	5
1885–86	England	5
	Scotland	5
1886–87	Scotland	6
1887–88	England	6
1888–89	Scotland	5
1889–90	Scotland	5
	England	5
1890–91	England	6
1891–92	England	6
1892–93	England	6
1893–94	Scotland	5
1894–95	England	5
1895–96	Scotland	5
1896–97	Scotland	5
1897–98	England	6
1898–99	England	6
1899–1900	Scotland	6
1900–01	England	5
1901–02	Scotland	5
	England	4
1902–03	Ireland	4
	Scotland	4
1903–04	England	5
1904–05	England	5
1905–06	England	4
	Scotland	4
1906–07	Wales	5
1907–08	Scotland	5
	England	5
1908–09	England	6
1909–10	Scotland	4
1910–11	England	5
1911–12	England	5
	Scotland	5
1912–13	England	4

Season	Winner	Pts.
1913–14	Ireland	5
1915–19	No contest	
1919–20	Wales	4
1920–21	Scotland	6
1921–22	Scotland	4
1922–23	Scotland	5
1923–24	Wales	6
1924–25	Scotland	6
1925–26	Scotland	6
1926–27	Scotland	4
	England	4
1927–28	Wales	5
1928–29	Scotland	6
1929–30	England	6
1930–31	Scotland	4
	England	4
1931–32	England	6
1932–33	Wales	5
1933–34	Wales	5
1934–35	England	4
	Scotland	4
1935–36	Scotland	4
1936–37	Wales	6
1937–38	England	4
	England	4
1938–39	Scotland	4
	Wales	4
1946–47	England	5
1947–48	England	5
1948–49	Scotland	5
1949–50	England	6
1950–51	Scotland	6
1951–52	Wales	5
	England	5
1952–53	England	4
	Scotland	4
1953–54	England	6

Season	Winner	Pts.
1954–55	England	6
	England	3
1955–56	Scotland	3
	Wales	3
	Ireland	3
1956–57	England	4
1957–58	England	4
	Ireland	4
1958–59	Ireland	4
	England	4
	England	4
1959–60	Scotland	4
	Wales	4
1960–61	England	6
1961–62	Scotland	6
1962–63	Scotland	6
	England	4
1963–64	Scotland	4
	Ireland	4
1964–65	England	4
1965–66	England	5
1966–67	Scotland	5
1967–68	England	5
1968–69	England	6
	England	4
1969–70	Scotland	4
	Wales	4
1970–71	England	4
1971–72	England	4
	Scotland	4
1972–73	England	6
1973–74	Scotland	4
	England	4
1974–75	England	4
1975–76	Scotland	6
1976–77	Scotland	5
1977–78	England	6
1978–79	England	5

Countries are bracketed when equal on points

INTERNATIONAL MATCHES

SCOTLAND UNDER-21 3 U.S.A. 1

At Aberdeen (6,000), September 17, 1978

Scotland.—Thomson (St. Mirren) Sneddon (Celtic), Gillespie (Coventry), Orr (Morton), McLeish (Aberdeen), McLeod (Dumbarton), Melrose (Patrtick), Jardine (Kilmarnock), McCluskey (Celtic), Bannon (Hearts), Lindsay (Motherwell).

U.S.A.—Brcic; Pollihan, Myernick, Droege, Fowles, Davis, Russell, Bandov, Prost, Nanchoff (L), Etherington.

Scorers: Scotland-Melrose, Orr, McLeod. U.S.A.—Etherington.

DENMARK UNDER-21 1 ENGLAND UNDER-21 2

European Under-21 Champiojnship

At Hvidovre (1,800), September 19, 1978

Denmark.—Neilsen; Olzyck, Sorensen, Petersen, Madsen, Ziegler, Schafer, Ostergaard, Anderson sub. (Birkedel), Eriksen, sub. (Garly), Berggren.

England.—Parkes (Q.P.R.); Wright (Everton), Sansom (C. Palace), Williams (Southampton), Hazell (Wolves), Futcher P (Man. City), Owen (Man. City), Reeves (Norwich), Regis (W.B.A.), Hoddle (Tottenham), Rix (Arsenal).

Scorers: Denmark—Sorensen (pen). England—Hoddle, Hazell.

DENMARK 3 ENGLAND 4

European Championship

In Copenhagen (47,600), September 20, 1978.

Denmark.—Jensen; Nielsen (F), Munk Jensen, Rontved, Lerby, Arnesen, Nielsen (C), Lund, Simonsen, Nielsen (B), sub. (Hansen A), Kristensen.

Engand.—Clemence (Liverpool), Mills (Ipswich), Neal (Liverpool), Watson (Man. City), Hughes (Liverpool), Wilkins R (Chelsea), Keegan (SV Hamburg), Coppell (Man. Utd), Brooking (West Ham), Latchford (Everton), Barnes (Man. City).

Scorers: Denmark—Simonsen (pen), Arnesen, Rontved. England—Keegasn 2, Latchford, Neal.

AUSTRIA 3 SCOTLAND 2

European Championship

In Vienna (72,000) September 20, 1978

Austria.—Fuchsbichler; Sara, Obermayer, Pezzey, Strasser, Prohaska, sub. (Oberacher), Weber, Jara, Schachner, Kreuz, Kranki.

Scotland.—Rough (Partick); Kennedy (Aberdeen), McQueen (Man. Utd.), Buchan (Man. Utd.), Donachie (Man. City), Gemmill (Nottm. For.), Hartford (Man. City), Souness (Liverpool), Jordan (Man. Utd.), sub. Graham (Leeds), Gray (A. Villa), Dalglish (Liverpool).

Scorers: Austria—Pezzey, Schachner, Kreuz. Scotland—McQueen, Gray.

REPUBLIC OF IRELAND 0 NORTHERN IRELAND 0

European Championship

In Dublin (55,000), September 20, 1978

R. of Ireland.—Kearns (Walsall); Grealish (Orient), Holmes (Tottenham), Lawrenson (Brighton), Synott (Shamrock), Brady (Arsenal), Daly (Derby), Stapleton (Arsenal), sub. Walsh (Everton), Heighway (Liverpool), sub. Givens (Birmingham), Giles (Shamrock), McGee (Q.P.R.).

N. Ireland.—Jennings (Arsenal); Rice (Arsenal), Nelson (Arsenal), Nicholl (Southampton), Hunter (Ipswich), sub. Hamilton (Millwall), Nicholl (Man. Utd.), O'Neill (Nottm. For.), McCreery (Man. Utd.), Armstrong (Tottenham), McIlroy (Man. Utd.), Spence (Blackpool), sub. Cochrane (Burnley).

SCOTLAND UNDER-21 5 NORWAY UNDER-21 1

European Under-21 Championship

At Easter Road (Edinburgh), 9,911, October 24, 1978.

Scotland.—Thomson (St. Mirren); Narey (Dundee Utd.), Stewart (Dundee Utd.), Wark. (Ipswich), sub. Redford (Dundee), McNichol (Brentford), Orr (Morton), McCluskey (Celtic), Bannon (Hearts), MacLeod A (Hibs.), Aitken (Celtic), Melrose (Partick), sub. MacLeod M (Dumbarton).

Norway.—Haugvaldstad; Iversen, Fkaelberg, Gran, Giske, Andersson, Myhre, Kujedal, Davidson, Jacobsen, Helvik.

Scorers: Scotland—Stewart, McCluskey 2, Melrose, Wark. Norway—Jacobsen.

REPUBLIC OF IRELAND 1 ENGLAND 1

European Championship

In Dublin (55,000) October 25, 1978

R. of Ireland.—Kearns (Walsall); Mulligan (W.B.A.), Holmes (Tottenham), Lawrenson (Brighton), O'Leary (Arsenal), sub. Gregg (Bohemians), Brady (Arsenal), Daly (Derby), Grealish (Orient), McGee (Q.P.R.) sub. Stapleton (Arsenal), Ryan (Brighton), Givens (Birmingham).

England.—Clemence (Liverpool); Neal (Liverpool), Mills (Ipswich), Wilkins R (Chelsea), Watson (Man City), sub. Thompson (Liverpool), Hughes (Liverpool), Keegan (SV Hamburg), Coppell (Man. Utd.), Latchford (Everton), Brooking (West Ham), Barnes (Man. City), sub. Woodcock (Nottm. For.).

Scorers: R. of Ireland—Daly. England—Latchford.

WALES 7 MALTA 0

At Wrexham (11,475) October 25, 1978.

Wales.—Davies (Wrexham); Stevenson (Leeds), Jones (Wrexham), Phillips (A. Villa), Page (Birmingham), Thomas (Wrexham), Harris (Leeds), Flynn (Leeds), Edwards (Chester), James (Swansea), Cartwright (Wrexham), sub. O'Sullivan (Brighton).

Malta.—Gatti; Cianter, Farrgia sub. (Consiglio), Toretell, Schembri, Holland, Magro, Aquilina, sub. (Spiteri-Gonzi), Xuereb (G), Xuereb (R), Sychell.

Scorers: Wales—Edwards 4, O'Sullivan, Thomas, Flynn.

NORTHERN IRELAND 2 DENMARK 1

European Championship

In Belfast (25,000), October 25, 1978

N. Ireland.—Jennings (Arsenal); Rice (Arsenal), Nelson (Arsenal), Nicholl (Man. Utd.), Hunter (Ipswich), McCreery (Man. Utd.), McIlroy (Man Utd.), O'Neill (Nottm. For.), Armstrong (Tottenham), Morgan (Sparta Rotterdam), sub. Spence (Blackpool), sub. Anderson (Peterborough), Cochrane (Middlesbrough).

Denmark.—Kjaer; Nielsen (F), Rontved, Larsen, Andersen, Rasmussen, Nielsen (C), Bjerg, Agerbeck sub. (Sorensen), Jensen, Kristensen.

Scorers: N. Ireland—Spence, Anderson. Denmark—Jensen.

SCOTLAND 3 NORWAY 2

European Championship

At Hampden Park (60,000), October 25, 1978

Scotland.—Stewart (Middlesbrough); Donachie (Man. City), Gray F (Leeds), Souness (Liverpool), McQueen (Man. Utd.), Buchan (Man. Utd.), Dalglish (Liverpool), Gemmill (Nottm. For.), Gray (Aston Villa), Hartford (Man. City), Graham (Leeds).

Norway.—Jacobsen (T.R.); Pedersen, Kordahl, Birkelund, Grondalen, Aas, Johansen, Jacobsen (T), Thoresen, Okland, Mathisen.

Scorers: Scotland—Dalglish 2, Gemmill (pen). Norway—Aas, Okland.

SCOTTISH LEAGUE 1 IRISH LEAGUE 1

At Motherwell (4,427), November 1, 1978

Scottish League.—Rough (Partick); Narey (Dundee Utd.), Burns (Celtic), Stevens (Motherwell), Hegerty (Dundee Utd.), Thomson (Morton), Houston (Partick), Bannon (Hearts), Pettigrew (Motherwell), McAdam (Celtic), sub. Somner (Partick), Marinello (Motherwell).

Irish League.—Barclay; Kennedy, Cromiė, Walsh, Rafferty, Cleary , Sloan, Dornan, Armstrong, Dickson, Murray.

Scorers: Scottish League—Pettigrew. Irish League—Armstrong.

CZECHOSLOVAKIA B 0 ENGLAND B 1

In Prague (5,000), November 28, 1978

Czechoslovakia.—Caloun; Mazura, Vaclavicek, Macela, Koubek, Nemec, Novak, Rott, Licka, Briza, Dvorak.

England.—Corrigan (Man. City); Gidman (A. Villa), Sansom (C. Palace), Talbot (Ipswich), Greenhoff B (Man. Utd.) sub. Hazell (Wolves), Lyons (Everton), Cunningham (W.B.A.), Daley (Wolves, Sunderland (Arsenal), Mortimer (A. Villa), sub. Owen (Man. City), Flanagan (Charlton), sub. Regis (W.B.A.).

Scorer: England—Daley

PORTUGAL UNDER-21 0 SCOTLAND UNDER-21 3

European Under-21 Championship

In Portugal (2,000), November 28, 1978

Portugal.—Jorge; Lavo, Silva, Ainho, Tobica, Pereirinha, Manuel, Antonia, Jorge, Fontes, Folha.

Scotland.—Stewart (Middlesbrough); Stewart (Dundee Utd.), Dawson (Rangers), Wark (Ipswicn), McNicholl (Brentford), Orr (Morton), McCluskey (Celtic), Bannon (Hearts), MacLeod (Hibs.), Aitken (Celtic), Melrose (Partick), sub. MacLeod (Celtic).

Scorers: Scotland—McCluskey, MacLeod 2 (1 a pen.).

ENGLAND 1 CZECHOSLOVAKIA 0

At Wembley (92,000), November 29, 1978.

England.—Shilton (Nottm. For.), Anderson (Nottm. For.), Cherry (Leeds), Thompson (Liverpool), Watson (Man. City), Wilkins R. (Chelsea), Keegan (SV Hamburg), Coppell (Man. Utd.), Woodcock (Nottm. For.), sub. Latchford (Everton), Currie (Leeds), Barnes (Man. City).

Czechoslovakia.—Michakiki; Barmos, Vojacek, Jurkemik, Gogh, Stambacher, Kozak, Gajdusek, Jarusek sub. (Panenka), Masny, Nehoda.

Scorer: England—Coppell.

BULGARIA 0 NORTHERN IRELAND 2

European Championship

In Sofia, (30,000), November 29, 1978

Bulgaria.—Goranov; Grancharov, Stankov (P), Karaskolev, Dimitrov, Sretkov, Gochev, Slavkov, Mlandenov, sub. (Dzevizov), Panov, Stankov (A), sub. (Svetkov).

N. Ireland—Jennings (Arsenal); Hamilton (Swindon), Nichol J. (Man Utd.), Nichol C. (Southampton), Nelson (Arsenal), O'Neill (Nottm. For.), McCreery (Man. Utd.), McIlroy (Man. Utd.), sub. Moreland (Derby), Cochrane (Middlesbrough), sub. McGrath (Man. Utd.), Armstrong (Tottenham), Caskey (Derby).

Scorers: N. Ireland—Armstrong, Caskey.

PORTUGAL 1 SCOTLAND 0

European Championship
In Lisbon (60,000), November 29, 1978.

Portugaı.—Bento; Artur, Humberto, Alhinho, Alberto, Pietra, Alves, Oliveira, sub. (Eurico), Costa, sub. (Sheu), Gomes, Nene.
Scotalnd.—Rough (Partick); Kennedy (Aberdeen), McQueen (Man. Utd.), Buchan (Man. Utd.), Gray F (Leeds), sub. Donachie (Man. City, Narey (Dundee Utd.), Gemmill (Nottm. For.), Hartford (Man. City), Dalglish (Liverpool), Jordan (Man. Utd.), sub. Wallace (Coventry), Robertson (Nottm. For.).

Scorer: Portugal—Alberto.

WALES 1 TURKEY 0

European Championship
At Wrexham (11,794), November 29, 1978.

Wales.—Davies (Wrexham); Stevenson (Leeds), Jones (Wrexham, Phillips (Swansea), Yorath (Coventry), Thomas (Man. Utd.), Harris (Leeds), Flynn (Leeds), Deacy (Berlingen), Dwyer (Cardiff), James (Burnley).

Turkey.—Senol; Turgay, Erdoan, Cem, Necati, Fatih, Necdet, Mehmeteski, Sedat, Onder, Ahmet.

Scorer: Wales—Deacy.

WALES UNDER-21 0 ENGLAND UNDER-21 1

At Swansea (5,642), February 6, 1979.

Wales.—Thomas M (Bristol Rovers); Jones (Bristol Rovers), Aizlewood (Luton), Phillips (Swansea), Dwyer (Cardiff), Nicholas (C. Palace), Lowndes (Newport), Clark (Derby), Walsh (C. Palace), Charles (Swansea), Thomas G (Leeds), sub. Doyle (Preston).

England.—Bailey (Man. Utd.), sub. Woods (Nottm. For.); Owen (Man. City), Gilbert (C. Palace), sub. Osman (Ipswich), Wright (Everton), Cowans (A. Villa), Sansom (C. Palace), Statham (W.B.A.), Blissett (Watford); Robson (W.B.A.), Reeves (Norwich), Hoddle (Tottenham).

Scorer: England—Hoddle.

ENGLAND 4 NORTHERN IRELAND 0

European Championship
At Wembley (92,000), February 7, 1979.

England.—Clemence (Liverpool); Neal (Liverpool), Mills (Ipswich), Currie (Leeds), Watson (Man. City), Hughes (Liverpool), Keegan (SV Hamburg), Coppell (Man. Utd.), Latchford (Everton), Brooking (West Ham), Barnes (Man. City).

N. Ireland.—Jennings (Arsenal), Rice (Arsenal), Nelson (Arsenal), Nicholl J (Man. Utd.), Nicholl C. (Southampton), McCreery (Man. Utd.), O'Neill (Nottm. For.), McIlroy (Man. Utd.), Armstrong (Tottenham), Caskey (Derby), sub. Spence (Blackpool), Cochrane (Middlesbrough), sub. McGrath (Man. Utd).

Scorers: England—Keegan, Latchford 2, Watson.

NORTHERN IRELAND 2 BULGARIA 0

European Championship

In Belfast (18,700), May 2, 1979.

Northern Ireland.—Jennings (Arsenal), Hamilton (Swindon), Nelson (Arsenal), Nicholl J (Man. Utd.), Nicholl C. (Southampton), sub. Moreland (Derby), McCreery (Man. Utd.), O'Neill (Nottm. For.), McIlroy (Man. Utd.), Armstrong (Tottenham), Caskey (Derby), sub. Spence (Blackpool), Cochrane (Middlesbrough).

Bulgaria.—Stojanov; Vassilev, Ivkoiv, Bonev, Kolev, Rainov, Zdravkov, sub. (Iley), Sredkov, Djevizov, Panov, Zvetkov.

Scorers: N. Ireland Nicholl (C), Armstrong.

REPUBLIC OF IRELAND 2 DENMARK 0

Eropean Championship

In Dublin (28,000), May 2, 1979

R. of Ireland.—Peyton (Fulham); Gregg (Bohemians), Holmes (Tottenham), Mulligan (W.B.A.), Martin (Newcastle), Brady (Arsenal), Daly (Derby), Hayes (Southampton), sub. Walsh (Q.P.R.), Stapleton (Arsenal), Giles (Shamrock), Givens (Birmingham).

Denmark.—Kjar; Nielsen (F), Rontved, Larsen, Lerby, Olsen, Lund, Arsesson, Simmonsen, Nielsen (B), Elkjer.

Scorers: R. of Ireland—Daly, Givens.

WALES 0 WEST GERMANY 2

European Championship

At Wrexham (29,500), May 2, 1979.

Wales.—Davies (Wrexham); Page (Birmingham), Berry (Wolves), Phillips (Swansea), Jones (Wrexham), Mahoney (Middlesbrough), Yorath (Coventry), sub. James (Swansea), Thomas (Man. Utd.), Harris (Leeds), Edwards (Chester), sub. Toshack (Swansea), Curtis (Swansea).

West Germany.—Maier; Kaltz, Stielike, Foerster, Dietz, Rummanigge, Bonhof, Zimmermann, Cullmann, Fischer, Allobs.

Scorers: West Germany—Zimmermann, Fischer.

BULGARIA 1 REPUBLIC OF IRELAND 0

European Championship

In Sofia (20,000), May 19, 1979

Bulgaria.—Filipov, Grancharov, Ivkov, Vassilev, Iliev, Zdravkov, Voinov, Borissov, Zhelyazkov, Panov, Zvetkov.

R. of Ireland.—Peyton (Fulham), Gregg (Bohemians), Holmes (Tottenham), sub. Mulligan (W.B.A.), Martin (Newcastle), O'Leary (Arsenal), Brady (Arsenal), Daly (Derby), Walsh (Q.P.R.), sub. McGee (Q.P.R.), Heighway (Liverpool), Giles (Shamrock), Givens (Birmingham).

Scorer: Bulgaria—Zvetkov.

REPUBLIC OF IRELAND 1 WEST GERMANY 3

In Dublin (20,000), May 22, 1979

R. of Ireland.—Peyton (Fulham), Gregg (Bohemians), Martin (Newcastle), O'Leary (Arsenal), Mulligan (W.B.A.), Grealish (Orient), Giles (Shamrock), Brady (Arsenal), Stapleton (Arsenal), Givens (Birmingham), sub. O'Callaghan (Stoke), Ryan (Brighton).

West Germany.—Maier, Kaltz, Cullmann, Forster (K), Forster (B), Schuster, Rummenigge, Zimmermann, Heoness, Allofs, Muller.

Scorers: R. of Ireland—Ryan. West Germany—Rummenigge, Kelsch, Heoness.

REPUBLIC OF IRELAND 0 ARGENTINA 0

In Dublin (25,000), May 29, 1979

R. of Ireland.—Peyton (Fulham), Gregg (Bohemians), Martin (Newcastle), O'Leary (Arsenal), Mulligan (W.B.A.), Grealish (Orient), Giles (Shamrock), Brady (Arsenal), Stapleton (Arsenal), sub. O'Callagham (Stoke), Walsh (Q.P.R.), Givens (Birmingham), sub. McGee (Q.P.R.).

Argentina.—Fillol, Villaverde, Tarantini (sub. Gallego), Olguin, Oviedo, Troossero, Houseman, Barbas, Reinalie (sub. Maradona), Valencia, Ferotti, (sub. Outes).

SCOTLAND 1 ARGENTINA 3

At Hampden Park (61,918), June 2, 1979

Scotland.—Rough (Partick), (sub. Wood (Everton)), Burley (Ipswich), Hegarty (Dundee Utd), Hansen (Liverpool), Munro (St. Mirren), Narey (Dundee Utd), Wark (Ipswich), Hartford (Man. City), (sub. Gray (F) (Leeds), Graham (Leeds), Dalglish (Liverpool), McGarvey (Liverpool).

Argentina.—Fillol, Villaverde (sub. Tressere), Olguin, Passarella, Tarantini, Barbas, Gallego, Maradona, Valencia, Houseman, (sub. Outes), Luque.

Scorers: Scotland—Graham Argentina—Luque 2, Maradona.

MALTA 0 WALES 2

European Championship

In Valleta (9,000), June 2, 1979

Malta.—Scriberras, Buckingham, Edwin, Farrugia, Holland, Buttigeg, Emanuel Farrugia, Magro, Xuereb (L), (sub. Aquilina), Spiteri-Gonzi (sub. Fabri), Xuereb (R), Xuereb (G).

Wales.—Davies (Wrexham), Stevenson (Leeds), Jones (Wrexham), Mahoney (Middlesbrough), Nicholas (C. Palace), Phillips (Swansea), Harris (Leeds), (sub. Thomas (Man. Utd.), Flynn (Leeds), (sub. Dwyer (Cardiff), James (Swansea), Toshack (Swansea), Curtis (Leeds).

Scorers: Wales—Nicholas, Flynn.

BULGARIA UNDER–21 1 ENGLAND UNDER–21 3

At Pernik (10,000), June 5, 1979

European Under–21 Championship

Bulgaria.—Laftschis, Balewski, Marinon, Tetschev, Dimitrov, Kotschev, Valkov, Marmkov, Mladenov, Stavkov, Milkov.

England.—Bailey (Man. Utd.), Sansom (C. Palace), Statham (W.B.A.), Williams (Southampton), Gilbert (C. Palace), Wright (Everton), Reeves (Norwich), Hoddle (Tottenham), (sub. Robson (W.B.A.), Deehan (Aston Villa), (sub. Blissett (Watford), Owen (W.B.A.), Regis (W.B.A.).

Scorers: Bulgaria—Valkov. England—Reeves 2, Regis.

BULGARIA 0 ENGLAND 3

European Championship
In Sofia (40,000), June 6, 1979

Bulgaria.—Filipov, Gruncherov, Ivakov, Boney, Iliev, Zdravkov, (sub. Bonev), Voinev, (sub. Gochev), Borissov, Zhelyakov, Panov, Tavatkuv.

England.—Clemence (Liverpool), Neal (Liverpool), Watson (Man. City), Thompson (Liverpool), Mills (Ipswich), Coppell (Man. Utd.), Wilkins (R) (Chelsea), Brooking (West Ham Utd.), Barnes (Man. City), (sub. Woodcock (Nottm. Forest), Latchford (Everton), (sub. Francis (Nottm. Forest), Keegan (SV Hamburg).

Scorers: England—Keegan, Watson, Barnes.

DENMARK 4 NORTHERN IRELAND 0

European Championship
In Copenhagen (16,800) June 6, 1979

Denmark.—Kiaer, Haigaard, Ziegler, Busk, Andersen, Olsen, Arnesen, Lerby, Norregaar, Simonsen, Elkjaer.

N. Ireland.—Jennings (Arsenal), Rice (Arsenal), Nelson (Arsenal), Nicholl (Man. Utd.), Hunter (Ipswich), McCreery (Man. Utd.), O'Neill (Nottm. Forest), McIlroy (Man. Utd.), Hamilton (Swindon), Spence (Blackpool), Armstrong (Tottenham).

Scorers: Denmark—Elkjaer 3, Simonsen.

NORWAY UNDER–21 2 SCOTLAND UNDER–21 2

In Hangesund, June 7, 1979

NORWAY 0 SCOTLAND 4

European Championship
In Oslo (17,269), June 7, 1979

Norway.—Jacobsen, Karisen, Groendalen, Kordahl, Pedersen, Aas, Albertsen, Thunberg, Mathisen, Oklund, Thoresen.

Scotland.—Rough (Partick), Burley (Ipswich), (sub. Hegarty (Dundee Utd.), Munro (St. Mirren), Burns (Nottm. Forest), McQueen (Man. Utd.), Hartford (Man. City), Graham (Leeds), Dalglish (Liverpool), Jordan (Man. Utd.), Gemmill (Nottm. Forest), Robertson (Nottm. Forest).

Scorers: Scotland—Jordan, Dalglish, Robertson, McQueen.

SWEDEN UNDER-21 1 ENGLAND UNDER-21 2

In Vasteras, June 9, 1979

Sweden.—Ravelli (T), Magnus Andersson, Ahlund, Mansson, Ravelli (A), Johansson, Mikael Andersson, Schiller, (sub. Gustavsson), Nilson, (sub. Westergren), Jingblad, (sub. Sunesson), Holmgren.

England.—Woods (Nottm. Forest), Sansom (C. Palace), Statham (W.B.A.), Robson (W.B.A.), Osman (Ipswich), Butcher (Ipswich), Reeves (Norwich), Cowans (Aston Villa), (sub. Williams (Southampton), Blissett (Watford), Rix (Arsenal), (sub. Owen (W.B.A.), Regis (W.B.A.), (sub. Deehan (Aston Villa).

Scorers: Sweden—Nilsson. England—Robson, Regis.

SWEDEN 0 ENGLAND 0

In Stockholm, June 10, 1979

Sweden.—Moller, Borg, Erlandsson, Arviddson, Arran, Tortensson, Linderoth, Nordgren, Cervin, Gronhagen, Johansson (S), sub. Wernersson, Nilsson.

England.—Shilton (Nottm. Forest), Anderson (Nottm. Forest), Hughes (Liverpool), Watson (Man. City), (sub. Thompson (Liverpool), Cherry (Leeds), McDermott (Liverpool), (sub. Wilkins (R) (Chelsea), Keegan (SV Hamburg), Currie (Leeds), (sub. Brooking (West Ham), Francis (Nottm. Forest), Woodcock (Nottm. Forest), Cunningham (W.B.A.)

AUSTRIA B 0 ENGLAND B 1

(Abandoned after 60 minutes)

In Klagenfurt (2,000), June 12, 1979

Austria.—Saria, Gisinger, Auer, Bauer, Ulmer, Dihanfch, Drabits, sub. Pilcher Ritter, sub. Pigel, Stelnkogler, Brauneder, Zuenelli.

England.—Corrigan (Man. City), Anderson (Nottm. Forest), Sansom (C. Palace), Williams (Southampton), Wright (Everton), Butcher (Ipswich), Hoddle (Tottenham), Robson (W.B.A.), Reeves (Norwich), Woodcock (Nottm. Forest), Rix (Arsenal).

Scorer: England—Robson.

AUSTRIA 4 ENGLAND 3

In vienna (31,000), June 13, 1979

Austria.—Koncilla, Sara, Obermeyer, Pezzey, Baumeister, Prohaska, Hattenberger, Jara, Weizl, sub. Shacner, Kreix, Schachner.

England.—Shilton (Nottm. Forest), sub. Clemence (Liverpool), Neal (Liverpool), Mills (Ipswich), Thompson (Liverpool), Watson (Man. City), Wilkins (R) (Chelsea), Keegan (SV Hamburg), Coppell (Man. Utd.), Latchford (Everton), sub. Francis (Nottm. Forest), Brooking (West Ham Utd.), Barnes (Man. City), sub. Cunningham (W.B.A.).

Scorers: Austria—Pezzey 2, Weizl 2. England—Keegan, Coppell, Wilkins.

European Championship Groups
involving British International teams

GROUP ONE

	P	W	D	L	F	A	Pts
England	4	3	1	0	12	4	7
N. Ireland	6	3	1	2	6	9	7
Eire	5	1	3	1	6	5	5
Denmark	6	1	2	3	13	13	4
Bulgaria	5	1	1	3	3	9	3

GROUP TWO

	P	W	D	L	F	A	Pts
Portugal	4	3	1	0	5	2	7
Austria	5	2	2	1	7	5	6
Scotland	4	2	0	2	9	6	4
Belgium	4	0	4	0	3	3	4
Norway	5	0	1	4	3	11	1

GROUP SEVEN

	P	W	D	L	F	A	Pts
Wales	4	3	0	1	10	2	6
W. Germany .	3	1	2	0	2	0	4
Turkey	3	1	1	1	2	2	3
Malta	4	0	1	3	1	11	1

SCOTTISH CUP FINAL

RANGERS 0 HIBERNIAN 0

At Hampden Park (50,610), May 12, 1979

Rangers.—McCloy, Jardine, Dawson, Johnstone, Jackson, MacDonald, (Miller), McLean, Russell, Parlane, Smith, Cooper.

Hibernian.—McArthur, Brazil, Duncan, Bremner, Stewart, McNamara, Hutchinson, (Rae), MacLeod, Campbell, Callachan, Higgins.

First Replay

RANGERS 0 HIBERNIAN 0

At Hampden Park (33,504), May 16, 1979

Rangers.—McCloy, Jardine, Dawson, Johnstone, Jackson, Macdonald, McLean, (Miller), Russell, Parlane, Smith, Cooper.

Hibernian.—McArthur, Brazil, Duncan, Brenmer, Stewart, McNamara, Rae, MacLeod, Campbell, Callachan, Higgins.

Second Replay

RANGERS 3 HIBERNIAN 2

(After extra-time. Score 2–2 at 90 mins)

At Hampden Park (30,602), May 28, 1979

Rangers.—McCloy, Jardine, Dawson, Johnstone, Jackson, Watson, (Miller), McLean, (Smith), Russell, Parlane, MacDonald, Cooper.

Hibernian.—McArthur, Brazil, Duncan, Bremner, Stewart, McNamara, Rae, MacLeod, Campbell, Callachan, (Brown), Higgins, (Hutchinson).

Scorers: Rangers—Johnstone 2, Duncan (own goal). Hibernian—Higgins, MacLeod (pen).

RESULTS OF ALL MATCHES

ENGLAND v. SCOTLAND

Played 96; England won 37; Scotland 38; drawn 22

Year	Venue	E	S
1872	Glasgow	0	0
1873	The Oval	4	2
1874	Glasgow	1	2
1875	The Oval	2	2
1876	Glasgow	0	3
1877	The Oval	1	3
1878	Glasgow	2	7
1879	The Oval	5	4
1880	Glasgow	4	5
1881	The Oval	1	6
1882	Glasgow	1	5
1883	Sheffield	2	3
1884	Glasgow	0	1
1885	The Oval	1	1
1886	Glasgow	1	1
1887	Blackburn	2	3
1888	Glasgow	5	0
1889	The Oval	2	3
1890	Glasgow	1	1
1891	Blackburn	2	1
1892	Glasgow	4	1
1893	Richmond	5	2
1894	Glasgow	2	2
1895	Everton	3	0
1896	Glasgow	1	2
1897	Crystal Palace	1	2
1898	Glasgow	3	1
1899	Birmingham	2	1
1900	Glasgow	1	4
1901	Crystal Palace	2	2
1902	Birmingham	2	2
1902†	Glasgow	1	1
1903	Sheffield	1	2
1904	Glasgow	1	0
1905	Crystal Palace	1	0
1906	Glasgow	1	2
1907	Newcastle	1	1
1908	Glasgow	1	1
1909	Crystal Palace	2	0
1910	Glasgow	0	2
1911	Everton	1	1
1912	Glasgow	1	1
1913	Stamford Bridge	1	0
1914	Glasgow	1	3
1915-6-7-8	Not Played		
1919	Everton	2	2
1919*	Glasgow	4	3
1919-20	Sheffield	5	4
1920-1	Glasgow	0	3
1921-2	Birmingham	0	1
1922-3	Glasgow	2	2
1923-4	Wembley	1	1
1924-5	Glasgow	0	2
1925-6	Manchester	0	1
1926-7	Glasgow	2	1
1927-8	Wembley	1	5
1928-9	Glasgow	1	5
1929-30	Wembley	5	2
1930-1	Glasgow	0	2
1931-2	Wembley	3	0
1932-3	Glasgow	1	2
1933-4	Wembley	3	0
1934-5	Glasgow	0	2
1935-6	Wembley	1	1
1936-7	Glasgow	1	3
1937-8	Wembley	0	1
1938-9	Glasgow	2	1
1945-6*	Glasgow	0	1
1946-7	Wembley	1	1
1947-8	Glasgow	2	0
1948-9	Wembley	1	3
1949-50	Glasgow	1	0
1950-1	Wembley	2	3
1951-2	Glasgow	2	1
1952-3	Wembley	2	2
1953-4	Glasgow	4	2
1954-5	Wembley	7	0
1955-6	Glasgow	1	2
1956-7	Wembley	2	1
1958-9	Wembley	1	0
1959-60	Glasgow	1	1
1960-1	Wembley	9	3
1961-2	Glasgow	0	2
1962-3	Wembley	1	2
1963-4	Glasgow	0	1
1964-5	Wembley	2	2
1965-6	Glasgow	4	3
1966-7	Wembley	2	3
1967-8	Glasgow	1	1
1968-9	Wembley	4	1
1969-70	Glasgow	0	0
1970-1	Wembley	3	1
1971-2	Glasgow	1	0
1972-3	Wembley	1	0
1973-4	Glasgow	0	2
1974-5	Wembley	5	1
1975-6	Glasgow	1	2
1976-7	Wembley	1	2
1977-8	Glasgow	1	0
1978-9	Wembley	3	1

* Unofficial "Victory" matches are not included in analyses

† Ibrox disaster; Match declared unofficial

ENGLAND v. WALES

Played 91; England won 60; Wales 12; drawn 19

		E	W
1879	The Oval	2	1
1880	Wrexham	3	2
1881	Blackburn	0	1
1882	Wrexham	3	5
1883	The Oval	5	0
1884	Wrexham	4	0
1885	Blackburn	1	1
1886	Wrexham	3	1
1887	The Oval	4	0
1888	Crewe	5	1
1889	Stoke	4	1
1890	Wrexham	3	1
1891	Sunderland	4	1
1892	Wrexham	2	0
1893	Stoke	6	0
1894	Wrexham	2	0
1895	London	1	1
1896	Cardiff	9	1
1897	Sheffield	4	0
1898	Wrexham	3	0
1899	Bristol	1	1
1900	Cardiff	1	1
1901	Newcastle	6	0
1902	Wrexham	0	0
1903	Portsmouth	2	1
1904	Wrexham	2	2
1905	Liverpool	3	1
1906	Cardiff	1	0
1907	Fulham	1	1
1908	Wrexham	7	1
1909	Nottingham	2	0
1910	Cardiff	1	0
1911	Millwall	3	0
1912	Wrexham	2	0
1913	Bristol	4	3
1914	Cardiff	2	0
1915-18	Not Played		
1919*	Cardiff	1	2
1919*	Stoke	2	0
1919-20	Highbury	1	2
1920-1	Cardiff	0	0
1921-2	Liverpool	1	0
1922-3	Cardiff	2	2
1923-4	Blackburn	1	2
1924-5	Swansea	2	1
1925-6	Selhurst Park	1	3
1926-7	Wrexham	3	3
1927-8	Burnley	1	2
1928-9	Swansea	3	2
1929-30	Stamford B.	6	0
1930-1	Wrexham	4	0
1931-2	Liverpool	3	0
1832-3	Wrexham	0	0
1833-4	Newcastle	1	2
1934-5	Cardiff	4	0
1935-6	Wolverhampton	1	2
1936-7	Cardiff	1	2
1937-8	Middlesbrough	2	1
1938-9	Cardiff	2	4
1945-6*	West Bromwich	0	1
1946-7	Manchester	3	0
1947-8	Cardiff	3	0
1948-9	Villa Park	1	0
1949-50	Cardiff	4	1
1950-1	Sunderland	4	2
1951-2	Cardiff	4	1
1952-3	Wembley	5	2
1953-4	Cardiff	4	1
1954-5	Wembley	3	2
1955-6	Cardiff	1	2
1956-7	Wembley	3	1
1957-8	Cardiff	4	0
1958-9	Birmingham	2	2
1959-60	Cardiff	1	1
1960-1	Wembley	5	1
1961-2	Cardiff	1	1
1962-3	Wembley	4	0
1963-4	Cardiff	4	0
1964-5	Wembley	2	1
1965-6	Cardiff	0	
1966-7	Wembley	5	1
1967-8	Cardiff	3	0
1968-9	Wembley	2	1
1969-70	Cardiff	1	1
1970-1	Wembley	0	0
1971-2	Cardiff	3	0
1972-3	Wembley	3	0
1973-4	Cardiff	2	0
1974-5	Wembley	3	0
1975-6	Cardiff	1	0
1976	Cardiff (century)	2	1
1976-7	Wembley	0	1
1977-8	Cardiff	1	3
1978-9	Wembley	0	0

ENGLAND v. IRELAND

Played 86; England won 67; Ireland 6; drawn 13

		E	I
1882	Belfast	13	0
1883	Liverpool	7	0
1884	Belfast	8	1
1885	Manchester	4	0
1886	Belfast	6	1
1887	Sheffield	7	0
1888	Belfast	5	1
1889	Liverpool	6	1
1890	Belfast	9	1
1891	Wolverhampton	6	1
1892	Belfast	2	0
1893	Birmingham	3	1

1894	Belfast	2	2
1895	Derby	9	0
1896	Belfast	2	0
1897	Nottingham	6	0
1898	Belfast	3	2
1899	Sunderland	13	2
1900	Dublin	2	0
1901	Southampton	3	0
1902	Belfast	1	0
1903	Wolverhampton	4	0
1904	Belfast	3	1
1905	Middlesbrough	1	1
1906	Belfast	5	0
1907	Liverpool	1	0
1908	Belfast	3	1
1909	Bradford (Park Ave)	4	0
1910	Belfast	1	1
1911	Derby	2	1
1912	Dublin	6	1
1913	Belfast	1	2
1914	Middlesbrough	0	3
1915-19	Not Played		
1919-20	Belfast	1	1
1920-1	Sunderland	2	0
1921-2	Belfast	1	1
1922-3	West Bromwich	2	0
1923-4	Belfast	1	2
1924-5	Liverpool	3	1
1925-6	Belfast	0	0
1926-7	Liverpool	3	3
1927-8	Belfast	0	2
1928-9	Liverpool	2	1
1929-30	Belfast	3	0
1930-1	Sheffield	5	1
1931-2	Belfast	6	2
1932-3	Blackpool	1	0
1933-4	Belfast	3	0
1934-5	Liverpool	2	1
1935-6	Belfast	3	[illegible]
1936-7	Stoke	3	1
1937-8	Belfast	5	1
1938-9	Manchester	7	0
1945-6*	Belfast	[illegible]	0
1946-7	Belfast	[illegible]	2
1947-8	Liverpool	2	2
1948-9	Belfast	6	2
1949-50	Manchester	9	2
1950-1	Belfast	4	1
1951-2	Birmingham	2	0
1952-3	Belfast	2	2
1953-4	Liverpool	3	1
1954-5	Belfast	2	0
1955-6	Wembley	3	0
1956-7	Belfast	1	1
1957-8	Wembley	2	3
1958-9	Belfast	3	3
1959-60	Wembley	2	1
1960-1	Belfast	5	2
1961-2	Wembley	1	1
1962-3	Belfast	3	1
1963-4	Wembley	8	3
1964-5	Belfast	4	3
1965-6	Wembley	2	1
1966-7	Belfast	2	0
1967-8	Wembley	2	0
1968-9	Belfast	3	1
1969-70	Wembley	3	1
1970-1	Belfast	1	0
1971-2	Wembley	0	1
1972-3	Goodison Park	2	1
1973-4	Wembley	1	0
1974-5	Belfast	0	0
1975-6	Wembley	4	1
1976-7	Belfast	2	1
1977-8	Wembley	1	0
1978-9	Belfast	2	0

* Unofficial "Victory" matches are not included in analyses

SCOTLAND v. WALES

Played 94; Scotland won 56; Wales 16; drawn 22

		S	W
1876	Glasgow	4	0
1877	Wrexham	2	0
1878	Glasgow	9	0
1879	Wrexham	3	0
1880	Glasgow	5	1
1881	Wrexham	5	1
1882	Glasgow	5	0
1883	Wrexham	3	0
1884	Glasgow	4	1
1885	Wrexham	8	1
1886	Glasgow	4	1
1887	Wrexham	2	0
1888	Edinburgh	5	1
1889	Wrexham	0	0
1890	Paisley	5	0
1891	Wrexham	[illegible]	3
1892	Edinburgh	8	1
1893	Wrexham	6	0
1894	Kilmarnock	5	2
1895	Wrexham	2	2
1896	Dundee	4	0
1897	Wrexham	2	2
1898	Motherwell	5	2
1899	Wrexham	6	0
1900	Aberdeen	5	2
1901	Wrexham	1	1
1902	Greenock	5	1
1903	Cardiff	1	0
1904	Dundee	1	1
1905	Wrexham	1	3

1906	Edinburgh	0	2
1907	Wrexham	0	1
1908	Dundee	2	1
1909	Wrexham	2	3
1910	Kilmarnock	1	0
1911	Cardiff	2	2
1912	Tynecastle	1	0
1913	Wrexham	0	0
1914	Glasgow	0	0
1915-19	Not Played		
1919-20	Cardiff	1	1
1920-1	Aberdeen	2	1
1921-2	Wrexham	1	2
1922-3	Paisley	2	0
1923-4	Cardiff	0	2
1924-5	Tynecastle	3	1
1925-6	Cardiff	3	0
1926-7	Glasgow	3	0
1927-8	Wrexham	2	2
1928-9	Ibrox	2	2
1929-30	Cardiff	4	2
1930-1	Glasgow	1	1
1931-2	Wrexham	3	2
1932-3	Edinburgh	2	5
1933-4	Cardiff	2	3
1934-5	Aberdeen	3	2
1935-6	Cardiff	1	1
1936-7	Dundee	1	2
1937-8	Cardiff	1	2
1938-9*	Edinburgh	3	2
1945-6*	Glasgow	2	0
1946-7	Wrexham	1	3
1947-8	Glasgow	1	2
1948-9	Cardiff	3	1
1949-50	Glasgow	2	0
1950-1	Cardiff	3	1
1951-2	Glasgow	0	1
1952-3	Cardiff	2	1
1953-4	Glasgow	3	3
1954-5	Cardiff	1	0
1955-6	Glasgow	3	0
1956-7	Cardiff	2	2
1957-8	Glasgow	1	1
1958-9	Cardiff	3	0
1959-60	Glasgow	1	1
1960-1	Cardiff	0	2
1961-2	Glasgow	2	0
1962-3	Cardiff	3	2
1963-4	Glasgow	2	1
1964-5	Cardiff	2	3
1965-6	Glasgow	4	1
1966-7	Cardiff	1	1
1967-8	Glasgow	3	2
1968-9	Wrexham	5	3
1969-70	Glasgow	0	0
1970-1	Cardiff	0	0
1971-2	Glasgow	1	0
1972-3	Wrexham	2	0
1973-4	Glasgow	2	0
1974-5	Cardiff	2	2
1975-6	Glasgow	3	1
1976-7	Wrexham	0	0
1977	(W. Cup) Liverpool	2	0
1977-8	Glasgow	1	1
1978-9	Cardiff	0	3

SCOTLAND v. IRELAND

Played 84, Scotland won 59; Ireland 13; drawn 12

		S	I
1884	Belfast	5	0
1885	Glasgow	8	2
1886	Belfast	7	2
1887	Belfast	4	1
1888	Belfast	10	2
1889	Glasgow	7	0
1890	Belfast	4	1
1891	Glasgow	2	1
1892	Belfast	3	2
1893	Glasgow	6	1
1894	Belfast	2	1
1895	Glasgow	3	1
1896	Belfast	3	3
1897	Glasgow	5	1
1898	Belfast	3	0
1899	Glasgow	9	1
1900	Belfast	3	0
1901	Glasgow	11	0
1902	Belfast	5	1
1903	Glasgow	0	2
1904	Dublin	1	1
1905	Glasgow	4	0
1906	Dublin	1	0
1907	Glasgow	3	0
1908	Dublin	5	0
1909	Glasgow	5	0
1910	Belfast	0	1
1911	Glasgow	2	0
1912	Belfast	4	1
1913	Dublin	2	1
1914	Belfast	1	1
1915-19	Not Played		
1919	Glasgow	2	1
1919	Belfast	0	0
1919-20	Glasgow	3	0
1920-1	Belfast	2	0
1921-2	Glasgow	2	1
1922-3	Belfast	1	0
1923-4	Glasgow	2	0
1924-5	Belfast	3	0
1925-6	Glasgow	4	0
1926-7	Belfast	2	0
1927-8	Glasgow	0	1
1928-9	Belfast	7	3
1929-30	Glasgow	7	3
1930-1	Belfast	0	0

1931-2	Glasgow	3	1
1932-3	Belfast	4	0
1933-4	Glasgow	1	2
1934-5	Belfast	1	2
1935-6	Edinburgh	2	1
1936-7	Belfast	3	1
1937-8	Aberdeen	1	1
1938-9	Belfast	2	0
1945-6	Belfast	3	2
1946-7	Glasgow	0	0
1947-8	Belfast	0	2
1948-9	Glasgow	3	2
1949 50	Belfast	8	2
1950-1	Glasgow	6	1
1951-2	Belfast	3	0
1952-3	Glasgow	1	1
1953-4	Belfast	3	2
1954-5	Glasgow	2	2
1955-6	Belfast	1	2
1956-7	Glasgow	1	0
1957-8	Belfast	1	1
1958-9	Glasgow	2	2
1959-60	Belfast	4	0
1960-1	Glasgow	5	2
1961-2	Belfast	6	1
1962-3	Glasgow	5	1
1963-4	Belfast	1	4
1964-5	Glasgow	3	2
1965-6	Belfast	2	3
1966-7	Glasgow	2	1
1967-8	Belfast	0	1
1968-9	Glasgow	1	1
1969-70	Belfast	1	0
1970-1	Glasgow	0	1
1971-2	Glasgow	2	0
1972-3	Glasgow	1	2
1973-4	Glasgow	0	1
1974-5	Glasgow	3	0
1975-6	Glasgow	3	0
1976-7	Glasgow	3	0
1977-8	Glasgow	1	1
1978-9	Glasgow	1	0

WALES v. IRELAND

Played 86; Wales won 40; Ireland 26; drawn 19

		W	I
1882	Wrexham	7	1
1883	Belfast	1	0
1884	Wrexham	6	0
1885	Belfast	8	2
1886	Wrexham	5	0
1887	Belfast	1	4
1888	Wrexham	11	0
1889	Belfast	3	1
1890	Shrewsbury	5	2
1891	Belfast	2	7
1892	Bangor	1	1
1893	Belfast	3	4
1894	Swansea	4	1
1895	Belfast	2	2
1896	Wrexham	6	1
1897	Belfast	3	4
1898	Llandudno	0	1
1899	Belfast	0	1
1900	Llandudno	2	0
1901	Belfast	1	0
1902	Cardiff	0	3
1903	Belfast	0	2
1904	Bangor	0	1
1905	Belfast	2	2
1906	Wrexham	4	4
1907	Belfast	3	2
1908	Aberdare	0	1
1909	Belfast	3	2
1910	Wrexham	4	1
1911	Belfast	2	1
1912	Cardiff	2	3
1913	Belfast	1	0
1914	Wrexham	1	2
1915-19	Not Played		
1919-20	Belfast	2	2
1920-1	Swansea	2	0
1921-2	Belfast	1	1
1922-3	Wrexham	0	3
1923-4	Belfast	1	0
1924-5	Wrexham	0	0
1925-6	Belfast	0	3
1926-7	Cardiff	2	2
1927-8	Belfast	2	2
1928-9	Wrexham	2	2
1929-30	Belfast	0	7
1930-1	Wrexham	3	2
1931-2	Belfast	0	4
1932-3	Wrexham	4	1
1933-4	Belfast	1	1
1934-5	Wrexham	3	1
1935-6	Belfast	2	3
1936-7	Wrexham	4	1
1937-8	Belfast	0	1
1938-9	Wrexham	3	1
1945-6*	Cardiff	0	1
1946-7	Belfast	1	2
1947-8	Wrexham	2	0
1948-9	Belfast	2	0
1949-50	Wrexham	0	0
1950-1	Belfast	2	1
1951-2	Swansea	3	0
1952-3	Belfast	3	2
1953-4	Wrexham	1	2
1954-5	Belfast	3	2
1955-6	Cardiff	1	1
1956-7	Belfast	0	0
1957-8	Cardiff	1	1
1958-9	Belfast	1	4
1959-60	Wrexham	3	2
1960-1	Belfast	5	1

1961-2	Cardiff	4 ...0	1970-1	Belfast	0 ...1
1962-3	Belfast	4 ...1	1971-2	Wrexham	0 ..0
1963-4	Swansea	2 ...3	1972-3	Goodison Park	0 ...1
1964-5	Belfast	5 ...0	1973-4	Wrexham	1 . 0
1965-6	Cardiff	1 ...4	1974-5	Belfast	0 ..1
1966-7	Belfast	0 ...0	1975-6	Swansea	1 ..0
1967-8	Wrexham	2 ...0	1976-7	Belfast	1 ..1
1968-9	Belfast	0 ...0	1977-8	Wrexham	1 ..0
1969-70	Swansea	1 ...0	1978-9	Belfast	1 .1

* Unofficial "Victory' match, not included in analyses

ENGLAND v. REST OF WORLD

1963—Wembley	England 2	Rest of World 1

(F.A. Century Match)

v. ARGENTINA

1951—Wembley	England 2	Argentina 1
1953—Buenos Aires	*England 0	Argentina 0
1962—Chile (W. Cup)	England 3	Argentina 1
1964—Rio de Janeiro	England 0	Argentina 1
1966—Wembley (W. Cup)	England 1	Argentina 0
1974—Wembley	England 2	Argentina 2
1977—Buenos Aires	England 1	Argentina 1

*Abandoned after 20 mins play. Rain

v. AUSTRALIA

		E	A			E	A
1925	Brisbane	5	1	1937	Newcastle (Aus.)	3	4
1925	Sydney	2	1	1951	Sydney	4	1
1925	Maitland	8	2	1951	Sydney	17	0
1925	Sydney	5	0	1951	Brisbane	4	1
1925	Melbourne	2	0	1951	Sydney	6	1
1937	Sydney	4	5	1951	Newcastle (Aus.)	5	0
1937	Brisbane	4	0				

v. AUSTRIA

		E	A			E	A
1903	Vienna	0	0	1952	Vienna	3	2
1906	Vienna	11	0	1958	Gothenburg (W. C.)	2	2
1908	Vienna	6	1	1961	Vienna	1	3
1909	Vienna	8	1	1962	Wembley	3	1
1903	Stamford Bridge	4	3	1965	Wembley	2	3
1936	Vienna	1	2	1967	Vienna	1	0
1951	Wembley	1	2	1973	Wembley	7	0
				1979	Vienna	3	4

v. BELGIUM

		E	B			E	B
1921	Brussels	2	...0	1931	Brussels	4	...1
1923	Highbury	6	...1	1936	Brussels	2	...3
1923	Antwerp	2	...2	1948	Brussels	5	...2
1924	West Bromwich	4	...0	1950	Brussels	4	...1
1926	Antwerp	5	...3	1952	Wembley	5	...0
1927	Brussels	9	...1	1954	Basle (W. Cup)	4	...4
1928	Antwerp	3	...1	1964	Wembley	2	...2
1929	Brussels	5	...1	1970	Brussels	3	...1

v. BOHEMIA

1908—Prague	England	4	Bohemia	0

v. BRAZIL

		E	B			E	B
1956	Wembley	4	...2	1969	Rio de Janeiro	1	...2
1958	Gothenburg (W. C.)	0	...0	1970	Guadalajara (W. C.)	0	...1
1959	Rio de Janeiro	0	...2	1976	Los Angeles	0	...1
1962	Chile (W. Cup)	1	...3	1977	Rio de Janeiro	0	...0
1963	Wembley	1	...1	1978	Wembley	1	...1
1964	Rio de Janeiro	1	...5				

v. BULGARIA

		E	B			E	B
1962	Chile (W. Cup)	0	...0	1974	Sofia	1	...0
1968	Wembley	1	...1	1979	Sofia (Nat. C.	3	...0

v. CHILE

1950—Rio (W. Cup)	England	2	Chile	0
1953—Santiago	England	2	Chile	1

v. COLOMBIA

1970—Bogota	England	4	Colombia	0

v. CYPRUS

1975—Wembley	England	5	Cyprus	0
1975—Nicosia	England	2	Cyprus	0

v. CZECHOSLOVAKIA

		E	C			E	C
1934	Prague	1	...2	1970	Guadalajara (W. C.)	1	...0
1938	Tottenham	5	...4	1973	Prague	1	...1
1963	Bratislava	4	...2	1975	Wembley	3	...0
1966	Wembley	0	...0	1975	Bratislava (Nat. C.)	1	...2
				1978	Wembley (Nat. C.)	1	...0

v. DENMARK

1949—Copenhagen	England 0	Denmark 0
1956—Copenhagen	England 5	Denmark 1
1957—Wolves (W. Cup) ..	England 5	Denmark 2
1957—C'hagen (W. Cup)	England 4	Denmark 1
1966—Copenhagen	England 2	Denmark 0
1978—C'hagen (Nat. C.) ..	England 4	Denmark 3

v. EAST GERMANY

	E	EG		E	EG
1963 Leipzig	2	...1	1974 Leipzig	1	..1
1970 Wembley	3	...1			

v. ECUADOR

1970—Quito	England 2	Ecuador 0

v. F.I.F.A.

1938—Highbury	England 3	F.I.F.A. 0
1953—Wembley	England 4	F.I.F.A. 4

v. FINLAND

1937—Helsinki	England 8	Finland 0
1956—Helsinki	England 5	Finland 1
1966—Helsinki	England 3	Finland 0
1976—Helsinki (W. Cup)	England 4	Finland 1
1977—Wembley (W. Cup)	England 2	Finland 1

v. FRANCE

	E	F		E	F
1923 Paris	4	...1	1947 Highbury	3	...0
1924 Paris	3	...1	1949 Paris	3	...1
1925 Paris	3	...2	1951 Highbury	2	...2
1927 Paris	6	...0	1955 Paris	0	...1
1928 Paris	5	...1	1958 Wembley	4	...0
1929 Paris	4	...1	1962 Sheffield (Nat. C.)	1	...1
1931 Paris	2	...5	1963 Paris (Nat. C.)	2	...5
1933 Tottenham	4	...1	1966 Wembley (W. Cup)	2	...0
1938 Paris	4	...2	1969 Wembley	5	...0
1946 Paris	1	...2			

v. GERMANY or WEST GERMANY

	E	G		E	G
1901 Tottenham	12	...0	1966 Wembley	1	...0
1901 Manchester	10	...0	1966 Wembley (W. C. F.)	4	...2
1930 Berline	3	...3	1968 Hanover	0	...1
1935 Tottenham	3	...0	1970 Leon (W. Cup)	2	...3
1939 Berlin	6	...3	1972 Wembley (Nat. C.)	1	...3
1955 Wembley	3	...1	1972 Berlin (Nat. Cup) ..	0	...0
1958 Berlin	3	...1	1975 Wembley	2	...0
1965 Nuremberg	1	...0	1978 Munich	1	...2

v. GREECE

1971—Wembley	England 3	Greece 0
1971—Athens	England 2	Greece 0

v. HUNGARY

		E	H			E	H
1934	Budapest	1	2	1960	Budapest	0	2
1936	Highbury	6	2	1962	Chile (W. Cup)	1	2
1954	Wembley	3	6	1965	Wembley	1	0
1954	Budapest	1	7	1978	Wembley	4	1

v. ITALY

		E	I			E	I
1933	Rome	1	1	1961	Rome	2	2
1934	Highbury	3	2	1973	Turin	0	2
1939	Milan	2	2	1973	Wembley	0	1
1948	Turin	4	0	1976	New York	3	2
1950	Tottenham	2	0	1976	Rome (W. Cup)	0	2
1952	Florence	1	1	1977	Wembley (W. C.)	2	0
1958	Wembley	2	2				

v. LUXEMBOURG

		E	L			E	L
1926	Luxembourg	5	2	1977	Wembley (W. C.)	5	0
1960	L'bourg (W. Cup)	0	0	1977	L'bourg (W. Cup)	2	0
1961	Highbury (W. Cup)	4	1				

v. MALTA

1971—Valeletta	England 1	Malta 0
1971—Wembley	England 5	Malta 0

v. MEXICO

1959—Mexico City	England 1	Mexico 2
1961—Wembley	England 8	Mexico 0
1966—Wembley (W. Cup)	England 2	Mexico 0
1969—Mexico City	England 0	Mexico 0

v. NETHERLANDS

1935—Amsterdam	England 1	Netherlands 0
1947—Huddersfield	England 8	Netherlands 2

1964—Amsterdam	England 1	Netherlands	1
1969—Amsterdam	England 1	Netherlands	0
1970—Wembley	England 0	Netherlands	0
1977—Wembley	England 0	Netherlands	2

v. NORWAY

1937—Oslo	England 6	Norway	0
1939—Newcastle	England 4	Norway	0
1949—Oslo	England 4	Norway	1
1966—Oslo	England 6	Norway	1

v. PERU

1959—Lima	England 1	Peru	4
1962—Lima	England 4	Peru	0

v. POLAND

1966—Everton	England 1	Poland	1
1966—Katowice	England 1	Poland	0
1973—Katowice (W. Cup)	England 0	Poland	2
1973—Wembley (W. Cup)	England 1	Poland	1

v. PORTUGAL

		E	P
1947	Lisbon	10	0
1950	Lisbon	5	3
1951	Liverpool	5	2
1955	Oporto	1	3
1958	Wembley	2	1
1961	Lisbon (W. Cup)	1	1
1961	Wembley (W. Cup)	2	0
1964	Lisbon	4	3
1964	Sao Paulo	1	1
1966	Wembley (W. C.)	2	1
1969	Wembley	1	0
1974	Liston	0	0
1975	Wembley (Nat. C.)	0	0
1975	Lisbon (Nat. C.)	1	1

v. REPUBLIC OF IRELAND

		E	I
1947	Dublin	1	0
1950	Everton	0	2
1957	Wembley (W. Cup)	5	1
1957	Dublin (W. Cup)	1	1
1964	Dublin	3	1
1977	Wembley	5	0
1978	Dublin (Nat. C.)	1	1

v. RUMANIA

1939—Bucharest	England 2	Rumania	0
1968—Bucharest	England 0	Rumania	0
1969—Wembley	England 1	Rumania	1
1970—Guadalajara (W.C.)	England 1	Rumania	0

v. SOUTH AFRICA

Year	Venue	E	SA
1910	Durban	3	0
1910	Johannesburg	6	2
1910	Capetown	6	3
1920	Durban	3	1
1920	Johannesburg	3	1
1920	Capetown	9	1
1929	Durban	3	2
1929	Johannesburg	2	1
1929	Capetown	3	1
1939	Johannesburg	3	0
1939	Durban	8	2
1939	Johannesburg	2	1

v. SOVIET UNION

Year—Venue		E		SA
1958—Moscow	England	1	Soviet Union	1
1958—G'burg (W. Cup)	England	2	Soviet Union	2
1958—G'burg (W. Cup)	England	0	Soviet Union	1
1958—Wembley	England	5	Soviet Union	0
1967—Wembley	England	2	Soviet Union	2
1968—Rome (W. Cup)	England	2	Soviet Union	0
1973—Moscow	England	2	Soviet Union	1

v. SPAIN

Year	Venue	E	S
1929	Madrid	3	4
1931	Highbury	7	1
1950	Rio (W. Cup)	0	1
1955	Madrid	1	1
1956	Wembley	4	1
1960	Madrid	0	3
1960	Wembley	4	2
1965	Madrid	2	0
1967	Wembley	2	0
1968	Wembley (Nat. C.)	1	0
1968	Madrid (Nat. Cup)	2	1

v. SWEDEN

Year	Venue	E	S
1923	Stockholm	4	2
1923	Stockholm	3	1
1937	Stockholm	4	0
1948	Highbury	4	2
1949	Stockholm	1	3
1956	Stockholm	0	0
1959	Wembley	2	3
1965	Gothenburg	2	1
1968	Wembley	3	1
1979	Sweden	0	0

v. SWITZERLAND

Year	Venue	E	S
1933	Berne	4	0
1938	Zurich	1	2
1946†	Chelsea	4	1
1947	Zurich	0	1
1949	Highbury	6	0
1952	Zurich	3	0
1954	Basle (W. Cup)	2	0
1962	Wembley	3	1
1963	Basle	8	1
1971	Basle (Nat. C.)	3	2
1971	Wembley	1	1
1975	Basle	2	1
1978	Wembley	0	0

v. URUGUAY

1953—Montevideo	England	1	Uruguay	2
1954—Basle (W. Cup)	England	2	Uruguay	4
1964—Wembley	England	2	Uruguay	1
1966—Wembley (W. Cup)	England	0	Uruguay	0
1969—Montevideo	England	2	Uruguay	1
1977—Montevideo	England	0	Uruguay	0

v. U.S.A.

1950—Belo H. (W. Cup)	England	0	U.S.A.	1
1953—New York	England	6	U.S.A.	3
1959—Los Angeles	England	8	U.S.A.	1
1964—New York	England	10	U.S.A.	0

v. YUGOSLAVIA

		E	Y
1939	Belgrade	1	2
1951	Highbury	2	2
1954	Belgrade	0	1
1957	Wembley	3	0
1958	Belgrade	0	5
1960	Wembley	3	3
1965	Belgrade	1	1
1966	Wembley	2	0
1968	Florence (Nat. C.)	0	1
1972	Wembley	1	1
1974	Belgrade	2	2

ENGLAND "B" TEAM RESULTS

1947	Switzerland "B" (A)	0	0
1948	Switzerland "B" (A)	5	1
1949	Finland (A)	4	0
1949	Holland (A)	4	0
1950	Italy "B" (A)	0	5
1950	Holland (A)	0	3
1950	Luxembourg (A)	5	0
1950	Switzerland (H)	5	0
1952	Holland (A)	1	0
1952	France "B" (A)	1	7
1953	Scotland "B" (A)	2	2
1954	Scotland "B" (H)	2	2
1954	Germany "B" (A)	1	1
1954	Yugoslavia "B" (A)	1	2
1954	Switzerland "B" (A)	0	2
1955	Germany "B" (H)	1	1
1955	Yugoslavia (H)	5	1
1956	Switzerland (H)	4	1
1956	Scotland (A)	2	2
1957	Scotland (H)	4	1
1978	W. Germany (A)	2	1
1978	Czechoslovakia (A)	1	0

GREAT BRITAIN v. REST OF EUROPE (F.I.F.A.)

1947—Glasgow	Great Britain	6	Rest of Europe	1
1955—Belfast	Great Britain	6	Rest of Europe	1
1955—Belfast	Great Britain	1	Rest of Europe	4

SCOTLAND v. ARGENTINA

1977—Buenos Aires	Scotland	1	Argentina	1

v. AUSTRIA

1931—Austria	Scotland	0	Austria	5
1933—Glasgow	Scotland	2	Austria	1
1937—Vienna	Scotland	1	Austria	2
1951—Glasgow	Scotland	0	Austria	1
1951—Vienna	Scotland	0	Austria	4
1954—Zurich (W. Cup)	Scotland	0	Austria	1
1955—Vienna	Scotland	4	Austria	1
1956—Glasgow	Scotland	1	Austria	1
1960—Vienna	Scotland	1	Austria	4
1963—Glasgow	*Scotland	4	Austria	1
1968—Glasgow (W. Cup) .	Scotland	2	Austria	1
1969—Vienna (W. Cup) ...	Scotland	0	Austria	2
1978—Vienna (Nat. Cup) .	Scotland	2	Austria	3

Abandoned after 79 mins.

v. BELGIUM

1946—Glasgow	*Scotland	2	Belgium	2
1947—Brussels	Scotland	1	Belgium	2
1948—Glasgow	Scotland	2	Belgium	0
1951—Brussels	Scotland	5	Belgium	0
1971—Liege (Nat. Cup) ...	Scotland	0	Belgium	3
1971—Aberdeen (Nat. C.) ..	Scotland	1	Belgium	0
1974—Bruges	Scotland	1	Belgium	2

v. BRAZIL

1966—Glasgow	Scotland	1	Brazil	1
1972—Rio de Janeiro	Scotland	0	Brazil	1
1973—Glasgow	Scotland	0	Brazil	1
1974—Frankfurt (W. Cup)	Scotland	0	Brazil	0
1977—Rio de Janeiro	Scotland	0	Brazil	2

v. BULGARIA

1978—Glasgow	Scotland	2	Bulgaria	1

v. CHILE

1977—Santiago	Scotland	4	Chile	2

v. CYPRUS

1968—Nicosia (W. Cup) ..	Scotland	5	Cyprus	0
1969—Glasgow (W. Cup) .	Scotland	8	Cyprus	0

v. CZECHOSLOVAKIA

1937—Prague	Scotland	3	Czechoslovakia	1
1938—Glasgow	Scotland	5	Czechoslovakia	0

1961—Bratislava (W. C.) ..	Scotland 0	Czechoslovakia 4
1961—Glasgow (W. Cup) .	Scotland 3	Czechoslovakia 2
1961—Burssels (W. Cup) .	*Scotland 2	Czechoslovakia 4
1972—Rio de Janeiro	Scotland 0	Czechoslovakia 0
1973—Glasgow (W. Cup) .	Scotland 2	Czechoslovakia 1
1973—Bratislava	Scotland 0	Czechoslovakia 1
1977—Prague (W. Cup) ...	Scotland 0	Czechoslovakia 2

* World Cup play-off

v. DENMARK

1961—Glasgow	Scotland 3	Denmark 1
1962—Copenhagen	Scotland 3	Denmark 1
1968—Copenhagen	Scotland 1	Denmark 0
1971—Glasgow (Nat. C.) .	Scotland 1	Denmark 0
1971—C'hagen (Nat. Cup)	Scotland 0	Denmark 1
1972—C'hagen (W. Cup) .	Scotland 4	Denmark 1
1972—Glasgow (W. Cup) .	Scotland 2	Denmark 0
1975—C'hagen (Nat. Cup)	Scotland 1	Denmark 0
1975—Glasgow (Nat. C.) .	Scotland 3	Denmark 1

v. EAST GERMANY

1975—Glasgow	Scotland 3	East Germany 0
1977—East Berlin	Scotland 0	East Germany 1

v. FINLAND

1954—Helsinki	Scotland 2	Finland 1
1964—Glasgow (W. Cup) .	Scotland 3	Finland 1
1965—Helsinki (W. Cup) ..	Scotland 2	Finland 1
1977—Glasgow	Scotland 6	Finland 0

v. FRANCE

1930—Paris	Scotland 2	France 0
1932—Paris	Scotland 3	France 1
1948—Paris	Scotland 0	France 3
1949—Glasgow	Scotland 2	France 0
1950—Paris	Scotland 1	France 0
1958—Orebro (W. Cup) ...	Scotland 1	France ....?

v. GERMANY

1929—Berlin	Scotland 1	Germany 1
1936—Glasgow	Scotland 2	Germany 0

v. HUNGARY

1939—Glasgow	Scotland 3	Hungary 1
1955—Glasgow	Scotland 2	Hungary 4
1955—Budapest	Scotland 1	Hungary 3
1958—Glasgow	Scotland 1	Hungary 1
1960—Budapest	Scotland 3	Hungary 0

v. IRAN

1978—Argentina (W. C.) ..	Scotland 1	Iran 1

v. ITALY

1931—Rome	Scotland 0	Italy 2
1965—Glasgow (W. Cup) .	Scotland 1	Italy 0
1965—Naples (W. Cup) ...	Scotland 0	Italy 3

v. LUXEMBOURG

1947—Luxembourg	Scotland 6	Luxembourg 0

v. NETHERLANDS

1929—Amsterdam	Scotland 2	Netherlands 0
1938—Amsterdam	Scotland 3	Netherlands 1
1959—Amsterdam	Scotland 2	Netherlands 1
1966—Glasgow	Scotland 0	Netherlands 3
1968—Amsterdam	Scotland 0	Netherlands 0
1971—Amsterdam	Scotland 1	Netherlands 2
1978—Argentina (W. C.) ..	Scotland 3	Netherlands 2

v. NORWAY

1954—Glasgow	Scotland 1	Norway 0
1954—Oslo	Scotland 1	Norway 1
1963—Bergen	Scotland 3	Norway 4
1963—Glasgow	Scotland 6	Norway 1
1974—Oslo	Scotland 2	Norway 1
1978—Glasgow (Nat. Cup)	Scotland 3	Norway 2
1979—Oslo	Scotland 4	Norway 0

v. PARAGUAY

1958—N'koping (W. Cup) .	Scotland 2	Paraguay 3

v. PERU

1972—Glasgow	Scotland 2	Peru 0
1978—Argentina (W. C.) ..	Scotland 1	Peru 3

v. POLAND

1948—Warsaw	Scotland 2	Poland 1
1960—Glasgow	Scotland 2	Poland 3
1965—Chorzow (W. Cup) .	Scotland 1	Poland 1
1965—Glasgow (W. Cup) .	Scotland 1	Poland 2

v. PORTUGAL

1950—Lisbon	Scotland 2	Portugal 2
1955—Glasgow	Scotland 3	Portugal 0
1959—Lisbon	Scotland 0	Portugal 1
1966—Glasgow	Scotland 0	Portugal 1
1971—Lisbon (Nat. Cup) ..	Scotland 0	Portugal 2
1971—Glasgow (W. Cup) .	Scotland 2	Portugal 1
1975—Glasgow	Scotland 1	Portugal 0
1978—Lisbon (Nat. Cup) ..	Scotland 0	Portugal 1

v. REPUBLIC OF IRELAND

1961—Glasgow (W. Cup) .	Scotland 4	R. of Ireland 1
1961—Dublin (W. Cup) ...	Scotland 3	R. of Ireland 0
1963—Dublin	Scotland 0	R. of Ireland 1
1969—Dublin	Scotland 1	R. of Ireland 1

v. RUMANIA

1975—Bucharest (Nat. C.)	Scotland 1	Rumania 1
1975—Glasgow (Nat. C.)	Scotland 1	Rumania 1

v. SOVIET UNION

1967—Glasgow	Scotland 0	Soviet Union 2
1971—Moscow	Scotland 0	Soviet Union 1

v. SPAIN

1957—Glasgow (W. Cup) .	Scotland 4	Spain 2
1957—Madrid (W. Cup) ...	Scotland 1	Spain 4
1963—Madrid	Scotland 6	Spain 2
1965—Glasgow	Scotland 0	Spain 0
1975—Glasgow (Nat. C). .	Scotland 1	Spain 2
1975—Valencia (Nat. C). ..	Scotland 1	Spain 1

v. SWEDEN

1952—Stockholm	Scotland 1	Sweden 2
1953—Glasgow	Scotland 1	Sweden 3
1975—Gothenburg	Scotland 1	Sweden 1
1977—Glasgow	Scotland 3	Sweden 1

v. SWITZERLAND

1931—Geneva	Scotland 3	Switzerland 2
1946—Glasgow	†Scotland 3	Switzerland 1
1948—Berne	Scotland 1	Switzerland 2
1950—Glasgow	Scotland 3	Switzerland 1
1957—Basle (W. Cup)	Scotland 2	Switzerland 1
1957—Glasgow (W. Cup) .	Scotland 3	Switzerland 2
1973—Berne	Scotland 0	Switzerland 1
1976—Glasgow	Scotland 1	Switzerland 0

v. TURKEY

1960—Ankara	Scotland 2	Turkey 4

v. URUGUAY

1954—Basle (W. Cup)	Scotland 0	Uruguay 7
1962—Glasgow	Scotland 2	Uruguay 3

v. U.S.A.

1952—Glasgow	Scotland 6	U.S.A. 0

v. WEST GERMANY

1957—Stuttgart	Scotland 3	West Germany 1
1959—Glasgow	Scotland 3	West Germany 2
1960—Hanover	Scotland 2	West Germany 2
1969—Glasgow	Scotland 1	West Germany 1
1969—Hamburg (W. Cup)	Scotland 2	West Germany 3
1973—Glasgow	Scotland 1	West Germany 1
1974—Frankfurt	Scotland 1	West Germany 2

v. YUGOSLAVIA

1955—Belgrade	Scotland 2	Yugoslavia 2
1957—Glasgow	Scotland 2	Yugoslavia 0
1958—Vasteras (W. Cup)	Scotland 1	Yugoslavia 1
1972—Rio de Janeiro	Scotland 2	Yugoslavia 2
1974—Frankfurt (W. Cup)	Scotland 1	Yugoslavia 1

v. ZAIRE

1974—Dortmund (W.Cup)	Scotland 2	Zaire 0

WALES v. AUSTRIA

1954—Vienna	Wales 0	Austria 2
1955—Wrexham	Wales 1	Austria 2
1975—Vienna (Nat. Cup)	Wales 1	Austria 2
1975—Wrexham (Nat. C.)	Wales 1	Austria 0

v. BELGIUM

1949—Liege	Wales 1	Belgium 3
1950—Cardiff	Wales 5	Belgium 1

v. BRAZIL

1958—G'burg (W. Cup) ...	Wales 0	Brazil 1
1961—Rio de Janeiro	Wales 1	Brazil 3
1962—Sao Paulo	Wales 1	Brazil 3
1966—Rio de Janeiro	Wales 1	Brazil 3
1966—Belo Horizonte	Wales 0	Brazil 1

v. CHILE

1966—Santiago	Wales 0	Chile 2

v. CZECHOSLOVAKIA

1957—Cardiff (W. Cup) ...	Wales 1	Czechoslovakia 0
1957—Prague (W. Cup) ...	Wales 0	Czechoslovakia 2
1971—Cardiff (Nat. Cup) ..	Wales 1	Czechoslovakia 3
1971—Prague (Nat. Cup) .	Wales 0	Czechoslovakia 1
1977—Wrexham (W. Cup)	Wales 3	Czechoslovakia 0
1977—Prague (W. Cup) ...	Wales 0	Czechoslovakia 1

v. DENMARK

1964—C'hagen (W. Cup) .	Wales 0	Denmark 1
1965—Wrexham (W. Cup)	Wales 4	Denmark 2

v. EAST GERMANY

1957—Leipzig (W. Cup) ...	Wales 1	East Germany 2
1957—Cardiff (W. Cup) ...	Wales 4	East Germany 1
1969—Dresden (W. Cup) .	Wales 1	East Germany 2
1969—Cardiff (W. Cup) ...	Wales 1	East Germany 3

v. FINLAND

1971—Helsinki	Wales 1	Finland 0
1971—Swansea	Wales 3	Finland 0

v. FRANCE

1933—Paris	Wales 1	France 1
1939—Paris	Wales 1	France 2
1953—Paris	Wales 1	France 6

v. GREECE

1964—Athens (W. Cup) ...	Wales 0	Greece 2
1965—Cardiff (W. Cup) ...	Wales 4	Greece 1

v. HUNGARY

1958—Sanviken (W. Cup)	Wales 1	Hungary 1
1958—Stockholm (W.C.) .	Wales 2	Hungary 1
1961—Budapest	Wales 2	Hungary 3
1962—Budapest (Nat. C.) .	Wales 1	Hungary 3
1963—Cardiff (Nat. C.)	Wales 1	Hungary 1
1975—Cardiff (Nat. C.)	Wales 2	Hungary 0
1975—Budapest (Nat. C.) .	Wales 2	Hungary 1

v. IRAN

1978—Teheran	Wales 1	Iran 0

v. ISRAEL

1958—Tel Aviv (W. Cup) ..	Wales 2	Israel 0
1958—Cardiff (W. Cup) ...	Wales 2	Israel 0

v. ITALY

1965—Florence	Wales 1	Italy 4
1968—Cardiff (W. Cup) ...	Wales 0	Italy 1
1969—Rome (W. Cup)	Wales 1	Italy 4

v. KUWAIT

1977—Wrexham	Wales 0	Kuwait 0
1977—Kuwait	Wales 0	Kuwait 0

v. LUXEMBOURG

1975—Swansea	Wales 5	Luxembourg 0
1975—Luxembourg	Wales 3	Luxembourg 1

v. MALTA

1978—Wrexham (Nat. Cup)	Wales 7	Malta 0
1979—Valetta (Nat. Cup) .	Wales 2	Malta 0

v. MEXICO

1968—Stockholm (W.C.) .	Wales 1	Mexico 1
1972—Mexico City	Wales 1	Mexico 2

v. POLAND

1972—Cardiff (W. Cup) ...	Wales 2	Poland 0
1973—Katowice (W. Cup)	Wales 0	Poland 3

v. PORTUGAL

1949—Lisbon	Wales 2	Portugal 3
1951—Cardiff	Wales 2	Portugal 1

v. REST OF UNITED KINGDOM

1951-8—Cardiff	Wales 3	Rest of U.K. 2
1969—Cardiff	Wales 0	Rest of U.K. 1

v. RUMANIA

1971—Cardiff (Nat. Cup) ..	Wales	0	Rumania	0
1971—Bucharest (Nat. C.)	Wales	0	Rumania	2

v. SOVIET UNION

1965—Moscow (W. Cup) .	Wales	1	Soviet Union	2
1965—Cardiff (W. Cup) ...	Wales	2	Soviet Union	1

v. SPAIN

1961—Cardiff (W. Cup) ...	Wales	1	Spain	2
1961—Madrid (W. Cup) ...	Wales	1	Spain	1

v. SWEDEN

1958—Stockholm (W.C.)	Wales	2	Sweden	0

v. SWITZERLAND

1949—Berne	Wales	0	Switzerland	4
1951—Wrexham	Wales	3	Switzerland	2

v. TURKEY

1978—Wrexham (Nat. Cup)	Wales	1	Turkey	0

v. WEST GERMANY

1968—Cardiff	Wales	1	West Germany	3
1969—Frankfurt	Wales	1	West Germany	2
1977—Cardiff	Wales	0	West Germany	2
1977—Dortmund	Wales	1	West Germany	1
1979—Wrexham (Nat. C.)	Wales	0	West Germany	2

v. YUGOSLAVIA

1953—Belgrade	Wales	2	Yugoslavia	5
1955—Cardiff	Wales	1	Yugoslavia	3
1976—Zagreb (Nat. Cup) .	Wales	0	Yugoslavia	2
1976—Cardiff (Nat. Cup) ..	Wales	1	Yugoslavia	1

REPUBLIC OF IRELAND v. ARGENTINA

1979—Dublin	R. of Ireland	0	Argentina	0

REPUBLIC OF IRELAND v. AUSTRIA

1962—Dublin	R. of Ireland	2	Austria	3
1963—Vienna	R. of Ireland	0	Austria	0
1963—Dublin	R. of Ireland	3	Austria	2
1966—Vienna	R. of Ireland	0	Austria	1
1968—Dublin	R. of Ireland	2	Austria	2
1971—Dublin (Nat. Cup)	R. of Ireland	1	Austria	4
1971—Austria (Nat. Cup)	R. of Ireland	0	Austria	6

v. BELGIUM

1966—Brussels	R. of Ireland	3	Belgium	2

v. BRAZIL

1974—Rio de Janeiro	R. of Ireland	1	Brazil	2

v. BULGARIA

1977—Sofia (W. Cup)	R. of Ireland		Bulgaria	2
1977—Dublin (W. Cup)	R. of Ireland	0	Bulgaria	0
1979—Sofia (Nat. Cup)	R. of Ireland	0	Bulgaria	1

v. CHILE

1974—Recife	R. of Ireland	1	Chile	2
1974—Santiago	R. of Ireland	2	Chile	1

v. CZECHOSLOVAKIA

1961—Dublin (W. Cup)	R. of Ireland	1	Czechoslovakia	3
1961—Prague (W. Cup)	R. of Ireland	1	Czechoslovakia	7
1967—Dublin (Nat. Cup)	R. of Ireland	0	Czechoslovakia	2
1967—Prague (Nat. Cup)	R. of Ireland	2	Czechoslovakia	8
1969—Dublin (W. Cup)	R. of Ireland	1	Czechoslovakia	2
1969—Prague (W. Cup)	R. of Ireland	0	Czechoslovakia	3

v. DENMARK

1956—Dublin (W. Cup)	R. of Ireland	2	Denmark	1
1957—C'hagen (W. Cup)	R. of Ireland	2	Denmark	0
1968—Dublin (W. Cup)	*R. of Ireland	1	Denmark	1
1969—C'hagen (Nat. Cup)	R. of Ireland	0	Denmark	2
1969—Dublin (W. Cup)	R. of Ireland	1	Denmark	1
1978—C'hagen (Nat. Cup)	R. of Ireland	3	Denmark	3

* Abandoned after 15 mins. Fog

v. ECUADOR

1972—Natal.	R. of Ireland	3	Ecuador	2

v. FRANCE

1951—Belfast	R. of Ireland	2	France	2
1972—Dublin (W. Cup)	R. of Ireland	2	France	1
1973—Paris (W. Cup)	R. of Ireland	1	France	1
1977—Paris (W. Cup)	R. of Ireland	0	France	2
1977—Dublin (W. Cup)	R. of Ireland	1	France	0

v. HUNGARY

1969—Dublin	R. of Ireland	1	Hungary	2
1969—Budapest (W. Cup)	R. of Ireland	0	Hungary	4

v. ICELAND

1962—Dublin	R. of Ireland	4	Iceland	1
1962—Reykjavik	R. of Ireland	1	Iceland	1

v. IRAN

1972—Recife	R. of Ireland	2	Iran	1

v. ITALY

1971—Florence (N. Cup)	R. of Ireland	0	Italy	3
1971—Dublin (Nat. Cup)	R. of Ireland	1	Italy	2

v. NORTHERN IRELAND

1978—Dublin (Nat. Cup)	R. of Ireland	0	N. Ireland	0

v. NORWAY

1960—Dublin	R. of Ireland	3	Norway	1
1964—Oslo	R. of Ireland	3	Norway	1
1973—Oslo	R. of Ireland	1	Norway	1
1976—Dublin	R. of Ireland	3	Norway	0
1978—Oslo	R. of Ireland	0	Norway	0

v. POLAND

1964—Cracow	R. of Ireland	2	Poland	3
1964—Dublin	R. of Ireland	3	Poland	2
1968—Dublin	R. of Ireland	2	Poland	2
1968—Katowice	R. of Ireland	0	Poland	1
1970—Dublin	R. of Ireland	1	Poland	2
1970—Dublin	R. of Ireland	0	Poland	2
1973—Katowice	R. of Ireland	0	Poland	2

1973—Dublin	R. of Ireland 1	Poland 0
1976—Warsaw	R. of Ireland 2	Poland 0
1977—Dublin	R. of Ireland 0	Poland 0
1978—Lodz	R. of Ireland 0	Poland 3

v. PORTUGAL

1972—Recife	R. of Ireland 1	Portugal 2

v. SOVIET UNION

1972—Dublin (W. Cup)	R. of Ireland 1	Soviet Union 2
1973—Moscow (W. Cup)	R. of Ireland 0	Soviet Union 1
1975—Dublin	R. of Ireland 3	Soviet Union 0
1975—Kiev	R. of Ireland 1	Soviet Union 2

v. SCOTLAND

1961—Glasgow	R. of Ireland 1	Scotland 4
1961—Dublin	R. of Ireland 0	Scotland 3
1963—Dublin	R. of Ireland 1	Scotland 0
1969—Dublin	R. of Ireland 1	Scotland 1

v. SPAIN

1964—Seville	R. of Ireland 1	Spain 5
1964—Dublin	R. of Ireland 0	Spain 2
1965—Dublin (W. Cup)	R. of Ireland 1	Spain 0
1965—Seville (W. Cup)	R. of Ireland 1	Spain 4
1965—Paris (W. Cup)	R. of Ireland 0	Spain 1
1966—Dublin (Nat. Cup)	R. of Ireland 0	Spain 0
1966—Valencia (N. Cup)	R. of Ireland 0	Spain 2
1977—Dublin	R. of Ireland 0	Spain 1

v. SWEDEN

1970—Dublin (Nat. Cup)	R. of Ireland 1	Sweden 1
1970—Malmo (Nat. Cup)	R. of Ireland 0	Sweden 1

v. SWITZERLAND

1975—Dublin (Nat. Cup)	R. of Ireland 2	Switzerland 1
1975—Berne (Nat. Cup)	R. of Ireland 0	Switzerland 1

v. TURKEY

1966—Dublin (Nat. Cup)	R. of Ireland 2	Turkey 1
1967—Ankara (Nat. Cup)	R. of Ireland 1	Turkey 2

1975—Izmir (Nat. Cup)	R. of Ireland	1	Turkey	1
1975—Dublin (Nat. Cup)	R. of Ireland	4	Turkey	0
1977—Ankara	R. of Ireland	3	Turkey	3
1978—Dublin	R. of Ireland	4	Turkey	0

v. URUGUAY

1974—Montevideo	R. of Ireland	0	Uruguay	2

v. WEST GERMANY

1966—Dublin	R. of Ireland	2	West Germany	4
1970—Berlin	R. of Ireland	1	West Germany	2
1979—Dublin	R. of Ireland	1	West Germany	3

NORTHERN IRELAND v. ALBANIA

1965—Belfast (W. Cup)	N. Ireland		Albania	1
1965—Tirana (W. Cup)	N. Ireland	1	Albania	1

v. ARGENTINA

1958—Halmstad (W. Cup)	N. Ireland	1	Argentina	3

v. BELGIUM

1977—Liege (W. Cup)	N. Ireland	0	Belgium	2
1977—Belfast (W. Cup)	N. Ireland	3	Belgium	0

v. BULGARIA

1973—Sofia (W. Cup)	N. Ireland	0	Bulgaria	3
1973—Sheffield (W. Cup)	N. Ireland	0	Bulgaria	0
1979—Belfast (Nat. Cup)	N. Ireland	2	Bulgaria	0

v. CYPRUS

1971—Nicosia (Nat. Cup)	N. Ireland	3	Cyprus	0
1971—Belfast (Nat. Cup)	N. Ireland	5	Cyprus	0
1973—Nicosia (W. Cup)	N. Ireland	0	Cyprus	1
1973—Craven C. (W. Cup)	N. Ireland	3	Cyprus	0

v. CZECHOSLOVAKIA

1958—Halmstad (W. Cup)	N. Ireland	1	Czechoslovakia	0
1958—Malmo (W. Cup)	N. Ireland	2	Czechoslovakia	1

v. DENMARK

1978—Belfast (Nat. Cup)	N. Ireland	2	Denmark	1
1979—Copenhagen (N. C.)	N. Ireland	0	Denmark	4

v. FRANCE

1958—Norrkoping (W. C.)	N. Ireland	0	France	4

v. GREECE

1961—Athens (W. Cup)	N. Ireland	0	Greece	2
1961—Belfast (W. Cup)	N. Ireland	2	Greece	0

v. ICELAND

1977—Belfast (W. Cup)	N. Ireland	2	Iceland	0
1977—Reykjavik (W. Cup)	N. Ireland	0	Iceland	1

v. ISRAEL

1968—Jaffa	N. Ireland	3	Israel	2
1976—Tel Avv	N. Ireland	1	Israel	1

v. ITALY

1957—Rome (W. Cup)	N. Ireland	1	Italy	1
1957—Belfast	N. Ireland	2	Italy	2
1958—Belfast (W. Cup)	N. Ireland	2	Italy	1
1961—Bologna	N. Ireland	2	Italy	3

v. NETHERLANDS

1961—Rotterdam	N. Ireland	0	Netherlands	4
1965—Belfast (W. Cup)	N. Ireland	2	Netherlands	1
1965—Rotterdam (W. C.)	N. Ireland	0	Netherland	0
1977—Rotterdam (W.C.)	N. Ireland	2	Netherlands	2
1977—Belfast (W. Cup)	N. Ireland	0	Netherlands	

v. NORWAY

1975—Oslo (Nat. Cup)	N. Ireland	1	Norway	2
1975—Belfast	N. Ireland	3	Norway	0

v. POLAND

1962—Katowice	N. Ireland	2	Poland	0
1962—Belfast	N. Ireland	2	Poland	0

v. PORTUGAL

1957—Lisbon (W. Cup)	N. Ireland	1	Portugal	
1957—Lisbon (W. Cup)	N. Ireland	3	Portugal	0
1973—Coventry (W. Cup)	N. Ireland	1	Portugal	
1973—Lisbon (W. Cup)	N. Ireland	1	Portugal	

v. REPUBLIC OF IRELAND

1978—Dublin (Nat. Cup)	N. Ireland	0	R. of Ireland	0

v. SPAIN

1958—Madrid	N. Ireland	2	Spain	6
1963—Bilbao	N. Ireland	1	Spain	1
1963—Belfast	N. Ireland	0	Spain	1
1970—Seville (N. Cup)	N. Ireland	0	Spain	3
1972—Hull (Nat. Cup)	N. Ireland	1	Spain	1

v. SWEDEN

1975—Stockholm (N. C.)	N. Ireland	2	Sweden	0
1975—Belfast (Nat. Cup)	N. Ireland		Sweden	2

v. SWITZERLAND

1964—Belfast (W. Cup)	N. Ireland	1	Switzerland	0
1964—Lausanne (W. Cup)	N. Ireland	1	Switzerland	2

v. TURKEY

1968—Belfast (W. Cup)	N. Ireland	4	Turkey	1
1968—Istanbul (W. Cup)	N. Ireland	3	Turkey	0

v. URUGUAY

1964—Belfast	N. Ireland	3	Uruguay	0

v. USSR

1969—Belfast (W. Cup)	N. Ireland	0	USSR	0
1969—Moscow (W. Cup)	N. Ireland	0	USSR	2
1971—Moscow (Nat. Cup)	N. Ireland	0	USSR	1
1971—Belfast (Nat. Cup)	N. Ireland	1	USSR	

v. WEST GERMANY

1958—Malmo (W. Cup)	N. Ireland	2	West Germany	2
1960—Belfast (W. Cup)	N. Ireland	3	West Germany	4
1961—Berlin (W. Cup)	N. Ireland	1	West Germany	2
1966—Belfast	N. Ireland	0	West Germany	2
1977—Cologne	N. Ireland	0	West Germany	5

v. YUGOSLAVIA

1975—Belfast (Nat. Cup)	N. Ireland	1	Yugoslavia	0
1975—Belgrade (N. Cup)	N. Ireland	0	Yugoslavia	1

LEAGUE ROLL CALL

The following statistics were supplied by the clubs concerned

CLUB DIRECTORY

Players' appearances and scorers 1978-79

FIRST DIVISION

ARSENAL

Ground: Avenell Road, Highbury, London N5 1BU.
Telephone: 01-226 0304
Colours: Red shirts, with white sleeves, white shorts, red stockings.

Brady, L. 37
Devine, J. 7
Gatting, S. 19
Harvey, J. 1
Heeley, M. 6
Jennings, P. 39
Baron, P. 3
Nelson, S. 38
O'Leary, D. 37
Price, D. 39
Rice, P. 39
Rix, G. 39
Stapleton, F. 41
MacDonald, M. 4
Stead, K. 1
Sunderland, A. 37
Talbot, B. 20
Vaessen, P. 1
Walford, S. 26
Young, W. 33

League Goalscorers—Stapleton 17, Brady 13, Sunderland 9, Price 8, Rix 3, MacDonald 2, Nelson 2, O'Leary 2, Walford 2, Gatting 1, Heeley 1, Rice 1.

Average Home League Gate— 36,377
All-time Record Attendance— 73,295 v. Sunderland (Division 1) March 9, 1935.

ASTON VILLA

Ground: Villa Park, Birmingham B6 6HE
Telephone: 021-327 6604
Colours: Shirts: claret with blue sleeves, claret and light blue collar and cuffs and trimmings, shorts: white claret and light blue vertical stripes, stockings: light blue, claret and white tops.

Carrodus, F. 6
Cowans, G. 34
Craig, T. 23
Cropley, A. 15
Deehan, J. 25
Evans, A. 36
Gibson, C. 11
Gidman, J. 36
Gray, A. 15
Gregory, J. 38
Linton, I. 4
Little, B. 24
McNaught, K. 32
Mortimer, D. 38
Ormsby, B. 2
Phillips, L. 3
Rimmer, J. 42
Shelton, G. 19
Smith, G. 6
Swain, K. 24
Ward, J. 1
Williams, G. 21
Young, W. 3

League Goalscorers—Deehan 9, Gregory 7, Shelton 7, Gray 6, Evans (A) 6, Cowans 4, Swain 4, Gidman, 3, Mortimer 3, Craig 2, Cropley 2, Little 1, McNaught 1, Opponents 4.

Average Home League Gate— 32,838
All-time Record Attendance— 76,588 v. Derby, (F.A. Cup 6th Rd), March 2, 1946.

BIRMINGHAM CITY

Ground: St. Andrews, Birmingham, B9 4NH.
Telephone: 021-772 0101/2689.
Colours: Blue/white/white.

Ainscow, A. 27
Barrowclough, S. ... 26
Bertschin, K............ 9
Broadhurst, K........ 13
Buckley, A. 24
Calderwood, J....... 24
Dark, T.................. 2
Dennis, M. 31
Dillon, K. 35
Emmanuel, G. 12
Pendrey, G. 9
Fox, J. 13
Francis, T. 8
Freeman, N. 29
Gallagher, J........41
Givens, D...........38
Howard, P. 5
Ivey, P. 3
Lynex, S. 2
Montgomery, J.... 13
Page, M. 32
Rathbone, M...........2
Rioch, B. 3
Tarantini, A. 23
Towers, T. 31
Van Denhauwe, P..... 7

League Goalscorers—Buckley 8, Givens 7, Francis 3, Gallagher 3, Ainscow 2, Barrowclough 2, Bertschin 2, Dillon 2, Towers 2, Broadhurst 1, Calderwood 1, Dark 1, Lynex 1, Tarantini 1, Opponents 1.
Average Home League Gate—20,163
All-time Record Attendance—66,844 v. Everton (F.A. Cup) February 11, 1939.

BOLTON WANDERERS

Ground: Burnden Park, Manchester Road, Bolton BL3 2QR
Telephone: Bolton 389200
Colours: White shirts, navy blue shorts, white stockings.

Allardyce, S.......... 18
Burke, D. 19
Dunne, A. 24
Gowling, A. 36
Graham, M.............9
Greaves, R. 41
Jones, P............31
McDonagh, J. 42
McNab, N. 22
Morgan, W.........41
Nicholson, P. 34
Nowak, T.............1
Reid, P................ 14
Smith, B. 18
Train, R. 5
Walsh, M............. 42
Whatmore, N. 23
Worthington, F. 42

League Goalscorers—Worthington 24, Gowling 15, McNab 3, Whatmore 3, Morgan 2, Allardyce 1, Burke 1, Greaves 1, Jones (P) 1, Smith 1, Walsh 1, Opponents 1.

Average Home League Gate—23,647
All-time Record Attendance— 69,912 v. Manchester City (F.A. Cup) February 18th, 1933.

BRISTOL CITY

Ground: Ashton Gate, Bristol BS3 2EJ.
Telephone: Bristol 632812
Colours: Red shirts, with white trim, white shorts, red socks with white trim.

Bain, J. 3
Cashley, R..............2
Collier, G. 9
Cooper, T. 11
Cormack, P. 15
Garland, C. 4
Gillies, D. 27
Gow, G. 38
Hunter, N. 39
Mabbutt, K.........26
Mann, J. 23
Meijer, G. 9
Pritchard, H. 1
Ritchie, T...........39
Rodgers, D. 36
Royle, J............... 40
Shaw, J. 40
Sweeney, G.......... 42
Tainton, T. 39
Whitehead, C........ 22

League Goalscorers—Mabbutt 9, Ritchie 9, Royle 7, Gow 5, Rodgers 5, Cormack 3, Meijer 2, Whitehead 2, Garland 1, Gillies 1, Mann 1, Tainton 1, Hunter 1.

Average Home League Gate— 22,306
All-time Record Attendance— 43,335 v. Preston North End (F.A. Cup) February 16, 1935.

CHELSEA

Ground: Stamford Bridge, Fulham Road, London SW6 1HS
Telephone: 01-385 5545/6/7
Colours: Royal blue shirts, royal blue shorts, white stockings.

Aylott, T. 13	Garner, W. 1	Osgood, P. 9
Bannon, E. 19	Harris, R. 38	Phillips, J. 7
Bonetti, P. 16	Hay, D. 8	Sitton, J. 11
Borota, P. 12	Isles, R. 7	Stanley, G. 32
Britton, I. 9	Johnson, G. 1	Stride, D. 32
Bumstead, J. 6	Langley, T. 40	Swain, K. 15
Chivers, G. 5	ington, R. 10	Walker, C. 23
Docherty, J. 2	Locke, G. 8	Wicks, S. 23
Droy, M. 14	McKenzie, D. 15	Wilkins, G. 28
Fillery, M. 6	Nutton, M. 15	Wilkins, R. 35
Frost, L. 2		

League Goalscorers—Langley 15, Stanley 5, McKenzie 4, Swain 4, Walker 4, Wilkins, R. 3, Osgood 2, Bannon 1, Bumstead 1, Johnson 1, Wicks 1, Wilkins, G. 1, Opponents 2.
Average Home League Gate— 23,816
All-time Record Atendance— 82,905 v. Arsenal (Div. 1) OO $\frac{3}{4}$ $\frac{3}{4}$ $\frac{3}{4}$.

COVENTRY CITY

Ground: Highfield Road Stadium, Highfield Road, Coventry CV2 4GU.
Telephone: Coventry 57171
Colours: Sky blue with navy and white trim strip.

Bannister, G. 3	Gooding, R. 3	Nardiello, D. 16
Blair, A. 26	Green, A. 6	Osgood, K. 11
Blyth, J. 6	Hagan, J. 12	Powell, B. 38
Beck, J. 5	Hateley, M. 1	Roberts, B. 17
Coop, M. 36	Holton, J. 34	Sealey, L. 36
Dyson, P. 2	Hunt, S. 21	Thompson, G. 20
Ferguson, M. 16	Hutchison, T. 42	Wallace, I. 38
Gillespie, G. 14	McDonald, R. 42	Yorath, T. 20

League Goalscorers—Wallace 15, Thompson 8, Powell 8, Ferguson 7, Hunt 6, Hutchison 6, McDonald 4, Beck 1, Green 1, Blair 1, Bannister 1.

Average Home League Gate— 22,637
All-time Record Attendance—51,457 v. Wolverhampton W. (Division Two) April 29, 1967.

DERBY COUNTY

Ground: The Baseball Ground, Shaftesbury Cres., Derby.
Telephone: 40105
Colours: White shirts, blue shorts, blue socks.

Bartlett, P. 3	Duncan, J. 17	Middleton, J. 26
Buckley, S............. 42	Emson, P.............7	Moreland, V. 27
Carter, S. 29	George, C. 8	Nish, D. 6
Clayton, J. 1	Greenwood, R. 19	Powell, S............. 41
Crawford, A.......... 12	Hill, G................ 12	Rioch, B. 7
Caskey, W. 22	Langan, D. 40	Ryan, G.................6
Clark, J. 17	McCaffery, A. 7	Todd, C..................4
Daly, G. 37	McFarland, R. 24	Webb, D.................9
Daniel, P. 6	McKellar, D. 16	Wicks, S............. 19

League Goalscorers—Daly 13, Duncan 5, Buckley 4, Caskey 3, McFarland 3, Crawford 3, Powell 3, George 2, Greenwood 1, Nish 1, Carter 1, Hill 1, Webb 1, Daniel 1, Opponents 2.
Average Home League Gate—21554
All-time Record Attendance—41826 v. Tottenham (20/9/69) (Division 1) September 20, 1969.

EVERTON

Ground: Goodison Park, Liverpool L4 4EL.
Telephone: 051-521 2020
Colours: Royal blue shirts with blue and white stripe down sleeve, white shorts, blue stockings.

Barton, J. 9	Kenyon, R. 3	Ross, ... 26
Darracott, T. 7	Kidd, B. 9	Telfer, G. 10
Dobson, M. 40	King, A. 40	Thomas, D. 33
Eastoe, P...............7	Latchford, R. 36	Todd, C............... 29
Heard, P................9	Lyons, ...37	Walsh, M............. 18
Higgins, M. 20	Nulty, G. 13	Wood, G. 42
Jack, R. 1	Pejic, M. 19	Wright, W............ 39
Jones, D............. 11	Robinson, N. 4	

League Goalscorers—King 13, Latchford 12, Ross 6, Lyons 5, Dobson 4, Kidd 2, Telfer 2, Thomas 2, Wright 2, Higgins 1, Jack 1, Nulty 1, Walsh 1.

Average Home League Gate— 35,460
All-time Record Attendance— 78,299 v. Liverpool (Division 1), September 18, 1948.

IPSWICH TOWN

Ground: Portman Road, Ipswich, IP1 2DA.
Telephone: Ipswich 219211
Colours: Royal Blue and white.

Beattie, K. 19	Mariner, P..........33	Wark, J. 42
Brazil, A. 14	Mills, M. 42	Whymark, T............8
Burley, G. 38	Muhren, A. 41	Woods, C. 41
Butcher, T............ 21	Osman, R. 39	Cooper, P. 41
Parkin, T................3	Gates, E. 20	Sivell, L.................1
Geddis, D. 6	Talbot, B. 21	Hunter, A...............4
Thijssen, F. 16	Lambert, M. 1	Tibbott, L............ 12

League Goalscorers—Mariner 13, Brazil 9, Muhren 8, Gates 7, Wark 6, Woods 5, Talbot 3, Butcher 2, Mills 2, Osman 2, Beattie 1, Burley 1, Geddis 1, Thijssen 1, Whymark 1, Opponents 1.
Average Home League Gate—21,644
All-time Record Attendance—38,010 v. Leeds United (F.A. Cup 6th Round), March 8, 1975.

LEEDS UNITED

Ground: Elland Road, Leeds LS11 0ES.
Telephone: Leeds 716037
Colours: All white with blue and yellow collar and trim.

Cherry, T. 38
Currie, T. 32
Flynn, B. 41
Graham, A. 39
Gray, E. 25
Gray, F................ 41
Hampton, P. 4
Hankin, R............ 29
Harris, C............ 29
Hart, P.............. 40
Harvey, D. 39
Hawley, J. 29
Hird, K.............. 13
Lorimer, P.............. 3
Madeley, P........... 39
Parkinson, K. 3
Stevenson, B. 14
Thomas, G. 1
Stewart, D. 3

League Goalscorers—Hawley 16, Hankin 9, Graham 9, Currie 7, Cherry 6, Gray (F) 6, Hart 4, Gray (E) 4, Flynn 3, Harris 3, Madeley 1, Stevenson 1, Opponents 1.

Average Home League Gate—29,630
All-time Record Attendance— 57,892 v. Sunderland (F.A. Cup) March 15, 1967.

LIVERPOOL

Ground: Anfield Road, Liverpool 4.
Telephone: 051-263 2361
Colours: All red strip with white trim.

Case, J. 37
Clemence, R. 42
Dalglish, K. 42
Fairclough, D. 3
Hansen, A........... 34
Heighway, S. 26
Hughes, E. 15
Johnson, D. 26
Kennedy, A. 37
Kennedy, R. 42
Lee, S.................. 1
McDermott, T. 34
Neal, P. 42
Souness, G. 42
Thompson, P. 39

League Goalscorers—Dalglish 21, Johnson 15, Kennedy (R) 10, McDermott 9, Souness 8, Case 7, Neal 5, Heighway 4, Kennedy (A) 3, Fairclough 2, Hansen 1.

Average Home League Gate—46,504.
All-time Record Attendance— 61,905 v. Wolverhampton W. (F.A. Cup), February 2, 1952.

MANCHESTER CITY

Ground: Maine Road, Moss Side, Manchester M14 7WN.
Telephone: 061-226 1191
Colours: Sky blue shirts shorts and stockings with white diamond trim.

Barnes, P............. 29
Bell, C. 10
Booth, T. 20
Channon, M. 36
Clements, K.......... 15
Corrigan, J. 42
Denya, K. 11
Donachie, W......... 38
Futcher, P.......... 24
Futcher, R.......... 10
Hartford, A. 39
Henry, T. 13
Keegan, G............ 4
Kidd, B. 19
Owen, G............. 34
Palmer, R. 10
Power, P. 32
Ranson, R. 8
Reid, N. 7
Silkman, B. 12
Viljoen, C............. 16
Watson, D. 33

League Goalscorers—Channon 11, Owen 11, Kidd 7, Futcher (R) 7, Denya 6, Palmer 4, Hartford 3, Power 3, Silkman 3, Watson 1, Barnes 1, Opponents 1.

Average Home League Gate— 36,223
All-time Record Attendance— 84,569 v. Stoke (F.A. Cup) March 3, 1934.

MANCHESTER UNITED

Ground: Old Trafford, Manchester M16 0RA.
Telephone: 061-872 1661
Colours: shirts, red and white, shorts white, stockings black and red with red and white band.

Albiston, A. 32
Bailey, G. 28
Buchan, M. 37
Connell, T. 2
Coppell, S. 42
Greenhoff, B. 32
Greenhoff, J. 33
Grimes, A. 5
Houston, S. 21
Jordan, J. 30
Macari, L. 31
McCrerry, D. 14
McIlroy, S. 40
McQueen, G. 36
Moran, K. 1
Nicholl, J. 19
Paterson, S. 1
Ritchie, A. 16
Roche, P. 14
Sloan, T. 3
Thomas, M. 25

League Goalscorers—Coppell 11, Greenhoff (J) 11, Ritchie 9, Jordan 6, Macari 6, McIlroy 6, McQueen 6, Buchan 2, Greenhoff (B) 2, Thomas 1.

Average Home League Gate— 46,430
All-time Record Attendance— 76,962 (F.A. Cup Semi-Final) Wolves v. Grimsby, March 25, 1939.

MIDDLESBROUGH

Ground: Ayresome Park, Middlesbrough.
Telephone: Middlesbrough 89659
Colour: Shirts red with three white stripes down sleeves, shorts: red with three white stripes down sides.

Armstrong, D. 42
Ashcroft, W. 33
Bailey, I. 18
Bell, C. 1
Boam, S. 40
Burns, M. 31
Cochrane, T. 18
Craggs, J. 41
Cummins, S. 11
Hodgson, D. 13
Jankovic, B. 4
Johnson, P. 21
Johnston, C. 1
McAndrew, T. 38
Mahoney, J. 40
Mills, D. 17
Platt, J. 15
Proctor, M. 31
Ramage, A. 14
Shearer, D. 2
Stewart, J. 27
Woof, W. 4

League Goalscorers—Burns 14, Armstrong 11, Proctor 9, Ashcroft 6, Mills 6, Cochrane 3, Woof 1, Cummins 1, Hodgson 1, Shearer 1, McAndrew 1, Boam 1, Jankovic 1, Opponents 1.

Average Home League Gate— 18,458
All-time Record Attendance— 53,596 v. Newcastle U. (Division 1) September 13, 1977.

NORWICH CITY

Ground: Carrow Road, Norwich, Norfolk.
Telephone: Norwich 612131
Colours: Yellow and green.

Baker, C. 2	Hansbury, R. 18	Peters, M. 39
Bennett, D. 1	Hoadley, P. 39	Powell, T. 42
Bond, K. 42	Keelan, K. 22	Reeves, K. 38
Chivers, M. 11	Lythgoe, P. 3	Robb, D. 5
Davies, I. 27	McGuire, M. 24	Robson, K. 29
Downs, G. 3	Mendham, P. 8	Ryan, J. 25
Evans, D. 4	Neighbour, J. 34	Sullivan, C. 10
Fashanu, J. 15	Paddon, G. 18	Symonds, R. 19
Forbes, D. 4		

League Goalscorers—Peters 10, Ryan 9, Reeves 8, Fashanu 5, Chivers 4, Robson 4, Bond 2, Davies 2, Neighbour 2, Evans 1, Paddon 1, Powell 1, Robb 1, Opponents 1.

Average Home League Gate— 18,667
All-time Record Attendance— 43,984 v. Leicester City (F.A. Cup) March 30, 1963.

NOTTINGHAM FOREST

Ground: City Ground, Nottingham, NG2 5FJ.
Telephone: 0602-868236
Colours: Red shirts, white shorts, red stockings.

Anderson, V. 40	Francis, T. 19	O'Hare, J. 9
Barrett, C. 11	Gemmill, A. 24	O'Neill, M. 28
Birtles, G. 35	Gunn, B. 1	Robertson, J. 42
Bowyer, I. 26	Lloyd, L. 36	Shilton, P. 42
Burns, K. 25	Mills, G. 4	Withe, P. 1
Clark, F. 20	McGovern, J. 36	Woodcock, A. 36
Elliott, S. 4	Needham, D. 23	

League Goalscorers—Birtles 15, O'Neill 10, Woodcock 9, Robertson 9, Francis 6, Bowyer 4, Needham 2, Anderson 1, Mills 1, Barrett 1, Gemmill 1, Opponents 2.

Average Home League Gate— 29,587
All-time Record Attendance— 49,945 v. Manchester U. Division 1, October 28, 1967.

QUEENS PARK RANGERS

Ground: Rangers Stadium, South Africa Road, London W12 7PA.
Telephone: 01-743 2618
Colours: Blue and white hooped shirts, white shorts with three blue stripes.

Abbott, R. 2	Francis, G. 31	McGee, P. 21
Allen, C. 9	Gillard, I. 38	Parkes, P. 24
Bowles, S. 30	Goddard, P. 23	Richardson, D. 18
Busby, M. 35	Hamilton, B. 11	Roeder, G. 27
Clement, D. 29	Harkouk, R. 15	Shanks, D. 41
Cunningham, T. 9	Hollins, J. 41	Wallace, B. 5
Eastoe, P. 26	Howe, E. 38	Walsh, M. 10
Elsey, C. 3	James, L. 1	

League Goalscorers—Busby 6, Goddard 6, Allen 4, Roeder 4, Eastoe 3, McGee 3, Gillard 3, Houkouk 3, Shanks 3, Walsh 3, Francis 2, Hamilton 2, Bowles 1, Clement 1, Howe 1.

Average Home League Gate— 15,570
All-time Record Attendance— 35,353 v. Leeds (Division 1) April 28, 1974.

SOUTHAMPTON

Ground: The Dell, Milton Road, Southampton.
Telephone: Southampton 23408/28108
Colours: Red and white striped shirts, black shorts, white socks.

Andruszewski, E.	10	Golac, I.	36	Pickering, M.	3
Baker, G.	20	Hayes, A.	13	Waldron, M.	42
Ball, A.	42	Hebberd, T.	16	Wells, P.	20
Boyer, P.	42	Holmes, N.	38	Williams, O.	6
Curran, E.	25	MacDougall, E.	10	Williams, S.	37
Funnell, A.	2	Nicholl, C.	38		
Gennoe, T.	23	Peach, D.	39		

League Goalscorers—Holmes 8, Boyer 7, Waldron 6, MacDougall 5, Baker 5, Peach 5, Nicholl 3, Hayes 3, Ball 2, Hebbard 2, Opponents 1.

Average Home League Gate—21,356
Attendance— 31,044 v. Manchester U., (Division 1) October 8, 1969.

TOTTENHAM HOTSPUR

Ground: White Hart Lane, 748 High Road, Tottenham, N.17.
Telephone: 01-808 2046
Colours: White shirts, blue shorts, white socks.

Aleksic, M.	5	Hoddle, G.	34	Moores, I.	2
Ardiles, O.	38	Holmes, J.	33	Naylor, T.	22
Armstrong, G.	7	Jones, C.	17	Perryman S.	42
Beavon, S.	1	Kendall, M.	23	Pratt, J.	37
Daines, B.	14	Lacy, J.	35	Smith, G.	1
Duncan, J.	2	Lee, C.	27	Taylor, P.	32
Falco, M.	1	McAllister, D.	38	Villa, R.	26
Galvin, T.	1	McNab, N.	2		
Gorman, J.	15	Miller, P.	7		

League Goalscorers—Taylor 10, Lee 8, Hoddle 7, Jones 5, Pratt 4, Ardilles 3, Villa 2, Duncan 1, Armstrong 1, McAllister 1, Perryman 1, Falco 1, Holmes 1, Opponents 3.

Average Home League Gate—34,862.
All-time Attendance Record— 75,038 v. Sunderland (F.A. Cup) March 5, 1938.

WEST BROMWICH ALBION

Ground: The Hawthorns, Halfords Lane, West Bromwich B71 4LF.
Telephone: 021-553 0095
Colours: Navy Blue and white striped shirts, white shorts.

Batson, B. 41	Godden, T. 42	Robertson, A. 39
Bennett, M. 1	Johnston, W. 3	Robson, B. 41
Brown, A. 41	Martin, M. 1	Statham, D. 39
Brown, T. 29	Mills, D. 15	Trewick, J. 19
Cantello, L. 32	Regis, C. 38	Wile, J. 42
Cunningham, L. 39		

League Goalscorers—Brown (A), 18, Regis 13, Brown (T) 10, Cunningham 9, Robson 7, Cantello 3, Trewick 3, Mills 3, Wile 2, Statham 1, Summerfield 1, Opponents 2.

Average Home League Gate— 26,600
All-time Record Attendance— 64,815 v. Arsenal (F.A. Cup) March 6, 1937.

WOLVERHAMPTON WANDERERS

Ground: Molineux Grounds, Wolverhampton, West Midlands, WV1 4QR.
Telephone: Wolverhampton 24053
Colours: Gold shirts, black shorts, gold socks.

Arkwright, I. 3	Clarke, W. 5	Moss, C. 1
Bell, N. 17	Daley, S. 39	Palmer, G. 41
Berry, G. 30	Daniel, P. 40	Parkin, D. 42
Black, J. 1	Eves, M. 17	Patching, M. 11
Bradshaw, P. 39	Hazell, R. 12	Pierce, G. 3
Brazier, C. 6	Hibbitt, K. 37	Rafferty, W. 24
Carr, W. 36	McAlle, J. 37	Richards, J. 19

League Goalscorers—Richards 9, Daley 6, Hibbitt 6, Daniel 5, Carr 3, Bell 3, Berry 3, Rafferty 2, Eves 2, Patching 1, Clarke 1, Opponents 3.

Average Home League Gate— 20,796
All-time Record Attendance— 61,315 v. Liverpool (F.A. Cup), February 11, 1939.

SECOND DIVISION

BLACKBURN ROVERS

Ground: Ewood Park, Blackburn.
Telephone: Blackburn 55432/3/4
Colours: Blue and white halves (shirts), white shorts.

Aston, J.	14	Fowler, M.	34	Parkes, T.	12
Bailey, J.	39	Garner, S.	32	Parkin, T.	13
Birchenall, A.	19	Gregory, D.	5	Radford, J.	23
Brothston, N.	36	Hird, K.	22	Ramsbottom, N.	10
Butcher, J.	32	Keeeley, G.	26	Rathbone, M.	15
Coughlin, R.	11	McKenzie, D.	13	Round, P.	22
Craig, J.	30	Metcalfe,	25	Taylor, R.	6
Curtis, J.	2	Morley, B.	4	Waddington,	15
Fazackerley, D.	38	Morris, P.	4	Wagstaffe,	2

League Goalscorers— Garner 8, Hird 6, Radford 6, Craig 5, Fazackerley 3, Gregory 3, Aston 2, Brotherston 2, McKenzie 2, Metcalfe 1, Round 1, Taylor 1, Waddington 1.

Average Home League Gate— 8,643
All-time Record Attendance— 61,783 v. Bolton F.A. Cup, March 2 1979.

BRIGHTON AND HOVE ALBION

Ground: Goldstone Ground, Old Shoreham Road, Hove.
Telephone: Brighton 739535
Colours: Blue and white striped shirts, blue shorts, white socks.

Cattlin, C.	27	Moseley, G.	17	Steele, E.	25
Chivers, M	3	O'Sullivan, P.	37	Tiler, K.	17
Clark, P.	28	Poskett, M.	21	Towner, T.	4
Horton, B.	39	Rollings, A.	37	Ward, P.	27
Lawrenson, M	39	Ryan, G.	34	Williams, G.	42
Maybank	35	Sayer P	26	Winstanley, G.	4

League Goalscorers—Horton, 11, Maybank 10, Ward 10, Poskett 9, Ryan 9, Sayer 5, Clark 4 Rollings 3 Lawrenson 2, Williams 2, Chivers 1, O'Sullivan 1, Dono erts 5

Average Home League Gate—22,143.
All-time Record Attendance— 36,747 v. Fulham (Division 2) December 27, 958

BRISTOL ROVERS

Ground: The Bristol Stadium, New Stadium Road, Eastville, Bristol BS5 6NN.
Telephone: 511050
Colours: Blue and white quarters

Aitken, P.	31	England, M.	1	Prince, F.	26
Barry, M.	12	Gould, B.	3	Randall, P.	21
Bater, P.	35	Harding, S.	15	Shaw, M.	1
Brown, K.	1	Jones, V.	20	Staniforth, D.	29
Clarke, G.	2	Lythgoe, P.	6	Taylor, S.	41
Day, G.	24	Mabbutt, G.	7	Thomas, M.	42
Dennehy, M.	29	Palmer, D.	1	Williams, D.	42
Emmanuel, G.	20	Petts, G.	8	White, S.	23

League Goalscorers—Randall 13, White 10, Williams 10, Stamforth 6, Gould 2, Prince 2, Aitken, 1, Barry 1, Hendrie 1, Jones 1, Opponents 1.

Average Home League Gate— 7,198
All-time Record Attendance— 38,472 v. Preston N.E. (F.A. Cup), 30 January 1960.

BURNLEY

Ground: Turf Moor, Brunshaw Road, Burnley, Lancs. BB10 4BX.
Telephone: 0282-27777
Colours: Claret and blue

Arins, A.	7	Jakub, Y.	13	Robinson, P.	8
Brennan, I.	38	James, L.	37	Scott, D.	35
Cochrane, T.	6	Kindon, S.	37	Smith, M.	9
Fletcher, P.	36	Morley, A.	12	Stevenson, A.	42
Hall, B.	25	Noble, P.	41	Thompson, J.	41
Ingham, W.	37	Rodaway, W	39	Young, K.	1

League Goalscorers—Noble 14, Ingham 9, Fletcher 9, Brennan 4, Kindon 3, Morley 2, Hall 2, Smith 1, Thomson 1, Scott 1, Robinson 1.

All-time Record Attendance— 54,775 v. Huddersfield T. (F.A. Cup) February 23, 1924.

CAMBRIDGE UNITED

Ground: Abbey Stadium, Newmarket Road, Cambridge CB5 8LL.
Telephone: Teversham 2170/3555
Colours: Amber/black shirts, black shorts, black socks with amber tops.

Adams, S.	1	Garner, W.	26	Smith, N.	1
Biley, A.	41	Graham, P.	31	Spriggs, S.	40
Buckley, I.	26	Howard, T.	15	Streete, F.	13
Christie, D.	21	Key, R.	1	Stringer, D.	36
Corbin, K.	6	Leach, M.	19	Sweetzer, G.	1
Fallon, S.	42	O'Neill, T.	2	Webster, M.	41
Finney, T.	42	Smith, L.	40		

League Goalscorers—Biley 20, Finney 8, Garner 3, Christie 3, Cozens 2, Spriggs 2, Streete 1, Murray 1,Buckley 1, Leach 1, Opponents 2.

Average Home League Gate— 6,896
All-time Record Attendance— 11,406 v. West Ham (Division 1) April 7, 1979.

CARDIFF CITY

Ground: Ninian Park, Sloper Road, Cardiff CF1 8SX.
Telephone: Cardiff 398636/7/8
Colours: Blue shirts with yellow/white stripe on chest, blue shorts, blue stockings with single yellow stripe on turn donw.

Attley, B.	8	Evans, T.	30	Moore, R.	18
Bishop, R.	26	Giles, D.	4	Pethard, F.	14
Barber, C.	2	Grapes, S.	22	Platt, J.	4
Buchanan, J.	36	Harris, G.	1	Pontin, K.	27
Burns, M.	6	Healey, R.	32	Roberts, D.	28
Byrne, G.	2	Jones, L.	14	Stevens, G.	32
Campbell, A.	40	Larmour, A.	15	Sullivan, C.	19
Davies, J.	4	Lewis, J.	13	Thomas, R.	22
Dwyer, P.	39	Micallef, T.	1	Went, P.	3

League Goalscorers—Buchanan 16, Stevens 13, Evans 7, Bishop (R) 6, Dwyer 4, Moore 4, Roberts 2, Sullivan 1, Went 1, Opponents 2

Average Home League Gate—9,259.
All-time Record Attendance— 61,566 Wales v. England (International) October 14, 1961.

CHARLTON ATHLETIC

Ground: The Valley, London SE7 2AW.
Telephone: 01-858 3711/2
Colours: Red, white, red.

Berry, L.	36	Hales, D.	20	Robinson, M.	35
Brisley, T.	29	Johns, N.	10	Shaw, P.	33
Campbell, D.	39	Madden, L.	37	Shipperley, D.	33
Churchouse, G.	9	Peacock, K.	25	Tydeman, R.	21
Dugdale, A.	4	Penfold, M.	4	Warman, P.	11
Flanagan, M.	25	Powell, C.	21	Wood, J.	32
Gritt, S.	38				

League Goalscorers—Robinson 15, Flanagan 13, Hales 8, Brisley 3, Gritt 3, Madden 3, Shipperley 3, Campbell 2, Peacock 2, Tydeman 2, Warman 2, Berry 1, Powell 1, Shaw 1, Opponents 1.

Average Home League Gate— 9,563
All-time Record Attendance— 75,031 v. Aston Villa (F.A. Cup) February 12, 1938.

CRYSTAL PALACE

Ground: Selhurst Park, London SE25.
Telephone: 01-653 2223
Colours: White shirts with 4inch diagonal band red over blue, white shorts, white socks.

Burridge, J.	42	Hazell, T.	5	Sansom, K.	42
Cannon, J.	41	Hilaire, V.	25	Sealy, T.	4
Chatterton, N.	13	Hinshelwood, P.	31	Smillie, N.	3
Elwiss, M.	19	Kember, S.	29	Swindlehurst, D.	40
Fenwick, T.	20	Murphy, J.	40	Walsh, I.	30
Gilbert, W.	41	Nicholas, P.	37		

League Goalscorers—Swindlehurst 14, Walsh 8, Elwiss 7, Hilaire 6, Murphy 5, Chatterton 3, Nicholas 3, Cannon 2, Gilbert 1, Hinshelwood 1, Smillie 1.

Average Home League Gate—23,347
Attendance— 51,801 v. Burnley (Division 2) May 11, 1979.

FULHAM

Ground: Craven Cottage, Stevenage Road, Fulham, SW6 6HH.
Telephone: 01-736 6561
Colours: White shirts, Black shorts, white socks.

Banton, G.	7	Gale, T.	36	Mahoney, T.	7
Beck, J.	32	Greenaway, B.	16	Margerrison, J.	24
Boyd, G.	3	Guthrie, C.	34	Marinello, P.	9
Bullivant, T.	28	Hatter, S.	5	Mason, T.	4
Davies, G.	32	Kitchen, P.	17	Money, R.	42
Digweed, P.	2	Lock, K.	39	Peyton, G.	40
Evans, R.	36	Lovell, M.	2	Strong, L.	41
Evanson, J.	22				

League Goalscorers—Guthrie 13, Davies 9, Margerrison 6, Kitchen 5, Greenaway 3, Lock 3, Evans 2, Gale 2, Beck 1, Evanson 1, Mahoney 1, Money 1, Strong 1, Opponents 2.

Average Home League Gate— 10,084
All-time Record Attendance— 49,335 v. Millwall (Division 2) October 8, 1938.

LEICESTER CITY

Ground: City Stadium, Filbert Street, Leicester LE2 7FL.
Telephone: Leicester 57111.
Colours: Blue shirts, white trim, white shorts and socks.

Armstrong, G.	3	Hughes, B.	18	Rofe, D.	39
Buchanan, D.	17	Kelly, E.	26	Sims, S.	8
Carr, E.	2	Kember, S.	8	Smith, B.	17
Christie, T.	23	Lee, A.	1	Wallington, M.	42
Davies, R.	8	Lineker, G.	7	Webb, D.	4
Duffy, M.	7	May, L.	36	Weller, K.	16
Goodwin, M.	23	O'Neill, J.	23	Welsh, P.	4
Grewcock, N.	1	Peake, A.	17	White, W.	1
Henderson, M.	31	Ridley, J.	17	Whitworth, S.	29
				Williams, T.	32

League Goalscorers—Christie 8, Smith 6, Buchanan 5, Henderson 4, May 4, Hughes 3, Weller 3, Davies 2, Peake 2, Williams 2, Duffy 1, Goodwin 1, Grewcock 1, Lineker 1.

Average Home League Gate—14,187.
All-time Record Attendance— 47,298 v. Tottenham (F.A. Cup) February 18, 1928.

LUTON TOWN

Ground: 70/72 Kenilworth Road, Luton, Beds.
Telephone: 0582-411622
Colours: Shirts: orange with white and navy vertical stripes down left side, shorts: navy blue, stockings: orange with navy blue and white turnover.

Aleksic, M.	14	Hatton, B.	41	Sherlock, S.	2
Aizlewood, M.	39	Hill, R.	38	Silkman, B.	3
Birchenall, A.	8	Ingram, G.	2	Stephens, K.	24
Boersma, P.	1	Jones, G.	6	Stein, B.	3
Carr, D.	13	Lawson, D.	5	Taylor, S.	15
Donaghy, M.	40	Moss, D.	29	Turner, W.	31
Findlay, J.	23	Phillipson-Masters, F.	10	West, A.	37
Fuccillo, L.	16	Price, P.	34		

League Goalscorers—Moss 13, Hatton 11, Stein 10, Fuccillo 7, Turner 5, West 4, Hill 3, Price 2, Taylor 2, Opponents 2.

Average Home League Gate— 8,792
All-time Record Attendance— 30,069 v. Blackpool (F.A. Cup) March 4, 1959.

MILLWALL

Ground: The Den, Cold Blow Lane, New Cross, London SE14 5RH.
Telephone: 01-639 3143/4
Colours: Blue shirts with white trim, white shorts with blue trim.

Allen, P.	4	Gale, I.	4	Moore, J.	11
Blyth, M.	13	Gregory, D.	23	O'Callaghan, K.	7
Chambers, B.	26	Hamilton, B.	12	Roberts, P.	1
Chatterton, N.	27	Hamilton, J.	1	Pearson, I.	8
Coleman, P.	2	Hazell, A.	7	Seasman, J.	35
Cross, R.	1	Lee, T.	4	Tagg, A.	26
Cuff, P.	42	Kitchener, B.	40	Towner, A.	25
Dibble, C.	5	Mehmet, D.	20	Walker, P.	38
Donaldson, D.	41	Mitchell, J.	32		

League Goalscorers—Seasman 9, Mitchell 6, Walker 5, Mehmet 4, Chambers 4, Chatterton 4, Kitchener 3, Hamilton (B), 2, Towner 1, Tagg 1, Lee 1, Opponents 2.

Average Home League Gate— 7,001
All-time Record Attendance— 48,672 v. Derby County (F.A. Cup), February 20, 1937.

NEWCASTLE UNITED

Ground: St. James' Park, Newcastle-upon-Tyne NE1 4ST.
Telephone: 0632 28361

Barker, A.	5	Hardwick, S.	31	Nicholson, G.	5
Barton, D.	20	Hibbitt, T.	40	Pearson, J.	9
Bird, J.	28	Kelly, P.	15	Robinson, S.	4
Blackley, J.	28	Mahoney, M.	3	Scott, S.	2
Brownlie, J.	34	Manners, P.	2	Shoulder, A.	24
Carr, K.	8	McGhee, M.	4	Suggett, C.	20
Cassidy, T.	19	Martin, M.	24	Walker, N.	18
Connolly, J.	34	Mitchell, K.	26	Withe, P.	39
Guy, A.	2	Nattrass, I.	21		

League Goalscorers—Withe 14, Shoulder 11, Connolly 8, Bird 3, Pearson 3, Barton 2, Walker 2, McGhee 2, Nattrass 2, Cassidy 1, Mitchell 1, Robinson 1, Martin 1.

Average Home League Gate— 20,493
All-time Record Attendance— 68,386 v. Chelsea, (Division 1), September 3 1930.

NOTTS. COUNTY

Ground: Meadow Lane Ground, Nottingham.
Telephone: 0602-868494
Colours: Black and white striped shirts, black shorts.

Benjamin, T. 24	Mair, G. 4	McVay, D. 3
Stubbs, B. / Blockley, J. .... 42 / 27	Mann, A. 37 37	Richards, P. ....
Green, R. 6	McCulloch, I. 42	Vinter, M. 41
Hooks, P. 36	McManus, E. 42	Wood, G. 2
Hunt, D. 36		

League Goalscorers—Vinter 13, Hooks 11, McCulloch 8, O'Brien 5, Blockley 3, Mann 3, Hunt 2, Masson 2, Mair 1.

Average Home League Gate— 8809
All-time Record Attendance— 47,310 v. York City (F.A. Cup) March 12, 1955.

OLDHAM ATHLETIC

Ground: Boundary Park, Oldham OL1 2PA.
Telephone: 061-624 4972
Colours: Blue shirts, white shorts, white stockings.

Atkinson, P. 1	Heaton, P. 29	McDonnell, P. 42
Barnett, D. 2	Hicks, K. 35	Sinclair, N. 2
Barnard, M. 2	Hilton, M. 20	Stainrod, S. 14
Bell, G. 23	Holt, D. 5	Steel, J. 21
Blair, R. 35	Hoolikin, G. 2	Taylor, S. 16
Chapman, L. 42	Hurst, J. 41	Valentine, C. 12
Edwards, S. 32	Jordan, T. 12	Wood, I. 36
Gardner, S. 33	Keegan, G. 20	Young, A. 37
Halom, V. 31		

League Goalscorers— Young 10, Heaton 5, Stainrod 5, Taylor 5, Hicks 4, Halom 4, Steel 4, Chapman 3, Hilton 3, Bell 2, Wood 2, Blair 1, Hurst 1, Valentine 1, Hoolickin 1, Opponents 1.

Average Home League Gate— 7,049
All-time Record Attendance— 47,671 v. Sheffield Wed. (F.A. Cup) January 25, 1930.

ORIENT

Ground: Leyton Stadium, Brisbane Road, Leyton, London E10 5NE.
Telephone: 01-539 2223/4
Colours: White shirts and shorts with red vertical stripes.

Banjo, T. 13	Gray, M. 1	Mayo, J. 40
Bennett, P. 6	Gray, N. 42	Moores, I. 30
Chiedozie, J. 33	Grealish, T. 39	Roffey, B. 39
Clarke, D. 4	Hughton, H. 33	Smith, M. 1
Coates, R. 30	Jackson, J. 42	Went, P. 37
Fisher, B. 37	Kitchen, P. 22	Whittle, A. 10
Godfrey, K. 3		

League Goalscorers—Moores 13, Mayo 11, Kitchen 7, Chiedozie 6, Grealish 5, Coates 3, Hughton 2, Went 2, Whittle 1, Banjo 1.

Average Home League Gate— 7323
All-time Record Attendance— 34,345 v. West Ham United (F.A. Cup) January 25, 1966.

PRESTON NORTH END

Ground: Deepdale, Preston, PR1 6RU.
Telephone: Preston 795919
Colours: All white strip with blue trim.

Baxter, M. 37
Bell, G. 10
Bruce, A. 40
Burns, F. 21
Cameron, D. 36
Cochrane, J. 2
Coleman, G. 37
Cross, G. 5
Doyle, S. 25
Elliott, S. 5
Haslegrave, S. 41
McMahon, J. 8
O'Riordan, D. 32
Potts, E. 25
Robinson, M. 36
Smith, A. 1
Spavin, A. 2
Taylor, B. 29
Thomson, R. 13
Tunks, R. 42
Uzelac, S. 7
Wilson, H. 8

League Goalscorers—Bruce 21, Robinson 13, Coleman 7, Potts 5, Baxter 4, Thomson 4, Doyle 2, Bell 1, Cochrane 1, Haslegrave 1.

Average Home League Gate—12,117
All-time Record Attendance— 42,684 v. Arsenal (Division 1) April 23, 1938.

SHEFFIELD UNITED

Ground: Bramall Lane, Sheffield S2 4SU.
Telephone: 738955
Colours: Red and white with thin black vertical stripes.

Anderson, P. 28
Benjamin, I. 1
Brown, D. 7
Calvert, C. 21
Conroy, S. 41
Cutbush, J. 26
Finnieston, S. 23
Flood, J. 5
Franks, C. 15
Garner, P. 19
Hamson, G. 41
Harwood, R. 2
Johns, N. 1
Jones, P. 1
Guy, M. 12
Keeley, A. 10
Kenworthy, T. 37
McPhail, J. 15
Matthews, J. 31
Renwick, C. 6
Rioch, B. 8
Sabella, A. 39
Smith, T. 2
Speight, M. 39
Stainrod, S. 9
Tibbott, L. 12
Varadi, I. 6
Woodward, A. 5

League Goalscorers—Anderson 12, Matthews 5, Finnieston 4, Varadi 4, Hamson 4, Sabella 3, Kenworthy 3, Stainrod 3, Speight 2, Guy 2, Benjamin 2, Garner 1, Franks 1, Calvert 1, McPhail 1, Smith 1, Brown 1, Rioch 1, Opponents 1.

Average Home League Gate— 16,369
All-time Record Attendance— 68,287 v. Leeds United (F.A. Cup) February 15, 1936.

STOKE CITY

Ground: Victoria Ground, Stoke-on-Trent, Staffordshire.
Colours: Red and white striped shirts and white shorts.

Busby, V. 9
Conroy, G. 3
Cook, J. 1
Crooks, G. 38
Dodd, A. 33
Doyle, M. 40
Fox, P. 1
Heath, A. 1
Irvine, S. 41
Jones, R. 41
Johnsen, P. 7
Johnson, P. A. 2
Kendall, H. 40
McGroarty, J. 3
Marsh, J. 24
O'Callaghan, B. 40
Randall, P. 20
Richardson, P. 40
Scott, G. 37
Smith, D. 39
Waddington, S. 2

League Goalscorers—O'Callaghan 15, Crooks 12, Irvine 7, Richardson 6, Busby 6, Randall 5, Smith 2, Kendall 2, Doyle 1, McGroarty 1, Opponents 1.

Average Home League Gate— 19,114
All-time Record Attendance— 51,380 v. Arsenal (Division 1) March 29, 1937.

SUNDERLAND

Ground: Roker Park Ground, Grantham Road, Roker, Sunderland.

Arnott, K.	15	Docherty, M.	28	Kerr, R.	3
Ashurst, J.	13	Elliott, S.	41	Lee, R.	33
Bolton, J.	32	Entwistle, W.	36	Rostron, W.	34
Brown, A.	27	Gilbert, T.	13	Rowell, G.	32
Buckley, M.	30	Greenwood, R.	8	Siddall, B.	41
Chisholm, G.	33	Gregoire, R.	2	Watson,	1
Clarke, J.	37	Henderson, M.	30	Whitworth,	10
Coady, M.	3				

League Goalscorers—Rowell 21, Entwistle 12, Rostron 11, Lee 6, Brown 6, Docherty 5, Bolton 3, Clarke 2, Greenwood 2, Ashurst 1, Gilbert 1.

Average Home League Gate— 25,454
All-time Record Attendance— 75,118 v. Derby County (F.A. Cup) March 8, 1933.

WEST HAM

Ground: Boleyn Ground, Green Street, Upton Park, London E13.
Telephone: 01-472 2740
Colours: Claret and blue.

Bonds, W.	39	Ferguson, R.	11	McDowell, J.	26
Brooking, T.	21	Holland, P.	39	Parkes, P.	18
Brush, P.	42	Jennings, W.	2	Pike, G.	10
Cross, D.	40	Lampard, F.	28	Robson, B.	41
Curbishley, L.	26	Martin, A.	22	Taylor, A.	10
Day, M.	13	Morgan, N.	1	Taylor, T.	32
Devonshire, A.	41				

League Goalscorers—Robson 24, Cross 17, Devonshire 5, Bonds 4, Holland 3, Lampard 3, Taylor (A) 3, Brooking 2, McDowell 2, Pike 2, Curbishley 1, Martin 1, Opponents 3.

Average Home League Gate—25,778
All-time Record Attendance— 39,202 v. Eintracht Frankfurt (Cup Winners Cup) April 14, 1976.

WREXHAM

Ground: Racecourse Ground, Mold Road, Wrexham, Clwyd LL11 2AN.
Telephone: Wrexham 262129
Colours: Red shirts (white trim), white shorts and stockings (red trim).

Buxton, S.	14	Giles, D.	23	Niedzwieki, E.	6
Cartwright, L.	25	Griffiths, A.	6	Roberts, I.	4
Cegielski, W.	30	Hill, A.	18	Roberts, J.	40
Davis, G.	22	Jones, J.	30	Shinton, R.	37
Davies, D.	36	Jones, F.	4	Sutton, M.	41
Dwyer, A.	29	Kenworthy, S.	2	Thomas, M.	16
Evans, M.	5	Lyons, J.	33	Whittle, G.	26
Fox, S.	22	McNeil, R.	31	Williams, P.	6

League Goarscorers—Lyons 11, Whittle 7, Shinton 6, Thomas 5, McNeil 3, 7Average Home League Gate— Approx. 10,000
All-time Record Attendance— 34,445 v. Manchester United (F.A. Cup) January 26, 1957.

THIRD DIVISION

BLACKPOOL

Ground: Bloomfield Road, Blackpool FY1 6JJ.
Telephone: 46118
Colours: Shirts: tangerine, white stripe on sleeves, white collar and cuffs, shorts: white with tangerine stripe, stockings: tangerine with two white lines on top.

Bissell, S.	1	Jones, G.	11	Sermanni, T.	6
Bowey, K.	1	Kellow, T.	25	Spence, D.	42
Chandler, J.	18	Kerr, R.	7	Suddaby, P.	42
Davidson, V.	23	Malone, R.	29	Thompson, M.	38
Gardner, P.	22	May, J.	4	Tong, D.	2
Hall, J.	1	McEwan, S.	46	Wagstaffe, D.	17
Hesford, I.	33	Milligan, L.	2	Waldron, A.	5
Hockaday, D.	13	Pashley, T.	36	Weston, J.	29
Holden, M.	2	Ronson, W.	31	Wilson, B.	7

League Goalscorers—Spence 16, Kellow 11, McEwan 5, Hockaday 4, Davidson 3, Jones 3, Chandler 5, Weston 4, Ronson 3, Suddaby 2, Malone 1, Thompson 1, Wilson 1, Wagstaffe 1, Opponents 1.

Average Home League Gate— 5,647
All-time Record Attendance— 39,118 Manchester United Div. 1 April, 1952.

BRENTFORD

Ground: Griffin Park, Braemar Road, Brentford, Middlesex, TW8 0NT.
Telephone: 01-560 2021
Colours: Shirts: red/white vertical stripes; shorts: black, stockings: black with red and white hooped tops.

Allder, D. S. 17	Glover, A. R. 18	Rolph, G. L. 1
Allen, M. 5	Graham, J. J. 35	Salman, D. M. M. 39
Baldwin, T. ... .-	Graham, W. V. 8	Shrubb, P. J. 39
Bond, L. A. 35	Kruse, P. K. 45	Silman, D. A. 1
Booker, R. 2	McCulloch, A. 39	Smith, D. 22
Carlton, D. G. 36	McNichol, J. A. 32	Smith, N. P. 2
Eames, W. A. 2	Phillips, S. E. 46	Tucker, W. B. 43
Fraser, J. 21	Porter, T. J. 11	Walker, J. P. 2
Frost, L. 5		

League Goalscorers—McCulloch, 14, Phillips 14, Smith 8, Kruse 4, McNichol 4, Carlton 2, Glover 2, Shrubb 2, Eames 1, Graham 1, Salman 1.

Average Home League Gate— 7,455
All-time Record Attendance— 39,626 v. Preston North End (F.A. Cup), March 5, 1938.

BURY

Ground: Gigg Lane, Bury
Telephone: 061-764 4881
Colours: White shirts, royal blue shorts.

Bailey, A. 15	Johnson, S. 3	Robins, I. 4
Beamish, K. 35	Hilton, P. 6	Rowland, A. 7
Constantine, D. 16	Keenan, G. 5	Stanton, B. 36
Farrell, P. 8	Kennedy, K. 33	Ritson, J. 31
Forrest, J. 44	Latchford, D. 2	Taylor, G. 45
Gregory, D. 36	Lugg, R. 45	Tucker, W. 37
Hatton, D. 12	Madden, C. 4	Wilson, D. 46
Hamstead, G. 10	Mullen, S. 2	Whitehead, A. 24

League Goalscorers—Beamish 16, Gregory 10, Wilson 7, Whitehead 3, Stanton 4, Tucker 2, Farrell 2, Ritson 2, Lugg 2, Keenan 1, Rowland 1, Robins 1, Kennedy 1, Constantine 1, Hatton 1, Hilton 1, Taylor 2, Madden 1, Opponents 1.

Average Home League Gate— 3,771
All-time Record Attendance— 35,000 v. Bolton Wanderers (F.A. Cup), January 9, 1960.

CARLISLE UNITED

Ground: Brunton Park, Carlisle, Cumbria, CA1 1LL.
Telephone: Carlisle 26237
Colours: Shirts: blue with broad vertical stripe piped with red, shorts: white, stockings: red.

Bannon, P. 2	Ludlam, S. 38	Parker, R. 46
Bonnyman, P. 45	Lumby, J. 22	Ross, A. 1
Collins, A. 3	McCartney, M. 44	Swinburne, T. 45
Hamilton, J. 31	MacDonald, I. 41	Tait, M. 45
Hoolickin, S. 46	McLean, D. 6	
Kemp, D. 45	McVitie, G. 46	

League Goalscorers—Kemp 18, Tait 7, Bonnyman 7, Lumby 6, McCartney 5, Ludlam 3, McVitie 2, Parker 1, MacDonald 1, Hamilton 1, Opponents 2.

Average Home League Gate— 5,204
All-time Record Attendance— 27,500 v. Birmingham City (F.A. Cup) January 5, 1957 and v. Middlesbrough (F.A. Cup) February 7, 1970.

CHESTER

Ground: The Stadium, Sealand Road, Chester.
Telephone: Chester 371376
Colours: Royal blue and white stripes.

Burns, D.	7	Jones, B.	26	Phillips, R.	40
Delgado, R.	15	Livermore, D.	39	Raynor, P.	36
Edwards, I.	39	Lloyd, B.	41	Rush, I.	1
Felix, G.	8	Millington, G.	5	Storton, T.	46
Henderson, P.	25	Mellor, I.	21	Sutcliffe, P.	11
Howat, I.	5	Nickeas, M.	33	Walker, J.	31
Jeffries, D.	40	Oakes, A.	37		

League Goal Scorers— Edwards, 20, Phillips, 10, Henderson 7, Mellor 6, Oakes 4, Raynor 4, Jones 2, Delgado 1, Walker 1, Jeffries 1, Libermore 1.

Average Home League Gate—4,022
All-time Record Attendance— 20,500 v. Chelsea (F.A. Cup) January 16, 1952.

CHESTERFIELD

Ground: Recreation Ground, St. Margaret's Drive, Chesterfield, Derbyshire.
Telephone: Chesterfield 32318
Colours: Royal blue shirts, white shorts, white socks.

Burton, K.	40	Heppolette, R.	13	Pollard, G.	1
Cammack, S.	13	Higgins, A.	1	Prophett, C.	35
Chamberlain, G.	1	Hunter, L.	40	Salmons, G.	37
Cottam, J.	36	Kowalski, A.	42	Simpson, G.	10
Dearden, B.	1	Letheren, G.	34	Tartt, C.	42
Fern, R.	39	Moss, E.	22	Tingay, P.	12
Flavell, B.	27	O'Neill, S.	23	Walker, P.	37

League Goalscorers—Fern 11, Walker 9, Kowalski 5, Moss 5, Salmons 5, Cammack 4, Simpson 3, Cottam 2, Flavell 2, Burton 1, Prophett 1, Tartt 1, Opponents 2.

Average Home League Gate—4,756
All-time Record Attendance—30,968 v. Newcastle United (Division 2) April 7, 1939.

COLCHESTER UNITED

Ground: Layer Road Ground, Colchester.
Telephone: Colchester 74042
Colours: Blue and white vertical striped shirts, blue shorts, white stockings.

Allinson, I.	44	Evans, A.	8	Packer, M.	40
Bunkell, R.	10	Foley, S.	34	Rowles, E.	19
Cook, M.	46	Gough, R.	42	Sharkey, P.	5
Cotton, R. A.	1	Hodge, R.	31	Walker, M.	46
Dowman, S.	37	Lee, T.C.	27	Wignall, S.	42
Dyer, P.D.	37	Leslie, S.	3	Wright, S.	34

League Goalscorers—Gough 16, Lee 11, Foley 6, Allinson 5, Wignall 4, Rowles 4, Hodge 3, Dyer 2, Dowman 2, Evans 2, Cook 1, Packer 1, Wright 1, Bunkell 1, Opponents 1.

Average Home League Gate— 3,409
All-time Record Attendance— 19,072 v. Reading (F.A. Cup) November 27, 1948.

EXETER CITY

Ground: St. James Park, Exeter.
Telephone: Exeter 54073
Colours: White with three red stripes on sleeves, white shorts and stockings.

Bowker, K.	26	Hore, K.	44	Pearson, I.	18
Delve, J.	42	Ingham, F.	2	Randell, C.	38
Forbes, R.	7	Kellow, T.	17	Roberts, L.	43
Giles, J.	43	Main, I.	13	Rogers, P.	11
Hatch, P.	45	Neville, S.	36	Sims, J.	25
Hodge, B.	4	Mitchell, T.	10	Templeman, J.	45
Holman, H.	6	O'Keefe, J.	33	Williams, O.	2

League Goalscorers— Bowker 11, Sims 11, Neville 9, Kellow 7, Delve 6, Roberts 3, Randell 3, Rogers 3, Pearson 3, Hatch 2, Templeman 1, Holman 1, Giles 1.

Average Home League Gate—4,415
All-time Record Attendance— 20,984 v. Sunderland (F.A. Cup) March 4, 1931.

GILLINGHAM

Ground: Priestfield Stadium, Gillingham.
Telephone: Medway 51854
Colours: Blue shirts, white shorts.

Armstrong, G.	24	Knight, G.	3	Walker, P.	4
Barker, M.	22	Nicholl, T.	43	Weatherly, M.	46
Crabbe, J.	34	Overton, J.	43	Westwood, D.	43
Funnell, A.	12	Price, K.	41	White, D.	26
Hillyard, R.	46	Richardson, D.	28	Williams, N.	1
Hughes, B.	38	Sharpe, J.	37	Young, C.	6
Jolley, T.	9				

League Goalscorers—Westwood 18, Price 14, Funnell 7, Jolley 5, Nicholl 4, Richardson 4, White 3, Crabbe 2, Hughes 2, Overton 2, Weatherly 2, Armstrong 1, Barker 1.

Average Home League Gate— 7,123
All-time Record Attendance— 23,002 v. Q.P.R. (F.A. Cup) January 10, 1948.

HULL CITY

Ground: Boothferry Park, Hull, HU4 6TE.
Telephone: 0482-52195
Colours: Black and amber striped shirts, black shorts, amber stockings.

Bannister, B. 43	Galvin, C. 15	Nisbet, G. 46
Blackburn, E. 18	Hawker, D. 22	Roberts, G. 18
Croft, S. 24	Horswill, M. 40	Skipper, P. 16
de Vries, R. 29	Hood, D. 15	Stewart, D. 2
Dobson, I. 22	Haigh, P. 45	Warboys, A. 14
Edwards, K. 46	Lord, M. 23	Wealands, S. 28
Farley, J. 33	McDonald, R. 8	

League Goalscorers—Edwards 24, Bannister 15, Horswill 6, Galvin 4, Roberts 3, Lord 3, Skipper 2, McDonald 2, Warboys 2, Nisbet 1, Haigh 1, Farley 1, Stewart 1, Hawker 1.

Average Home League Gate— 5,238
All-time Record Attendance— 55,019 v. Manchester Utd. (F.A. Cup) February 26, 1949.

LINCOLN CITY

Ground: Sincil Bank, Lincoln LN5 8LD.
Telephone: 22224/5
Colours: Red and white stripes.

Burrows, D. 1	Harford, M. 28	Sivell, L. 2
Cockerill, G. 34	Hobson, G. 27	Smith, M. 17
Cooper, T. 35	Hubbard, P. 21	Sunley, D. 28
Creane, G. 2	Hughes, D. 13	Turner, C. 5
Cross, G. 19	Jones, A. 1	Turner, I. 7
Eden, A. 1	Laybourne, K. 17	Tynan, T. 9
Fleming, J. 27	Leigh, D. 29	Ward, J. 32
Grotier, P. 32	Loxley, T. 1	Watson, G. 21
Guest, B. 39	McCalliog, J. 9	Wigginton, C. 19
Harding, A. 17	Neale, P. 11	Wright, B. 3

League Goalscorers—Cockerill 6, Fleming 6, Harford 5, Hobson 5, Sunley 4, Ward 4, Watson 2, Wigginton 2, Cooper 1, Harding 1, Laybourne 1, Leigh 1, Neale 1, Tynan 1.

Average Home League Gate— 3,173
All-time Record Attendance— 23,196 v. Derby County, November 15, 1967.

MANSFIELD TOWN

Ground: Field Mill Ground, Quarry Lane, Mansfield.
Telephone: Mansfield 23567
Colours: Amber shirts, blue shorts, amber socks.

Allen, R. 26	Foster, B. 39	Miller, J. 28
Arnold, R. 28	Foster, C. 9	Moss, E. 12
Austin, T. 16	Goodwin, D. 26	New, M. 18
Bird, K. 44	Gratton, J. 1	Phillips, I. 3
Carter, M. 18	Hamilton, N. 16	Sxby, G. 14
Coffey, M. 2	Hodgson, G. 6	Saxby, M. 46
Curtis, B. 33	McClelland, J. 33	Syrett, D. 23
Dawkins, D. 26	Martin, D. 33	Wood, I. 6

League Goalscorers—Curtis 6, Allen 5, Austin 5, Bird 4, Goodwin 4, Syrett 4, Saxby (M) 4, Miller 4, Carter 4, Martin 3, Moss 2, Saxby (G) 1, McClelland 1, Hamilton 1, Opponents 3.
Average Home Leauge Gate—5,157

All-time Record Attendance— 24,467 v. Nottingham Forest (F.A. Cup) January 10, 1953.

OXFORD UNITED

Ground: Manor Ground, Headington, Oxford.
Telephone: Oxford 61503
Colours: Yellow and blue shirts, blue shorts with yellow stripe, yellow and blue stockings.

Berry, P.	16	Foley, P.	31	Milkins, J.	7
Bodel, A.	40	Graydon, R.	18	Seacole, J.	45
Briggs, G.	39	Hodgson, G.	31	Taylor, L.	46
Burton, R.	39	Jeffrey, W.	40	Watson, G.	9
Curran, H.	1	Kingston, A.	3	White, A.	3
Doyle, J.	5	McGrogan, H.	21	Curran, H.	2
Duncan, C.	43	McIntosh, M.	23	Stott, I.	2
Fogg, D.	44				

League Goalscorers—Foley 9, Seacole 8, Graydon 5, Berry 4, Duncan 3, Fogg 3, McGrogan 3, Bodel 2, Hodgson 2, Jeffrey 1, Sweetzer 1, Taylor 1, White 1, Opponents 1.

Average Home League Gate— 4,373
All-time Record Attendance— 22,730 v. Preston North End (F.A. Cup), February 29, 1964.

PETERBOROUGH UNITED

Ground: London Road Ground, Peterborough.
Telephone: 63947, commercial office 69760
Colours: Blue with white trimmings.

Anderson, T.	23	Doyle, B.	41	Robson, T.	29
Butlin, B.	30	Green, B.	30	Ross, I.	45
Byatt, D.	2	Gynn, M.	9	Sargent, G.	9
Carmichael, J.	25	Guy, A.	13	Slough, A.	10
Collins, S.	5	Hindley, P.	30	Sharkey, P.	11
Chard, P.	5	Holman, H.	9	Smith, T.	15
Cooke, J.	18	McEwan, B.	32	Styles, A.	32
Cliss, T.	15	McLennan,	1	Quow, T.	5
Cunningham, D.	4	Robertson, A.	12	Robson, T.	29
				Waugh, K.	46

League Goalscorers—Butlin 5, Cooke 5, Slough 4, Robson 4, Guy 4, Doyle 3, McEwan 2, Sargent 2, Smith 2, Cliss 2, Gynn 2, Robertson 1, Anderson 1, Styles 1, Cunningham 1, Holman 1, Ross 1, Chard 1, Opponents 2.

Average Home League Gate— 4,194
All-time Record Attendance— 30,096 v. Swansea (F.A. Cup) February 20, 1965.

PLYMOUTH ARGYLE

Ground: Home Park, Plymouth
Telephone: 52561/2/3
Colours: Green shirts (black and white trim), white shorts, black and white trim.

Bason, B. 36	Graves, M. 10	McNeil, B. 27
Binney, F. 43	Harrison, C. 24	Perrin, S. 23
Brennan, S. 6	Hodge, M. 38	Rogers, A. 37
Burns, T. 8	Hodges, K. 12	Silkman, B. 14
Chapman, L. 4	James, T. 15	Taylor, B. 8
Clarke, C. 35	Johnson, B. 33	Trusson, M. 27
Fear, K. 27	Levy, A. 1	Upton, C. 3
Forde, C. 5	Megson, G. 42	Uzzell, J. 21
Foster, G. 28		

League Goalscorers—Binney 27, Johnson 11, Megson 7, Trusson 4, Bason 4, Fear 3, Clarke 3, Perrin 3, Silkman 2, Harrison 1, Rogers 1, Opponents 1.

Average Home League Gate— 7,779
All-time Record Attendance— 43,596 v. Aston Villa (Division 2) October 10, 1936.

ROTHERHAM UNITED

Ground: Millmoor Ground, Rotherham.
Telephone: 2434
Colours: Red shirts with white collars and sleeves, white shorts, red socks.

Breckin, J. 45	Green, J. 46	Rhodes, M. 20
Carr, P. 18	Gwyther, D. 41	Smith, D. 31
Crawford, A. 39	McAllister, T. 45	Stancliffe, P. 33
Dawson, R. 7	Mountford, R. 1	Vaughan, I. 1
Flynn, J. 29	Phillips, T. 46	Winn, S. 6
Finney, R. 41	Pugh, D. 3	Young, T. 8
Forrest, G. 46		

League Goalscorers—Gwyther 14, Phillips 14, Finney 9, Smith 3, Crawford 2, Carr 1, Dawson 1, Green 1, Rhodes 1, Flynn 1, Breckin 1, Opponents 1.

Average Home League Gate— 4,466
All-time Record Attendance— 25,000 v. Sheffield Wednesday, (Division 2) January 26, 1952 and Sheffield United, (Division 2) December 13, 1952.

SHEFFIELD WEDNESDAY

Ground: Hillsborough, Sheffield S6 1SW.
Telephone: 0742-343123
Colours: Royal blue/white.

Blackhall, R. 21	Johnson, J. 37	Rushbury, D. 36
Bolder, R. 19	Leman, D. 16	Shirtliff, P. 26
Cox, B. 4	Lowey, J. 29	Smith, M. 20
Curran, E. 12	Mullen, J. 35	Sterland, M. 1
Dowd, H. 7	Nimmo, I. 8	Taylor, K. 5
Fleming, I. 6	Owen, G. 14	Turner, C. 23
Grant, D. 26	Pickering, M. 35	Tynan, T. 8
Hornsby, B. 44	Porterfield, I. 45	Wylde, R. 36

League Goalscorers—Hornsby 16, Wylde 14, Nimmo 4, Lowey 3, Owen 3, Johnson 3, Porterfield 2, Curran 1, Fleming 1, Grant 1, Mullen 1, Rushbury 1, Sterland 1, Shirtliff 1, Tynan 1.

Average Home League Gate— 10,817
All-time Record Attendance— 72,841 v. Manchester City (F.A. Cup) February 17, 1934.

SHREWSBURY TOWN

Ground: Gay Meadow, Shrewsbury.
Telephone: 0743-56068
Colours: Blue/amber stripes.

Atkins, I.	44	Hayes, S.	21	Loughnane, P.	3
Biggins, S.	44	Keay, J.	27	Maguire, P.	41
Birch, T.	13	King, J.	39	Mulhearn. K.	26
Chapman, S.	24	Larkin, T.	25	Turner, G.	32
Cross, S.	14	Leonard, C.	26	Tong, D.	35
Griffin, C.	46	Lindsay, J.	26	Wardle, R.	20

League Goalscorers—Maguire 13, Atkins 11, Biggins 9, King 6, Turner 5, Tong 5, Chapman 4, Griffin 2, Cross 2, Keay 2, Birch 2.

Average Home League Gate— 6,098
All-time Record Attendance— 18,917 v. Walsall (Division 3) April 26, 1961.

SOUTHEND UNITED

Ground: Roots Hall, Victoria Avenue, Southend-on-Sea, Essex, SS2 6NQ.
Telephone: 0702-40707
Colours: Blue shirts with red and white trim, white shorts with blue trim, white stockings with red and blue trim.

Abbott, P.	7	Horn, G.	7	Polycarpou, A.	21
Cawston, M.	39	Hull, J.	1	Pountney, R.	40
Cusack, D.	37	Laverick, M.	29	Stead, M.	38
Dudley, P.	46	Moody, A.	34	Townsend, N.	1
Fell, G.	22	Morris, C.	44	Walker, J.	11
Goodwin, S.	2	Otulakowski, A.	9	Yates, S.	42
Hadley, A.	33	Parker, D.	43		

League Goalscorers— Parker 10, Fell 7, Morris 7, Laverick 6, Polycarpou 5, Pountney 5, Dudley 3, Moody 3, Stead 2, Abbott 1, Cusack 1, Yates 1.

Average Home League Gate— 6,344
All-time Record Attendance— 31,036 v. Liverpool (F.A. Cup) January 10, 1979.

SWANSEA CITY

Ground: The Vetch Field, Swansea, W. Glamorgan, Wales.
Telephone: Swansea 42855/6
Colours: White with black motifs.

Attley, B. 20	Crudgington, G. 46	Morris, S. 5
Bartley, D. 39	Curtis, A. 34	Phillips, L. 28
Baker, M. 3	Evans, W. 36	Reeves, P. 2
Boersma, P. 15	James, A. 1	Smith, T. 31
Bruton, D. 7	James, R. 44	Stevenson, N. 38
Callaghan, I. 39	Marustik, C. 1	Toshack, J. 25
Charles, J. 38	Moore, K. 14	Waddle, A. 40

League Goalscorers—Waddle 19, James (R) 14, Curtis 13, Toshack 13, Charles 12, Baker 2, Bartley 2, Stevenson 2, Smith 2, Boersma 1, Attley 1, Moore 1, Opponents 1.

Average Home League Gate— 13,474
All-time Record Attendance— 32,796 v. Arsenal.

SWINDON TOWN

Ground: The County Ground, Swindon, Wiltshire.
Telephone: 0793-22118
Colours: Red shirts, white shorts and red socks.

Aizlewood, S. 39	Gilchrist, P. 10	Mayes, A. 21
Allan, J. 24	Guthrie, C. 6	Miller, I. 44
Bates, P. 34	Hamilton, B. 18	Ogden, C. 22
Carter, R. 46	Kamara, C. 22	Rowland, A. 28
Cunningham, D. 1	Lewis, R. 5	Stroud, K. 44
Ford, A. 6	McHale, R. 46	Trollope, N. 16
	McLaughlin, J. 18	Williams, B. 16

League Goalscorers—Bates 14, Rowland 12, Mayes 11, Carter 10, Gilchrist 6, McHale 6, Miller 4, Kamara 3, Aizlewood 2, Williams 2, Hamilton 1, McLaughlin 1, Opponents 2.

Average Home League Gate— 7,754
All-time Record Attendance— 32,000 v. Arsenal (F.A. Cup) January 15, 1972.

TRANMERE ROVERS

Ground: Prenton Park, Prenton Road West, Birkenhead, Merseyside.
Telephone: 051-608 4194
Colours: Shirts white with 4" diagonal royal blue stripe from left shoulder, shorts white, socks royal blue.

Bramhall, J. 35	Griffiths, I. 3	Parlios, M. 21
Cahill, P. 5	Johnson, D. 42	Parry, L. 46
Cliff, E. 6	Kerr, J. 22	Peplow, S. 23
Craven, S. 26	McAuley, H. 41	Postlewaite, D. 31
Eaton, S. 1	Mathias, R. 45	Thomas, J. 10
Evans, ... 46	Moore, R. 26	West, G. 4
Flood, E. 40	O'Neil, T. 32	Whittingham, S. 3
		Williams, J. 1

League Goalscorers— Evans 10, Moore 8, Peplow 8, Kerr 6, Bramhall 2, O'Neil 2, Craven 2, Thomas 2, Cliff 1, Parry 1, Postlewaite 1, Parlios 1, Opponent 1.

Average Home Leage Gate— 2,186
All-time Record Attendance— 24,424 v. Stoke City (F.A. Cup) February 5, 1972.

WALSALL

Ground: Fellows Park, Walsall WS2 9DB.
Telephone: 0922-22791
Colours: Red shirts with white collar, shorts: white with red and green stripe down side, Stockings: green with red top having white band.

Birch, A.	45	Kelly, J.	18	Serella, D.	43
Caswell, B.	41	McDonough, R.	31	Syrett, D.	11
Clarke, K.	1	Macken, A.	42	Rees, M.	7
Green, R.	1	Mower, K.	1	Turner, I.	21
Harrison, C.	30	Paul, I.	13	Waddington, P.	1
Jones, S.	15	Penn, D.	9	Waddington, S.	33
Kearns, M.	24	Sbragia, R.	32	Williams, J.	7
King, J.	34				

League Goalscorers—Austin 13, Birch 9, Buckley 5, McDonough 7, King 3, Penn 3, Sbragia 3, Syrett 3, Waddington (S) 3, Kelly 2, Caswell 1, Serella 1, Williams 1, Opponents 2.

Average Home League Gate— 4,101
All-time Record Attendance— 25,453 v. Newcastle United (Div. 2) August 29, 1961.

WATFORD

Ground: Vicarage Road Stadium, Watford, Herts.
Telephone: Watford 49747/8/9
Colours: Yellow shirts with red/black trim, red shorts with yellow/black strip, red socks yellow/black top.

Blissett, L.	41	Harrison, S.	23	Pritchett, K.	22
Booth, I.	37	Jenkins, R.	46	Rankin, A.	30
Bolton, I.	43	Joslyn, R.	45	Sherwood, S.	16
Downes, B.	37	Mayes, A.	5	Sims, S.	13
Ellis, S.	6			Mercer, K.	9
Garner, A.	43	Pollard, B.	33	Train, R.	20

League Goalscorers—Jenkins 29, Blissett 21, Bolton 9, Joslyn 8, Garner 4, Pollard 4, Downes 2, Mercer 2, Pritchett 2, Sims 1, Train 1.

Average Home League Gate— 14,424
All-time Record Attendance— 34,099 v. Manchester United (F.A. Cup) February 3, 1969.

FOURTH DIVISION

ALDERSHOT

Ground: Recreation Ground, High Street, Aldershot.
Colours: Red shirts, with blue and white trim. White shorts with blue and red trim, red socks with blue and white trim.

Brodie, M.	38	Hooper, W.	3	McGregor, A.	41
Crosby, M.	30	Howitt, D.	28	Scott, P.	9
Dixon, W.	36	Johnson, G.	46	Shanahan, T.	14
Dungworth, J.	46	Jopling, J.	39	Tomlin, D.	9
Earls, M.	3	Longhorn, D.	30	Wooler, A.	31
Edwards, N.	31	Needham, A.	29	Youlden, T.	43

League Goalscorers—Dungworth 26, Needham 10, Brodie 6, Shanahan 4, Dixon 3, Edwards 2, Longhorn 2, McGregor 2, Wooler 2, Crosby 1, Howitt 1, Jopling 1, Tomlin 1, Opponents 2.

Average Home League Gate— 4,185
All-time Record Attendance— 19,138 v. Carlisle Utd. (F.A. Cup) September 9, 1970.

BARNSLEY

Ground: Oakwell Ground, Grove Street, Barnsley S71 1ET.
Telephone: 0226-84113
Colours: Red shirts, white shorts, white stockings.

Bell, D.	32	Joicey, B.	6	Pugh, G.	42
Chambers, P.	45	Little, A.	40	Reed, G.	1
Clarke, A.	34	McCarthy, M.	46	Riley, G.	34
Collins, J.	46	Millar, A.	43	Saunders, J.	46
Copley, G.	1	Peachey, J.	12	Speedie, D.	5
Graham, T.	27	Prendergast, M.	1	Springett, P.	45

League Goalscorers—Bell 18, Clarke 12, Graham 12, Little 7, Millar 4, Pugh 4, Joicey 3, Riley 3, Peachey 2, McCarthy 2, Chambers 1, Collins 1, Saunders 2, Opponents 2.

Average Home League Gate— 11,048
All-time Record Attendance— 42,056 v. Stoke C. (F.A. Cup) February 15, 1936.

BOURNEMOUTH

Ground: Dean Court Ground, Bournemouth.
Telephone: Bournemouth 35381
Colours: Red and white

Allen, K.	46	Butler, M.	28	Lennard, D.	18
Barton, F.	22	Cunningham, J.	39	MacDougall, T.	29
Benjafield, B.	2	Ferns, P.	14	Massey, S.	28
Benson, J.	1	Finnigan, T.	3	Miller, K.	46
Borthwick, G.	42	Holder, P.	15	Scott, J.	19
Brown, K.	28	Impey, J.	38	Showers, D.	14
Brown, R.	45	Johnson, P.	21	Weeks, G.	3
Butler, G.	6				

League Goalscorers—Butler (M) 8, MacDougall 8, Massey 6, Brown (K) 5, Scott 4, Johnson 3, Barton 2, Brown (R) 2, Lennard 2, Showers 2, Borthwick 1, Finnigan 1, Impey 1, Opponents 2.

Average Home League Gate— 3,759
All-time Record Attendance— 28,799 v. Manchester United, March 2, 1957.

BRADFORD CITY

Ground: Valley Parade Ground, Bradford BD8 7DY.
Telephone: 02741-306062
Colours: All white, with claret and amber motifs side arms sleeves, side shorts.

Baines, S.	43	Jackson, D.	9	Reaney, P.	33
Bates, M.	30	Jackson, P.	8	Robertson, L.	14
Cook, J.	8	Johnson, R.	24	Smith, S.	21
Cooke, J.	16	Martinez, E.	15	Szabo, T.	8
Dolan, T.	40	McNiven, D.	42	Watson, G.	28
Downsborough, P.	25	Middleton, J.	23	Wood, M.	42
Hutchins, D.	37	Podd, C.	39	Gilliver, A.	1

League Goalscorers—McNiven 15, Dolan 10, Baines 10, Cooke 7, Hutchin 5, Robertson 3, Wood 3, Jackson (D) 3, Martinez 2, Cook 1, Szabo 1, Jackson (P) 1, Johnson 1.

Average Home League Gate— 3,927
All-time Record Attendance— 39,146 v. Burnley (F.A. Cup) March 11, 1911.

CREWE ALEXANDRA

Ground: Gresty Road, Crewe.
Telephone: Crewe 3014
Colours: Red shirts, white shorts, red and white socks.

Bevan, P.	44	Hughes,	12	Robertson, J.	32
Bowles, P.	45	Nelson, D.	31	Spence, C.	1
Brand, A.	1	Nicholls, P.	10	Tully, K.	6
Caswell, P.	21	Purdie, B.	39	Warnock, N.	20
Cheetham, H.	22	Rafferty, K.	21	White, E.	1
Coyne, P.	32	Rimmer, W.	20	Wilkinson, N.	25
Davies, D.	38	Rogan, M.	3	Wilshaw, S.	20
Dulson, G.	28	Roberts, I.	34		

League Goalscorers—Coyne 16, Bowles 8, Davies 8, Nelson 5, Purdie 2, Bevan 1, Warnock 1, Wilshaw 1, Opponents 1.

Average Home Leage Gate—1,990
All-time Record Attendance— 20,000 v. Tottenham (F.A. Cup) January 30, 1960.

DARLINGTON

Ground: Feethams Road, Darlington.
Telephone: Darlington 65097/67712
Colours: White shirts with red trim, black shorts, black socks.

Burleigh, M. 42	Hedley, G. 14	Peachey, J. 13
Cochrane, J. 39	Lyons, B. 26	Probert, E. 19
Crosson, D. 14	Maitland, L. 19	Seal, J. 35
Craig, D. 44	Nattress, C. 45	Stone, J. 41
Ferguson, R. 30	Owers, P. 4	Taylor, P. 2
Hague, N. 34	Paterson, T. 7	Walsh, A. 32
		Wann, J. 46

League Goalscorers—Stone 9, Walsh 9, Seal 8, Ferguson 6, Peachey 6, Lyons 2, Paterson 2, Wann 2, Cochrane 1, Hague 1, Hedley 1, Maitland 1, Nattress 1.

Average Home League Gate—1,814.
All-time Record Attendance— 21,023 v. Bolton (League Cup) November 14, 1960.

DONCASTER ROVERS

Ground: Belle Vue Ground, Doncaster DN4 5HT
Telephone: Doncaster 55281
Colours: Shirts: red with white trimmings, shorts: white, stockings: red with white trimmings.

Austin, R. 2	Hemsley, E. 8	Packer, P. 3
Bentley, D. 34	Habbin, R. 18	Peacock, D. 46
Bowden, P. 7	Laidlaw, J. 38	Pugh, D. 31
Bradley, D. 42	Lally, P. 31	Reed, S. 11
Cannell, S. 11	Lewis, J. 34	Robinson, F. 6
Cork, D. 7	Lister, S. 9	Snodin, G. 34
Cox, M. 11	Meagan, T. 30	Taylor, B. 13
Flanagan, S. 14	Olney, K. 32	Jones, C. 4
French, M. 36	Owen, R. 31	

League Goalscorers—Owen 10, Laidlaw 7, Lewis 5, French 5, Cox 3, Bradley 3, Snodin 3, Bentley 2, Habbin 2, Jones 2, Packer 2, Cork 1, Olney 1, Pugh 1, Reed 1, Taylor 1, Opponents 1.

Average Home League Gate— 3,004
All-time Record Attendance— 37,149 v. Hull Div. 3 (N)October 2, 1948.

GRIMSBY TOWN

Ground: Blundell Park, Cleethorpes, DN35 7PY.
Telephone: 0472-61420/61803
Colours: Black and white vertical striped shirts; black shorts; red socks.

Barker, G. 28	Drinkell, K. 20	Moore, D. 30
Batch, N. 46	Ford, T. 43	Moore, K. 46
Brolly, M. 44	Lester, M. 30	Partridge, M. 7
Crombie, D. 46	Liddell, G. 21	Waters, J. 46
Cumming, R. 31	Mawer, S. 15	Wiggington, C. 18
Donovan, T. 4	Mitchell, R. 24	Young, M. 7

League Goalscorers—Ford 16, Cumming 10, Waters 10, Brolly 8, Drinkell 7, Lester 7, Moore, (K) 7, Liddell 6, Donovan 3, Mitchell 2, Barker 1, Crombie 1, Young 1, Opponents 3.

Average Home League Gate—6,221
All-time Record Attendance— 31,657 v. Wolverhampton W. (F.A. Cup), February 20, 1937.

HALIFAX TOWN

Ground: Shay Ground, Halifax, W. Yorks, HX1 2YS.
Telephone: Halifax 53423
Colours: Blue and white.

Bell, D. 11	Hutt, G. 31	Mountford, R. 27
Bradley, L. 24	Johnson, K......... 42	Nixon, J. 24
Bullock, M. 12	Johnston, J. 6	Prendergast, M........4
Burke, P. 31	Kennedy, M........ 31	Sidebottom, A..... 21
Campbell, R.......... 22	Kilner, J. 21	Smith, S.............. 40
Carroll, J. 13	Lawson, J. 12	Stafford, A. 8
Dunleavy, C.......... 46	Leonard, M. 25	Trainer, J... 30
Firth, F................ 35		

League Goalscorers—Johnson 9, Mountford 4, Bell 3, Bradley 3, Campbell 3, Dunleavy 2, Firth 2, Sidebottom 2, Trainer 2, Bullock 2, Burke 2, Carroll 1, Lawson 1, Nixon 1, Prendergast 1, Opponents 1.

Average Home League Gate— 1,820
All-time Record Attendance— 36,885 v. Tottenham (F.A. Cup) February 14, 1953.

HARTLEPOOL UNITED

Ground: Victoria Ground, Clarence Road, Hartlepool.
Telephone: 72584
Colours: Blue and white stripes, white shorts, blue stockings.

Ayre, W. 41	Harding, A. 15	Newton, R. 23
Brooks, S............. 33	Hogan, R. 22	Norton, D. 8
Crumplin, I. 26	Houchen, K. 39	Platt, J................ 13
Edgar, E. 3	Larkin, G. 1	Richardson, G. 19
Evans, D................1	Linacre, J. 45	Smith, G. 43
Gorry, M.............. 41	Loadwick, D. 27	Smith, T. 15
Guy, K. 7	Lawrence, M. 34	Watson, J. 11
Goldthorpe, W....... 36	Malone, R. 3	

League Goalscorers—Houchen 13, Lawrence 9, Newton 8, Goldthorpe 6, Ayre 5, Crumplin 5, Linacre 5, Norton 2, Brooks 1, Harding 1, Hogan 1, Smith (T) 1.

Average Home League Gate—2,994
All-time Record Attendance— 17,426 v. Manchester United (F.A. Cup) January 5, 1959.

HEREFORD UNITED

Ground: Edgar Street, Hereford.
Telephone: 0432-4037
Colours: Shirts: white with red and black trim, shorts: black with red and white trim, stockings: black.

Barton, F. 4	Holmes, K..........25	Powell, W..............8
Bailey, M. 16	Holmes, W. 17	Price, C. 28
Bowston, B. 1	Hughes, T. 43	Spiring, P. 28
Burrows, P........... 33	Hunt, P. 12	Stephens, K.......... 29
Cornes, S. 21	Jones, D............26	Thomas, V. 12
Crompton, S. 8	Knight, L. 2	White, W............. 15
Emery, S. 43	Layton, J. 37	Feeley, A. 28
Gould, R.............. 39	McGrellis, F........ 11	Phillips, S. 8
Hendry, I. 14	Marshall, J........ 14	Strong, S.... 10

League Goalscorers—Gould 13, Jones 8, Spiring 5, Emery 4, Holmes 3, Holmes 3, White 3, McGrellis 3, Powell 2, Barton 1, Burrows 1, Bailey 1, Layton 1, Stephens 1, Crompton 1, Thomas 1, Opponents 2.

Average Home League Gate— 3,368
All-time Record Attendance— 18,114 v. Sheffield Wednesday, January 1958.

HUDDERSFIELD TOWN

Ground: Leeds Road, Huddersfield.
Telephone: Huddersfield 20335
Colours: Blue/white stripes, white shorts and socks.

Armstrong, T.	15	Gray, T.	22	Ridley, J.	2
Bielby, P.	29	Gartland, P.	4	Robins, I.	37
Branagan, J.	13	Hanvey, K.	32	Sandercock, P.	36
Brook, D.	1	Hart, P.	46	Starling, A.	45
Brown, M.	42	Holmes, I.	31	Sutton, D.	39
Cowling, D.	25	Howey, P.	10	Topping, C.	23
Fletcher, P.	31	Lillis, M.	11	Taylor, R.	1

League Goalscorers—Robins 17, Fletcher 12, Holmes 12, Bielby 5, Campbell 3, Hanvey 2, Sutton 1, Gray 1, Cowling 1, Hart 1, Armstrong 1.

Average Home League Gate— 3,750
All-time Record Attendance— 67,037 v. Arsenal (F.A. Cup) February 27, 1932.

NEWPORT COUNTY

Ground: Somerton Park, Newport, Gwent.
Telephone: 277543
Colours: Amber shirts, black shorts, amber socks.

Armstrong, K.	3	Jones, R.	2	Sinclair, C.	14
Bailey, N.	20	Lee, T.	1	Thompson, T.	26
Brown, J.	2	Lowndes, S.	43	Tynan, T.	20
Bruton, D.	34	McGeady, J.	2	Vaughan, N.	23
Byrne, T.	26	Moore, K.	21	Walden, R.	40
Clark, B.	1	Oakes, K.	33	Walker, R.	6
Cosslett, M.	1	Plumley, G.	45	Warriner, S.	16
Davies, G.	38	Relish, J.	20	Williams, M.	3
Goddard, H.	46			Woods, E.	19

League Goalscorers—Goddard 18, Lowndes 8, Tynan 7, Bruton 5, Oakes 5, Moore 4, Sinclair 4, Vaughan 4, Woods 2, Walden 2, Williams 1, Bailey 1, Clark 1, Davies 1, Thompson 1, Warriner 1, Opponents 1.

Average Home League Gate—3,732
All-time record attendance—24,268 v. Cardiff City (Div. 3(S) October 16, 1937.

NORTHAMPTON TOWN

Ground: County Ground, Abington Avenue, Northampton.
Telephone: Northampton 31553
Colours: White shirts, claret trim, white shorts, white socks with two claret rings round turnover.

Ashenden, R. 2
Bower, K. 2
Bryant, S. 28
Christie, D. 15
Cordice, N. 34
Farrington, J. 46
Froggatt, J. 42
Geidmintis, T. 45
Jayes, C. 28
Liddle, P. 3
Matthews, ... 13
McCaffrey, J. 25
Mead, P. 38
Poole, A. 18
Reilly, G. 42
Robertson, S. 38
Saunders, P. 24
Waldock, D. 3
Walker, R. 10
Wassell, K. 10
Williams, K. 45
Wollett, A. 23

League Goalscorers—Reilly 19, Froggatt 13, Farrington 8, Robertson 5, McCaffrey 4, Bryant 3, Christie 3, Mead 3, Williams 2, Cordice 1, Geidmintis 1, Liddle 1, Opponents 1.

Average Home League Gate— 2,895
All-time Record Attendance— 24,523 v. Fulham (Division 1) April 23, 1966.

PORTSMOUTH

Ground: Fratton Park, Frogmore Road, Portsmouth, Hampshire.
Telephone: Portsmouth 731204/5
Colours: Blue shirts, with white trim on collar and cuffs, white shorts, red socks.

Barnard, L. 29
Bryant, S. 16
Davey, S. 46
Denyer, P. 43
Ellis, P. 44
Foster, S. 36
Garwood, C. 37
Hemmerman, J.... 37
Knight, A. .... -
Lathan, J. 45
Mellor, P. 46
McIlwraith, J. 26
Piper, S. 14
Pullar, D. 40
Showers, D. 20
Viney, K. 39
Roberts, T. 3

League Goalscorers—Garwood 15, Hemmerman 14, Davey 7, Barnard 7, Denyer 6, Lathan 4, Foster 2, Showers 2, Viney 2, Hand 1, Wilson 1, Pullar 1.

Average Home League Gate— 10,123
All-time Record Attendance— 51,385 v. Derby Co. (F.A. Cup) February 26, 1949.

PORT VALE

Ground: Vale Park, Burslem, Stoke-on-Trent ST6 1AW.
Telephone: 0782-814134
Colours: White shirts, black trim, black shorts, white socks black hoop.

Beech, K. 27
Beamish, K. 6
Bentley, W. 34
Bloor, A. 6
Bromage, R. 21
Chamberlain, N. 26
Chamberlain, M. 10
Connaughton, J. 19
Dance, T. 26
Delgado, R. 30
Elsby, I. 5
Farrell, P. 28
Froggatt, J. 2
Griffiths, N. 26
Hawkins, G. 40
Harris, D. 10
Healy, F. 22
Keenan, G. 32
Proudlove, A. 5
Ridley, J. 7
Sinclair, B. 19
Sproson, P. 29
Stenson, G. 10
Sutcliffe, P. 8
Todd, K. 42
Tully, K. 8
Wilkinson, N. 7
Wright, B. 46

League Goalscorers—Wright 16, Todd 8, Chamberlain (N) 6, Beamish 4, Farrell 4, Beech 3, Bromage 2, Healy 2, Sinclair 2, Hawkins 2, Chamberlain (M) 1, Keenan 1, Sutcliffe 1, Tully 1, Griffiths 1, Bloor 1, Opponents 2.

Average Home League Gate— 3,286
All-time Record Attendance— 50,000 v. Aston Villa (F.A. Cup) February 2, 1960.

READING

Ground: Elm Park, Norfolk Road, Reading.
Telephone: Reading 57878/9/0
Colours: Blue and white hoops, white shorts, white socks.

Alexander, J.	15	Hicks, M.	46	Sanchez, L.	35
Bennett, P.	45	Kearney, M.	31	Shipley, G.	11
Bowman, R.	34	Kearns, O.	19	Wanklyn, W.	13
Death, S.	46	Lewis, A.	40	White, M.	46
Earles, P.	37	Peters, G.	45	Williams, J.	1
Hetzke, S.	42				

League Goalscorers—Earles 14, Kearns 11, Kearney 11, Bowman 10, Hetzke 9, Alexander 8, Lewis 4, Sanchez 4, Bennett 1, Hicks 1, Peters 1, Shipley 1, Opponents 1.

Average Home League Gate—7,383.
All-time Record Attendance— 33,042 v. Brentford (F.A. Cup) February 19, 1927.

ROCHDALE

Ground: Spotland, Rochdale.
Telephone: 44648
Colours: Blue shirts with white trim, white shorts, with blue trim, blue stockings.

Ashworth, P.	9	Hilditch, M.	18	Owen, T.	39
Bannon, I.	14	Hoy, R.	37	Price, J.	8
Collins, J.	6	Jones, C.	20	Scaife, R.	32
Creamer, P.	17	Milne, M.	3	Scott, R.	29
Esser, D.	35	Morrin, T.	1	Shyne, C.	10
Felgate, D.	33	Mullington, P.	8	Slack, A.	1
Hallows, P.	18	Oliver, E.	6	Snookes, E.	35
Hart, B.	37	O'Loughlin, N.	43	Taylor, B.	25

League Goalscorers—Owen 12, Hoy 10, Jones 10, Esser 4, Hilditch 3, Scott 2, Scaife 2, Snookes 1, O'Loughlin 1, Oliver 1, Taylor 1.

Average Home League Gate— 1,770
All-time Record Attendance— 24,231 v. Notts. County (F.A. Cup) December 10, 1969.

SCUNTHORPE UNITED

Ground: Old Show Ground, Scunthorpe, South Humberside, DN15 7RH.
Telephone: Scunthorpe 2954
Colours: Shirts Red with white collar and cuffs, shorts, red, stockings: red.

Bloomer, B.	3	Earl, S.	23	Kilmore, K.	44
Couch, G.	14	Gibson, D.	14	Oates, R.	45
Crawford, G.	46	Grimes, V.	45	O'Donnell, J.	33
Czuczman, M.	39	Hall, D.	9	Peacock, J.	26
Davy, S.	12	Kavanagh, E.	37	Pilling S.	29
Deere, S.	45	Keeley, N.	25	Wigg, R.	17

League Goalscorers—Kilmore 16, Earl 8, Pilling 6, Grimes 5, Couch 5, Oates 3, Wigg 3, Kavanagh 2, Keeley 2, Bloomer 1, Deere 1, Gibson 1, Opponents 1.

Average Home League Gate— 2,721
All-time Record Attendance— 23,935 v. Portsmouth (F.A. Cup) January 30, 1954.

STOCKPORT COOUNTY

Ground: Edgeley Park, Stockport, Cheshire SK3 9DD.
Telephone: Stockport 8888/9
Colours: Sky blue and white stripes, dark blue shorts, white socks with blue trim.

Armstrong, G.	34	Goodfellow, J.	2	Rogan, M.	24
Bradd, L.	45	Henson, P.	34	Rutter, J.	45
Cahill, P.	3	Lawson, D.	18	Smith, G.	18
Cassidy, A.	4	Lee, S.	45	Seddon, A.	1
Connor, J.	1	Loadwick, D.	11	Summerbee, M.	33
Edwards, P.	41	Park, T.	29	Sumner, A.	3
Fogarty, K.	20	Prudham, E.	19	Thorpe, A.	37

League Goalscorers—Lee 20, Bradd 18, Henson 5, Thompson 4, Park 4, Edwards 2, Prudham 2, Halford 1, Summerbee 1, Opponents 1.

Average Home League Gate— 4,142
All-time Record Attendance— 27,833 v. Liverpool (F.A. Cup) February 11, 1950.

TORQUAY UNITED

Ground: Plainmoor, Torquay.
Telephone: Torquay 38666
Colours: White, blue, white.

Boulton, C.	11	Dunne, J.	43	Raper, K.	21
Clarke, S.	4	Green, M.	33	Ritchie, S.	17
Cox, M.	2	Johnson, B.	5	Turner, J.	46
Coffill, P.	27	Lawrence, L.	42	Twitchin, I.	45
Cooper, S.	28	Murphy, D.	37	Vassallo, B.	1
Davies, R.	39	Parsons, L.	13	Wilson, A.	38
Darke, P.	33	Payne, J.	38		

League Goalscorers—Lawrence 17, Cooper 14, Murphy 10, Green 3, Davies 3, Coffill 3, Cox 2, Wilson 2, Johnson 2, Raper 1, Payne 1.

Average Home League Gate— 2,669
All-time Record Attendance— 21,736 v. Huddersfield (F.A. Cup) January, 20, 1955.

WIGAN ATHLETIC

Ground: Springfield Park, Wigan.
Telephone: Wigan 44433
Colours: Blue and white vertical striped shirts, blue shorts white stockings.

Brown, J.	42	Gay, G.	1	Seddon, I.	1
Brownbill, D.	20	Gillibrand, I.	7	Smart, K.	40
Corrigan, F.	45	Gore, T.	46	Ward, N.	44
Crompton, A.	7	Grew, M.	4	Wilkie, J.	3
Curtis, J.	8	Hinnigan, J.	40		
Davids, N.	10	Houghton, P.	23	Wright, J.	46
Fretwell, D.	33	Moore, M.	40		

League Goalscorers—Houghton 13, Purdie 11, Moore 9, Wright 7, Brownbill 6, Hinnigan 5, Corrigan 4, Ward 4, Gore 2, Smart 1, Opponents 1.

Average Home League Gate— 6,701
All-time Record Attendance— 27,500 v. Hereford United, December 1953.

WIMBLEDON

Ground: Durnsford Road, Wimbledon, London SW19.
Telephone: 01-946 6311/2/3
Colours: Yellow and blue shirts, blue shorts, yellow and blue socks.

Bowgett, P.	11	Downes, W.	3	Haverson, P.	26
Briley, L.	26	Driver, P.	3	Ketteridge, S.	15
Bryant, J.	27	Dziadulewicz, M.	1	Knowles, R.	23
Connell, R.	2	Eames, T.	26	Leslie, J.	44
Cork, A.	45	Galliers, S.	44	Parsons, S.	34
Cowley, F.	3	Galvin, D.	33	Perkins, S.	26
Cunningham, T.	15	Goddard, R.	45	Priddy, P.	1
Denny, P.	24	Harwood, L.	1	Summerill, P.	5
Donaldson, D.	23				

League Goalscorers—Cork 22, Leslie 19, Denny 7, Parsons 7, Knowles 5, Cunningham 3, Galliers 3, Bryant, 2 Galvin 2, Ketteridge 2, Downes 1, Driver 1, Eames 1, Haverson 1, Opponents 2

Average Home League Gate— 3,712
All-time Record Attendance— 18,000 v. H.M.S. Victory (F.A. Amateur Cup 1932-33).

YORK CITY

Ground: Bootham Crescent, York, YO3 7AQ.
Telephone: York 24447
Colours: Red shirts, blue shorts, red socks.

Bainbridge, P.	2	Loggie, D.	36	Staniforth, G.	45
Brown, G.	24	McDonald, I.	43	Stronach, P.	22
Clements, A.	46	Neenan, J.	22	Walsh, J.	38
Collier, G.	5	Pugh, D.	31	Warnock, N.	1
Faulkner, S.	44	Randall, K.	37	Wellings, B.	10
Ford, G.	32	Scott, P.	11	Young, A.	11
Kay, R.	46				

League Goalscorers—Staniforth 15, Randall 10, Loggie 8, McDonald 6, Ford 4, Clements 2, Stronach 2, Wellings 2, Faulkner 1, Opponents 1.

Average Home League Gate— 2,929
All-time Record Attendance— 28,123 v. Huddersfield (F.A. Cup) March 5, 1938.

SCOTTISH LEAGUE ROLL CALL

PREMIER DIVISION

ABERDEEN

Ground: Pittodrie Park, Aberdeen.
Telephone: Aberdeen 21428
Colours: Scarlet shirts, white collars and cuffs, scarlet shorts, red socks.

Archibald, S. 30
Clark, R. 23
Considine, J. 3
Cooper, N. 3
Davidson, D. 7
Fleming, I. 4
Gardiner, J. 2
Garner, W. 12
Hamilton, D. 9
Harper, J. 25
Jarvie, D. 24
Kennedy, J. 32
Leighton, J. 11
McGhee, M. 11
McLeish, A. 18
McLelland, C. 25
McMaster, J. 24
Miller, W. 34
Ritchie, S. 1
Rougvie, D. 16
Scanlon, I. 22
Strachan, G. 26
Sullivan, D. 32
Watson, A. 2

League Goalscorers—Harper 18, Archibald 13, Strachan 5, Sullivan 5, Jarvie 4, McGhee 4, Davidson 2, McMaster 2, Scanlon 2, Cooper 1, Fleming 1, McLeish 1.

CELTIC

Ground: Celtic Park
Telephone: 041-554 2710
Colours: Green and white hooped shirts, white shorts.

Aitken, R. 36
Baines, R. 7
Bonnar, P. 2
Burns, T. 27
Casey, J. 1
Conn, A. 12
Conroy, M. 20
Davidson, V. 12
Doyle, J. 23
Edvaldsson, J. 34
Filippi, J. 19
Glavin, R. 9
Latchford, P. 27
Lennox, R. 6
Lynch, A. 27
McAdam, T. 24
McCluskey, G. 16
McDonald, R. 18
McGrain, D. 18
McLeod, M. 23
Provan, D. 30
Sneddon, A. 4

League Goalscorers—Lynch 7, McAdam 7, Conn 6, Aitken 5, McCluskey 5, Conroy 4, Lennox 4, Provan 4, Burns 3, Glavin 3, McLeod 3, Davidson 2, Doyle 2, McDonald 2, McGrain 2, Edvaldsson 1, Opponents 1.

DUNDEE UNITED

Ground: Tannadice Park.
Telephone: Dundee 86104
Colours: All tangerine with black facings.

Addison, D. 24
Dodds, D. 19
Frye, D. 5
Hegarty, P. 36
Holt, J. 26
Honeyman, G. 2
Kirkwood, W. 32
Kopel F. 11
McAlpine, H. 36
Narey, D. 36
Payne, G. 19
Phillip, I. 9
Robinson, R. 8
Smith, W. 5
Stark, D. 30
Stewart, R. 34
Sturrock, P. 31

League Goalscorers—Kirkwood 11, Dodds 10, Sturrock 6, Narey 5, Hegarty 4, Stewart 4, Addison 3, Fleming 3, Payne 3, Holt 5ee3 eee3 ents 1.

HEARTS OF MIDLOTHIAN

Ground: Tynecastle Park.
Telephone: 031-337 6132
Colours: Maroon shirts, white trim and white shorts, maroon socks.

Allan, T. 16
Bannon, E. 19
Black, J. 10
Brough, J. 2
Brown, J. 22
Busby, D. 25
Craig, J. 14
Dunlop, R. 18
Fraser, C. 36
Gibson, W. 33
Jeffries, J. 26
Kidd, J. 29
Liddell, F. 31
McCall, W. 1
McLeod, T. 2
McNicoll, D. 15
McQuade, D. 13
More, C. 4
O'Connor, D. 18
O'Sullivan, D. 2
Park, D. 2
Prentice, R. 6
Robertson, M. 27
Rodger, P. 2
Scott, W. 3
Shaw, G. 8
Stewart, R. 4
Tierney, L. 8

League Goalscorers—O'Connor 8, Busby 6, Gibson 6, Bannon 5, McQuade 4, Robertson 4, Fraser 3, Park 1, Shaw 1.

HIBERNIAN

Ground: Easter Road Park
Telephone: 031-661 2159
Colours: Green shirts with white collars and sleeves, white shorts, green and white socks.

Brazil, A. 17
Bremner, D. 31
Brown, S. 10
Callachan, R. 33
Campbell, C. 16
Carrol, P. 1
Duncan, A. 35
Fleming, R. 11
Higgins, A. 21
Hutchinson, R. 19
Kilgour, J. 5
Lambie, J. 4
McArthur, J. 18
McDonald M. 18
McLeod, A. 36
McNamara, J. 35
Mathisen, S. 2
Murray, W. 6
O'Brien, G. 2
Rae, G. 24
Refvik, I. 5
Smith, R. 17
Stewart, G. 27
Temperley, W. 3

League Goalscorers—Callachan 9, McLeod 8, Rae 7, Bremner 5, Higgins 4, Hutchinson 4, Campbell 3, Brazil 1, Duncan 1, Stewart 1, Temperley 1, Opponents 1.

MORTON

Ground: Cappielow Park.
Telephone: Greenock 23571
Colours: Blue and white hooped shirts, white shorts and socks.

Anderson, G. 12
Baines, R. 14
Brcic, D. 6
Connachan, D. 16
Evans, B. 15
Hayes, D. 28
Holmes, J. 35
Hutchison, R. 16
McLaren, W. 18
McLean, J. 1
McNeill, J. 21
Miller, J. 33
Orr, N. 35
Rae, D. 1
Ritchie, A. 35
Rooney, J. 26
Russell, R. 23
Scott, A. 24
Thomson, R. 30
Tolmie, J. 7

League Goalscorers—Ritchie 22, Thomson 11, Russell 5, McNeill 4, Scott 3, Tolmie 3, Anderson 1, Hutchison 1, Ronney 1, Opponents 1.

MOTHERWELL

Ground: Fir Park
Telephone: Motherwell 63229
Colours: Amber strip with claret and white trim.

Boyd, J. 9
Capaldi, J. 3
Carberry, W. 9
Carr, R. 6
Clinging, I. 29
Dempsey, J. 10
Donnelly, J. 14
Hare, W. 1
Irvine, W. 9
Kane, T. 2
Kennedy, I. 5
Larnach, M. 27
Latchford, D. 8
Leonard, M. 2
Lindsay, J. 7
McLaren, S. 12
McLeod, I. 21
McVie, W. 16
Mackin, A. 7
Marinello, P. 14
Meikle, R. 1
Millar, P. 13
Mungall, S. 1
Pettigrew, W. 30
Rafferty, R. 4
Rennie, S. 28
Shanks, M. 10
Smith, J. 14
Sommerville, J. 3
Stevens, G. 31
Wark, J. 33
Wilson, P. 18

League Goalscorers—Pettigrew 6, Stevens 6, Clinging 5, Irvine 4, Larnach 4, Lindsay 1, McLaren 1, Marinello 1, Millar 1, Wilson 1, Opponents 1.

PARTICK THISTLE

Ground: Firhill Park, Glasgow, N.W.
Telephone: 041-946 2673
Colours: Red and yellow shirts, broad vertical stripes, black shorts, red socks.

Anderson, A. 17
Campbell, J. 30
Craig, J. 1
Doyle, J. 4
Gibson, I. 21
Houston, R. 31
Love, J. 13
McAdam, C. 22
McDonald, I. 1
Mackie, G. 1
McKinnon, D. 35
McLean, A. 1
McQuade, D. 1
Marr, J. 29
Melrose, J. 29
O'Hara, A. 26
Park, D. 30
Rough, A. 35
Sheed, R. 1
Somner, D. 31
Thomson, W. 1
Whittaker, B. 36

League Goalscorers—Somner 11, Melrose 9, O'Hara 8, Houston 4, McAdam 4, Park 2, Anderson 1, Gibson 1, Sheed 1.

RANGERS

Ground: Ibrox Park.
Telephone: 041-427 0159
Colours: Royal blue shirts, white shorts, black socks.

Cooper, D. 26
Dawson, A. 23
Forsyth, A. 16
Forsyth, T. 17
Jackson, C. 28
Jardine, A. 35
Johnstone, D. 31
McCloy, P. 36
McDonald, A. 33
McLean, T. 34
Miller, A. 10
Morris, E. 1
Parlane, D. 21
Russell, R. 36
Smith, G. 32
Strickland, D. 1
Urquhart, W. 6
Watson, K. 11

League Goalscorers—Smith 11, Johnstone 9, Cooper 5, McDonald 5, Forsyth (A) 4, Russell 4, Urquhart 4, Watson 2, Dawson 1, Jackson 1, Robertson 1, McLean 1, Opponents 1.

ST. MIRREN

Ground: St. Mirren Park.
Telephone: 041-889 2558
Colours: Black and white strips, white shorts and socks.

Abercrombie, W. 30
Beckett, A. 12
Bone, J. 33
Copland, J. 36
Docherty, B. 1
Dunlop, A. 36
Fitzpatrick, T. 36
Hyslop, D. 3
McGarvey, F. 33
McLean, A. 2
Munro, I. 34
Mowat, J. 1
Richardson, L. 28
Sharp, R. 2
Stark, W. 32
Thomson, W. 34
Torrance, R. 14
Weir, J. 4
Young, J. 25

League Goalscorers—McGarvey 13, Stark 9, Bone 7, Torrance 6, Fitzpatrick 3, Abercrombie 2, Hyslop 2, Copland 1, Richardson 1, Young 1.

FIRST DIVISION

AIRDRIEONIANS

Ground: Broomfield Park.
Telephone: Airdrie 62067
Colours: White shirts with red diamond, white shorts, black socks.

Anderson, N. 26
Black, J. 22
Clark, A. 38
Cowan, M. 17
Curran, J. 1
Docherty, A. 7
Goldthorp, J. 31
Gordon, J. 3
Henderson, W. 1
Irwin, J. 2
Jonquin, P. 25
Kirkland, B. 5
Lapsley, J. 38
McCann, K. 14
McCormack, J. 3
McCulloch, J. 7
McGarr, E. 28
McGuire, W. 34
McKeown, R. 7
McVeigh, J. 11
March, J. 25
Newman, A. ....
Poulton, M. 7
Ross, J. 2
Short, M. 8
Smith, J. 18
Veitch, T. 14
Walker, T. 30
Wilson, W. 1

League Goalscorers—Clark 24, Goldthorp 15, McGuire 8, Lapsley 6, McVeigh 4, March 4, McCann 2, Jonquin 1, McCormack 1, McCulloch 1, McKeown 1, Short 1, Smith 1, Walker 1, Kirkland 1.

ARBROATH

Ground: Gayfield Park.
Telephone: Arbroath 72157
Colours: Maroon shirts white shorts, maroon socks.

Cargill, T. 39
Carson, J. 31
Edwards, A. 6
Fettes, A. 27
Fletcher, J. 30
Follon, N. 6
Gavine, W. 28
Grant, I. 1
Kidd, A. 37
Kydd, L. 19
Lister, J. 39
McKenzie, A. 39
Mitchell, J. 4
Mylles, S. 16
Newman, A. 3
Rylance, D. 39
Smith, J. 2
Wells, W. 15
Wilson, T. 14
Yule, T. 32

League Goalscorers—Yule 10, Mylles 8, Gavine 7, Kidd 7, Fletcher 5, Wilson 4, Carson 2, Kydd 2, McKenzie 1, Mitchell 1, Opponents 1.

AYR UNITED

Ground: Somerset Park.
Telephone: Ayr 63435
Colours: White shirts, with black facings, black shorts, white socks.

Brown, J.	1	McAllister, W.	39	Masterton, D.	17
Christie, G.	32	McCall, W.	10	Northcote, R.	1
Connor, R.	27	McColl, B.	33	Phillips, G.	22
Cramond, G.	39	McCutcheon, D.	8	Reilly, R.	1
Fleeting, R.	16	McIlwraith, J.	1	Scott, J.	1
Hannah, R.	4	McLuaghlin, B.	38	Sproat, H.	38
Hyslop, D.	5	McLelland, S.	20	Wells, D.	33
Kelly, J.	16	McSherry, J.	27		

League Goalscorers—McLaughlin 19, Phillips 14, Christie 6, McCall 5, McCutcheon 5, McSherry 5, Masterton 5, Cramond 4, Wells 2, McAllister 1, McLelland 1, Reilly 1, Opponents 1.

CLYDE

Ground: Shawfield Stadium.
Telephone: 041-647 6329
Colours: White shirts, with red facings, black shorts.

Ahern, B.	38	Henderson, I.	3	Martin, J.	12
Arrol, J.	37	Hood, N.	30	Mitchell, W.	1
Brogan, J.	29	Kean, J.	13	Nelson, J.	1
Clougherty, M.	37	Kinnear, B.	33	O'Neill, W.	34
Anderson, E.	38	McCabe, G.	32	Thorburn, W.	6
Ferris, R.	7	McGettrick, J.	13	Ward, J.	14
Grant, A.	23	Marshall, G.	26	Young, W.	2

League Goalscorers—Ward 10, Ahern 8, Grant 8, Hood 7, Marshall 7, O'Neill 4, McCabe 3, Kean 2, Brogan 1, Anderson 1, Ferris 1.

CLYDEBANK

Ground: Kilbowie Park.
Telephone: 041-952 2887
Colours: White shirts with red and black vertical strips on the left breast and red stripes on sleeves, white shorts, white socks.

Abel, G.	37	Gallacher, J.	36	McCulloch, D.	5
Bannon, W.	1	Gervaise, T.	1	McDougall, F.	36
Brown, D.	4	Given, J.	37	McIntyre, J.	2
Bryan, J.	3	Gourlay, I.	4	McLaughlin, J.	12
Colgan, G.	37	Hall, N.	38	Miller, B.	37
Fallon, J.	38	Houston, D.	38	Ross, J.	1
Fanning, J.	24	McCormack, J.	39		

League Goalscorers—Miller 28, McDougall 25, McCormack 10, Hall 3, Houston 3, Colgan 2, Given 2, Brown 1, Fallon 1, Fanning 1, McIntyre 1, McLaughlin 1.

DUMBARTON

Ground: Boghead Park.
Telephone: Dumbarton 62569
Colours: White shirts with gold horizontal band between two black bands, white shorts and socks.

Anderson, I. 1	Gallacher, B.......... 33	McNeill, D. 21
Blair, R. 27	Gallacher, J. 39	Muir, J. 9
Brown, A. 26	Hunter, A. 15	Sharpe, G. 4
Campbell, J. 12	McCluskey, P. 38	Sinclair, G. 27
Coyle, J. 24	McLean, H. 14	Whiteford, D. 18
Coyle, T. 7	McLeod, A. 17	Whiteford, J. 11
Findlay, W. 9	McLeod, M. 27	Williams, L. 24
Fyfe, G. 26		

League Goalscorers—Blair 8, Gallacher (B) 8, Whiteford (D) 7, Fyfe 7, Brown 4, McNeill 3, Coyle 3, Whiteford (J) 3, McCluskey 2, McLean 2, McLeod (M) 2, Sinclair 2, Muir 2, Findlay 1, Sharpe 1.

DUNDEE

Ground: Dens Park.
Telephone: Dundee 81604
Colours: Dark blue shirts and shorts, red socks.

Barr, J. 21	McGhee, J. 20	Redford, I. 35
Caldwell, A. 13	McKinnon, D. 1	Schaedler, E. 27
Davidson, A. 3	McLaren, S. 21	Scott, J. 1
Donaldson, A. 39	McPhail, I. 2	Scrimgeour, B. 3
Glennie, R. 37	Millar, P. 16	Shirra, J. 28
Lamb, A. 23	Murphy, J. 10	Sinclair, E. 27
McDougall, I. 9	Phillip, I. 7	Watson, J. 34
McGeachie, G. 3	Pirie, W. 31	Williamson, W. 19

League Goalscorers—Pirie 16, Redford 15, Sinclair 10, Shirra 5, McLaren 4, Williamson 4, Lamb 2, McGhee 2, Murphy 2, Barr 1, Caldwell 1, Glennie 1, McDougall 1, Phillip 1, Schaedler 1, Opponents 2.

HAMILTON ACADEMICALS

Ground: Douglas Park.
Telephone: Hamilton 23108
Colours: Red and white hooped shirts white shorts and socks.

Alexander, E. 38	Grant, J. 23	McManus, M. 20
Dempsey, J. 39	Howe, S. 3	McQuade, W. 5
Fairlie, J. 36	Howie, N. 33	Morrison, J. 7
Ferguson, R. 39	Kellaghan, J. 32	O'Donnell, J. 2
Frew, J. 34	McCulloch, A. 14	Reilly, J. 1
Glavin, T... . 14	McDougall, J. 1	Weir, J. 5
Gormley, J. . ..1	McDowall, D. 10	Wright, B. 17
Graham, R. 38	McGrogan, J. 9	Young, A. 10

League Goalscorers—Graham 18, Fairlie 14, Howie 10, Glavin 3, Morrison 3, Wright 3, Dempsey 2 McCulloch 2, McManus 2, McDowall 1, McGrogan 1, O'Donnell 1.

KILMARNOCK

Ground: Rugby Park.
Telephone: Kilmarnock 25184
Colours: White shirts with blue and white centre panel, white shorts and socks.

Armstrong, K. 4
Bourke, J. 27
Cairney, J. 26
Clark, J. 32
Clarke, P. 37
Docherty, J. 8
Gibson, I. 24
Hughes, W. 8
Jardine, I. 27
McCulloch, A. 39
McDowall, J. 5
McLean, A. 38
Mauchlen, A. 21
Maxwell, G. 33
Murdoch, W. 1
Provan, D. 5
Robertson, A. 37
Street, R. 11
Taylor, W. 2
Welsh, F. 8

League Goalscorers—Bourke 21, Maxwell 11, Cairney 9, Gibson 9, Street 5, Clark (J) 3, Hughes 3, Docherty 2, Jardine 2, McDicken 2, McDowall 2, Clarke (P) 1, Provan 1.

MONTROSE

Ground: Links Park.
Telephone: Montrose 3200
Colours: Royal blue shirts and shorts, white socks.

Beardie, W. 9
Cormack, R. 5
Daun, D. 10
D'Arcy, B. 36
D'Arcy, D. 34
Downie, C. 1
Ford, J. 25
Georgeson, W. 19
Gorman, D. 24
Hair, I. 30
Johnston, W. 22
Joss, K. 7
Livingstone, R. 18
Lowe, M. 35
McIntosh, J. 21
Miller, R. 20
Mitchell, J. 1
Moffat, J. 15
Murray, T. 24
Newman, A. 1
Robb, D. 28
Shirran, J. 10
Taylor, K. 11
Walker, A. 20
Wright, A. 1

League Goalscorers—Murray 11, Robb 9, Miller 7, Georgeson 5, Livingstone 4, Lowe 4, McIntosh 4, Hair 3, Cormack 1, D'Arcy (B) 1, D'Arcy (D) 1, Ford 1, Wright 1, Opponents 2.

QUEEN OF THE SOUTH

Ground: Palmerston Park.
Telephone: Dumfries 4853
Colours: Royal blue shirts, with white facings, white shorts, royal blue socks.

Alexander, J. 2
Ball, A. 17
Boyd, C. 36
Bryce, T. 31
Carson, J. 3
Clark, D. 7
Clark, R. 39
Cloy, G. 26
Coughlin, J. 29
Dempster, J. 28
Dickson, G. 7
Dickson, P. 31
Ferrie, B. 6
Halley, P. 33
Hewitson, D. 1
Lyle, W. 5
McCann, J. 9
McChesney, I. 33
McLaren, W. 1
McMillan, W. 8
Mitchell, I. 23
Muldoon, J. 2
O'Hara, J. 12
Pollock, M. 15
Poulton, M. 10
Robertson, J. 1
Shields, J. 5
Thorburn, R. 9

League Goalscorers—Bryce 13, Coughlin 7, Dempster 6, Dickson (P) 4, McChesney 3, Boyd 2, Mitchell 2, Clark (R) 1, Dickson (G) 1, Halley 1, McCann 1, Pollock 1, Shields 1, Opponents 2.

RAITH ROVERS

Ground: Stark's Park.
Telephone: Kirkcaldy 3514
Colours: Royal blue shirts, white shorts and socks.

Candlish, C. 37	Hunter, D. 4	Pettie, G. 5
Duncan, R. 26	McComb, L. 5	Taylor, J. 15
Ford, R. 12	McDermott, M. ... 39	Thomson, D. 24
Forrest, G. 11	McDonough, B. ... 20	Thomson, R. 19
Forsyth, A. 31	McFarlane, T. 22	Urquhart, D. 38
Harrow, A. 38	Murray, T. 18	Wallace, G. 34
Houston, T. 30	Myles, J. 1	

League Goalscorers—Wallace 14, Harrow 10, Forrest 6, Duncan 2, McDonough 2, Thomson (D) 2, Candlish 1, Ford 1, Hunter 1, McComb 1, McFarlane 1, Murray 1, Myles 1, Pettie 1, Taylor 1, Thomson (R) 1, Urguhart 1, Opponents 3.

ST. JOHNSTONE

Ground: Muirton Park.
Telephone: Perth 26961
Colours: Royal blue shirts with white trim, white shorts and socks.

Brannigan, A. 14	McCoist, J. 4	Redford, J. 7
Brogan, J. 36	MacKay, J. 11	Robertson, D. 18
Fitzpatrick, J. 7	McLellan, L. 8	Ross, D. 5
Geoghegan, A. 21	McNeill, T. 35	Rutherford, D. 39
Gray, H. 9	Montgomery, S. 6	Salisbury, A. 4
Hamilton, G. 20	Muir, L. 36	Thomas, W. 11
Hamilton, J. 12	O'Brien, J. 3	Ward, P. 7
Houston, D. 8	O'Connor, D. 10	Weir, J. 32
Lawson, M. 20	Pelosi, J. 31	Wright, J. 9
McCall, W. 5		

League Goalscorers—Brogan 14, Lawson 11, Rutherford 7, Brannigan 5, Pelosi 4, Ward 4, McNeill 3, Muir 3, Hamilton (G) 1, Hamilton (J) 1, O'Connor 1, Redford 1, Thomas 1, Opponents 4.

STIRLING ALBION

Ground: Annfield Park.
Telephone: Stirling 3584
Colours: All red strip.

Armstrong, G. 39	Heggie, S. 16	Nicol, G. 31
Arthur, G. 2	Irving, J. 5	Skilling, A. 4
Beaton, R. 2	Kennedy, A. 34	Steedman, D. 34
Brown, J. 12	Kennedy, J. 10	Steele, J. 15
Browning, I. 21	Lowe, J. 6	Thomson, R. 11
Burns, J. 6	McGibbon, W. 13	Ward, J. 1
Dick, G. 1	McLeod, J. 1	Watson, G. 23
Duffin, R. 11	McPhee, M. 33	Young, G. 37
Gray, R. 18	Moffat, A. 38	Young, R. 5

League Goalscorers—Steele 8, Kennedy (A) 5, Armstrong 4, McPhee 4, Heggie 3, Watson 3, Gray 2, Brown 1, Browning 1, Irving 1, Kennedy (J) 1, Lowe 1, McGibbon 1, Nicol 1, Thomson 1, Opponents 1.

PLAYING STAFFS 1979-80

These lists, which were supplied by the clubs concerned, were the latest available to us when going to press. Certain players have since changed clubs.

DIVISION ONE

ARSENAL

	Height ft.	in.	Weight st.	lb.	Previous Club	Birthplace
Goalkeepers						
Barron, Paul	6	2	13	0	Plymouth A.	London
Jennings, Pat	6	0	12	6	Tottenham H.	Newry
Defenders						
Devine, John	5	10	11	4	——	Dublin
Flight, Keith	5	10	11	7	——	Woolwich
Gatting, Steve	6	0	12	0	——	Middlesex
Nelson, Sammy	5	10	11	0	——	Belfast
O'Leary, David	6	2	12	6	——	London
Rice, Pat	5	8	11	7	——	Belfast
Stead, Kevin	5	10	11	0	Tottenham H.	West Ham
Walford, Steve	6	1	11	7	Tottenham H.	Highgate
Young, Willie	6	3	14	3	Tottenham H.	Edinburgh
Midfield						
Brignall, Steve	5	$7\frac{1}{2}$	10	8	——	Kent
Brady, Liam	5	7	10	7	——	Dublin
Cant, Clifford	5	9	11	3	——	London
Harvey, Jimmy	5	9	11	4	Glenavon	Lurgan
Heeley, Mark	5	6	9	0	Peterborough	Peterborough
Powling, Richie	5	8	11	6	——	London
Price, David	5	11	12	2	——	Caterham
Rix, Graham	5	9	11	0	——	Doncaster
Talbot, Brian	5	8	11	9	Ipswich T.	Ipswich
Forwards						
Macdonald, Malcolm	5	$10\frac{1}{2}$	13	2	Newcastle Utd.	Fulham
Stapleton, Frank	5	11	12	7	——	Dublin
Sunderland, Alan	5	9	11	$6\frac{1}{2}$	Wolves	Mexborough

Also under contract: Dermott Drummy, Brian McDermott, Nicky sullivan

ASTON VILLA

	Height ft.	in.	Weight st.	lb.	Previous Club	Birthplace
Goalkeepers						
Rimmer, Jimmy	5	11	11	12	Arsenal	Southport
Spink, Nigel	6	1	13	10	——	Chelmsford
Defenders						
Evans, Allan	6	1	12	9	Dunfermline	Dunfermline
Evans, David	5	10	12	1	——	West Bromwich
Gibson, Colin	5	8	10	10	Aston Villa	Bridport
Gidman, John	5	10	11	0	Liverpool	Liverpool

Gregory, John	6	1	11	0	Northampton	Scunthorpe
McNaught, Ken	5	11	11	11	Everton	Kirkcaldy
Ormsby, Brendan	6	0	11	3	——	Birmingham
Williams, Gary	5	10½	11	5	——	Wolverhampton
Midfield						
Carrodus, Frank	5	9	10	11	Manchester City	Manchester
Cowans, Gordon	5	8	9	2	——	Co. Durham
Craig, Tommy	5	7½	11	7	Newcastle Utd.	Aberdeen
Cropley, Alex	5	8	10	0	Arsenal	Aldershot
Deacy, Eamonn	5	7	10	10	Galway Rovers	Ireland
Jenkins, Lee	5	10	11	9	——	Birmingham
Mortimer, Dennis	5	10	12	0	Coventry City	Liverpool
Stirland, Gary	5	9	11	7	——	Middlesborough
Forwards						
Cunningham, David	5	5	9	5	Swindon	Kirkcaldy
Deehan, John	5	11	11	13	——	Solihull
Gray, Andy	5	10	11	5	Dundee Utd.	Glasgow
Linton, Ivor	5	10	10	13	——	West Bromwich
Little, Brian	5	8	11	2	——	Durham
O'Dowd, Adrian	5	11	11	0	——	Solihull
Ready, Kevin	5	11	12	0	Gt. Yarmouth	Wymondham
Shaw, Gary	5	10	10	4	——	Birmingham
Shelton, Gary	5	7	10	0	Walsall	Nottingham
Swain, Ken	5	11	11	7	Chelsea	Liverpool
Ward, Joe	6	0	12	5	Clyde	Glasgow
Young, Willie	5	9	10	12	Arthurlie	Glasgow

BOLTON WANDERERS

	Height ft.	in.	Weight st.	lb.	Previous Club	Birthplace
Goalkeepers						
Felgate, David,	6	1	12	12	——	Blaenau Ffestiniog
McDonagh, James	6	0	13	12	Rotherham Utd.	Rotherham
Poole, Terence	6	1	13	0	Huddersfld. Tn.	Chesterfield
Defenders						
Allardyce, Samuel	6	1½	14	0	——	Dudley
Burke, David, Ian	5	10	10	7	——	Liverpool
Graham, Michael	5	10	11	13	——	Lancaster
Heaney, Roy	5	7½	11	11	——	Liverpool
Nicholson, Peter	6	0	12	5	Blackpool	Cleator Moor
Midfield						
Greaves, Roy	5	10	12	3	——	Farnworth
Jones, Paul Bernard	6	1½	13	10	——	Ellesmere Port
McNab, Neil	5	9	11	5	Spurs	Greenock
Reid, Peter	5	7	11	10	——	Huyton
Smith, Brian	5	7	11	7	——	Bolton
Walsh, Michael	6	0	12	0	——	Manchester
Wilson, Philip	5	6	10	4	——	Hemsworth
Forwards						
Carter, Michael	5	8½	11	0	——	Warrington
Gowling, Alan, Edwin	6	2	12	1	Newcastle Utd.	Stockport
Keighley, John, Paul	5	7½	10	5	——	Rochester
Moores, James, Craig	5	7	9	10	——	Macclesfield
Morgan, William	5	8	11	2	Burnley	Glasgow
Nowak, Tadeusz	6	0	11	2	Warsaw Legia	Trzcinsko, Polano
Thompson, Christopher	5	10	11	10	——	Walsall
Whatmore, Neil	5	9½	11	4	——	Ellesmere Port
Worthington, Frank	6	0½	12	9	Leicester	Halifax

BRIGHTON AND HOVE ALBION

	Height ft.	in.	Weight st.	lb.	Previous Club	Birthplace
Goalkeepers						
Moseley, Graham	6	0	11	8	Derby Co.	Manchester
Steele, Eric	5	11	11	3	Peterborough Utd.	Newcastle
Defenders						
Cattlin, Chris	5	11½	12	5	Coventry C.	Milnrow
Kerslake, Mick	5	10	11	1	Fulham	Bethnal Green
Lawrenson, Mark	5	10	10	10	Preston N. E.	Preston
Rollings, Andy	6	0	11	8	Norwich C.	N. Weston
Tiler, Ken	5	11	10	12	Chesterfield	Sheffield
Williams, Gary	5	10	11	0	Preston N. E.	Liverpool
Winstanley, Graham	5	11	11	3	Carlisle Utd.	Croxdale
Midfield						
Clark, Paul	5	10	12	5	Southend U.	S. Benfleet
Geard, Glen	5	7	10	3	——	Brighton
Horton, Brian	5	10	11	4	Port Vale	Hednesford
O'Sullivan, Peter	5	7	10	0	Manchester Utd.	Colwyn Bay
Sayer, Peter	5	6	10	2	Cardiff City	Cardiff
Forwards						
Chivers, Martin	6	1½	12	12	Servette	Southampton
Maybank, Teddy	5	10	10	12	Fulham	London
Poskett, Malcolm	6	0	11	2	Hartlepool Utd.	Middlesbrough
Ring, Michael	5	10	11	0	——	Brighton
Ryan, Gerry	5	10	10	12	Derby County	Dublin
Ward, Peter	5	7	10	3	——	Derby

BRISTOL CITY

	Height ft.	in.	Weight st.	lb.	Previous Club	Birthplace
Goalkeepers						
Cashley, Ray	5	11	13	11	——	Bristol
Mogg, David	5	10	10	5	——	Bristol
Shaw, John	6	1	13	2	Leeds Utd.	Stirling
Defenders						
Gillies, Donnie	5	10	11	10	Morton	Glencoe
Hay, Alan	5	11	11	3	Bolton	Montrose
Hunter, Norman	5	11	12	8	Leeds Utd.	Eighton Banks
Merrick, Geoff	5	8	10	8	——	Bristol
Rodgers, David	6	2	15	1	——	Bristol
Stevens, Paul	5	7	10	12	——	Bristol
Sweeney, Gerry	5	8	10	8	Morton	Renfrew
Whitehead, Clive	5	10	12	8	——	Birmingham
Midfield						
Cormack, Peter	5	9	11	0	Liverpool	Edinburgh
Gow, Gerry	5	8	10	8	——	Glasgow
Jantunen, Pertti	5	9	10	9	Eskilstuna	Lahti
Mabbutt, Kevin	5	8	11	1	——	Bristol
Mann, Jimmy	5	9	11	12	Leeds Utd.	Goole
Tainton, Trevor	5	7	11	10	——	Bristol

	Height ft.	in.	Weight st.	lb.	Previous Club	Birthplace
Forwards						
Chandler, Ricky	5	10	11	2	——	Bristol
Doyle, Ian	5	9	11	0	——	Torquay
Garland, Chris	5	9	11	12	Leicester	Bristol
Meijer, Geert	6	0	12	8	Ajax	Amsterdam
Penny, Shaun	5	8	11	1	——	Bristol
Pritchard, Howard	5	10	11	10	——	Cardiff
Ritchie, Tom	6	2	11	2	——	Bowness
Royle, Joe	6	1	14	2	Man. City	Liverpool

COVENTRY CITY

	Height ft.	in.	Weight st.	lb.	Previous Club	Birthplace
Goalkeepers						
Blyth, Jim	6	1¼	13	3	Preston N. E.	
Sealey, Les	6	1	11	6½	——	Bethnal Green
Murcott, Steve	5	11	11	10	——	Birmingham
Defenders						
Barnes, David	5	9	10	10	——	Paddington
Collier, Gary	6	0	11	5	Bristol C.	Bristol
Coop, Mick	5	11	11	5½	——	Leamington
Dyson, Paul	6	2	13	7	——	Birmingham
Hagan, Jim	6	0	11	10	Larne	Monkstown
Holton, Jim	6	1¼	13	7	Sunderland	Lesmahagow
Jacobs, Steve	5	7	11	0	——	London
Jones, David	5	9	12	0	Everton	Liverpool
McDonald, Bobby	5	9	11	5½	Aston Villa	Aberdeen
Oakey, Graham	5	7	9	10	——	Worcester
Osgood, Keith	5	11	11	2	Tottenham	Ealing
Roberts, Brian	5	8¼	11	3½	——	Manchester
Whitton, Steve	6	0	11	0	——	East Ham
Midfield						
Blair, Andy	5	8½	10	10	——	Bedworth
Gooding, Ray	5	8	11	4½	——	Hartlepool
Gillespie, Gary	6	2	12	1	Falkirk	Scotland
Hutchinson, Tommy	5	11½	11	2	Blackpool	Cardenden
Phillips, Nicky	5	8	11	0	——	London
Powell, Barry	5	7½	10	0	Wolves	Kenilworth
Thomas, Danny	5	6	10	6	——	Worksop
Yorath, Terry	5	10½	12	3	Leeds Utd.	Cardiff
Forwards						
Bannister, Gary	5	7½	10	1	——	Warrington
Bodak, Peter	5	6	10	0	——	Birmingham
Ferguson, Mick	6	1½	12	8½	——	Newcastle
Hateley, Mark	6	1	11	0	——	Derby
Haywood, Clive	5	8	11	6	——	Ramsgate
Hunt, Steve	5	7	11	6	N. Y. Cosmos	Birmingham
Nardiello, Don	5	10	10	11	——	Cardinganshire
Thompson, Gary	6	0	12	9	——	Birmingham
Wallace, Ian	5	7½	10	9	Dumbarton	Glasgow

CRYSTAL PALACE

	Height ft.	in.	Weight st.	lb.	Previous Club	Birthplace
Goalkeepers						
Burridge, John	5	10	12	2	Aston Villa	Custon
Fry, David	6	0	12	4	——	Bournemouth
Horn, Robert	6	0	13	0	——	Westminster
Defenders						
Boyle, Terry	5	10	12	2	Tottenham H.	Ammerford
Cannon, Jim	6	0	13	2	——	Glasgow
Dare, Kevin	5	9	11	2	——	Finchley
Evans, Ian	6	2	12	7	Q.P.R.	Egham
Gilbert, Billy	5	11	12	2	——	Lewisham
Hazell, Tony	5	10	12	12	Millwall	High Wycombe
Hinshelwood, Paul	5	11	12	0	——	Bristol
Nicholas, Peter	5	8½	10	11	——	Newport
Sansom, Kenny	5	7	11	7	——	Camberwell
Sparks, Chris	5	10	10	8	——	Islington
Midfield						
Fenwick, Terry	5	9½	10	0	——	Camden
Graham, George	5	11	12	6	Portsmouth	Bargeddie
Kember, Steve	5	8	10	8	Leicester C.	Croydon
Lovell, Steve	6	0	11	12	——	Swansea
Lowe, Garry	5	10	11	1	——	Manchester
Murphy, Jerry	5	9	10	12	——	Stepney
Paul, Tony	5	9	11	0	——	Islington
Smillie, Neil	5	6	10	7	——	Barnsley
Forwards						
Carter, Les	5	9	10	10	——	Farnborough
Elwiss, Mike	6	0	12	6	Preston N. E.	Doncaster
Hilaire, Vince	5	6	9	8	——	Forest Hill
Leahy, Steve	5	7	10	6	——	Battersea
Sealy, Tony	5	6½	10	12	Southampton	London
Swindlehurst, David	6	2	13	5	——	Edgware
Walsh, Ian	5	9½	11	6	——	St. Davids

DERBY COUNTY

	Height ft.	in.	Weight st.	lb.	Previous Club	Birthplace
Goalkeepers						
Cherry, Steve	5	11			School	Nottingham
McKellar, David	6	0			Ardrossan	Irvine
Middleton, John	6	3			Nottm. For.	Skegness
Defenders						
Blades, Stephen	5	8			School	Peterborough
Buckley, Steven	5	9			Luton	Brinsley
Falconer, Keith	5	10			School	Newcastle
Langan, David	5	9			School	Dublin
McCaffery, Aidan	5	11			Newcastle	Newcastle
McFarland, Roy	5	11			Tranmere	Liverpool
Moreland, Vic	6	0			Glentoran	Belfast
Rioch, Bruce	5	10			Everton	Aldershot
Sheridan, Frank	5	10			School	London
Webb, David	5	10			Leicester	London
Wicks, Steve	6	3			Chelsea	Reading

Midfield						
Bowers, Robert	5	7			Cliftonville	Belfast
Clark, Jonathan	5	10			Man. Utd.	Swansea
Daly, Gerard	5	10			Man. Utd.	Dublin
Powell, Steve	5	10			School	Derby
Spooner, Steve	5	9			School	London
Strikers						
Bartlett, Paul	5	7			School	Grimsby
Carter, Steve	5	7			Notts. County	Gt. Yarmouth
Caskey, Billy	5	10			Glentoran	Millisle
Chesters, Colin	5	10			School	Crewe
Clayton, John	6	0			Elgin	Elgin
Crawford, Andrew	5	10			School	Filey
Duncan, John	6	0			Tottenham	Dundee
Emson, Paul	6	0			Brigg	Grimsby
Greenwood, Roy	5	10			Sunderland	Leeds
Hill, Gordon	5	7			Man. Utd.	London
Murray, Kevin	5	10			School	Dundee

EVERTON

	Height ft.	in.	Weight st.	lb.	Previous Club	Birthplace
Goalkeepers						
Banner, Nicholas	6	1	11	3	——	Liverpool
Brand, Drew	6	0	11	1	——	Edinburgh
Wood, George	6	3	14	2	Blackpool	Douglas
Defenders						
Barton, John	5	10	10	12	Worcester	Birmingham
Deakin, Ray	5	9	10	13	——	Liverpool
Higgins, Mark	6	1	13	3	——	Buxton
Lyons, Mike	6	0	12	3	——	Liverpool
Pejic, Mike	5	6	10	4	Stoke C.	Chesterton
Ratcliffe, Kevin	5	11	12	7	——	Mancot
Robinson, Neil	5	7	9	12	——	Liverpool
Todd, Colin	5	9	11	9	Derby C.	Chester-le-Street
Wright, Billy	5	11	12	8	——	Liverpool
Midfield						
Dobson, Martin	6	0	11	9	Bolton W.	Blackburn
Heard, Pat	5	10	11	4	——	Hull
King, Andy	5	9	10	13	Luton T.	Luton
Lodge, Paul	5	8½	10	10	——	Liverpool
Murray, Martin	5	11	11	12	Home Farm	Dublin
Nulty, Geoff	5	10	11	7	Newcastle	Whiston
Ross, Trevor	5	9½	11	10	Arsenal	Asthon-U-Lyne
Forwards						
Anderson, John	5	9	10	8	——	Manchester
Barton, David	5	8	10	12	——	Adelaide
Eastoe, Peter	5	9	11	1	Q.P.R.	Tamworth
Jack, Ross	5	11	11	12	——	Inverness
Kidd, Brian	6	0	11	10	Manchester C.	Manchester
Latchford, Bob	6	0	12	1	Birmingham C.	Birmingham
McBride, Joe	5	8	10	6	——	Glasgow
Smallman, David	5	8	10	3	Wrexham	Connah's Quay
Telfer, George	5	10	11	7	——	Liverpool
Thomas, David	5	7½	11	5	Q.P.R.	Kirkby-in-Ashfield
Varadi, Imrie	5	8½	10	6	Sheffield U.	London

IPSWICH TOWN

	Height ft.	in.	Weight st.	lb.	Previous Club	Birthplace
Goalkeepers						
Baker, Kieron	6	0½	13	0	Bournemouth	Ryde, I. Of W.
Cooper, Paul	5	11	12	7	Birmingham C.	Cannock
Endersby, Scott	5	10	12	3	Kettering	Lewisham
Sivell, Laurie	5	8	11	0	——	Lowestoft
Defenders						
Beattie, Kevin	5	10½	12	4	——	Carlisle
Burley, George	5	9½	11	0	——	Cumnock
Butcher, Terry	6	4	14	0	——	Singapore
Crouch, Nigel	5	8	10	7	——	Ardleigh
Hunter, Allan	6	0	12	8	Blackburn R.	Sion Mills
Osman, Russell	6	0	11	10	——	Repton
Roberts, Dale	5	10½	11	5	——	Newcastle
Shields, Peter	5	7	10	11	——	Glasgow
Souter, Don	5	11	11	7	——	Hammersmith
Steggles, Kevin	6	0	11	10	——	Bungay
Mills, Mick	5	7½	11	9	——	Godalming
Midfield						
Burns, Ronnie	5	8	10	7	Coleraine	Londonderry
Muhren, Arnold	5	11	11	1	FC Twente	Volendam
Parkin, Tommy	5	7	10	4	——	Gateshead
Parkinson, Noel	5	7	10	6	——	Hull
Klug, Bryan	5	8	10	10	——	Coventry
Thijssen, Frans	5	11	11	2	FC Twente	Heumen
Osborne, Roger	5	9	10	11	——	Otley
Wark, John	5	10½	12	0	——	Glasgow
McCall, Steve	5	11	11	3	——	Carlisle
Forwards						
Brazil, Alan	6	0	12	4	——	Glasgow
Gates, Eric	5	6	10	4	——	Ferryhill
Geddis, David	6	1	11	10	——	Carlisle
Lambert, Mick	5	9	12	0	——	Balsham
D'Avray, Mich	6	1	12	0	——	Johannesburg
Hubbick, David	5	7½	10	10	——	Jarrow
Mariner, Paul	5	11½	12	2	Plymouth	Bolton
Turner, Robin	5	9	10	8	——	Carlisle
Woods, Clive	5	9	10	8	——	Norwich
Wharton, Tony	5	8	11	0	——	Beverley

LEEDS UNITED

	Height ft.	in.	Weight st.	lb.	Previous Club	Birthplace
Goalkeepers						
Harvey, David	5	11	12	3	——	Leeds
Lukic, John	6	0	9	0	——	Chesterfield
Smith, Henry	6	1½	11	12	——	Lanarkshire
Defenders						
Cherry, Trevor	5	9½	11	6	Huddersfield	Huddersfield
Firm, Neil	6	2½	11	2	——	Bradford
Gray, Frank	5	9½	11	8	——	Glasgow
Hampton, Peter	5	7	10	11	——	Oldham
Hart, Paul	6	0	12	0	Blackpool	Manchester
Hird, Kevin	5	6	9	9	Blackburn	Colne

Madeley, Paul	6	0	12	6	——	Leeds
Parker, Neil	5	6	10	13	——	Blackburn
Reynard, Duncan	5	8	11	10	——	Gosport
Tyerman, Barry	5	7	8	7	——	S. Shields
Parkinson, Keith	5	11½	11	2	——	Preston
Stevenson, Byron	6	1	11	0	——	Llanelli
Midfield						
bennett, David	5	8½	9	6	——	Rotherham
Currie, Tony	5	10½	12	9	Sheff. Utd.	Edgware
Daly, Peter	5	7	10	0	——	Hamilton
Flynn, Brian	5	3½	8	8	Burnley	Port Talbot
McGhie, Billy	5	9	11	1	——	Lanark
Reid, David	5	10	11	5	——	Glasgow
Savill, Peter	5	9	11	5	——	Bacup
Whyte, David	5	8	11	2	——	Dunfermline
Forwards						
Clarke, Alan	5	9	9	10	——	Dublin
Graham, Arthur	5	7½	11	10	Aberdeen	Glasgow
Gray, Eddie	5	11	12	6	——	Glasgow
Hankin, Ray	6	2	13	10	Burnley	Wallsend
Harris, Carl	5	9	11	5	——	Neath
Hawley, John	6	1	13	5	Hull City	Withernsea
Porthouse, Phil	5	9	10	0	——	Jarrow
Reid, David	6	0	11	5	——	——
Thomas, Gwyn	5	8	11	0	——	Swansea

LIVERPOOL

	Height ft.	in.	Weight st.	lb.	Previous Club	Birthplace
Goalkeepers						
Clemence, Ray	6	0	12	9	Scunthorpe U.	Skegness
Ogrizovic, Steve	6	3	14	7	Chesterfield	Mansfield
Defenders						
Ainsworth, Jeff	5	9	11	7	——	Liverpool
Carroll, Derek	5	6	9	12	Dundalk	Dublin
Hansen, Alan	6	1	13	0	Partick Thistle	Alloa
Harper, Alan	5	8	9	7	——	Liverpool
Hughes, Emlyn	5	10½	12	9	Blackpool	Barrow
Irwin, Colin	6	0	12	6	——	Liverpool
Kennedy, Alan	5	9½	11	10	Newcastle Utd.	Sunderland
Kettle, Brian	5	9	12	13	——	Prescott
Neal, Phil	5	11	12	2	Northampton T.	Irchester
Thompson, Phil	6	0	11	8	——	Liverpool
Midfield						
Braddish, Synan	5	7	10	11	Dundalk	Dublin
Case, Jimmy	5	9	12	7	——	Liverpool
Kennedy, Ray	5	11	13	3	Arsenal	Seaton Delaval
Lee, Sammy	5	7	10	1	——	Liverpool
McDermott, Terry	5	9	12	13	Newcastle Utd.	Liverpool
Sheddy, Kevin	5	8½	10	10	Hereford Utd.	Builth Wells
Souness, Graeme	5	11	12	13	Middlesbrough	Edinburgh
Forwards						
Dalglish, Kenny	5	8	11	13	Glasgow Celtic	Glasgow
Duff, Brian	5	10	10	12	Dundalk	Dublin
Fairclough, David	5	11	11	1	——	Liverpool
Gayle, Howard	5	10½	10	9	——	Liverpool
Heighway, Steve	5	10½	11	2	——	Dublin
Johnson, David	5	10	12	4	Ipswich Town	Liverpool

McCartney, Gary	5	9	10	2	——	Belfast
McGarvey, Frank	5	10	10	7	St. Mirren	Kilsyth
Russell, Colin	5	7	10	7	——	Liverpool
Savage, Robert	5	7	11	1	——	Liverpool
Williams, Jimmy	5	6½	9	2	——	Liverpool

Also under contract: John Brown, Alexander Cribley, Craig LeCornu

MANCHESTER CITY

	Height ft.	in.	Weight st.	lb.	Previous Club	Birthplace
Goalkeepers						
Corrigan, Joe	6	4½	14	0	——	Manchester
MacRae, Keith	6	0	11	11	Motherwell	Glasgow
Defenders						
Booth, Tommy	6	1	11	12	——	Manchester
Clements, Kenny	6	1	12	6	——	Manchester
Donachie, Willie	5	9	11	3	——	Glasgow
Futcher, Paul	6	0	11	5	Luton	Chester
Ranson, Ray	5	9	10	10	——	St. Helens
Reid, Nick	5	10	10	12	——	Manchester
Watson, Dave	5	11	11	7	Sunderland	Nottingham
Midfield						
Bell, Colin	5	11	11	6	Bury	Hesleden
Hartford, Asa	5	7	10	6	West Brom.	Clydebank
Henry, Tony	5	11	11	12	——	Newcastle
Power, Paul	5	11	10	13	——	Manchester
Silkman, Barry	5	8	10	13	Plymouth	London
Viljoen, Colin	5	8	10	10	Ipswich	Johannesburg
Forwards						
Barnes, Peter	5	10	11	4	——	Manchester
Bennett, Dave	5	10	10	7	——	Manchester
Channon, Mike	6	0	11	6	Southampton	Orcheston
Deyna, Kazimerz	5	11	11	2	Legia Warsaw	Poland
Palmer, Roger	5	10	10	10	——	Manchester

MANCHESTER UNITED

	Height ft.	in.	Weight st.	lb.	Previous Club	Birthplace
Goalkeepers						
Bailey, Gary	6	1	12	0	——	Ipswich
Pears, Stephen	5	10¾	11	5	——	Brandon
Roche, Paddy	6	1½	11	3	Shelbourne	Dublin
Defenders						
Albiston, Arthur	5	7½	10	10	——	Edinburgh
Buchan, Martin	5	10¼	12	4	Aberdeen	Aberdeen
Connell, Tom	5	9¾	11	1	Coleraine	Newry
Davies, Alan	5	7½	10	3	——	Manchester
Duxbury, Mike	5	9¼	10	6	——	Accrington
Houston, Stewart	5	11	12	3	Brentford	Dunoon
Keen, Nigel	5	8½	10	13	——	Barrow
Knox, Barry	5	7½	10	3	Sunderland	Gateshead
McQueen, Gordon	6	3½	13	8½	Leeds United	Kilbirnie
Moran, Kevin	5	10½	12	6	——	Dublin
Nicholl, Jimmy	5	9½	11	11½	——	Hamilton
Roberts, Chris	5	7	10	12	——	Bangor
Rogers, Martyn	5	9¼	11	5½	——	Nottingham

Midfield						
Greenhoff, Brian	5	10½	12	2	——	Barnsley
Grimes, Ashley	6	0	10	12	——	Dublin
Haggett, David	6	0	11	1	——	Merthyr
Macari, Lou	5	5¾	10	10	Glasgow Celtic	Edinburgh
McCreery, David	5	6½	10	6	——	Belfast
McDermott, Kel	5	6	9	10	——	Belfast
McIlroy, Sammy	5	9¾	11	8	——	Belfast
Micklewhite, Gary	5	6½	9	10½	——	Southwark
Sloan, Tom	5	6	9	9	Ballymena	Ballymena
Thomas, Mike	5	6	10	10	Wrexham	Mochdre
Forwards						
Coppell, Steve	5	7½	10	12	Tranmere Rovers	Liverpool
Greenhoff, Jimmy	5	9	12	0	Stoke City	Barnsley
Jordan, Joe	6	0¾	12	8	Leeds United	Carluke
McGrath, Chris	5	9½	10	11	Millwall (loan)	Belfast
Lynam, Chris	5	5	9	3	——	Manchester
Paterson, Steve	6	1½	13	2½	——	Elgin
Reynolds, Andy	5	3½	9	4	——	Neath
Ritchie, Andy	5	9½	11	12½	——	Manchester
Pearson, Stuart	5	9	12	2½	Hull City	Hull
Worrall, Gary	5	9	10	1½	——	Salford
Wray, Andy	5	7½	9	6	——	Beverley

MIDDLESBROUGH

	Height ft.	in.	Weight st.	lb.	Previous Club	Birthplace
Goalkeepers						
Platt, James	6	1	12	6	Ballymena	Ballymoney
Brown, David	6	0	12	2	Juniors	Hartlepool
Stewart, James	6	2	12	8	Kilmarnock	Kilwinning
Defenders						
Angus, Michael					Juniors	Middlesbrough
Bailey, Ian	5	9	10	10	Juniors	Middlesbrough
Boam, Stuart	6	2	13	5	Mansfield	Kirkby
Craggs, John	5	9	12	5	Newcastle	Flinthill
Johnson, Peter	5	9	11	2	Juniors	Harrogate
McAndrew, Anthony	6	0	11	8	Juniors	Glasgow
Ramage, Alan	6	2	13	0	Juniors	Guisborough
Stokoe, Ian	5	11	11	7	Juniors	Prudhoe
Peters, Jeffrey					Juniors	Wideopen
Midfield						
Armstrong, David	5	9	11	0	Juniors	Durham
Askew, William	5	6	9	4	Juniors	Lumleu
Bell, Charles	5	7	10	2	Juniors	Guisborough
Hedley, Graeme	5	11	10	7	Juniors	Easington
Johnston, Craig	5	9	10	12	Lake McQuarry	Johannesburg
Mahoney, John	5	8	11	2	Stoke	Cardiff
Proctor, Mark					Juniors	Middlesborough
Forwards						
Bell, Anthony					Juniors	Middlesborough
Cummins, Stanley	5	5	9	2	Juniors	Ferryhill
Hodgson, David	5	10	11	0	Juniors	Gateshead
Woof, William	5	10	11	10	Juniors	Gateshead

NORWICH CITY

	Height ft.	in.	Weight st.	lb.	Previous Club	Birthplace
Goalkeepers						
Baker, Clive	5	9	11	0	Junior	N. Walsham
Hansbury, Roger	5	11	12	0	Junior	Barnsley
Defenders						
Bond, Kevin	6	0	12	6	Junior	London
Bird, Kevan	5	10	11	9	Lowestoft	Beccles
Carter, Robert	5	10	11	8	Junior	Kings Lynn
Davies, Ian	5	8	10	12	Junior	Bristol
Forbes, Duncan	5	11	11	9	Colchester	Edinburgh
Halsey, Mark	5	7	11	0	Junior	Romford
Hoadley, Phil	5	11	12	2	Orient	Battersea
Jones, David	6	1	12	8	Notts. F.	Gosport
Nightingale, Mark	5	10	11	6	Crystal P.	Salisbury
Powell, Tony	5	11	10	7	Bournemouth	Bristol
Symonds, Richard	5	10	10	7	Junior	Dereham
Midfield						
Bennett, David	5	11	11	6	Man. City	Oldham
Evans, Douglas	5	10			Junior	Swansea
McGuire, Michael	5	7	10	7	Coventry	Blackpool
Mendham, Peter	5	10	11	6	Junior	Kings Lynn
Mountford, Peter	5	8	11	2	Junior	Stoke-on-Trent
Paddon, Graham	5	9	11	7	West Ham	Manchester
Peters, Martin	5	11	12	4	Spurs	London
Steele, William	5	8	11	0	Junior	Kirkmuirhill
Forwards						
Cordice, Alan	5	10	10	7	Maidenh'd	West Indies
Downs, Greg	5	9	10	7	Junior	Carlton
Fashanu, Justin	6	1	12	6	Junior	London
Goble, Stephen	5	7	11	0	Junior	West Runton
Lythgoe, Philip	5	9	11	0	Junior	Norwich
Neighbour, Jimmy	5	8	11	10	Spurs	Chingford
Reeves, Kevin	5	10	11	4	Bournemouth	Burley
Robson, Keith	5	10	10	4	Cardiff C.	Hetton le Hole
Shepherd, Greg	5	11	11	9	Musselburgh	Musselburgh

NOTTINGHAM FOREST

	Height ft.	in.	Weight st.	lb.	Previous Club	Birthplace
Goalkeepers						
Shilton, Peter	6	0	12	10	Stoke City	Leicester
Woods, Chris	6	0	12	0	——	Lincolnshire
Defenders						
Anderson, Viv	5	11	10	4	——	Nottingham
Barrett, Colin	5	11	11	7	Man. City	Stockport
Burns, Kenny	5	$10\frac{1}{2}$	11	0	Birmingham C.	Glasgow
Clark, Frank	6	0	12	2	Newcastle Utd.	Durham
Gunn, Bryn	5	9	10	5	——	Corley
Lloyd, Larry	6	2	12	4	Coventry C.	Bristol
Needham, David	6	1	12	7	Q.P.R.	Leicester
Midfield						
Bowyer, Ian	5	11	11	2	Orient	Ellesmere Port
Burke, Steve	5	9	10	7	——	Nottingham
Gemmill, Archie	5	6	11	2	Derby Co.	Paisley
McGovern, John	5	10	10	13	Leeds Utd.	Montrose

	Height ft.	in.	Weight st.	lb.	Previous Club	Birthplace
O'Hare, John	5	8½	11	7	Leeds Utd.	Renton
Robertson, John	5	8	10	9	——	Uddiston
Forwards						
Birtles, Gary	5	11	10	12	——	Nottingham
Francis, Trevor	5	11	11	7	Birmingham C.	Plymouth
Mills, Gary	5	11	11	5	——	Nottingham
O'Neill, Martin	5	10	11	3	Distillery	Kilrea
Woodcock, Tony	5	10	11	0	——	Nottingham

SOUTHAMPTON

	Height ft.	in.	Weight st.	lb.	Previous Club	Birthplace
Goalkeepers						
Wells, Peter	6	1	13	0	Nottingham F.	Nottingham
Gennoe, Terence	6	2½	13	5	——	Shrewsbury
Harrison, Mark	6	¼	12	3½	——	London
Defenders						
Arnold, Paul	5	9	11	0	——	Bournemouth
Coak, Timothy	5	4¾	10	4	——	Southampton
Peach, David	5	9	11	6	Gillingham	Bedford
Waldron, Malcolm	6	0	12	4	——	Emsworth
Andruszewski, Manny	5	10	11	9	——	Eastleigh
Phillipson-Masters, Forbes	6	1	12	10	——	Bournemouth
Nicholl, Chris	6	2	12	9	Aston V.	Wilmslow
Whitlock, Mark	5	11	11	8½	——	Portsmouth
Golac, Ivan	5	11	12	10	——	Yugoslavia
Midfield						
Holmes, Nick	5	11	12	3	——	Southampton
Baker, Graham	5	8½	10	2½	——	Southampton
Ball, Alan	5	6	10	6	Arsenal	Farnworth
Williams, Steve	5	10½	11	8	——	London
Pratt, Wayne	5	8	9	9	——	Southampton
McGrath, Martin	5	10	11	11	——	London
Forwards						
Shipley, George	5	7¾	9	10	——	Newcastle-on-Tyne
Dawtry, Kevin	5	6	9	13¼	——	Southampton
Hayes, Austin	5	5½	9	10	——	London
Hebberd, Trevor	5	11½	11	4	——	Winchester
Boyer, Phil	5	8	11	2	Norwich C.	Nottingham
Williams, Oshor	5	10	11	3	——	Stockton
George, Charles	5	11	12	0	Derby C.	London
Puckett, David	5	7	9	12	——	Southampton
O'Donoghue, Mike	5	9	11	9	——	London

STOKE CITY

	Height ft.	in.	Weight st.	lb.	Previous Club	Birthplace
Goalkeepers						
Jones, Roger	5	10½	12	13	Newcastle	Upton-on-Severn
Fox, Peter	5	10½	12	11	Sheff. Wed.	Scunthorpe
Defenders						
Bowers, Ian	5	8¾	10	2	——	Stoke-on-Trent
Brissett, Trevor	5	9	11	7	——	Stoke-on-Trent
Dodd, Alan	5	10¼	11	11	——	Stoke-on-Trent
Doyle, Mike	6	1	12	0	Man. C	Manchester
Johnson, Paul	5	9	10	12	——	Stoke-on-Trent

Morgan, Andrew	5	8¾	11	7	——	Stoke-on-Trent
Pejic, Melvin	5	7½	10	6	——	Stoke-on-Trent
Smith, Denis	6	0	12	2	——	Stoke-on-Trent
Midfield						
Heath, Adrian	5	4½	8	11	——	Stoke-on-Trent
Irvine, Sammy	5	6	10	7	Shrewsbury	Glasgow
Johnson, Paul	5	6½	12	2	——	Stoke-on-Trent
Kendall, Howard	5	7½	10	13	Birmingham	Ryton-on-Tyne
McGroarty, James	5	6¼	9	9	Finn Harps	Londonderry
Richardson, Paul	5	10¼	11	10	Chester	Nottingham
Simpson, Gary	5	5¼	9	13	——	Sheffield
Forwards						
Busby, Viv	6	0	11	12	Norwich City	High Wycombe
Barron, Tom	5	6½	9	10	——	Dublin
Chapman, Lee	6	1½	12	10	——	Lincoln
Cook, Jeff	5	9	11	12	Helenic	Hartlepool
Crooks, Garth	5	8¼	11	0	——	Stoke-on-Trent
O'Callaghan, Bren	6	3	13	12	Doncaster	Bradford
Randall, Paul	5	11½	12	2	Bristol Rovers	Liverpool

TOTTENHAM HOTSPUR

	Height ft.	in.	Weight st.	lb.	Previous Club	Birthplace
Goalkeepers						
Aleksic, Milija	6	0	13	11	Luton T.	Stafford
Daines, Barry	6	0	13	4	——	Witham
Kendall, Mark	6	¼	13	5	——	Tredegar
Defenders						
Holmes, Jimmy	5	10¾	12	3	Coventry C.	Dublin
Hughton, Chris	5	7¾	11	5	——	Forest Gate
Lacy, John	6	3	12	4	Fulham	Liverpool
McAllister, Don	5	10	12	11	Bolton W.	Radcliffe
Naylor, Terry	5	10	11	10	——	Islington
Smith, Gordon	5	9	12	1	Aston Villa	Glasgow
Mazzon, Georgio	5	10	11	5	——	London
Midfield						
Ardiles, Osvaldo	5	6	9	10	Hurucan	Cordoba
Beavon, Stuart	5	6½	9	12½	——	Wolverhampton
Hazard, Mike	5	7	10	5	——	Sunderland
Hoddle, Glenn	6	1	12	3	——	Hayes
Miller, Paul	6	½	12	2	——	Stepney
Perryman, Steve	5	8	11	6	——	Ealing
Pratt, John	5	8	11	3	——	Hackney
Forwards						
Armstrong, Gerry	5	11½	13	4	Bangor City	Belfast
Brooke, Garry	5	6	10	5	——	Bethnal Green
Falco, Mark	6	0	12	0	——	Hackney
Galvin, Tony	5	9	11	5	Goole Town	Huddersfield
Jones, Chris	5	11	11	9	——	Jersey
Lee, Colin	6	0	12	6	Torquay U.	Torquay
Taylor, Peter	5	7	12	2	Crystal Palace	Rochford
Villa, Ricardo	6	0	12	5	Racing Club	Buenos Aires

WEST BROMWICH

	Height ft.	in.	Weight st.	lb.	Previous Club	Birthplace
Goalkeepers						
Godden, Tony	6	0	11	12	——	Gillingham

Grew, Mark	5	11	11	7	——	Bilston
Stewart, David	6	1	12	2	Leeds Utd.	Glasgow
Defenders						
Anderson, John	5	9	11	0	——	Dublin
Batson, Brendon	5	11	11	11	Cambridge Utd	West Indies
Bennett, Martyn	5	11	11	8	——	Birmingham
Hodgson, Vernon	5	10	11	11	——	Birmingham
Robertson, Alistair	5	11	11	10	——	Philipstoun
Wile, John	6	1	11	9	Peterborough	Sherburn
Midfield						
Brown, Tony	5	9	11	0	——	Oldham
Cantello, Len	5	10	11	2	——	Newton Heath
Loveridge, John	5	7	10	13	——	Wolverhampton
Moses, Remi	5	7	10	10	——	Birmingham
Robson, Bryan	5	9	11	7	——	Chester-le-Street
Trewick, John	5	8	11	5	——	Bedlington
Forwards						
Brown, Alistair	6	0	11	7	Leicester C.	Mussleburgh
Cunningham, Laurie	5	11	11	0	Orient	London
Cross, Nicky	5	9	11	0	——	Birmingham
Cowdrill, Barry	5	11	11	5	——	Birmingham
Monaghan, Derek	5	9	10	13	——	Bromsgrove
Mills, David	5	10	11	0	Middlesbrough	Middlesbrough
Summerfield, Kevin	5	11	10	8	——	Walsall
Regis, Cyrille	6	0	12	3	——	French Guyana

WOLVERHAMPTON WANDERERS

	Height ft.	in.	Weight st.	lb.	Previous Club	Birthplace
Goalkeepers						
Bradshaw, Paul	6	2½	12	1	Blackburn	Altrincham
Pierce, Gary	6	1⅛	13	4½	Huddersfield	Bury
Defenders						
Berry, George	6	¾	11	12	——	Germany
Brazier, Colin	6	1½	10	13½	——	Birmingham
Daniel, Peter	5	8½	11	3	Hull	Hull
Fleming, Christopher	5	7¾	9	5¾	——	Bangor
Hazell, Robert	5	11⅝	14	2½	——	Jamaica
Humphrey, John	5	9½	10	13	——	Wembley
McAlle, John	6	0	11	3	——	Liverpool
Palmer, Geoff	5	11	11	9	——	Cannock
Parkin, Derek	5	9½	11	9	Huddersfield	Newcastle
Midfield						
Arkwright, Ian	5	7¼	10	4¼	——	Barnsley
Black, John	5	8½	10	10½	——	Glasgow
Carr, Willie	5	6¾	10	7½	Coventry	Glasgow
Daley, Steve	5	11⅛	11	13½	——	Barnsley
Hibbitt, Kenny	5	10⅛	12	0	Bradford PA	Bradford
Moss, Paul	5	8¾	10	3	——	Birmingham
Patching, Martin	5	11¾	11	2	——	Rotherham
Atkinson, Hugh	5	11½	11	9½	——	Dublin
Forwards						
Bell, Norman	6	0⅛	13	2	——	Sunderland
Clarke, Wayne	5	11¼	10	6¾	——	Willenhall
Eves, Mel	5	10½	10	1	——	Wednesbury
Matthews, Michael	5	7½	10	12½	——	Hull
Rafferty, Billy	6	0	12	6	Carlisle	Port Glasgow
Richards, John	5	9¾	11	9	——	Warrington
Moss, Craig,	5	7½	10	8	——	Birmingham

DIVISION TWO

BIRMINGHAM CITY

	Height ft.	in.	Weight st.	lb.	Previous Club	Birthplace
Goalkeepers						
Coton, Tony	6	1	11	13	——	Tamworth, Staffs.
Freeman, Neil	6	3	14	4	Southend	Northampton
Defenders						
Brady, Paul	5	10	11	2	——	Birmingham
Broadhurst, Kevan	5	10	11	2	——	Dewsbury
Calderwood, Jimmy	5	9½	11	0	——	Glasgow
Dennis, Mark	5	8½	9	0	——	Streatham
Gallagher, Joe	6	1½	11	3	——	Liverpool
Page, Malcolm	5	9	10	11	——	Knucklas
Pendrey, Garry	5	9½	11	0	——	Birmingham
Van Den Hauwe, Pat	5	10½	11	2	——	Dendermonde, Belg.
Ainscow, Alan	5	7½	9	3½	Blackpool	Bolton
Buckley, Alan	5	6	9	11	Walsall	Mansfield
Dark, Trevor	5	9	11	1	——	Carshalton
Dillon, Kevin	5	11½	10	13	——	Sunderland
Towers, Tony	5	9	11	2½	Sunderland	Manchester
Forwards						
Barrowclough, Stewart	5	8	9	0	Newcastle	Barnsley
Bertschin, Keith	6	0	11	8	Ipswich	Enfield
Givens, Don	6	1	12	0	Q.P.R.	Limerick
Ivey, Paul	5	10½	11	0	——	Westminster
Lynex, Steve	5	9	11	0	Shamrock Rvrs.	West Bromwich

BRISTOL ROVERS

	Height ft.	in.	Weight st.	lb.	Previous Club	Birthplace
Goalkeepers						
Jones, Glyn	6	0	13	1	Juniors	Newport
Thomas, Martin	6	1	12	11	Juniors	Senghenydd
Defenders						
Aitken, Peter	5	11	12	1	Juniors	Penarth
Bater, Phil	5	10½	11	0	Juniors	Cardiff
England, Mike	6	0	10	10	Juniors	Bristol
Harding, Steve	6	1	14	4	Bristol City	Bristol
Hughes, Mark	6	0	11	4	Juniors	Port Talbot
Jones, Vaughan	5	8½	11	0	Juniors	Tonyrefail
Malpas, Mike	6	0	12	2	Juniors	Bristol
Palmer, Dave	5	9	11	0	Juniors	Bristol
Pulis, Tony	5	10	10	8	Juniors	Newport
Shaw, Jeff	5	11	10	5	Juniors	Bargoed
Taylor, Stuart	6	4½	14	6	Juniors	Bristol
Midfield						
Dean, Steve	5	7	9	10	Poole Town	Poole
Emmanuel, Gary	5	9	10	8	Birmingham C.	Swansea
Hendrie, Paul	5	6	9	8	Portland Timbers	Kilsythe
Griffiths, Ashley	5	9	10	6	Juniors	Barry
Prince, Frank	5	9	11	7	Juniors	Penarth
Shaw, Martin	5	7	9	12	Juniors	Bristol
Williams, Dave	5	9	11	10	Juniors	Cardiff
Williams, Geraint	5	7	10	8	Juniors	Treorchy

Forwards						
Brown, Keith	5	9	11	2	Juniors	Bristol
Clarke, Gary	5	8	10	10	Juniors	Boston, Lincs.
Dennehy, Miah	5	9	10	13	Walsall	Cork, Eire
Mabbutt, Gary	5	10	10	8	Juniors	Bristol
Petts, Paul	5	10	11	2	Juniors	Hackney
Staniforth, Dave	6	0	12	1	Sheffield Utd.	Chesterfield
White, Steve	5	11	11	11	Juniors	Bristol

BURNLEY

	Height ft.	in.	Weight st.	lb.	Previous Club	Birthplace
Goalkeepers						
Stevenson, Alan	6	1	12	3	Chesterfield	——
Norman, Anthony	6	1	11	11	Schoolboy	——
O'Rourke, William	6	0	12	8	Schoolboy	——
Defenders						
Arins, Anthony	5	11	11	8	Schoolboy	——
Brennan, Ian	5	10	11	5	Schoolboy	——
Thomson, James	5	11½	12	0	Chelsea	——
Higgins, Robert	6	1	12	10	Schoolboy	——
Scott, Derek	5	8	11	10	Schoolboy	——
Rodaway, William	5	9	12	13	Schoolboy	——
Robinson, Peter	6	1	12	6	Schoolboy	——
McAdam, Steven	5	11	11	9	Portadown	——
Overson, Richard	5	11	12	2	Schoolboy	——
Tait, David	5	9	12	0	Schoolboy	——
Midfield						
Robertson, Stuart	5	4	10	0	Schoolboy	——
Noble, Peter	5	9	10	6	Newcastle	——
Ingham, William	5	6	9	10	Schoolboy	——
Jakub, Yanek	5	6	9	5	Schoolboy	——
Burke, Marshall	5	7	9	3	Schoolboy	——
Hall, Brian	5	7	10	6	Plymouth	——
Cavener, Philip	5	7	10	0	Schoolboy	——
Dixon, Paul	5	9	11	0	Schoolboy	——
Tate, Jeffrey	5	7	10	0	Schoolboy	——
Forwards						
McGregor, Neil	5	6	10	9	Schoolboy	——
Gardiner, James	5	10	11	10	Portadown	——
Fletcher, Paul	5	10	12	10	Bolton	——
Morley, Anthony	5	7	10	0	Preston	——
Kindon, Stephen	6	0	12	12	Wolves	——
James, Leighton	5	10	11	10	Derby	——
Young, Kevin	5	8	10	0	Schoolboy	——
Smith, Malcolm	5	8	11	0	Middlesbrough	——
Pickerill, Stuart	5	8	10	10	Schoolboy	——

CAMBRIDGE UNITED

	Height ft.	in.	Weight st.	lb.	Previous Club	Birthplace
Goalkeepers						
Key, Richard	6	0	12	4	Exeter C.	Coventry
Webster, Malcolm	5	11	12	6	Southend U.	Rossington
Defenders						
Buckley, Ian	5	8	11	0	Stockport Co.	Oldham
Fallon, Steve	6	1	11	2	——	Whittlesey
Smith, Lindsay	5	11	11	1	Colchester U.	London
Stringer, David	5	10	11	9	Norwich C.	Gt. Yarmouth

Midfield						
Christie, Derrick	5	8	10	10	Northampton T.	Bletchley
Graham, Peter	5	10	10	4	Lincoln C.	Barnsley
Howard, Trevor	5	7	10	10	Bournemouth	Kings Lynn
Leach, Mike	6	0	12	0	In America	London
Spriggs, Steve	5	2	9	0	Huddersfield T.	Doncaster
Forwards						
Avery, Roger					——	Cambridge
Biley, Alan	5	8	10	9	Luton T.	Leighton Buzzard
Cozens, John	6	0	12	0	Peterborough U.	London
Garner, Bill	6	0	12	0	Chelsea	Leicester
Finney, Tom	5	11	11	8	Sunderland	Belfast
Murray, Jim	5	7	10	8	——	Scotland
O'Neill, Tom	5	7	10	11	——	Glasgow
Streete, Floyd	6	1	12	8	——	West Indies
Sweetzer, Gordon	6	0	11	8	Brentford	Toronto

Also under contract: Nigel Smith

CARDIFF CITY

	Height ft.	in.	Weight st.	lb.	Previous Club	Birthplace
Goalkeepers						
Davies, John	6	3	13	2	——	
Healey, Ron	5	11½	13	0	Man City	Manchester
Defenders						
Dwyer, Phil	6	0	13	0	——	Cardiff
Harris, Gary	5	9½	13	0	——	
Jones, Linden	5	6	10	8	——	New Tredegar
Leach, Phil	5	11	11	6	——	Cardiff
Miller, Paul	5	11	11	3	——	Cardiff
Pontin, Keith	6	1½	12	7	——	Pontyclun
Piper, Dean	5	9	11	5	——	Newport
Roberts, Dave	5	11	12	7	Hull City	Southampton
Thomas, Rod	6	2½	13	1	Derby C.	Neath
Sullivan, Colin	5	8	11	0	Norwich	Saltash
Midfield						
Buchanan, John	5	8	11	0	Northampton	Dingwell
Campbell, Alan	5	8	11	7	Birmingham	
Grapes, Steve	5	7	10	11	Norwich	Norwich
Joseph, Antone	5	9	11	½	——	Manchester
Parson, Tony	5	8	9	12	——	Cardiff
Lewis, John						Tredegar
Forwards						
Bishop, Ray	5	7	9	12	Cheltenham	Hengoed
Evans, Tony	5	8½	10	8	Blackpool	Liverpool
Davies, Paul					——	
Micallef, Constantinous	5	5	11	4	——	Cardiff
Moore, Ronnie					Tranmere	Liverpool
Sherman, Robert	5	10	9	11½	——	Aberystwyth
Stevens, Gary						Birmingham

CHARLTON ATHLETIC

	Height ft.	in.	Weight st.	lb.	Previous Club	Birthplace
Goalkeepers						
Wood, Jeffrey	6	1	10	9	Harlow T.	London

Defenders						
Berry, Leslie	6	2	11	13	——	London
Campbell, David	6	1	11	8	——	Edinburgh
Dugdale, Alan	5	8	12	6	Coventry C.	Liverpool
Madden, Lawrence	6	0	12	6	Arsenal	London
Newson, Mark	5	9½	11	0	——	London
Shaw, Peter	6	2	13	10	Staines T.	Northolt
Shipperley, David	6	3	14	0	Gillingham	Hillingdon
Warman, Philip	5	6	11	0	——	Bromley
Midfield						
Brisley, Terence	5	6	10	6½	Millwall	London
Churchouse, Gary	5	9	11	8	Windsor & Eton	Wembley
Gritt, Steven	5	10	10	10	Bournemouth	Bournemouth
Tydeman, Richard	6	1¾	12	8	Gillingham	Gillingham
Forwards						
Ambrose, Leroy	5	7½	10	8	——	St. Vincent
Booth, Anthony	5	7½	10	3	——	Biggin Hill
Flanagan, Michael	5	9½	11	8	Tottenham	Ilford
Hales, Derek	5	10	11	2	West Ham Utd.	Lower Halstow
Robinson, Martin	5	8	11	5½	Tottenham	Ilford

CHELSEA

	Height ft.	in.	Weight st.	lb.	Previous Club	Birthplace
Goalkeepers						
Borota, Petar	6	0	12	7	Belgrade	Belgrade
Isles, Bob	6	1	12	7	Weymouth	Leicester
Phillips, John	5	11½	11	7	Aston Villa	Shrewsbury
Defenders						
Chivers, Gary	5	11	11	7	Juniors	Stockwell
Droy, Micky	6	4½	15	5	Slough Town	Highbury
Harris, Ron	5	8	11	7	Juniors	Hackney
Jenkins, Iori	5	10	11	7	Juniors	Neath
Locke, Gary	5	11	11	5	Juniors	Park Royal
Nutton, Michael	5	11	10	12	Juniors	St. John's Wood
Penny, Clive	5	8	10	0	Juniors	Neath
Sitton, John	6	0	12	2	Juniors	Hackney
Sparrow, John	5	10	12	0	Juniors	Bethnal Green
Stride, David	5	9	11	5	Juniors	Lymington
Wilkins, Graham	5	6½	10	2	Juniors	Hillingdon
Midfield						
Bannon, Eamonn	5	10	11	7	Hearts	Edinburgh
Bumstead, John	5	7	10	0	Juniors	Rotherhithe
Britton, Ian	5	5	9	7	Juniors	Dundee
Fillery, Michael	5	10	11	12	Juniors	Mitcham
Hales, Kevin	5	7	10	4	Juniors	Dartford
Hay, David	5	11	11	7	Celtic	Paisley
Osgood, Peter	6	2	12	9	Philadelphia Fury	Windsor
Stanley, Garry	5	9½	10	8	Juniors	Burton-on-Trent
Wilkins, Ray	5	7	10	10	Juniors	Hillingdon
Clare, Jimmy	5	8	9	9	Juniors	Islington
Forwards						
Aylott, Trevor	6	1	13	10	Juniors	Bermondsey
Docherty, Jim	5	10	10	5	E. Stirling	Broxburn
Frost, Lee	5	8½	10	7	Juniors	Elephant & Castle
Johnson, Gary	5	11	11	7	Juniors	Peckham
Langley, Tommy	5	11	11	7	Juniors	Elephant & Castle
Sully, Chris	5	8	10	0	Juniors	Camberwell
Stewart, David	5	8	9	3	Hull City	Belfast

Walker, Clive	5	8½	11	4	Juniors	Oxford
Wilson, Richard	5	8	10	7	Juniors	Orpington

FULHAM

	Height ft.	in.	Weight st.	lb.	Previous Club	Birthplace
Goalkeepers						
Peyton, Gerry	6	2	13	10	Burnley	Nottingham
Digweed, Perry	6	0	11	0	——	London
Defenders						
Money, Richard	5	10	11	0	Scunthorpe	Lowestoft
Evans, Ray	6	0	12	7	Millwall	London
Strong, Les	5	11	10	8	——	London
Gale, Tony	6	2	13	1	——	London
Hatter, Steve	6	2	13	10	——	London
Lock, Kevin	6	0	11	6	West Ham	London
Banton, Geoff	6	1	12	10	Plymouth	Ashton-under-Lyne
Mason, Tommy	5	9	10	4	——	London
Midfield						
Beck, John					Coventry	London
Boyd, Gordon	5	8	10	4	Glasgow R.	Glasgow
Bullivant, Terry	5	8	10	11	——	London
Evanson, John	5	11	11	10	Blackpool	Newcastle
Lovell, Mark	5	9	11	5	——	London
Margerrison, John	6	0	12	10	Tottenham	London
Day, Clive	6	0	11	0	——	Essex
Corner, Brian	5	7	9	3	——	Scotland
Forwards						
Gibson, Brian	5	9	10	0	——	Scotland
Guthrie, Chris	6	2			Swindon	Dilston-on-Tyne
Davies, Gordon	5	8	10	10	Merthyr	Merthyr
Greenaway, Brian	5	10	10	1	——	London
Mahoney, Tony	5	11	12	3	——	London

LEICESTER CITY

	Height ft.	in.	Weight st.	lb.	Previous Club	Birthplace
Goalkeepers						
Humphries, Stephen	5	11½	12	9½	——	Rockford
Rafter, Sean	6	1¼	12	11	Southend	Sleaford
Wallington, Mark	6	1	14	4¼	Walsall	Sleaford
Defenders						
Carr, Everton	5	7	11	0	——	
Convey, Steven	5	10¼	10	1	——	Belfast
Farmer, Kevin	6	0	12	1	——	
Geddes, Paul	6	1½	12	2	——	
Hamilton, Steven	5	8½	10	2½	——	Leicester
May, Larry	6	½	12	4	——	Sutton Coldfield
O'Boyle, Rory	5	10½	10	9	——	
O'Neill, John	6	0	12	13	——	Derry
Ratcliffe, Mark	5	11	12	12	——	
Ridley, John	6	1½	12	5	Port Vale	Consett
Rofe, Denis	5	7½	11	4	Orient	Leicester
Smith, Ian	5	9	10	3	——	
Welsh, Peter	6	1	12	8½	——	Coatbridge
Williams, Tommy	5	11	11	0	——	Leicester

Midfield						
Geddes, Andy	5	8½	11	10	——	
Goodwin, Mark	5	9½	10	11	——	Sheffield
Kelly, Eddie	5	9½	12	2½	Q.P.R.	Glasgow
Peake, Andy	5	10½	10	7	——	
Ramsey, Paul	5	9	10	8	——	
Smith, Bobby	5	8	11	9	Hibernian	Edinburgh
Wilson, Ian	5	7½	10	10½	——	
Forwards						
Allen, John	6	1	13	1½	——	
Brotherton, Alan	6	1½	12	5	——	
Buchanan, Dave	5	7½	10	2½	——	
Christie, Trevor	6	1	12	6	——	Newcastle
Cole, Frankie	5	5½	9	2	——	
Duffy, Mick	5	10	11	9½	——	
Edmunds, Paul	5	8	10	10	——	
Grewcock, Neil	5	7	10	12	——	
Henderson, Martin	6	0	12	10¼	Rangers	Glasgow
Hughes, Billy	5	8½	11	10	Derby	Coatbridge
Kirk, David	5	5½	9	12	——	
Lee, Alan	5	11	12	5	——	
Lineker, Gary	5	9½	10	8	——	
McShane, Patrick	6	1½	11	3½	——	

LUTON TOWN

	Height ft.	in.	Weight st.	lb.	Previous Club	Birthplace
Goalkeepers						
Finlay, John	6	1	14	1	Aston Villa	Blairgowrie
Judge, Alan	5	11	11	5½	——	Kingsbury
Defenders						
Aizilewood, Mark	6	0	11	4	Newport	Newport
Carr, David	5	10	11	8	——	Luton
Donaghy, Mal	5	10	12	7	Larne	Belfast
Goodyear, Clive	5	11	11	4	——	Lincoln
Harriott, Leslie	5	7	11	9	——	Luton
Johnson, Robert	5	6	9	12	——	Bedford
Jones, Graham	6	0	12	7	——	Worsley
Murphy, Thomas	5	8½	11	5	——	Waterford, Eire
Price, Paul	5	11	11	12	——	St. Albans
Sisman, Gary	5	7½	11	1	——	Stevenage
Stephens, Kirk	5	8¾	11	8	Stafford R.	Coventry
Woodward, John	5	5¾	8	13½	——	London
Midfield						
Birchenall, Alan	6	0	12	8	Blackburn	Eastham
Cosby, Alan	5	5½	8	13	——	Luton
Fuccillo, Pasquale	5	9½	11	12¼	——	Bedford
Hill, Ricky	5	10½	13	0	——	Paddington
Madden, Neil	5	5½	9	4	——	Luton
Turner, Wayne	5	8¼	11	15¾	——	Luton
West, Alan	5	8½	10	7½	Burnley	Hyde
Forwards						
Conquest, Martin	5	8¾	10	7	——	Leighton Buzzard
Bunn, Frank	5	10	10	12½	——	Birmingham
Hatton, Bob	5	11	12	0	Blackpool	Hull
Heath, Seamus					——	Belfast
Heale, Gary	5	11	11	6¾	——	Canvey Island
Ingram, Godfrey	5	6¾	10	4	——	Luton
Moss, David	5	9	11	7	Swindon	Witney

	Height ft.	in.	Weight st.	lb.	Previous Club	Birthplace
Pearson, Andy	5	5	9	9	——	Newmarket
Stein, Brian	5	9½	11	6	——	St. Albans
Taylor, Steve	5	9	11	2	Oldham	Royton

NEWCASTLE UNITED

	Height ft.	in.	Weight st.	lb.	Previous Club	Birthplace
Goalkeepers						
Baldwin, Kevin	6	0	12	8	——	Gateshead
Carr, Devin	6	2	13	6	Burnley	Morpeth
Hardwick, Steven	5	11	13	0	Chesterfield	Mansfield
Defenders						
Barton, David	6	0	11	7	——	Bishop Auckland
Bird, John	6	0	12	3	Preston N.E.	Doncaster
Brownlie, John	5	10			Hibernian	Caldercruix
Fairless, Stephen	5	8			——	Wingate
Halliday, Bruce	5	10			——	Sunderland
Kelly, Peter	5	8	9	10	——	Glasgow
Mitchell, Kenneth	5	11	11	12	——	Sunderland
Mulgrove, Keith	5	9	10	12	——	Haltwhistle
Midfield						
Nattrass, Irving	5	11	12	4	——	Fishburn
Armstrong, Robin	5	10	10	13	——	Newburn
Cassidy, Thomas	5	11	13	3	Glentoran	Belfast
Ferguson, Brian	5	10			Mansfield	
Hibbitt, Terry					Birmingham	Bradford
Manners, Peter	5	10	10	12	——	Sunderland
Martin, Mick	5	10			W.B.A.	Dublin
Pugh, Kevin	5	0¾			——	Corbridge
Scott, James	5	8	11	0	——	Newcastle
Suggett, Colin	5	8			Norwich	Washington
Walker, Nigel	5	12	11	11	——	Gateshead
Wharton, Kenneth	5	7½			——	Newcastle
Forwards						
Connolly, John					Birmingham	Glasgow
Latty, Brian					——	Seaton Delaval
MacFarlane, Craig	6	0	12	12	Dunfermline Jub. A.J.	Dunfermline
Nicholson, Gary	5	7½			——	Newcastle
Pearson, James	5	11½			Everton	Falkirk
Robinson, Stuart	5	9	10	7	——	Middlesbrough
Shoulder, Alan	5	5			Blyth Spartans	Bishop Auckland
Withe, Peter	6	2			Nottm. Forest	Liverpool

NOTTS. COUNTY

	Height ft.	in.	Weight st.	lb.	Previous Club	Birthplace
Goalkeepers						
King, Colin	6	1	13	0	Clydebank	Edinburgh
McManus, Eric	6	0	11	2	Coventry	Limavvady, N.I.
Defenders						
Benjamin, Triston	6	0	11	1	——	St. Kitts
Blockley, Jeff	6	0½	12	6	Leicester City	Leicester
McVay, David	6	1	11	11	——	Workington
O'Brien, Raymond	5	9	11	0	Man. Utd.	Sherbourne
Wood, Garry	5	10	11	3	Kettering T.	Corby
Richards, Pedro	5	8	10	8	——	London
Stubbs, Brian	6	2	12	0	——	Keyworth, Notts.

Midfield						
Hunt, David	5	11	11	0	Derby Co.	Leicester
Mair, Gordon	5	9	10	6	——	Coatbridge
Mann, Arthur	5	9	10	10	Man. City	Burntisland
Masson, Donald	5	8	10	12	Derby Co.	Banchory
Richards, Lloyd	5	8	11	0	——	Derby
Smith, David	5	4	10	6		Nottingham
Forwards						
Green, Ricky	6	0	10	9	Chesterfield	Scunthorpe
Hooks, Paul	5	8	10	11	——	Wallsend
McCulloch, Iain	5	10	11	0	Kilmarnock	Kilmarnock
Vinter, Michael	5	9	11	0		Boston

OLDHAM ATHLETIC

	Height ft.	in.	Weight st.	lb.	Previous Club	Birthplace
Goalkeepers						
McDonnell, Peter	6	1	13	0	Liverpool	Kendal
Platt, John	5	10	11	7	——	Ashton
Defenders						
Blair, Ronald	5	9	11	0	——	Coleraine
Edwards, Stephen	5	9	10	7	——	Birkenhead
Hicks, Keith	6	0	12	4	——	Oldham
Hoolikin, Gary	5	11	11	1	——	Middleton
Wood, Ian	5	9	11	1	——	Bury
Midfield						
Halom, Victor	5	10	10	10	Sunderland	Burton-on-Trent
Holt, David	5	10	11	0	Bury	Padiham
Hurst, John	5	10	12	7	Everton	Blackpool
Keegan, Gerrard	5	7	10	2	Manchester City	Manchester
Valentine, Carl	5	9	10	7	——	Manchester
Gardner, Steven	5	10	10	5	Ipswich	Hemsworth
Hilton, Mark	5	9	10	3	——	Middleton
Forwards						
Atkinson, Paul					——	Otley
Heaton, Paul					——	Manchester
Jordan, Timothy					——	Rochdale
Sinclair, Nicholas					——	Stockport
Stainrod, Simon	5	10	11	1	——	Sheffield Utd.
Steel, James						

ORIENT

	Height ft.	in.	Weight st.	lb.	Previous Club	Birthplace
Goalkeepers						
Jackson, John	6	2	13	10	C. Palace	London
Scott, Lloyd	6	0	12	3	——	Stepney
Defenders						
Bennett, Peter	5	11	12	2	West Ham	Hillingdon
Bright, Mickey	5	10	12	4	——	Chelmsford
Fisher, Bobby	5	8½	10	7	——	Wembley
Gray, Nigel	6	3	13	4	——	Fulham
Henney, Chris	5	10	11	0	——	Forest Gate
Hughton, Henry	5	7½	11	10	——	Stratford
Kane, John	5	10	11	5	——	Hackney
Roffey, Bill	5	11	12	13	C. Palace	Stepney
Taylor, Tommy	6	0	13	7	West Ham	Hornchurch
Went, Paul	5	11	14	4	Cardiff C.	Bromley by Bow
Hamberger, Steve	6	0	12	0	Walthamstow Avenue	Hackney

Midfield						
Banjo, Tunji	5	9	11	0	———	Kensington
Coates, Ralph	5	7	12	2	Tottenham	Hetton Le Hole
Gealish, Tony	5	7	11	6	———	Paddington
Whittle, Alan	5	6	11	2	Sheffield Utd.	Liverpool
Forwards						
Blackhall, Mark	6	0	12	0	———	Upney
Chiedozie, John	5	6	10	10	———	Nigeria
Godfrey, Kevin	5	10½	10	11	———	Kennington
Gray, Mark	5	9½	11	4	Fulham	Tenby
Mayo, Joe	6	2	13	6	West Brom	Tipton
Moores, Ian	6	2	14	4	Tottenham	Chesterton

PRESTON NORTH END

	Height ft.	in.	Weight st.	lb.	Previous Club	Birthplace
Goalkeepers						
Kilner, John	6	0	11	5	Apprentice	Bolton
Litchfield, Peter	6	2	13	7	Droylsden	Manchester
Tunks, Roy	6	½	13	11	Rotherham	Wuppertall, W. Germany
Defenders:						
Baxter, Michael	6	1	12	2	Apprentice	Birmingham
Blackley, John	5	10	13	1	Newcastle Utd.	Falkirk
Cameron, Daniel	5	6½	11	3	Sheff. Wed.	Dundee
O'Riordan, Donald	6	0	11	12	Tulsa USA	Dublin
Taylor, Brian	5	10	11	7	Plymouth A.	Gateshead
Uzelac, Steven	5	11	12	11	Doncaster	Doncaster
Wilson, Harry	5	10	11	8	Brighton	Hetton-Le-Hole
Midfield						
Bell, Graham	5	9	10	6	Oldham Ath.	Middleton
Burns, Francis	5	9	10	10	Southampton	Coatbridge
Coleman, Gordon	5	9	10	12	Amateur	Nottingham
Doyle, Stephen	5	9½	11	1	Apprentice	Neath, Glam.
Haslegrave, Sean	5	8	10	5	Notts. For.	Stoke
McAteer, Andrew	5	9½	10	12	Apprentice	Preston
Spavin, Alan	5	7½	11	9	Wash. Dips (USA)	Lancaster
Forwards						
Bruce, Alex	5	8	11	1	New. Utd.	Dundee
Cochrane, Ian	5	10	11	3	Apprentice	Bellshill
Elliott, Stephen	5	11	11	10	Notts. For.	Haltwistle
Houston, Graham	5	8	10	4	Amateur	Gibraltar
Potts, Eric	5	6	10	5	Brighton	Liverpool
Robinson, Michael	6	0	12	12	Apprentice	Leicester
Thomson, Richard	5	8	10	9	Apprentice	Edinburgh

QUEENS PARK RANGERS

	Height ft.	in.	Weight st.	lb.	Previous Club	Birthplace
Goalkeepers						
Hucker, Peter	6	3	14	6	——	Hampstead
Richardson, Derek	6	3	15	6	Chelsea	Hackney
Defenders						
Abbott, Ron	6	2	11	10	——	Lambeth
Gillard, Ian	6	1	13	10	——	Hammersmith

Howe, Ernie	6	2½	12	12	Fulham	Chiswick
Roeder, Glenn	6	1½	12	8	Orient	Woodford
Shanks, Don	5	10	11	11	Luton	Hammersmith
Wilkins, Jon	5	10	11	8	——	Neath
Midfield						
Busby, Martin	6	1½	13	6	Notts County	High Wycombe
Elsey, Carl	5	10	11	6	Pembroke Boro	Pembroke
Hollins, John	5	8	11	7	Chelsea	Guildford
Richards, Craig	5	7½	11	8	——	Neath
Wallace, Barry	5	9½	11	4	West Ham	London
Walsh, Mick	5	9	11	5	Everton	Chorley
Forwards						
Allen, Clive	5	10	11	0	——	London
Bowles, Stan	5	11	11	8	Carlisle Utd	Manchester
Goddard, Paul	5	10	11	0	——	Harlington
Hamilton, Billy	6	3	11	10	Linfield	Belfast
Harkouk, Rachid	6	1	12	10	C. Palace	London
McGee, Paul	5	10¼	12	5	Sligo Rovers	Sligo

SHREWSBURY TOWN

	Height ft.	in.	Weight st.	lb.	Previous Club	Birthplace
Goalkeepers						
Mulhearn, Ken	6	1	12	13	Man. City	Liverpool
Wardle, Robert	5	11	10	12	Bristol C.	Leeds
Defenders						
Jones, Trevor	5	8	10	8	——	Shrewsbury
King, John	5	10	11	8	——	Glasgow
Larkin, Tony	5	10	11	12	Wrexham	Liverpool
Leonard, Carleton	5	9	10	5	——	Oswestry
Midfield						
Atkins, Ian	6	0	11	7	——	Birmingham
Griffin, Colin	6	0	11	7	Derby	Dudley
Hayes, Stephen	6	0	11	10	——	Smethwick
Lindsay, James	5	7	12	0	Hereford	Hamilton
Roberts, Michael	5	8	10	6	——	Birmingham
Tong, David	5	8½	10	9	——	Blackpool
Turner, Graham	5	11	11	13	Chester	Ellesmere Port
Forwards						
Birch, Trevor	5	11	11	13	Liverpool	Ormskirk
Biggins, Stephen	6	0	11	12	——	Walsall
Cross, Stephen	5	10	10	6	——	Wolverhampton
Maguire, Paul	5	9	11	0	——	Glasgow

SUNDERLAND

	Height ft.	in.	Weight st.	lb.	Previous Club	Birthplace
Goalkeepers						
Siddall, Barry	6	1	14	7	Bolton	Ellesmere Port
Watson, Ian	5	10	11	3	——	North Shields

Defenders						
Ashurst, Jack	6	0	11	5	——	Alexandria
Bolton, Joseph	5	11	12	10	——	Barley Mow
Clarke, Jeffrey	6	0½	13	2	——	Hemsworth
Coady, Michael	5	11	10	11	——	Dipton
Duncan, John	5	10½	11	0	——	South Shields
Elliott, Shaun	5	11	11	1	——	Haltwistle
Gilbert, Timothy	5	9	11	1	——	South Shields
Henderson, Michael	5	10	11	8	——	Newcastle
Weir, Alan	5	8¼	10	10	——	South Shields
Midfield						
Arnott, Kevin	5	10	11	8	——	Bensham
Buckley, Michael	5	5	9	6	Everton	Manchester
Chisholm, Gordon	6	0	10	10	——	Glasgow
Docherty, Michael	5	7	10	12	Burnley	Preston
Hamilton, David	5	6½	8	13	——	South Shields
Lee, Robert	6	1½	13	10	Leicester	Leicester
Main, John	5	7½	9	5	——	Glasgow
Forwards						
Brown, Alan	5	11	12	6	——	Easington
Crawford, Colin	5	8	11	6	——	Doach
Entwistle, Wayne	5	9½	11	11	Bury	Bury
Gregoire, Roland	5	9	10	12	Halifax	Liverpool
Hutton, Vince	5	7½	10	7	——	Newcastle
Roddy, Joseph	5	9	11	4	——	Stockton
Rowell, Gary	5	8¾	11	1	——	Sunderland
Rostron, John	5	6¼	11	1	Arsenal	Sunderland

SWANSEA CITY

	Height ft.	in.	Weight st.	lb.	Previous Club	Birthplace
Goalkeepers						
Crudgir gton, Geoff	5	11½	12	12½	Aston Villa	Wolverhampton
Defenders						
Bartley, Daniel	5	8½	11	4½	Bristol C.	Paulton
Evans, Wyndham	5	9½	12	11½	——	Llanelli
Morris, Stephen	5	11¼	11	2½	——	Swansea
Smith, Tommy	5	11	13	2½	Liverpool	Liverpool
Stevenson, Nigel	6	0½	11	12½	——	Swansea
Midfield						
Attley, Brian	5	9	9	12	Cardiff	Cardiff
Boersma, Philip	5	9½	11	11	Luton T.	Liverpool
Callaghan, Ian	5	6	10	12	Liverpool	Liverpool
James, Anthony	5	8½	10	0½	——	Swansea
Marustik, Chris	5	8	11	11½	——	Swansea
Phillips, Leighton	5	10	10	11½	Aston Villa	Briton Ferry
Reeves, Peter	5	8½	10	7	Coventry	Swansea
Forwards						
Baker, Mark	5	9	11	4½	——	Swansea
Charles, Jeremy	6	1	12	3	——	Swansea
James, Robbie	5	11	12	1½	——	Swansea
Toshack, John	6	2	12	12½	Liverpool	Cardiff
Waddle, Alan	6	3½	13	11½	Leicester	Wallsend

WATFORD

	Height ft.	in.	Weight st.	lb.	Previous Club	Birthplace
Goalkeepers						
Rankin, Andy	6	0	12	0	Everton	Liverpool
Sherwood, Steve	6	3	15	0	Chelsea	Selby
Defenders						
Bolton, Ian	6	0	11	9	Notts Co.	Leiceste
Garner, Alan	6	0	12	4	Luton	Lambeth
Harrison, Steve	5	7	11	1½	Vancouver Whitecaps	Blackpool
Pritchett, Keith	5	9	11	2	Brentford	Glasgow
Sims, Steve	6	0	13	6	Leicester C.	Lincoln
Stirk, John	5	6	9	11	Ipswich	Consett
Midfield						
Booth, Dennis	5	7½	10	5	Lincoln C.	Stenley Common
How, Trevor	5	10	12	2	——	Amersham
Joslyn, Roger	5	10	11	2	Aldershot	Colchester
Train, Ray	5	4	9	7	Bolton W.	Nuneaton
Forwards						
Blissett, Luther	5	11	12	0	——	Jamaica
Cassells, Keith	5	10	11	2	——	London
Downes, Bobby	5	10	11	5	Rochdale	Bloxwich
Jenkins, Ross	6	2	12	2	Crystal Palace	Kensington
Mercer, Keith	5	10	11	7	——	Lewisham
Pollard, Brian	5	5	9	6	York City	York

WEST HAM UNITED

	Height ft.	in.	Weight st.	lb.	Previous Club	Birthplace
Goalkeepers						
Day, Mervyn	6	2	14	12	——	Chelmsford
Ferguson, Bobby	5	10½	12	7	Kilmarnock	Ardrossan
Parkes, Phil	6	2½	14	0	Q.P.R.	Sedgeley
Defenders						
Brignull, Philip	5	10	11	6	——	Stratford
Brush, Paul	5	11	11	7	——	Plaistow
Cowie, George	5	9	11	0	Buckie Rovers	Buckie
Lampard, Frank	5	11	12	9	——	West Ham
Landsdowne, Billy	6	0	12	0	——	Epping
McDowell, John	5	10	12	4	——	East Ham
Martin, Alvin	6	1	12	6	——	Bootle
Taylor, Tommy	6	1	14	0	Orient	Hornchurch
Midfield						
Bonds, Billy	6	½	12	12	Charlton Ath.	Woolwich
Brooking, Trevor	6	½	13	8	——	Barking
Curbishley, Alan	5	9	11	6	——	Forest Gate
Devonshire, Alan	5	10½	10	8	——	London
Holland, Pat	5	10	11	6	——	Limehouse
Morgan, Nicky	5	10	12	0	——	Plaistow
Moseley, Gary	5	10	11	4	Tonbridge	Farnborough
Pike, Geoff	5	6	11	0	——	Clapton
Forwards						
Cross, David	6	½	12	0	W.B.A.	Bury
Jennings, Billy	5	9	10	2	Watford	Hackney
Robson, Bryan	5	6	11	12	Sunderland	Sunderland
Taylor, Alan				6	Rochdale	Lancaster
Thomson, Brian	5	7	10	4	——	Morecambe

WREXHAM

	Height ft.	in.	Weight st.	lb.	Previous Club	Birthplace
Goalkeepers						
Davies, Dai	6	1	13	10	Everton	Ammansford
Niedzsiecki, Eddie	6	1	11	0	——	Conway
Defenders						
Davis, Gareth	5	10½	11	7	——	Bangor
Dwyer, Alan	5	7	10	7	——	Liverpool
Evans, Mickey	5	9½	11	2	——	Gaesws
Hill, Alan	5	11	11	4	——	Chester
Jones, Joey	5	10	11	7	Liverpool	Llandudno
Kenworthy, Steve	6	1	11	6	——	Wrexham
Roberts, John	6	0	12	2	Birmingham C.	Swansea
Midfield						
Cartwright, Les	5	9	10	13	Coventry C.	Aberdare
Cegielski, Wayne	6	0	12	0	Tottenham H.	Bedwellty
Fox, Steve	5	7½	11	2	Birmingham C.	Tamworth
Giles, David	5	5	10	4	Cardiff C.	Cardiff
Sutton, Mel	5	10	10	10	Cardiff C.	Birmingham
Forwards						
Buxton, Steve	5	5	9	8	——	Birmingham
Lyons, John	5	11	11	12	——	Burckley
McNeil, Dixie	5	10	11	7	Hereford Utd.	Melton Mowbray
Shinton, Bobby	5	10	11	7	Cambridge U.	West Bromwich
Whittle, Graham	5	9	10	3	——	Liverpool
Williams, Peter	5	8	10	11	——	Johnstown

DIVISION THREE

BARNSLEY

	Height ft.	in.	Weight st.	lb.	Previous Club	Birthplace
Goalkeeper						
Springett, Peter	5	10	11	6	Sheff. W.	Fulham
Defenders						
Chambers, Philip	5	8	11	4	——	Barnsley
Collins, John	5	9	11	0	Sheff. W.	Rhymney
McCarthy, Michael	6	1	13	0	——	Barnsley
Midfield						
Little, Alan	5	10	12	3	Southend	Co. Durham
Millar, Alistair	5	8	10	7	——	Glasgow
Pugh, Graham	5	8	11	2	Chester	Chester
Speedie, David	5	7	10	4	——	Doncaster
Forwards						
Bell, Derek	5	8	11	5	Halifax	Wyberton
Clarke, Allan	6	0	11	1	Leeds Utd.	Willenhall
Graham, Tommy	5	9	10	7	Aston Villa	Glasgow
Reed, Graham	5	10	11	10	——	Barnsley
Riley, Glyn	5	8	11	11	——	Barnsley

BLACKBURN ROVERS

	Height ft.	in.	Weight st.	lb.	Previous Club	Birthplace
Goalkeeper						
Butcher, John	6	2	12	3	——	Newcastle

Defenders						
Bailey, John	5	8	10	9	——	Liverpool
Fazackerley, Dereck	5	11	11	6	——	Preston
Keeley, Glen	5	10	12	0	Newcastle	Barking
Morley, Brian	5	7	11	3	——	Fleetwood
Parkin, Timothy	6	1	12	10	——	Penrith
Rathbone, Michael	5	10	11	13	Birmingham	Birmingham
Round, Paul	6	0	11	0	——	Blackburn
Waddington, John	5	11	11	7	Liverpool	Darwen
Midfield						
Brotherston, Noel	5	8	10	8	Tottenham	Belfast
Coughlin, Russell	5	8	11	6	Man. City	Swansea
Fowler, Martin	5	10	11	8	Huddersfield	York
Metcalfe, Stuart	5	7	9	0	——	Blackburn
Parkes, Tony	5	10	11	0	——	Sheffield
Forwards						
Aston, John	5	10	11	12	Mansfield	Manchester
Garner, Simon	5	8	11	3	——	Boston
Craig, Joe	5	9	11	2	Celtic	Alloa
McKenzie, Duncan	5	9	11	0	Chelsea	Grimsby
Morris, Peter	5	7	9	8	Preston	Farnworth
Wagstaffe, David	5	8	10	8	Blackpool	Manchester

BLACKPOOL

	Height		Weight			
	ft.	in.	st.	lb.	Previous Club	Birthplace
Goalkeeper						
Hesford, Iain	6	1½	12	9	——	Noola, Kenya
Defenders						
Fleming, Robert	5	9	10	12	——	Edinburgh
Gardner, Paul	5	9½	11	8	——	Southport
Malone, Richard	6	0	12	2	Hartlepool	Ayr
May, Jonathan	5	11	11	4	——	Crosby
McEwan, Stanley	5	11	12	2	——	Cambusnethan
Pashley, Terence	5	8	12	2	Burnley	Chesterfield
Suddaby, Peter	5	11½	11	10	Wycombe W.	Stockport
Thompson, Maxwell	6	1	12	2	Liverpool	Liverpool
Wilson, Brian	5	11	11	9	——	Newcastle
Midfield						
Bowey, Keith	5	6	9	8	——	Newcastle
Coyle, Patrick	5	10	10	13	——	Dublin
Hall, James	5	9	9	3	——	Bootle
Jackson, Brian	5	8½	11	2	Southport	Liverpool
Kerr, Robert	5	4½	9	3	Sunderland	Alexandria
Ronson, William	5	7	9	13	——	Fleetwood
Sermanni, Thomas	5	8	11	2	Albion Rovers	Glasgow
Tynan, Robert	5	10	11	0	Tranmere Rovers	Liverpool
Weston, James	5	9	10	11	Skelmersdale U.	Whiston
Forwards						
Chandler, Jeffrey	5	7	10	2	——	London
Hockaday, David	5	10	10	13	——	Billingham
Howarth, Carl	5	9	9	10	——	Blackpool
Jones, Garry	5	9	10	2	Bolton W.	Manchester
Kellow, Anthony	5	10	12	0	Exeter City	Falmouth
Rowland, Shaun	5	10	11	5	——	Doncaster
Spence, Derek	5	9	11	8	Olympiakas	Belfast

BRENTFORD

	Height ft.	in.	Weight st.	lb.	Previous Club	Birthplace
Goalkeepers						
Bond, Leonard	6	0	12	7	Bristol City	Ilminster, Somerset
Porter, Trevor	5	11	11	6	Slough Town	Guildford, Surrey
Defenders						
Fraser, John	5	10	10	7	Fulham	London
Johns, Dean	5	7	10	5	——	Harrow, Middx.
Kruse, Patrick	5	11	12	10	Torquay Utd.	London
McNichol, James	6	0	12	10	Luton Town	Glasgow
Salman, Danis	5	10	11	8	——	Cyprus
Tucker, William (Barry)	6	6	10	12	Northampton Town	Swansea
Midfield						
Carlton, David	5	10½	11	7	Northampton Town	London
Glover, Allan	5	8½	11	8	Orient	Windsor, Berks.
Graham, Jack	5	7	11	4	Guildford City	Glasgow
Graham, William	6	8½	10	7	Northampton Town	Co. Armagh, Ireland
Shrubb, Paul	5	7¾	10	4	Hellenic, S. Africa	Guildford, Surrey
Walker, James (Paul)	5	6	10	10	——	London
Forwards						
Allder, Douglas	5	10	11	7	Watford	Hammersmith
Booker, Robert	6	2½	12	4	——	Watford
McCulloch, Andrew	6	2	13	6	Oxford Utd.	Northampton
Phillips, Stephen	5	6	10	6	Northampton Town	London
Smith, Dean	5	10	11	9	Leicester City	Leicester

BURY

	Height ft.	in.	Weight st.	lb.	Previous Club	Birthplace
Goalkeepers						
Forrest, John	5	9	11	6	——	Bury
Latchford, David	6	2	12	9	——	Birmingham
Defenders						
Bailey, Anthony	5	10	11	2	Oldham A.	Burton
Constantine, David	5	8	10	7	Hyde United	Ashton
Kennedy, Keith	5	7	10	8	Newcastle U.	Sunderland
Ritson, John	5	8	10	5	Bolton W.	Liverpool
Tucker, Bill	5	11	11	10	Hereford U.	Kidderminster
Midfield						
Whitehead, Alan	6	2	12	0	——	Bury
Lugg, Raymond	5	9	10	10	Crewe A.	Jarrow
Stanton, Brian	5	7	10	7	——	Liverpool
Wilson, Danny	5	7	10	3	Wigan A.	Wigan
Madden, Craig	5	8	10	2	——	Manchester
Forwards						
Beamish, Kenneth	6	0	12	6	Port Vale	Bebbington
Gregory, David	5	9	11	6	Stoke City	Peterborough
Johnson, Steve	6	0	12	9	——	Liverpool
Mullen, Steve	5	7	10	2	Darwen	Scotland
Hilton, Paul	6	1	11	6	——	Oldham

CARLISLE UNITED

	Height ft.	in.	Weight st.	lb.	Previous Club	Birthplace
Goalkeepers						
Swinburne, Trevor	6	0	13	2	Sunderland	East Rainton
Harrison, Anthony					Southport	Gateshead
Defenders						
Collins, Andrew	5	10	11	0	Local Reserves	Carlisle
Hoolickin, Stephen	5	10	12	5	Bury	Manchester
McCartney, Michael	5	8½	11	0	W.B.A.	Edinburgh
MacDonald, Ian	6	2	13	0	St. Johnstone	Rinteln
Parker, Robert	5	9	10	6	Coventry	Coventry
Midfield						
Bonnyman, Philip	6	0	12	2	Hamilton Ac.	Glasgow
Fell, Geoffrey					Local Reserves	Carlisle
Hamilton, James	5	9	11	4	Bristol Rovers	Glasgow
Ludlam, Stephen	5	6	10	8	Sheff. Utd.	Chesterfield
McVitie, George	5	9	12	0	Oldham	Carlisle
Sawyers, Keith	5	9	10	6	Local Reserves	Banbury
Tait, Michael	5	10	12	2	Oxford	Willington Quay
Forwards						
Bannon, Paul					Bridgend	Dublin
Kemp, David	5	9	11	9	Portsmouth	Harrow
Lumby, James	5	10	12	0	Scunthorpe	Grimsby

CHESTER

	Height ft.	in.	Weight st.	lb.	Previous Club	Birthplace
Goalkeepers						
Lloyd, Brian	6	2	12	7	Wrexham	Rhyl
Millington, Grenville	5	10	11	6	Brighton	Queensferry
Defenders						
Burns, David	5	8	10	6	——	Ellesmere Port
Jeffries, Derek	5	11	11	3	Crystal Palace	Manchester
Needham, Paul	5	10	10	7	——	Buxton
Nickeas, Mark	5	11	10	11	Plymouth A.	Southport
Raynor, Paul	5	11	11	0	——	Chester
Storton, Trevor	6	1	12	4	Liverpool	Keighley
Walker, James	5	9	10	10	Peterborough	Winsford
Midfield						
Gendall, Richard	5	11	11	6	——	Wrexham
Livermore, Doug	5	9	10	5	Cardiff C.	Liverpool
Oakes, Alan	6	0	12	10	Manchester C.	Winslow
Phillips, Ron	5	9	11	3	Bury	Worsley
Ruggiero, John	5	11	11	4	Brighton	Stoke
Forwards						
Edwards, Ian	6	1	12	5	W.B.A.	Wrexham
Henderson, Peter	6	0	12	11	——	C Chester
Howat, Ian	5	10	11	2	——	Wrexham
Jones, Brynley	5	10	11	0	——	St. Asaph
Lewis, Paul	5	7	11	7	——	Shotton
Mellor, Ian	6	1	10	12	Brighton	Manchester
Prestidge, David	5	9	10	6	——	Queensferry
Sutcliffe, Peter	5	6	9	5	Port Vale	Manchester

CHESTERFIELD

	Height ft.	in.	Weight st.	lb.	Previous Club	Birthplace
Goalkeepers						
Letheren, Glan	6	2½	13	7½	Leeds Utd.	Llanelli
Tingay, Philip	5	10	11	4	Amateur	Chesterfield
Defenders						
Burton, Ken	5	9	11	0	Sheff. Wed.	Sheffield
Chamberlain, Glyn	5	9	11	4	Burnley	Chesterfield
Cottam, John	5	11½	12	12	Notts. For.	Warsop
Hunter, Les	6	2	12	1	Schoolboy	Middlesbro'
O'Neill, Sean	5	9½	11	6	Leeds Utd	Belfast
Pollard, Gary	6	1	11	12	Schoolboy	Staveley
Prophett, Colin	6	0	11	10	Norwich	Crewe
Tartt, Colin	5	10½	11	4	Port Vale	Liverpool
Midfield						
Dearden, Bill	5	10	11	0	Sheff. Utd.	Oldham
Flavell, Bobby	5	9	11	0	Halifax	Berwick
Heppolette, Ricky	5	10	11	5	Preston	Bashawhl
Higgins, Andy	6	3½	12	8	Schoolboy	Bolsover
Kowolski, Andy	5	11	11	4	Amateur	Mansfield
Salmons, Geoff	6	0	12	7	Sheff. Utd.	Mexbro'
Forwards						
Cammack, Steve	5	9½	11	3	Sheff. Utd	Sheffield
Fern, Rodney	5	10	11	12	Luton	Burton-on-Trent
Moss, Ernie	6	2	13	0	Mansfield	Hollingwood
Simpson, Gary	6	1	12	12	Schoolboy	Chesterfield
Walker, Phil	6	0	12	0	Amateur	Sutton-in-Ashfield

COLCHESTER UNITED

	Height ft.	in.	Weight st.	lb.	Previous Club	Birthplace
Goalkeepers						
Hamilton, Bobby	5	10	12	7	Ipswich	Irvine
Walker, Mike	6	0	13	5	Watford	Colwyn Bay
Defenders						
Cook, Michael	5	8	11	11	Orient	Enfield
Dowman, Steve	5	11	12	5	——	Manor Park
Dyer, Paul	5	8	12	7	Notts. County	Leicester
Packer, Michael	5	8	11	10	Watford	London
Wignall, Steve	5	11	11	12	Doncaster	Liverpool
Wright, Steve	6	0	10	11	——	Clacton
Midfield						
Bunkell, Ray	5	8	10	11	Swindon	Tottenham
Cotton, Russell	5	10	11	8	——	Wellington, Salop
Foley, Steve	5	11½	12	5	——	Clacton
Hodge, Bobby	5	10	11	5	Exeter	Exeter
Leslie, Steve	5	8	11	6	——	Hornsey
Forwards						
Allinson, Ian	5	10	11	10	——	Hitchin
Evans, Tony	5	8	10	8	——	Colchester
Gough, Robert	5	7	10	13	Southport	Birmingham
Lee, Trevor	6	1	12	3	Millwall	Lewisham
Rowles, Eddie	5	9	11	4	Darlington	Gosport

EXETER CITY

	Height ft.	in.	Weight st.	lb.	Previous Club	Birthplace
Goalkeeper						
O'Keefe, Vince	6	2	12	7	A.P.Leamington	Birmingham
Defenders						
Templeman, John	5	11	11	10	Brighton	Yapton
Hore, John	5	7½	10	12	Plymouth Arg.	St. Dennis
Giles, James	6	0	13	4	Charlton A.	Kidlington
Roberts, Lee	5	11	11	7	Shrewsbury	Wolverhampton
Ireland, Roy	5	10	11	0	——	Exeter
Midfield						
Hatch, Peter	5	11	11	6	Oxford U.	Henley on Thames
Randell, Colin	5	9	10	10	Plymouth Arg.	Skewen
Delve, John	5	8	11	0	Plymouth Arg.	Hazelworth
Forwards						
Bowker, Keith	5	9	11	5	Cambridge U.	West Bromwich
Sims, John	6	0	12	12	Notts. C.	Belper
Rogers, Peter	5	8	11	0	Bath City	Bristol
Neville, Steve	5	10	10	10	Southampton	Walthamstow
Pearson, Ian	5	10	11	3	Millwall	Leeds

GILLINGHAM

	Height ft.	in.	Weight st.	lb.	Previous Club	Birthplace
Goalkeepers						
Hillyard, Ron	5	11	11	4	York City	Rotherham
Wheatley, Steve	5	10	11	0	Junior	Durham
Defenders						
Barker, Mick	5	11	12	0	Newcastle	Newcastle
Bruce, Steve	6	0	11	4	Junior	Durham
Ford, Colin	5	9	10	8	Junior	Welling
Hobday, Peter	6	0	12	0	Junior	W. Germany
Overton, John	5	11	11	4	Aston Villa	Rotherham
Sharpe, John	5	10	11	2	Southampton	Portsmouth
Weatherly, Mark	6	0	12	2	Junior	Ramsgate
Young, Charlie	6	1	11	12	Aston Villa	Nicosia
Midfield						
Armstrong, Gary	5	8	10	12	Junior	London
Crabbe, John	5	8	10	12	Southampton	Weymouth
Hughes, Billy	5	11	11	0	Junior	Folkestone
Knight, Graham	5	11	11	12	Junior	Chatham
Nicholl, Terry	5	10	11	0	Southend	Wilmslow
White, Dean	5	10	12	0	Chelsea	Hastings
Forwards						
Funnell, Tony	5	8	10	4	Southampton	Eastbourne
Jolley, Terry	5	11	10	4	Junior	London
Price, Ken	5	11	11	10	Southend	Wolverhampton
Richardson, Damien	6	0	11	12	Shamrock	Dublin
Walker, Pat	5	9	11	0	Junior	Carlow, Eire
Westwood, Danny	5	10	11	0	Q.P.R.	London

GRIMSBY TOWN

	Height ft.	in.	Weight st.	lb.	Previous Club	Birthplace
Goalkeepers						
Batch, Nigel	5	10½	12	5	Derby C.	Huddersfield
Wainman, Harry	6	0	13	6	——	Hull
Defenders						
Mawer, Shaun	5	7	10	8	——	Ulceby
Moore, David	4	10	12	13	——	Grimsby
Moore, Kevin	5	11	11	8	——	Grimsby
Wigginton, Clive	6	1	12	9	Lincoln City	Sheffield
Young, Martin	6	0	11	8	——	Grimsby
Midfield						
Collins, David	5	7	10	10	——	Grimsby
Cumming, Bobby	5	8	11	4	——	Airdrie
Mitchell, Bobby	5	8	11	0	Blackburn R.	South Shields
Waters, Joe	5	5	10	6	Leicester C.	Limerick
Forwards						
Brolly, Michael	5	9	10	4	Bristol C.	Kilmarnock
Drinkell, Kevin	5	11	12	2	——	Grimsby
Donovan, Terry	5	10	10	8	——	Liverpool
Ford, Tony	5	8	12	4	——	Grimsby
Lester, Michael	5	10	11	7	Washington Diplomats	Manchester
Liddell, Garry	5	9½	11	2	Leeds U.	Bannockburn

HULL CITY

	Height ft.	in.	Weight st.	lb.	Previous Club	Birthplace
Goalkeepers						
Blackburn, Edwin	5	9	10	5	——	Houghton
Boyd, William	5	10½	11	0	——	Bellshill
Wealands, Jeff	6	0½	12	0	Darlington	Darlington
Defenders						
de Vries, Roger	5	8½	11	5	——	Hull
Nisbet, Gordon	5	10	12	2	W.B.A.	Wallsend
Haigh, Paul	5	10	11	6	——	Scarborough
Croft, Stuart	5	11	11	5	——	Ashington
Dobson, Ian	5	10	11	1	——	Hull
Skipper, Peter	5	11	12	6½	——	Hull
McDonald, Robert	6	3	13	5	——	Hull
Lord, Malcolm	5	7½	11	10	——	Driffield
Horswill, Michael	5	10½	11	0	Plymouth	Anfield Plain
Roberts, Garreth	5	4	10	2	——	Hull
Hood, Derek	5	10½	11	4	——	Washington
Hawker, David	5	7	9	12	——	Hull
McLaren, Stephen	5	7½	9	4	——	
Marwood, Brian	5	7	9	13	——	Easington
Forwards						
Edwards, Keith	5	7	8	3	Sheffield Utd.	Stockton
Bannister, Bruce	5	7½	11	5	Plymouth	Bradford
Warboys, Alan	6	½	13	7	Fulham	Goldthorpe
Farley, John	5	7	9	12	Wolverhamton W.	Stockton
Norrie, Craig	5	10½	10	11½	——	Hull
Leadbeater, David	5	7	10	5½	——	

MANSFIELD TOWN

	Height ft.	in.	Weight st.	lb.	Previous Club	Birthplace
Goalkeepers						
Arnold, Rod	5	9	11	3	Wolves	Wolverhampton
New, Martin	6	0	11	12	Arsenal	Swindon
Defenders						
Bird, Kevin	5	10½	12	2	Doncaster R.	Doncaster
Burrows, Adrian	5	11	11	12	——	Sutton
Dawkins, Derek	5	10	11	5	Leicester C.	London
Curtis, Bob	5	9½	11	3	Charlton Ath.	Shirebrook
Foster, Barry	5	8	11	7	——	Worksop
Foster, Colin	5	10	12	2	——	Nottingham
McClelland, John	6	2	12	5	Bangor City	Belfast
Saxby, Mick	6	0	11	0	——	Clipstone
Wood, Ian	6	1½	13	8	——	Kirkby-in-Ashfield
Midfield						
Curtis, Bob	5	9½	11	3	Charlton Ath.	Shirebrook
Hamilton, Neville	5	9	11	4	Leicester C.	Leicester
Morris, Peter	5	8	11	3	Norwich C.	Mansfield
Saxby, Gary	5	8	10	3	——	Clipstone
Forwards						
Allen, Russell	5	10	11	7	Tranmere R.	Smethwick
Austin, Terry	6	1	11	10	Walsall	Isleworth
Goodwin, David	5	11	12	9	Stoke City	Stoke
Miller, John	5	8	12	3	Norwich C.	Ipswich

MILLWALL

	Height ft.	in.	Weight st.	lb.	Previous Club	Birthplace
Goalkeepers						
Cuff, Pat	6	0	12	4	Middlesbrough	Middlesbrough
Gleasure, Peter	5	11	12	3	——	Luton
Defenders						
Blyth, Mel	6	1	12	2	Southampton	Norwich
Coleman, Phil	5	11	11	9	——	London
Donaldson, Dave	5	10	13	9	Arsenal	London
Kitchener, Barry	6	1½	14	7½	——	Dagenham
Tagg, Tony	6	2¼	13	4	Q.P.R.	Epson
Roberts, Paul	5	7½	10	2½	——	London
Gregory, David	5	7	9	13	——	Essex
Midfield						
Allen, Peter	5	9¼	11	11½	Orient	Hove
Chambers, Brian	5	9¼	11	4	Luton Town	Newcastle
Chatterton, Nicky	5	9	11	4	Crystal Palace	Norwood
Dibble, Chris	5	10	10	4	——	Surrey
Gale, Ian	5	8	10	0	——	Slough
Kinsella, Tony	5	8	9	10½	——	Essex
Mehmet, David	5	8	10	4	——	London
Walker, Phil	5	9¼	12	2¼	——	London
Massey, Andy	5	10	10	3	——	London
Forwards						
McKenna, Alan	5	9½	10	9	——	Edinburgh
Mitchell, John	5	11	12	0¼	Fulham	London
O'Callaghan, Kevin	5	8¼	10	9	——	London
Seasman, John	5	9	11	8	Luton Town	Liverpool
Towner, Tony	5	6	10	0	Brighton & Hove	Brighton
Horrix, Dean	5	10	10	5½	——	Slough

OXFORD UNITED

	Height ft.	in.	Weight st.	lb.	Previous Club	Birthplace
Goalkeepers						
Burton, Royston	5	10	12	2	——	Wantage
Foyster, Stephen	6	3	12	0	——	Norwich
Milkins, John	6	0½	13	7½	Portsmouth	Dagenham
Defenders						
Bodel, Andy	5	11	11	13	——	Clydebank
Briggs, Gary	6	3	12	7	Middlesbrough	Leeds
Doyle, John	5	9	10	7	——	Oxford
Fogg, David	5	10½	11	0	Wrexham	Liverpool
Kingston, Andy	5	11	11	2	——	Oxford
McIntosh, Malcolm	5	8	11	0	——	Oxford
Watson, Gary	6	2	11	7	——	Easington
Midfield						
Duncan, Colin	5	10	11	4	——	Plymouth
Hodgson, Gordon	6	0	12	3	Mansfield	Newcastle
Jeffrey, Billy	5	10	11	6	——	Clydebank
Taylor, Les	5	9	10	9	——	North Shields
Forwards						
Berry, Paul	6	0	12	7	——	Oxford
Emsden, Phil	6	0	11	10	——	Oxford
Foley, Peter	5	11	10	7	——	Bicester
Graydon, Raymond	5	8	11	0	Washington Dip.	Bristol
McGrogan, Hughie	5	9	11	0	——	Dumbarton
Merry, Nick	5	8	10	7	——	Chipping Norton
Seacole, Jason	5	10	11	0	——	Oxford
Sweetzer, Jimmy	5	9½	11	0	——	Woking
White, Archie	5	7	10	8	——	Glasgow

PLYMOUTH ARGYLE

	Height ft.	in.	Weight st.	lb.	Previous Club	Birthplace
Goalkeepers						
Hodge, Martin	6	2	12	13	——	Southport
Hards, Neil	6	0	12	7	——	Portsmouth
Defenders						
Bason, Brian	5	9	11	1	Chelsea	Epsom
Clarke, Colin	6	1½	13	0	Oxford United	Glasgow
Cooper, Leigh	5	7	10	8	——	Reading
Foster, George	5	10	11	2	——	Plymouth
Hodges, Kevin	5	7	10	0	——	Bridport
James, Tyrone	6	3	11	0	Fulham	Paddington
McNeill, Brian	5	9	10	12	Bristol City	Newcastle-on-Tyne
Uzzell, John	5	10	11	0	——	Plymouth
Midfield						
Brennan, Stephan	5	9	11	0	Crystal Palace	London
Elliott, William	5	10	11	6	——	Poole
Fear, Keith	5	7	10	8	Bristol City	Bristol
Harrison, Chris	5	8	10	6	——	Launceston
Megson, Gary	5	10	11	0	——	Manchester
McCormick, Steve	5	7	9	7	Manchester City	Manchester

Forwards						
Ball, Gary	5	8	9	8	——	St. Austell
Binney, Frederick	5	10	12	2	Brighton	Plymouth
Forde, Clevere	5	7	12	0	Hounslow	London
Graves, Mark	5	9	10	11	——	Middlesex
Johnson, Brian	5	10	11	6	——	London
Levy, Tony	5	10	9	10	——	London
Perrin, Steven	6	1	12	3	Crystal Palace	London
Rogers, Alan	5	10	9	10	——	Plymouth
Trusson, Michael	5	11	11	10	——	Northolt
Upton, Colin	5	7	10	9	——	Reading

READING

	Height ft.	Height in.	Weight st.	Weight lb.	Previous Club	Birthplace
Goalkeeper						
Death, Steve	5	8	11	7	West Ham	Norton
Defenders						
Bennett, Paul	6	0	12	6	Southampton	Southampton
Henderson, Stewart	5	8	11	8	Brighton	Bridge Allan
Hetzke, Steve	6	2	11	10	——	Marlborough
Hicks, Martin	6	3	13	6	Charlton Ath.	Stratford-on-Avon
Moreline, Dave	5	9	10	8	Fulham	Stepney
Peters, Gary	6	0	12	3	Guildford C.	Carshalton
White, Mark	5	9	11	0	Sheffield Wed.	Sheffield
Midfield						
Bowman, Richie	5	6	10	7	Charlton Ath.	Lewisham
Lewis, Alan	5	8	10	12	Brighton	Oxford
Sanchez, Lawrie	5	11	11	9	——	Reading
Wanklyn, Wayne	5	7	10	7	——	Hull
Forwards						
Alexander, John	5	11	10	11	Millwall	Liverpool
Earles, Pat	5	7	11	6	Southampton	Titchfield
Kearney, Mike	6	0	12	0	Chester	Glasgow
Kearns, Oliver	6	0	12	0	Banbury	Banbury
Williams, Jerry	5	11	11	10	——	Didcot

ROTHERHAM UNITED

	Height ft.	Height in.	Weight st.	Weight lb.	Previous Club	Birthplace
Goalkeepers						
McAlister, Tom	6	0	11	1	Sheff. Utd.	Clydebank
Mountford, Raymond	6	3	12	7	Man. Utd.	Goldthorpe
Defenders						
Breckin, John	5	10	12	1	——	Rotherham
Flynn, John	6	0	11	7	Sheff. Utd.	Workington
Forrest, Gerry	5	8½	10	1	——	
Galloway, Steve	5	10	10	3	——	Stockton
Green, John	5	11½	12	10½	——	Rotherham
Stancliffe, Paul	6	2	13	13½	——	Sheffield
Taylor, Ashley	5	9	9	9½	——	Sheffield
Midfield						
Carr, Peter	5	9	9	12½	——	Rawmarsh
Moon, Richard	5	9	11	3½	——	Maltby
Smith, David	5	8	11	13	Lincoln C.	Thornby
Nix, Peter	5	7½	9	9½	——	Rotherham
Rhodes, Mark	5	8½	11	1½	——	Sheffield

Forwards						
Crawford, Alan	5	8	9	7	——	Rotherham
Dawson, Richard	5	8½	12	2	——	Chesterfield
Evans, Stewart	6	4	11	10	——	Rawmarsh
Gwyther, David	5	11½	13	5½	Halifax T.	Birmingham
Philips, Trevor	5	6½	11	0	——	Barnsley
Winn, Stephen	5	9½	11	9	——	Thornby

SHEFFIELD UNITED

	Height ft.	in.	Weight st.	lb.	Previous Club	Birthplace
Goalkeepers						
Conroy, Steve	5	11	12	2	——	Chesterfield
Johns, Nicky	6	1	12	3	Tampa Bay	Bristol
Defenders						
Cutbush, John	5	7½	10	7	Fulham	Malta
Franks, Colin	5	11	12	8	Watford	Wembley
Garner, Paul	5	8¾	10	8	Huddersfield Town	Doncaster
Jones, Phil	6	0½	12	4	——	Mansfield
Keeley, Andy	5	10	11	5	Tottenham Hotspur	Basildon
Kenworthy, Tony	5	8	10	8	——	Leeds
Mathews, John	5	11½	11	13½	Arsenal	London
McGarry, Brian	5	9¾	11	6	Bromsgrove	Birmingham
McPhail, John	5	10½	12	6	Dundee	Dundee
Renwick, Craig	5	10½	11	2½	East Stirling	Lanark
Tibbott, Les	5	10	11	7	Ipswich Town	Ipswich
Midfield						
Benjamin, Ian	6	0	11	10½	——	Nottingham
Guy, Mike	5	9	11	1½	Coleraine	Limavady
Hamson, Gary	5	9½	10	12	——	Nottingham
Harwood, Richard	5	7	10	12	——	Sheffield
Sabella, Alex	5	8	10	13	River Plate	Buenos Aires
Speight, Mick	5	10½	12	3	——	Upton
Rioch, Bruce					Derby County	
Forwards						
Anderson, Peter	5	9	11	9	Tampa Bay	
Brown, Dougie	5	9	12	4	Clydebank	Airdrie
Flood, John	5	7	9	8½	——	Glasgow
Finnieston, Steve	5	11	12	0	Chelsea	London
Larner, Keith	5	7	10	7	Letchworth	Bushey
McKee, Steve	5	8¾	10	4	Linfield	Belfast

SHEFFIELD WEDNESDAY

	Height ft.	in.	Weight st.	lb.	Previous Club	Birthplace
Goalkeepers						
Bolder, Robert	6	1	13	7	——	Dover
Cox, Brian	6	0	12	7	——	Sheffield
Turner, Christopher	5	11	11	0	——	Sheffield
Defenders						
Blackhall, Raymond					Newcastle	Ashington
Dowd, Hugh	6	1	12	11	Glenavon	Lurgan
Grant, David	6	0	12	11	——	Sheffield
Mullen, James	5	10	11	9	——	Jarrow
Pickering, Michael					Southampton	Mirfield
Shirtliff, Peter	5	11	12	0	——	Sheffield
Smith, Mark	6	0½	12	6	——	Sheffield

Midfield						
Hornsby, Brian	5	8	10	7	Shrewsbury	Peterborough
Johnson, Jeffrey	5	8	11	7	Crystal P.	Cardiff
Porterfield, Ian	5	11	12	7	Sunderland	Dunfermline
Taylor, Kevin	5	7	11	7	———	Wakefield
Forwards						
Curran, Terry					Southampton	Kinsley
Fleming, Ian					Aberdeen	Maybole
Leman, Denis	5	5	10	9	Man. City	Newcastle
Lowey, John					Man. Utd.	Manchester
Nimmo, Ian	5	11	11	7	———	Boston
Owen, Gordon	5	8	10	1	———	Barnsley
Strutt, Brian	5	9½	10	7	———	Malta
Wylde Rodger	6	1	12	0	———	Sheffield

SOUTHEND UNITED

	Height ft.	in.	Weight st.	lb.	Previous Club	Birthplace
Goalkeepers						
Cawston, Mervyn	6	2	12	2	Chicago Sting	Norwich
Horn, Graham	6	2	13	11	Kettering	Westminster
Defenders						
Cusack, David	6	2	13	11	Sheffield W.	Thurcroft
Hadley, Tony	6	0	11	11	———	Rochford
Moody, Alan	5	11	11	12	Middlesbrough	Middlesbrough
Stead, Mickey	5	7	11	10	Tottenham H.	London
Walker, John	6	0	11	10	———	Rochford
Yates, Stephen	6	0	12	11	Leicester	Ashby
Midfield						
Dudley, Phil	5	7	10	0	———	Basildon
Goodwin, Steve	5	7	11	6	Norwich	Chadderton
Hull, Jeff	5	6	9	2	———	Rochford
Laverick, Mickey	5	9	10	10	Mansfield	Trimdon
Otulakowski, Anton	5	7	10	7	West Ham	Dewsbury
Forwards						
Abbott, Peter	6	1	12	2	Crewe	Rotherham
Fell, Gerry	5	11	11	12	Brighton	Newark
Franklin, Graham	5	8	11	4	Lowestoft	Bicester
Morris, Colin	5	6	10	2	Burnley	Blyth
Parker, Derrick	5	7	10	2	———	Islingto ı
Poutney, Ron	5	6	9	7	Bilston	Bilston

SWINDON TOWN

	Height ft.	in.	Weight st.	lb.	Previous Club	Birthplace
Goalkeepers						
Allan, James	6	1	12	4	Apprentice	Inverness
Ogden, Christopher	5	10½	12	5	Oldham Ath.	Oldham
Roberts, Kevin	6	0	12	9	Weston Rovers	Bristol
Defenders						
Aizlewood, Stephen	5	11½	13	7	Newport Co.	Newport
Ford, Andrew	5	10	12	0	Southend Utd.	Minehead
Lewis, Russell	5	10	13	0	Everwarm F.C.	Neath
McLaughlin, John	5	8	10	10	Colchester	Edmonton, London
Norman, Kenneth	5	9	10	6	Apprentice	Longlevens
Stroud, Kenneth	5	9½	11	13	Apprentice	London
Trollope, John	6	0	12	2	Apprentice	Wroughton

	Height ft.	in.	Weight st.	lb.	Previous Club	Birthplace
Midfield						
Carter, Roy	6	0	10	9	Hereford Utd.	Torpoint
Hamilton, Bryan	5	8	11	4	Millwall	Belfast
Kamara, Christopher	6	1½	11	11	Middlesbrough	Portsmouth
Mchale, Raymond	5	7½	12	7	Halifax Town	Sheffield
Williams, Brian	5	7	12	0	Q.P.R.	Manchester
Forwards						
Abbley, Stephen	5	11	10	6	Local Football	Liverpool
Bates, Philip	6	0	11	7	Shrewsbury	West Bromwich
Dornan, Peter	6	1	12	2	Linfield	Belfast
Gilchrist, Paul	5	11	11	4	Portsmouth	Dartford
Mayes, Alan	5	6	10	7	Watford	Edmonton, London
Miller, Ian	5	9	11	5	Doncaster Rov.	Perth
Rowland, Andrew	5	10½	11	11	Bury	Derby

WIMBLEDON

	Height ft.	in.	Weight st.	lb.	Previous Club	Birthplace
Goalkeeper						
Goddard, Ray	5	10	11	9	Millwall	London
Defenders						
Bowgett, Paul	6	1			Spurs	Stevenage
Cunningham, Tommy	6	0	11	3	Q.P.R.	London
Eames, Terry	5	10	11	1	Crystal P.	Croydon
Haverson, Paul					Q.P.R.	Chigwell
Harwood, Lee					Southampton	
Perkins, Stephen	5	11	11	0	Q.P.R.	
Midfield						
Briley, Leslie	5	7	9	11	Hereford	London
Denny, Paul	5	9	10	8	Southend	Croydon
Downes, Walter					——	London
Dziadulewicz, Mark					Southend	
Galliers, Steven	5	6	9	7	Chorley	Chorley
Ketteridge, Steven	5	9	10	7	Derby	Stevenage
Forwards						
Cork, Alan	6	0			Derby	Derby
Driver, Philip					Luton T.	
Leslie, John	5	8	11	2	Charlton	London
Knowles, Ray					——	London
Parsons, Stephen	6	0	12	7	——	London

DIVISION FOUR

ALDERSHOT

	Height ft.	in.	Weight st.	lb.	Previous Club	Birthplace
Goalkeepers						
Dodds, Kenneth	5	11	11	4	Sunderland	Portsmouth
Johnson, Glen	6	2	13	6	Doncaster	Barrow
Defenders						
Edwards, Nigel	5	11	11	10	Chester	Wrexham
Howitt, Dave	5	11	11	8	Workington	Birmingham
Jopling, Joe	6	0	12	13	Leic. City	South Shields
Scott, Peter	5	9	11	4	York City	Liverpool
Wooler, Alan	5	10	11	0	West Ham	Poole
Youlden, Tommy	6	0¼	12	9	Reading	London

Midfield						
Crosby, Malcolm	5	9½	11	0	——	South Shields
Dixon, Will	5	8	10	6	Swindon T.	London
Green, Adrian	6	0	10	9	Leic. City	Leicester
Longhorn, Dennis	5	11	11	0	Sheffield U.	Hythe, S'ton.
Forwards						
Bambridge, Steve	5	11	10	12	——	London
Brodie, Murray	5	11½	12	13	Leic. City	Glasgow
Dungworth, John	6	0	10	7	Oldham A.	Rotherham
French, Micky	5	11	12	2	Doncaster R.	
Lucas, Brian	5	7	10	12	——	Farnborough
McGregor, Alex	5	10	10	8	West Ham U.	Glasgow
Needham, Andy	5	11	11	6	Blackburn R.	Oldham
Shanahan, Terry	5	10	11	0	Bournemouth	London
Smith, Gareth, (App.)						
Tomlin, Dave	5	10	11	9	Torquay Utd.	Nuneaton

BOURNEMOUTH

	Height ft.	Height in.	Weight st.	Weight lb.	Previous Club	Birthplace
Goalkeeper						
Allen, Kenny	6	5	12	1	Bath City	Middlesbrough
Defenders						
Allen, Kevin	5	10	11	5	——	Ryde
Brown, Roger	6	1	11	10	AP Leamington	Tamworth
Bryant, Jeff	6	0	11	8	Wimbledon	Redhill
Butler, Geoff	5	7	11	0	Norwich C.	Middlesbrough
Cunningham, Ian	5	11	10	11	——	Glasgow
Ferns, Phil	5	11	11	2	——	Liverpool
Impey, John	6	0	12	7	Cardiff C.	Exeter
Miller, Keith	5	9½	10	10	West Ham	Lewisham
Moore, Jon	5	11½	11	3	Millwall	Cardiff
Midfield						
Benjafield, Brian	5	8	11	1	——	Barton-on-Sea
Borthwick, Gary	5	7	10	4	Barnet	Slough
Brown, Kenny	5	8	9	0	Barnsley	Barnsley
Heffernan, Tom	6	0	11	8	Tottenham	Dublin
Holder, Phil	5	4	11	6	C. Palace	Kilburn
Forwards						
Butler, Mick	5	9	10	0	Huddersfield	Barnsley
MacDougall, Ted	5	10	11	11	Southampton	Inverness
Massey, Steve	5	11	11	0	Stockport	Stockport
Scott, Joey	5	10	12	3	Falmouth Tn.	Plymouth

BRADFORD CITY

	Height ft.	Height in.	Weight st.	Weight lb.	Previous Club	Birthplace
Goalkeepers						
Downsborough, Peter	5	10½	13	4	Swindon	Halifax
Smith, Stephen	6	0	12	5	Birmingham	Chepstow
Defenders						
Baines, Stephen	6	0	12	12	Huddersfield	Newark
Jackson, Peter	6	1	11	8	——	Bradford
Podd, Ceril	5	9	10	0	——	St. Kitts
Watson, Gary	5	8	10	6	——	Bradford
Wood, Mick					Blackburn	Bury
Reaney, Paul	5	9	11	7½	Leeds	Fulham

Midfield						
Bates, Mick	5	7	10	7	Walsall	Doncaster
Dolan, Terry	6	1	11	3	Huddersfield	Bradford
Robertson, Lammond	5	10	11	2	Peterborough	Paisley
Gallagher, Barry					——	Bradford
Forwards						
Hutchins, Donald	5	7	10	2	Plymouth	Middlesbrough
Martinez, Eugene					——	Chelmsford
McNiven, David	5	6	11	4	Leeds	Stonehouse

CREWE ALEXANDRA

	Height ft.	in.	Weight st.	lb.	Previous Club	Birthplace
Goalkeeper						
Rafferty, Kevin	6	0	11	8	——	Crewe
Defenders						
Beavon, Paul	5	11	11	4	Swansea C.	Shrewsbury
Dulson, Garry	5	10	11	10	Port Vale	Nottingham
Cheetham, Hughie	5	9	10	9	——	Manchester
Wilkinson, Neil	5	10	11	4	Port Vale	Manchester
Midfield						
Bowles, Paul	6	0	13	0	Manchester Utd.	Manchester
Davies, Dai	6	0	13	0	Swansea C.	Rhondda Valley
Mayman, Paul	5	8	10	5	——	Crewe
Forwards						
Coyne, Peter	5	9½	11	0	Manchester Utd.	Hartlepool
Nelson, Dennis	5	8	10	6	Reading	Edinburgh
Purdie, Bernard	5	9	10	9	Chester	Wrexham
Warnock, Neil	5	9	10	10	York City	Sheffield

DARLINGTON

	Height ft.	in.	Weight st.	lb.	Previous Club	Birthplace
Goalkeepers						
Burleigh, Martin	5	10	13	1	Carlisle U.	Durham
Owers, Phil	5	11	10	9	Gillingham	Shildon
Defenders						
Cochrane, Jimmy	5	9	11	0	Middlesborough	Glasgow
Craig, Derek	6	0	11	9	Newcastle Utd.	Durham
Hague, Neil	6	½	12	7	Rotherham U.	Rotherham
Nattress, Clive	6	0	12	4½	Blackpool	Durham
Stone, John	6	0	12	2	York	Carlinstow
Midfield						
Crosson, David	5	9	11	11	Newcastle Utd.	Durham
Lyons, Barry	5	7	10	8	York City	Nottingham
Maitland, Lloyd	5	7	11	2	Huddersfield T.	Birmingham
Probert, Eric	5	7½	10	9½	Notts County	South Kirby
Taylor, Philip	5	9	10	12	York City	Sheffield
Wann, Dennis	5	8	10	11	York City	Blackpool
Forwards						
Ferguson, Ronnie	6	0	12	5	Sheffield Wed.	Accrington
Patterson, Thomas	5	10	11	0	Bournemouth	Newcastle
Peachey, John	6	0	12	1	Barnsley	Cambridge
Seal, Jimmy	5	10	11	8	York City	Pontefract
Walsh, Alan	6	0	11	0	Middlesbrough	Hartlepool

DONCASTER ROVERS

	Height ft.	in.	Weight st.	lb.	Previous Club	Birthplace
Goalkeeper						
Peacock, Dennis	6	3	14	0	Nottingham Forest	Lincoln
Defenders						
Bentley, David	5	8½	10	0	Chesterfield	Worksop
Bradley, David	5	11	12	0	Manchester Utd.	Salford
Flanagan, Shaun	5	3	9	7	——	
Lister, Stephen					——	Doncaste
Midfield						
Cork, David	5	6	9	5	Manchester Utd.	Doncaster
Lally, Patrick	5	10	10	9	Swansea City	Paddington
Lewis, Frederick	5	10	11	4	Blackburn Rovers	Long Ear Eaton
Meagan, Thomas	5	9	10	0	——	Wallasey
Snodin, Glyn	5	5	9	0	——	Rotherham
Forwards						
Packer, Leslie					——	Sunderland
Pugh, Daral	5	7	9	0	——	

HALIFAX TOWN

	Height ft.	in.	Weight st.	lb.	Previous Club	Birthplace
Goalkeeper						
Leonard, Michael	5	11½	11	4	——	Carshalton
Defenders						
Burke, Peter	6	1	12	12	Barnsley	Rotherham
Dunleavy, Chris	5	10	12	7	Chester	Liverpool
Hutt, Geoff	5	8	12	0	York C.	Hazelwood
Midfield						
Kennedy, Mick	5	9	11	5	——	Salford
Forwards						
Bullock, Mick	5	10½	12	10	Orient	Stoke-on-Trent
Firth, Francis	5	10	11	0	Huddersfield	Dewsbury
Johnson, Kevin	5	6	10	4	Huddersfield	Doncaster
Mountford, Bob	5	11	12	4	Huddersfield	Stoke-on-Trent
Stafford, Andrew	6	2	11	10	Blackburn	Littleboro

HARTLEPOOL UNITED

	Height ft.	in.	Weight st.	lb.	Previous Club	Birthplace
Goalkeepers						
Richardson, Graham	5	9	12	4	——	Sedgefield
Watson, John	6	1	11	10	Huddersfield	Halifax
Defenders						
Ayre, William	5	10	12	2	Scarborough	Ryton
Brooks, Steve	6	0	12	8	Southport	
Gorry, Martin	5	9	12	4	Newcastle	Derby
Goldthorpe, Wayne	6	0	12	10	Huddersfield	Staincross
Norton, David	5	8	11	10	Whickham	Whickham
Brown, Philip	5	11	10	12	——	Hartlepool
Leighton, Edward	5	10½	11	0	——	Hartlepool
Normanton, Graham	5	10	11	8	——	Hartlepool
Duncan, Anthony	5	9	11	10	——	Hartlepool

Midfield						
Hogan, Roy	5	5½	10	12	——	Hartlepool
Lawrence, Mark	6	1	11	10	——	Middlesbrough
Linacre, John	5	10	10	12	Whitby Town	Middlesbrough
Loadwick, Derek	5	9	11	0	Stockport Co.	Middlesbrough
Smith, George	5	9	11	2	Swansea	Newcastle
Lowe, Kenneth	5	10	10	10	——	Billingham
Forwards						
Crumplin, Ian	5	10	11	10	Blue Star	Newcastle
Evans, Dave	5	11	11	8	——	Peterlee
Harding, Alan	5	9	10	10	Lincoln	Sunderland
Houchen, Keith	6	1	11	2	——	Middlesbrough
Larkin, Gordon	5	10	10	12	——	Hartlepool
Newton, Robert	5	11	11	2	Huddersfield	Chesterfield

HEREFORD UNITED

	Height ft.	in.	Weight st.	lb.	Previous Club	Birthplace
Goalkeepers						
Hughes, Thomas	6	1½	12	5	Aston V.	Dalmuir
Knight, Lyndon	6	1	11	6	App/Pro	Lydbrook
Defenders						
Price, Chris	5	7	10	2	App/Pro	Hereford
Marshall, Julian	6	3	13	0	Amateur	Swansea
Bailey, Michael	5	8	11	7	Minnosota Kicks	Wisbech
Bouston, Bryan	5	7	10	9	App/Pro	Hereford
Burrows, Philip	5	8	10	13	Plymouth	Stockport
Cornes, Stuart	6	0	11	1	App/Pro	Usk
Dixon, David	6	2	12	2	App/Pro	Hereford
Layton, John	6	0	12	13	Amateur	Hereford
Thomas, Valmore	5	8	10	6	Coventry C.	Worksop
Midfield						
Emery, Stephen	5	9	11	2	App/Pro	Hereford
Hendry, Ian	5	8	10	7	Aston V.	
Holmes, Kyle	5	7	10	9	App/Pro	Abergavenny
Hunt, Paul	5	9	11	8	Amateur	Hereford
Spiring, Peter	5	8	10	13	Luton T.	Glastonbury
Forwards						
Gould, Bobby	5	11			Bristol Rov.	Coventry
Holmes, William	5	10	11	2	Wimbledon	Balham
Jones, David	6	2	14	0	Telford U.	Chirk
McGrellis, Frank	5	10	11	7	Coventry C.	Falkirk
Stephens, Kenneth	5	7½	10	12	Bristol Rov.	Bristol
White, Winstone	5	10	11	4	Leicester C.	Leicester
Powell, Wayne	5	11	11	0	Bristol R.	Newport

HUDDERSFIELD TOWN

	Height ft.	in.	Weight st.	lb.	Previous Club	Birthplace
Goalkeepers						
Starling, Alan	6	1	13	4	Northampton	Barking
Taylor, Richard	6	0	12	9	——	Huddersfield

Defenders						
Branagan, James	5	9½	11	2	Oldham	Davyhulme
Brook, Nicholas App.	5	8½	10	5	—	Huddersfield
Brown, Malcolm	6	2	13	3	Bury	Salford
Gartland, Paul	5	10	12	5	—	Shipley
Gibson, Paul	5	8	10	6	—	Huddersfield
Sandercock, Philip	5	9½	11	7	Torquay	Plymouth
Shepherd, John App.	6	0	12	0	—	Bradford
Midfield						
Armstrong, Terrence	5	9½	11	7	—	Barnsley
Hanvey, Keith	6	0	12	7	Grimsby	Manchester
Hart, Peter	5	10	12	7	—	Mexborough
Holmes, Ian	5	6	11	0	York	Wombwell
Lillis, Mark	6	0	12	2	—	Manchester
Mellor, Robert	6	0	12	2	—	Huddersfield
Sutton, David	6	1	12	0	Plymouth	Tarlaton
Topping, Christopher	6	1	12	10	York	Bubwith
Forwards						
Bielby, Paul	5	8	11	10	Hartlepool	Darlington
Brook, Daryl	5	9	10	5	—	Huddersfield
Cowling, David	5	7	10	6	Doncaster	Doncaster
Fletcher, Peter	6	1	12	0	Stockport	Manchester
Gray, Terence	5	8	10	0	—	Bradford
Robins, Ian	5	9	11	4	Bury	Bury
Smith, Thomas	5	10	11	6	Sheffield U.	Wolverhampton

LINCOLN CITY

	Height ft.	Height in.	Weight st.	Weight lb.	Previous Club	Birthplace
Goalkeepers						
Grothier, Peter	5	11½	12	9½	West Ham U.	London
Fox, Kevin	5	11½	11	1	—	Sheffield
Defenders						
Laybourne, Keith	5	10½	11	1	—	Sunderland
Smith, Mick	6	0½	12	0	—	Sunderland
Loxley, Tony	6	3½	13	0	—	Nottingham
Wright, Billy	5	9	12	4	Birmingham C.	Birmingham
Cooper, Terry	5	11	11	6¾	Notts. Co.	Cwmbran, Newport
Guest, Brendan	6	0	11	7	—	Nottingham
Ward, Stephen	5	10	10	5¼	—	Chapel Town
Midfield						
Fleming, John	5	7	10	11½	Oxford U.	Nottingham
Watson, Graham	5	9	11	6½	Cambridge U.	Doncaster
Cockerill, Glenn	5	11	11	8	—	Cleethorpes
Neale, Philip	5	9	11	2	—	Scunthorpe
Hughes, David	5	9	12	0	Aston Villa	Birmingham
Forwards						
Harford, Mick	6	2	13	3	—	Sunderland
Eden, Alan	5	7	10	12	—	Sunderland
Ward, John	5	11	10	10½	—	Lincoln
Sunley, David	5	10	11	6	Hull City	Lingdale
Hobson, Gordon	5	7	10	1½	—	Sheffield
Burrows, David	5	6	10	2	—	Bilsthorpe Mansfield

NEWPORT COUNTY

	Height ft.	in.	Weight st.	lb.	Previous Club	Birthplace
Goalkeepers						
Dowler, Mike	5	8	11	0	Hereford	Caldicot
Plumley, Gary	6	0	12	0	Leicester	Leicester
Defenders						
Bruton, Dave	6	2	14	0	Swansea	Gloucester
Davies, Grant	5	10	11	0	Preston	Barrow-in-Furness
Oakes, Keith	5	10	12	2	Peterborough	Bedworth
Relish, John	5	8	12	0	Bury	Liverpool
Thompson, Trevor	5	9	10	12	West Brom	N. Shields
Walden, Richard	6	0	12	10	Sheffield Wed.	Hereford
Midfield						
Warriner, Steve	5	7	10	0	Liverpool	Liverpool
Bailey, Neil	5	6	11	0	Burnley	Billinge
Lowndes, Steve	5	7	10	7	——	Cwmbran
Vaughan, Nigel	5	5	9	10	——	Newport
Forwards						
Aldridge, John	5	10	11	0	South Liverpool	Liverpool
Goddard, Howard	5	10	12	0	Bournemouth	Over Wallop
Moore, Kevin	5	9	11	4	Bury	Blackpool
Tynan, Thomas	5	10	13	0	Lincoln City	Liverpool
Brown, Jeremy	5	8	9	0	——	Cwmbran

NORTHAMPTON TOWN

	Height ft.	in.	Weight st.	lb.	Previous Club	Birthplace
Goalkeepers						
Jayes, Carl	6	0	12	3	Leicester	Leicester
Poole, Andrew	6	0	12	5	Mansfield	Chesterfield
Defenders						
Walker, Ricky	5	9	11	2	Coventry	Northampton
Perkins, Glenn	5	8	11	3	App.	Brixworth
Woollett, Alan	5	11	11	3	Leicester	Leicester
McNichol, James	6	3	12	6	App.	Greenock
Saunders, Paul	5	10	11	5	Watford	Watford
Waldock, Desmond	5	10	11	5	App.	
Midfield						
Williams, Keith	5	8	11	3	Aston Villa	Birmingham
Ashenden, Russell	5	7	10	0	N.T.F.C.	Thurrock
Farrington, John	5	10	10	6	Cardiff	Lynmouth
Leonard, Gary	5	9	10	9	App.	Northampton
Forwards						
Corcoran, Stephen	5	10½	11	0	App.	Coventry
Reilly, George	6	2	11	10	Corby T.	Bellshill
Frogatt, John	5	11	12	7	Port Vale	Sutton in Ashfield
McCaffrey, James	5	7	9	11	Portsmouth	Luton
Bowen, Keith	6	0	11	0	——	Northampton

PETERBOROUGH UNITED

	Height ft.	in.	Weight st.	lb.	Previous Club	Birthplace
Goalkeepers						
Overton, Paul	6	2	13	3	Ipswich	Soham
Waugh, Keith	6	0	12	5½	Sunderland	Sunderland

Defenders						
Carmichael, Jack	5	10	13	2½	Arsenal	Newcastle
Collins, Steven	5	10	11	3	——	Stamford
Smith, Anthony	5	11	11	12	Newcastle	Sunderland
Winters, John	5	11	11	4½	——	Wisbech
Midfield						
Chard, Philip	5	10	11	3½	——	Corby
Doyle, Robert	5	11	11	12	Barnsley	Dumbarton
Gynn, Michael	5	3	10	6	——	Peterborough
McEwan, Billy	5	10	11	6	Mansfield	Lanarkshire
Slough, Alan	5	10	11	8	Fulham	Luton
Sharkey, Pat	5	5	12	1	Colchester	Omagh
Forwards						
Anderson, Trevor	5	8½	10	13	Swindon	Belfast
Butlin, Barry	5	11½	11	9½	Nottingham F.	Roslington
Cooke, Joseph	5	11	12	8	Bradford City	Dominica
Cliss, Tony	5	7	10	2	——	March
Guy, Alan	5	6	12	3	Newcastle	Jarrow
Quow, Trevor	5	5	10	6	——	Peterborough
Robson, Tommy	5	8	10	7½	Newcastle	Gateshead

PORTSMOUTH

	Height ft.	in.	Weight st.	lb.	Previous Club	Birthplace
Goalkeepers						
Mellor, Peter	6	1¾	14	0	Hereford	Prestbury
Knight, Alan	6	1	12	6	——	Balham
Defenders						
Ellis, Peter	5	9	11	2	——	Portsmouth
Foster, Stephen	6	1¼	12	8	——	Portsmouth
Piper, Stephen	5	10¾	11	10	Brighton	Brighton
Viney, Keith	5	11	11	12	Portsmouth	Portsmouth
Roberts, Trevor			85.8		——	
Midfield						
Denyer, Peter	5	10	11	9	——	Hazelmere
Lathan, John	5	7	11	0	Carlisle	Sunderland
McIlwraith, James	5	9	10	4	Bury	Troon
Bryant, Stephen	5	8	10	6	Northampton	Islington
Forwards						
Davey, Stephen	5	8½	10	3	Hereford	Plymouth
Garwood, Colin	5	8	10	13	Colchester	Heacham
Pullar, David	5	10½	10	11	——	Durham
Showers, Derek	5	11	11	4	Bournemouth	Merthyr Tydfil
Barnard, Leigh	5	9	9	10	——	Worsley
Hemmerman, Jeffrey	5	11	11	0	Port Vale	Hull

PORT VALE

	Height ft.	in.	Weight st.	lb.	Previous Club	Birthplace
Goalkeeprs						
Connaughton, Patrick John	6	0	12	5	Man. Utd.	Wigan
Dance, Trevor	5	11	11	10	——	Durham
Defenders						
Keenan, Gerry	5	9	11	0	Bury	Liverpool
Griffiths, Neil	5	11	11	10	Chester	Stoke
Delgado, Bob	6	0	12	2	Chester	Cardiff
Hawkins, Graham	6	0	13	4	Blackburn	Darlaston

Bloor, Alan	6	2	13	7	Stoke C.	Stoke
Sproson, Phil	6	0	12	0	——	Stoke
Leese, Bill	6	1	12	6	——	Stoke
Bentley, Bill	5	11	13	5	Stoke C.	Stoke
Midfield						
Beech, Ken	5	7	10	2	——	Stoke
Healy, Felix	5	10	12	0	Finn Harps	Londonderry
Farrell, Peter	5	7	10	9	Bury	Liverpool
Bromage, Russ	5	11	11	5	——	Stoke
Stenson, Ged	5	7	10	2	Everton	Bootle
Elsby, Ian	5	8	9	10	——	Stoke
Bennett, Paul	5	9	9	9	——	Liverpool
Forwards						
Chamberlain, Neville	5	8	11	5	——	Stoke
Chamberlain, Mark	5	9	9	8	——	Stoke
Sinclair, Brian	5	6	9	6	Blackpool	Liverpool
Wright, Bernie	6	1	13	0	Bradford C.	Birmingham
Todd, Ken	5	7	9	9	Wolves	Durham
Tully, Kevin	5	10	12	4	Crewe	Manchester

ROCHDALE

	Height ft.	in.	Weight st.	lb.	Previous Club	Birthplace
Goalkeeper						
Slack, Andy	5	9	10	7	——	Bury
Defenders						
Bannon, Ian	6	0	11	10	——	Bury
Hallows, Paul	5	8	10	9	Bolton	Chester
Hart, Brian	6	0	11	0	——	Bolton
Snookes, Eric	5	10	11	0	Preston	Birmingham
Taylor, Brian	6	0	11	9	Doncaster	Hodthorpe
Wright, Graham	5	8	10	4	——	Manchester
Midfield						
Collins, Doug	5	8	10	0	Grimsby	Newton
Esser, David	5	6	10	2	Everton	Bowdon
Oliver, Ted	5	7	10	0	——	Manchester
O'Loughlin, Nigel	5	9	10	10	Shrewsbury	Rochdale
Scaife, Robert	6	0	12	4	Hartlepool	Northampton
Forwards						
Ashworth, Phil	5	11	11	7	Southport	Burnley
Hilditch, Mark	5	11	11	8	Rochdale	Shaw
Hoy, Bobby	5	7	10	0	York	Halifax
Jones, Chris	5	11	11	8	Doncaster	Altrincham
Stanley, Nicholas	5	9	10	4	——	Bolton

SCUNTHORPE UNITED

	Height ft.	in.	Weight st.	lb.	Previous Club	Birthplace
Goalkeepers						
Crawford, Graeme	6	$1\frac{1}{2}$	13	0	York	Falkirk
Gordon, James	5	11	12	5	Lincoln	
Defenders						
Davy, Stephen	5	$8\frac{1}{2}$	10	2	——	Norwich
Oates, Robert	5	$11\frac{1}{2}$	11	7	——	Leeds
O'Donnel, Jon	5	$9\frac{1}{2}$	12	8	Hartlepool	Leeds
Peacock, John	5	$8\frac{1}{2}$	10	2	——	Leeds
Pilling, Stuart	5	9	10	2	Hull City	Sheffield

	Height ft.	in.	Weight st.	lb.	Previous Club	Birthplace
Midfield						
Deere, Stephen	6	1½	12	10	Hull City	Burnham
Kavanagh, Eamon	5	9½	11	10	Workington	
Keeley, Nolan	5	10½	10	12	——	Fakenham
Hall, David	5	8½	11	0	——	Doncaster
Forwards						
Gibson, David	5	5½	9	10	Hull	
Grimes, Vince	5	9½	11	10	Hull	Scunthorpe
Couch, Geoffrey	5	10½	10	6	——	Scunthorpe
Kilmore, Kevin	5	10	10	9	——	Scunthorpe
Earl, Steven	5	9	12	4		

STOCKPORT CO.

	Height ft.	in.	Weight st.	lb.	Previous Club	Birthplace
Goalkeepers						
Lawson, David	6	0¾	11	0	Luton	Newcastle
Rogan, Mike	5	11	12	0	Workington	Fleetwood
Defenders						
Rutter, John	5	7	10	7	Exeter C.	Warrington
Thorpe, Andy	5	10	10	10	——	Stockport
Edwards, Paul	5	10	10	4	Oldham A.	Crompton
Smith, Nigel	5	10	10	8	Non Contract	Manchester
Connor, James	6	0	11	0	——	Stockport
Midfield						
Henson, Phil	5	10	9	12	Sheffield W.	Manchester
Galvin, Chris	5	10	12	3	Hull C.	Huddersfield
Summerbee, Mike	5	10½	11	4	Blackpool	Preston
Forwards						
Armstrong, George	5	6	11	2	Leicester C.	Hebburn
Bradd, Les	6	0	12	12	Notts. C.	Buxton
Lee, Stuart	5	7	9	0	Wrexham	Manchester
Prudham, Eddie	5	8½	10	6	Carlisle	Gateshead

TORQUAY UNITED

	Height ft.	in.	Weight st.	lb.	Previous Club	Birthplace
Goalkeepers						
Turner, John	6	0	12	10	Reading	Peterlee
Defenders						
Boulton, Clinton	6	0	11	7	Port Vale	Stoke
Bowden, Alan	5	8	11	0	——	Torquay
Dunne, Jimmy	5	10	10	0	Fulham	Eire
Payne, Jess	6	2	11	0	Leicester	Leicester
Green, Mike	6	1	10	7	Plymouth A.	Carlisle
Ritchie, Steve	5	8	11	0	Aberdeen	Bo'ness
Twitchin, Ian	5	8	10	0	——	Teignmouth
Midfield						
Davies, Roy	5	8	11	7	Reading	London
Forwards						
Clarke, Stuart	5	9	11	0	——	Torquay
Coffill, Peter	5	8	10	0	Watford	London
Cooper, Steve	5	10	11	7	Stourbridge	Stourbreidge
Lawrence, Les	6	3	11	7	Telford	Wolverhampton
Murphy, Donal	5	10	11	0	Coventry	Dublin

TRANMERE ROVERS

	Height ft.	in.	Weight st.	lb.	Previous Club	Birthplace
Goalkeepers						
Johnson, Dick	6	1	12	10	——	Liverpool
West, Gordon	6	1	14	0	Everton	Darfield
Defenders						
Bramhall, John	6	2	13	6	——	Warrington
Eaton, Stephen	6	0	11	13	——	Liverpool
Flood, Eddie	5	7	10	0	Liverpool	Liverpool
Mathias, Ray	5	9	11	4	——	Liverpool
Parry, Leslie	5	11	11	0	——	Wallasey
Postlethwaite, Dennis	6	½	12	1	——	Birkenhead
Williams, John	6	2	13	6	——	Liverpool
Midfield						
Cliff, Eddie	5	10	11	5	Notts Co.	Liverpool
Craven, Steve	5	10	11	0	——	Birkenhead
Evans, Cliff	5	10	10	9	——	Birkenhead
Griffiths, Ian	5	6	10	2	——	Birkenhead
O'Neill, Tommy	5	6½	10	4	Southport	St. Helens
Palios, Mark	5	8	10	13	——	Birkenhead
Peplow, Steve	5	8	10	4	Nottingham F.	Liverpool
Forwards						
Kerr, John	6	1	12	5	——	Birkenhead
McAuley, Hugh	5	7	9	7	Charlton Ath.	Bootle
Whittingham, Stephen	5	10	11	8	——	Birkenhead

WALSALL

	Height ft.	in.	Weight st.	lb.	Previous Club	Birthplace
Goalkeepers						
Green, Ron	6	2½	13	12	Alvechurch	Birmingham
Kearns, Mick	6	3	13	12	Oxford U.	Banbury
Turner, Ian	6	0	12	10	Southampton	Middlesbrough
Defenders						
Caswell, Brian	5	10	10	7	——	Wednesbury
Harrison, Colin	5	10	11	8	——	Pelsall
Macken, Tony	5	7	12	0	Derby	Dublin
Mower, Ken	6	0	12	2	——	Walsall
Paul, Ian	5	10	11	8	——	Wolverhampton
Sbragia, Ricky	6	0	11	0	Birmingham C.	Lennoxtown
Serella, Dave	5	9	10	10	Notts. F.	Kings Lynn
Midfield						
Birch, Alan	5	5	10	2	——	West Bromwich
Jones, Steve	6	1	12	1	Q.P.R.	Eastbourne
King, Jeff	5	9	10	7	Derby	Faulthouse
Waddington, Steve	5	4	8	10	Stoke City	Crewe
Forwards						
Kelly, Jimmy	5	6	9	1	W'ton Wand.	Aldergrove NI
McDonough, Roy	6	1	12	2	Birmingham C.	Solihull
Penn, Don	5	11	11	8	——	Smethwick
Syrett, Dave	5	11	11	13	Mansfield T.	Salisbury
Waddington, Paul	5	8	11	4	——	Warley
Williams, Jimmy	5	8	12	2	Worc. City	Wolverhampton

WIGAN ATHLETIC

	Height ft.	in.	Weight st.	lb.	Previous Club	Birthplace
Goalkeeper						
Brown, John	5	11	13	0	Stockport Co.	Bradford
Defenders						
Davids, Neil	6	0¾	13	9	Swansea C.	Bingley
Fretwell, David	5	9	10	9	Bradford C.	Normanton
Gillibrand, Ian	5	8	11	0	——	Blackburn
Hart, Nigel	6	0	11	7	——	Manchester
Hinnigan, Joseph	6	0	12	0	——	Liverpool
Smart, Kevin	5	7	10	8	Plymouth A.	High Heaton
Midfield						
Corrigan, Frank	5	10	11	7	——	Liverpool
Gore, Thomas	5	7	11	0	Tranmere R.	Liverpool
Wright, Jeffrey	5	11	11	7	——	Alston
Purdie, Ian	5	8½	11	0	Motherwell	Motherwell
Forwards						
Brownbill, Derek	5	9	10	10	Port Vale	Liverpool
Crompton, Alan	5	9	10	8	Blackburn R.	Manchester
Houghton, Peter	5	11	12	7	——	Liverpool
Moore, Michael	5	9½	10	11	Port Vale	Chorley
Quinn, Anthony	5	11	11	0	Liverpool	——
Wilkie, John	5	7	10	7	Morton	Dundee

YORK CITY

	Height ft.	in.	Weight st.	lb.	Previous Club	Birthplace
Goalkeepers						
Brown, Graham	6	0	12	7	Portland	Matlock
Neenan, Joseph	6	2	11	9	——	Manchester
Defenders						
Clements, Andy	6	0	11	10	Bolton	Swinton
Faulkner, Steve	6	3	13	2	Sheffield U.	Sheffield
Harrison, John	5	8	10	13	——	York
James, Steve	6	0	12	8	Manchester U.	Coseley
Kay, Roy	5	10	11	7	Celtic	Edinburgh
Kamara, Alan	5	8	10	13	——	Sheffield
Walsh, Jimmy	5	10	11	2	Watford	London
Midfield						
Byrne, John	6	0	11	7	——	Manchester
Ford, Gary	5	9	10	13	——	York
Ferebee, Stewart	5	11	10	12	——	Carshalton
McDonald, Ian	5	9	11	4	Mansfield	Barrow
Pugh, David	5	9	11	7	Rotherham	Newport
Stronach, Peter	5	9	11	2	Sunderland	Sunderland
Forwards						
Loggie, David	6	0	12	6	Burnley	Newcastle
Randall, Kevin	5	11	12	8	Mansfield	Ashton-under-Lyne
Staniforth, Gordon	5	6	9	12	Hull	Hull
Wellings, Barry	5	6	9	12	Everton	Liverpool

FOOTBALL LEAGUE—DIVISION ONE
Results for 1978—79

	Arsenal	Aston Villa	Birmingham	Bolton W.	Bristol City	Chelsea	Coventry	Derby County	Everton	Ipswich	Leeds United
Arsenal	–	1–1	3–1	1–0	2–0	5–2	1–1	2–0	2–2	4–1	2–2
Aston Villa	5–1	–	1–0	3–0	2–0	2–1	1–1	3–3	1–1	2–2	2–2
Birmingham City	0–0	0–1	–	3–0	1–1	1–1	0–0	1–1	1–3	1–1	0–1
Bolton Wanderers	4–2	0–0	2–2	–	1–2	2–1	0–0	2–1	3–1	2–3	3–1
Bristol City	1–3	1–0	2–1	4–1	–	3–1	5–0	1–0	2–2	3–1	0–0
Chelsea	1–1	0–1	2–1	4–3	0–0	–	1–3	1–1	0–1	2–3	0–3
Coventry City	1–1	1–1	2–1	2–2	3–2	3–2	–	4–2	3–2	2–2	0–0
Derby County	2–0	0–0	2–1	3–0	0–1	1–0	0–2	–	0–0	0–1	0–1
Everton	1–0	1–1	1–0	1–0	4–1	3–2	3–3	2–1	–	0–1	1–1
Ipswich Town	2–0	0–2	3–0	3–0	0–1	5–1	1–1	2–1	0–1	–	2–3
Leeds United	0–1	1–0	3–0	5–1	1–1	2–1	1–0	4–0	1–0	1–1	–
Liverpool	3–0	3–0	1–0	3–0	1–0	2–0	1–0	5–0	1–1	2–0	1–1
Manchester City	1–1	2–3	3–1	2–1	2–0	2–3	2–0	1–2	0–0	1–2	3–0
Manchester United	0–2	1–1	1–0	1–2	1–3	1–1	0–0	0–0	1–1	2–0	4–1
Middlesbrough	2–3	2–0	2–1	1–1	0–0	7–2	1–2	3–1	1–2	0–0	1–0
Norwich City	0–0	1–2	4–0	0–0	3–0	2–0	1–0	3–0	0–1	0–1	2–2
Nottingham Forest	2–1	4–0	1–0	1–1	2–0	6–0	3–0	1–1	0–0	1–0	0–0
Q.P.R.	1–2	1–0	1–3	1–3	1–0	0–0	5–1	2–2	1–1	0–4	1–4
Southampton	2–0	2–0	1–0	2–2	2–0	0–0	4–0	1–2	3–0	1–2	2–2
Tottenham Hotspur	0–5	1–4	1–0	2–0	1–0	2–2	1–1	2–0	1–1	1–0	1–2
W.B.A.	1–1	1–1	1–0	4–0	3–1	1–0	7–1	2–1	1–0	2–1	1–2
Wolverhampton W.	1–0	0–4	2–1	1–1	2–0	0–1	1–1	4–0	1–0	1–3	1–1

Read across for home results, down for away results

FOOTBALL LEAGUE—DIVISION ONE
Results for 1978—79

Liverpool	Manchester City	Manchester United	Middlesbrough	Norwich City	Q.P.R.	Southampton	Tottenham Hotspur	West Bromwich	Wolverhampton W.		
1–0	1–1	1–1	0–0	1–1	2–1	5–1	1–0	1–0	1–2	0–1	Arsenal
3–1	1–1	2–2	0–2	1–1	1–2	3–1	1–1	2–3	0–1	1–0	Aston Villa
0–3	1–2	5–1	1–3	1–0	0–2	3–1	2–2	1–0	1–1	1–1	Birmingham City
1–4	2–2	3–0	0–0	3–2	0–1	2–1	2–0	1–3	0–1	3–1	Bolton Wanderers
1–0	1–1	1–2	1–1	1–1	1–3	2–0	3–1	0–0	1–0	0–1	Bristol City
0–0	1–4	0–1	2–1	3–3	1–3	1–3	1–2	1–3	1–3	1–2	Chelsea
0–0	0–3	4–3	2–1	4–1	0–0	1–0	4–0	1–3	1–3	3–0	Coventry City
0–2	1–1	1–3	0–3	1–1	1–2	2–1	2–1	2–2	3–2	4–1	Derby County
1–0	1–0	3–0	2–0	2–2	1–1	2–1	0–0	1–1	0–2	2–0	Everton
0–3	2–1	3–0	2–1	1–1	1–1	2–1	0–0	2–1	0–1	3–1	Ipswich Town
0–3	1–1	2–3	3–1	2–2	1–2	4–3	4–0	1–2	1–3	3–0	Leeds United
–	1–0	2–0	2–0	6–0	2–0	2–1	2–0	7–0	2–1	2–0	Liverpool
1–4	–	0–3	1–0	2–2	0–0	3–1	1–2	2–0	2–2	3–1	Manchester City
0–3	1–0	–	3–2	1–0	1–1	2–0	1–1	2–0	3–5	3–2	Manchester United
0–1	2–0	2–2	–	2–0	1–3	0–2	2–0	1–0	1–1	2–0	Middlesbrough
1–4	1–1	2–2	1–0	–	1–1	1–1	3–1	2–2	1–1	0–0	Norwich City
0–0	3–1	1–1	2–2	2–1	–	0–0	1–0	1–1	0–0	3–1	Nottingham Forest
1–3	2–1	1–1	1–1	0–0	0–0	–	0–1	2–2	0–1	3–3	Q.P.R.
1–1	1–0	1–1	2–1	2–2	0–0	1–1	–	3–3	1–1	3–2	Southampton
0–0	0–3	1–1	1–2	0–0	1–3	1–1	0–0	–	1–0	1–0	Tottenham H.
1–1	4–0	1–0	2–0	2–2	0–1	2–1	1–0	0–1	–	1–1	W.B.A.
0–1	1–1	2–4	1–3	1–0	1–0	1–0	2–0	3–2	0–3	–	Wolverhampton W.

FOOTBALL LEAGUE—DIVISION TWO
Results for 1978—79

	Blackburn	Brighton & H. A.	Bristol Rovers	Burnley	Cambridge United	Cardiff	Charlton	Crystal Palace	Fulham	Leicester	Luton
Blackburn	–	1–1	0–2	1–2	1–0	1–4	1–2	1–1	2–1	1–1	0–0
Brighton & H. A.	2–1	–	3–0	2–1	0–2	5–0	2–0	0–0	3–0	3–1	3–1
Bristol Rovers	4–1	1–2	–	2–0	2–0	4–2	5–5	0–1	3–1	1–1	2–0
Burnley	2–1	3–0	2–0	–	1–1	0–0	2–1	2–1	5–3	2–2	2–1
Cambridge United	0–1	0–0	1–1	2–2	–	5–0	1–1	0–0	1–0	1–1	0–0
Cardiff City	2–0	3–1	2–0	1–1	1–0	–	1–4	2–2	2–0	1–0	2–1
Charlton	2–0	0–3	3–0	1–1	2–3	1–1	–	1–1	0–0	1–0	1–2
Crystal Palace	3–0	3–1	0–1	2–0	1–1	2–0	1–0	–	0–1	3–1	3–1
Fulham	1–2	0–1	3–0	0–0	5–1	2–2	3–1	0–0	–	3–0	1–0
Leicester City	1–1	4–1	0–0	2–1	1–1	1–2	0–3	1–1	1–0	–	3–0
Luton Town	2–1	1–1	3–2	4–1	1–1	7–1	3–0	0–1	2–0	0–1	–
Millwall	1–1	1–4	0–3	0–2	2–0	2–0	0–2	0–3	0–0	2–0	0–2
Newcastle United	3–1	1–3	3–0	3–1	1–0	3–0	5–3	1–0	0–0	1–0	1–0
Notts County	2–1	1–0	2–1	1–1	1–1	1–0	1–1	0–0	1–1	0–1	3–1
Oldham Athletic	5–0	1–3	3–1	2–0	4–1	2–1	0–3	0–0	0–2	2–1	2–0
Orient	2–0	3–3	1–1	2–1	3–0	2–2	2–1	0–1	1–0	0–1	3–2
Preston North End	4–1	1–0	1–1	2–2	0–2	2–1	6–1	2–3	2–2	4–0	2–2
Sheffield United	0–1	0–1	1–0	4–0	3–3	2–1	2–1	0–2	1–1	2–2	1–1
Stoke City	1–2	2–2	2–0	3–1	1–3	2–0	2–2	1–1	2–0	0–0	0–0
Sunderland	0–1	2–1	5–0	3–1	0–2	1–2	1–0	1–2	1–1	1–1	1–0
West Ham United	4–0	0–0	2–0	3–1	5–0	1–1	2–0	1–1	0–1	1–1	1–0
Wrexham	2–1	0–0	0–1	0–1	2–0	1–2	1–1	0–0	1–1	0–0	2–0

FOOTBALL LEAGUE—DIVISION TWO
Results for 1978—79

Millwall	Newcastle United	Notts County	Oldham	Orient	Preston	Sheffield United	Stoke City	Sunderland	West Ham	Wrexham	
1–1	1–3	3–4	0–2	3–0	0–1	2–0	2–2	1–1	1–0	1–1	Blackburn Rovers
3–0	2–0	0–0	1–0	2–0	5–1	2–0	1–1	2–0	1–2	2–1	Brighton & H. A.
0–3	2–0	2–2	0–0	2–1	0–1	2–1	0–0	0–0	0–1	2–1	Bristol Rovers
0–1	1–0	2–1	1–0	0–1	1–1	1–1	0–3	1–2	3–2	0–0	Burnley
2–1	0–0	0–1	3–3	3–1	1–0	1–0	0–1	0–2	0–0	1–0	Cambridge United
2–1	2–1	2–3	1–3	1–0	2–2	4–0	1–3	1–1	0–0	1–0	Cardiff City
2–4	4–1	1–1	2–0	0–2	1–1	3–1	1–4	1–2	0–0	1–1	Charlton
0–0	1–0	2–0	1–0	1–1	0–0	3–1	1–1	1–1	1–1	1–0	Crystal Palace
1–0	1–3	1–1	1–0	2–2	5–3	2–0	2–0	2–2	0–0	0–1	Fulham
0–0	2–1	0–1	2–0	5–3	1–1	0–1	1–1	1–2	1–2	1–1	Leicester City
2–2	2–0	6–0	6–1	2–1	1–2	1–1	0–0	0–3	1–4	2–1	Luton Town
–	2–1	0–1	2–3	2–0	0–2	1–1	3–0	0–1	2–1	2–2	Millwall
1–0	–	1–2	1–1	0–0	4–3	1–3	2–0	1–4	0–3	2–0	Newcastle United
1–1	1–2	–	0–0	1–0	0–0	4–1	0–1	1–1	1–0	1–1	Notts County
4–1	1–3	3–3	–	0–0	2–0	1–1	1–1	0–0	2–2	1–0	Oldham Athletic
2–1	2–0	3–0	0–0	–	2–0	1–1	0–1	3–0	0–2	0–1	Orient
0–0	0–0	1–1	1–1	1–1	–	2–2	0–1	3–1	0–0	2–1	Preston North End
0–2	1–0	5–1	4–2	1–2	0–1	–	0–0	3–2	3–0	1–1	Sheffield United
2–0	0–0	2–0	4–0	3–1	1–1	2–1	–	0–1	2–0	3–0	Stoke City
3–2	1–1	3–0	3–0	1–0	3–1	6–2	0–1	–	2–1	1–0	Sunderland
3–0	5–0	5–2	3–0	0–2	3–1	2–0	1–1	3–3	–	1–1	West Ham United
3–0	0–0	3–1	2–0	3–1	2–1	4–0	0–1	1–2	4–3	–	Wrexham

Read across for home results, down for away results

FOOTBALL LEAGUE—DIVISION THREE
Results for 1978—79

	Blackpool	Brentford	Bury	Carlisle United	Chester	Chesterfield	Colchester United	Exeter City	Gillingham	Hull City	Lincoln City	Mansfield Town	
Blackpool	–	0–1	1–2	3–1	3–0	0–0	2–1	1–1	2–0	3–1	2–0	2–0	
Brentford	3–2	–	0–1	0–0	6–0	0–3	1–0	0–0	0–2	1–0	2–1	1–0	
Bury	1–3	2–3	–	2–2	1–1	3–1	2–2	4–2	2–2	1–1	2–2	0–0	
Carlisle United	1–1	1–0	1–2	–	1–1	1–1	4–0	1–1	1–0	2–2	2–0	1–0	
Chester	4–2	3–1	1–1	1–2	–	3–0	2–2	3–0	1–1	2–1	5–1	1–1	
Chesterfield	1–3	0–0	2–1	2–3	3–1	–	2–1	0–1	0–2	1–2	1–3	1–0	
Colchester United	3–1	1–1	0–0	2–1	2–1	0–0	–	2–2	2–2	2–1	2 0	1–0	
Exeter City	3–0	2–2	2–1	3–2	0–1	3–1	2–1	–	0–0	3–1	3–2	0–0	
Gillingham	2–0	0–0	3–3	0–0	1–0	2–1	3–0	2–0	–	2–0	4–2	0–0	
Hull City	0–0	1–0	4–1	1–1	3–0	1–1	1–0	1–0	0–1	–	0–0	3–0	
Lincoln City	1–2	1–0	1–4	1–1	0–0	0–1	0–0	0–1	2–4	4–2	–	0–1	
Mansfield Town	1–1	2–1	3–0	1–0	2–0	2–1	1–1	1–1	1–1	0–2	2–0	–	
Oxford United	1–0	0–1	0–0	5–1	0–0	1–1	2–0	3–2	1–1	1–0	2–1	3–2	
Peterborough United	1–2	3–1	2–2	0–0	2–1	0–0	1–2	1–1	1–1	3–0	0–1	1–2	
Plymouth Argyle	0–0	2–1	3–0	2–0	2–2	1–1	1–1	4–2	2–1	3–4	2–1	1–4	
Rotherham United	2–1	1–0	2–1	1–3	0–1	1–0	1–0	2–1	1–1	0–2	2–0	2–0	
Sheffield Wednesday	2–0	1–0	0–0	0–0	4–0	0–0	2–1	2–1	2–3	0–0	1–2		
Shrewsbury	2–0	1–0	1–0	0–0	1–0	1–1	2–0	4–1	1–1	1–0	2–0	2–2	
Southend United	4–0	1–1	0–0	1–1	0–1	2–0	1–1	0–1	0–1	3–0	2–0	1–1	
Swansea City	1–0	2–1	2–0	0–0	2–2	2–1	4–1	1–0	3–1	5–3	3–0	3–2	
Swindon Town	0–1	2–0	2–1	0–0	2–0	1–0	–	1–2	1–1	3–1	2–0	6–0	1–0
Tranmere Rovers	0–2	0–1	0–0	1–1	6–2	1–1	1–5	2–2	1–1	1–3	0–0	1–2	
Walsall	2–1	2–3	0–1	1–2	2–1	0–1	2–2	2–2	0–1	1–2	4–1	1–1	
Watford	5–1	2–0	3–3	2–1	1–0	2–0	0–3	1–0	1–0	4–0	2–0	1–1	

FOOTBALL LEAGUE—DIVISION THREE
Results for 1978—79

Oxford United	Peterborough United	Plymouth Argyle	Rotherman United	Sheffield Wed.	Shrewsbury	Southend United	Swansea City	Swindon Town	Tranmere Rovers	Walsall	Watford	
1–0	0–0	0–0	1–2	0–1	5–0	1–2	1–3	5–2	2–0	2–1	1–1	Blackpool
3–0	0–0	2–1	1–0	2–1	2–3	3–0	1–0	1–2	2–0	1–0	3–3	Brentford
1–1	1–0	1–2	3–2	0–0	3–0	3–3	0–1	0–1	1–0	1–1	1–2	Bury
0–1	4–1	1–1	1–1	0–0	1–1	0–0	2–0	2–0	2–0	1–0	1–0	Carlisle United
4–1	1–1	0–0	0–1	2–2	0–0	0–1	2–0	2–0	1–1	2–1	2–1	Chester
1–1	3–1	1–3	1–0	3–3	2–1	3–2	2–1	1–1	5–2	0–0	0–2	Chesterfield
1–1	4–2	2–1	0–0	1–0	1–0	1–1	2–2	3–2	1–0	2–0	0–1	Colchester United
2–0	1–0	1–0	2–0	2–2	0–1	0–0	2–1	1–2	3–0	3–1	0–0	Exeter City
2–1	1–0	2–0	0–0	0–0	2–0	1–0	2–0	2–2	3–2	3–1	2–3	Gillingham
0–1	1–1	2–1	1–0	1–1	1–1	2–0	2–2	1–1	2–1	4–1	4–0	Hull City
2–2	0–1	3–3	3–0	1–2	1–2	1–1	2–1	0–3	2–1	1–1	0–5	Lincoln City
1–1	1–1	5–0	0–1	1–1	2–2	1–1	2–2	0–1	0–0	1–3	0–3	Mansfield Town
–	0–2	3–2	1–0	1–1	0–1	0–0	0–2	0–1	0–0	2–1	1–1	Oxford United
1–1	–	2–1	1–1	2–0	0–2	0–1	2–0	2–1	1–0	0–3	0–1	Peterborough United
0–1	3–2	–	2–0	2–0	1–1	1–1	2–2	2–0	2–2	1–0	1–1	Plymouth Argyle
0–0	1–1	1–0	–	0–1	1–2	2–1	0–1	1–3	3–2	4–1	2–1	Rotherham United
1–1	3–0	2–3	2–1	–	0–0	3–2	0–0	2–1	1–2	0–2	2–3	Sheffield Wednesday
0–0	2–0	2–0	3–1	2–2	–	2–0	3–0	0–0	2–1	1–1	1–1	Shrewsbury
2–0	0–0	2–1	2–1	2–1	0–1	–	0–2	5–3	0–1	1–0	1–0	Southend United
1–1	4–1	2–1	4–4	4–2	1–1	3–2	–	1–2	4–3	2–2	3–2	Swansea City
2–0	3–1	1–3	1–0	3–0	2–1	1–0	0–1	–	4–1	4–1	2–0	Swindon Town
1–0	1–0	2–1	1–1	1–1	2–2	1–2	1–2	1–1	–	0–0	1–1	Tranmere Rovers
0–1	4–1	2–1	0–1	0–2	1–1	1–1	1–1	4–1	2–0	–	2–4	Walsall
4–2	1–2	2–2	2–2	1–0	2–2	2–0	0–2	2–0	4–0	3–1	–	Watford

Read across for home results, down for away results

FOOTBALL LEAGUE—DIVISION FOUR
Results for 1978—79

	Aldershot	Barnsley	Bournemouth	Bradford City	Crewe Alexandra	Darlington	Doncaster Rovers	Grimsby Town	Halifax Town	Hartlepool United	Hereford United	Huddersfield Town
Aldershot	–	1–0	1–0	6–0	3–0	1–1	2–1	2–0	1–0	1–1	2–0	1–0
Barnsley	2–0	–	1–0	0–1	3–1	1–1	3–0	2–1	4–2	1–0	2–1	1–0
Bournemouth	0–1	0–2	–	1–0	0–1	2–2	7–1	0–0	1–0	0–1	1–1	2–0
Bradford City	0–2	1–2	2–1	–	6–0	0–0	1–0	1–3	3–0	1–2	2–1	1–1
Crewe Alexandra	1–1	0–2	1–0	1–2	–	1–1	2–4	0–3	1–0	0–1	0–0	3–3
Darlington	2–1	0–0	0–0	1–1	1–1	–	3–2	0–1	2–1	0–1	2–1	1–0
Doncaster Rovers	1–1	2–2	1–1	2–0	2–0	2–3	–	0–1	1–1	0–0	1–0	0–2
Grimsby Town	0–0	2–0	1–0	5–1	2–2	7–2	3–4	–	2–1	0–1	1–1	2–1
Halifax Town	1–1	0–2	0–2	2–0	0–0	0–2	0–0	1–2	–	2–4	1–0	2–3
Hartlepool United	2–2	1–1	0–0	2–2	2–2	0–2	3–4	1–0	3–1	–	2–1	2–0
Hereford United	1–1	1–1	0–0	3–1	6–1	1–0	2–0	0–1	2–2	1–0	–	3–0
Huddersfield Town	0–0	1–0	2–1	0–0	0–0	2–2	2–1	2–0	2–0	2–0	2–3	–
Newport County	1–2	1–1	2–0	2–4	1–2	2–1	3–0	1–1	2–0	3–2	4–1	2–1
Northampton Town	2–3	0–1	4–2	1–0	3–1	4–1	3–0	1–2	2–1	1–1	2–1	2–3
Portsmouth	1–1	0–1	1–1	0–1	3–0	3–0	4–0	1–3	3–1	3–0	1–0	1–0
Port Vale	1–1	3–2	1–2	2–1	2–2	2–1	1–3	1–1	0–1	2–0	1–1	1–0
Reading	4–0	1–0	1–0	3–0	3–0	1–0	3–0	4–0	1–0	3–1	3–0	1–1
Rochdale	1–1	0–3	2–1	1–0	2–1	2–1	2–0	2–5	1–1	1–1	0–2	0–2
Scunthorpe United	2–0	0–1	1–0	3–2	0–1	1–0	0–0	2–1	1–0	3–1	4–2	3–1
Stockport County	2–2	0–0	1–0	1–0	4–3	3–0	0–1	2–1	1–2	4–0	0–2	3–1
Torquay	2–1	3–2	0–1	1–2	3–0	1–0	2–1	3–1	2–0	4–1	1–0	2–1
Wigan Athletic	3–2	1–1	1–0	1–3	1–0	2–2	1–0	0–3	1–0	2–2	0–0	2–1
Wimbledon	3–1	1–1	4–0	2–1	1–1	2–0	3–2	0–1	2–1	3–1	2–0	2–1
York City	1–1	0–1	2–1	2–2	1–0	5–2	1–1	0–0	2–0	1–1	1–0	1–3

FOOTBALL LEAGUE—DIVISION FOUR
Results for 1978—79

	Newport County	Northampton Town	Portsmouth	Port Vale	Reading	Rochdale	Scunthorpe United	Stockport County	Torquay	Wigan Athletic	Wimbledon	York City
Aldershot	2–3	2–0	0–2	1–1	1–2	1–0	2–0	3–2	1–0	1–0	1–1	1–0
Barnsley	1–0	1–1	1–1	6–2	3–1	0–3	4–1	4–4	1–2	0–0	3–1	3–0
Bournemouth	3–1	0–0	3–1	3–1	0–0	3–1	0–0	3–1	1–0	2–1	1–2	1–2
Bradford City	1–3	3–0	2–0	2–3	2–3	1–0	1–1	1–1	3–1	1–1	1–0	2–1
Crewe Alexandra	0–1	2–4	0–0	1–5	0–2	1–2	0–2	2–2	6–2	1–1	1–2	0–1
Darlington	1–0	0–0	2–0	4–0	1–2	0–2	2–2	0–1	1–2	1–1	1–1	0–1
Doncaster Rovers	0–0	2–0	2–3	1–3	2–2	1–0	0–0	2–0	1–0	0–1	1–0	1–2
Grimsby Town	1–0	4–3	1–0	1–0	1–2	4–0	1–1	2–1	3–0	3–1	2–2	3–0
Halifax Town	1–2	2–2	2–0	0–3	0–0	2–1	2–3	2–1	1–0	1–2	2–1	0–1
Hartlepool United	0–0	2–0	1–1	1–2	0–0	5–1	1–1	1–3	3–2	1–1	1–1	1–1
Hereford United	0–3	4–3	0–1	1–0	0–0	2–2	3–1	1–0	3–1	0–0	0–0	1–0
Huddersfield Town	0–1	1–0	2–0	3–2	1–1	1–0	3–2	0–0	1–1	1–1	3–0	1–0
Newport County	–	2–1	1–2	1–0	3–2	0–0	2–0	1–2	1–1	2–1	1–3	1–1
Northampton Town	3–1	–	0–2	1–0	2–2	1–0	1–0	2–2	1–2	2–4	1–1	1–0
Portsmouth	2–1	1–0	–	2–0	4–0	1–1	0–0	1–1	1–0	1–0	0–0	1–1
Port Vale	1–1	2–2	0–0	–	0–3	1–1	2–2	2–1	1–2	2–1	1–0	0–0
Reading	2–1	5–1	2–0	0–0	–	2–0	0–1	3–3	1–0	2–0	1–0	3–0
Rochdale	1–0	4–1	0–2	0–1	1–0	–	1–0	2–0	1–0	0–2	0–0	1–2
Scunthorpe United	2–3	0–3	2–2	2–0	0–3	0–4	–	1–0	2–2	0–1	2–0	2–3
Stockport County	1–1	2–1	4–2	0–0	0–0	3–0	0–2	–	0–1	0–1	0–1	2–0
Torquay	2–0	0–1	2–1	2–2	1–1	1–1	0–1	1–0	–	1–1	1–6	3–0
Wigan Athletic	2–3	2–0	2–0	5–3	3–0	3–0	1–0	2–0	3–1	–	1–2	1–1
Wimbledon	0–0	4–1	2–4	1–0	1–0	3–2	3–1	2–0	5–0	2–1	–	2–1
York City	1–2	1–0	5–3	4–0	0–1	2–1	1–0	1–0	0–0	0–1	1–4	–

Read across for home results, down for away results

SCOTTISH LEAGUE—PREMIER DIVISION
Results for 1978—79

	Aberdeen	Celtic	Dundee United	Hearts	Hibernian	Morton	Motherwell	Partick Thistle	Rangers	St. Mirren
		4–1	1–0	1–2	4–1	3—1	4–0	1–1	0–0	1–1
Aberdeen	–	1–1	0–2	5–0	0–0	1–2	8–0	2–1	2–1	1–2
	0–0		1–1	4–0	0–1	0–0	1–2	1–0	3–1	2–1
Celtic	1–0	–	2–1	1–0	3–1	3–0	2–1	2–0	4–2	2–1
	1–1	1–0		3–1	0–0	1–2	2–1	2–0	3–0	1–1
Dundee United	2–2	2–1	–	2–1	2–1	4–1	2–1	2–1	1–2	2–0
	1–4	2–0	2–0		1–1	1–1	3–2	0–1	0–0	1–1
Heart of Midlothian	0–0	0–3	0–3	–	1–2	0–1	3–0	0–2	3–2	1–2
	2–1	2–2	1–1	1–2		1–1	2–2	0–0	0–0	1–0
Hibernian	1–1	2–1	1–0	1–1	–	1–1	4–0	1–0	2–1	0–2
	2–1	1–2	3–1	3–2	3–0		1–2	1–0	2–2	1–3
Morton	0–1	1–0	3–1	2–2	2–2	–	6–0	2–2	0–2	1–0
	1–1	1–5	0–1	0–1	2–3	1–1	0–1	1–2	1–2	1–2
Motherwell	1–1	3–4	0–4	3–2	0–3	3–3	–	1–1	2–0	0–3
	1–2	2–3	1–1	3–2	2–1	2–1	2–0		1–0	2–1
Partick Thistle	0–1	1–2	1–2	2–0	6–1	2–1	0–0	–	0–2	3–1
	1–1	1–1	1–1	5–3	2–1	3–0	4–1	0–0		0–1
Rangers	2–0	1–0	1–0	4–0	1–0	1–1	3–0	1–0	–	1–0
	2–1	0–2	1–3	4–0	1–0	0–0	0–1	1–0	0–1	
St. Mirren	2–2	0–1	2–1	2–1	2–3	3–1	1–0	1–1	1–2	–

SCOTTISH LEAGUE—DIVISION ONE
Results for 1978—79

	Airdrieonians	Arbroath	Ayr United	Clyde	Clydebank	Dumbarton	Dundee
		1–1	2–4		1–1		0–2
Airdrieonians	–	2–0	2–0	2–2	1–3	3–6	2–4
			4–1	0–2		1–1	
Arbroath	3–3	–	2–3	2–0	1–1	1–1	0–1
						2–5	0–1
Ayr United	0–0	3–0	–	2–0	4–3	1–0	1–2
	2–1		0–1		1–2		
Clyde	2–3	1–0	0–5	–	0–1	1–0	2–1
		5–2	3–1			1–1	
Clydebank	4–1	2–2	0–1	1–4	–	3–1	2–1
	1–1			3–0			0–0
Dumbarton	0–1	0–1	2–0	0–0	1–2	–	3–2
		2–0		2–0	2–0		
Dundee	1–0	0–2	2–2	2–0	2–1	2–0	–
		3–1		3–3			
Hamilton Academicals	2–0	2–0	3–1	2–0	1–0	5–0	1–2
	2–0						1–1
Kilmarnock	1–0	3–1	1–2	1–0	0–0	0–0	2–1
				2–2	1–3	0–2	
Montrose	2–2	3–0	4–6	4–0	1–2	2–1	0–2
	1–3	1–1	1–0			0–2	
Queen of the South	1–5	2–2	0–1	3–0	2–1	1–3	3–1
		1–0	0–0		4–2		2–4
Raith Rovers	2–0	1–2	2–0	1–2	1–2	0–0	1–2
	0–2			1–1		2–2	0–2
St. Johnstone	1–3	1–1	4–2	0–1	2–3	2–2	3–2
	1–2			1–4	0–0		1–0
Stirling Albion	2–1	2–1	1–2	3–2	2–3	1–1	0–1

Read across for home results, down for away results

SCOTTISH LEAGUE—DIVISION ONE
Results 1978—79

Hamilton Academicals	Kilmarnock	Montrose	Queen of the South	Raith Rovers	St. Johnstone	Stirling Albion	
4–1		1–1		3–0			
2–1	4–1	8–2	4–1	0–1	0–1	2–1	Airdrieonians
	3–2	1–3			3–0	1–0	
3–0	0–1	4–0	1–1	0–5	3–1	0–0	Arbroath
1–2	0–0	5–0			1–0	0–1	
2–1	2–1	5–0	1–1	3–0	4–2	2–0	Ayr United
	1–1		3–0	3–1			
2–3	1–2	2–4	3–0	1–1	6–4	0–0	Clyde
4–1	2–1		2–0		1–0		
3–1	1–2	1–0	3–1	2–1	3–0	5–2	Clydebank
2–0	0–3			1–3		0–1	
3–0	1–3	4–1	4–1	3–0	2–0	0–2	Dumbarton
1–1		1–1	5–0				
4–3	0–0	1–0	4–0	2–0	1–1	2–1	Dundee
	2–3		3–2		2–1	1–1	
–	1–0	3–1	0–0	1–1	2–1	2–0	Hamilton Academicals
		2–2	3–1	3–0	3–2		
4–0	–	4–1	0–0	2–1	3–1	5–0	Kilmarnock
1–1				0–0		1–1	
2–4	0–4	–	6–1	1–1	1–3	0–2	Montrose
		1–3			1–1	1–2	
3–3	2–1	2–1	–	2–1	1–2	3–2	Queen of the South
0–1			4–0				
2–0	1–3	3–1	3–0	–	0–0	1–2	Raith Rovers
		3–2		1–1		0–0	
0–0	0–0	4–0	5–2	3–0	–	0–2	St. Johnstone
	1–4			0–1			
0–0	0–0	0–1	4–1	3–0	1–5	–	Stirling Albion

SCOTTISH LEAGUE—DIVISION TWO
Results for 1978—79

	Albion Rovers	Alloa	Berwick Rangers	Brechin City	Cowdenbeath	Dunfermline Ath.	East Fife
		1–2		3–2		1–1	
Albion Rovers	–	2–1	0–2	2–2	1–1	1–0	2–0
				1–1	2–4	1–1	0–0
Alloa	2–6	–	2–1	1–0	4–0	2–0	4–3
	2–0	0–1		2–0		2–2	
Berwick Rangers	5–1	3–2	–	1–0	4–1	0–0	1–2
					1–1	1–6	
Brechin City	1–1	4–2	1–2	–	2–1	0–0	1–1
	4–1		1–3				1–0
Cowdenbeath	3–1	5–1	1–2	0–0	–	1–1	1–1
					3–0		5–1
Dunfermline Athletic	2–1	2–2	1–0	1–1	2–0	–	1–1
	0–2		2–4	0–0			
East Fife	1–2	3–0	2–1	1–0	0–1	2–1	–
	3–3	3–2				1–1	0–1
East Stirling	0–1	3–1	1–4	3–2	4–1	0–2	2–1
			6–0	2–0	2–1	1–1	0–1
Falkirk	2–1	1–0	1–1	3–0	0–3	4–1	2–5
	1–1	2–1			4–2		3–1
Forfar Athletic	1–1	2–0	2–2	2–2	2–0	1–2	1–1
		0–1	0–5				
Meadowbank Thistle	2–0	1–1	0–1	0–3	0–2	1–3	1–3
			0–1		1–1		
Queen's Park	2–0	0–1	1–1	1–1	1–2	0–1	1–1
	3–2	0–2			1–1		1–2
Stenhousemuir	2–3	0–1	0–2	4–2	0–0	1–2	2–2
	3–1	0 0	1–0				
Stranraer	0–1	4–0	1–5	4–2	2–4	1–0	2–4

SCOTTISH LEAGUE —DIVISION TWO
Results for 1978—79

East Stirling	Falkirk	Forfar Ath.	Meadowbank Thistle	Queen's Park	Stenhousemuir	Stranraer	
	1–1		1–2	4–0			
1–1	0–0	3–0	2–0	1–0	0–1	2–1	Albion Rovers
	3–3			1–0		2–1	
2–2	2–0	2–0	1–1	1–1	2–1	0–1	Alloa
5–2		2–4			6–1		
5–1	1–1	1–0	0–0	1–1	3–2	1–1	Berwick Rangers
1–1		3–2	2–2	2–1	1–3		
3–1	1–4	1–0	2–1	1–1	2–1	1–2	Brechin City
1–2			2–1			2–0	
2–1	1–1	2–1	4–1	2–2	1–2	3–1	Cowdenbeath
		2–1	2–1	0–3	1–0	6–1	
2–1	1–1	2–2	1–0	2–2	2–1	3–0	Dunfermline Athletic
			2–2	3–2		2–0	
5–0	1–0	1–2	2–3	3–0	3–0	0–2	East Fife
		1–1		4–2			
–	1–1	3–1	4–1	4–2	1–3	4–1	East Stirling
2–0					1–0		
1–1	–	1–0	6–0	1–0	1–1	2–0	Falkirk
	1–0				1–1	1–3	
4–0	1–4	–	2–3	2–1	0–0	2–0	Forfar Athletic
3–1	1–2	0–0			2–0		
3–1	1–1	1–0	–	0–4	1–2	0–1	Meadowbank Thistle
	0–3	1–1	1–1			0–1	
4–0	1–2	0–1	3–0	–	0–0	2–1	Queen's Park
0–2				1–2		4–1	
5–0	1–2	1–1	2–0	5–1		1–2	Stenhousemuir
1–0	1–0		3–1				
6–2	2–1	0–3	1–0	0–2	0–1	–	Stranraer

Read across for home results, down for away results

NORTHERN RUGBY FOOTBALL LEAGUE

FIRST DIVISION

Sunday, August 19
COUNTY CUP COMPETITIONS
First Round

Sunday, August 26
COUNTY CUP COMPETITIONS
Second Round

Sunday, September 2
Blackpool B. v. Salford
Hull v. Castleford
Hunslet v. Bradford N.
Leigh v. Widnes
St. Helens v. Warrington
Wakefield T. v. Wigan
Workington T. v. Hull K.R.
York v. Leeds

Friday, September 7
Castleford v. Blackpool B.
Salford v. St. Helens

Saturday, September 8
Leeds v. Leigh

Sunday, September 9
Bradford N. v. Wakefield T.
Hull K.R. v. Hunslet
Warrington v. York
Widnes v. Workington T.
Wigan v. Hull

Saturday/Sunday
September 15/16
JOHN PLAYER TROPHY
First Round

Workington T. v. Leigh

Friday, September 21
Salford v. Leeds

Sunday, September 23
Blackpool B. v. Hull
Hull K.R. v. Warrington
Hunslet v. Wigan
Leigh v. Castleford
St. Helens v. Bradford N.
Wakefield T. v. Workington T.
York v. Widnes

Saturday/Sunday
September 29/30
JOHN PLAYER TROPHY
Second Round

Sunday, October 7
Bradford N. v. York
Hull v. Hull K.R.
Leeds v. St. Helens
Wakefield T. v. Blackpool B.
Warrington v. Salford
Widnes v. Castleford
Wigan v. Leigh
Workington T. v. Hunslet

Wednesday, October 10
Hull K.R. v. Wakefield T

Friday, October 12
Castleford v. Warrington

Sunday, October 14
Blackpool B. v. Leeds
Hull v. Bradford N.
Hunslet v. Wakefield T.
Leigh v. Workington T.
St. Helens v. Hull K.R.
Salford v. Widnes
York v. Wigan

Saturday, October 20
Leeds v. Warrington

Sunday, October 21
Bradford N. v. Salford
Hull K.R. v. York
Hunslet v. Blackpool B.
Wakefield T. v. Leigh
Widnes v. Hull
Wigan v. Castleford
Workington T. v. St. Helens

Friday, October 26
Castleford v. Leeds
Salford v. Hull K.R.

Sunday, October 28
Blackpool B. v. Widnes
Hull v. Wigan
Leigh v. Hunslet
St. Helens v. Wakefield T.
Warrington v. Bradford N.
York v. Workington T.

Saturday, November 3
Leeds v. Hull

Sunday, November 4
Bradford N. v. Leigh
Hull K.R. v. Castleford
Hunslet v. St. Helens
Wakefield T. v. York
Widnes v. Warrington
Wigan v. Blackpool B.
Workington T. v. Salford

Friday, November 9
Castleford v. Hunslet
Salford v. Wigan

Saturday, November 10
Leeds v. Widnes

Sunday, November 11
Blackpool B. v. Hull K.R.
Hull v. Wakefield T.
St. Helens v. Leigh
Warrington v. Workington T.
York v. Bradford N.

Sunday, November 18
Bradford N. v. Widnes
Hull K.R. v. Leeds
Hunslet v. Hull
Leigh v. York
St. Helens v. Blackpool B.
Wakefield T. v. Salford
Wigan v. Warrington
Workington T. v. Castleford

Friday, November 23
Salford v. Hunslet

Saturday, November 24
Leeds v. Workington T.

Sunday, November 25
Blackpool B. v. Leigh
Castleford v. Bradford N.
Hull v. St. Helens
Warrington v. Wakefield T.
Widnes v. Wigan
York v. Hull K.R.

Sunday, December 2
Hull K.R. v. Widnes
Hunslet v. Warrington
Leigh v. Hull
St. Helens v. Castleford
Wakefield T. v. Leeds
Wigan v. Bradford N.
Workington T. v. Blackpool B.
York v. Salford

Friday, December 7
Castleford v. Leigh
Salford v. Workington T.

Saturday, December 8
Leeds v. Wigan

Sunday, December 9
Blackpool B. v. York
Bradford N. v. Hull K.R.
Hull v. Hunslet
Warrington v. St. Helens
Widnes v. Wakefield T.

Sunday, December 16
Bradford N. v. Leeds
Hull K.R. v. Blackpool B.
Hunslet v. Salford
Leigh v. St. Helens
Wakefield T. v. Hull
Workington T. v. Warrington
York v. Castleford

Friday, December 21
Castleford v. Widnes

Saturday, December 22
Leeds v. York

Sunday, December 23
Blackpool B. v. Wigan
St. Helens v. Workington T.
Salford v. Bradford N.
Wakefield T. v. Hull K.R.
Warrington v. Hunslet

Boxing Day,
Wednesday, December 26
Bradford N. v. Blackpool B.
Castleford v. Wakefield T.
Leeds v. Hunslet
Leigh v. Warrington
Widnes v. Salford
Wigan v. St. Helens

Sunday, December 30
Blackpool B. v. Workington T
Hull K.R. v. Salford
Hunslet v. Castleford
Wakefield T. v. Warrington
Wigan v. Widnes
York v. Hull

New Year's Day,
Tuesday, January 1
Bradford N. v. Castleford
St. Helens v. Widnes
Salford v. Leigh
Warrington v. Wigan

Friday, January 4
Castleford v. St. Helens

Saturday, January 5
Leeds v. Hull K.R.

Sunday, January 6
Hull v. Blackpool B.
Leigh v. Wakefield T.
Widnes v. Bradford N.
Wigan v. Hunslet
Workington T. v. York

Sunday, January 13
Blackpool B. v. Castleford
Bradford N. v. Hull
Hull K.R. v. Wigan
Hunslet v. Workington T.
St. Helens v. Salford
Wakefield T. v. Widnes
Warrington v. Leeds
York v. Leigh

Friday, January 18
Castleford v. York
Salford v. Blackpool B.

Sunday, January 20
Bradford N. v. St. Helens
Hull v. Warrington
Leigh v. Hull K.R.
Widnes v. Hunslet
Wigan v. Wakefield T.
Workington T. v. Leeds

Friday, January 25
Castleford v. Hull

Saturday, January 26
Leeds v. Salford

Sunday, January 27
Hull K.R. v. Bradford N.
St. Helens v. York
Wakefield T. v. Hunslet
Warrington v. Blackpool B.
Widnes v. Leigh
Wigan v. Workington T.

Friday, February 1
Salford v. Castleford

Sunday, February 3
Blackpool B. v. St. Helens
Bradford N. v. Warrington
Hull v. Leeds
Hunslet v. Hull K.R.
Leigh v. Wigan
Workington T. v. Widnes
York v. Wakefield T.

Saturday/Sunday
February 9/10
STATE EXPRESS CHALLENGE CUP
First Round

Sunday, February 17
Castleford v. Workington T.
Hull v. Salford
Leigh v. Bradford N.
St. Helens v. Hunslet
Warrington v. Hull K.R.
Widnes v. Leeds
York v. Blackpool B.

Saturday/Sunday
February 23/24
STATE EXPRESS CHALLENGE CUP
Second Round

Saturday, March 1
Leeds v. Castleford

Sunday, March 2
Hull K.R. v. Workington T.
Hunslet v. Leigh
Wakefield T. v. Bradford N.
Warrington v. Hull
Widnes v. Blackpool B.
Wigan v. York

Friday, March 7
Castleford v. Hull K.R.
Salford v. Wakefield T.

Sunday, March 9
Blackpool B. v. Warrington
Bradford N. v. Hunslet
Hull v. Widnes
Leigh v. Leeds
Workington T. v. Wigan
York v. St. Helens

Friday, March 14
Castleford v. Salford

Saturday, March 15
Leeds v. Wakefield T.

Sunday, March 16
Blackpool B. v. Hunslet
Hull K.R. v. Leigh
St. Helens v. Hull
Widnes v. York
Workington T. v. Bradford N

Friday, March 21
Salford v. York

Saturday, March 22
Leeds v. Blackpool B.

Sunday, March 23
Hull v. Workington T.
Hunslet v. Widnes
Wakefield T. v. St. Helens
Warrington v. Castleford
Wigan v. Hull K.R.

Friday, March 28
Salford v. Warrington

Sunday, March 30
Bradford N. v. Wigan
Hull v. Leigh
St. Helens v. Leeds
Widnes v. Hull K.R.
Workington T. v. Wakefield
York v. Hunslet

Good Friday, April 4
Hull K.R. v. Hull
Leeds v. Bradford N.
Leigh v. Salford
St. Helens v. Wigan
Warrington v. Widnes

Sunday, April 6
Blackpool B. v. Bradford N.
Hunslet v. Leeds
Wakefield T. v. Castleford
Widnes v. St. Helens

Easter Monday, April 7th
Hull v. York
Warrington v. Leigh
Wigan v. Salford

Friday, April 11
Castleford v. Wigan
Salford v. Hull

Sunday, April 13
Bradford N. v. Workington T.
Leigh v. Blackpool B.
York v. Warrington

Sunday, April 20
Blackpool B. v. Wakefield T.
Hull K.R. v. St. Helens
Hunslet v. York
Wigan v. Leeds
Workington T. v. Hull

SECOND DIVISION

Sunday, August 19

COUNTY CUP COMPETITIONS
First Round

Sunday, August 26

COUNTY CUP COMPETITIONS
Second Round

Sunday, September 2
Batley v. Whitehaven
Doncaster v. Oldham
Halifax v. Featherstone R.
Huyton v. Bramley
Keighley v. Huddersfield
Rochdale H. v. Barrow
Swinton v. Dewsbury

Friday, September 7
Bramley v. Batley

Sunday, September 9
Barrow v. Swinton
Dewsbury v. Doncaster
Featherstone R. v. Keighley
Huddersfield v. Rochdale H.
Oldham v. Huyton
Whitehaven v. Halifax

Saturday/Sunday September 15/16

JOHN PLAYER TROPHY
First Round

Sunday, September 23
Batley v. Oldham
Doncaster v. Huddersfield
Halifax v. Swinton
Huyton v. Featherstone R.
Keighley v. Barrow
Rochdale H. v. Dewsbury
Whitehaven v. Bramley

Saturday/Sunday September, 29/30

JOHN PLAYER TROPHY Second Round

Friday, October 5
Bramley v. Rochdale H.

Sunday, October 7
Barrow v. Halifax
Dewsbury v. Huyton
Doncaster v. Keighley
Huddersfield v. Whitehaven
Oldham v. Featherstone R.
Swinton v. Batley

Sunday, October 14
Batley v. Dewsbury
Featherstone R. v. Barrow
Halifax v. Bramley
Huyton v. Huddersfield
Keighley v. Swinton
Rochdale H. v. Doncaster
Whitehaven v. Oldham

Sunday, October 21
Barrow v. Huyton
Dewsbury v. Featherstone R.
Doncaster v. Halifax
Huddersfield v. Batley
Keighley v. Rochdale H.
Oldham v. Bramley
Swinton v. Whitehaven

Sunday, October 28
Batley v. Keighley
Bramley v. Barrow
Featherstone v. Huddersfield
Huyton v. Doncaster
Oldham v. Halifax
Rochdale H. v. Swinton
Whitehaven v. Dewsbury

Sunday, November 4
Barrow v. Batley
Dewsbury v. Bramley
Featherstone R. v. Doncaster
Halifax v. Keighley
Huddersfield v. Oldham
Rochdale H. v. Whitehaven
Swinton v. Huyton

Sunday, November 11
Batley v. Halifax
Bramley v. Huddersfield
Featherstone R. v. Swinton
Huyton v. Rochdale H.
Keighley v. Dewsbury
Oldham v. Barrow
Whitehaven v. Doncaster

Sunday, November 18
Barrow v. Featherstone R.
Dewsbury v. Halifax
Doncaster v. Bramley
Huddersfield v. Keighley
Huyton v. Whitehaven
Rochdale H. v. Batley
Swinton v. Oldham

Sunday, November 25
Batley v. Doncaster
Bramley v. Swinton
Featherstone R. v. Rochdale H.
Halifax v. Barrow
Keighley v. Huyton
Oldham v. Dewsbury
Whitehaven v. Huddersfield

Sunday, December 2
Barrow v. Dewsbury
Batley v. Featherstone R.
Doncaster v. Whitehaven
Huddersfield v. Bramley
Huyton v. Oldham
Rochdale H. v. Halifax
Swinton v. Keighley

Sunday, December 9
Barrow v. Huddersfield
Bramley v. Keighley
Dewsbury v. Swinton
Featherstone R. v. Huyton
Halifax v. Doncaster
Oldham v. Batley
Whitehaven v. Rochdale H.

Sunday, December 16
Dewsbury v. Oldham
Doncaster v. Batley
Huddersfield v. Featherstone R.
Huyton v. Halifax
Keighley v. Whitehaven
Rochdale H. v. Bramley
Swinton v. Barrow

Boxing Day, Wednesday, December 26
dBarrow v. Whitehaven
Bramley v. Featherstone R.
Dewsbury v. Batley
Huddersfield v. Halifax
Oldham v. Rochdale H.

Sunday, December 30
Batley v. Barrow
Doncaster v. Dewsbury
Featherstone R. v. Oldham
Keighley v. Halifax
Swinton v. Bramley
Whitehaven v. Huyton

New Year's Day
Tuesday, January 1
Halifax v. Huddersfield

Sunday, January 6
Barrow v. Keighley
Bramley v. Huyton
Dewsbury v. Rochdale H.
Featherstone R. v. Whitehaven
Halifax v. Batley
Huddersfield v. Doncaster
Oldham v. Swinton

Sunday, January, 13
Batley v. Bramley
Halifax v. Dewsbury
Huyton v. Barrow
Keighley v. Oldham
Rochdale H. v. Featherstone R.
Swinton v. Doncaster

Sunday, January 20
Batley v. Swinton
Rochdale H. v. Huddersfield

Sunday, January 27
Barrow v. Rochdale H.
Bramley v. Halifax
Dewsbury v. Keighley
Doncaster v. Huyton
Oldham v. Huddersfield
Swinton v. Featherstone R.
Whitehaven v. Batley

Sunday, February 3
Batley v. Huyton
Doncaster v. Barrow
Featherstone R. v. Dewsbury
Halifax v. Whitehaven
Huddersfield v. Swinton
Keighley v. Bramley

Saturday/Sunday
February, 9/10
STATE EXPRESS CHALLENGE CUP
First Round

Sunday, February 17
Doncaster v. Featherstone R.

Saturday/Sunday
February, 23/24
STATE EXPRESS CHALLENGE CUP
Second Round

Sunday, March 2
Barrow v. Oldham
Huyton v. Batley
Rochdale H. v. Keighley
Swinton v. Huddersfield
Whitehaven v. Featherstone R.

Sunday, March 9
Bramley v. Doncaster
Dewsbury v. Barrow
Halifax v. Rochdale H.
Huyton v. Swinton
Keighley v. Batley
Oldham v. Whitehaven

Sunday, March 16
Batley v. Rochdale H.
Bramley v. Dewsbury
Doncaster v. Swinton
Featherstone R. v. Halifax
Huddersfield v. Huyton
Oldham v. Keighley

Sunday, March 23
Barrow v. Bramley
Dewsbury v. Huddersfield
Halifax v. Oldham
Rochdale H. v. Huyton
Whitehaven v. Keighley

Sunday, March 30
Bramley v. Whitehaven
Huddersfield v. Barrow
Keighley v. Featherstone R.
Oldham v. Doncaster
Swinton v. Rochdale H.

Good Friday,
April 4
Rochdale H. v. Oldham

Sunday, April 6
Doncaster v. Rochdale H.
Featherstone R. v. Bramley
Huddersfield v. Dewsbury
Huyton v. Keighley
Swinton v. Halifax

Easter Monday,
April 7
Whitehaven v. Barrow

Sunday, April, 13
Barrow v. Doncaster
Batley v. Huddersfield
Dewsbury v. Whitehaven
Halifax v. Huyton

Sunday, April 20
Bramley v. Oldham
Featherstone R. v. Batley
Huyton v. Dewsbury
Keighley v. Doncaster
Whitehaven v. Swinton

RUGBY FOOTBALL LEAGUE PRINCIPAL DATES 1979/80

August	19	County Cups (Round 1)
	26	County Cups (Round 2)
	29	County Championship — Cumbria v. Yorkshire
September	2	League Season begins
	5	County Championship — Lancashire v. Cumbria
	12	County Championship — Yorkahire v. Lancashire
	15—16	John Player Trophy (1st Round)
	29—30	John Player Trophy (2nd Round)
October	20—21	John Player Trophy (3rd Round)
	27	Esso Yorkshire Cup Final
November	3	John Player Trophy (Semi-Final 1)
	17	John Player Trophy (Semi-Final 2)
	25	Great Britain V. France (Under 24)
December	1	John Player Trophy Final
	8	Forshaws Lancashire Cup Final
	18	BBC2 Floodlit Fianl
1980		
January	13	France v. Great Britain (Under 24)
	20	France v. Great Britain (Colts)
	26	Wales v. France (European Championship)
February	9—10	State Express Challenge Cup (Round 1)
	23—24	State Express Challenge Cup (Round 2)
Marcn	8—9	State Express Challenge Cup (Round 3)
	16	France v. England (European Championship)
	22	State Express Challenge Cup (Semi-Final 1)
	29	State Express Challenge Cup (Semi-Final 2)
	30	Great Britain v. France (Colts)
Aprii	20	League Season ends
	27	Premiership Round 1
May	3	State Express Challenge Cup Final at Wembley
	10—11	Premiership Semi-Finals
	17	Premiership Final

THE NORTHERN RUGBY FOOTBALL LEAGUE

DIVISION 1

	P.	W.	D.	L.	F.	A.	Pts.
Hull K.R.	30	23	0	7	616	344	46
Warrington	30	22	0	8	521	340	44
Widnes	30	21	2	7	480	322	44
Leeds	30	19	1	10	555	370	39
St. Helens	30	16	2	12	485	379	34
Wigan	30	16	1	13	484	411	33
Castleford	30	16	1	13	498	469	33
Bradford N.	30	16	0	14	523	416	32
Workington T.	30	13	3	14	378	345	29
Wakefield T.	30	13	1	16	382	456	27
Leigh	30	13	1	16	406	535	27
Salford	30	11	2	17	389	435	24
Barrow	30	9	2	19	368	536	20
Featherstone R.	30	8	1	21	501	549	17
Rochdale H.	30	8	0	22	297	565	16
Huddersfield	30	7	1	22	314	725	15

SECOND DIVISION

Hull	26	26	0	0	702	175	52
New Hunslet	26	21	1	4	454	218	43
York	26	17	1	8	426	343	35
Blackpool B.	26	15	3	8	321	272	33
Halifax	26	15	2	9	312	198	32
Dewsbury	26	15	0	11	368	292	30
Keighley	26	12	2	12	357	298	26
Bramley	26	12	1	13	375	342	25
Oldham	26	10	1	15	297	435	21
Whitehaven	26	8	3	15	297	408	19
Swinton	26	7	2	17	349	452	16
Doncaster	26	7	0	19	259	547	14
Huyton	26	3	3	20	261	513	9
Batley	26	4	1	21	194	479	9

STATE EXPRESS CHALLENGE CUP

First Round

	Pts.		Pts.
Barrow	10	York	7
Dewsbury	15	Blackpool B.	6
Huddersfield	11	Whitehaven	9
Hull	17	Leeds	6
Hull K.R.	23	New Hunslet	15
Huyton	2	Keighley	14
Leigh Miners Welfare	10	Leigh	23
Oldham	23	Ace Amateurs	5
Rochdale H.	15	Batley	0
St. Helens	34	Doncaster	9
Salford	6	Bramley	6
Swinton	2	Bradford N.	8
Wakefield T.	10	Featherstone R.	7
Warrington	9	Castleford	15
Widnes	12	Workington T.	5
Wigan	9	Halifax	6

First Round Replay

Bramley	2	Salford	2

First Round Second Replay

Bramley	7	Salford	5

(at Swinton)

Second Round

Barrow	25	Leigh	2
Bradford N.	14	Hull K.R.	7
Castleford	31	Dewsbury	15
Huddersfield	31	Bramley	12
Keighley	12	Hull	33
Oldham	7	Wakefield T.	19
Rochdale H.	10	St. Helens	11
Widnes	21	Wigan	5

Third Round

Bradford N.	8	Hull	8
Castleford	6	St. Helens	10
Huddersfield	0	Widnes	14
Wakefield T.	8	Barrow	5

Third Round Replay

12Hull	4	Bradford N.	8

Semi-Finals

Bradford N.	11	Widnes	14

(at Swinton)

St. Helens	7	Wakefield T.	9

(at Leeds)

Final at Wembley

Wakefield T.	3	Widnes	12

PREMIERSHIP TROPHY 1979

First Round

	Pts.		Pts.
Hull K.R.	17	Bradford N.	18
Leeds	21	St. Helens	10
Warrington	17	Castleford	10
Widnes	8	Wigan	12

Semi-Finals

Leeds	20	Wigan	10
Warrington	11	Bradford N.	14

Final at Huddersfield

Bradford N.	2	Leeds	24

JOHN PLAYER TROPHY

First Round

	pts.		pts.
Barrow	8	Bradford N.	26
Castleford	18	Swinton	10
Doncaster	2	Wigan	30
Huddersfield	10	Widnes	21
Hull K.R.	67	Oldham	11
Keighley	20	York	4
Leigh	13	Huyton	13
Leigh Miners Welfare	9	Halifax	21
Milford Arms	5	Dewsbury	38
New Hunslet	7	Hull	17
St. Helens	16	Leeds	11
Salford	25	Rochdale H.	7
Wakefield T.	27	Batley	2
Warrington	14	Blackpool B.	4
Whitehaven	3	Featherstone R.	9
Workington T.	17	Bramley	8

First Round Replay

Huyton	8	Leigh	10

Second Round

Castleford	20	Workington T.	9
Featherstone R.	0	Warrington	7
Hull	12	Bradford N.	18
Hull K.R.	16	Salford	14
Keighley	9	Wigan	5
Leigh	17	Dewsbury	8
Wakefield T.	15	Halifax	10
Widnes	11	St. Helens	10

Third Round

Bradford N.	16	Wakefield T.	13
Hull K.R.	23	Castleford	10
Keighley	4	Widnes	15
Warrington	27	Leigh	0

Semi-Finals

Warrington	9	Hull K.R.	5
Widnes	21	Bradford N.	3

Final at St. Helens

Warrington	4	Widnes	16

B.B.C. 2 FLOODLIT TROPHY 1978-79

St. Helens	7	Widnes	13

FORSHAWS LANCASHIRE CUP 1978

First Round

Barrow	13	Leigh	17
St. Helens	14	Rochdale H.	14
Salford	30	Oldham	15
Warrington	18	Swinton	4
Whitehaven	15	Blackpool B.	12
Widnes	43	Huyton	6
Workington T.	14	Wigan	2

First Round Replay

Rochdale H.	8	St. Helens	8

First Round Second Replay

St. Helens	28	Rochdale H.	9

(at Wigan)

Second Round

Leigh	21	St. Helens	4
Whitehaven	6	Salford	19
Widnes	17	Warrington	10

Workington T. BYE

Semi-Finals

Salford	8	Workington T.	9
Widnes	28	Leigh	14

Widnes	15	Workington T.	13

ESSO YORKSHIRE CUP 1978

First Round

	Pts.		Pts.
Batley	8	Halifax	24

Final at Wigan

Bradford N.	24	Leeds	23
Bramley	4	Hull	13
Castleford	18	Dewsbury	11
Doncaster	5	Keighley	20
Featherstone R.	23	Huddersfield	8
Wakefield T.	11	Hull K.R.	16
York	25	New Hunslet	19

Second Round

Bradford N.	28	Hull K.R.	17
Featherstone R.	8	Hull	20
Halifax	20	Castleford	8
York	13	Keighley	6

Semi-Finals

Bradford N.	12	Hull	7
Halifax	2	York	4

Final at Leeds

Bradford N.	18	York	8

COUNTY CHAMPIONSHIP

	Pts.		Pts.
Yorkshire	37	Cumbria	9
(Played at Hull)			
Lancashire	23	Yorkshire	7
(Played at Widnes)			
Cumbria	16	Lancashire	15
(Played at Whitehaven)			

AUSTRALIAN TOUR OF BRITAIN 1978

		Pts.		Pts.	
30th Sept.	Blackpool B	1	Australia	39	
1st Oct.	Cumbria	4	Australia	47	at Barrow
4th Oct.	Great Britain Under-21	8	Australia	30	at Hull K.2
8th Oct.	Bradford N.	11	Australia	21	
11th Oct.	Warrington	15	Australia	12	
15th Oct.	Wales	3	Australia	8	at Swanaea
17th Oct.	Leeds	19	Australia	25	
21st Oct.	GREAT BRITAIN	9	AUSTRALIA	15	at Wigan
25th Oct.	Widnes	11	Australia	10	
29th Oct.	Hull	2	Australia	34	
1st Nov.	Salford	2	Australia	14	
5th Nov.	GREAT BRITAIN	18	AUSTRALIA	14	at Bradford
8th Nov.	Wigan	2	Australia	28	
12th Nov.	St. Helens	4	Australia	26	
14th Nov.	York	2	Australia	29	
18th Nov.	GREAT BRITAIN	6	AUSTRALIA	23	at Leeds

EUROPEAN CHAMPIONSHIP 1979

4th Feb.	France 15 pts. v.	Wales	8 pts.	Narbonne
16th Mar.	Wales 7 pts. v.	England	15 pts.	Widnes
24 th Mar.	England 12 pts.	Warrington		

FINAL TABLE

	P.	W.	L.	F.	A.	Pts.
England	2	2	—	27	13	4
France	2	1	1	21	20	2
Wales	2	—	2	15	30	0

LEAGUE CHAMPIONS

1901–2	Broughton R.	43 pts.
1902–3	Halifax	49 „
1903–4	Bradford	54 „
1904–5	Oldham	51 „
1905–6	Leigh	80.00
1906–7	Halifax	83.35
1907–8	Hunslet	79.28
1908–9	Wigan	87.50
1909–10	Oldham	88.23
1910–11	Oldham	83.82
1911–12	Huddersfield	87.50
1912–13	Huddersfield	87.50
1913–14	Salford	76.68
1914–15	Huddersfield	88.28
1919–20	Hull	75.00
1920–1	Hull	75.00
1921–2	Wigan	70.81
1922–3	Hull K.R.	73.61
1923–4	Batley	70.83
1924–5	Hull K.R.	77.94
1925–6	Wigan	80.26
1926–7	Swinton	78.98
1927–8	Swinton	79.16
1928–9	Huddersfield	73.68
1929–30	Huddersfield	68.42
1930–1	Swinton	64 pts.
1931–2	St. Helens	60 „
1932–3	Salford	64 „
1933–4	Wigan	52 „
1934–5	Swinton	61 „
1935–6	Hull	61 „
1936–7	Salford	61 „
1937–8	Hunslet	53 „
1938–9	Salford	63 „
1945–6	Wigan	60 „
1946–7	Wigan	59 „
1947–8	Warrington	61 „
1948–9	Huddersfield	54 „
1949–50	Wigan	63 „
1950–1	Workington T.	54 „
1951–2	Wigan	55 „
1952–3	St. Helens	66 „
1953–4	Warrington	61 „
1954–5	Warrington	60 „
1955–6	Hull	70 „
1956–7	Oldham	66 „
1957–8	Hull	56 „
1958–9	St. Helens	63 „
1959–60	Wigan	56 „
1960–1	Leeds	60 „
1961–2	Huddersfield	52 „
1962–3	Div. 1–Swinton	45 „
1962–3	Div. 2–Hunslet	44 „
1963–4	Div. 1–Swinton	50 „
1963–4	Div. 2–Oldham	43 „
1964–5	Halifax	45 „
1965–6	St. Helens	57 „
1966–7	Wakefield T.	54 „
1967–8	Wakefield T.	49 „
1968–9	Leeds	60 „
1969–70	St. Helens	47 „
1970–1	St. Helens	58 „
1971–2	Leeds	58 „
1972–3	Dewsbury	46 „
1973–4	Salford	47 „
1974–5	St. Helens	53 „
1975–6	Salford	45 „
1976–7	Featherstone R.	44 „
1977–8	Widnes	50 „
1978–9	Hull K.R.	46 „

CHALLENGE CUP WINNERS

Year	*Winners*	G.	T.	P.	*Runners up*	G.	T.	P.	*Venue*
1897	Batley	1	2	8	St. Helens	0	1	3	Headingley
1898	Batley	2	1	7	Bradford	0	0	0	Headingley
1899	Oldham	2	5	19	Hunslet	3	1	9	Fallowfield
1900	Swinton	2	4	16	Salford	1	2	8	Fallowfield
1901	Batley	0	2	6	Warrington	0	0	0	Headingley
1902	Broughton R.	5	5	25	Salford	0	0	0	Rochdale
1903	Halifax	2	1	7	Salford	0	0	0	Headingley
1904	Halifax	1	2	8	Warrington	0	1	3	Salford
1905	Warrington	0	2	6	Hull K.R.	0	0	0	Headingley
1906	Bradford	1	1	5	Salford	0	0	0	Headingley
1907	Warrington	4	3	17	Oldham	0	1	3	Broughton
1908	Hunslet	4	2	14	Hull	0	0	0	Huddersfield
1909	Wakefield T.	1	5	17	Hull	0	0	0	Headingley
1910	Leeds	2	1	7	Hull	2	1	7	Huddersfield
1910	Leeds (replay)	7	4	26	Hull	3	2	12	Huddersfield
1911	Broughton R.	2	0	4	Wigan	0	0	0	Salford
1912	Dewsbury	1	2	8	Oldham	1	1	5	Headingley
1913	Huddersfield	0	3	9	Warrington	1	1	5	Headingley

1914	Hull 0	2	6	Wakefield T.......0	0	0	Halifax
1915	Huddersfield...5	9	37	St. Helens 0	1	3	Oldham
1920	Huddersfield...3	5	21	Wigan 2	2	10	Headingley
1921	Leigh 2	3	13	Halifax 0	0	0	Broughton
1922	Rochdale R.....2	2	10	Hull 0	3	9	Headingley
1923	Leeds...........5	6	28	Hull 0	1	3	Wakefield
1924	Wigan 3	5	21	Oldham 2	0	4	Rochdale
1925	Oldham 2	4	16	Hull K.R. 0	1	3	Leeds
1926	Swinton........3	1	9	Oldham 0	1	3	Rochdale
1927	Oldham 4	6	26	Swinton...........2	1	7	Wigan
1928	Swinton........1	1	5	Warrington 0	1	3	Wigan
1929	Wigan 2	3	13	Dewsbury.........1	0	2	Wembley
1930	Widnes.........2	2	10	St. Helens 0	1	3	Wembley
1931	Halifax 3	4	22	York 1	2	8	Wembley
1932	Leeds...........4	1	11	Swinton...........4	0	8	Wigan
1933	Huddersfield...6	3	21	Warrington 4	3	17	Wembley
1934	Hunslet 1	3	11	Widnes...........1	1	5	Wembley
1935	Castleford 1	3	11	Huddersfield.....1	2	8	Wembley
1936	Leeds...........3	4	18	Warrington 1	0	2	Wembley
1937	Widnes.........3	4	18	Keighley 1	0	5	Wembley
1938	Salford 2	1	7	Barrow 2	0	4	Wembley
1939	Halifax 4	4	20	Salford 0	1	3	Wembley
1940	No competition						
1941*	Leeds 2	5	19	Halifax 1	0	2	Bradford
1942*	Leeds 3	3	15	Halifax 5	0	10	Bradford
1943*	Dewsbury 2	4	16	Leeds.............3	1	9	*(Dews. won on*
	Dewsbury......0	0	0	Leeds.............3	0	6	*agg.* 16–15)
1944*	Bradford N. 0	0	0	Wigan 0	1	3	*(Brad. won on*
	Bradford N. 1	2	8	Wigan 0	0	0	*agg.* 8–3)
1945*	Huddersfield ...2	1	7	Bradford N. 2	0	4	*(Hudd. won on*
	Huddersfield...0	2	6	Bradford N. 1	1	5	*agg.* 13–9)
1946	Wakefield T....2	3	13	Wigan 0	4	12	Wembley
1947	Bradford N. 1	2	8	Leeds.............2	0	4	Wembley
1948	Wigan 1	2	8	Bradford N. 0	1	3	Wembley
1949	Bradford N. 3	2	12	Halifax 0	0	0	Wembley
1950	Warrington 5	3	19	Widnes...........0	0	0	Wembley
1951	Wigan 2	2	10	Barrow 0	0	0	Wembley
1952	Workington T...3	4	18	Featherstone R. .2	2	10	Wembley
1953	Huddersfield...3	3	15	St. Helens 2	2	10	Wembley
1954†	Warrington.....1	2	8	Halifax 2	0	4	Wembley
1955	Barrow 6	3	21	Workington......3	2	12	Wembley
1956	St. Helens 2	3	13	Halifax 1	0	2	Wembley
1957	Leeds...........0	3	9	Barrow 2	1	7	Wembley
1958	Wigan 2	3	13	Workington......3	1	9	Wembley
1959	Wigan 6	6	30	Hull 5	1	13	Wembley
1960	Wakefield T....7	8	38	Hull 1	1	5	Wembley
1961	St. Helens 3	2	12	Wigan 3	0	6	Wembley
1962	Wakefield T....3	2	12	Huddersfield.....0	2	6	Wembley
1963	Wakefield T....5	5	25	Wigan 2	2	10	Wembley
1964	Widnes.........2	3	13	Hull K.R. 1	1	5	Wembley
1965	Wigan 4	4	20	Hunslet 5	2	16	Wembley
1966	St. Helens 6	3	21	Wigan 1	0	2	Wembley
1967	Featherstone R.4	3	17	Barrow 3	2	12	Wembley
1968	Leeds...........4	1	11	Wakefield T.......2	2	10	Wembley
1969	Castleford 1	3	11	Salford 3	0	6	Wembley
1970	Castleford 2	1	7	Wigan 1	0	2	Wembley
1971	Leigh 9	2	24	Leeds.............2	1	7	Wembley
1972	St. Helens 5	2	16	Leeds.............5	1	13	Wembley
1973	Featherstone R.9	5	33	Bradford N. 4	2	14	Wembley
1974	Warrington 9	2	24	Featherstone R. .3	1	9	Wembley

1975	Widnes.........6	0	14	Warrington 2	1	7	Wembley
1976	St. Helens 5	4	20	Widnes...........3	0	5	Wembley
1977	Leeds...........4	3	16	Widnes...........2	1	7	Wembley
1978	Leeds...........3	3	14	St. Helens 3	2	12	Wembley
1979	Widnes.......		12	Wakefield T.		3	Wembley

* War-time competition in which not all the clubs took part.
† After a draw (4–4) at Wembley.

COUNTY CUP WINNERS

LANCASHIRE

1905	Wigan	1931	Salford	1958	Oldham
1906	Broughton R.	1932	Warrington	1959	Warrington
1907	Oldham	1933	Oldham	1960	St. Helens
1908	Wigan	1934	Salford	1961	St. Helens
1909	Wigan	1935	Salford	1962	St. Helens
1910	Oldham	1936	Salford	1963	St. Helens
1911	Rochdale H.	1937	Warrington	1964	St. Helens
1912	Wigan	1938	Wigan	1965	Warrington
1913	Oldham	1939	Swinton	1966	Wigan
1914	Rochdale H.	1940–4	No comp.	1967	St. Helens
1918	Rochdale H.	1945	Widnes	1968	St. Helens
1919	Oldham	1946	Wigan	1969	Swinton
1920	Broughton R.	1947	Wigan	1970	Leigh
1921	Warrington	1948	Wigan	1971	Wigan
1922	Wigan	1949	Wigan	1972	Salford
1923	St. Helens R.	1950	Wigan	1973	Wigan
1924	Oldham	1951	Wigan	1974	Wigan
1925	Swinton	1952	Leigh	1975	Widnes
1926	St. Helens	1953	St. Helens	1976	Widnes
1927	Swinton	1954	Barrow	1977	Widnes
1928	Wigan	1955	Leigh	1978	Workington T.
1929	Warrington	1956	Oldham	1979	Widnes
1930	St. Helens	1957	Oldham		

YORKSHIRE

1905	Hunslet	1932	Leeds	1956	Wakefield T.
1906	Bradford	1933	York	1957	Huddersfield
1907	Hunslet	1934	Leeds	1958	Leeds
1908	Halifax	1935	Leeds	1959	Featherstone
1909	Huddersfield	1936	York	1960	Wakefield T.
1910	Wakefield T.	1937	Leeds	1961	Wakefield T.
1911	Huddersfield	1938	Huddersfield	1962	Hunslet
1912	Batley	1939	Featherstone R.	963	Halifax
1913	Huddersfield	1940	Bradford N.	964	Wakefield T.
1914	Huddersfield	1941	Bradford N.	1965	Bradford N.
1919 (May)	Hud'field	1942	Dewsbury	1966	Hull K.R.
1919 (Nov.)	Hud'field	1943	Bradford N.	1967	Hull K.R.
1920	Hull K.R.	1944	Halifax	1968	Leeds
1921	Leeds	1945	Bradford N.	1969	Hull
1922	York	1946	Wakefield T.	1970	Leeds
1923	Hull	1947	Wakefield T.	1971	Hull K.R.
1924	Wakefield T.	1948	Bradford N.	1972	Leeds
1925	Dewsbury	1949	Bradford N.	1973	Leeds
1926	Huddersfield	1950	Huddersfield	1975	Hull K.R.
1927	Dewsbury	1951	Wakefield T.	1976	Leeds
1928	Leeds	1952	Huddersfield	1977	Leeds
1929	Hull K.R.	1953	Bradford N.	1978	Castleford
1930	Leeds	1954	Halifax	1979	Bradford N
1931	Huddersfield	1955	Halifax		